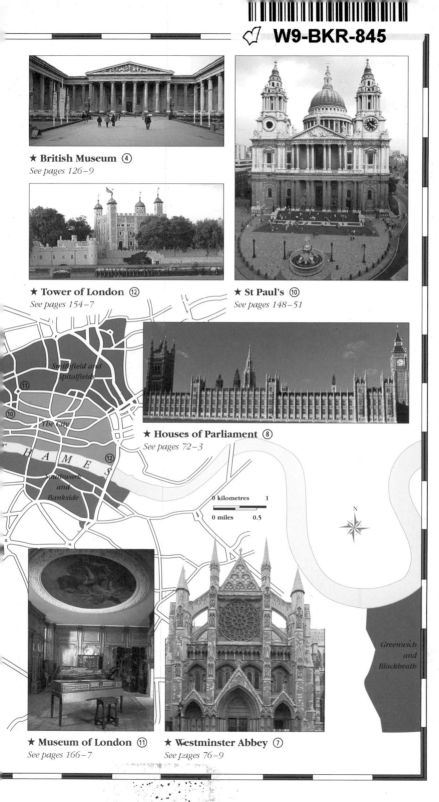

★ **British Museum** ④
See pages 126–9

★ **Tower of London** ⑫
See pages 154–7

★ **St Paul's** ⑩
See pages 148–51

★ **Houses of Parliament** ⑧
See pages 72–3

Smithfield and Spitalfields

The City

T H A M E S

Southwark and Bankside

0 kilometres   1

0 miles   0.5

N

Greenwich and Blackheath

★ **Museum of London** ⑪
See pages 166–7

★ **Westminster Abbey** ⑦
See pages 76–9

EYEWITNESS *TRAVEL GUIDES*

LONDON

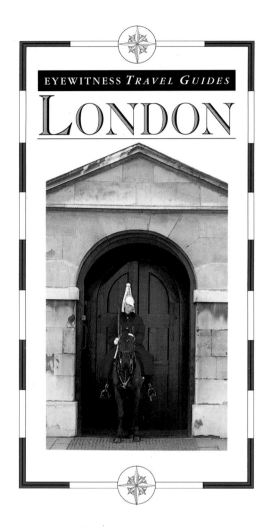

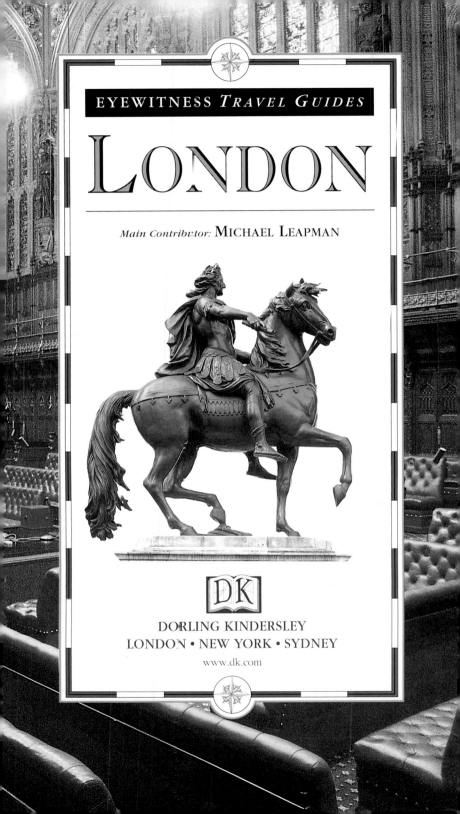

EYEWITNESS TRAVEL GUIDES

LONDON

Main Contributor: MICHAEL LEAPMAN

DK

DORLING KINDERSLEY
LONDON • NEW YORK • SYDNEY

www.dk.com

A DORLING KINDERSLEY BOOK

www.dk.com

PROJECT EDITOR Jane Shaw
ART EDITOR Sally Ann Hibbard
EDITOR Tom Fraser
DESIGNERS Pippa Hurst, Robyn Tomlinson
DESIGN ASSISTANT Clare Sullivan

MANAGING EDITOR Douglas Amrine
MANAGING ART EDITOR Geoff Manders
SENIOR EDITOR Georgina Matthews
SERIES DESIGN CONSULTANT Peter Luff
EDITORIAL DIRECTOR David Lamb
ART DIRECTOR Anne-Marie Bulat

PRODUCTION CONTROLLER Hilary Stephens
PICTURE RESEARCH Ellen Root
DTP EDITOR Siri Lowe

CONTRIBUTORS
Christopher Pick, Lindsay Hunt

MAPS
Andrew Heritage, James Mills-Hicks, Chez Picthall,
John Plumer (Dorling Kindersley Cartography)

PHOTOGRAPHERS
Philip Enticknap, John Heseltine,
Stephen Oliver

ILLUSTRATORS
Brian Delf, Trevor Hill, Robbie Polley

•

This book was produced with the assistance of
Websters International Publishers.

Film outputting bureau PLS (London)
Reproduced by Colourscan (Singapore)
Printed and bound by Dai Nippon Printing Co., (Hong Kong) Ltd.

First published in Great Britain in 1993
by Dorling Kindersley Limited
9 Henrietta Street, London WC2E 8PS
Reprinted with revisions 1994, 1995, 1996, 1997, 1999, 2000

Copyright 1993, 2000 © Dorling Kindersley Limited, London

**The information in every
Eyewitness Travel Guide is checked annually.**
Every effort has been made to ensure that this book is as up-to-
date as possible at the time of going to press. Some details,
however, such as telephone numbers, opening hours, prices,
gallery hanging arrangements and travel information are liable to
change. The publishers cannot accept responsibility for any
consequences arising from the use of this book.
We value the views and suggestions of our readers very highly.
Please write to: Editorial Director, Eyewitness Travel Guides
Dorling Kindersley, 9 Henrietta Street, London WC2E 8PS.

CONTENTS

Portrait of Sir Walter Raleigh (1585)

INTRODUCING LONDON

Bedford Square doorway (1775)

The Broadwalk at Hampton Court (c.1720)

Beefeater at the Tower of London

Bandstand in St James's Park

Houses of Parliament

St Paul's Church: Covent Garden

How to Use this Guide

THIS EYEWITNESS TRAVEL GUIDE helps you get the most from your stay in London with the minimum of practical difficulty. The opening section, *Introducing London,* locates the city geographically, sets modern London in its historical context and describes the regular highlights of the London year. *London at a Glance* is an overview of the city's specialities. *London Area by Area* takes you round the city's areas of interest. It describes all the main sights with maps, photographs and detailed illustrations. In addition, five planned walk routes take you to parts of London you might otherwise miss.

Well-researched tips on where to stay, eat, shop, and on entertainments are in *Travellers' Needs. Children's London* lists highlights for young visitors, and *Survival Guide* tells you how to do anything from posting a letter to using the Underground.

LONDON AREA BY AREA
The city has been divided into 17 sightseeing areas, each with its own section in the guide. Each section opens with a portrait of the area, summing up its character and history and listing all the sights to be covered. Sights are numbered and clearly located on an *Area Map.* After this comes a largescale *Street-by-Street Map* focusing on the most interesting part of the area. Finding your way about the area section is made simple by the numbering system. This refers to the order in which sights are described on the pages that complete the section.

Sights at a Glance
lists the sights in the area by category: Historic Streets and Buildings, Churches, Museums and Galleries, Monuments, Parks and Gardens.

The area covered in greater detail on the *Street-by-Street Map* is shaded red.

Numbered circles
pinpoint all the listed sights on the area map. St Margaret's Church, for example, is ❻

1 The Area Map
For easy reference, the sights in each area are numbered and located on an Area Map. *To help the visitor, the map also shows Underground and mainline stations and car parks.*

Photographs of facades and distinctive details of buildings help you to locate the sights.

Colour-coding
on each page makes the area easy to find in the book.

Travel tips help you reach the area quickly by public transport.

2 The Street-by-Street Map
This gives a bird's eye view of the heart of each sightseeing area. The most important buildings are picked out in stronger colour, to help you spot them as you walk around.

A locator map shows you where you are in relation to surrounding areas. The area of the *Street-by-Street Map* is shown in red.

A suggested route
for a walk takes in the most attractive and interesting streets in the area.

St Margaret's Church is shown on this map as well.

Red stars indicate the sights that no visitor should miss.

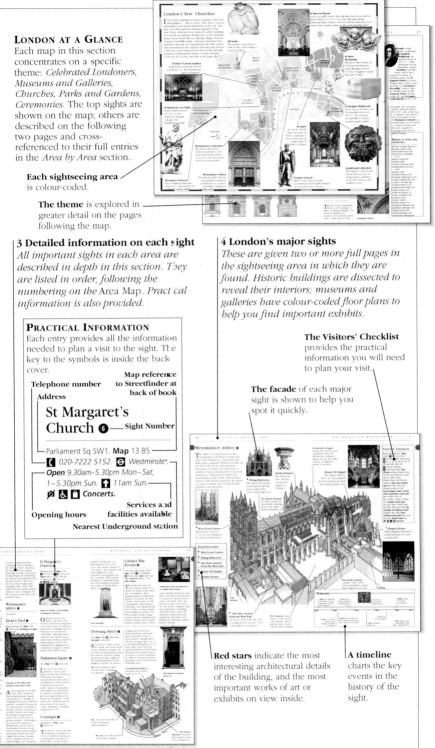

LONDON AT A GLANCE

Each map in this section concentrates on a specific theme: *Celebrated Londoners, Museums and Galleries, Churches, Parks and Gardens, Ceremonies.* The top sights are shown on the map; others are described on the following two pages and cross-referenced to their full entries in the *Area by Area* section.

Each sightseeing area is colour-coded.

The theme is explored in greater detail on the pages following the map.

3 Detailed information on each sight

All important sights in each area are described in depth in this section. They are listed in order, following the numbering on the Area Map. Practical information is also provided.

PRACTICAL INFORMATION

Each entry provides all the information needed to plan a visit to the sight. The key to the symbols is inside the back cover.

Telephone number

Map reference to Streetfinder at back of book

Address

St Margaret's Church ⑥ — Sight Number

Parliament Sq SW1. **Map** 13 B5.

020-7222 5152. Westminster.

Open 9.30am–5.30pm Mon–Sat, 1–5.30pm Sun. 11am Sun.

Concerts.

Opening hours

Services and facilities available

Nearest Underground station

4 London's major sights

These are given two or more full pages in the sightseeing area in which they are found. Historic buildings are dissected to reveal their interiors; museums and galleries have colour-coded floor plans to help you find important exhibits.

The Visitors' Checklist provides the practical information you will need to plan your visit.

The facade of each major sight is shown to help you spot it quickly.

Red stars indicate the most interesting architectural details of the building, and the most important works of art or exhibits on view inside.

A timeline charts the key events in the history of the sight.

INTRODUCING
LONDON

Putting London on the Map

Lowdon, the capital of the United
Kingdom, is a city of seven million
people covering 620 sq miles (1,606 sq
km) of southeast England. It is built on
the River Thames and is at the centre of
the UK road and rail networks. From
London visitors can easily reach the
country's other main tourist attractions.

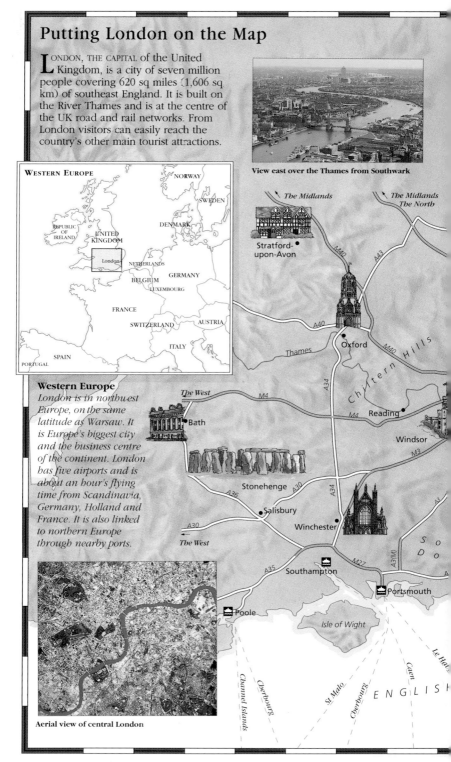

View east over the Thames from Southwark

WESTERN EUROPE

NORWAY

SWEDEN

DENMARK

REPUBLIC
OF
IRELAND

UNITED
KINGDOM

London

NETHERLANDS

GERMANY

BELGIUM

LUXEMBOURG

FRANCE

SWITZERLAND

AUSTRIA

ITALY

SPAIN

PORTUGAL

The Midlands

The Midlands
The North

Stratford-
upon-Avon

M40

A43

A40

Oxford

M40

Chiltern Hills

Thames

Western Europe

*London is in northwest
Europe, on the same
latitude as Warsaw. It
is Europe's biggest city
and the business centre
of the continent. London
has five airports and is
about an hour's flying
time from Scandinavia,
Germany, Holland and
France. It is also linked
to northern Europe
through nearby ports.*

The West

M4

Bath

M4

Reading

Windsor

M3

Stonehenge

A36

A30

A34

A3

Salisbury

Winchester

A30

The West

S
o
o
D
o

A35

M27

Southampton

A3(M)

A

Portsmouth

Poole

Isle of Wight

Le Hav

Channel Islands

Cherbourg

St Malo

Cherbourg

Caen

E N G L I S H

Aerial view of central London

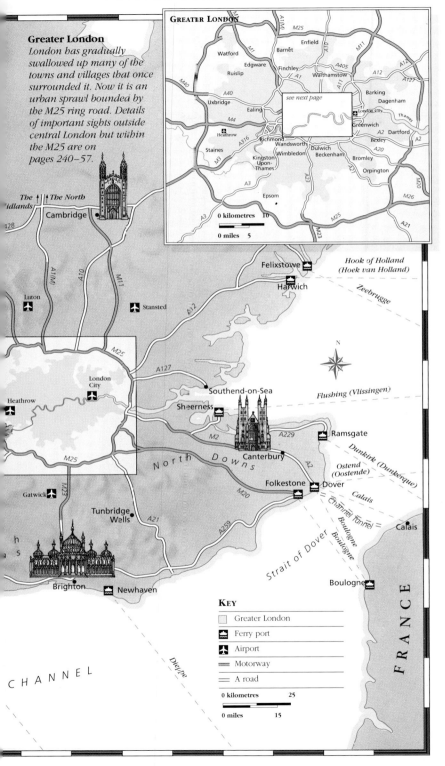

Greater London

London has gradually swallowed up many of the towns and villages that once surrounded it. Now it is an urban sprawl bounded by the M25 ring road. Details of important sights outside central London but within the M25 are on pages 240–57.

GREATER LONDON

Watford Enfield Barnet Edgware Finchley Walthamstow Ruislip Barking Dagenham Uxbridge Ealing London City Greenwich Dartford Heathrow Richmond Wandsworth Bexley Staines Wimbledon Dulwich Beckenham Bromley Kingston-Upon-Thames Orpington Epsom

see next page

0 kilometres 10
0 miles 5

The Midlands The North Cambridge

Luton Stansted Felixstowe Harwich Hook of Holland (Hoek van Holland) Zeebrugge

London City Heathrow Southend-on-Sea Sheerness Flushing (Vlissingen) Ramsgate Canterbury Dunkirk (Dunkérque) Ostend (Oostende) Folkestone Dover Calais

Gatwick Tunbridge Wells Channel Tunnel Boulogne Calais

Brighton Newhaven Strait of Dover Boulogne

North Downs FRANCE

KEY

Greater London
Ferry port
Airport
Motorway
A road

0 kilometres 25
0 miles 15

CHANNEL Dieppe

Central London

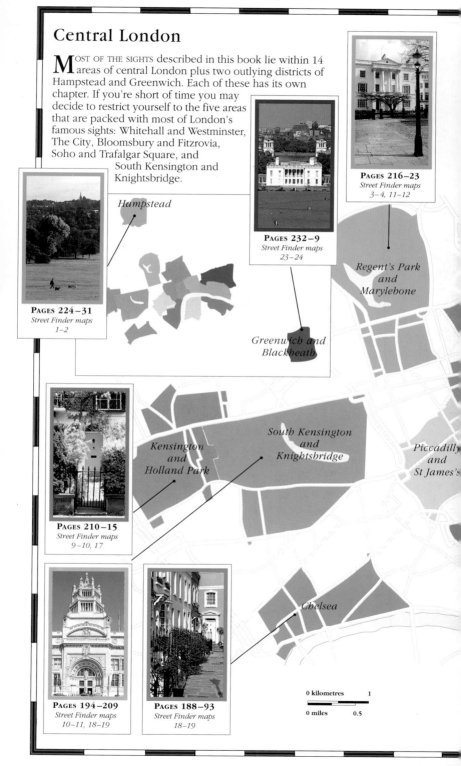

MOST OF THE SIGHTS described in this book lie within 14 areas of central London plus two outlying districts of Hampstead and Greenwich. Each of these has its own chapter. If you're short of time you may decide to restrict yourself to the five areas that are packed with most of London's famous sights: Whitehall and Westminster, The City, Bloomsbury and Fitzrovia, Soho and Trafalgar Square, and South Kensington and Knightsbridge.

PAGES 216–23
Street Finder maps
3–4, 11–12

Hampstead

PAGES 232–9
Street Finder maps
23–24

Regent's Park and Marylebone

PAGES 224–31
Street Finder maps
1–2

Greenwich and Blackheath

Kensington and Holland Park

South Kensington and Knightsbridge

Piccadilly and St James's

PAGES 210–15
Street Finder maps
9–10, 17

Chelsea

PAGES 194–209
Street Finder maps
10–11, 18–19

PAGES 188–93
Street Finder maps
18–19

0 kilometres 1

0 miles 0.5

PAGES 98–109
Street Finder maps
12–13

PAGES 120–31
Street Finder maps
4–5, 13

PAGES 110–19
Street Finder maps
13–14

PAGES 132–41
Street Finder maps
5–6, 13–14

PAGES 160–71
Street Finder maps
6–7, 14, 16

PAGES 142–59
Street Finder maps
14–16

N

Bloomsbury
and
Fitzrovia

Smithfield
and
Spitalfields

oho and
rafalgar
Square

Holborn
and the
Inns of Court

Covent
Garden
and the
Strand

The City

RIVER THAMES

Southwark
and Bankside

South Bank

Whitehall
and
Westminster

PAGES 68–85
Street Finder maps
13, 20–1

PAGES 86–97
Street Finder maps
12–13, 20

PAGES 180–7
Street Finder maps
13–14, 21–2

PAGES 172–9
Street Finder maps
6, 16

THE HISTORY OF LONDON

The griffon: the City of London's symbol

IN 55 BC, JULIUS CAESAR'S Roman army invaded England, landed in Kent and marched north-west until it reached the broad River Thames at what is now Southwark. There were a few tribes-men living on the opposite bank but no major settlement. However, by the time of the second Roman invasion 88 years later, a small port and mercantile community had been established there. The Romans bridged the river and built their administrative headquarters on the north bank, calling it Londinium – a version of its old Celtic name.

LONDON AS CAPITAL

London was soon the largest city in England and, by the time of the Norman Conquest in 1066, it was the obvious choice for national capital.

Settlement slowly spread beyond the original walled city, which was virtually wiped out by the Great Fire of 1666. The post-Fire rebuilding formed the basis of the area we know today as the City but, by the 18th century, London enveloped the settlements around it. These included the royal city of Westminster which had long been London's religious and political centre. The explosive growth of commerce and industry during the 18th and 19th centuries made London the biggest and wealthiest city in the world, creating a prosperous middle class who built the fine houses that still grace parts of the capital. The prospect of riches also lured millions of the dispossessed from the countryside and from abroad. They crowded into insanitary dwellings, many just east of the City, where docks provided employment.

By the end of the 19th century, 4.5 million people lived in inner London and another 4 million in its immediate vicinity. Bombing in World War II devastated many central areas and led to substantial rebuilding in the second half of the 20th century, when the docks and other Victorian industries disappeared.

The following pages illustrate London's history by giving snapshots of significant periods in its evolution.

A map of 1580 showing the City of London and, towards the lower left corner, the City of Westminster

A 15th-century manuscript showing the Tower of London with London Bridge in the background

Roman London

1st-century Roman coin

W HEN THE ROMANS invaded Britain in the 1st century AD, they already controlled vast areas of the Mediterranean, but fierce opposition from local tribes (such as Queen Boadicea's Iceni) made Britain difficult to control. The Romans persevered however, and had consolidated their power by the end of the century. Londinium, with its port, developed into a capital city; by the 3rd century, there were some 50,000 people living there. But, as the Roman Empire crumbled in the 5th century, the garrison pulled out, leaving the city to the Saxons.

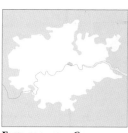

EXTENT OF THE CITY

☐ *125 AD*   ☐ *Today*

Site of present-day Museum of London

Public Baths
Bathing was an important part of Roman life. This pocket-sized personal hygiene kit (including a nail pick) and bronze pouring dish date from the 1st century.

Roman fort

Site of present-day St Paul's

Basilica

Forum

Temple of Mithras
Mithras protected the good from evil. This 2nd-century head was in his temple.

LONDINIUM
Roman London was an important centre on the site of the present-day City (see pp142–159). On the Thames, it was in a good position to trade with the rest of the Empire.

Forum and Basilica
About 200 m (600 ft) from London Bridge was the forum (the chief market and meeting place) and the basilica (the town hall and court of justice).

TIMELINE

55 BC Julius Caesar invades Britain		**200** City wall built	**410** Roman troops begin to leave
	AD 61 Boadicea attacks		
	100	200	300	400

AD 43 Claudius establishes Roman London and builds the first bridge

☐ **Roman London**

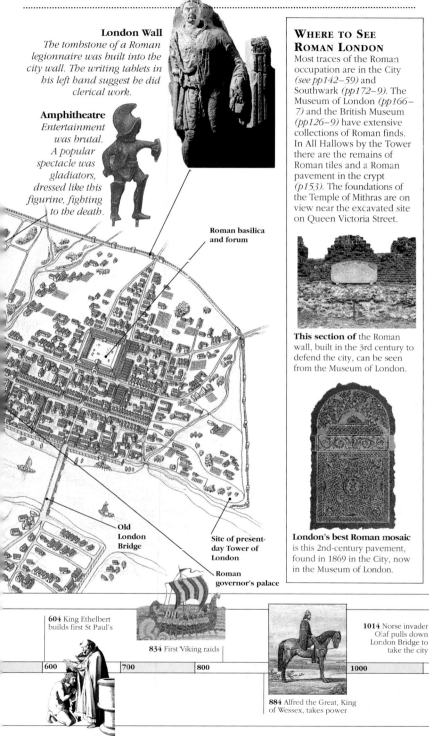

London Wall
The tombstone of a Roman legionnaire was built into the city wall. The writing tablets in his left hand suggest he did clerical work.

Amphitheatre
Entertainment was brutal. A popular spectacle was gladiators, dressed like this figurine, fighting to the death.

Roman basilica and forum

Old London Bridge

Site of present-day Tower of London

Roman governor's palace

WHERE TO SEE ROMAN LONDON

Most traces of the Roman occupation are in the City *(see pp142–59)* and Southwark *(pp172–9)*. The Museum of London *(pp166–7)* and the British Museum *(pp126–9)* have extensive collections of Roman finds. In All Hallows by the Tower there are the remains of Roman tiles and a Roman pavement in the crypt *(p153)*. The foundations of the Temple of Mithras are on view near the excavated site on Queen Victoria Street.

This section of the Roman wall, built in the 3rd century to defend the city, can be seen from the Museum of London.

London's best Roman mosaic is this 2nd-century pavement, found in 1869 in the City, now in the Museum of London.

604 King Ethelbert builds first St Paul's

834 First Viking raids

884 Alfred the Great, King of Wessex, takes power

1014 Norse invader Olaf pulls down London Bridge to take the city

600   700   800   1000

Medieval London

THE HISTORIC DIVISION between London's centres of commerce (the City) and government (Westminster) started in the mid-11th century when Edward the Confessor established his court and sited his abbey *(see pp76–9)* at Westminster. Meanwhile, in the City, tradesmen set up their own institutions and guilds, and London appointed its first mayor. Disease was rife, however, and the population never rose much above its Roman peak of 50,000. The Black Death (1348) reduced the population by half.

EXTENT OF THE CITY

☐ *1200*   ☐ *Today*

St Thomas à Becket
As Archbishop of Canterbury he was murdered in 1170, at the request of Henry II with whom he was quarrelling. Thomas was made a saint and pilgrims visited his Canterbury shrine.

LONDON BRIDGE
The first stone bridge was built in 1209 and lasted 600 years. It was the only bridge across the Thames in London until Westminster Bridge (1750).

The Chapel of St Thomas, erected the year the bridge was completed, was one of its first buildings.

Iron railings

Houses and shops
projected over both sides of the bridge. Shopkeepers made their own merchandise on the premises and lived above their shops. Apprentices did the selling.

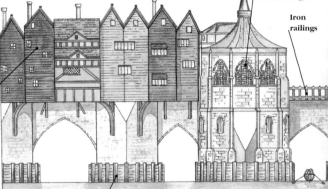

THE CORPORATION OF
THE HOUSE OF
RICHARD
WHITTINGTON
MAYOR OF LONDON
STOOD ON THIS SITE
1423
THE CITY OF LONDON

Dick Whittington
The 15th-century trader was thrice mayor of London (see p39).

The piers were made from wooden stakes rammed into the river bed and filled with rubble.

Stag Hunting
Such sports were the chief recreation of wealthy landowners.

The arches ranged from 4.5 m (15 ft) to 10 m (35 ft) in width.

TIMELINE

1042 Edward the Confessor becomes king	**1086** Domesday Book, England's first survey, published		**1191** Henry Fitzalwin becomes London's first mayor	**1215** King John's Magna Carta gives City more powers
1050	1100	1150	1200	1250
	1066 William I crowned in Abbey	**1176** Work starts on the first stone		**1240** First parliament sits at Westminster
	1065 Westminster Abbey completed	London Bridge		

Chivalry
*Medieval knights were idealized
for their courage and honour.
Edward Burne-Jones (1833–
98) painted George, patron
saint of England, rescuing a
maiden
from this
dragon*

Geoffrey Chaucer
*The poet and customs controller
(see p39), is best remembered for
Canterbury Tales which creates a rich
picture of 14th-century England.*

WHERE TO SEE MEDIEVAL LONDON

There were only a few
survivors of the Great Fire
of 1666 *(see pp22–3)* – the
Tower *(pp154–7)*,
Westminster Hall *(p72)*
and Abbey *(pp76–9)*, and
a few churches *(p46)*. The
Museum of London
(pp166–7) has artefacts
while the Tate *(pp82–5)*
and National Gallery
(pp104–7) have paintings.
Manuscripts, including the
Domesday Book, are at
the British Library *(p129)*
and the Public Record
Office *(p137)*.

The Tower of London was
started in 1078 and became
one of the few centres of
royal power in the largely
self-governing City.

A 14th-century rose
window is all that remains
of Winchester Palace near
the Clink *(see p177)*.

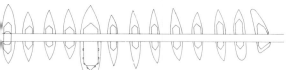

Plan of the Bridge
*The bridge had 19 arches to span the
river making it, for many years, the
longest stone bridge in England.*

---

*Many 13th-century pilgrims
went to Canterbury.*

	1348 Black Death kills thousands	**1394** Westminster Hall remodelled by Henry Yevele	*The Great Seal of Richard I shows us what medieval kings looked like.*
1350		**1400**	**1450**
	1381 Peasant's Revolt defeated	**1397** Richard Whittington becomes mayor	**1476** William Caxton sets up first printing press at Westminster

Elizabethan London

IN THE 16TH CENTURY the monarchy was stronger than ever before. The Tudors established peace throughout England, allowing art and commerce to flourish. This renaissance reached its zenith under Elizabeth I as explorers opened up the New World, and English theatre, the nation's most lasting contribution to world culture, was born.

Curtain

SHAKESPEARE'S GLOBE
Elizabethan theatres were built of wood and only half covered, so plays had to be cancelled in bad weather.

EXTENT OF THE CITY

▨ *1561*	☐ *Today*

A balcony on the stage was part of the scenery.

The apron stage had a trap door for special effects.

Death at the Stake
The Tudors dealt harshly with social and religious dissent. Here Bishops Latimer and Ridley die for so-called heresy in 1555, when Elizabeth's sister, Mary I, was queen. Traitors could expect to be hung, drawn and quartered.

In the pit, below the level of the stage, commoners stood to watch the play.

Hunting and Hawking
Popular 16th-century pastimes are shown on this cushion cover.

TIMELINE

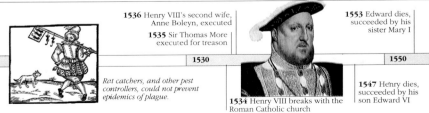

1536 Henry VIII's second wife, Anne Boleyn, executed

1535 Sir Thomas More executed for treason

1553 Edward dies, succeeded by his sister Mary I

1530

1550

Rat catchers, and other pest controllers, could not prevent epidemics of plague.

1547 Henry dies, succeeded by his son Edward VI

1534 Henry VIII breaks with the Roman Catholic church

☐ **Elizabethan London**

The galleries were for rich theatre-goers who could watch from the comfort of seats.

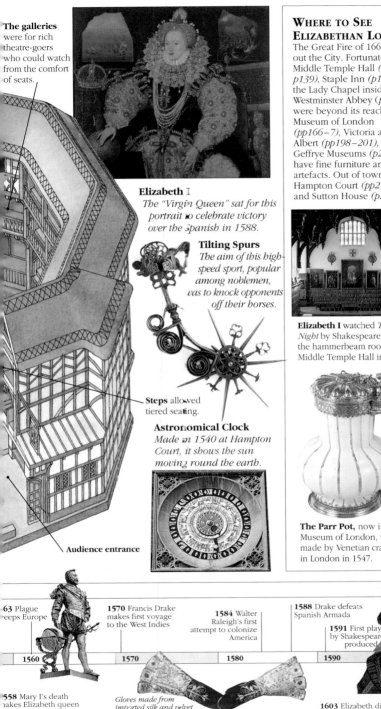

Elizabeth I
The "Virgin Queen" sat for this portrait to celebrate victory over the Spanish in 1588.

Tilting Spurs
The aim of this high-speed sport, popular among noblemen, was to knock opponents off their horses.

Steps allowed tiered seating.

Astronomical Clock
Made in 1540 at Hampton Court, it shows the sun moving round the earth.

Audience entrance

WHERE TO SEE ELIZABETHAN LONDON

The Great Fire of 1666 wiped out the City. Fortunately, Middle Temple Hall *(see p139)*, Staple Inn *(p141)* and the Lady Chapel inside Westminster Abbey *(pp76–9)* were beyond its reach. The Museum of London *(pp166–7)*, Victoria and Albert *(pp198–201)*, and Geffrye Museums *(p244)* have fine furniture and artefacts. Out of town are Hampton Court *(pp250–3)* and Sutton House *(p244)*.

Elizabeth I watched *Twelfth Night* by Shakespeare under the hammerbeam roof of Middle Temple Hall in 1603.

The Parr Pot, now in the Museum of London, was made by Venetian craftsmen in London in 1547.

63 Plague sweeps Europe

558 Mary I's death makes Elizabeth queen

1560

1570 Francis Drake makes first voyage to the West Indies

Gloves made from imported silk and velvet

1570

1584 Walter Raleigh's first attempt to colonize America

1580

1588 Drake defeats Spanish Armada

1591 First play by Shakespeare produced

1590

1603 Elizabeth dies, James I accedes

Restoration London

CIVIL WAR HAD BROKEN OUT in 1642 when the mercantile class demanded that some of the monarch's power be passed to Parliament. The subsequent Commonwealth was dominated by Puritans under Oliver Cromwell. The Puritans outlawed simple pleasures, such as dancing and theatre, so it was small wonder that the restoration of the monarchy under Charles II in 1660 was greeted with rejoicing and the release of pent-up creative energies. The period was, however, also marked with two major tragedies: the Plague (1665) and the Great Fire (1666).

EXTENT OF THE CITY

☐ *1680*   ☐ *Today*

St Paul's was destroyed in the fire that raged as far east as Fetter Lane *(map 14 E1).*

London Bridge itself survived, but many of the buildings on it were burned down.

Oliver Cromwell
He led the Parliamentarian army and was Lord Protector of the Realm from 1653 until his death in 1658. At the Restoration, his body was dug up and hung from the gallows at Tyburn, (near Hyde Park see p207).

Charles I's Death
The king was beheaded for tyranny on a freezing day (30 January 1649) outside Banqueting House (see p80).

Charles I
His belief in the Divine Right of Kings angered Parliament and was one of the causes of civil war.

TIMELINE

1623 Shakespeare's first folio published

1625 James I dies, succeeded by his son Charles I

1642 Civil war starts when Parliament defies king

1620   **1640**   **1650**

1605 Guy Fawkes leads failed attempt to blow up the King and Parliament

Feathered helmet worn by Royalist cavaliers

1649 Charles I executed, Commonwealth established

☐   **Restoration London**

THE HISTORY OF LONDON

Newton's Telescope
*Physicist and astronomer
Sir Isaac Newton
(1642–1727) dis-
covered the law
of gravity.*

Samuel Pepys
*His exuberant diaries
tell us much about
courtly life of the time.*

**The Tower of
London** was
just out of the
fire's reach.

THE GREAT FIRE OF 1666

*An unidentified Dutch artist painted this view of the fire
that burned for 5 days, destroying 13,000 houses.*

The Plague
*During 1665, carts
collected the dead
and took them to
communal graves
outside the city.*

WHERE TO SEE RESTORATION LONDON

Wren's churches and his St Paul's Cathedral *(see p47 and pp148–51)* are, with Inigo Jones's Banqueting House *(p80)*, London's most famous 17th-century buildings. On a more modest scale are Lincoln's Inn *(p136)* and Cloth Fair *(p165)*. There is a fine period interior at the Museum of London *(pp166–7)*. The British Museum *(pp126–9)* and the Victoria and Albert *(pp198–201)* have pottery, silver and textile collections.

Ham House *(p248)* was built in 1610 but much enlarged later in the century. It has the finest interior of its time in England.

Peter Paul Rubens painted the ceiling in 1636 for Inigo Jones's Banqueting House *(p80)*. This is one of its panels.

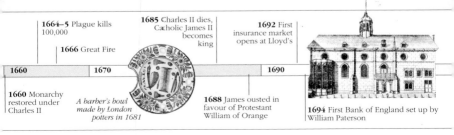

1664–5 Plague kills 100,000

1666 Great Fire

1685 Charles II dies, Catholic James II becomes king

1692 First insurance market opens at Lloyd's

1660   **1670**   **1690**

1660 Monarchy restored under Charles II

A barber's bowl made by London potters in 1681

1688 James ousted in favour of Protestant William of Orange

1694 First Bank of England set up by William Paterson

Georgian London

George I (reigned 1714–27)

THE FOUNDATION of the Bank of England in 1694 spurred the growth of London and, by the time George I came to the throne in 1714, it had become an important financial and commercial centre. Aristocrats with West End estates began laying out elegant squares and terraces to house newly-rich merchants. Architects such as the Adam brothers, John Soane and John Nash developed stylish medium-scale housing. They drew inspiration from the great European capitals, as did English painters, sculptors, composers and craftsmen.

EXTENT OF THE CITY

☐ *1810*   ☐ *Today*

Manchester Square was laid out in 1776–8.

Portman Square was on the town's outskirts when it was started in 1764.

Great Cumberland Place
Built in 1790, it was named after a royal duke and military commander.

Grosvenor Square
Few of the original houses remain on one of the oldest and largest Mayfair squares (1720).

Docks
Purpose-built docks handled the growth in world trade.

TIMELINE

1714 George I becomes king

1727 George II becomes king

1717 Hanover Square built, start of West End development

1720

1729 John Wesley (1703–91) founds the Methodist Church

1740

1759 Kew Gardens established

1768 Royal Academy of Art established

1760

1760 George III becomes king

17

John Nash
Stylish Nash shaped 18th-century London with variations on Classical themes, such as this archway in Cumberland Terrace, near Regent's Park.

WHERE TO SEE GEORGIAN LONDON

The portico of the Theatre Royal, Haymarket *(see pp326–7)* gives a taste of the style of fashionable London in the 1820s. In Pall Mall *(p92)* Charles Barry's Reform and Travellers' Clubs are equally evocative. Most West End squares have some Georgian buildings, while Fournier Street *(p170)* has good small-scale domestic architecture. The Victoria and Albert Museum (V&A *pp198–201*) has silver, as do the London Silver Vaults *(p141)* where it is for sale. Hogarth's pictures, at the Tate *(pp82–5)* and Sir John Soane's Museum *(pp136–7)*, show the social conditions.

This English long case clock (1725), made of oak and pine with Chinese designs, is in the V&A.

GEORGIAN LONDON

The layout of much of London's West End has remained very similar to how it was in 1828, when this map was published.

Captain Cook
This Yorkshire-born explorer discovered Australia during a voyage round the world in 1768–71.

Berkeley Square
Built in the 1730s and 1740s in the grounds of the former Berkeley House, several characteristic original houses remain on its west side.

Ironwork
Crafts flourished. This ornate railing is on Manchester Square.

Signatories of the American Declaration of Independence

1811 George III goes mad, his son George is made Regent

1820 George III dies, Prince Regent becomes George IV

1830 George IV dies, brother William IV is king

| 1800 | 1810 | 1820 | 1830 |

1776 Britain loses American colonies with Declaration of Independence

1802 Stock Exchange formally established

1829 London's first horse bus

Victorian London

MUCH OF LONDON TODAY is Victorian. Until the early 19th century, the capital had been confined to the original Roman city, plus Westminster and Mayfair to the west, ringed by fields and villages such as Brompton, Islington and Battersea. From the 1820s these green spaces filled rapidly with terraces of houses for the growing numbers attracted to London by industrialization. Rapid expansion brought challenges to the city. The first cholera epidemic broke out in 1832, and in 1858 came the Great Stink, when the smell from the Thames became so bad that Parliament had to go into recess. But Joseph Bazalgette's sewerage system (1875), involving banking both sides of the Thames, eased the problem.

Queen Victoria in her coronation year (1838)

EXTENT OF THE CITY

☐ 1900   ☐ Today

The building was 560 m (1,850 ft) long and 33 m (110 ft) high.

Nearly 14,000 exhibitors came from all over the world, bringing more than 100,000 exhibits.

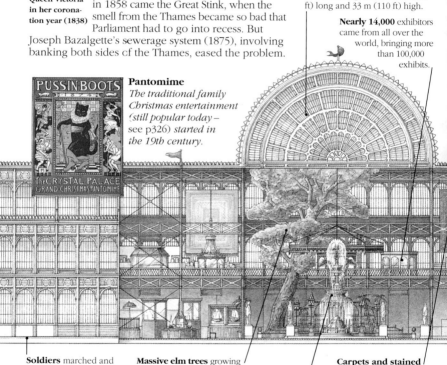

Pantomime
The traditional family Christmas entertainment (still popular today – see p326) started in the 19th century.

PUSS IN BOOTS

The CRYSTAL PALACE GRAND CHRISTMAS PANTOMIME

Soldiers marched and jumped on the floor to test its strength before the exhibition opened.

Massive elm trees growing in Hyde Park were left standing and the exhibition was erected around them.

The Crystal Fountain was 8 m (27 ft) high.

Carpets and stained glass were hung from the galleries.

TIMELINE

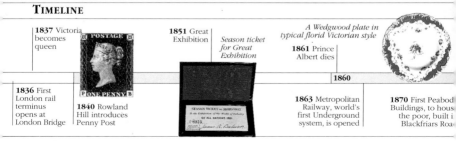

1837 Victoria becomes queen

1851 Great Exhibition

Season ticket for Great Exhibition

A Wedgwood plate in typical florid Victorian style

1861 Prince Albert dies

1860

POSTAGE

ONE PENNY

1836 First London rail terminus opens at London Bridge

1840 Rowland Hill introduces Penny Post

1863 Metropolitan Railway, world's first Underground system, is opened

1870 First Peabody Buildings, to house the poor, built in Blackfriars Road

☐ Victoria's reign

Railways
By 1900 fast trains, such as this Scotch Express, *were crossing the country.*

WHERE TO SEE VICTORIAN LONDON
Grandiose buildings best reflect the spirit of the age, notably the rail termini, the Kensington Museums *(see pp194–209)* and the Royal Albert Hall *(p203)*. Leighton House *(p214)* has a well-preserved interior. Pottery and fabrics are in the Victoria and Albert Museum, and the London Transport Museum *(p114)* has buses, trams and trains.

Telegraph
Newly-invented communications technology, like this telegraph from 1840, made business expansion easier.

Crystal Palace
Between May and October 1851, six million people visited Joseph Paxton's superb feat of engineering. In 1852 it was dismantled and reassembled in south London where it remained until destroyed by fire in 1936.

The Victorian Gothic style suited buildings like the Public Record Office *(p137)*.

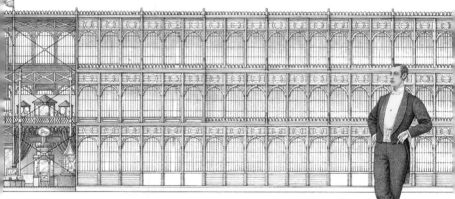

GREAT EXHIBITION OF 1851
The exhibition, held in the Crystal Palace in Hyde Park, celebrated industry, technology and the expanding British Empire.

Formal Dress
Under Victoria, elaborate men's attire was replaced by more restrained evening wear.

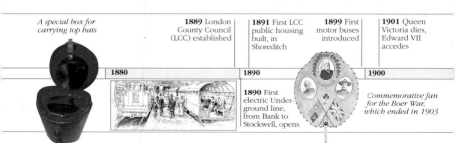

A special box for carrying top hats

1889 London County Council (LCC) established

1891 First LCC public housing built, in Shoreditch

1899 First motor buses introduced

1901 Queen Victoria dies, Edward VII accedes

1880

1890

1900

1890 First electric Underground line, from Bank to Stockwell, opens

Commemorative fan for the Boer War, which ended in 1903

London Between the World Wars

**Art Deco china
by Clarice Cliff**

THE SOCIETY THAT emerged from World War I grasped eagerly at the innovations of early 20th-century London – the motor car, the telephone, commuter transport. The cinema brought transatlantic culture, especially jazz and swing music. Victorian social restraints were discarded as people flocked to dance in restaurants, clubs and dance halls. Many left the crowded inner city for new suburban estates. Then came the 1930s global Depression, whose effects had barely worn off when World War II began.

EXTENT OF THE CITY

☐ *1938*   ☐ *Today*

Formal evening wear, including hats for both sexes, was still compulsory when going to smart West End night spots.

Commuting
London's new outer suburbs were made popular by the underground railway. In the north was "Metroland", named after the Metropolitan line which penetrated Hertfordshire.

High Fashion
The sleek flowing new styles contrasted with the fussy elaboration of the Victorians and Edwardians. This tea gown is from the 1920s.

A LONDON STREET SCENE
Maurice Greiflenhagen's painting (1926) captures the bustle of London after dark.

TIMELINE

Medals, like this from 1914, were struck during the campaign for women's votes.

1910

1910
George V succeeds Edward VII

Cavalry was still used in the Middle Eastern battles of World War I (1914–18).

1921 North Circular Road links northern suburbs

1922 First BBC national radio broadcast

1920

☐ **Interwar period**

Early Cinema
London-born Charlie Chaplin (1889–1977), seen here in City Lights, *was a popular star of both silent and talking pictures.*

Seven new theatres were built in central London from 1924 to 1931.

George VI
Oswald Birley painted this portrait of the king who became a model for wartime resistance and unity.

Early motor buses had open tops, like the old horse-drawn buses.

Communications
The radio provided home entertainment and information. This is a 1933 model.

Throughout the period newspaper circulations increased massively. In 1930 *The Daily Herald* sold 2 million copies a day.

WORLD WAR II AND THE BLITZ
World War II saw large-scale civilian bombing for the first time, bringing the horror of war to Londoners' doorsteps. Thousands were killed in their homes. Many people took refuge in underground stations and children were evacuated to the safety of the country.

WOMEN OF BRITAIN
COME INTO THE FACTORIES

As in World War I, women were recruited for factory work formerly done by men who were away fighting.

Bombing raids in 1940 and 1941 (the Blitz) caused devastation all over the city.

1929 US stock market crash brings world Depression

1939 World War II begins

1927 First talking pictures

1936 Edward VIII abdicates to marry US divorcée Wallis Simpson. George VI accedes

1940 Winston Churchill becomes Prime Minister

Postwar London

MUCH OF LONDON was flattened by World War II bombs. Afterwards, the chance for imaginative rebuilding was missed – some badly designed postwar developments are already being razed. But, by the 1960s, London was such a dynamic world leader in fashion and popular music that *Time* magazine dubbed it "swinging London". Skyscrapers sprang up, but some stayed empty as 1980s boom gave way to 1990s recession.

The Beatles
The Liverpool pop group, pictured in 1965, had rocketed to stardom two years earlier with songs of appealing freshness and directness. The group symbolized carefree 1960s London.

Margaret Thatcher
Britain's first woman Prime Minister (1979–90) promoted the market-led policies that fuelled the 1980s boom.

Festival of Britain
After wartime, the city's morale was lifted by the Festival, marking the 1851 Great Exhibition's centenary (see pp26–7).

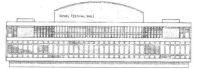

The Royal Festival Hall (1951) was the Festival's centrepiece and is still a landmark *(see pp184–5).*

Telecom Tower (1964), at 180 m (580 ft) high, dominates the Fitzrovia skyline.

The Lloyd's Building (1986) is Richard Rogers's Post-Modernist emblem *(see p159).*

TIMELINE

1948 Olympic Games held in London	**1952** George VI dies; his daughter Elizabeth II accedes	*Minis became a symbol of the 1960s; small and manoeuvrable, they typified the go-as-you-please mood of the decade.*				
1945	1950	1955	1960	1965	1970	1975
1951 Festival of Britain	**1954** Food rationing, introduced during World War II, abolished		**1963** National Theatre founded at the Old Vic		**1977** Queen's silver jubilee; work starts on Jubilee line underground	
1945 End of World War II			**1971** New London Bridge built			

Postwar London

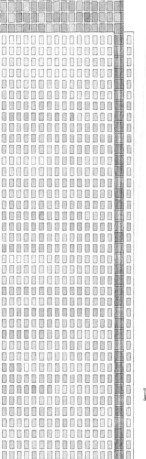

Canada Tower (1991) is London's tallest building, and was designed by César Pelli *(see p245).*

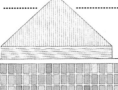

Docklands Light Railway
In the 1980s, new, driver-less trains started to transport people to the developing Docklands.

POST-MODERN ARCHITECTURE

The new wave of archi-tects since the 1980s are reacting against the bleak and stark shapes of the Modernists. Some, like Richard Rogers, are masters of high-tech, emphasizing structural features in their designs. Others, Terry Farrell for example, adopt a more playful approach using pastiches of Classical features such as columns.

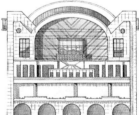

Charing Cross (1991) has Terry Farrell's glasshouse on top of the Victorian station *(see p119).*

YOUTH CULTURE

With their new-found mobility and spending power, young people assumed an influence in the development of British popular culture in the years after World War II. Music, fashion and design were increasingly geared to their rapidly changing tastes.

Punks were a phenomenon of the 1970s and 1980s. Their clothes, music, hair and habits were designed to shock.

The Prince of Wales
As heir to the throne, he is outspokenly critical of much of London's recent architecture. He prefers Classical styles.

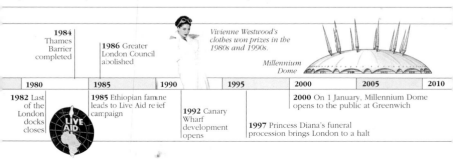

1984 Thames Barrier completed

1986 Greater London Council abolished

Vivienne Westwood's clothes won prizes in the 1980s and 1990s.

Millennium Dome

1980 | 1985 | 1990 | 1995 | 2000 | 2005 | 2010

1982 Last of the London docks closes

1985 Ethiopian famine leads to Live Aid relief campaign

1992 Canary Wharf development opens

2000 On 1 January, Millennium Dome opens to the public at Greenwich

1997 Princess Diana's funeral procession brings London to a halt

Kings and Queens in London

LONDON HAS BEEN the royal capital of England since 1066, when William the Conqueror began a tradition of holding coronations in Westminster Abbey. Since then, successive kings and queens have left their mark on London and many of the places described in this book have royal associations: Henry VIII hunted at Richmond, Charles I was executed on Whitehall and the young Queen Victoria rode on Queensway. Royalty is also celebrated in many of London's traditional ceremonies – for more details on these turn to pages 52–5.

1413–22
Henry V

1509–47
Henry VIII

1399–1413
Henry IV

1485–1509
Henry VII

1066–87 William the Conqueror

1087–1100 William II

1100–35 Henry I

1135–54 Stephen

1327–77 Edward III

1483–5
Richard III

1050	1100	1150	1200	1250	1300	1350	1400	1450	1500
NORMAN		**PLANTAGENET**					**LANCASTER**	**YORK**	**TUDO**
1050	1100	1150	1200	1250	1300	1350	1400	1450	1500

1154–89 Henry II

1189–99 Richard I

1199–1216 John

1216–72 Henry III

1307–27
Edward II

1272–1307 Edward I

1461–70
and
1471–83
Edward IV

1422–61
and 1470–1
Henry VI

1377–99 Richard II

Matthew Paris's 13th-century chronicle showing Kings Richard I, Henry II, John and Henry III

1483 Edward V

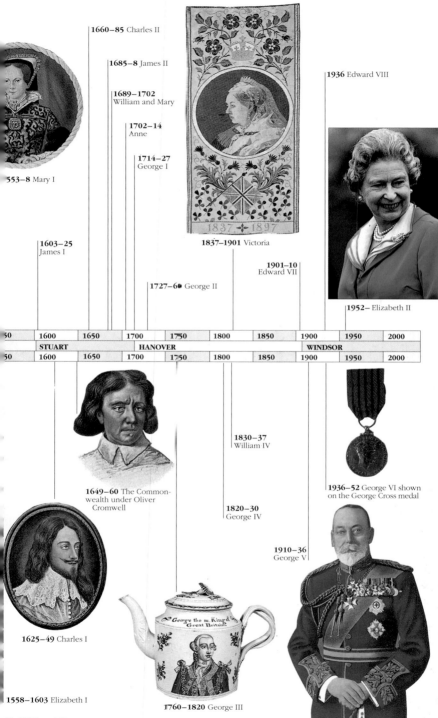

1660–85 Charles II

1685–8 James II

1689–1702 William and Mary

1702–14 Anne

1714–27 George I

1936 Edward VIII

553–8 Mary I

1603–25 James I

1837–1901 Victoria

1901–10 Edward VII

1727–60 George II

1952– Elizabeth II

50	1600	1650	1700	1750	1800	1850	1900	1950	2000
	STUART		HANOVER				WINDSOR		
50	1600	1650	1700	1750	1800	1850	1900	1950	2000

1830–37 William IV

1649–60 The Commonwealth under Oliver Cromwell

1936–52 George VI shown on the George Cross medal

1820–30 George IV

1910–36 George V

1625–49 Charles I

1760–1820 George III

1558–1603 Elizabeth I

47–53 Edward VI

LONDON AT A GLANCE

THERE ARE NEARLY 300 places of interest described in the Area by Area section of this book. These range from the cheerful Museum of the Moving Image *(see p184)* to gruesome Old St Thomas's Operating Theatre *(p176)*, and from ancient Charterhouse *(p164)* to modern Canary Wharf *(p245)*. To help you make the most of your stay, the following 20 pages are a time-saving guide to the best London has to offer. Museums and galleries, churches, and parks and gardens each have a section, and there are guides to famous Londoners and ceremonies in London. Each sight mentioned is cross-referenced to its own full entry. Below are the ten top tourist attractions to start you off.

LONDON'S TOP TEN TOURIST ATTRACTIONS

St Paul's
See pp148–51.

Hampton Court
See pp254–7.

Changing the Guard
Buckingham Palace, see pp94–5.

British Museum
See pp126–9.

National Gallery
See pp104–7.

Westminster Abbey
See pp76–9.

Madame Tussaud's
See p220.

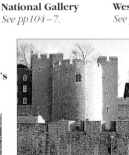

Houses of Parliament
See pp72–3.

Tower of London
See pp154–7.

Victoria and Albert Museum
See pp198–201.

Westminster Bridge and the Houses of Parliament

Celebrated Visitors and Residents

Many famous Londoners are famous for *being* Londoners – Samuel Pepys, Christopher Wren, Dr Samuel Johnson, Charles Dickens and countless others (*see pp38–9*). However, as a centre of international culture, commerce and politics, the English capital has also always attracted celebrated people from overseas. Some famous visitors were escaping war or persecution at home, others came to work or study, or as tourists. In some cases, their association with London is little-known and surprising.

Mary Seacole *(1805–81)*
The Jamaican-born writer and nurse in the Crimean War lodged first in Tavistock Street, then Cambridge Street, Paddington.

Regent's Park and Marylebone

Richard Wagner *(1813–83)*
In 1877 the German opera composer lived at No. 12 Orme Square, Bayswater, from where he would walk across the park to conduct at the Royal Albert Hall (see p203).

South Kensington and Knightsbridge

Kensington and Holland Park

Henry James *(1843–1916)*
The American novelist lived at No. 3 Bolton Street, Mayfair then at No. 34 de Vere Gardens, Kensington (1886–92). He died at Carlyle Mansions, Cheyne Walk.

Dwight Eisenhower *(1890–1969)*
During World War II he planned the North African invasion in a house on Grosvenor Square, Mayfair.

Chelsea

Mark Twain *(1835–1910)*
Huckleberry Finn's American creator lived from 1896 until 1897 at No. 23 Tedworth Square.

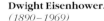

Jenny Lind *(1827–87)*
The "Swedish Nightingale" lived for a time at No. 189 Old Brompton Road, Kensington.

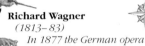

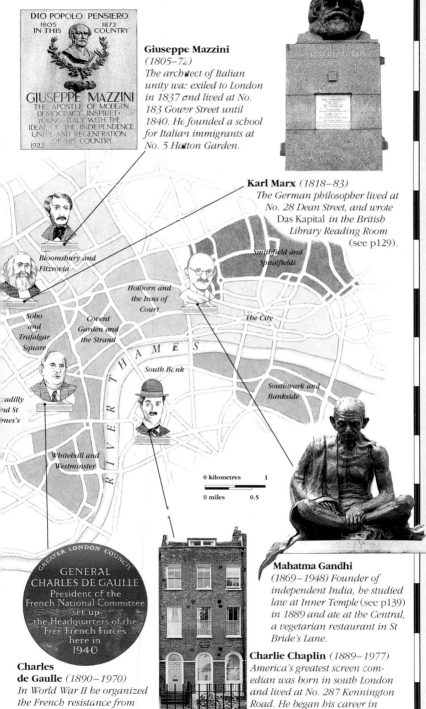

DIO POPOLO PENSIERO
1805   1872
IN THIS   COUNTRY

GIUSEPPE MAZZINI
THE APOSTLE OF MODERN
DEMOCRACY, INSPIRED
YOUNG ITALY WITH THE
IDEAL OF THE INDEPENDENCE,
UNITY AND REGENERATION
OF HIS COUNTRY
1922

Giuseppe Mazzini
(1805–72)
*The architect of Italian
unity was exiled to London
in 1837 and lived at No.
183 Gower Street until
1840. He founded a school
for Italian immigrants at
No. 5 Hatton Garden.*

WORKERS OF ALL LANDS
UNITE

Karl Marx *(1818–83)*
*The German philosopher lived at
No. 28 Dean Street, and wrote*
Das Kapital *in the British
Library Reading Room
(see p129).*

*Bloomsbury and
Fitzrovia*

*Smithfield and
Spitalfields*

*Holborn and
the Inns of
Court*

The City

*Soho
and
Trafalgar
Square*

*Covent
Garden and
the Strand*

South Bank

*Southwark and
Bankside*

*adilly
nd St
mes's*

*Whitehall and
Westminster*

0 kilometres   1

0 miles   0.5

GREATER LONDON COUNCIL

GENERAL
CHARLES DE GAULLE
President of the
French National Committee
set up
the Headquarters of the
Free French Forces
here in
1940

Mahatma Gandhi
*(1869–1948) Founder of
independent India, he studied
law at Inner Temple (see p139)
in 1889 and ate at the Central,
a vegetarian restaurant in St
Bride's Lane.*

Charlie Chaplin *(1889–1977)*
*America's greatest screen com-
edian was born in south London
and lived at No. 287 Kennington
Road. He began his career in
London's music halls.*

**Charles
de Gaulle** *(1890–1970)*
*In World War II he organized
the French resistance from
Carlton House Terrace.*

Remarkable Londoners

Venus Venticordia by Dante Gabriel Rossetti

LONDON HAS ALWAYS been a gathering place for the most prominent and influential people of their times. Some of these figures have come to London from other parts of Britain or from countries further afield; others have been Londoners, born and bred. All of them have left their mark on London, by designing great and lasting buildings, establishing institutions and traditions, and by writing about or painting the city they knew. Most of them have also had an influence on their times that spread out from London to the rest of the world.

Caricature of the Duke of Wellington

ARCHITECTS AND ENGINEERS

John Nash's Theatre Royal Haymarket (1821)

A NUMBER OF people who built London still have works standing. Inigo Jones (1573–1652), London-born, was the father of English Renaissance architecture. He was also a landscape painter and a stage designer. Jones lived and worked at Great Scotland Yard, Whitehall, then the residence of the royal architect – the post in which he was later succeeded by Sir Christopher Wren (1632–1723).

Wren's successors as the prime architects of London were his protégé Nicholas Hawksmoor (1661–1736) and James Gibbs (1682–1754). Succeeding generations each produced architects who were to stamp their genius on the city: in the 18th century the brothers Robert (1728–92) and James Adam (1730–94), then John Nash (1752–1835), Sir Charles Barry (1795–1860), Decimus Burton (1800–81), and the Victorians Alfred Waterhouse (1830–1905),

Norman Shaw (1831–1912) and Sir George Gilbert Scott (1811–78). The engineer Sir Joseph Bazalgette (1819–91) built London's sewer system and the Thames Embankment.

ARTISTS

P AINTERS IN LONDON, as elsewhere, often lived in enclaves, for mutual support and because they shared common priorities. During the 18th century, artists clustered around the court at St James's to be near their patrons. Thus both William Hogarth (1697–1764) and Sir Joshua Reynolds (1723–92) lived and worked in Leicester Square, while Thomas Gainsborough (1727–88) lived in Pall Mall. (Hogarth's Chiswick house was his place in the country.)

Later, Cheyne Walk in Chelsea, with its river views, became popular with artists, including the masters J M W Turner (1775–1851), James McNeill Whistler (1834–1903), Dante Gabriel Rossetti (1828–82), Philip Wilson Steer (1860–1942) and the sculptor

HISTORIC LONDON HOMES

Four writers' homes that have been recreated and are open to visitors are those of the romantic poet **John Keats** (1795–1821), where he fell in love with Fanny Brawne; the historian **Thomas Carlyle** (1795–1881); the lexicographer **Dr Samuel Johnson** (1709–84); and the prolific and popular novelist **Charles Dickens** (1812–70). The house that the architect **Sir John Soane** (1753–1837) designed for himself remains largely as it was when he died, as does the house where the psychiatrist **Sigmund Freud** (1856–1939) settled after fleeing from the Nazis before the outbreak of World War II.

The Hyde Park Corner house of the **Duke of Wellington** (1769–1852), hero of the Battle of Waterloo, has been lovingly refurbished. Finally, the rooms of Sir Arthur Conan Doyle's fictional detective **Sherlock Holmes** have been created in Baker Street.

Dickens House

Carlyle's House

PLAQUES

All over London the former homes of well-known figures are marked by plaques. Look out for these, especially in Chelsea, Kensington and Mayfair, and see how many names you recognize.

SIR WINSTON CHURCHILL Lived in a house on this site 1921–1924
No. 3 Sussex Square, Kensington

HISTORIC HOUSE GEORGE ORWELL 1903–1950 NOVELIST & ESSAYIST LIVED AT 27b 1945 LONDON BOROUGH OF ISLINGTON
No. 27b Lawford Road, Islington

LCC ROBERT FALCON SCOTT ANTARCTIC EXPLORER (1868–1912) Lived here
No. 56 Oakley Street, Chelsea

Sir Jacob Epstein (1880–1959). Augustus John (1879–1961) and John Singer Sargent (1856–1925) had studios in Tite Street. John Constable (1776–1837) is best known as a Suffolk painter but lived for a while at Hampstead, from where he painted many fine views of the heath.

WRITERS

GEOFFREY CHAUCER (c.1345–1400), author of *The Canterbury Tales*, was born in Upper Thames Street, the son of an innkeeper. Both the playwrights William Shakespeare (1564–1616) and Christopher Marlowe (1564–93) were associated with the theatres in Southwark, and may have lived nearby.

The poets John Donne (1572–1631) and John Milton (1608–74) were both born in Bread Street in the City. Donne, after a profligate youth, became Dean of St Paul's. The diarist Samuel Pepys (1633–1703) was born off Fleet Street.

The young novelist Jane Austen (1775–1817) lived briefly off Sloane Street, near the Cadogan Hotel, where the flamboyant Oscar Wilde (1854–1900) was arrested in 1895 for homosexuality. Playwright George Bernard Shaw (1856–1950) lived at No. 29 Fitzroy Square in Bloomsbury. Later the same house was home to Virginia Woolf (1882–1941) and

George Bernard Shaw

became a meeting place for the Bloomsbury Group of writers and artists, which included Vanessa Bell, John Maynard Keynes, E M Forster, Roger Fry and Duncan Grant.

LEADERS

IN LEGEND, a penniless boy named Dick Whittington came to London with his cat seeking streets paved with gold, and later became Lord Mayor. In fact, Richard Whittington (c.1360?–1423), Lord Mayor three times between 1397 and 1420 and one of London's most celebrated early politicians, was the son of a noble. Sir Thomas More (1478–1535), a Chelsea resident, was Henry VIII's chancellor until they quarrelled over the king's break with the Catholic church and Henry ordered More's execution. More was canonized in 1935. Sir Thomas Gresham (1519?–79) founded the Royal Exchange. Sir Robert Peel (1788–1850) started the London police force, who were known as "bobbies" after him.

ACTORS

NELL GWYNNE (1650–87) won more fame as King Charles II's mistress than as an actress. However, she did appear on stage at Drury Lane Theatre; she also sold oranges there. The Shakespearean actor Edmund Kean (1789–1833) and the great

tragic actress Sarah Siddons (1755–1831) were more distinguished players at Drury Lane. So were Henry Irving (1838–1905) and Ellen Terry (1847–1928), whose stage partnership lasted 24 years. Charlie Chaplin (1889–1977, born in Kennington, had a poverty-stricken childhood in the slums of London.

In the 20th century, a school of fine actors blossomed at the Old Vic, including Sir John Gielgud (1904–), Sir Ralph Richardson (1902–83), Dame Peggy Ashcroft (1907–91) and Laurence (later Lord) Olivier (1907–89), who was appointed the first director of the National Theatre.

Laurence Olivier

WHERE TO FIND HISTORIC LONDON HOMES

London's Best: Museums and Galleries

L ONDON'S MUSEUMS ARE FILLED with an astonishing diversity of treasures from all over the world. This map highlights 15 of the city's most important galleries and museums whose exhibits cater to most interests. Some of these collections started from the legacies of 18th- and 19th-century explorers, traders and collectors. Others specialize in one aspect of art, history, science or technology. A more detailed overview of London's museums and galleries is on pages 42–3.

British Museum
This Anglo-Saxon helmet is part of a massive collection of antiquities.

Wallace Collection
Frans Hals's Laughing Cavalier *is a star attraction in this museum of art, furniture, armour and* objets d'art.

Royal Academy of Arts
Major international art exhibitions are held here, and the renowned Summer Exhibition, when works are on sale, takes place every year.

Regent's Park and Marylebone

Kensington and Holland Park

South Kensington and Knightsbridge

Picca an St Jar

Science Museum
Newcomen's steam engine of 1712 is just one of many exhibits that cater for both novice and expert.

Chelsea

Natural History Museum
All of life is here, with vivid displays on everything from dinosaurs (like this Triceratops skull) to butterflies.

Victoria and Albert
It is the world's largest museum of decorative arts. This Indian vase is 18th-century.

0 kilometres 1
0 miles 0.5

National Portrait Gallery

Important British figures are documented in paintings and photographs. This is Vivien Leigh, by Angus McBean (1954).

National Gallery

The world-famous paintings in its collection are mainly European and date from the 15th to the 19th centuries.

Museum of London

London's history since prehistoric times is told with exhibits like this 1920s lift door.

Tower of London

Crown Jewels and the Royal Armouries are here. This armour was worn by a 14th-century Italian knight.

Design Museum

New inventions and prototypes sit next to familiar, everyday objects from past and present.

Bloomsbury and Fitzrovia

Smithfield and Spitalfields

Holborn and the Inns of Court

The City

Soho and Trafalgar Square

Covent Garden and the Strand

THAMES

Southwark and Bankside

South Bank

Whitehall and Westminster

RIVER THAMES

Courtauld Institute

Well-known works, such as Manet's Bar at the Folies Bergère, line its galleries.

Tate Gallery

Two outstanding national collections, of British art from 1550 and of international modern art, are housed here.

Imperial War Museum

It uses displays, film and special effects to recreate 20th-century battles. This is one of the earliest tanks.

Museum of the Moving Image

Actors and life-sized models, like this film director, bring the cinema to life.

Exploring Museums and Galleries

Austin Mini, exhibited at the Design Museum

LONDON BOASTS astonishingly rich and diverse museums, the product, in part, of centuries at the hub of world-wide trade and a far-flung Empire. The world-renowned collections cannot be missed, but do not neglect the city's range of smaller museums. From buses to fans, these cover every imaginable speciality and are often more peaceful than their grander counterparts.

Geffrye Museum: Art Nouveau Room

ANTIQUITIES AND ARCHAEOLOGY

SOME OF THE most celebrated artefacts of ancient Asia, Egypt, Greece and Rome are housed in the **British Museum**. Other antiquities, including books, manuscripts, paintings, busts and gems, are displayed in **Sir John Soane's Museum**, which is one of the most idiosyncratic to be found in London.

The **Museum of London** contains much of archaeological interest from all periods of the city's history.

FURNITURE AND INTERIORS

THE MUSEUM OF LONDON recreates typical domestic and commercial interiors from the Roman period right up to the present day. The **Victoria and Albert Museum** (or V&A) contains complete rooms rescued from now vanished buildings, plus a magnificent collection of furniture ranging from the 16th century to work by contemporary designers.

Design Museum display of chairs

Eclectic collection at Sir John Soane's Museum

On a more modest scale, the **Geffrye Museum** consists of fully-furnished period rooms dating from 1600 to the 1990s. Writers' houses, such as the **Freud Museum**, give insights into the furniture of specific periods, while the **Linley Sambourne House** offers visitors a perfectly preserved example of a late Victorian interior.

COSTUME AND JEWELLERY

THE V&A'S VAST collections include English and European clothes of the last 400 years, and some stunning jewellery from China, India and Japan. The priceless Crown Jewels, at the **Tower of London**, should also not be missed. **Kensington Palace** Court Dress Collection opens a window on Court uniforms and protocol from about 1750. The **Theatre Museum** has displays of costumes, props and other memorabilia, while the **British Museum** displays ancient Aztec, Mayan and African costume.

CRAFTS AND DESIGN

ONCE AGAIN, the **Victoria and Albert Musuem** (V&A) is the essential first port of call; its collections in these fields remain unrivalled. The **William Morris Gallery** shows every aspect of the 19th-century designer's work within the Arts and Crafts movement. For more modern craft and design, the **Design Museum** focuses on mass-produced goods, while the **Crafts Council Gallery** displays (and sometimes sells) contemporary British craftwork.

MILITARY ARTIFACTS

THE NATIONAL ARMY MUSEUM uses vivid models and displays to narrate the history of the British Army from the reign of Henry VII to to the present. The crack regiments of Foot Guards, who are the elite of the British Army, are the main focus of the **Guards' Museum**. The Royal Armouries in the **Tower of London**, Britain's oldest public museum, hold part of the national collection of arms and armour; the **Wallace Collection** also has a display. In the **Imperial War Museum** re-creations of World War I trenches and the 1940 Blitz show war as it really was. The **Florence Nightingale Museum** illustrates the hardships of 19th-century warfare.

TOYS AND CHILDHOOD

TEDDY BEARS, toy soldiers, dolls' houses and Dinky cars are just some of the toys in the **London Toy and Model Museum**. Pollock's **Toy Museum** offers a similar collection, including Eric, "the oldest known teddy-bear". The **Bethnal Green Museum of Childhood** and the **Museum of London** are slightly more formal, but still fun, and illustrate aspects of the social history of childhood.

SCIENCE AND NATURAL HISTORY

COMPUTERS, ELECTRICITY, space exploration, industrial processes, and transport are all featured at the **Science Museum**. Transport enthusiasts are also catered for at the **London Transport Museum**. There are other specialized museums, too, such as the **Faraday Museum**, of the development of electricity; the **Kew Bridge Steam Museum**; and the **Museum of the Moving Image**. The **National Maritime Museum** and the Royal Observatory chart both maritime history and the creation of GMT, by which the world still sets its clocks.

Samson and Delilah (1620) by Van Dyck at the Dulwich Picture Gallery

The **Natural History Museum** mixes displays of animal and bird life with ecological exhibits The **Museum of Garden History** is devoted to the favourite British pastime.

Imperial War Museum

VISUAL ARTS

THE PARTICULAR STRENGTHS of the **National Gallery** are early Renaissance Italian and 17th-century Spanish painting and a wonderful collection of Dutch masters. The **Tate Gallery** specializes in 20th-century art from both Europe and America, and British paintings of all periods; the Clore Gallery is devoted to the work of Turner. The **V&A** is strong on European art of 1500–1900 and British art of 1700–1900. The **Royal Academy** and the **Hayward**

Stone Dancer (1913) by Gaudier-Brzeska at the Tate Gallery

Gallery specialize in major temporary exhibitions. The **Courtauld Institute** contains Impressionist and Post-Impressionist works, while the **Wallace Collection** has 17th-century Dutch and 18th-century French paintings. The **Dulwich Picture Gallery** includes works by Rembrandt, Rubens, Poussin and Gainsborough. **Kenwood House** is home to paintings by Reynolds, Gainsborough and Rubens in fine Adam interiors. Details of temporary exhibitions are in listings magazines *(see p324).*

London's Best: Churches

IT IS WORTH stopping to look at London's churches and going in, if they're open. They have a special atmosphere unmatched elsewhere in the city, and they can often yield an intimate glimpse of the past. Many churches have replaced earlier buildings in a steady succession, dating back to pre-Christian times. Some began life in outlying villages beyond London's fortified centre, and were absorbed into suburbs when the city expanded in the 18th century. The memorials in the capital's churches and church-yards are a fascinating record of local life, liberally peppered with famous names. A more detailed overview of London churches is on pages 46–7.

All Souls
This plaque comes from a tomb in John Nash's Regency church of 1824.

St Paul's Covent Garden
Inigo Jones's Classical church was known as "the handsomest barn in England".

Regent's Park and Marylebone

Bloomsbury and Fitzrovia

Soho and Trafalgar Square

Piccadilly and St James's

St Martin-in-the-Fields
James Gibbs's church of 1722–6 was originally thought "too gay" for Protestant worship.

South Kensington and Knightsbridge

0 kilometres   1
0 miles   0.5

Whitehall Westmins

Westminster Cathedral
The Italian-Byzantine Catholic cathedral's red-and-white brick exterior conceals a rich interior of multicoloured marbles.

Westminster Abbey
The famous abbey has the most glorious medieval architecture in London, and highly impressive tombs and monuments.

Brompton Oratory
This sumptuous Baroque church was decorated with works by Italian artists.

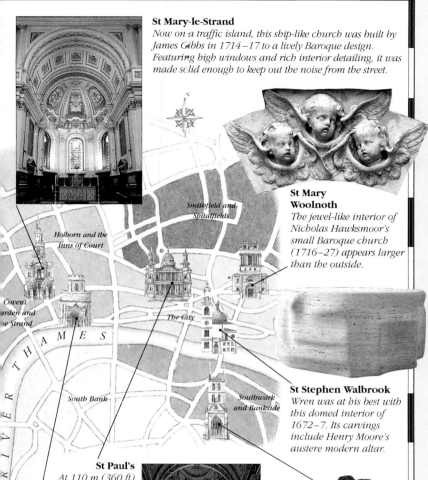

St Mary-le-Strand
Now on a traffic island, this ship-like church was built by James Gibbs in 1714–17 to a lively Baroque design. Featuring high windows and rich interior detailing, it was made solid enough to keep out the noise from the street.

Smithfield and Spitalfields

Holborn and the Inns of Court

Covent Garden and the Strand

The City

St Mary Woolnoth
The jewel-like interior of Nicholas Hawksmoor's small Baroque church (1716–27) appears larger than the outside.

South Bank

Southwark and Bankside

St Stephen Walbrook
Wren was at his best with this domed interior of 1672–7. Its carvings include Henry Moore's austere modern altar.

St Paul's
At 110 m (360 ft) high, the dome of Wren's cathedral is the world's second largest after St Peter's in Rome.

Temple Church
Built in the 12th and 13th centuries for the Knights Templar, it is one of the few circular churches to survive in England.

Southwark Cathedral
This largely 13th-century priory church was not designated a cathedral until 1905. It has a fine medieval choir.

RIVER THAMES

Exploring Churches

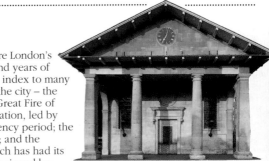

THE CHURCH SPIRES that puncture London's skyline span nearly a thousand years of the city's history. They form an index to many of the events that have shaped the city – the Norman Conquest (1066); the Great Fire of London (1666); the great restoration, led by Wren, that followed it; the Regency period; the confidence of the Victorian era; and the devastation of World War II. Each has had its effect on the churches, many designed by the most influential architects of their times.

St Paul's, Covent Garden

MEDIEVAL CHURCHES

THE MOST FAMOUS old church to survive the Great Fire of 1666 is the superb 13th-century **Westminster Abbey**, the church of the Coronation, with its tombs of British monarchs and heroes. Less well known are the well-hidden Norman church of **St Bartholomew-the-Great**, London's oldest church, (1123), the circular **Temple Church** founded in 1160 by the Knights Templars and **Southwark Cathedral**, set amid Victorian railway lines and warehouses. **Chelsea Old Church** is a charming village church near the river.

CHURCHES BY JONES

INIGO JONES (1573–1652) was Shakespeare's contemporary, and his works were almost as revolutionary as the great dramatist's. Jones's Classical churches of the 1620s and 1630s shocked a public used to conservative Gothic finery. By far the best-known is **St Paul's Church** of the 1630s, the centrepiece of Jones's Italian-style piazza in Covent Garden. **Queen's Chapel, St James** was built in 1623 for Queen Henrietta Maria, the Catholic wife of Charles I. It was the first Classical church in England and has a magnificent interior but is, unfortunately, usually closed to the public.

CHURCHES BY HAWKSMOOR

NICHOLAS HAWKSMOOR (1661–1736) was Wren's most talented pupil, and his churches are among the finest

SPIRES

Look out for London's richly-decorated church steeples. Here are four of the city's most distinctive to get you started.

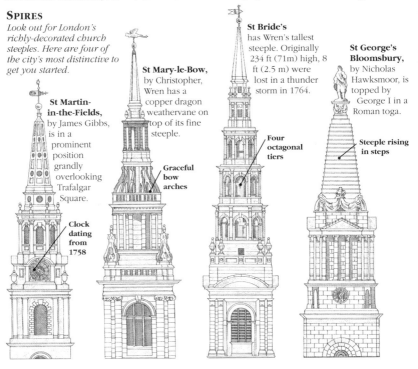

St Martin-in-the-Fields, by James Gibbs, is in a prominent position grandly overlooking Trafalgar Square.

Clock dating from 1758

St Mary-le-Bow, by Christopher, Wren has a copper dragon weathervane on top of its fine steeple.

Graceful bow arches

St Bride's has Wren's tallest steeple. Originally 234 ft (71m) high, 8 ft (2.5 m) were lost in a thunder storm in 1764.

Four octagonal tiers

St George's Bloomsbury, by Nicholas Hawksmoor, is topped by George I in a Roman toga.

Steeple rising in steps

Baroque buildings to be found in Britain. **St George's, Bloomsbury** (1716–31) has an unusual centralized plan and a pyramid steeple topped by a statue of King George I. **St Mary Woolnoth** is a tiny jewel of 1716–27, and further east **Christ Church, Spitalfields** is a Baroque tour-de-force of 1714–29, now being restored.

Among Hawksmoor's East End churches are the stunning **St Anne's, Limehouse** and **St Alfege**, of 1714–17, which is across the river in Greenwich. The tower on this temple-like church was added later by John James in 1730.

St Anne's, Limehouse

CHURCHES BY GIBBS

JAMES GIBBS (1682–1754) more conservative than his Baroque contemporaries such as Hawksmoor, and he also kept his distance from the Neo-Classical trend so popular after 1720. His idiosyncratic London churches were enormously influential. **St Mary-le-Strand** (1714–17) is an island church which appears to be sailing down the Strand. The radical design of **St Martin-in-the-Fields** (1722–6) predates its setting, Trafalgar Square, by a hundred years.

REGENCY CHURCHES

THE END OF the Napoleonic Wars in 1815 brought a flurry of church building. The need for churches in London's new suburbs fused with a Greek Revival. The

CHRISTOPHER WREN

Sir Christopher Wren (1632–1723) was leader among the many architects who helped restore London after the Great Fire of London. He devised a new city plan, replacing the narrow streets with wide avenues radiating from piazzas. His plan was rejected, but he was commissioned to build 52 new churches; 31 have survived various threats of demolition and the bombs of World War II, although six are shells. Wren's great masterpiece is the massive St Paul's, while nearby is splendid **St Stephen Walbrook**, his domed church of 1672–77. Other landmarks are **St Bride's**, off Fleet Street, said to have inspired the traditional shape of wedding cakes, **St Mary-le-Bow** in Cheapside and **St Magnus Martyr** in Lower Thames Street. Wren's own favourite was **St James's, Piccadilly** (1683–4). Smaller gems are **St Clement Danes**, Strand (1680–82) and **St James, Garlickhythe** (1674–87).

results may lack the exuberance of Hawksmoor, but they have an austere elegance of their own. **All Souls, Langham Place** (1822–4), at the north end of Regent Street, was built by the Prince Regent's favourite, John Nash, who was ridiculed at the time for its unusual combination of design styles. Also worth visiting is **St Pancras**, a Greek Revival church of 1819–22, which is typical of the period.

VICTORIAN CHURCHES

LONDON HAS SOME of the finest 19th-century churches in Europe. Grand and colourful, their riotous decoration is in marked contrast to the chaste Neo-Classicism of the preceding Regency era. Perhaps the best of the capital's late Victorian churches is **Westminster Cathedral**, a

stunningly rich, Italianate Catholic cathedral built in 1895–1903, with architecture by J F Bentley and *Stations of the Cross* reliefs by Eric Gill. **Brompton Oratory** is a grand Baroque revival, based on a church in Rome and filled with magnificent furnishings from all over Catholic Europe.

WHERE TO FIND THE CHURCHES

Brompton Oratory

London's Best: Parks and Gardens

SINCE MEDIEVAL TIMES London has had large expanses of green. Some of these, such as Hampstead Heath, were originally common land, where small-holders could graze their animals. Others, such as Richmond Park and Holland Park, were royal hunting grounds or the gardens of large houses; several still have formal features dating from those times. Today you can cross much of central London by walking from St James's Park in the east to Kensington Gardens in the west. Purpose-built parks, like Battersea, and botanical gardens, like Kew, appeared later.

Hampstead Heath
This breezy, open space is located in the midst of north London. Nearby Parliament Hill offers views of St Paul's, the City and the West End.

Kensington Gardens
This plaque is from the Italian Garden, one of the features of this elegant park.

Holland Park
The former grounds of one of London's grandest homes are now its most romantic park.

Kew Gardens
The world's premier botanic garden is a must for anyone with an interest in plants, exotic or mundane.

Richmond Park
The biggest royal park in London remains largely unspoiled, with deer and magnificent river views.

0 kilometres   1

0 miles   0.5

Regent's Park
*In this civilized park
surrounded by fine
Regency buildings, you
can stroll around the
rose garden, visit the
open-air theatre, or
simply sit and admire
the view.*

Greenwich Park
*Its focal point is the National
Maritime Museum, well worth
a visit for its architecture as
well as its exhibits. There
are also fine views.*

Hyde Park
*The Serpentine is one of the
highlights of a park which also
boasts restaurants, an art
gallery and
Speakers' Corner.*

Regent's
Park and
Marylebone

Bloomsbury
and Fitzrovia

Holborn
and the
Inns of
Court

Smithfield
and Spitalfields

Soho and
Trafalgar
Square

Piccadilly

The City

R I V E R T H A M E S

The
South-
bank

Southwark
and Bankside

Whitehall and
Westminster

N

Greenwich
and Blackheath

Green Park
*Its leafy paths are favoured
by early-morning joggers
from the Mayfair hotels.*

St James's Park
*People come here to feed
the ducks, or watch the
pelicans. A band plays
throughout the summer.*

Battersea Park
*Visitors can hire a
rowing boat for the
best view of the
Victorian landscaping
around the lake.*

Exploring Parks and Gardens

LONDON HAS ONE of the the world's greenest city centres, full of tree-filled squares and grassy parks. From the intimacy of the Chelsea Physic Garden, to the wild, open spaces of Hampstead Heath, every London park has its own charm and character. For those looking for a specific outdoor attraction – such as sports, wildlife or flowers – here is a list of the most interesting London parks.

Camilla japonica

FLOWER GARDENS

THE BRITISH are famed for their gardens and love of flowers and this is reflected in several of London's parks. Really keen gardeners will find all they ever wanted to know at **Kew Gardens** and the **Chelsea Physic Garden**, which is especially strong on herbs. Closer to the centre of town, **St James's Park** boasts some spectacular flower beds, filled with bulbs and bedding plants, which are changed every season. **Hyde Park** sports a magnificent show of daffodils and crocuses in the spring and London's best rose garden is Queen Mary's in **Regent's Park**. **Kensington Gardens'** flower walk has an exemplary English mixed border, and there is also a delightful small 17th-century garden at the **Museum of Garden History**.

Battersea Park also has a charming flower garden, and indoor gardeners should head to the **Barbican Centre's** well-stocked conservatory.

FORMAL GARDENS

THE MOST SPECTACULAR formal garden is at **Hampton Court**, which has a network of gardens from different periods, starting with Tudor. The gardens at **Chiswick**

Embankment Gardens

House remain dotted with their 18th-century statuary and pavilions. Other restored gardens include 17th-century **Ham House**, and **Osterley Park**, whose 18th-century layout was retraced through the art of dowsing. **Fenton House** has a really fine walled garden; **Kenwood** is less formal, with its woodland area. **The Hill** is great in summer. The sunken garden at **Kensington Palace** has a formal layout and **Holland Park** has flowers around its statues.

RESTFUL CORNERS

LONDON'S SQUARES are cool, shady retreats but, sadly, many are reserved for key-holders, usually residents of the surrounding houses. Of those open to all, **Russell Square** is the largest and most secluded. **Berkeley Square** is open but barren. **Green Park**, with its shady trees and deck chairs, offers a cool picnic spot right in central London. The Inns of Court provide some really pleasant havens: **Gray's Inn** gardens, **Middle Temple**

Sunken garden at Kensington Palace

GREEN LONDON

In Greater London there are 1,700 parks covering a total of 67 sq miles (174 sq km). This land is home to some 2,000 types of plant and 100 bird species who breed in the trees. Trees help the city to breathe, manufacturing oxygen from the polluted air. Here are some of the species you are most likely to see in London.

The London plane, now the most common tree in London, grows along many streets.

The English oak grows all over Europe. The Royal Navy used to build ships from it.

gardens and **Lincoln's Inn Fields**. **Soho Square**, which is surrounded by streets, is more urban and animated.

MUSIC IN SUMMER

STRETCHING OUT on the grass or in a deck chair to listen to a band is a British tradition. Military and other bands give regular concerts throughout the summer at **St James's** and **Regent's Parks** and also at **Parliament Hill Fields**. The concert schedule will usually be found posted up close to the bandstand in the park.

Open-air festivals of classical music are held in the summer in several parks (see p331).

WILDLIFE

THERE IS A LARGE and well-fed collection of ducks and other water birds, even including a few pelicans, in **St James's Park**. Duck lovers will also appreciate **Regent's**, **Hyde** and **Battersea Parks**, as well as **Hampstead Heath**. Deer roam in **Richmond** and **Greenwich Parks**. For a wide variety of captive animals, **London Zoo** is in **Regent's Park** and there are aviaries or aquariums at several parks and gardens, including **Kew Gardens** and **Syon House**.

Geese in St James's Park

HISTORIC CEMETERIES

In the late 1830s a ring of private cemeteries was established around London to ease the pressure on the monstrously overcrowded and unhealthy burial grounds of the inner city. Today some of these (notably **Highgate Cemetery** and Kensal Green – Harrow Road W10) are worth visiting for their air of repose and their Victorian monuments. **Bunhill Fields** is earlier; it was first used during the plague of 1665.

Kensal Green cemetery

Boating pond at Regent's Park

SPORTS

CYCLING IS NOT universally encouraged in London's parks, and footpaths tend to be too bumpy to allow much rollerskating. However, most parks have tennis courts, which normally have to be reserved in advance with the attendant. Rowing boats may be hired at **Hyde**, **Regent's** and **Battersea Parks**, among others. Athletics tracks are at both Battersea Park and also **Parliament Hill**. The public may swim at the ponds on **Hampstead Heath** and in the Serpentine in Hyde Park. Hampstead Heath is also ideal kite-flying territory.

WHERE TO FIND THE PARKS

The common beech has a close relation, the copper beech, with reddish purple leaves.

The horse chestnut's hard round fruits are used by children for a game called conkers.

London's Best: Ceremonies

MUCH OF LONDON'S rich inheritance of tradition and ceremony centres on royalty. Faithfully enacted today, some of these ceremonies date back to the Middle Ages, when the ruling monarch had absolute power and had to be protected from opponents. This map shows the venues for some of the most important ceremonies in London. For more details on these and other ceremonies please turn to pages 54–5; information on all sorts of events taking place in London throughout the year can be found on pages 56–9.

St James's Palace and Buckingham Palace
Members of the Queen's Life Guard stand at Horse Guard's Arch. The Guard is changed daily at 11am.

Bloomsbu and Fitzro

Soho and Trafalgar Square

South Kensington and Knightsbridge

Piccadilly and St James's

Hyde Park
Royal Salutes are fired by six guns of the King's Troop Royal Horse Artillery on royal anniversaries and ceremonial occasions.

Whitehall and Westminster

Chelsea

Chelsea Hospital
In 1651 Charles II hid from parliamentary forces in an oak tree. On Oak Apple Day, Chelsea Pensioners decorate his statue with oak leaves and branches.

Horse Guards
At Trooping the Colour, the most elaborate of London's royal ceremonies, the Queen salutes as a battalion of Foot Guards parades its colours before her.

The City and Embankment
At the Lord Mayor's Show, pikemen and musketeers escort the newly elected Lord Mayor through the City in a gold state coach.

Holborn and the
Inns of Court

vent
en and
Strand

The City

R I V E R   T H A M E S

South Bank

Southwark and
Bankside

The Cenotaph
On Remembrance Sunday the Queen pays homage to the nation's war dead.

0 kilometres   1

0 miles   0.5

Tower of London
In the nightly Ceremony of the Keys, a Yeoman Warder locks the gates. A military escort ensures the keys are not stolen.

Houses of Parliament
Each autumn the Queen goes to Parliament in the Irish State Coach, to open the new parliamentary session.

Attending London's Ceremonies

ROYALTY AND COMMERCE provide the two principal sources of London's rich calendar of ceremonial events. Quaint and old-fashioned these events may be, but what may seem arcane ritual has real historical meaning – many of the capital's ceremonies originated in the the Middle Ages.

ROYAL CEREMONIES

ALTHOUGH THE Queen's role is now largely symbolic, the Guard at Buckingham Palace still actively patrols the palace grounds. The impressive ceremony of **Changing the Guard** – dazzling uniforms, shouted commands, martial music – consists of the Old Guard, which forms up in the palace forecourt, going off duty and handing over to the New Guard. The Guard consists of three officers and 40 men when the Queen is in residence, but only three officers and 31 men when she is away. The ceremony takes place in full public view, right in front of the palace. The Guard is also changed at Horse Guards and on Tower Green, at the Tower of London.

One of the Queen's Life Guards

A Queen's Guard in winter

The **Ceremony of the Keys** at the Tower of London is one of the capital's most timeless ceremonies. After each of the Tower gates has been locked, the last post is sounded by a trumpeter before the keys are secured in the Queen's House.

The Tower of London and Hyde Park are also the scene of **Royal Salutes** which take place on birthdays and other occasions throughout the year. At such times 41 rounds are fired in Hyde Park at noon, and 62 rounds at the Tower at 1pm. The spectacle in Hyde Park is a stirring one as 71 horses and six 13-pounder cannons swirl into place and the roar of the guns begins.

The combination of pageantry, colour and music makes the annual **Trooping the Colour** the high point of London's ceremonial year. The Queen takes the Royal Salute, and after her troops have marched past, she leads them to Buckingham Palace where a second march past takes place. The best place to watch this spectacle is from the Horse Guards Parade side of St James's Park.

Bands of the Household Cavalry and the Foot Guards stage the ceremony of **Beating the Retreat** at Horse Guards Parade. This takes place three or four evenings a week in the fortnight leading up to **Trooping the Colour**

The spectacular **State Opening of Parliament**, when the Queen opens the annual parliamentary session in the House of Lords – usually in November – is not open to the general public, although it is now televised. The huge royal procession, which moves from Buckingham Palace to Westminster, is, however, a magnificent sight, with the Queen travelling in the highly ornate Irish State Coach drawn by four horses.

MILITARY CEREMONIES

THE CENOTAPH in Whitehall is the setting for a ceremony held on **Remembrance Sunday**, to give thanks to those who died fighting in the two World Wars.

National **Navy Day** is commemorated by a parade down the Mall, followed by a service held at Nelson's Column in Trafalgar Square.

Royal salute, Tower of London

Changing the Guard, Tower of London

Silent Change Ceremony at Guildhall for the new Lord Mayor

CEREMONIES IN THE CITY

NOVEMBER IS THE focus of the City of London's ceremonial year. At the **Silent Change** in Guildhall, the outgoing Lord Mayor hands over symbols of office to the new Mayor in a virtually wordless ceremony. The following day sees the rumbustious **Lord Mayor's Show**. Accompanying the Lord Mayor in his gold state coach a procession of bands, decorated floats and military detachments makes its way through the City from Guildhall past the Mansion House to the Law Courts, and back again along the Embankment.

Lord Mayor's chain of office

Many of the ceremonies that take place in the City are linked to the activities of the Livery Companies *(see p152).* These include the Worshipful Companies of **Vintners' and Distillers'** annual celebration of the wine harvest and the Stationers' **Cakes and Ale Sermon**, held in St Paul's. Cakes and ale are provided according to the will of a 17th-century stationer.

NAME-DAY CEREMONIES

EVERY 21 MAY **King Henry VI**, who was murdered in the Tower of London in 1471, is still remembered by the members of his two famous foundations, Eton College and King's College, Cambridge, who meet for a ceremony at the Wakefield Tower where he was killed. **Oak Apple Day** commemorates King Charles II's lucky escape from the Parliamentary forces of Oliver Cromwell in 1651. The King managed to conceal himself in a hollow oak tree, and today Chelsea Pensioners honour his memory by decorating his statue at Chelsea Hospital with oak leaves and branches. On 18 December, the diarist **Dr Johnson** is commemorated in an annual service held at Westminster Abbey.

INFORMAL CEREMONIES

EACH JULY, six guildsmen from the Company of Watermen compete for the prize in **Doggett's Coat and Badge Race**. In autumn, the **Pearly Kings and Queens**, representatives of east London's traders, meet at St Martin-in-the-Fields. In March children are given oranges and lemons at the **Oranges and Lemons service** at St Clement Danes Church. In February, clowns take part in a service for **Joseph Grimaldi** (1779–1837) at the Holy Trinity Church in Dalston E8.

Pearly Queen

WHERE TO FIND THE CEREMONIES

Beating the Retreat
Horse Guards *p80*, date arranged during first two weeks of June.
Cakes and Ale Sermon
St Paul's *pp148–51*, Ash Wed.
Ceremony of the Keys
Tower of London *pp154–7*, 9.30pm daily. Tickets from the Tower, but book well in advance.
Changing the Guard
Buckingham Palace *pp94–5*, Apr–Jul: 11.30am daily; Aug–Mar: alternate days. Horse Guards *p80*, 1pm daily. Tower of London *pp154–7*, noon daily.
Doggett's Coat and Badge Race
From London Bridge to Cadogan Pier, Chelsea *pp189–93*, July.
Dr Johnson Memorial
Westminster Abbey *pp76–9*, 18 Dec.
Joseph Grimaldi Memorial
Holy Trinity Church, Dalston E8, 7 Feb.
King Henry VI Memorial
Wakefield Tower, Tower of London *pp154–7*, 21 May.
Lord Mayor's Show
The City *pp143–53*, second Sat Nov.
Navy Day
Trafalgar Sq *p102*, 21 Oct.
Oak Apple Day
Royal Hospital *p193*, Thu after 29 May.
Oranges and Lemons Service
St Clement Danes *p138*, March.
Pearly Kings and Queens Harvest Festival
St Martin-in-the-Fields *p102*, autumn.
Remembrance Sunday
Cenotaph *p74*, Sun nearest 11 Nov.
Royal Salutes
Hyde Park *p207*, royal anniversaries and other state occasions.
Silent Change
Guildhall *p159*, second Fri Nov.
State Opening of Parliament, Houses of Parliament *pp72–3*, Oct–Nov. Procession from Buckingham Palace *pp94–5* to Westminster.
Trooping the Colour
Horse Guards *p80*, 2nd Sat Jun (rehearsals on previous two Sats). Limited tickets from headquarters Household Division, Horse Guards.
Vintners' and Distillers' Wine Harvest
St Olave's Church, Hart St EC3, second Tue Oct.

LONDON THROUGH THE YEAR

SPRINGTIME IN London carries an almost tangible air of a city waking up to longer days and outdoor pursuits. The cheerful yellow of daffodils studs the parks, and less-hardy Londoners turn out for their first jog of the year to find themselves puffing in the wake of serious runners in training for the Marathon. As spring turns into summer, the royal parks reach their full glory, and in Kensington Gardens nannies gather to chat under venerable chestnut trees. As autumn takes hold, those same trees are ablaze with red and gold and Londoners' thoughts turn to afternoons in museums and art galleries, followed by tea in a café. The year draws to a close with Guy Fawkes parties and shopping in the West End. Contact the London Tourist Board (*see p345*) or check the listings magazines (*p325*) for details of seasonal events.

SPRING

THE WEATHER during the spring months may be raw, and an umbrella is a necessary precaution. Druids celebrate the Spring Equinox in a subdued ceremony on Tower Hill. Painters compete to have their works accepted by the Royal Academy. Footballers close their season with the FA Cup Final at Wembley, while cricketers don their sweaters to begin theirs. Oxford and Cambridge Universities row their annual boat race along the Thames, and Marathon runners pound the streets.

Runners in the London Marathon passing Tower Bridge

MARCH

Chelsea Antiques Fair (*second week*), Chelsea Old Town Hall, King's Rd SW3.
Ideal Home Exhibition (*second week*), Earl's Court, Warwick Rd SW5. It is a long-established show with the latest in domestic gadgetry and state-of-the-art technology.
Oranges and Lemons Service, St Clement Danes (*p55*). Service for schoolchildren; each child is given an orange and a lemon.
Oxford v Cambridge boat race (*Sat before Easter, or Easter*), Putney to Mortlake (*p337*).
Spring Equinox celebration (*21 Mar*), Tower Hill EC3. Subdued pagan ceremony with modern-day druids.

EASTER

Good Fri and following Mon are public holidays. **Easter parades**, Covent Garden (*p114*), Battersea Park (*p251*).

Kite flying, Blackheath (*p239*) and Hampstead Heath (*p230*).
Easter procession and hymns (*Easter Mon*), Westminster Abbey (*pp76–9*). One of London's most evocative religious celebrations.
International Model Railway Exhibition (*Easter weekend*), Royal Horticultural Hall, Vincent Sq SW1. Of real interest to everyone, not just railway enthusiasts.

A London park in the spring

APRIL

Queen's Birthday gun salutes (*21 Apr*), Hyde Park, Tower of London (*p54*).
London Marathon (*Sun in Apr or May*), Greenwich to Westminster (*p337*).

MAY

First and last Mon are public holidays.
FA Cup Final, Wembley. Football season's climax (*p336*).
Henry VI Memorial (*p55*).
Beating the Bounds (*Ascension Day*), throughout the City. Young boys selected from the City parish beat certain buildings, marking the parish boundaries.
Oak Apple Day, at the Royal Hospital, Chelsea (*p55*).
Funfairs (*late May public hol weekend*), various commons.
Chelsea Flower Show (*late May*), Royal Hospital, Chelsea.
Beating the Retreat (*p54*).
Royal Academy Summer Exhibition (*May–Jul*), Piccadilly (*p90*).

AVERAGE DAILY HOURS OF SUNSHINE

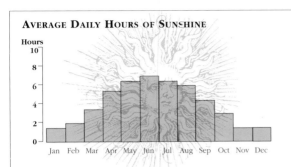

Hours
10
8
6
4
2
0

Jan Feb Mar Apr May Jun Jul Aug Sep Oct Nov Dec

Sunshine Chart
London's longest and hottest days fall between May and August. In the height of summer, daylight hours can extend from well before 5am to after 9pm. Daytime is much shorter in the winter, but London can be stunning in the winter sunshine.

SUMMER

L ONDON'S SUMMER season is packed full of indoor and outdoor events. The weather is very unreliable, even at the height of summer, but unless you are notably unlucky there should be enough fine days to sample what is on offer.

The selection includes many traditional events, such as the Wimbledon tennis championships and the cricket test matches at Lord's and the Oval. Well out of view from the general public and prying photographers, the Queen holds garden parties for favoured subjects in the splendid grounds of Buckingham Palace. The summer public holiday is also marked with funfairs in some of London's parks.

JUNE

Morris dancing *(Wed eves, all summer)*, Westminster Abbey *(pp76–9)*. Traditional English folk-dancing.
Coronation Day gun salutes *(2 Jun)*, Hyde Park and Tower of London *(p54)*.
Ceramics fair, Dorchester Hotel, Park Lane W1.
Fine Art and Antiques fair, Olympia, Olympia Way W14.
Trooping the Colour, Horse Guards *(p54)*.
Charles Dickens memorial service *(9 Jun)*, Westminster Abbey *(pp76–9)*. Celebration of London's famous author.
Duke of Edinburgh's Birthday gun salutes *(10 Jun)*, Hyde Park and Tower of London *(p54)*.
Wimbledon Lawn Tennis Championships *(two weeks in late Jun; p336)*.

Revellers at Notting Hill Carnival

Cricket test match, Lord's *(p336)*.
Open-air theatre season *(throughout the summer)*, Regent's Park and Holland Park. Shakespeare, Shaw and others offer the perfect opportunity for a picnic *(p326)*.
Open-air concerts, Kenwood, Hampstead Heath, Crystal Palace, Marble Hill, St James's Park *(p331)*.
Street theatre festival *(Jun–Jul)*, Covent Garden *(p114)*. Street performers of every kind gather to flaunt their various talents.
Summer festivals *(late Jun)*, Greenwich, Spitalfields and Primrose Hill. Contact the London Tourist Board *(p345)* or see the listings magazines *(p325)* for times and venues of all these events.

JULY

Summer festivals, City of London and Richmond.
Sales. Price reductions across London's shops *(p311)*.

Doggett's Coat and Badge Race *(p55)*.
Hampton Court Flower Show, Hampton Court Palace *(pp254–7)*.
Royal Tournament *(mid-Jul)*, Earl's Court, Warwick Rd SW5. Impressive military spectacle put on by members of the combined armed forces.
Capital Radio Jazz Festival, Royal Festival Hall *(p184)*.
Henry Wood Promenade Concerts *(late Jul–Sep)*, Royal Albert Hall *(p203)*.

AUGUST

Last Mon is a public holiday.
Queen Mother's Birthday gun salutes *(4 Aug)*, Hyde Park and Tower of London *(p54)*.
Notting Hill Carnival *(late Aug holiday weekend)*. A celebration organized mainly by the area's various ethnic communities *(p215)*.
Funfairs *(Aug holiday)*, throughout London's parks.

Regimental band, St James's Park

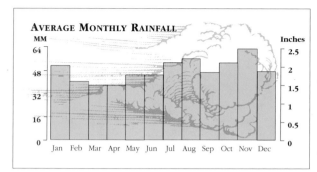

Rainfall Chart
*London's average
monthly rainfall
remains much the
same throughout the
year. July and August,
the capital's warmest
months, are also two
of its wettest. Rain is
less likely in spring,
but visitors should be
prepared for a shower
at any time of year.*

AUTUMN

THERE IS A SENSE of purpose
about London in autumn.
The build-up to the busiest
shopping season, the start of
the academic year, and the new
parliamentary session, opened
by the Queen, inject some life
into the colder months. The
cricket season comes to an
end in mid-September, while
food-lovers may be interested
in the spectacular displays of
fresh fish that are laid out in
the vestry of St Mary-at-the-
Hill, celebrating the harvest
of this island nation.

Memories of a more turbu-
lent opening of Parliament
are revived on 5 November,
when there are bonfires and
firework to commemorate the
failure of a conspiracy led by
Guy Fawkes to blow up the
Palace of Westminster in
1605. A few days later the
dead of two World Wars are
commemorated at a cere-
mony held in Whitehall.

Pearly Kings gathering for the harvest festival at St Martin-in-the-Fields

SEPTEMBER

**National Rose Society
Annual Show**, Royal Horticultural Hall, Vincent Sq W1.
Chelsea Antiques Fair
(third week), Chelsea Old
Town Hall, King's Road SW3.
Last Night of the Proms
(late Sep), Royal Albert Hall
(p203).

OCTOBER

Pearly Harvest Festival
(3 Oct), St Martin-in-the-Fields
(p55).
Punch and Judy Festival
(3 Oct), Covent Garden WC2.
Celebration of puppet duo.
Horse of the Year Show
(early Oct), Wembley *(p337)*.
London's equestrian showpiece.
Harvest of the Sea *(second
Sun)*, St Mary-at-Hill Church
(p152).
**Vintners' and Distillers'
Wine Harvest** *(p55)*.
Navy Day *(p54)*.

**State Opening of Parlia-
ment** *(p54)*.

NOVEMBER

Guy Fawkes Night *(5 Nov)*.
Listings magazines give details
of firework displays *(p324)*.
Remembrance Day Service
(p54).
Silent Change *(p55)*.
Lord Mayor's Show *(p55)*.
London to Brighton veteran
car run *(first Sun)*. Starts in
Hyde Park *(p207)*.
Christmas lights *(late Nov–
6 Jan)*, West End *(p313)*.

London-to-Brighton veteran car run

Autumn colours in a London park

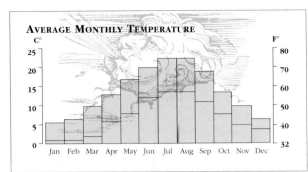

AVERAGE MONTHLY TEMPERATURE

Temperature Chart
The chart shows the average minimum and maximum temperatures for each month. Top temperatures averaging 22° C (75° F) belie London's reputation for year-round chilliness, although November through to February sees icy conditions.

WINTER

SOME OF THE most striking images of London are drawn from winter: paintings of frost fairs in the 17th and 18th centuries, when the River Thames froze over completely; and Claude Monet's views of the river and its bridges.

For centuries thick "pea-souper" fogs were an inevitable part of winter, until the Clean Air Act of 1956 barred coal-burning in open grates.

Christmas trees and lights twinkle everywhere – from the West End shopping streets to construction sites. The scent of roasting chestnuts pervades as street pedlars sell them from glowing mobile braziers.

Seasonal menus feature roast turkey, mince pies and rich, dark Christmas pudding. Traditional fare in theatres includes colourful family pantomimes (where the customary cross-dressing between the sexes baffles many visitors – *p326*) and popular ballets such as *Swan Lake* or *The Nutcracker*.

Skaters use the open-air rink at the Broadgate Centre in the City, and sometimes it is safe to venture on to the frozen lakes in the parks.

Winter in Kensington Gardens

DECEMBER

Oxford v Cambridge rugby union match *(mid-Dec)*, Twickenham *(p337)*.
Dr Johnson memorial service *(18 Dec)*, Westminster Abbey *(p55)*.

CHRISTMAS AND NEW YEAR

25–26 Dec and 1 Jan are public hols. There is no train service on Christmas Day.
Carol services *(each*

evening on the lead up to Christmas)*, Trafalgar Square *(p102)*, St Paul's *(pp148–51)*, Westminster Abbey *(pp76–9)* and other churches.
Turkey auction *(24 Dec)*, Smithfield Market *(p164)*.
Christmas Day swim Serpentine, Hyde Park *(p207)*.
New Year's Eve celebrations *(31 Dec)*, Trafalgar Square, St Paul's.

JANUARY

Sales *(p311)*.
International Boat Show, Earl's Court, Warwick Rd SW5.
International Mime Festival *(mid Jan–early Feb)*, various venues.
Charles I Commemoration *(last Sun)*, procession from St James's Palace *(p91)* to Banqueting House *(p80)*.
Chinese New Year *(late Jan–early Feb)*, Chinatown *(p108)* and Soho *(p109)*.

FEBRUARY

Clowns' Service *(first Sun)*, Dalston *(p55)*.
Queen's Accession gun salutes *(6 Feb)*, 41-gun salute Hyde Park; 62-gun salute Tower of London *(p54)*.
Pancake races *(Shrove Tue)*, Lincoln's Inn Fields *(p137)* and Covent Garden *(p114)*.

PUBLIC HOLIDAYS
New Year's Day (1 Jan); **Good Friday; Easter Monday; May Day** (first Monday in May); **Whit Monday** (last Monday in May); **August Bank Holiday** (last Monday in August); **Christmas** (25– 26 December).

Christmas illuminations in Trafalgar Square

A RIVER VIEW OF LONDON

IN OLD Celtic the word for river was *teme*, and the Romans adopted this as the name for the great waterway upon which they founded the city of *Londinium (see pp16–17)* nearly 2,000 years ago. The Roman settlers built their new city along the most easterly point at which the river could be bridged using the technology of the time. Since then, the Thames has continued to play a critical role in London's history. It was the route taken by the Viking invaders of the 8th and 9th centuries, the birthplace of the Royal Navy in Tudor times, and the artery for much of the country's commerce until well into the 1950s.

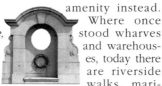

Decoration on Southwark Bridge

Now changing trade patterns have moved the big ships elsewhere, and the river has become the capital's foremost leisure amenity instead. Where once stood wharves and warehouses, today there are riverside walks, marinas, bars and restaurants.

One of the most interesting ways of seeing the capital is by boat, and several companies offer sightseeing cruises from central London. These vary in length from 30 minutes to four hours. The most popular section of the river to travel runs downstream from the Houses of Parliament to Tower Bridge. A river view gives you a very different perspective of London's major sites, including Traitors' Gate, the infamous river entrance to the Tower of London, which was used for prisoners brought from trial in Westminster Hall *(see pp72–3)*. You can also take longer journeys past the varied architectural styles found between Hampton Court and the Thames Barrier.

The Thames in London

Passenger boat services cover about 30 miles (50 km) of the Thames, from Hampton Court in the west to the Thames Barrier in the former Docklands of the east.

Houseboats at Chelsea

Kew Rail Bridge
Kew Bridge
Kew
Chiswick Bridge
Twickenham Rail Bridge
Twickenham Bridge
Richmond Bridge
Richmond
Teddington Foot Bridge
Kingston Bridge
Hampton Court

TOUR OPERATORS

Most of these services run from 1 April until the end of September, when they revert to winter schedules, but phone first because some change later. During the winter there are no upriver services.

A circular cruise on *Mercedes*

Westminster Pier
Map 13 C5.
🚇 *Westminster.*

Downriver to Tower Pier
📞 020-7515 1415.

Departures 10.20am, 10.40am, 11am, 11.30am and noon. Then every 20 minutes until 3pm. Then every 30 minutes until 5pm (every 30 minutes until 6pm then hourly until 9pm during peak season).
Duration 30 minutes.

Downriver to Greenwich
📞 020-7930 4097.
Departures every 30 minutes, 10.30am–4pm.
Duration 1 hour.

Downriver to the Thames Barrier
📞 020-7930 3373.
Departures 10.15am, 11.15am, 12.45pm, 1.45pm and 3.15pm.
Duration 75 mins each way.

Private party on a chartered boat

Upriver to Kew
📞 020-7930 4721.
Departures 10am, 10.15pm, 10.30am, 11.15am, noon and 2pm.
Duration about 90 minutes.

Upriver to Richmond
📞 020-7930 4721.
Departures 10.30am, 11.15am and noon.
Duration about 2 hours.

Upriver to Hampton Court
📞 020-7930 4721.
Departures 11.15am and noon.

The River Thames is at its most romantic at dusk. The view east from Waterloo Bridge shows St Paul's and the City on the north bank and the Oxo Tower on the south.

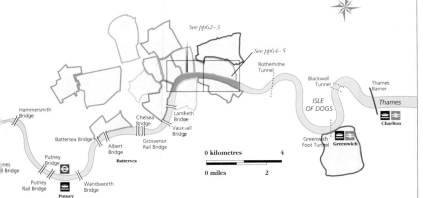

See pp62–3

See pp64–5

Rotherhithe
Tunnel

Blackwall
Tunnel

Thames
Barrier

ISLE
OF DOGS

Thames

Charlton

Hammersmith
Bridge

Chelsea
Bridge

Lambeth
Bridge

Vauxhall
Bridge

Battersea Bridge

Albert
Bridge

Grosvenor
Rail Bridge

Putney
Bridge

Battersea

Putney
Rail Bridge

Wandsworth
Bridge

Putney

nes
Bridge

Greenwich
Foot Tunnel

Greenwich

0 kilometres   4

0 miles   2

KEY

Underground station

Railway station

River boat stop

The river at Twickenham

The view from Richmond Hill

Open-decked boat

Duration *about 3 hours.*

Circular supper cruise
[020-7839 3572.
9pm Wed, Fri, Sun.
Duration *90 minutes.*

Circular evening cruise
[020-7930 2062.
7.30 and 8.30pm.
Duration *45 minutes.*

Charing Cross Pier
Map 13 C3.
Charing Cross,
Embankment.

*Downriver to
Tower Pier*
[020-7839 3572.
Departures *every 45
minutes, 10.30am–4pm.*
Duration *30 minutes.*

Downriver to Greenwich
[020-7839 3572.
Departures *every 45
minutes, 10.30am–3pm.*
Duration *1 hour.*

Circular evening cruise
[020-7839 3572.
6.30, 7.30 and 8.30pm.
Duration *45 minutes.*

Temple Pier
Map 14 D2. Temple.

Circular lunchtime cruise
[020-7839 3572.
12.15pm Mon–Sat.
Duration *1¼ hours.*

Tower Pier
Map 16 D3. Tower Hill.

Upriver to HMS Belfast
[020-8468 7201.
Departures *every 30
minutes, 10.30am–4pm.*

Downriver to Greenwich
[020-7839 3572.
Departures *every
45 minutes,
11am–4.15pm.*
Duration
30 minutes.

Sightseeing boat

Westminster Bridge to Blackfriars Bridge

UNTIL WORLD WAR II, this stretch of the Thames marked the division between rich and poor London. On the north bank were the offices, shops, luxury hotels and apartments of Whitehall and the Strand, the Inns of Court and the newspaper district. To the south were smoky factories and slum dwellings. After the war, the Festival of Britain in 1951 started the revival of the South Bank *(see pp181–7)* which now has some of the capital's most interesting modern buildings.

Savoy Hotel
This hotel is on the site of a medieval palace (p116).

Shell Mex House
Offices for the oil company were built in 1931 on the site of the vast Cecil Hotel.

Somerset House is an office complex built in 1786 *(p117).*

Cleopatra's Needle was made in ancient Egypt and given to London in 1819 *(p118).*

Embankment Gardens is the site of many open-air concerts held in the bandstand during the summer months *(p118).*

Waterloo Bridge

Charing Cross

Embankment

Charing Cross Pier

Festival Pier

Hungerford Railway Bridge

Charing Cross
The rail terminus is encased in a Post-Modernist office complex with many shops (p119).

The South Bank Centre was the site of the 1951 Festival of Britain and is London's most important arts complex. It is dominated by the Festival Hall, the National Theatre and the Hayward Gallery *(pp181–7).*

The Banqueting House is one of Inigo Jones's finest works, built as part of Whitehall Palace *(p80).*

The Ministry of Defence is a bulky white fortress completed in the 1950s.

Westminster

Westminster Bridge

London Aquarium
The former seat of London's government is now home to a state-of-the-art aquarium (p185).

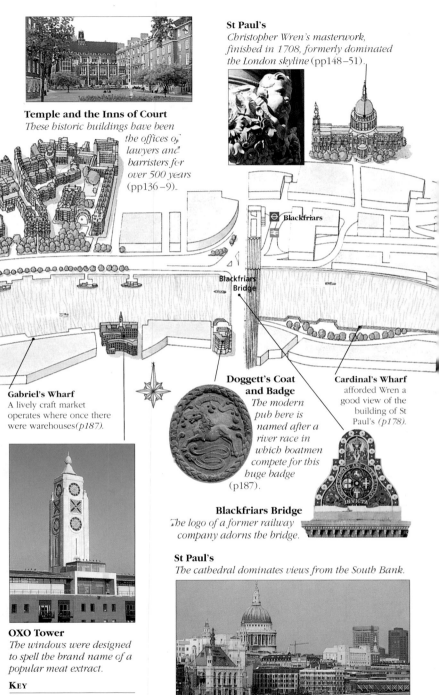

St Paul's
Christopher Wren's masterwork, finished in 1708, formerly dominated the London skyline (pp148–51).

Temple and the Inns of Court
These historic buildings have been the offices of lawyers and barristers for over 500 years (pp136–9).

Blackfriars

Blackfriars Bridge

Gabriel's Wharf
A lively craft market operates where once there were warehouses *(p187)*.

Doggett's Coat and Badge
The modern pub here is named after a river race in which boatmen compete for this huge badge (p187).

Cardinal's Wharf
afforded Wren a good view of the building of St Paul's *(p178)*.

Blackfriars Bridge
The logo of a former railway company adorns the bridge.

St Paul's
The cathedral dominates views from the South Bank.

OXO Tower
The windows were designed to spell the brand name of a popular meat extract.

KEY

Underground station
Railway station
River boat boarding point

Southwark Bridge to St Katharine's Dock

FOR CENTURIES THE STRETCH just east of London Bridge was the busiest part of the Thames, with ships of all sizes jostling for position to unload at the wharves on both banks. Then, in the 19th century, the construction of the docks to the east eased congestion. Today most landmarks on this section hark back to that commercial past.

Old Billingsgate
Notice the flying fish weather vanes on what was London's main fish market (p152).

Fishmongers' Hall
The hall (1834) of this ancient City guild dominates the view north from London Bridge (p152).

Monument
The Great Fire of 1666 started near this spot (p152).

A Custom House has been here since 1272. This version dates from 1825.

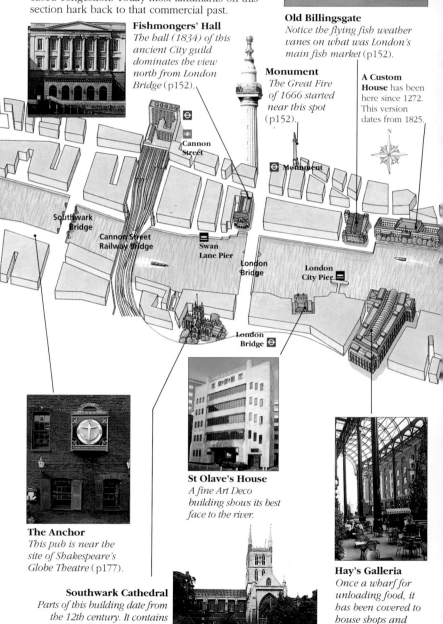

Cannon Street

Monument

Southwark Bridge

Cannon Street Railway Bridge

Swan Lane Pier

London Bridge

London City Pier

London Bridge

The Anchor
This pub is near the site of Shakespeare's Globe Theatre (p177).

St Olave's House
A fine Art Deco building shows its best face to the river.

Hay's Galleria
Once a wharf for unloading food, it has been covered to house shops and restaurants.

Southwark Cathedral
Parts of this building date from the 12th century. It contains memorials to Shakespeare (p176).

Southwark Wharves
Now there are walkways with river views where ships used to dock.

Tower Bridge
It still opens to let tall ships pass, but not as often as it did when cargo vessels came through (p153).

Tower of London
Look out for Traitors' Gate, where prisoners would be taken into the Tower by boat (pp154–7).

St Katharine's Dock
The former dock is now a lively attraction for visitors. Its yacht marina is a highlight (p158).

Tower Pier

Tower Bridge

Victorian warehouses on Butlers Wharf have been converted into apartments.

HMS Belfast
The World War II cruiser has been a museum since 1971 (p179).

Design Museum
Opened in 1989, this ship-like building is a shining example of Docklands' renaissance (p179).

LONDON AREA BY AREA

WHITEHALL AND WESTMINSTER

WHITEHALL AND WESTMINSTER have been at the centre of political and religious power in England for a thousand years. King Canute, who ruled at the beginning of the 11th century, was the first monarch to have a palace on what was then an island in the swampy meeting point of the Thames and its vanished tributary, the Tyburn. Canute built his palace beside the church that, some 50 years later, Edward the Confessor would enlarge into England's greatest abbey, giving the area its name. (A minster is an abbey church.) Over the following centuries the offices of state were established in the vicinity. All this is still reflected in Whitehall's heroic statues and massive government buildings. But, to its north, Trafalgar Square marks the start of the West End entertainment district.

Horse Guard on Whitehall

SIGHTS AT A GLANCE

Historic Streets and Buildings

Houses of Parliament *pp72–3* **1**
Big Ben **2**
Jewel Tower **3**
Dean's Yard **5**
Parliament Square **7**
Downing Street **9**
Cabinet War Rooms **10**
Banqueting House **11**
Horse Guards **12**
Queen Anne's Gate **14**
St James's Park Station **16**
Blewcoat School **17**

Churches, Abbeys and Cathedrals

Westminster Abbey *pp76–9* **4**
St Margaret's Church **6**
Westminster Cathedral **18**
St John's, Smith Square **19**

Museums and Galleries

Guards' Museum **15**
Tate Gallery *pp82–5* **20**

Theatres

Whitehall Theatre **13**

Monuments

Cenotaph **8**

GETTING THERE

Rail services and the Victoria, District and Circle lines all serve the area. Bus numbers 3, 11, 12, 24, 29, 53, 77, 77A, 88, 109, 159, 170 and 184 go to Whitehall; 2, 2B, 16, 25, 36A, 38, 39, 52, 52A, 73, 76, 135, 507 and 510 serve Victoria.

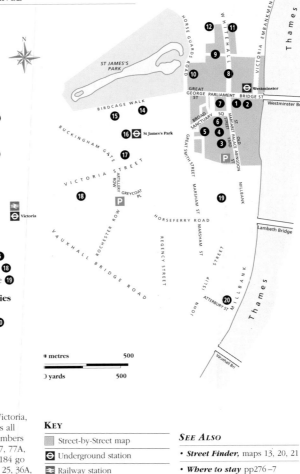

KEY

	Street-by-Street map
⊖	Underground station
⇌	Railway station
P	Parking

SEE ALSO

- *Street Finder,* maps 13, 20, 21
- *Where to stay* pp276–7
- *Restaurants* pp292–4

Looking down Whitehall towards Big Ben

Street-by-Street: Whitehall and Westminster

COMPARED WITH MANY capital cities, London has little monumental architecture designed to overawe with pomp. Here, at the historic seat both of the government and of the established church, it most closely approaches the broad, stately avenues of Paris, Rome and Madrid. On weekdays the streets are crowded with members of the civil service, as most of their work is based in this area. At weekends, however, it is deserted, apart from tourists visiting some of London's most famous sights.

Earl Haig, the British World War I chief, was sculpted by Alfred Hardiman in 1936.

Downing Street
British Prime Ministers have lived here since 1732 ❾

★ **Cabinet War Rooms**
Now open to the public, these were Winston Churchill's World War II headquarters ❿

Central Hall is a florid example of the Beaux Arts style, built in 1911 as a Methodist meeting hall. In 1946 the first General Assembly of the United Nations was held here.

★ **Westminster Abbey**
The Abbey is London's oldest and most important church ❹

The Sanctuary
was a medieval safe-place for those escaping the law.

Dean's Yard
Westminster School was founded here in 1540 ❺

Richard I's Statue, by Carlo Marochetti (1860), depicts the 12th-century *Coeur de Lion* (Lionheart).

Jewel Tower
Kings once stored their most valuable possessions here ❸

The Burghers of Calais
is a cast of Auguste Rodin's original in Paris.

★ **Horse Guards**
A mounted guard is ceremonially changed here twice a day ⓬

To Trafalgar Square

Dover House, a stately mansion dating from 1787, now houses the Scottish Office.

LOCATOR MAP
See Central London Map pp12–13

★ **Banqueting House**
Inigo Jones designed this elegant building, which has a Rubens ceiling, in 1622 ⓫

Cenotaph
Edward Lutyens's war memorial dates from 1920 ⑧

Richmond House is William Whitfield's prize-winning 1980s building for the Department of Health.

The Treasury is where the nation's finances are administered.

Norman Shaw Buildings were the Victorian site of New Scotland Yard, the Metropolitan Police HQ.

Westminster Pier is a starting point for river excursions.

Westminster station

Boadicea, the English queen who resisted the Romans, was portrayed by Thomas Thornycroft in the 1850s.

STAR SIGHTS

★ **Westminster Abbey**

★ **Houses of Parliament and Big Ben**

★ **Banqueting House**

★ **Cabinet War Rooms**

★ **Horse Guards**

Parliament Square
Statues of famous statesmen, such as Benjamin Disraeli and Winston Churchill, stand here ⑦

★ **Houses of Parliament and Big Ben**
These were designed by Barry in 1834 when the Palace of Westminster burned down ❶ ❷

St Margaret's Church
Society weddings often take place here, in Parliament's church ❺

KEY

– – – Suggested route

0 metres   100

0 yards   100

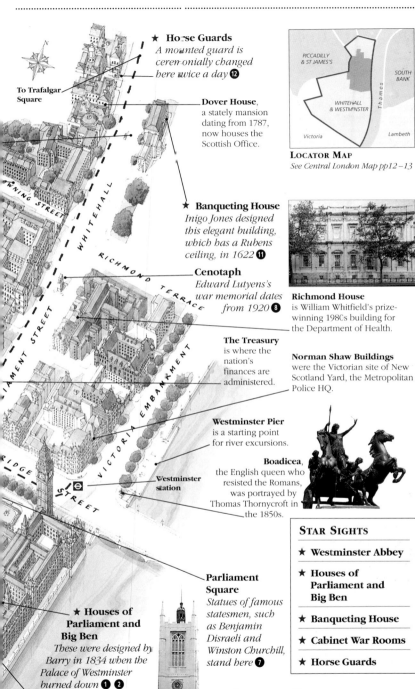

Houses of Parliament

Since 1512 the Palace of Westminster has been the seat of the two Houses of Parliament, called the Lords and the Commons. The Commons is made up of elected Members of Parliament (MPs) of different political parties; the party with the most MPs forms the Government, and its leader becomes Prime Minister. MPs from other parties make up the Opposition. Commons' debates can become heated and are impartially chaired by an MP designated as Speaker. The Commons formulates legislation which is first debated in both Houses before becoming law.

The mock-Gothic building was designed by Victorian architect Sir Charles Barry. Victoria Tower, on the left, contains 1.5 million Acts of Parliament passed since 1497.

★ **Commons' Chamber**
The room is upholstered in green. The Government sits on the left, the Opposition on the right, and the Speaker presides from a chair between them.

Big Ben
The vast bell was hung in 1858 and chimes on the hour; four smaller ones ring on the quarter hours (see p74).

Members' entrance

Star Features

★ Westminster Hall

★ Lords' Chamber

★ Commons' Chamber

★ **Westminster Hall**
The only surviving part of the original Palace of Westminster, it dates from 1097; its hammerbeam roof is from the 14th century.

Central Lobby
People who come to meet their MP wait here under a ceiling of rich mosaics.

Peers are members of the House of Lords – many receive their titles for services to their country. This is their lobby.

Royal Gallery
The Queen passes through here at the State Opening. It is lined with peers' desks.

St Stephen's entrance

★**Lords' Chamber**
At the State Opening of Parliament (see pp54–5) the Queen delivers a speech from the throne of the House of Lords, which outlines the Government's plans.

TIMELINE

1042 Work starts on first palace for Edward the Confessor	**1547** St Stephen's chapel becomes first Chamber of the House of Commons	**1642** Charles I tries to arrest five MPs but is forced to withdraw by the Speaker	**1941** Chamber of House of Commons destroyed by World War II bomb	

1000	1200	1400	1600	1800	2000

1087–1100 Westminster Hall built	**1512** After a fire, palace stops being a royal residence		**1870** Present building completed
The Mace: symbol of royal authority in the Commons	**1605** Guy Fawkes and others try to blow up the king and Houses of Parliament	**1834** Palace destroyed by fire; only Westminster Hall and the Jewel Tower survive	

Houses of Parliament ❶

See pp72–3.

Big Ben ❷

Bridge St SW1. **Map** 13 C5.
📞 020-7222 2219. 🚇 Westminster.
Not open to the public.

To BE PEDANTIC, Big Ben is not the name of the world-famous four-faced clock in the 106-m (320-ft) tower that rises above the Houses of Parliament, but of the resonant 14-tonne bell on which the hours are struck. It was named after Sir Benjamin Hall, Chief Commissioner of Works when the bell was hung in 1858. Cast at White-chapel, it was the second giant bell made for the clock, the first having become cracked during a test ringing. (The present bell also has a slight crack.) The clock is the largest in Britain, its four dials 7.5 m (23 ft) in diameter and the minute hand 4.25 m (14 ft) long, made in hollow copper for lightness. It has kept exact time for the nation more or less continuously since it was first set in motion in May 1859. The deep chimes have become a symbol of Britain all over the world and are broadcast daily on BBC radio.

Jewel Tower ❸

Abingdon St SW1. **Map** 13 B5.
📞 020-7222 2219. 🚇 Westminster.
Open Apr–Sep: 10am–6pm daily;
Oct–Mar: 10am–4pm daily.
Closed 24–26 Dec, for state occasions. **Adm charge.** 📷 🚻

THIS AND WESTMINSTER HALL *(see p72)* are the only vestiges of the old Palace of Westminster. The tower was built in 1366 as a stronghold for Edward III's treasure and is today a small museum

containing relics relating to the palace, pottery dug from the moat, and fascinating drawings of some of the best losing designs for rebuilding the Houses of Parliament after the fire of 1834.

The tower served as the weights and measures office from 1869 until 1938 and another display relates to that era. Alongside are the remains of the moat and a medieval quay.

Westminster Abbey ❹

See pp76–9.

Dean's Yard ❺

Broad Sanctuary SW1. **Map** 13 B5.
🚇 Westminster. **Buildings not open** to the public.

Entrance to the Abbey and cloisters from Dean's Yard

AN ARCH NEAR the west door of the Abbey leads into this secluded grassy square, surrounded by a jumble of buildings from many different periods. A medieval house on the east side has a distinctive dormer window and backs on to Little Dean's Yard, where the monks' living quarters used to be. Dean's Yard is private property. It belongs to the Dean and Chapter of Westminster and is close to Westminster School, whose famous former pupils include poet John Dryden and playwright Ben Jonson. Scholars are, by tradition, the first to acknowledge a new monarch.

St Margaret's Church ❻

Parliament Sq SW1. **Map** 13 B5.
📞 020-7222 5152. 🚇 Westminster.
Open 9.30am–3.45pm Mon–Fri,
9.30am–1.45pm Sat, 2–5pm Sun.
⛪ 11am Sun. 📷 ♿ 📷 **Concerts.**

Statue of Charles I overlooking St Margaret's doorway

OVERSHADOWED by the Abbey, this early-15th-century church has long been a favoured venue for political and society weddings, such as Winston and Clementine Churchill's. Although much restored, the church retains some Tudor features, notably a stained-glass window that celebrates the engagement of Catherine of Aragon to Arthur, Henry VIII's eldest brother.

Parliament Square ❼

SW1. **Map** 13 B5. 🚇 Westminster.

LAID OUT IN THE 1840s to provide a more open aspect for the new Houses of Parliament, the square became Britain's first official roundabout in 1926. Today it is hemmed in by heavy traffic. Statues of statesmen and soldiers are dominated by Winston Churchill in his greatcoat, glowering at the House of Commons. On the north side Abraham Lincoln sits in front of the mock-Gothic Middlesex Guildhall, completed in 1913.

Cenotaph ❽

Whitehall SW1. **Map** 13 B4.
🚇 Westminster.

THIS SUITABLY BLEAK and pale monument, completed in 1920 by Sir Edwin Lutyens to commemorate the dead of World War I, stands in the middle of Whitehall. On Remembrance Day every year – the Sunday nearest 11 November – the monarch and other dignitaries place wreaths of red poppies on the Cenotaph. This solemn ceremony, commemorating the 1918 armistice, honours the victims of World Wars I and II (see pp 54 – 5).

The Cenotaph

Cabinet War Rooms ❿

Clive Steps, King Charles St SW1. **Map** 13 B5. 020-7930 6961. ⊖ Westminster. **Open** Apr–Sep: 9.30am–6pm; Oct–Mar: 10am–6pm daily (last adm: 5.15pm). **Closed** 24–26 Dec. **Adm charge.** 🖸 ⚅ 🗍

THIS INTRIGUING slice of 20th-century history is a warren of cellar rooms below the Government Office Building north of Parliament Square. It is where the War Cabinet – first under Neville Chamberlain, then Winston Churchill – met during World War II when German bombs were falling on London. The War Rooms include living quarters for key ministers and military leaders and a sound-proofed Cabinet

Telephones in the Map Room of the Cabinet War Rooms

Room, where many strategic decisions were taken. All rooms are protected by a layer of concrete about a metre (3 ft) thick. They are laid out as they were when the war ended, complete with period furniture, including Churchill's desk, some old-fashioned communications equipment and maps with markers for plotting complex military strategy.

Downing Street ❾

SW1. **Map** 13 B4. ⊖ Westminster. **Not open** to the public.

SIR GEORGE DOWNING (1623 – 84) spent part of his youth in the American colonies. He was the second graduate from the nascent Harvard College before returning to fight for the Parliamentarians in the English Civil War. In 1680 he

bought some land near Whitehall Palace and built a street of houses. Four of these survive, though they are much altered. George II gave No. 10 to Sir Robert Walpole in 1732. Since then it has been the official residence of the Prime Minister and contains offices as well as a private apartment. In 1989, for security reasons, iron gates were erected at the Whitehall end.

The famous front door of No. 10

No. 12, the Whips' Office, is where Party campaigns are organized.

Government policy is decided in the Cabinet Room at No. 10.

No. 11 is the Chancellor of the Exchequer's official residence.

No. 10 is the official home of the Prime Minister.

The Prime Minister entertains official guests in the State Dining Room.

Westminster Abbey ❹

THE ABBEY is world-famous as the resting-place of Britain's monarchs, and as the setting for coronations and other great pageants. Within its walls can be seen some of the most glorious examples of medieval architecture in London. It also contains one of the most impressive collections of tombs and monuments in the world. Half national church, half national museum, the abbey occupies a unique place in the British national consciousness.

North Entrance
The stonework here, like this carving of a dragon, is Victorian.

★ **Flying Buttresses**
The massive flying buttresses help transfer the great weight of the 31-m (102-ft) high nave.

The North Transept
has three chapels on the east side containing some of the Abbey's finest monuments.

★ **West Front Towers**
These towers, built in 1734–45, were designed by Nicholas Hawksmoor.

STAR FEATURES

★ **West Front Towers**

★ **Flying Buttresses**

★ **The Nave viewed from the West End**

★ **The Lady Chapel**

★ **Chapter House**

Main entrance

★ **The Nave viewed from the West End**
At 10 m (35 ft) wide, the nave is comparatively narrow, but it is the highest in England.

The Cloisters, built mainly in the 13th and 14th centuries, used to link the Abbey church with the other buildings.

St Edward's Chapel
houses not only the royal
Coronation Chair and
Edward the Confessor's
shrine, but also the tombs
of many of England's
medieval monarchs.

★ **The Lady Chapel**
*The chapel, built in
1503–12, has a superb
vaulted ceiling and choir
stalls dating from 1512.*

★ **Chapter House**
*This octagonal structure is
worth seeing for its 13th-
century tiles.*

The South Transept
contains "Poets' Corner",
where memorials to famous
literary figures can be seen.

Museum

TIMELINE

1000	1200	1400	1600	1800	2000

1050 New Benedic-
tine abbey church
begun by Edward
the Confessor

1376 Henry
Yevele begins
rebuilding the
nave

*13th-century
tile from the
Chapter House*

1838 Queen
Victoria's
coronation

1245 New abbey
begun to the
designs of Henry
of Rheims

1269 Body of Edward
the Confessor moved to
new shrine in the abbey

1734 West
towers begun

1540 Monastery
dissolved

1953 Most recent
coronation in the
abbey: Elizabeth II's

A Guided Tour of Westminster Abbey

THE ABBEY'S INTERIOR presents an exceptionally diverse array of architectural and sculptural styles. These range from the austere French Gothic of the nave to the stunning complexity of Henry VII's Tudor chapel and the riotous invention of the later 18th-century monuments. Many English monarchs were buried here; some of their tombs are deliberately plain, while others are lavishly decorated. At the same time, there are monuments to a number of Britain's greatest public figures – ranging from politicians to poets – crowded into the aisles and transepts.

② Lady Nightingale's Memorial
The North Transept chapels contain some of the abbey's finest monuments – this one, by Roubiliac, is for Lady Nightingale (1761).

Main entrance

HISTORICAL PLAN OF THE ABBEY
The first abbey church was established as early as the 10th century, when St Dunstan brought a group of Benedictine monks to the area. The present structure dates largely from the 13th century; the new, French-influenced design was begun in 1245 at the behest of Henry III. Because of its unique role as the royal coronation church, the abbey survived Henry VIII's mid-16th-century onslaught on Britain's monastic buildings.

KEY

- Built before 1400
- Added in 15th century
- Built in 1503–19
- Completed in 1745
- Restored after 1850

① The Nave
The nave is 10.5 m (35 ft) wide and 31 m (102 ft) high. It took 150 years to build.

The Choir houses a gilded 1840s screen, which contains remnants of the 13th-century original.

The Jericho Parlour, added in the early 16th century, contains some fine panelling.

The Jerusalem Chamber has a 17th-century fireplace, fine tapestries and an interesting painted ceiling.

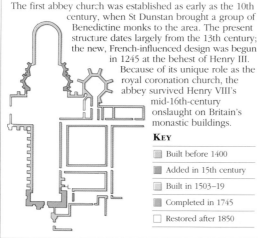

⑧ Tomb of the Unknown Warrior
This plain but moving memorial serves to commemorate the many thousands killed in World War I who had no formal resting place. One un-named soldier is actually buried here.

The Deanery is where the monastery's abbot used to live.

CORONATION
The abbey has been the fittingly sumptuous setting for all royal coronations since 1066. The last occupant of the Coronation Chair was the present monarch, Elizabeth II. She was crowned in 1953 in the first televised coronation.

The Chapel of St John the Baptist is full of tombs dating from the 14th to the 19th centuries.

③ **Coronation Chair**
Constructed in 1301, this is the chair on which monarchs have been crowned since 1308.

The St Faith Chapel contains works of art that date back to the 13th century.

④ **Tomb of Elizabeth I**
Inside Henry VII's Chapel you will find Elizabeth I's (reigned 1558–1603) huge tomb. It also houses the body of her sister, "Bloody" Mary I.

⑤ **Henry VII Chapel**
The undersides of the choir stalls, dating from 1512, are beautifully carved with exotic and fantastic creatures.

⑥ **St Edward's Chapel**
The shrine of the Saxon king Edward the Confessor and the tombs of many medieval monarchs are here.

The Pyx Chamber's gaunt columns date from the 11th century.

Dean's Yard entrance

KEY

– – – Tour route

⑦ **Poets' Corner**
Take time to explore the memorials to countless literary giants, such as Shakespeare and Dickens, which are gathered here.

Banqueting House ⓫

Whitehall SW1. **Map** 13 B4. ☎ 020-7839 8919. 🚇 *Charing Cross, Embankment, Westminster.* **Open** *10am–5pm Mon–Sat (last adm: 4.30).* **Closed** *public hols, 24 Dec–2 Jan, at short notice for ceremonies.* **Adm charge.** 🎧 📷 **Video presentations.**

THIS DELIGHTFUL BUILDING is of great architectural importance. It was the first in central London to embody the Classical Palladian style that designer Inigo Jones brought back from his travels in Italy. Completed in 1622, its disciplined stone facade marked a startling change from the Elizabethans' fussy turrets and unrestrained external decoration. It was the sole survivor of the fire that destroyed most of the old Whitehall Palace in 1698.

The ceiling paintings by Rubens, a complex allegory on the exaltation of James I, were commissioned by his son, Charles I, in 1630. This blatant glorification of royalty was despised by Oliver Cromwell and the Parliamentarians, who executed King Charles I on a scaffold outside Banqueting House in 1649. Ironically, Charles II celebrated his restoration to the throne here 20 years later. The building is occasionally used for official functions.

Mounted sentries stationed outside Horse Guards

Horse Guards ⓬

Whitehall SW1. **Map** 13 B4. ☎ 0891-505 452. 🚇 *Westminster, Charing Cross.* **Open** *8am–6pm daily.* **Changing of the Guard** *11am Mon–Sat, 10am Sun.* **Dismounting Ceremony** *4pm daily. Times for both are subject to change (phone for details).* **Trooping the Colour** *see* **Ceremonial London** *pp52–5.*

ONCE HENRY VIII'S tiltyard (tournament ground), the Changing of the Guard still takes place here every day. The elegant buildings, completed in 1755, were designed by William Kent. On the left is the Old Treasury, also by Kent, and the back of Dover House, completed in 1758 and now used as the Scottish Office.

Nearby is a trace of the "real tennis" court where Henry VIII is said to have played the ancient precursor of modern lawn tennis. On the opposite side, the view is dominated by the ivy-covered Citadel. This is a bomb-proof structure that was erected in 1940 beside the Admiralty. During World War II it was used as a communications headquarters by the Navy.

Whitehall Theatre ⓭

Whitehall SW1. **Map** 13 B3. ☎ 020-7369 1735. 🚇 *Charing Cross.* **Open** *for performances only. See* **Entertainment** *pp326–7.*

Detail of a Whitehall Theatre box

BUILT IN 1930, the plain white front seems to emulate the Cenotaph *(see p74)* at the other end of the street, but, inside, the theatre boasts some excellent Art Deco detailing. From the 1950s to the 1970s it was noted for staging a wide range of farces.

Queen Anne's Gate ⓮

SW1. **Map** 13 A5. 🚇 *St James's Park.*

THE SPACIOUS terraced houses at the west end of this well-preserved enclave date from 1704 and are notable for the ornate canopies over their front doors. At the other end are houses built some 70 years later, sporting blue plaques that record former residents, such as Lord Palmerston, the Victorian Prime Minister. Until recently, the British Secret Service, MI5, was allegedly based in this unlikely spot. A small statue of Queen Anne stands in front of the wall separating Nos. 13 and 15. To the west, situated at the corner of Petty France, Sir Basil Spence's Home Office building (1976)

Panels from the Rubens ceiling, Banqueting House

is an architectural incongruity. Cockpit Steps, leading down to Birdcage Walk, mark the site of a 17th-century venue for the popular, yet blood-thirsty, sport of cockfighting.

Guards Museum ⓯

Birdcage Walk SW1. **Map** 13 A5.
📞 020-7930 4466 x 3271. 🚇 St James's Park. **Open** 10am– 4pm daily. **Closed** 25 Dec, 1 Jan, ceremonies. **Adm charge.** 📷 ♿ 🚻

ENTERED FROM Birdcage Walk, the museum is under the parade ground of Wellington Barracks, head-quarters of the five Guards regiments. A must for military buffs, the museum uses tableaux and dioramas to illustrate various battles in which the Guards have taken part, from the English Civil War (1642– 8) to the present. Weapons and row after row of colourful uniforms are on display, as well as a fascinating collection of models.

St James's Park Station ⓰

55 Broadway SW1. **Map** 13 A5.
🚇 St James's Park.

Epstein sculpture outside St James's Park Station

THE STATION is built into Broadway House, Charles Holden's 1929 headquarters for London Transport. It is notable for its sculptures by Jacob Epstein and reliefs by Henry Moore and Eric Gill.

Blewcoat School ⓱

23 Caxton St SW1. **Map** 13 A5. 📞 020-7222 2877. 🚇 St James's Park. **Open** 12am –5.30pm Mon– Wed, Fri, 10am –7pm Thu. **Closed** public hols.

Statue of a Blewcoat pupil above the Caxton Street entrance

A RED-BRICK GEM hemmed in by the office towers of Victoria Street, it was built in 1709 as a charity school to teach pupils how to "read, write, cast accounts and the catechism". It remained as a school until 1939, then became an army store during World War II and was bought by the National Trust in 1954. The beautifully proportioned interior now serves as a National Trust gift shop.

Westminster Cathedral ⓲

Ashley Place SW1. **Map** 20 F1. 📞 020-7798 9055. 🚇 Victoria. **Open** 5am–5pm daily (Dec–Mar: Thu–Sun only). **Adm charge** for bell tower lift (Apr– Oct: 9am–1pm, 2–4.30pm). 🕐 5.30pm Mon–Fri, 10.30am Sat, Sun, Sung Mass (phone to check for other services). 📷 ♿ 🚻 🚻 **Concerts**.

ONE OF LONDON'S rare Byzantine buildings, it was designed by John Francis Bentley for the Catholic diocese and completed in 1903 on the site of a former prison. Its 87-m (261-ft) high, red-brick tower, with horizontal stripes of white stone, stands out on the skyline in sharp contrast to the Abbey nearby. A restful piazza on the north side provides a good view of the

cathedral from Victoria Street. The rich interior decoration, with marble of varying colours and intricate mosaics, makes the domes above the nave seem incongruous. They were left bare because the project ran out of money before it could be completed.

Eric Gill's dramatic reliefs of the 14 Stations of the Cross, created during World War I, adorn the pier of the nave. The organ is one of the finest in Europe, and a series of concerts is held here every second Tuesday from June until September.

St John's, Smith Square ⓳

Smith Sq SW1. **Map** 21 B1. 📞 020-7222 1061. 🚇 Westminster, **Open** 10am–5pm Mon–Fri and for evening concerts. 🅿 🚻 🚻 **Concerts**. See **Entertainment** pp330 –1.

Premiere Ensemble at St John's, Smith Square

DESCRIBED BY artist and art historian Sir Hugh Casson as one of the masterpieces of English Baroque architecture, Thomas Archer's plump church, with its turrets at each corner, looks as if it is trying to burst from the confines of the square, and rather over-powers the pleasing 18th-century houses on its north side. It has an accident-prone history: completed in 1728, it was burned down in 1742, struck by lightning in 1773 and destroyed again by a World War II bomb in 1941. There is a reasonably priced restaurant in the basement – a rarity in this area – that is open daily for lunch and on the evenings of concerts.

Tate Gallery ⓴

See pp82–5.

Tate Gallery ⑳

O FFICIALLY NOW the Tate Gallery of British Art, the founding gallery of a series of Tates holds the world's largest collection of British works from the 16th to the 20th centuries. In the adjoining Clore Gallery is the magnificent Turner Bequest, left to the nation by the land-scape artist J M W Turner himself. The collection of international art once here is now at the Bankside branch *(see p178)*.

The portico of the Tate building, which dates from 1897, overlooks the Thames.

GALLERY GUIDE

Most of the collection is housed on the ground floor. Works on paper and temporary exhibitions are downstairs. The paintings are hung chronologically, tracing British art from 1550 to the present day, with 20th-century works occupying the east side of the gallery, all earlier works on the west side. Displays are changed frequently, to emphasize different aspects of the collection. Note that not all of the works illustrated here will be on show.

Stairs to lower galleries

★ Peace – Burial at Sea
This is J M W Turner's tribute to his friend and rival David Wilkie. It was painted in 1842, the year after Wilkie died at sea.

★ Flatford Mill (Scene on a Navigable River)
John Constable's works are among the best represented and most popular in the Tate. This painting of 1816–17 typifies his masterly use of shadow and light.

Stairs to lower galleries

KEY TO FLOORPLAN

☐	Sculpture Gallery
☐	Temporary exhibitions
☐	Paintings
☐	Clore Gallery (Turner)
☐	Non-exhibition space

Three Figures: Pink and Grey
J A M Whistler's work of 1868–78 is an example of his use of tonal shades and liquid forms.

THE ART OF GOOD FOOD

As well as a coffee bar, the Tate boasts a café and licensed restaurant on the lower floor decorated with a lavish mural by Rex Whistler. It tells the story of the inhabitants of the mythical Epicurania, and their pursuit of exotic foods to revive their jaded palates. The restaurant is well worth a visit for lunch, but it is not open for dinner.

VISITORS' CHECKLIST

Millbank SW1. **Map** 21 B2.
C 020-7887 8000.
Fi 020-7887 8008. **⊖** Pimlico.
▥ 77a, 88, C10 or 2, 2b, 3, 36, 36b, 159, 185, 507. **⊋** Victoria, Vauxhall. **Open** 10am–5.50pm daily. **Closed** 24–26 Dec, Good Fri, May Day. **Adm charge** for major exhibitions. **No charge** for permanent collections.
◘ & Atterbury St.
⊠ ⊓ ⊑ 🛈

Disabled entrance
on ground floor **&**

Entrance to
Clore Gallery
via Room 18

★ **Mares and Foals**
George Stubbs's work (from 1762–8) is characterized by perfect anatomical detail.

Stairs to lower
galleries

Main
entrance
to Clore
Gallery

Lady of Shalott (1888)
J W Waterhouse's work reflects the Pre-Raphaelite fascination with Arthurian myth.

Rotunda

Main entrance

**Standing by
the Rags** ★
*(1988–9)
Lucien Freud's
nude studies are
considered his finest
works, and this is a
superlative example.*

STAR PAINTINGS

★ **Mares and Foals by
George Stubbs**

★ **Burial at Sea by
J M W Turner**

★ **Flatford Mill by
John Constable**

★ **Standing by the Rags
by Lucien Freud**

Exploring the Tate's Collection

U NTIL 2000 THIS GALLERY housed two collections – international modern art and British art from the 16th century on. Modern works are now on display in the new gallery at Bankside (see p178).

Endymion Porter (1643–5) by William Dobson

THE TATE IN TRANSITION

W ITH THE TRANSFER of the modern collection, the Tate has taken the opportunity of upgrading and expanding its facilities, With £32 million of improvements for completion in 2001, the new galleries will hold the world's largest display of British art from Tudor times to the present day, with extra space for special exhibitions. The change means that the gallery is reverting to the purpose that Sir Henry Tate intended when he endowed it and presented it with his own collection of British art (mainly Victorian).

He had made his fortune in Liverpool in the 1870s by patenting a machine for cutting sugar into cubes. Occupying the site of the former Millbank prison, the gallery he funded opened as the national gallery of British art in 1897, two years before he died. In 1916 it also became home to the national collection of modern art but, as the number of acquisitions grew, space became a critical problem. Now the west side of the building can be devoted to works from 1500–1899, the east to the 20th century, with new works of merit constantly being added.

16TH- AND 17TH-CENTURY ART

F ORMAL PORTRAITS only began to appear during the 16th century, influenced by Hans Holbein, who brought Renais-

Ashley Cowper with his Wife and Daughter (1731) by William Hogarth

sance ideas and techniques from the continent. His meticulous, linear style is echoed in many early works, notably John Bettes' *A Man in a Black Cap* of 1545. Miniaturist Nicholas Hilliard is represented here by a rare and exquisite full-sized portrait of Elizabeth I. In the 17th century, under the influence of Van Dyck, a new, grandly elegant style of portraiture emerged. His *Lady of the Spencer Family* and Dobson's *Endymion Porter* are fine examples. Two non-portrait gems are Francis Barlow's *Monkeys and Spaniels Playing*, a charming early animal painting, and Jan Sibrecht's *Landscape with Rainbow, Henley-on-Thames* which marks the birth of the English landscape tradition.

Satan Smiting Job with Sore Boils (c.1826) by William Blake

18TH-CENTURY ART

A LONG WITH the early 18th-century illustrative paintings, the collection boasts some fine examples of "conversation pieces" (people in an informal setting). These include the doll-like *James Family* by Arthur Devis, and William Hogarth's vivid *The*

TURNER AT THE CLORE GALLERY

When J M W Turner (1775–1851) left his works to the nation, it was on condition that they were kept together. In 1910, a suite of rooms at the Tate was given over to some of his oil paintings, but it was not until the Clore Gallery was opened in 1987 that the entire bequest, including thousands of studies, came together. The gallery also houses Turner's watercolours including *A City on a River at Sunset*, part of his *Great Rivers of Europe* project.

A City on a River at Sunset **(1832)**

Strode Family at Breakfast. Hogarth was the leading figure in British art in the 18th century and his pictures, laced with sharp satire and social comment, remain popular today. From the late 18th century, the "Grand Style" of Joshua Reynolds can be compared with the feathery brushwork in the portraits of his now more highly-regarded rival, Thomas Gainsborough. The latter also produced some ravishing landscapes but the father of the English landscape was Richard Wilson, who painted some marvellous views of the Thames. George Stubbs is best known for painting horses: his *Mares and Foals in a Landscape* is here, as well as a pair of lyrical depictions of

rural pursuits, *Reapers* and *Haymakers*. Joseph Wright of Derby produced some powerful early industrial and scientific scenes.

Two Figures (Menhirs) (1964) by Barbara Hepworth

19TH-CENTURY ART

THE TATE HOLDS a large body of works by William Blake, the visionary genius of the 19th century, and his followers – chief among them Samuel Palmer, who painted intimate pastoral scenes imbued with mystic intensity. Constable and Turner, the two greatest landscape artists of their time, are also well represented, Turner in the dedicated Clore Gallery and Constable by sketches and full-scale paintings such as *Chain Pier, Brighton* and the famous *Flatford Mill*. Later in the century came the Pre-Raphaelites, with their highly coloured, emotionally

Recumbent Figure (1938) by Henry Moore

intense images. J E Millais' *Ophelia*, one of the paintings from Sir Henry Tate's original collection, is an outstanding example of the genre.

1945 Still Life by Ben Nicholson

20TH-CENTURY ART

AT THE START of the 20th century, British art was heavily influenced by developments in Europe, as it had been 300 years earlier. Wilson Steer and James Sickert were known as the British Impressionists

Mr and Mrs Clark and Percy (1970–1) by David Hockney

and Wyndham Lewis invented Vorticism, which derived from Cubism. Stanley Spencer developed a more ideosyncratic style. Ben Nicholson was among the leaders of the Abstract school of painting, but sculpture was the area in which British art gained an international reputation, notably in the works of Henry Moore, Barbara Hepworth and Anthony Caro. The effects of World War II can be seen in the paintings of the 1940s and '50s, from Paul Nash's war-torn landscapes to the disturbing images created by Francis Bacon. Richard Hamilton and Peter Blake and are the outstanding representatives of British Pop Art, and more recent painters represented include Lucien Freud, Patrick Heron, R B Kitaj and David Hockney. Controversial works of minimalist and conceptual art complete the displays, by artists such as Richard Long, Rachel Whiteread and Damian Hirst. A new suite of galleries will allow the work of up-and-coming British artists to be highlighted to an extent not possible before. Some modern British works of international importance are also on view at the Tate Gallery of Modern Art on Bankside.

PICCADILLY AND ST JAMES'S

Piccadilly is the main artery of the West End. Once called Portugal Street, it acquired its present name from the ruffs, or pickadills, worn by 17th-century dandies. St James's still bears traces of the 18th century, when it surrounded the royal residences, and denizens of the court and society shopped and disported

Buckingham Palace decorative lock

themselves there. Two shops in St James's Street – Lock the hatter and Berry Bros vintners – recall that era. Fortnum and Mason, on Piccadilly, has served high-quality food for nearly 300 years. Mayfair to the north is still the most fashionable address in London, while Piccadilly Circus marks the start of Soho.

SIGHTS AT A GLANCE

Historic Streets and Buildings

Piccadilly Circus ❶
Albany ❸
Burlington Arcade ❺
Ritz Hotel ❻
Spencer House ❼
St James's Palace ❽
St James's Square ❾
Royal Opera Arcade ❿
Pall Mall ⓫
The Mall ⓮
Marlborough House ⓯
Clarence House ⓱
Lancaster House ⓲
Buckingham Palace pp94–5 ⓳
Royal Mews ㉑
Wellington Arch ㉒
Shepherd Market ㉔

Museums and Galleries

Royal Academy of Arts ❹
Institute of Contemporary Arts ⓬
Queen's Gallery ⓴
Royal Mews ㉑
Apsley House ㉓
Faraday Museum ㉖

Churches

St James's Church ❷
Queen's Chapel ⓰

Parks and Gardens

St James's Park ⓭
Green Park ㉕

SEE ALSO

• *Street Finder*, maps 12, 13

• *Where to Stay* pp276–7

• *Restaurants* pp292–4

GETTING THERE

The Piccadilly line serves Hyde Park Corner, Piccadilly Circus, and Green Park. The Bakerloo and Jubilee lines serve Charing Cross, which is also a major railway terminus. The area is served by buses Nos. 6, 9, 15, 23 and 139.

KEY

▢	Street-by-Street map
⊖	Underground station
⇌	Railway station
P	Parking

Piccadilly Arcade with its many fine shops

Street-by-Street: Piccadilly and St James's

A<small>S SOON AS HENRY VIII</small> built St James's Palace in the 1530s, the area around it became the centre of fashionable London, and it has remained so ever since. The most influential people in the land strut importantly along its historic streets as they press on with the vital business of lunching in their clubs, discussing matters of pith and moment and brandishing their gold cards in the capital's most exclusive stores, or paying a visit to one of the many art galleries.

Albany
It has been one of London's smartest addresses since it opened in 1803 ❸

★Royal Academy of Arts
Sir Joshua Reynolds founded the Academy in 1768. Now it mounts large popular exhibitions ❹

★ Burlington Arcade
Uniformed beadles discourage unruly behaviour in this 19th-century mall ❺

Fortnum and Mason
was founded in 1707 by one of Queen Anne's footmen *(see p311).*

The Ritz
Named after César Ritz, and opened in 1906, it still lives up to his name ❻

Spencer House
An ancestor of Princess Diana built this house in 1766 ❼

St James's Palace
This Tudor palace is still the Court's official headquarters ❽

To the Mall

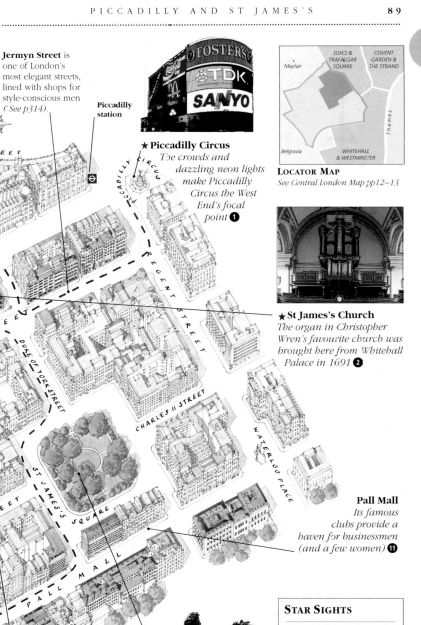

Jermyn Street is one of London's most elegant streets, lined with shops for style-conscious men *(See p314).*

Piccadilly station

★ **Piccadilly Circus**
The crowds and dazzling neon lights make Piccadilly Circus the West End's focal point ❶

LOCATOR MAP
See Central London Map pp12–13

★ **St James's Church**
The organ in Christopher Wren's favourite church was brought here from Whitehall Palace in 1691 ❷

Pall Mall
Its famous clubs provide a haven for businessmen (and a few women) ⓫

St James's Square
William III's statue dominates the square ❾

King Street is lined with art galleries, including Christie's, St James's.

STAR SIGHTS

★ **Burlington Arcade**

★ **Royal Academy**

★ **St James's Church**

★ **Piccadilly Circus**

KEY

– – – Suggested route

0 metres   100

0 yards   100

Piccadilly Circus ❶

W1. **Map** 13 A3. 🚇 *Piccadilly Circus.*

Alfred Gilbert's statue of Eros

FOR YEARS PEOPLE have congregated beneath the symbolic figure of Eros, originally intended as an angel of mercy but renamed after the Greek god of love. Poised delicately with his bow, Eros has become almost a trade mark for the capital. It was erected in 1892 as a memorial to the Earl of Shaftesbury, the Victorian philanthropist. Part of Nash's master plan for Regent's Street *(see p220)*, Piccadilly Circus has been considerably altered in recent years and consists chiefly of shopping malls. One of them can be found behind the facade of the London Pavilion (1885), once a popular music hall. The circus has London's gaudiest array of neon advertising signs marking the entrance to the city's lively entertainment district with cinemas, theatres, night clubs, restaurants and pubs.

St James's Church ❷

197 Piccadilly W1. **Map** 13 A3. 📞 *020-7734 4511.* 🚇 *Piccadilly Circus, Green Park.* **Open** 8am–7pm daily. **Craft market** 10am–6pm Wed–Sat, **antiques market** 10am–6pm Tue (except Easter). 🚫 during services. 🎵 **Concerts, lectures.**

AMONG THE many churches Wren designed *(see p47)*, this is said to be one of his favourites. It has been altered over the years and was half-wrecked by a bomb in 1940, but it maintains its essential features from 1684 – the tall, arched windows, thin spire (a 1966 fibreglass replica of the original) and a light, dignified interior. The ornate screen behind the altar is one of the finest works of the 17th-century master carver Grinling Gibbons, who also made the exquisite marble font, with a scene depicting Adam and Eve standing by the Tree of Life. Artist and poet William Blake and Prime Minister Pitt the Elder were both baptized here. More of Gibbons's carvings can be seen above the grandiose organ, made for Whitehall Palace chapel but installed here in 1691. Today the church has a full calendar of events, and runs the vegetarian Wren Coffee House.

Albany ❸

Albany Court Yard, Piccadilly W1. **Map** 12 F3. 🚇 *Green Park, Piccadilly Circus.* **Closed** to the public.

THESE DESIRABLE and discreet bachelor apartments, half hidden through an entrance off Piccadilly, were built in 1803 by Henry Holland. Notable residents have included the poet Lord Byron, novelist Graham Greene, two Prime Ministers (William Gladstone and Edward Heath) and the actor Terence Stamp. Married men were admitted in 1878 but could not bring their wives to live with them until 1919. Women are now allowed to live here in their own right.

Lord Byron lived in Albany

Royal Academy of Arts ❹

Burlington House, Piccadilly W1. **Map** 12 F3. 📞 *020-7300 8000.* 🚇 *Piccadilly Circus, Green Park.* **Open** 10am–6pm daily (last adm: 5.30pm). **Closed** 24–26 Dec, Good Fri. **Adm charge.** 🚫 ♿ 🎁 book in advance 📷 🍴 🛍 📠 **Lectures.**

Michelangelo's Madonnna and Child

THE COURTYARD in front of Burlington House, one of the West End's few surviving mansions from the early 18th century, is often crammed with people waiting to get into one of the prestigious visiting art exhibitions on show at the Royal Academy (founded 1768). The famous annual summer exhibition, which has now been held for over 200 years, comprises around 1,200 new works by both established and unknown painters, sculptors and architects. Any artist, regardless of background or talent, may submit work.

The airy Sackler Galleries (1991), designed by Norman Foster in the former diploma galleries, show visiting exhibitions. There are permanent items in the sculpture promenade outside the galleries, notably a Michelangelo relief of the Madonna and Child (1505). The exceptional permanent collection (not all on display) includes one work by each current and former Academician. There is a good shop on the first floor which sells cards and other items that are designed by Academy members for the RA.

Burlington Arcade ❺

Piccadilly W1. **Map** 12 F3. 🚇 *Green Park, Piccadilly Circus. See* **Shops and Markets** *p318.*

THIS IS ONE OF three 19th-century arcades of small shops which sell traditional British luxuries. (The others, the Piccadilly and Princes Arcades, are on the south side of Piccadilly). It was built for Lord Cavendish in 1819 to prevent passers-by throwing rubbish into his garden. The arcade is still patrolled by beadles who ensure that an atmosphere of refinement is maintained. They have the authority to eject anyone who sings, whistles, runs or opens an umbrella; those powers are infrequently invoked now, perhaps because the dictates of commerce take precedence over those of decorum.

Ritz Hotel ❻

Piccadilly W1. **Map** 12 F3. 📞 *020-7493 8181.* 🚇 *Green Park.* **Open** *to non-residents for tea or restaurant meals.* 👦👿 *See* **Where to Stay** *p282 and* **Restaurants and Pubs** *p306.*

CESAR RITZ, the famed Swiss hotelier who inspired the adjective "ritzy", had virtually retired by the time this hotel was built and named after him in 1906. The colonnaded frontal aspect of the imposing château-style building was meant to suggest Paris, where the very grandest and most fashionable hotels were to be

The exquisite Palm Room of Spencer House

found around the turn of the century. It still manages to maintain its Edwardian air of *fin de siècle* opulence and is a popular stop, among those who are suitably dressed, for genteel afternoon tea. The atmosphere of chic suavity is enhanced by the tea dances and fashion parades which are held in the Palm Court.

Spencer House ❼

27 St James's Pl SW1. **Map** 12 F4. 📞 *020-7499 8620.* 🚇 *Green Park.* **Open** *10.30am–5.30pm Sun (last adm 4.45pm).* **Closed** *Jan & Aug.* **Adm charge. Children** *under 10 not welcome.* 🚫👦👿 *compulsory.*

THIS PALLADIAN PALACE was finished in 1766 for the first Earl Spencer, an ancestor of the late Princess of Wales. Today it has been completely restored to its 18th-century splendour (thanks to an £18 million renovation project)

and contains an amazing selection of paintings and contemporary furniture; one of the real highlights is the beautifully decorated painted room. The house is open to the public for guided tours, receptions or meetings.

St James's Tudor gatehouse

St James's Palace ❽

The Mall SW1. **Map** 12 F4. 🚇 *Green Park.* **Not open** *to the public.*

BUILT BY HENRY VIII in the late 1530s on the site of a former leper hospital, it was a primary royal residence only briefly, mainly during the reign of Elizabeth I and during the late 17th and early 18th centuries. In 1952 Queen Elizabeth II made her first speech as queen here, and foreign ambassadors are still officially accredited to the Court of St James. Its northern gatehouse, seen from St James's Street, is one of London's most evocative Tudor landmarks. Behind it the palace buildings are now occupied by privileged Crown servants.

Afternoon tea served in the opulent Palm Court of the Ritz

Royal Opera Arcade

St James's Square 🄎

SW1. **Map** 13 A3. 🄎 *Green Park, Piccadilly Circus.*

ONE OF LONDON'S earliest squares, it was laid out in the 1670s and lined by exclusive houses for those whose business made it vital for them to live near St James's Palace. Many of the buildings date from the 18th and 19th centuries and have had many illustrious residents. During World War II Generals Eisenhower and de Gaulle both had headquarters here.

Today No. 10 on the north side is Chatham House (1736), home of the Royal Institute for International Affairs and, in the northeast corner, can be found the London Library (1896), a private lending library founded in 1841 by historian Thomas Carlyle *(see p192)* and others. The private gardens in the middle contain an equestrian statue of William III, here since 1808.

Royal Opera Arcade 🄎

SW1. **Map** 13 A3. 🄎 *Piccadilly Circus.*

LONDON'S FIRST shopping arcade, it was designed by John Nash and completed in 1818, behind the Haymarket Opera House (now called Her Majesty's Theatre). It beat the Burlington Arcade *(see p91)* by a year or so. Farlows sell shooting equipment, fishing tackle, including the famous Hunter's green Wellington boots, and a broad range of other essentials for traditional country living, from the Pall Mall side of this arcade.

Pall Mall 🄎

SW1. **Map** 13 A4. 🄎 *Charing Cross, Green Park.*

The Duke of Wellington (1842): a frequent visitor to Pall Mall

THIS DIGNIFIED street is named from the game of *palle-maille*, a cross between croquet and golf, which was played here in the early 17th century. For more than 150 years Pall Mall has been at the heart of London's clubland. Here exclusive gentlemen's clubs were formed to provide members with a refuge from their womenfolk.

The club houses now amount to a text book of the most fashionable architects of the era. From the east end, on the left is the colonnaded entrance to No. 116, Nash's United Services Club (1827). This was the favourite club of the Duke of Wellington and now houses the Institute of Directors. Facing it, on the other side of Waterloo Place, is the Athenaeum (No. 116), designed three years later by Decimus Burton, and long the power house of the British establishment. Next door are two clubs by Sir Charles Barry, architect of the Houses of Parliament *(see pp72–3)*; the Travellers' is at No. 106 and the Reform at No. 104. The clubs' stately interiors are well preserved but only members and their guests are admitted.

Institute of Contemporary Arts 🄎

The Mall SW1. **Map** 13 B3. 🄎 *020-7930 3647.* 🄎 *Charing Cross, Piccadilly Circus.* **Open** *noon–10.30pm Sun, noon–11pm Mon, noon–1am Tue–Sat.* **Closed** *Christmas week, public hols.* **Adm charge.** 🄎 *notify in advance.* 🄎
🄎 🄎 🄎 *Concerts, theatre, dance, lectures, films, exhibitions. See* **Entertainment** *pp332–3.*

THE INSTITUTE (ICA) was established in 1947 in an effort to offer British artists some of the facilities which were available to United States artists at the Museum of Modern Art in New York. Originally on Dover Street, it has been situated in John Nash's Classical Carlton House Terrace (1833) since 1968.

With its entrance on the Mall, this extensive warren contains a cinema, auditorium, bookshop, art gallery, bar and a fine restaurant. It also offers exhibitions, lectures, concerts, films and plays. Non-members have to pay a charge.

Institute of Contemporary Arts, Carlton House Terrace

St James's Park ⓫

SW1. **Map** *13 A4.* ☏ *020-7930 1793.* ⊖ *St James's Park.* **Open** *5am–midnight daily.* ⊡ **Open** *daily.* ♿ **Concerts** *twice daily at weekends and summer public hols, weather permitting.* **Bird collection**.

IN SUMMER office workers sunbathe between the dazzling flower beds of this, the capital's most ornamental park. In winter overcoated civil servants discuss affairs of state as they stroll by the lake and eye its ducks, geese and pelicans. Originally a marsh, the park was drained by Henry VIII and incorporated into his hunting grounds. Later Charles II redesigned it for pedestrian pleasures, with an aviary along its southern edge (hence Birdcage Walk, the street where the aviary was). It is still a popular place to take the air, with an appealing view of Whitehall rooftops. In the summer there are concerts on the bandstand.

The Mall ⓬

SW1. **Map** *13 A4.* ⊖ *Charing Cross, Green Park, Piccadilly Circus.*

THIS BROAD triumphal approach to Buckingham Palace was created by Aston Webb when he redesigned the front of the palace and the Victoria Monument in 1911 (*see picture p96*). It follows the course of the old path at the edge of St James's Park, laid out in the reign of Charles II when it became London's most fashionable promenade. On the flagpoles down both sides of the Mall fly national flags of foreign heads of state during official visits.

Marlborough House ⓭

Pall Mall SW1. **Map** *13 A4.* ☏ *020-7839 3411.* ⊖ *St James's Park, Green Park.* **Open** *one Sat in Sep only (phone for details).*

MARLBOROUGH HOUSE was designed by Christopher Wren (*see p47*) for the Duchess of Marlborough, and

finished in 1711. It was substantially enlarged in the 19th century and used by members of the Royal Family. From 1863 until he became Edward VII in 1903, it was the home of the Prince and Princess of Wales and the social centre of London. An Art Nouveau memorial in the Marlborough Road wall of the house commemorates Edward's queen, Alexandra. The building now houses the Commonwealth Secretariat.

Queen's Chapel ⓮

Marlborough Rd SW1. **Map** *13 A4.* ☏ *020-7930 4832.* ⊖ *Green Park.* **Open** *for Sun services only.*

THIS EXQUISITE WORK of the architect Inigo Jones was built for Charles I's French wife, Henrietta Maria, in 1627, and was the first Classical church in England. It was initially intended to be part

Queen's Chapel

of St James's Palace but is now separated from it by Marlborough Gate. George III married his queen, Charlotte of Mecklenburg-Strelitz (who was to bear him 15 children), here in 1761.

The interior of the chapel, with its wonderful Annibale Caracci altarpiece and glorious 17th-century fittings is, unfortunately, open only to regular worshippers during the spring and early summer.

Early summer in St James's Park

Buckingham Palace ⓳

Buckingham palace is the headquarters of the British monarchy. It doubles as an office and a home, and is also used for ceremonial state occasions such as banquets for visiting heads of state. About 300 people work at the palace. These include officers of the Royal Household, who organize The Queen's official affairs, as well as domestic staff.

John Nash converted the original Buckingham House into a palace for George IV (reigned 1820–30). Both he and his brother, William IV (reigned 1830–7), died before work was completed, and Queen Victoria was the first monarch to live at the palace. The present east front, facing the Mall, was added in 1913.

Music Room
State guests are presented and royal christenings take place in this room, which boasts a beautiful, original parquet floor by Nash.

The Picture Gallery houses a selection of The Queen's priceless collection of paintings.

The State Dining Room is where meals that are less formal than state banquets are held.

Kitchen and staff quarters

Blue Drawing Room
Imitation onyx columns, created by John Nash, decorate this room.

Private post office

Changing of the Guard
During the summer the palace guard is changed every day in a colourful ceremony.
(See p52–5.)

State Ballroom
The Georgian baroque ballroom is used for state banquets and investitures.

VISITORS' CHECKLIST

SW1. **Map** 12 F5. 020-739 1377. St James's Park, Victoria. 2B, 11, 16, 24, 25, 36, 38, 52, 73, 135, C1. Victoria. **State rooms open** *Aug–Sep: 9.30am– 5.30pm daily (last adm: 4.30pm).* **Adm charge.** **Changing of the Queen's Guard:** *May–Aug: 11.30am daily; Sep–Apr: alternate days but subject to change without notice.*

The garden is a haven for wild life and is overlooked by most of the lavishly decorated state rooms at the back of the palace.

The White Drawing Room is where The Royal Family assemble before passing into the State Dining Room or Ball Room.

A swimming pool lies in the palace grounds as does a private cinema.

The Throne Room is illuminated by seven magnificent chandeliers.

The Green Drawing Room is the first of the state rooms entered by guests at royal functions.

Queen's Audience Chamber
This is one of The Queen's 12 private rooms on the first floor of the palace.

The Royal Standard flies when The Queen is in residence.

WHO LIVES IN BUCKINGHAM PALACE?

The palace is the London residence of The Queen and her husband, the Duke of Edinburgh. Prince Edward also has an apartment here, as do Princess Anne and the Duke of York. About 50 domestic staff have rooms in the palace. There are more staff homes situated in the Royal Mews *(see p96)*.

View over Mall
Traditionally, The Royal Family waves to eager crowds from the palace balcony.

Clarence House ⓱

Stable Yard SW1. **Map** 12 F4.
🚇 *Green Park, St James's Park.*
Not open to the public.

OVERLOOKING THE MALL, it was designed in 1827 by John Nash for Queen Victoria's predecessor, William, Duke of Clarence who lived here after he became king in 1830. It is now the Queen Mother's London home.

Lancaster House ⓲

Stable Yard SW1. **Map** 12 F4.
🚇 *Green Park, St James's Park.*
Not open to the public.

Lancaster House

THIS ROYAL residence was built for the Duke of York by Benjamin Wyatt, architect of Apsley House, in 1825. In 1848 Chopin played here for Queen Victoria, Prince Albert and the Duke of Wellington. It is now a conference centre.

Buckingham Palace ⓳

See pp94–5.

Queen's Gallery ⓴

Buckingham Palace Rd SW1.
Map 12 F5. ☎ 020-7839 1377.
🚇 *St James's Park, Victoria.* **Closed** for refurbishment until 2002. **Adm** charge. 🚫 🎫

THE QUEEN POSSESSES one of the finest and most valuable collections of paintings in the world, rich in the work of such old masters

as Vermeer and Leonardo. (For 30 years her art adviser was Sir Anthony Blunt, until he was finally exposed as a Soviet spy in 1979 and then stripped of his knighthood.)

A selection of the works is on display in this small gallery (at the side of the Palace), which was used as a conservatory until 1962. The building was once also used as a chapel, and there is still an area which is entirely devoted to private worship and is screened off from the public. The exhibitions here are based on a specific theme and change regularly. A shop sells a variety of interesting royal memorabilia.

Royal Mews ㉑

Buckingham Palace Rd SW1.
Map 12 E5. ☎ 020-7839 1377.
🚇 *St James's Park, Victoria.*
Open noon–4pm Tue–Thu
last adm: 3.30pm). Subject to closure at short notice (phone first). **Adm charge.**
♿ 📷

ALTHOUGH OPEN for only a few hours a week, the mews is worth catching for all lovers of horses and of royal pomp. The stables and coach houses, designed by Nash in 1825, accommodate the horses and coaches used by the Royal Family on state occasions, as well as the Rolls-Royce limousines with transparent tops that allow their

Fabergé egg, Queen's Gallery

royal occupants to be seen. The star exhibit is the gold state coach, built for George III in 1761, with fine panels by Giovanni Cipriani. Among the other vehicles are the Irish state coach, bought by Queen Victoria for the State Opening of Parliament; the open-topped royal landau; and the glass coach which was used for royal weddings and for transporting foreign ambassadors. The elaborate horses' harnesses are also on display, and so are some of the splendid animals that wear them.

The mews remains open during the week of the Royal Ascot race meeting in June. For this event, however, the Mews vehicles go to the Berkshire course, where they transport the royal party past the grandstand before the first race.

The Victoria Monument outside Buckingham Palace

Wellington Arch ㉒

SW1. **Map** 12 D4. ⊖ Hyde Park
Corner. **Open** 5am–midnight daily.

AFTER NEARLY A century of
debate about what to do
with the patch of land that
lies in front of Apsley House,
a vast archway, designed by
Decimus Burton and called
Wellington Arch, was erected
in 1828. The sculpture, by
Adrian Jones, was added
later, in 1912. Before it was
installed on the arch Jones
had managed to seat eight
people for dinner in the
hollow, boat-shaped body of
one of the horses.

Until 1992 London's second
smallest police station (the
smallest can be found on
Trafalgar Square) used to be
located inside the arch, which
is sometimes referred to as
Constitution Arch.

Wellington Arch

Apsley House ㉓

149 Piccadilly W1. **Map** 12 D4.
☎ 020-7499 5676. ⊖ Hyde Park
Corner. **Open** 11am–5pm Tue–Sun (last
adm: 4.30pm). **Closed** 24–26 Dec, 1
Jan, Good Fri, May Day. **Adm charge**.
◎ ⅌ ♿ ☏ phone first.

APSLEY HOUSE, on the southeast corner of Hyde Park,
was completed by Robert
Adam for Baron Apsley in
1778. Fifty years later it was
enlarged and altered by the
architects Benjamin and Philip
Wyatt, to provide a suitably
grand home for the Duke of
Wellington, whose dual career
as politician and soldier
brought him victory against
Napoleon at Waterloo (1815),
and two terms as prime
minister (1828-30, 1834). It is
now a museum of Wellington
memorabilia and some of his

Interior of Apsley House

trophies, and is dominated by
Canova's startling, double life-
size statue of Napoleon, who
was Wellington's arch-enemy,
wearing only a fig leaf. This
once stood in the Louvre in
Paris. Most of the paintings
are of Wellington's contemporaries and victories, but
there are also some old
masters from his collection.
The few remaining Adam
interiors are worth seeing.

Shepherd Market ㉔

W1. **Map** 12 E4. ⊖ Green Park.

THIS BIJOU pedestrianized
enclave of small shops,
restaurants, and outdoor
cafes, between Piccadilly and
Curzon Street, was named
after Edward Shepherd, who
built it in the mid-18th
century. During the 17th
century the annual 15-day
May Fair (from which the
area's name is derived) was
held on this
site, and today Shepherd
Market is still very much
the centre of Mayfair.

Green Park ㉕

SW1. **Map** 12 E4. ☎ 020-7930
1793. ⊖ Green Park, Hyde Park
Corner. **Open** 5am–midnight daily.

ONCE PART OF Henry VIII's
hunting ground, it was,
like St James's Park, adapted
for public enjoyment by
Charles II in the 1660s and is
a natural, undulating
landscape of grass and trees

(with a good spring show of
daffodils). It was a favourite
site for duels during the 18th
century; in 1771 the poet
Alfieri was wounded here
by his mistress's husband,
Viscount Ligonier, but then
rushed back to the Haymarket
Theatre still in time to catch
the last act of a play. Today
the park is popular with
guests staying at the Mayfair
hotels as a place to jog.

Faraday Museum ㉖

The Royal Institution, 21 Albemarle St
W1. **Map** 12 F3. ☎ 020-7409 2992.
⊖ Green Park. **Open** 10am–4pm
Mon–Fri. **Closed** 124 Dec–7 Jan. **Adm
charge**. ◎ ☏ phone first. **Lectures**.

MICHAEL FARADAY was a
19th-century pioneer of
the uses of electricity. His
laboratory of the 1850s has
been reconstructed in the
basement here, and is on
display together with a small
museum showing some of
Faraday's scientific apparatus
together with personal effects.

Michael Faraday

SOHO AND TRAFALGAR SQUARE

SOHO HAS BEEN renowned for pleasures of the table, the flesh and the intellect ever since it was first developed in the late 17th century. For its first century the area was one of London's most fashionable, and Soho residents of the time have gone down in history for their extravagant parties.

Clock on Liberty department store

Today the area is the capital's best-known red light district, even though most of the prostitutes were forced from the streets by legislation in 1959. There is also a fertile sub-culture of artists and writers in the scruffy pubs, clubs and cafés.

Soho is one of London's most multi-cultural districts. The first immigrants were 18th-century Huguenots from France *(see Christ Church, Spitalfields p170).* They were followed by people from all over the rest of Europe, but today Soho is famous as a Chinatown.

SIGHTS AT A GLANCE

Historic Streets and Buildings
Trafalgar Square ❶
Admiralty Arch ❷
Leicester Square ❻
Shaftesbury Avenue ❽
Chinatown ❾
Charing Cross Road ❿
Soho Square ⓬
Carnaby Street ⓮

Shops and Markets
Berwick Street Market ⓭
Liberty ⓯

Churches
St Martin-in-the-Fields ❹

Museums and Galleries
National Gallery pp104–7 ❸
National Portrait Gallery ❺

Theatres
Palace Theatre ⓫
Theatre Royal ❼

GETTING THERE
This area is served by the Central, Piccadilly, Bakerloo, Victoria, Northern and Jubilee lines. Many buses pass through Trafalgar Square. Rail services run from Charing Cross.

KEY
▢ Street-by-Street map
🚇 Underground station
🚉 Railway station
🅿 Parking

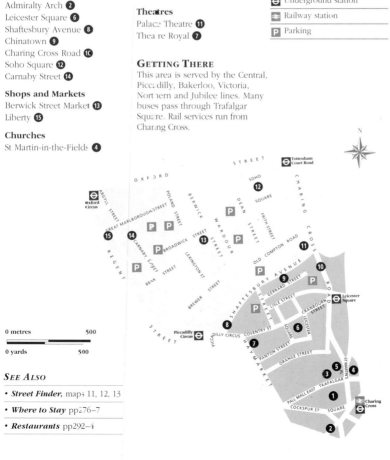

The fountains of Trafalgar Square

Street-by-Street: Trafalgar Square

Theatres, cinemas, night clubs and restaurants make this London's prime area for entertainment; there are also vast official buildings and narrow, shop-lined streets nearby.

To Tottenham Court Road station

Charing Cross Road
The shops here are a feast for booklovers ❿

Shaftesbury Avenue
Theatreland's main artery is lined with announcements for current shows ❽

★ **Chinatown**
An area of Chinese restaurants and shops, it is home to many Chinese-speaking people ❾

The Blue Posts pub stands on the site of a pick-up point for sedan chairs in the 18th century.

Guinness World of Records reveals the best, worst and most of anything and everything *(see p340).*

Mechanized pop stars wave from the balcony of Rock Circus, in the former London Pavilion.

Leicester Square
Film pioneer Charlie Chaplin stands in the traffic-free square ❻

The Theatre Royal
On the site of an older theatre, it is graced by a John Nash portico ❼

STAR SIGHTS

★ **National Gallery**

★ **National Portrait Gallery**

★ **St Martin-in-the-Fields**

★ **Chinatown**

★ **Trafalgar Square**

KEY

- - -   Suggested route

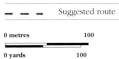

0 metres	100
0 yards	100

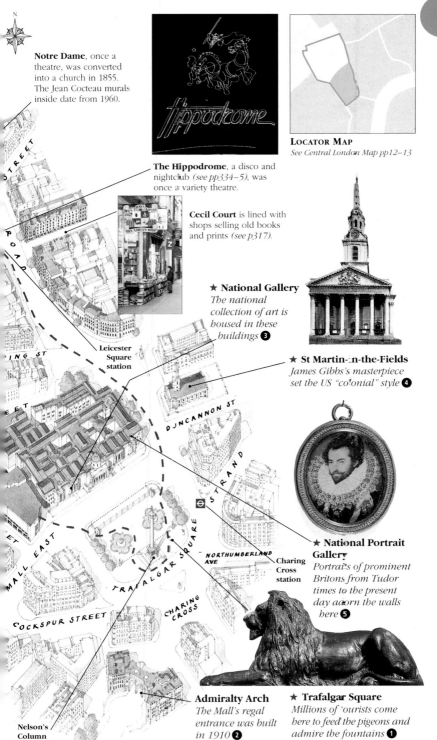

Notre Dame, once a theatre, was converted into a church in 1855. The Jean Cocteau murals inside date from 1960.

The Hippodrome, a disco and nightclub *(see pp334–5)*, was once a variety theatre.

Cecil Court is lined with shops selling old books and prints *(see p317)*.

LOCATOR MAP
See Central London Map pp12–13

★ **National Gallery**
The national collection of art is housed in these buildings ❸

★ **St Martin-in-the-Fields**
James Gibbs's masterpiece set the US "colonial" style ❹

Leicester Square station

DUNCANNON ST

★ **National Portrait Gallery**
Portraits of prominent Britons from Tudor times to the present day adorn the walls here ❺

Charing Cross station

NORTHUMBERLAND AVE

TRAFALGAR SQUARE

CHARING CROSS

MALL EAST

COCKSPUR STREET

Nelson's Column

Admiralty Arch
The Mall's regal entrance was built in 1910 ❷

★ **Trafalgar Square**
Millions of tourists come here to feed the pigeons and admire the fountains ❶

Trafalgar Square ●

WC2. **Map** 13 B3. ⊖ *Charing Cross.*

LONDON'S MAIN venue for rallies and outdoor public meetings, the square was conceived by John Nash and was mostly constructed during the 1830s. The 50-m (165-ft) column commemorates Admiral Lord Nelson, Britain's most famous sea lord, who died heroically at the Battle of Trafalgar against Napoleon in 1805. It dates from 1842; 14 stonemasons held a dinner on its flat top before the statue of Nelson was finally installed. Edwin Landseer's four impassive lions were added to guard its base 25 years later. The north side of the square is now taken up by the National Gallery and its annexe *(see pp104–7),* with Canada House on the west side, and South Africa House on the east. The restored Grand Buildings on the south side, with their fine arcade, were built in 1880 as the Grand Hotel. Today the pigeon-filled square is a popular rallying point for demonstrations, and for raucous New Year's Eve celebrations.

Nelson's statue overlooking the square

Admiralty Arch ●

The Mall SW1. **Map** 13 B3. ⊖ *Charing Cross.*

DESIGNED IN 1911, this triple archway was part of Aston Webb's scheme to rebuild the Mall as a grand processional route honouring Queen Victoria. The arch effectively seals the eastern end of the Mall, although traffic passes through the smaller side gates, and separates courtly London from the hurly-burly of Trafalgar Square. The central gate is opened only for royal processions, making a fine setting for the coaches and horses trotting through.

Filming *Howard's End* at Admiralty Arch

National Gallery ●

See pp104–7.

St Martin-in-the-Fields ●

Trafalgar Sq WC2. **Map** 13 B3. ☎ 020-7930 1862. ⊖ *Charing Cross.* **Open** 9am–6pm daily. ⛪ 11.30am Sun. & ▯ ☐ ♿ *London Brass Rubbing Centre* ☎ 020-7930 9306. **Open** 10am–6pm Mon–Sat, noon–6pm Sun. **Concerts** see **Entertainment** pp330–1.

THERE HAS BEEN a church on this site since the 13th century. Many famous people were buried here, including Charles II's mistress, Nell Gwynn, and the painters William Hogarth and Joshua Reynolds. The present church was designed by James Gibbs and completed in 1726. In architectural terms it was one of the most influential ever built; it was much copied in the United States where it became a model for the Colonial style of church-building. An unusual feature of St Martin's spacious interior is the royal box at gallery level on the left of the altar.
From 1914 until 1927 the crypt was opened as a shelter for homeless soldiers and down-and-outs; during World War II it was an air-raid shelter. Today it still plays a role, helping the homeless and providing a lunchtime soup kitchen for them. It also houses a café and a religious bookshop as well as the

London Brass Rubbing Centre. There is a good craft market in the yard outside *(see p323)* and regular lunch-time and evening concerts are held in the church.

National Portrait Gallery ●

2 St Martin's Place WC2. **Map** 13 B3. ☎ 020-7306 0055. ⊖ *Leicester Sq, Charing Cross.* **Open** 10am–6pm Mon–Sat, noon–6pm Sun. **Closed** Good Fri, May Day, 24–26 Dec, 1 Jan. ♿ & *Orange St entrance.* ▯ *during August.* ▯ ♿ **Lectures.**

TOO OFTEN IGNORED in favour of the National Gallery next door, this fascinating museum recounts Britain's development through portraits of its main characters, giving faces to names which are familiar from the history books. There are pictures of kings, queens, poets, musicians, artists, thinkers,

Rodrigo Moynihan's portrait of Margaret Thatcher (1984)

heroes and villains from all periods since the late 14th century. The oldest works, on the fourth floor, include a Hans Holbein cartoon of Henry VIII and paintings of several of his unfortunate wives. The Elizabethans, a floor higher, feature probably the only surviving portrait of Shakespeare taken from life. Lower floors continue the collection chronologically, with works from such artists as Van Dyck, Reynolds, Gainsborough and Sargent.

The 20th century is represented on the first floor where there are as many photographs as paintings. Here musicians Elton John and Mick Jagger, and fashion designers Mary Quant and Katherine Hamnett hang round the corner from the Royal Family and politicians, reflecting the range of public figures to which British culture now attaches importance.

The gallery also houses temporary exhibitions and has an excellent shop selling books on art and literature, as well as an extensive range of cards, prints and posters featuring pictures from the main collection.

Leicester Square 6

WC2. **Map** *13 B2.* 🚇 *Leicester Sq, Piccadilly Circus.*

IT IS HARD to imagine that this, the perpetually animated heart of the West End entertainment district, was once a fashionable place to live. Laid out in 1670 south of Leicester House, a long-gone royal residence, the square's early occupants included the scientist Isaac Newton and later the artists Joshua Reynolds and William Hogarth. Reynolds made his fortune painting high society in his elegant salon at No. 46. Hogarth's house, in the south-east corner, became the Hôtel de la Sablionère in 1801, probably the area's first public restaurant.

In Victorian times several of London's most popular music halls were established here, including the Empire (today

the cinema on the same site perpetuates the name) and the Alhambra, replaced in 1937 by the Art Deco Odeon. The centre of the square has recently been refurbished and includes a booth selling cut-price theatre tickets *(see pp320–7)*. There is also a statue of Charlie Chaplin (by John Doubleday), unveiled in 1981. The Shakespeare fountain dates from an earlier renovation in 1874.

Theatre Royal 7

Haymarket SW1. **Map** *13 A3.* 📞 *020-7930 8800.* 🚇 *Piccadilly Circus.* **Open** *performances only.*

THE FINE FRONTAGE of this theatre, with its portico of six Corinthian columns, dates from 1821, when John Nash designed it as part of his plan for a stately route from Carlton House to his new Regent's Park. The interior is equally grand.

Shaftesbury Avenue 8

W1. **Map** *13 A2.* 🚇 *Piccadilly Circus, Leicester Sq.*

THE MAIN ARTERY of London's theatreland, Shaftesbury Avenue has six theatres and two cinemas, all on its north side. This street was cut through an area of terrible slums between 1877 and 1886 in order to improve communications across the city's busy West End; it follows the route of a much earlier highway. It is named after the Earl of Shaftesbury (1801–85), whose attempts to improve housing conditions had helped some of the local poor. (The Earl is also commemorated by the Eros statue in Piccadilly Circus – *see p90.*) The Lyric Theatre, which was designed by C J Phipps, has been open for almost the same length of time as the avenue.

London's West End: the Globe Theatre (now known as the Gielgud)

National Gallery 🅳

Trafalgar Square facade

THE NATIONAL GALLERY has flourished since its inception in the early 19th century. In 1824 George IV persuaded a reluctant government to buy 38 major paintings, including works by Raphael and Rembrandt, and these became the start of a national collection. The collection grew over the years as rich benefactors contributed works and money. The main gallery building was designed in Neo-Classical style by William Wilkins and built in 1834–8. To its left lies the new Sainsbury Wing, financed by the grocery family and completed in 1991. It houses some spectacular early Renaissance art.

Stairs and lift to lower galleries

Orange St entrance ♿

Stairs to lower floor 👜 🚹

GALLERY GUIDE

Most of the collection is housed on one floor divided into four wings. The paintings hang chronologically, with the earliest works (1260–1510) in the Sainsbury Wing. The North, West and East Wings cover 1510–1600, 1600–1700 and 1700–1900. Lesser paintings of all periods are on the lower floor.

Link to main building

Stairs to lower floors 🖼 👜 🚹 🚹 ℹ️ 📷

★ **Leonardo Cartoon** (1510s)
The genius of Leonardo da Vinci glows through this chalk drawing of the Virgin and Child with St Anne and John the Baptist.

KEY TO FLOORPLAN

- ☐ Painting 1260–1510
- ☐ Painting 1510–1600
- ☐ Painting 1600–1700
- ☐ Painting 1700–1900
- ☐ Special exhibitions
- ☐ Non-exhibition space

Main entrance to Sainsbury Wing ♿

Doge Leonardo Loredan (1501)
Giovanni Bellini portrays this Venetian head of state as a serene father figure.

★ Rokeby Venus (1649)
*Diego Velázquez painted it
to match a lost
Venetian
nude.*

★ The Haywain (1821)
*John Constable brilliantly
caught the effect of distance
and the changing light and
shadow of a typically
English cloudy summer day
in this famous classic.*

VISITORS' CHECKLIST

Trafalgar Sq WC2. **Map** 13 B3.
020-7747 2885. Charing
Cross, Leicester Sq, Piccadilly
Circus. 3, 6, 9, 11, 12, 13,
15, 23, 24, 29, 53, 77a, 88, 91,
94, 109, 139, 159, 176.
Charing Cross. **Open** 10am–
6pm daily (8pm Wed). **Closed**
24–26 Dec, 1 Jan, Good Fri.
Orange St and Sainsbury
Wing entrances.
**Lectures, film presentations,
videos, exhibitions, events,
gallery guide on CD-Rom.**
www.nationalgallery.org.uk

Bathers at Asnières (1884)
*Georges Seurat experiments here
with millions of little dots of colour,
to create a Neo-Classical portrayal
of modern urban life.*

Stairs to
lower floor

★The Ambassadors
*The strange shape in the
foreground of this Hans
Holbein portrait (1533)
is a foreshortened skull,
a symbol of mortality.*

Trafalgar Square
entrance

★ Baptism of Christ
*Piero della Francesca
painted this tranquil
masterpiece (1450s) of
early Renaissance
perspective for a church
in his native Umbria.*

Arnolfini Marriage
*The woman in Jan van
Eyck's famous painting
(1434) is not pregnant –
her rotund shape
conforms to contemporary
ideas of female beauty.*

STAR PICTURES

★ **Baptism of Christ
by Piero della
Francesca**

★ **Cartoon by
Leonardo da Vinci**

★ **Rokeby Venus by
Diego Velázquez**

★ **The Ambassadors
by Hans Holbein**

★ **The Haywain by
John Constable**

Exploring the National Gallery

THE NATIONAL GALLERY IS London's leading art museum with over 2,200 paintings, most kept on permanent display. The Collection includes everything from early works by Giotto, in the 13th century, to 19th-century Impressionists, but its particular strengths are in Dutch, early Renaissance Italian and 17th-century Spanish painting. The bulk of the modern and British collections are housed in the Tate Gallery *(see pp82–5 and p178)*.

EARLY RENAISSANCE (1260–1510): ITALIAN AND NORTHERN PAINTING

THREE LUSTROUS PANELS from the *Maestà*, Duccio's great altarpiece in Siena cathedral, are among the earliest paintings here. Other Italian works of the period include his outstanding *Madonna*.

The fine *Wilton Diptych* portraying England's Richard II is probably by a French artist. It displays the lyrical elegance of the International Gothic style that swept Europe.

Italian masters of this style include Pisanello and Gentile da Fabriano, whose *Madonna* often hangs beside another, by Masaccio – both date from 1426. Also shown are works by Masaccio's pupil, Filippo Lippi, as well as Botticelli and Uccello. Umbrian paintings include Piero della Francesca's *Nativity* and *Baptism*, and an excellent collection of Mantegna, Bellini and other works from the Venetian and Ferrarese schools. Antonello da Messina's *St Jerome in his Study* has been mistaken for a van Eyck; it is not hard to see why, when you compare it with van Eyck's *Arnolfini Marriage*. Important

Netherlandish pictures, including some by Rogier van der Weyden and his followers, are also here, in the Sainsbury Wing.

HIGH RENAISSANCE (1510–1600): ITALIAN, NETHERLANDISH AND GERMAN PAINTING

Christ Mocked (1490–1500) by Hieronymus Bosch

SEBASTIANO DEL PIOMBO'S *The Raising of Lazarus* was painted, with Michelangelo's assistance, to rival Raphael's great *Transfiguration*, which hangs in the Vatican in Rome.

The Adoration of The Kings (1564) by Pieter Brueghel the Elder

These and other well-known names of the High (or late) Renaissance are extremely well represented, often with massive works. Look out for Parmigianino's *Madonna and Child with Saints*, Leonardo da Vinci's charcoal cartoon of the *Virgin and Child* (a full-sized drawing used for copying as a painting), and his second version of the *Virgin of the Rocks*. There are also tender and amusing works by Piero di Cosimo, and several Titians, including *Bacchus and Ariadne* – which the public found too bright and garish when it was first cleaned by the gallery in the 1840s.

The Netherlandish and German collections are weaker. Even so, they include *The Ambassadors*, a fine double portrait by Holbein; and Altdorfer's superb *Christ Taking Leave of his Mother*, bought by the gallery in 1980. There is also an Hieronymus Bosch of *Christ Mocked* (sometimes known as *The Crowning with Thorns*), and an excellent Brueghel, *The Adoration of the Kings*.

The Annunciation (1448) by Filippo Lippi

The Sainsbury Wing

Plans for this new wing, opened in 1991, provoked a storm of dissension. An incensed Prince Charles dubbed an early design "a monstrous carbuncle on the face of a much-loved friend". The final building, by Venturi, has drawn criticism from other quarters for being a derivative compromise.

This is where major changing exhibitions are held. It also houses the Micro Gallery, a computerized database of the Collection.

Dutch, Italian, French and Spanish Painting (1600–1700)

THE SUPERB DUTCH collection gives two entire rooms to Rembrandt. There are also works by Vermeer, Van Dyck (among them his equestrian portrait of King Charles I) and Rubens (including the popular *Chapeau de Paille*).

From Italy, the works of Carracci and Caravaggio are strongly represented, and Salvatore Rosa has a glowering self-portrait.

French works on show include a magnificent portrait of Cardinal Richelieu by Philippe de Champaigne. Claude's seascape, *The Embarkation of the Queen of Sheba*, hangs beside Turner's rival painting *Dido Building Carthage*, as Turner himself had instructed.

The Spanish school has works by Murillo, Velázquez, Zurbarán and others.

Young Woman Standing at a Virginal (1670) by Jan Vermeer

The Scale of Love (1715–18) by Jean Antoine Watteau

Venetian, French and English Painting (1700–1800)

ONE OF THE GALLERY's most famous 18th-century works is Canaletto's *The Stone-Mason's Yard*. Other Venetians here are Longhi and Tiepolo.

The French collection includes Rococo masters such as Chardin, Watteau and Boucher, as well as landscapists and portraitists.

Gainsborough's early, gauche *Mr and Mrs Andrews* and *The Morning Walk* are favourites with visitors; his rival, Sir Joshua Reynolds, is represented by some of his most Classical work and by more informal portraits.

English, French and German Painting (1800–1900)

THE GREAT AGE OF 19th-century landscape painting is amply represented here, with fine works by Constable and Turner as well as by the French artists Corot and Daubigny.

Of Romantic art, there is Géricault's vivid work, *Horse Frightened by Lightning*, and several interesting paintings by Delacroix. In contrast, the society portrait of *Mme Moitessier* by Ingres, though still Romantic, is more restrained and Classical.

Impressionists and other French avant-garde artists are well represented. High-lights include: *Waterlilies* by Monet, Renoir's *Umbrellas*, Van Gogh's *Sunflowers*, Seurat's *Bathers at Asnières* and Rousseau's *Tropical Storm with Tiger*.

With the opening of the Tate Bankside (see p178) in 2000, an exchange program is underway to move all 20th-century works out of the National Gallery.

Umbrellas (1881–6) by Pierre-Auguste Renoir

Chinatown **9**

Streets around Gerrard St W1.
Map 13 A2. ⊖ *Leicester Sq,
Piccadilly Circus.*

THERE HAS BEEN a Chinese community in London since the 19th century. Originally it was concentrated around the East End docks at Limehouse, where the opium dens of Victorian melodrama were sited. As the number of immigrants increased in the 1950s, many moved into Soho where they created an ever-expanding Chinatown. It contains scores of restaurants, and mysterious aroma-filled shops selling oriental produce. Three Chinese arches straddle Gerrard Street, where a vibrant, colourful street festival, held in late January, celebrates Chinese New Year *(see p59)*.

Charing Cross Road **10**

WC2. **Map** 13 B2. ⊖ *Leicester Sq.
See* **Shops and Markets** *p316.*

**Antiquarian books from the
shops on Charing Cross Road**

THE ROAD is a mecca for book-lovers, with a row of second-hand bookshops south of Cambridge Circus and, north of these, a clutch of shops that, between them, should be able to supply just about any recent volume. Visit the giants: chaotic Foyle's and busy Waterstones, and the smaller, specialist shops: try Zwemmer's for art books and Silver Moon for feminism. Sadly, huge rent rises have put this unique mix under threat. At the junction with New Oxford Street rises the 1960s skyscraper, Centre Point. It lay empty for nearly ten years after it was built, its owners finding this more profitable than renting it out.

At the Palace Theatre in 1898

Palace Theatre **11**

Shaftesbury Ave W1. **Map** 13 B2.
[Box office 020-7434 0909.
⊖ *Leicester Sq.* **Open** *for
performances only. See*
Entertainment *pp326–7.*

MOST WEST END theatres are disappointingly unassertive. This one, which dominates the west side of Cambridge Circus, is a splendid exception, with its sparkling terracotta exterior and opulent furnishings. Completed as an opera house in 1891, it became a music hall the following year. The ballerina Anna Pavlova made her London debut here in 1910. Now the theatre, owned by Andrew Lloyd Webber whose own musicals are all over London, stages hit shows such as *Les Miserables*.

Soho Square **12**

W1. **Map** 13 A1. ⊖ *Tottenham
Court Rd.*

SOON AFTER it was laid out in 1681 this enjoyed a brief reign as the most fashionable address in London. Originally it was called King Square, after Charles II whose statue was erected in the middle. The square went out of fashion by the late 18th century and is now surrounded by bland office buildings. The mock-Tudor garden shed in the centre was added much later in Victorian times.

Berwick Street Market **13**

W1. **Map** 13 A1. ⊖ *Piccadilly
Circus.* **Open** *9am–6pm Mon–Sat.
See* **Shops and Markets** *p322.*

THERE HAS BEEN a market here since the 1840s. Berwick Street trader Jack Smith introduced grapefruit to London in 1890. Today this is the West End's best street market, at its cheeriest and most crowded during the lunch hour. The freshest and least expensive produce for miles around is to be had here. There are also some interesting shops, including Borovick's which sells extraordinary fabrics, and a growing number of cafés and restaurants. At its southern end the street narrows into an alley on which Raymond's Revue Bar (the comparatively respectable face of Soho sleaze) has presented its festival of erotica since 1958.

Some of London's cheapest produce at Berwick Street Market

Carnaby Street ❶

W1. **Map** 12 F2. 🔵 *Oxford Circus.*

DURING THE 1960s this street was so much the centre of swinging London that the Oxford English Dictionary recognized the noun "Carnaby Street" as meaning "fashionable clothing for young people". Today the street is rather down-market and caters more for tourists than for the truly fashionable. England's oldest pipe maker, Inderwick's, founded in 1797, is situated at No. 45. There are some interesting young designers' shops in nearby backstreets, notably those on Newburgh Street *(see pp314–15)*.

Liberty's mock-Tudor facade

Liberty ❺

Regent St W1. **Map** 12 F2. 🔵 *Oxford Circus. See Shops and Markets p311.*

ARTHUR LASENBY LIBERTY opened his first shop, selling oriental silks, on Regent Street in 1875. Among his first customers were the artists Ruskin, Rossetti and Whistler. Soon Liberty prints and designs, by artists such as William Morris, influenced the Arts and Crafts movement of the late 19th and early 20th centuries. They are still very fashionable today.

The present mock-Tudor building with its country-house feel dates from 1925, and was built specifically to house the store.

Today the shop maintains its strong links with the East. The basement Oriental Bazaar and the top floor, which is crammed with period Art Nouveau and Arts and Crafts furniture, are particularly worth visiting.

The Heart of Soho

OLD COMPTON STREET is Soho's High Street. Its shops and restaurants reflect the variety of people who have lived in the area over the centuries. These include many great artists, writers and musicians.

Wheeler's opened in 1929 as part of the London-wide fish restaurant chain.

Ronnie Scott's opened in 1959, and nearly all the big names of jazz have played there *(see pp333–5).*

Bar Italia is a coffee shop situated under the room where John Logie Baird first demonstrated television in 1926. As a child, Mozart stayed next door with his family in 1764 and 1765.

The Coach and Horses pub has been a centre of bohemian Soho since the 1950s and is still popular.

Patisserie Valerie is a Hungarian-owned café serving delicious pastries *(see pp306–7).*

St Anne's Church Tower is all that remains after a bomb destroyed the church in 1940.

The French House was frequented by Maurice Chevalier and General de Gaulle.

The Palace Theatre has hosted many successful musicals.

COVENT GARDEN AND THE STRAND

THE OPEN-AIR cafés, street enter-tainers, stylish shops and markets make this area a magnet for vis-itors. At its centre is the Piazza, which sheltered a wholesale market until 1974. Since then, the pretty Victorian buildings here and in the surround-ing streets have been converted into one of the city's liveliest districts. In medieval times the area was occupied by a convent garden which supplied Westminster Abbey with produce. Then in the 1630s, Inigo Jones laid out the Piazza as London's first square, with its west side dominated by St Paul's Church.

The Piazza was commissioned as a residential develop-ment by the Earl of Bedford, owner of one of the mansions that lined the Strand. Before the Embankment was built, the Strand ran along the river.

Dried flowers from the Piazza

SIGHTS AT A GLANCE

Historic Streets and Buildings
The Piazza and Central Market ❶
Neal Street and Neal's Yard ❼
Savoy Hotel ⓭
Somerset House ⓯
Roman Bath ⓲
Bush House ⓳
Adelphi ㉒
Charing Cross ㉓

Museums and Galleries
London Transport Museum ❸
Theatre Museum ❹
Photographers' Gallery ⓫
Courtauld Gallery ⓰

Churches
St Paul's Church ❷
Savoy Chapel ⓮
St Mary-le-Strand ⓱

Monuments and Statues
Seven Dials ❾
Cleopatra's Needle ⓴

Famous Theatres
Theatre Royal ❺
Royal Opera House ❻
Adelphi Theatre ⓬
The London Coliseum ㉔

Parks and Gardens
Victoria Embankment Gardens ㉑

Historic Pubs, Shopping Arcades
Lamb and Flag ❿
Thomas Neal's ❽

GETTING THERE
Covent Garden, Leicester Square and Charing Cross Underground stations are all nearby. There are frequent buses: 9, 11, 15 and 30 to the Strand or 14, 19, 22b, 24, 29, 38 and 176 to Shaftesbury Avenue. Charing Cross rail station is a short walk.

KEY

▦	Street-by-Street map
⊖	Underground station
⇌	Railway station
P	Parking

SEE ALSO

- **Street Finder**, maps 13, 14
- **Where to Stay** pp276–7
- **Restaurants** pp292–4

The old vegetable market, now converted into shops and bars

Street-by-Street: Covent Garden

ONCE AN AREA of decaying streets and warehouses, Covent Garden came alive only after dark when the fruit and vegetable market traders went about their business. Now it is completely revitalized. Day and night visitors, residents and street-entertainers of every vocation throng the Piazza, much as they would have done several centuries ago.

★ Neal Street and Neal's Yard
Shops line this traffic-free area ❼

Covent Garden station

Thomas Neal's
This airy complex is full of designer shops and cafés ❽

Seven Dials
A replica of a 17th-century monument marks the crossroads ❾

Ching Court
is a post-modernist courtyard by architect Terry Farrell.

St Martin's Theatre
is home to the world's longest running play: *The Mousetrap*

Stanfords,
established in 1852, is the largest map and guide retailer in the world *(see p316–17)*.

Lamb and Flag
Parts of this pub, one of London's oldest, date from 1623 ❿

The Garrick Club is London's literary club.

New Row
is lined with little shops and cafés.

Goodwin's Court
was inhabited by a colony of tailors in the 18th century.

Rules
is frequented by the rich and famous for its typically English food *(see p295)*.

ALL THE WORLD'S A STAGE

GARRICK CLUB

★ The Piazza and Central Market
Performers of all kinds – jugglers, clowns, acrobats and musicians – entertain the crowds in the square ❶

LOCATOR MAP
See Central London Map pp12–13

Royal Opera House
Most of the world's greatest singers and dancers have appeared on its stage ❻

Bow Street Police Station
housed London's first police force, the Bow Street Runners, in the 18th century. It closed in 1992.

★ Theatre Museum
A collection of theatrical memorabilia is housed here ❹

Theatre Royal
The old theatre now shows extravagant musicals ❺

Boswells, now a coffee house, is where Dr Johnson first met his biographer, Boswell.

Jubilee Market
sells clothes and bric-a-brac.

★ St Paul's Church
Despite appearances, Inigo Jones's church faces away from the Piazza – the entrance is through a churchyard ❷

★ London Transport Museum
The history of the city's tube and buses is brought to life in this museum ❸

STAR SIGHTS

★ **The Piazza and Central Market**

★ **St Paul's Church**

★ **London Transport Museum**

★ **Theatre Museum**

★ **Neal Street and Neal's Yard**

KEY

– – – Suggested route

0 metres	100
0 yards	100

The Piazza and Central Market ❶

Covent Garden WC2. **Map** 13 C2.
🅴 Covent Garden. ♿ but cobbled
streets. **Street performers**
10am–dusk daily. See **Shops and
Markets** p323.

T HE 17TH-CENTURY architect
Inigo Jones originally
planned this area to be an
elegant residential square,
modelled on the piazza at
Livorno, northern Italy. Today
the buildings on and around
the Piazza are almost entirely
Victorian. The covered central
market was designed by
Charles Fowler in 1833 for
fruit and vegetable whole-
salers, the glass and iron roof
anticipating the giant rail
termini built later in the
century – for instance, St
Pancras (see p130) and
Waterloo (see p187). It now
makes a magnificent shell for
an array of small shops selling
designer clothes, books, arts,
crafts, decorative items and
antiques, all surrounded
by bustling market stalls
that overflow north into
the adjacent streets and
south into Jubilee Hall,
which was built in
1903.
  The colonnaded
Bedford Chambers, on
the north side, give a hint
of Inigo Jones's plan,
although even they are
not original: they were
rebuilt and partially
modified in 1879.
  Street entertain-
ment is a tradition of
the area; in 1662,
diarist Samuel Pepys wrote of
watching a Punch and Judy
show under the portico of St
Paul's Church.

**Punch and Judy
performer**

West entrance to St Paul's

St Paul's Church ❷

Bedford St WC2. **Map** 13 C2.
📞 020-7836 5221. 🅴 Covent
Garden. **Open** 9.30am–2.30pm
Mon, 9.30am–4.30pm Tue–Fri,
10am–1pm Sun. ✝ 11am Sun. ♿

I NIGO JONES built this church
(completed in 1633) with the
altar at the west end, so as to
allow his grand portico, with
its two square and two round
columns, to face east into the
new Piazza. Clerics objected to
this unorthodox arrangement,
and the altar was moved to its
conventional position at the
east end. Jones still went ahead
with his original exterior
design. Thus the church
is entered from the west,
and the east portico is
essentially a fake door,
used now as an
impromptu stage for
street entertainers. In
1795 the interior was
destroyed by fire but
was rebuilt in Jones's
airy, uncomplicated
style. Today the church is all
that is left of Jones's original
plan for the Piazza. St Paul's
has long been called "the
actors' church" and
plaques commemorate
distinguished men and
women of the theatre. A 17th-
century carving by Grinling
Gibbons, on the west screen,
is a memorial to the architect.

London Transport Museum ❸

The Piazza WC2. **Map** 13 C2.
📞 020-7379 6344. 🅴 Covent
Garden. **Open** 10am–6pm Sat–Thu,
11am–6pm Fri (last adm: 5.15pm).
Closed 24–26 Dec. **Adm charge**.
📷 ♿ 🛍 phone in advance. 🚻

London Transport Museum

Y OU DO NOT have to be a
train spotter or a collector
of bus numbers to enjoy this
exhibition. Since 1980 the
intriguing collection has been
housed in the picturesque
Victorian Flower Market,
which was built in 1872, and
features past and present
public transport.
  The history of London's
transport is in essence a social
history of the capital. Bus,
tram and underground route
patterns first reflected the
city's growth and then
promoted it: the northern and
western suburbs began to
develop only after their tube
connections were built. The
museum houses a fine
collection of 20th-century
commercial art. London's bus
and train companies have
been, and still are, prolific
patrons of contemporary
artists, and copies of some of
the finest posters on display
can be bought at the well-
stocked museum shop. They
include the innovative Art
Deco designs of E McKnight
Kauffer, as well as work by
renowned artists of the 1930s,
such as Graham Sutherland
and Paul Nash.
  This museum is excellent
for children. There are plenty
of hands-on exhibits, and
these include the opportunity
for children to put themselves
in the driver's seat of a
London bus, or a train from
the underground system.

A mid-18th-century view of the Piazza

Theatre Museum ❹

7 Russell St WC2. **Map** 13 C2.
(020-7836 7891. ❺ *Covent
Garden.* **Open** *10am–6pm Tue–Sun.*
Closed *25–26 Dec, 1 Jan & public hols.*
Adm charge. ♿ 🎥 🏛 *Studio
theatre performances, events.*

A LARGE GOLD statue of the
Spirit of Gaiety, which
once stood on the roof of
the long-gone Gaiety variety
theatre, lures you down into
the museum's subterranean
galleries with their fascinating
collection of theatrical
memorabilia. This includes
playbills, programmes, props
and costumes from historic
productions, bits of interior
decor from vanished theatres,
and paintings of actors and
scenes from plays. A display
illustrates the development of
theatre from Shakespeare's
time to the present, with
models of auditoriums
through the ages. Exhibitions
are held in the Gielgud and
Irving galleries and young
companies mount produc-
tions in the theatre inside.

Theatre Royal ❺

Catherine St WC2. **Map** 13 C2.
(020-7494 5040. ❺ *Covent
Garden, Holborn, Temple.* **Open**
*for performances and guided tours
(phone to check). See* **Entertainment**
pp326–7.

THE FIRST THEATRE on
this site was built in
1663 as one of only two
venues in London where
drama could legally be
staged. Nell Gwynn
acted here. Three of the
theatres built here since
then burned down,
including one designed
by Sir Christopher Wren
(see p47). The present
one, by Benjamin Wyatt,
was completed in 1812
and has one of the city's
largest auditoriums. In
the 1800s it was famous
for pantomimes – now it
stages block-buster
musicals. It is called the
Theatre Royal, Drury
Lane even though its
entrance is actually on
Catherine Street.

The Royal Opera House, designed by E M Barry in 1858

Royal Opera House ❻

Covent Garden WC2. **Map** 13 C2.
(020-7240 1200. ❺ *Covent
Garden.* **Open** *for performances only.
See* **Entertainment** *p330.*

THE FIRST THEATRE on this
site was built in 1732, and
staged plays as well as
concerts. However, like its
neighbour the Theatre Royal,
it proved prone to fire and
was destroyed in 1808 and
again in 1856. The present
opera house was designed in
1858 by E M Barry (son of the
architect of the Houses of
Parliament). John Flaxman's
portico frieze, of tragedy and
comedy, survived from the
previous building of 1809.

The Opera House has had
both high and low
points during its history.
In 1892, the first British
performance of
Wagner's *Ring* was
conducted here by
Gustav Mahler. Later,
during World War I, the
opera house was used
as a storehouse by the
government.

The siting of a fine
opera house next to a
busy, bustling produce
market was exploited to
great dramatic effect by
George Bernard Shaw in
1913 for his *Pygmalion*,
on which the musical
My Fair Lady is based.
The building is home to
the Royal Opera and
Royal Ballet Companies

– the best tickets cost over
£100 and are hard to acquire.
Nonetheless, severe financial
crises, caused by the building
of a new extension, mean that
its future is in the balance.

Neal Street and Neal's Yard ❼

Covent Garden WC2. **Map** 13 B1.
❺ *Covent Garden. See* **Shops and
Markets** *pp312–13.*

A specialist shop on Neal Street

IN THIS ATTRACTIVE street,
former warehouses from
the 19th century can be
identified by the hoisting
mechanisms high on their
exterior walls. The buildings
have been converted into a
number of shops, art galleries
and restaurants. Off Neal
Street is Neal's Yard, a mock-
rustic cornucopia for lovers of
farmhouse cheeses and yogurt,
salads, wholefoods, herbs and
fresh-baked breads. Brainchild
of the late Nicholas Saunders,
it remains an oasis of alternative values amid the growing
commercialism of the area.

Café at Thomas Neal's

Thomas Neal's ❽

Earlham St WC2. **Map** 13 B2.
🚇 Covent Garden. ♿ ground floor
only.

O PENED IN the early 1990s,
this upmarket shopping
complex offers an interesting
range of shops, selling designer
clothes and cosmetics, jewellery and accessories, antique
clothing and lace. There is a
coffee shop and restaurant on
the lower floor. The Donmar
Warehouse theatre *(see p328)*
is also part of the complex,
staging must-see productions
such as *The Blue Room*.

Seven Dials ❾

Monmouth St WC2. **Map** 13 B2.
🚇 Covent Garden, Leicester Sq.

T HE PILLAR at this junction of
seven streets incorporates
six sundials (the central spike
acted as a seventh). It was

Photographers' Gallery

installed in 1989 and is a copy
of a 17th-century monument.
The original was removed in
the 19th century because it
had become a notorious
meeting place for criminals.

Lamb and Flag ❿

33 Rose St WC2. **Map** 13 B2.
📞 020-7497 9504. 🚇 Covent
Garden, Leicester Sq. **Open** 11am–
11pm Mon–Thu, 11am–10.45pm Fri
& Sat, noon–10.30pm Sun. See
Restaurants and Pubs p309.

T HERE HAS BEEN an inn here
since the 16th century,
and the cramped bars are still
largely unmodernized. A
plaque commemorates the
satirist John Dryden who was
viciously attacked in the alley
outside in 1679, probably
because he lampooned the
Duchess of Portsmouth (one
of Charles II's mistresses) in
scurrilous verses.

Photographers' Gallery ⓫

5 & 8 Great Newport St WC2.
Map 13 B2. 📞 020-7831 1772.
🚇 Leicester Sq. **Open** 11am–6pm
Mon–Sat. 🖥 📷 ♿

T HIS ENTERPRISING gallery is
London's leading venue
for photographic exhibitions,
which change periodically.
There are occasional lectures
and theatrical events and you
can also browse in the good
specialized photographic
bookshop, buy original prints
or meet fellow enthusiasts in

the café. The plaque outside
commemorates Sir Joshua
Reynolds, the founder of the
Royal Academy *(see p90)*, who
lived here in the 18th century.

Adelphi Theatre ⓬

Strand WC2. **Map** 13 C3.
📞 020-7344 0055. 🚇 Charing
Cross, Embankment.
Open for performances only.
See **Entertainment** pp326–7.

B UILT IN 1806, the Adelphi
was opened by John
Scott, a wealthy tradesman,
who was helping to launch
his daughter on the stage. It
was remodelled in 1930 in Art
Deco style. Note the highly
distinctive lettering on the
frontage, and the well-kept
lobby and auditorium, with
their stylized motifs.

Adelphi Theatre (1840)

Savoy Hotel ⓭

Strand WC2. **Map** 13 C2.
📞 020-7836 4343. 🚇 Charing
Cross, Embankment. See **Where to
Stay** p285.

T HE SAVOY was opened in
1889 on the site of the
medieval Savoy Palace. One
of London's grandest hotels,
it pioneered en suite bathrooms and electric lighting.
The forecourt is the only
street in Britain where traffic
drives on the right. Attached
to the hotel are the Savoy
Theatre built for D'Oyly Carte
opera, Simpson's traditional
English restaurant specializing
in roast beef *(see p295)*, and
the Savoy Taylor's Guild with

Front entrance to the Savoy Hotel

its Art Nouveau shop front. Next door is Shell Mex House which replaced the Cecil Hotel while keeping its Strand facade.

Savoy Chapel **⑭**

Strand WC2. **Map** 13 C2.
(020-7836 7221. **⊖** Charing Cross, Embankment. **Open** 11.30am–3.30pm Tue–Fri. **Closed** Aug–Sep.
↑ 11am Sun. **∅** **☎** phone to book.

T HE FIRST SAVOY CHAPEL was founded during the 16th century as the chapel for the hospital established on the site of the old Savoy Palace.

Parts of the outside walls date from 1502, but most of the present building dates from the mid-19th century. In 1890 it was London's first church to be electrically lit. It became the chapel of the Royal Victorian Order in 1936, and is now a private chapel of the Queen. Nearby on Savoy Hill were the first studios of the BBC from 1922 until 1932.

Somerset House **⑮**

Strand WC2. **Map** 14 D2.
(020-7438 6622. **⊖** Temple, Embankment, Charing Cross.
Not open to the public.

T HE IMPOSING Classical compound by William Chambers was built during the 1770s on the site of the Renaissance palace of the Earls of Somerset. It was the first major building designed specifically as offices and is like four extremely grand mansions of the period grouped around a courtyard. Before the river embankment was built in the late 19th century, Somerset House stretched down to the water line. You can still see old mooring rings on the arched southern frontage. The courtyard is open to visitors but most of the interiors, still used by the Civil Service, are private. The exception is the block known as the Fine Rooms and built for the Royal Academy of Arts. It is now the Courtauld Institute.

Somerset House: Strand facade

Courtauld Gallery **⑯**

Courtauld Institute of Art, Somerset House, Strand WC2. **Map** 14 D2.
(020-7873 2526. **⊖** Temple, Embankment, Charing Cross. **Open** 10am–6pm Mon–Sat, noon–6pm Sun (last adm: 5.15pm). **Closed** 24–26 Dec, 1 Jan, Good Fri. **Adm charge.**
∅ **♿** **▯** **▯**

L ONDON'S MOST spectacular small collection of paintings has been housed here since 1990. The Institute was established in 1931 by the textile magnate Samuel Courtauld, and its holdings are based on his collection of Impressionist and Post-Impressionist paintings. Subsequent donations have made the collection more representative of post-Renaissance European art.

The early galleries display work by Botticelli, Brueghel, Bellini, Rubens and Tiepolo. The Impressionists remain the chief attraction, and this collection includes Manet's *Bar at the Folies-Bergère*, one of the two versions of *Le Déjeuner sur l'Herbe*, Van Gogh's *Self-Portrait with Bandaged Ear* and works by Renoir, Monet, Degas, Gauguin, Cézanne and Toulouse-Lautrec. The gallery also houses a fine collection of 20th-century British art.

Van Gogh's *Self-Portrait with Bandaged Ear* (1889) at the Courtauld

St Mary-le-Strand ⓱

The Strand WC2. **Map** 14 D2.
☎ *020-7836 3126.* ⊖ *Temple,
Holborn.* **Open** *10.30am–3.30pm
Mon–Fri,10am–1pm Sun.* ⛪ *11am
Sun, 1.05pm Tue & Thu.* 📷 ⛪

N OW BEACHED on a road
island at the east end of
the Strand, this pleasing
church was completed in
1717. It was the first public
building by James Gibbs, who
designed St-Martin-in-the-
Fields *(see p102).* Gibbs was
influenced by Christopher
Wren, but the exuberant
external decorative detail here
was inspired by the Baroque
churches of Rome, where
Gibbs studied. Its multi-
arched tower is layered like a
wedding cake, and culminates
in a cupola and lantern. St-
Mary-le-Strand is now the
official church of the Women's
Royal Naval Service.

St-Mary-le-Strand

Roman Bath ⓲

5 Strand Lane WC2. **Map** 14 D2.
☎ *020-7798 2063.* ⊖ *Temple,
Embankment, Charing Cross.* **Open**
only by prior request. ♿ *through
Temple Pl.*

T HIS LITTLE BATH and its
surround may be seen
from a full-length window on
Surrey Street, by pressing a
light switch on the outside
wall. It is almost certainly not
Roman, for there is no other

Bush House from Kingsway

evidence of Roman habitation
in the immediate area. It is
more likely to have been part
of Arundel House, one of
several palaces which stood
on the Strand from Tudor
times until the 17th century,
when they were demolished
for new building. In the 19th
century the bath was open to
the public for cold plunges,
believed to be healthy.

Bush House ⓳

Aldwych WC2. **Map** 14 D2.
⊖ *Temple, Holborn.* **Not open** *to
the public.*

S ITUATED AT THE CENTRE of the
Aldwych crescent, this Neo-
Classical building was first
designed as manufacturers'
showrooms by an American,
Irving T Bush, and completed
in 1935. It appears especially
imposing when viewed from
Kingsway, its dramatic north
entrance graced with various
statues symbolizing Anglo-
American relations. Since
1940 it has been used as radio
studios, and is the head-
quarters of the BBC World
Service, which is due to be
relocated to West London
within a few years.

Cleopatra's Needle ⓴

Embankment WC2. **Map** 13 C3.
⊖ *Embankment, Charing Cross.*

E RECTED IN HELIOPOLIS in
about 1500 BC, this
incongruous pink granite
monument is much older than
London itself. Its inscriptions

celebrate the deeds of the
pharaohs of ancient Egypt. It
was presented to Britain by
the then Viceroy of Egypt,
Mohammed Ali, in 1819 and
erected in 1878, shortly after
the Embankment was built. It
has a twin in New York's
Central Park, behind the
Metropolitan Museum of Art.
The bronze sphinxes, added
in 1882, are not Egyptian.

In its base is a Victorian
time capsule of artefacts of
the day, such as the day's
newspapers, a rail timetable
and photographs of 12
contemporary beauties.

Victoria Embankment Gardens ㉑

WC2. **Map** 13 C3. ⊖ *Embankment,
Charing Cross.* **Open** *7.30am–dusk
daily.* ♿ 🚻

T HIS NARROW SLIVER of a
public park, created when
the Embankment was built,
boasts well-maintained flower
beds, a clutch of statues of
British worthies (including the
Scottish poet Robert Burns)
and, in summer, a season of
concerts. Its main historical
feature is the water gate at its
north west corner, which was
built as a triumphal entry to
the Thames for the Duke of
Buckingham in 1626. It is a
relic of York House, which
used to stand on this site and
was the home first of the
Archbishops of York and then
of the Duke. It is still in its
original position and although
the water used to lap against
it, because of the Thames's
Embankment the gate is now
a good 100 m (330 ft) from
the river's edge.

Victoria Embankment Gardens

The new shopping and office block above Charing Cross

Adelphi ㉒

Strand WC2. **Map** 13 C3.
🚇 Embankment, Charing Cross.
Not open to the public.

John Adam Street, Adelphi

ADELPHI IS A PUN on
adelphoi, the Greek word
for brothers – this area was
once an elegant riverside
residential development
designed in 1772 by brothers
Robert and John Adam. The
name now refers to the Art
Deco office block, its entrance
adorned with N A Trent's
heroic reliefs of workers at
toil, which in 1938 replaced
the Adams' much admired
Palladian-style apartment
complex. That destruction is
now viewed as one of the
worst acts of 20th-century
official vandalism. A number
of the Adams' surrounding
buildings fortunately survive,
notably the ornate Royal
Society for the Encouragement of Arts, Manufactures

and Commerce just opposite.
In the same exuberant idiom
are Nos. 1–4 Robert Street,
where Robert Adam lived for
a time, and No. 7 Adam
Street, decorated with honey-
suckle reliefs.

Charing Cross ㉓

Strand WC2. **Map** 13 C3.
🚇 Charing Cross, Embankment.

THE NAME DERIVES from the
last of the 12 crosses
erected by Edward I to mark
the funeral route in 1290 of
his wife, Eleanor of Castile,
from Nottinghamshire to
Westminster Abbey. Today a
19th-century replica stands in
the forecourt of Charing
Cross station. Both the
cross and the Charing Cross
Hotel, built into the
station frontage, were
designed in 1863 by
E M Barry, architect
of the Royal Opera
House *(see p115)*.
Above the station
platforms has risen an
assertive shopping
centre and office
block, completed
in 1991. Designed
by Terry Farrell it
resembles a giant
ocean liner, with
portholes looking on
to Villiers Street. The
new building is best
seen from the river,
where it dominates
its neighbours. The
railway arches at the
rear of the station

have been modernized as a
suite of small shops and
cafés, as well as a new venue
for the Players Theatre, the
last repository of Victorian
music hall entertainment.

London
Coliseum ㉔

St Martin's Lane WC2. **Map** 13 B3.
📞 020-7836 0111. 🚇 Leicester Sq,
Charing Cross. **Open** for performances
and 🎭 (phone to arrange). 🚫 ♿
🔲 🎞 **Lectures**. See **Entertainment**
pp330–1.

LONDON'S LARGEST theatre
and one of its most
elaborate, this flamboyant
building, topped with a large
globe, was designed in 1904
by Frank Matcham and was
equipped with London's first
revolving stage. It was also
the first theatre in Europe to
have lifts. A former variety
house, it had a brief spell as
a cinema in 1961–8. Today it
is the home of the English
National Opera,
and well worth
visiting, if only
for the largely
unaltered
Edwardian
interior with its
gilded cherubs
and heavy
scarlet
curtains.

**London
Coliseum**

BLOOMSBURY AND FITZROVIA

SINCE THE BEGINNING OF the 20th century, Bloomsbury and Fitzrovia have been synonymous with literature, art and learning. The Bloomsbury Group of writers and artists were active from the early 1900s until the 1930s; the name Fitzrovia was invented by writers such as Dylan

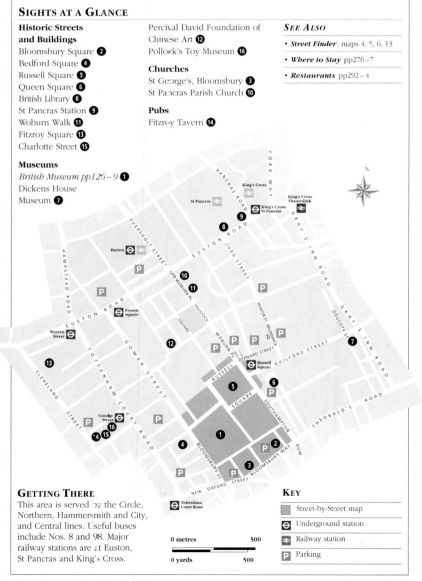

Carving in Russell Square

Thomas who drank in the Fitzroy Tavern. Bloomsbury still boasts the University of London, the British Museum and many fine Georgian squares. But it is now also noted for its Charlotte Street restaurants and the furniture and electrical shops lining Tottenham Court Road.

SIGHTS AT A GLANCE

Historic Streets and Buildings
Bloomsbury Square ❷
Bedford Square ❹
Russell Square ❺
Queen Square ❻
British Library ❽
St Pancras Station ❾
Woburn Walk ⓫
Fitzroy Square ⓭
Charlotte Street ⓯

Museums
British Museum pp126–9 ❶
Dickens House Museum ❼

Percival David Foundation of Chinese Art ⓬
Pollock's Toy Museum ⓰

Churches
St George's, Bloomsbury ❸
St Pancras Parish Church ❿

Pubs
Fitzroy Tavern ⓮

SEE ALSO

• *Street Finder*, maps 4, 5, 6, 13

• *Where to Stay* pp276–7

• *Restaurants* pp292–4

GETTING THERE

This area is served by the Circle, Northern, Hammersmith and City, and Central lines. Useful buses include Nos. 8 and 98. Major railway stations are at Euston, St Pancras and King's Cross.

KEY

▨	Street-by-Street map
⊖	Underground station
⇌	Railway station
P	Parking

0 metres   500

0 yards   500

A grand Georgian house in Bedford Square

Street-by-Street: Bloomsbury

THE BRITISH MUSEUM dominates Bloomsbury. Its earnestly intellectual atmosphere spills over into the surrounding streets, and to its north lies the main campus of London University. The area has been home to writers and artists, and is a traditional centre of the book trade. Most of the publishers have left, but there are still many book shops around.

The Senate House (1932) is the administrative headquarters of the University of London. It holds a priceless library.

RUSSELL SQUARE

MALET STREET

GOWER ST

MONTAGUE PLACE

BLOOMSBURY STREET

GREA

COATIC S

Bedford Square
Uniform doorways in this square (1775) are fringed in artificial stone ❹

★ British Museum
Designed in the mid-19th century, it is London's most popular attraction with some 5 million visitors a year ❶

STAR SIGHTS

★ British Museum

★ Russell Square

KEY

– – – Suggested route

0 metres   100

0 yards   100

Museum Street is lined with small cafés and shops selling old books, prints and antiques.

Pizza Express occupies a charming and little-altered Victorian dairy.

The Duke of Bedford's statue commemorates the fifth duke, Francis Russell (1765–1805). An avid farmer, he is shown with sheep and a plough.

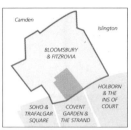

LOCATOR MAP
See Central London Map pp12–13

★ **Russell Square**
It was once part of the Duke of Bedford's estate, and is now a shady retreat on a hot day ❺

Bloomsbury Square
Laid out in 1660, it is graced by a statue of statesman Charles James Fox (1749–1806) ❷

To Holborn station

Sicilian Avenue is a small and unexpected pedestrian precinct from 1905, where colonnades evoke Roman architecture.

St George's, Bloomsbury
The tower on this typically flamboyant Hawksmoor church is modelled on the tomb of King Mausolus ❻

SOUTHAMPTON ROW

BEDFORD PLACE

MONTAGUE ST

STREET

RUSSELL

BLOOMSBURY PLACE

SSELL STREET

BLOOMSBURY WAY

BLOOMSBURY SQ

British Museum ❶

See pp126–9.

Bloomsbury Square ❷

WC1. **Map** 5 C5. 🚇 *Holborn.*

**Novelist Virginia Woolf, a
Bloomsbury resident**

T HIS IS THE OLDEST of the
Bloomsbury squares. It
was laid out in 1661 by the
Earl of Southampton, who
owned the land. None of the
original buildings survive and
its shaded garden is encircled
by a busy one-way traffic
system. (Unusually for central
London, you can nearly
always find a space in the car
park under the square.)

  The square has had many
famous residents; a plaque
commemorates members of
the literary and artistic
Bloomsbury Group, who
lived in the area during the
early decades of this century.
The group included novelist
Virginia Woolf, biographer
Lytton Strachey, and artists
Vanessa Bell, Duncan Grant
and Dora Carrington. Look
out for their individual
plaques throughout the area.

St George's, Bloomsbury ❸

Bloomsbury Way WC1. **Map** 13 B1.
📞 *020-7405 3044.* 🚇 *Holborn,
Tottenham Court Rd.* **Open** *9.30am–
5.30pm Mon–Fri, 9am–5pm Sun.* ⛪
10.30am Sun. **Recitals.**

A SLIGHTLY ECCENTRIC church,
St George's was designed
by Nicholas Hawksmoor,
Wren's pupil, and completed

in 1730. It was built as a
place of worship for the
prosperous residents of
newly-developed, fashionable
Bloomsbury. The layered
tower, modelled on the tomb
of King Mausolus (the original
mausoleum in Turkey) and
topped by a statue of George
I, was for a long time an
object of derision – the king
was thought to be presented
too heroically. There is some
good original plasterwork,
especially in the apse.

Bedford Square ❹

WC1. **Map** 5 B5. 🚇 *Tottenham
Court Rd, Goodge St.*

B UILT IN 1775, this is one of
the best-preserved of
London's 18th-century squares.
All the entrances to its brick
houses are adorned with
Coade stone, a hard-wearing
artificial stone made in

**A plaque in Bloomsbury Square
commemorating famous residents**

Lambeth (in south London) to
a formula that remained
secret for generations. The
stately houses were once
inhabited by the aristocracy.
Now all are offices, many of
them occupied until recently
by publishers most of whom
have since moved to less
expensive premises. A large
number of London's architects
have passed through the
Architectural Association at
Nos. 34–36, including
Richard Rogers who designed
the Lloyd's Building *(see p159).*

Bedford Square's lush private gardens

Russell Square **5**

WC1. **Map** 5 B5. 🚇 Russell Sq.
🕐 opening hours flexible.

ONE OF LONDON'S largest squares, the east side boasts perhaps the best of the Victorian grand hotels to survive in the capital. Charles Doll's Russell Hotel (see p284), which was opened in 1900, is a wondrous confection of red terracotta, with colonnaded balconies and prancing cherubs beneath the main columns. The exuberance is continued in the lobby, faced with marble of many colours.

The garden is open to the public. Poet T S Eliot worked at the west corner of the square, from 1925 until 1965, in what were the offices of publishers Faber and Faber.

The flamboyant Russell Hotel on Russell Square

Queen Square **6**

WC1. **Map** 5 C5. 🚇 Russell Sq.

IN SPITE OF being named after Queen Anne, the square contains a statue of Queen Charlotte. Her husband, George III, stayed at the house of a doctor here when he became ill with the hereditary disease that drove him mad before his death in 1820. Today the square is surrounded chiefly by hospital buildings and there are early Georgian houses on its west side.

Queen Charlotte's statue in Queen Square

Dickens House Museum **7**

48 Doughty St WC1. **Map** 6 D4.
📞 020-7405 2127. 🚇 Chancery Lane, Russell Sq. **Open** 10am–5pm Mon–Sat (last adm: 4.30pm). **Closed** some public hols. **Adm charge.** 🚫 📷

THE NOVELIST Charles Dickens lived in this early-19th-century terraced house for three of his most productive years (from 1837 to 1839). The popular works *Oliver Twist* and *Nicholas*

Nickleby were entirely written here, and *Pickwick Papers* was finished. Although Dickens had many London homes throughout his lifetime, this is the only one to have survived. In 1923 it was acquired by the Dickens Fellowship and it is now a well-conceived museum with some of the principal rooms laid out exactly as they were in Dickens's time. Others have been adapted to display a varied collection of articles associated with him. The exhibits include papers, portraits and pieces of furniture taken from his other homes as well as first editions of many of his best-known works. The most moving mementoes are of Mary Hogarth, the author's sister-in-law, who died, aged 17, a month after the family moved here.

British Library **8**

96 Euston Rd WC1. **Map** 5 B3. 📞 020-7412 7332. 🚇 King's Cross, St Pancras. **Open** 9.30am–6pm Mon–Fri (3pm Tue), 9.30am–5pm Sat, 11am–5pm Sun. **Closed** some public hols. 🚫 📷 phone for reservation 🖥 📷

LONDON'S MOST important building from the late 20th century houses the national collection of books, manu-scripts and maps, as well as the National Sound Archive. Designed in red brick by Sir Colin St John Wilson, it opened in 1998 after nearly 20 years under construction, involving controversial cost over-runs and technological problems, but is now widely admired.

A copy of nearly every printed book in the English language is held here – more than 15 million volumes in all – and can be consulted by anyone with a reader's ticket. In addition there are three exhibition galleries open to everyone. Here some of the Library's most precious items are on show, including Magna Carta, the Lindisfarne Gospels, a Gutenberg Bible and Shakespeare's First Folio. Running through six floors is a spectacular glass tower holding the 65,000 volumes of George III's library. Works of art include a statue of Sir Isaac Newton by Eduardo Paolozzi.

Page from the Lindisfarne Gospels

British Museum ●

THE BRITISH MUSEUM, founded in 1753, is the oldest museum in the world. Its rich collection of artefacts was started by the physician Sir Hans Sloane (1660–1753), who also helped establish the Chelsea Physic Garden

The museum's Classical Greek portico

(see p193). Over the years, Sloane's collection has been added to by gifts and purchases. It now contains treasures from all over the world – some, including many on these pages, were brought back by 18th- and 19th-century travellers and explorers. The main part of the present building (1823–50) is by Robert Smirke.

★ Egyptian Mummies
The ancient Egyptians preserved their dead in expectation of an afterlife. Animals that were believed to have sacred powers were also often mummified. This cat comes from Abydos on the Nile and dates from about 30 BC.

North entrance

North stairs

North stairs

West stairs

★ Elgin Marbles
Lord Elgin took these reliefs from the Parthenon in Athens. The British government bought them for the museum in 1816 (see p129).

Stairs to basement

KEY TO FLOORPLAN

- ☐ Early British collection
- ☐ Coins, medals, prints and drawings
- ☐ Medieval, Renaissance and Modern collection
- ☐ Western Asian collection
- ☐ Egyptian collection
- ☐ Greek and Roman collection
- ☐ Oriental collection
- ☐ Former British Library
- ☐ Temporary exhibitions
- ☐ Non-exhibition space

GALLERY GUIDE

Greek, Roman, Western Asian and Egyptian exhibits occupy the west side of the ground floor; the Oriental collection is on the north; the new Mexican Gallery is on the east. Temporary exhibitions are held throughout the museum and near the entrance in rooms 27 and 28.

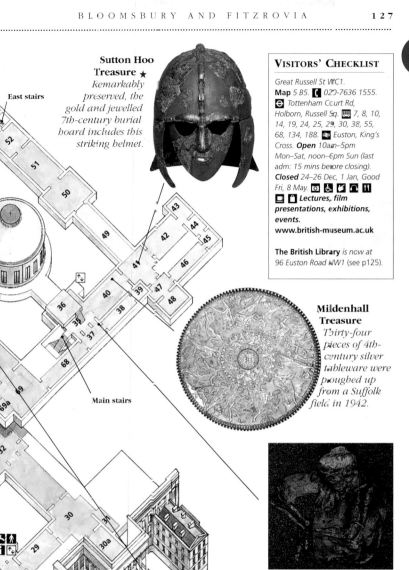

Sutton Hoo Treasure ★
Remarkably preserved, the gold and jewelled 7th-century burial hoard includes this striking helmet.

East stairs

VISITORS' CHECKLIST

Great Russell St WC1.
Map *5 B5.* [ ] *020-7636 1555.*
[ ] *Tottenham Court Rd, Holborn, Russell Sq.* [ ] *7, 8, 10, 14, 19, 24, 25, 29, 30, 38, 55, 68, 134, 188.* [ ] *Euston, King's Cross.* **Open** *10am–5pm Mon–Sat, noon–6pm Sun (last adm: 15 mins before closing).*
Closed *24–26 Dec, 1 Jan, Good Fri, 8 May.* [ ] [ ] [ ] [ ] [ ]
[ ] [ ] *Lectures, film presentations, exhibitions, events.*
www.british-museum.ac.uk

The British Library *is now at 96 Euston Road NW1 (see p125).*

Mildenhall Treasure
Thirty-four pieces of 4th-century silver tableware were ploughed up from a Suffolk field in 1942.

★ **Lindow Man**
The skin on this 2,000-year-old human body was preserved by the acids of a peat-bog in Cheshire. He was probably killed in an elaborate ritual.

Main stairs

Main entrance

Main stairs

Portland Vase
It was made in Italy or Egypt shortly before the birth of Christ. In 1845 a drunken visitor smashed it into 200 pieces. It was repaired and has been reassembled twice since then.

STAR EXHIBITS

★ **Elgin Marbles**

★ **Lindow Man**

★ **Egyptian Mummies**

★ **Sutton Hoo Treasure**

Exploring the British Museum's Collections

THE MUSEUM'S immense hoard of treasure spans two million years of world history and civilization. There are 94 galleries, covering 2.5 miles (4 km), which are divided into the following specialized sections.

Ornamental detail from a Sumerian Queen's lyre

PREHISTORIC AND ROMAN BRITAIN

1st-century BC bronze helmet dredged up from the Thames

SIX GALLERIES cover the period from man's first, prehistoric, efforts at tool-making in Africa's Olduvai Gorge up until Christianity overtook Britain's Roman overlords. The first exhibit, which stands at the top of the main stairs, is a vast mosaic of Christ, dating from Roman times, which was dug up in an English field.

The remains of an Iron Age human sacrifice are in Room 37: "Lindow Man", probably slain in the 1st century AD, lay preserved in a bog until 1984.

Rooms 38 and 39 contain superb Celtic artefacts; Room 40 houses the silver Mildenhall Treasure and many other fine Roman pieces, often made by British craftsmen.

MEDIEVAL, RENAISSANCE AND MODERN OBJECTS

THE SPECTACULAR Sutton Hoo ship treasure, the burial hoard of a 7th-century Anglo-Saxon king, is on display in Room 41; this superb gold and garnet jewellery has been preserved unblemished.

The medieval carved walrus-tusk chessmen from the island of Lewis off Scotland are in Room 42. Room 44 has a fine collection of clocks, watches and scientific instruments. Timepieces have inspired the most exquisite craftsmanship

and some grand designs – a 400-year-old table clock made for a Holy Roman Emperor is an ornate golden galleon that pitched, played music and fired a cannon. Room 45 is an Aladdin's cave housing part of Baron Ferdinand Rothschild's extraordinarily diverse treasure, all in one room. Artefacts from the Renaissance and later are on view in Room 47 and the museum's modern collection is in Room 48.

Gilded brass late-16th-century ship clock from Prague

WESTERN ASIA

THERE ARE 18 galleries on all three floors devoted to the Western Asian collections, which cover 7,000 years of history from an area stretching from Afghanistan to Phoenicia. The most prized part of the collection is probably the 7th-century BC Assyrian reliefs from King Ashurbanipal's palace at Nineveh, in Room 21. Two large human-headed bulls from 7th-century BC Khorsabad are in Room 16; there are more fine reliefs in Rooms 17, 19, 20 and 89. Room 19 also houses the famous inscribed Black

Obelisk of King Shalmaneser III. Room 51 houses part of the Oxus Treasure, a large hoard of gold and silver, buried for over 2,000 years. The museum's collection of clay cuneiform tablets are in Room 55. This was the first form of writing, developed when civilization began 5,000 years ago. Room 56 contains treasures from ancient Sumeria.

ANCIENT EGYPT

THE MUSEUM'S Egyptian sculptures are in Room 25, a giant gallery just off the front hall. The Rosetta Stone, the famous key to the Egyptian hieroglyphs, is near the main entrance. In a side gallery is a fine New Kingdom royal head in green schist, dated 1490 BC, with a wonderful tomb painting of a hunt on the far wall. Don't miss the bronze cat with its gold nose-ring, in the centre of the main hall; the huge statue of Rameses II is impossible to miss. The amazing mummies, jewellery and Coptic art are in Rooms 60–66 upstairs.

Part of a colossal granite statue to Rameses II, the 13th-century BC Egyptian monarch

GREECE AND ROME

THE GREEK and Roman collections, in 30 galleries, include the museum's most famous treasure, the Elgin Marbles in Room 8. These 5th-century BC reliefs from the Parthenon once made up a marble frieze, with sculptured pediments and panels, which went right round Athena's temple on the Acropolis in Athens. Much of it was ruined in battle in 1687, and most of what survived was removed between 1801 and 1804 by British diplomat Lord Elgin, and sold to the British nation.

Ancient Greek vase illustrating the mythical hero Hercules's fight with a bull

The Greek government wants it back. However, it is still here. You can hire a recorded commentary at the entrance. Don't miss the Nereid Monument in Room 7, or, in Room 12, the 350 BC sculpture and friezes from the Mausoleum at Halicarnassus, one of the Seven Wonders of the Ancient World. The 1st-century BC Portland Vase, which was smashed by a drunken visitor in 1845 and then lovingly reassembled, is located in the Roman Empire collection upstairs in Room 70.

ORIENTAL ART

THE BRITISH Museum's magnificent Chinese collection in Gallery 33 is noted for its fine porcelain and ancient Shang bronzes. Now opulently refurbished and featuring stunning beaten gold leaf walls, it houses the museum's Southeast Asian collections. Particularly well-renowned are the ceremonial ancient Chinese bronze vessels, with their enigmatic animal-head shapes. The fine Chinese ceramics range from delicate tea bowls to a model pony which is almost a

Statue of the Hindu God Shiva Nataraja, also known as the Lord of the Dance (11th century AD)

thousand years old. The far end of the gallery has one of the finest collections of Asian religious sculpture outside India. In room 33a are pretty sculpted reliefs which once covered the walls of the Buddhist temple at Amaravati, and which tell stories from the life of Buddha. Islamic art is in Room 34, with a stunning jade terrapin, found in a water tank. Room 91 usually houses temporary exhibitions, and Rooms 92–4 are the Japanese galleries, with a Classical teahouse in Room 92 and *netsuke* (small ivory carvings) gracing the lobby.

THE GREAT COURT

The Great Court scheme is the museum's £97 million project to mark the millennium. Designed by Sir Norman Foster, the Court (which is built around the former British Library Reading Room building) will be covered by a wide-span, light-weight roof made from enough glass to glaze 50 greenhouses, forming the city's first covered public square. A multi-level construction will contain a Centre for Education, temporary exhibition galleries, bookshops, cafés and restaurants. The Reading Room itself will be restored to its original interior decoration, to give visitors a taste of the atmosphere which Karl Marx, Mahatma Gandhi and George Bernard Shaw found so agreeable. Part of the Reading Room will become a study suite where those wishing to find out about the Museum's collections will have access to a library equipped with information technology running computerized catalogues and fascinating multimedia programmes.

The dome of the Great Court is wider than that of St Peter's in Rome.

A study suite allows visitors to learn about the museum and its exhibits.

The massive former Midland Grand Hotel above St Pancras Station

St Pancras Station ❾

Euston Rd NW1. **Map** 5 B2.
☎ 020-7387 7070 (British Rail enquiries). ⊖ King's Cross, St Pancras. **Open** 5am–11pm daily. See **Getting to London** pp358–9.

EASILY THE MOST spectacular of the three rail termini along Euston Road, its extravagant, frontage, in red-brick gingerbread Gothic, is technically not part of the station. It was really Sir George Gilbert Scott's Midland Grand Hotel, opened in 1874 with 250 bedrooms as one of the most sumptuous and up-to-date hotels of its time. In 1890 London's first smoking room for women was opened here. From 1935 until the early 1980s the building was used as offices; it is now being lavishly restored. The vast train shed behind it is an outstanding example of Victorian engineering, with a roof that is 210 m (700 ft) long and 30 m (100 ft) high.

St Pancras Parish Church ❿

Euston Rd NW1. **Map** 5 B3.
☎ 020-7388 1461. ⊖ Euston. **Open** 9am–noon Mon, 9.30am–6pm Wed–Sat, 9.30am–noon, 4–6.30pm Sun. ✝ 10am Sun 📷 ♿ **Recitals** Mar–Sep: 1.15pm Thu.

THIS IS A STATELY Greek revival church of 1822 by William Inwood and his son Henry, both great enthusiasts for Athenian architecture. The design is based on the Erectheum on the Acropolis in Athens, and even the wooden pulpit stands on miniature Ionic columns of its own. The long, galleried interior has a dramatic severity appropriate to the church's style. The female figures on the northern outer wall were originally taller than they are now; a chunk had to be taken out of the middle of each to make them fit under the roof they were meant to be supporting.

Figures on St Pancras Church

Woburn Walk ⓫

WC1. **Map** 5 B4. ⊖ Euston, Euston Sq.

A WELL-RESTORED street of bow-fronted shops, it was designed by Thomas Cubitt in 1822. The high pavement on the east side was to protect shop fronts from the mud thrown up by carriages. The poet W B Yeats lived at No. 5 from 1895 until 1919.

Percival David Foundation of Chinese Art ⓬

53 Gordon Sq WC1. **Map** 5 B4. ☎ 020-7387 3909. ⊖ Russell Sq, Euston Sq, Goodge St. **Open** 10.30am–5pm Mon–Fri. **Closed** public hols. 📷 📱

PARTICULARLY fascinating to those with a specialized interest in Chinese porcelain, but attractive also to the non-specialist, this is an important collection of exquisite wares made between the 10th and 18th centuries. Percival David presented his fine collection, much of it uniquely well preserved, to the University of London in 1950, and it is now administered by the School of Oriental and African Studies. The foundation includes a research library and, as well as the permanent collection, houses occasional special exhibitions of east Asian art.

Blue temple vase from David's collection

Fitzroy Square ⓭

W1. **Map** 4 F4. ⊖ Warren St, Great Portland St.

DESIGNED BY Robert Adam in 1794, the square's south and east sides survive in their original form, in dignified Portland stone. Blue plaques record the homes of many artists, writers and statesmen: George Bernard Shaw and Virginia Woolf both lived at No. 29 – although not at the same time. Shaw gave money to the artist Roger Fry to establish the Omega workshop at No. 33 in 1913. Here young artists were paid a fixed wage to produce Post-Impressionist furniture, pottery, carpets and paintings for sale to the public.

No. 29 Fitzroy Square

Fitzroy Tavern ⓮

16 Charlotte St W1. **Map** 4 F5.
(020-7580 3714. **⊖** Goodge St.
Open 11am–11pm Mon–Sat,
noon–10.30pm Sun. **&** See
Restaurants and Pubs pp308–9.

THIS TRADITIONAL PUB was a meeting place between World Wars I and II for a group of writers and artists who dubbed the area around Fitzroy Square and Charlotte Street "Fitzrovia". A basement "Writers and Artists Bar" contains pictures of former customers, including the writers Dylan Thomas and George Orwell, and the artist Augustus John.

Charlotte Street ⓯

W1. **Map** 5 A5. **⊖** Goodge St.

AS THE UPPER classes moved west from Bloomsbury in the early 19th century, a flood of artists and European immigrants moved in, turning the area into a northern appendage to Soho (see pp98–109). The artist John Constable lived and worked for many years at No. 76. Some of the new residents established small workshops

to service the clothing shops on Oxford Street and the furniture stores on Tottenham Court Road. Others set up reasonably-priced restaurants. The street still boasts a great variety of eating places. It is overshadowed from the north by the 180-m (580-ft) Telecom Tower, built in 1964 as a vast TV, radio and telecommunications aerial (see p30).

Telecom Tower

Pollock's Toy Museum ⓰

1 Scala St W1. **Map** 5 A5.
(020-7636 3452. **⊖** Goodge St.
Open 10am–5pm Mon–Sat. **Closed**
public hols. **Adm charge**. **🛈**

BENJAMIN POLLOCK was a renowned maker of toy theatres in the late 19th and early 20th centuries – the

novelist Robert Louis Stevenson was an enthusiastic customer. The museum opened in 1956 and the final room is devoted to stages and puppets from Pollock's theatres, together with a reconstruction of his workshop. This is a child-sized museum created in two largely unaltered 18th-century houses. The small rooms have been filled with a fascinating assortment of historic toys from all over the world. There are dolls, puppets, trains, cars, construction sets, a fine rocking horse and a splendid collection of mainly Victorian dolls' houses. Toy theatre performances are held here during school holidays and children can play games with boards and pieces lent free; but parents should beware – the exit leads through a very tempting toyshop.

Pearly king and queen dolls from Pollock's Museum

HOLBORN AND THE INNS OF COURT

THIS AREA IS traditionally home to the legal and journalistic professions. The law is still here, in the Royal Courts of Justice and the Inns of Court, but most national newspapers left Fleet Street in the 1980s. Several buildings here predate the Great Fire of 1666 (see pp22–3). These

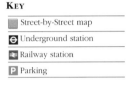

Royal crest at Lincoln's Inn

include the superb facade of Staple Inn, Prince Henry's Room, and the interior of Middle Temple Hall. Holborn used to be one of the capital's main shopping districts. Times have changed, but the jewellery and diamond dealers of Hatton Garden are still here, as well as the London Silver Vaults.

SIGHTS AT A GLANCE

Historic Buildings, Sights and Streets
Lincoln's Inn ②
Old Curiosity Shop ④
Law Society ⑤
Royal Courts of Justice ⑦
Fleet Street ⑨
Prince Henry's Room ⑩
Temple ⑪
Dr Johnson's House ⑭
Holborn Viaduct ⑯
Hatton Garden ⑱
Staple Inn ⑲
Gray's Inn ㉑

Museums and Galleries
Sir John Soane's Museum ①

Churches
St Clement Danes ⑥

St Bride's ⑫
St Andrew, Holborn ⑮
St Etheldreda's Chapel ⑰

Monuments
Temple Bar Memorial ⑧

Parks and Gardens
Lincoln's Inn Fields ③

Pubs
Ye Olde Cheshire Cheese ⑬

Shops
London Silver Vaults ⑳

KEY

▦	Street-by-Street map
⊖	Underground station
🚆	Railway station
P	Parking

GETTING THERE

This area is served by the Circle, Central, District, Metropolitan and Piccadilly lines. Buses 17, 18, 45, 46, 171, 243 and 259 are among many in the area, and trains run from a number of mainline stations inside or close to the area.

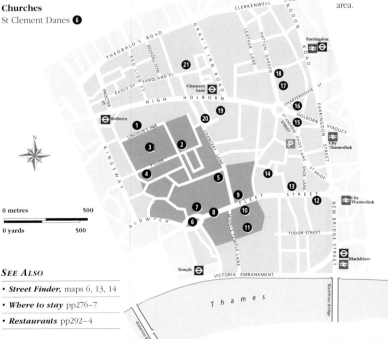

SEE ALSO

- **Street Finder,** maps 6, 13, 14
- **Where to stay** pp276–7
- **Restaurants** pp292–4

The Royal Courts of Justice on the Strand

Street-by-Street: Lincoln's Inn

T HIS IS CALM, dignified, legal London, packed with history and interest. Lincoln's Inn, adjoining one of the city's first residential squares, has buildings dating from the late 15th century. Dark-suited lawyers carry bundles of briefs between their offices here and the Neo-Gothic Law Courts. Nearby is the Temple, another historic legal district with a famous 13th-century round church.

★ **Sir John Soane's Museum**
The Georgian architect made this his London home and left it, with his collection, to the nation ❶

To Kingsway

★Lincoln's Inn Fields
The mock-Tudor archway, leading to Lincoln's Inn and built in 1845, overlooks the Fields ❸

Old Curiosity Shop
It is a rare 17th-century, pre-Great Fire building which is now a shop ❹

The Royal College of Surgeons was designed in 1836 by Sir Charles Barry. Inside there are laboratories for research and teaching as well as a museum of anatomical specimens.

STAR SIGHTS

- ★ **Sir John Soane's Museum**
- ★ **Temple**
- ★ **Lincoln's Inn Fields**
- ★ **Lincoln's Inn**

KEY

– – – Suggested route

0 metres   100

0 yards   100

Twinings have been selling tea from here since 1706. The doorway dates from 1787 when the shop was called the Golden Lion.

The Gladstone Statue was erected in 1905 to commemorate William Gladstone, the Victorian statesman who was Prime Minister four times.

LOCATOR MAP
See Central London Map pp12–13

★ Lincoln's Inn
The Court of Chancery sat here, in Old Hall, from 1835 until 1858. Sir John Taylor Coleridge was a well-known judge of the time ❷

Royal Courts of Justice
The country's main court for civil cases and appeals was built in 1882. It is made out of 35 million bricks faced with Portland stone ❼

Law Society
Look for the gold lions on the railings of this superb building ❺

Fleet Street
For two centuries this was the centre of the national press. Today the newspaper offices are gone ❾

El Vino s is a venerable wine bar, where journalists still mingle with lawyers.

Prince Henry's Room
There is an authentic 17th-century room in this former gatehouse ❿

St Clement Danes
Designed by Wren (1679), it is the Royal Air Force church ❻

Temple Bar Memorial
A griffin marks where the City of London meets Westminster ❽

★ Temple
It was built for the Knights Templar in the 13th century, but today lawyers stroll here ⓫

Wigged barristers on their way to their offices in Lincoln's Inn

Lincoln's Inn ❷

WC2. **Map** 14 D1. 020-7405 6360.
Holborn, Chancery Lane.
Grounds open 7am–7pm Mon–Fri.
Chapel open 12.30–2pm Mon–Fri.
Hall enquire at chapel. grounds
only.

SOME OF THE BUILDINGS in
Lincoln's Inn. the best-
preserved of London's Inns of
Court, go back to the late
15th century. The coat of
arms above the arch of the
Chancery Lane gatehouse is
Henry VIII's, and the heavy
oak door is of the same
vintage. Shakespeare's
contemporary, Ben Jonson, is
believed to have laid some of
the bricks of Lincoln's Inn
during the reign of Elizabeth I.
The chapel is early-17th-
century Gothic. Women were
not allowed to be buried here
until 1839, when the grieving
Lord Brougham petitioned to
have the rule changed so that
his beloved daughter could
be interred in the chapel, to
wait for him to join her.
  Lincoln's Inn has its share
of famous alumni. Oliver
Cromwell and John Donne,

Sir John Soane's Museum ❶

13 Lincoln's Inn Fields WC2.
Map 14 D1. 020-7430 0175.
Holborn. **Open** 10am–5pm
Tue–Sat, 6–9pm first Tue of month.
Closed 24–6 Dec, 1 Jan, Easter,
public hols. Sat 2.30pm.
ground floor only.

ONE OF THE MOST surprising
museums in London, this
house was left to the nation
by Sir John Soane in 1837,
with a far-sighted stipulation
that nothing at all should be
changed. One of Britain's
leading 19th-century architects,
responsible for designing the
Bank of England, Soane was
the son of a bricklayer. After
prudently marrying the niece
of a wealthy builder, whose
fortune he inherited, he
bought and reconstructed No.
12 Lincoln's Inn Fields. In
1813 he and his wife moved
into No. 13 and later, in 1824,
he rebuilt No. 14. Today, true
to Soane's wishes, the collections are much as he left
them – an eclectic gathering
of beautiful, peculiar and
often instructional objects.
  The building itself abounds
with architectural surprises
and illusions. In the main
ground floor room, with its
deep red and green
colouring, cunningly placed
mirrors play tricks with light
and space. The upstairs
picture gallery is lined with
layers of folding panels to
increase its capacity. The
panels open out to reveal
galleried extensions to the
room itself. Among other
works here are many of
Soane's own exotic designs,
including those for Pitshanger
Manor *(see p254)* and the
Bank of England *(see p147)*.
Here also is William Hogarth's
Rake's Progress series.
  In the centre of the low-
ceilinged basement an atrium
stretches up to the roof. A
glass dome lights galleries, on
every floor, that are laden
with Classical statuary.

A glass dome allows
light into the basement.

A vast sarcophagus
stands on the floor of
the crypt.

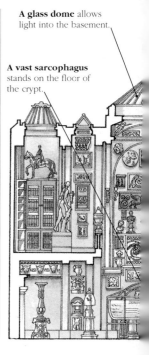

the 17th-century poet, were both students here, as was William Penn, founder of the US state of Pennsylvania.

Lincoln's Inn Fields ❸

WC2. **Map** 14 D1. 🚇 *Holborn.* **Open** *dawn–dusk daily.* **Public tennis courts** 📞 *020-7278 4444 (to book).*

T HIS USED TO BE a public execution site. Under the Tudors and the Stuarts, many religious martyrs, and those suspected of treachery to the Crown, perished here.

When the developer William Newton wanted to build here in the 1640s, students at Lincoln's Inn and other residents made him undertake that the land in the centre would remain a public area for ever. Thanks to this early environmental pressure group, lawyers today play tennis here throughout the summer, or read their briefs in the fresh air. In recent years it has also become the site of a "tent city" for some of London's homeless.

Old Curiosity Shop sign

Old Curiosity Shop ❹

13–14 Portsmouth St WC2. **Map** 14 D1. 🚇 *Holborn.*

W HETHER IT IS or is not the original for Charles Dickens's novel of the same name, this is a genuine 17th-century building and almost certainly the oldest shop in central London. With its overhanging first floor, it gives a rare impression of a London streetscape from before the Great Fire of 1666.

The Old Curiosity Shop maintains its retailing tradition, and currently operates as a shoe shop. A preservation order guarantees the long-term future of the building.

Law Society ❺

113 Chancery Lane WC2. **Map** 14 E1. 📞 *020-7242 1222.* 🚇 *Chancery Lane.* **Not open** *to the public.*

T HE HEADQUARTERS of the solicitors' professional body is, architecturally, one of the most interesting buildings in the legal quarter. The main part, dominated by four Ionic columns, was completed in 1832. More significant is the northern extension, an early work of Charles Holden, an Arts and Crafts enthusiast who later made his name as a designer of London underground stations. In his window arches the four seated figures depict truth, justice, liberty and mercy.

The building is on the corner of Carey Street, the site of the bankruptcy court whose name, corrupted to "Queer Street", entered the language to describe a state of destitution.

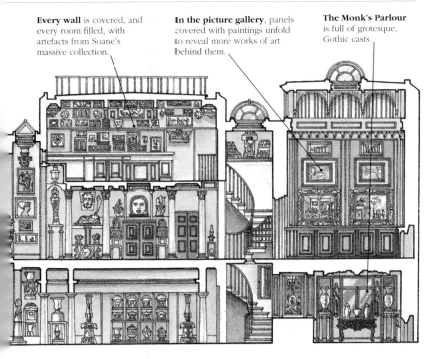

Every wall is covered, and every room filled, with artefacts from Soane's massive collection.

In the picture gallery, panels covered with paintings unfold to reveal more works of art behind them.

The Monk's Parlour is full of grotesque, Gothic casts.

St Clement Danes ❻

Strand WC2. **Map** 14 D2. 📞 *020-7242 8282.* 🚇 *Temple.* **Open** *8.30am–4.30pm Mon–Fri, 8.30am–3.30pm Sat, 8.30am–12.30pm Sun.* **Closed** *noon 25 Dec–27 Dec.* ✝ *11am Sun.* See **Ceremonial London** p55.

Cʜʀɪsᴛᴏᴘʜᴇʀ ᴡʀᴇɴ designed this wonderful church in 1680. Its name derives from an earlier church built here by the descendants of Danish invaders whom Alfred the Great had allowed to remain in London in the 9th century.

During the 17th, 18th and 19th centuries many people were buried in the crypt. The chain now hanging on the crypt wall was probably used to secure coffin lids against body snatchers who stole fresh corpses and sold them to the teaching hospitals.

St Clement Danes sits proudly isolated on a traffic island. It is now the Royal Air Force (RAF) church, and the interior decor is dominated by

Clock at the Victorian law courts

RAF symbols, memorials and monuments. Outside, to the east, is a statue (1910) of Dr Samuel Johnson *(see p140)* who, during the 18th century, often came to services here. The church's bells ring to the tune of the English nursery rhyme, *Oranges and Lemons* at 9am, noon, 3pm and 6pm daily, and there is an annual oranges and lemons service.

Royal Courts of Justice (the Law Courts) ❼

Strand WC2. **Map** 14 D2. 📞 *020-7936 6000.* 🚇 *Holborn, Temple, Chancery Lane.* **Open** *9.30am–4.30pm Mon–Fri.* **Closed** *public hols.* ♿ *limited.* ⬛

Kɴᴏᴛs ᴏғ demonstrators and television cameras can often be seen outside this sprawling and fanciful Victorian Gothic building, waiting for the result of a contentious case. These are the nation's main civil courts, dealing with such matters as divorce, libel, civil liability and appeals. Criminals are dealt with at the Old Bailey *(see p147)*, ten minutes' walk to the east. The public are admitted to all the court rooms and a list tells you which case is being heard in which court.

The massive, Gothic building was completed in 1882. It is said to contain 1,000 rooms and 5.6 km (3.5 miles) of corridors.

Temple Bar Memorial ❽

Fleet St EC4. **Map** 14 D2. 🚇 *Holborn, Temple, Chancery Lane.*

Tʜᴇ ᴍᴏɴᴜᴍᴇɴᴛ in the middle of Fleet Street, outside the Law Courts, dates from 1880 and marks the entrance to the City of London. On state occasions the monarch traditionally has to pause here and ask permission of the Lord Mayor to enter. Temple Bar, an archway designed by Wren, used to stand here. You can see what it used to look like from one of the four reliefs that surround the base of the present monument.

Fleet Street ❾

EC4. **Map** 14 E1. 🚇 *Temple, Blackfriars, St Paul's.*

Eɴɢʟᴀɴᴅ's ғɪʀsᴛ printing press was set up here in the late 15th century by William Caxton's assistant,

The griffon, symbol of the City, at the entrance to the City at Temple Bar

William Capon's engraving of Fleet Street in 1799

and Fleet Street has been a centre of London's publishing industry ever since. Playwrights Shakespeare and Ben Jonson were patrons of the old Mitre Tavern, now No. 37 Fleet Street. In 1702 the first newspaper, *The Daily Courant*, was issued from Fleet Street – conveniently placed for the City and Westminster which were the main sources of news. Later the street became synonymous with the Press.

The printing presses underneath the newspaper offices were abandoned in 1987, when new technology made it easy to produce papers away from the centre of town in areas such as Wapping and the Docklands. Today the newspapers have left their Fleet Street offices and only the agencies, Reuters and the Press Association, remain.

El Vino's wine bar, at the western end opposite Fetter Lane, is a traditional haunt of journalists and lawyers.

Prince Henry's Room ❿

17 Fleet St EC4. **Map** 14 E1.
(020 7936 2710. **⊖** Temple, Chancery Lane. **Open** 11am–2pm Mon–Sat. **Closed** public hols. 📷

BUILT IN 1610 as part of a Fleet Street tavern, this gets its name from the Prince of Wales's coat of arms and the initials PH in the centre of the ceiling. They were probably put there to mark the investiture as Prince of Wales of Henry, James I's eldest son who died before he became king.

The fine half-timbered front, alongside the gateway to Inner Temple, is original and so is some of the room's oak panelling. It contains an exhibition about the diarist Samuel Pepys.

Temple ⓫

Inner Temple, King's Bench Walk EC4. **Map** 14 E2. **(** 020-7797 8250. **⊖** Temple. **Open** 10am–4pm Mon–Fri. 📷 ♿
Middle Temple Hall, Middle Temple Lane EC4. **Map** 14 E2. **(** 020-7427 4800. **⊖** Temple. **Open** 10am–noon, 3–4pm Mon–Fri. **Closed** at short notice for functions. 🎥 📷

THIS EMBRACES TWO of the four Inns of Court, the Middle Temple and the Inner Temple. (The remaining two are Lincoln's and Gray's Inns – see p136 and p141.)

The name derives from the Knights Templar, a chivalrous order which used to protect

Effigies in Temple Church

pilgrims to the Holy Land. The order was based here until it was suppressed by the Crown because its power was viewed as a threat. Initiations probably took place in the crypt of Temple Church and there are 13th-century effigies of Knights Templar in the nave.

Among some other ancient buildings is the wonderful Middle Temple Hall. Its fine Elizabethan interior survives – Shakespeare's *Twelfth Night* was performed here in 1601. Behind Temple, peaceful lawns stretch lazily down towards the Embankment.

St Bride's ⓬

Fleet St EC4. **Map** 14 F2. **(** 020-7353 1301. **⊖** Blackfriars, St Paul's. **Open** 8am–5pm Mon–Fri (last adm: 4.45pm), 9am–4.30pm Sat, 9.30am–12.30pm, 5.30–7.30pm Sun. **Closed** public hols. 📷 ♿ ✝ 11.30am Sun. **Concerts.**

St Bride's, church of the Press

ST BRIDE'S IS ONE OF Wren's best-loved churches. Its position just off Fleet Street has made it the traditional venue for memorial services to departed journalists. Wall plaques commemorate Fleet Street journalists and printers.

The marvellous octagonal layered spire has been the model for tiered wedding cakes since shortly after it was added in 1703. Bombed in 1940, the interior was faithfully restored after World War II. The fascinating crypt contains remnants of earlier churches on the site, and a section of Roman pavement.

Ye Olde Cheshire Cheese ⓭

145 Fleet St EC4. **Map** 14 E1. 📞
020-7353 6170. 🚇 *Blackfriars.* **Open**
*11.30am–11pm Mon–Fri, noon–2.30pm,
5.30–11pm Sat, noon–3pm Sun. See*
Restaurants and Pubs *pp308–9.*

THERE HAS BEEN an inn here
for centuries; parts of this
building date back to 1667,
when the Cheshire Cheese
was rebuilt after the Great
Fire. The diarist Samuel Pepys
often drank here in the 17th
century, but it was Dr Samuel
Johnson's association with
"the Cheese" which made it
a place of pilgrimage for 19th-
century literati. These included
novelists Mark Twain and
Charles Dickens.
    It is one of the few pubs to
have kept the 18th-century
arrangement of small rooms
with fireplaces, tables and
benches, instead of knocking
them into larger bars.

Dr Johnson's House ⓮

17 Gough Sq EC4. **Map** 14 E1.
📞 020-7353 3745. 🚇 *Blackfriars,
Chancery Lane, Temple.* **Open**
*Apr–Sep: 11am–5.30pm Mon–Sat;
Oct–Mar: 11am–5pm Mon–Sat.*
Closed *24–26 Dec, 1 Jan, Good Fri,
public hols.* **Adm charge**. 📷 *small
charge.* 🚻 ♿ *for groups of more
than ten (call to arrange).*

DR SAMUEL JOHNSON was an
18th-century scholar
famous for the many witty
(and often contentious)

19th-century St Andrew schoolgirl

remarks that his biographer,
James Boswell, recorded and
published. Johnson lived here
from 1748 to 1759. He
compiled the first definitive
English dictionary (published
in 1755) in the attic, where
six scribes and assistants
stood all day at high desks.
    The house, built before
1700, is sparsely furnished
with 18th-century pieces and
a small collection of exhibits
relating to Johnson and the
times in which he lived. These
include a tea set belonging to
his friend Mrs Thrale and
pictures of the great man
himself, his contemporaries
and their houses.

St Andrew, Holborn ⓯

Holborn Circus EC4. **Map** 14 E1.
📞 020-7583 7394. 🚇 *Chancery
Lane.* **Open** *9am–4.30pm Mon–Fri.* 📷

THE MEDIEVAL CHURCH here
survived the Great Fire of
1666. In 1686 Christopher
Wren was, however, asked to
redesign it, and the lower part
of the tower is virtually all
that remains of the earlier
church. One of Wren's most
spacious churches, it was
gutted during World War II
but faithfully restored as the
church of the London trade
guilds. Benjamin Disraeli, the
Jewish-born Prime Minister,
was baptized here in 1817, at
the age of 12. In the 19th
century a charity school was
attached to the church.

Holborn Viaduct ⓰

EC1. **Map** 14 F1. 🚇 *Farringdon, St
Paul's, Chancery Lane.*

Civic symbol on Holborn Viaduct

THIS piece of Victorian
ironwork was erected in
the 1860s as part of a much-
needed traffic scheme. It is
best seen from Farringdon
Street which is linked to the
bridge by a staircase. Climb
up and see the status of City
heroes and bronze images of
Commerce, Agriculture,
Science and Fine Arts.

St Etheldreda's Chapel ⓱

14 Ely Place EC1. **Map** 6 E5. 📞 *020-
7405 1061.* 🚇 *Chancery Lane,
Farringdon.* **Open** *8am–6.30pm daily.*
📷 📹 *11.30am–2.30pm Mon–Fri.*

THIS IS A RARE 13th-century
survivor, the chapel and
crypt of Ely House, where the
Bishops of Ely lived until the

Reconstructed interior of Dr Johnson's house

Reformation. Then it was acquired by an Elizabethan courtier, Sir Christopher Hatton, whose descendants demolished the house but kept the chapel and turned it into a Protestant church. It passed through various hands and, in 1874, reverted to the Catholic faith.

Hatton Garden ⑱

EC1. **Map** 6 E5. 🚇 *Chancery Lane, Farringdon.*

BUILT ON LAND that used to be the garden of Hatton House, this is London's diamond and jewellery district. Gems ranging from the priceless to the mundane are traded from scores of small shops with sparkling window displays, and even from the pavements. One of the city's few remaining pawnbrokers is here – look for its traditional sign of three brass balls above the door.

Staple Inn ⑲

Holborn WC1. **Map** 14 E1.
☎ 020-7242 0106. 🚇 *Chancery Lane.* **Courtyard open** *9am–5pm Mon–Fri.* 📷

ONCE THE WOOL staple, where wool was weighed and taxed, the frontage overlooks Holborn and is the only real example of Elizabethan half-timbering left in central London. Although now much restored, it would still be recognizable by someone who had known it in 1586, when it was built. The shops at street level have the feel of the 19th century, and there are some 18th-century buildings in the courtyard.

London Silver Vaults ⑳

53–64 Chancery Lane WC2.
Map 14 D1. 🚇 *Chancery Lane. See* **Shops and Markets** *pp322–3.*

THE LONDON SILVER VAULTS originate from the Chancery Lane Safe Deposit Company, established in

Staple Inn, a survivor from 1586

1885. After descending a staircase you pass through formidable steel security doors and reach a nest of underground shops sparkling with antique and modern silverware. London silver makers have been renowned for centuries, reaching their peak in the Georgian era. The best examples sell for many thousands of pounds but most shops also offer modest pieces at realistic prices.

Coffee pot (1716): Silver Vaults

Gray's Inn ㉑

Gray's Inn Rd WC1. **Map** 6 D5.
☎ 020-7458 7800. 🚇 *Chancery Lane, Holborn.* **Grounds open** *6am– midnight daily.* 📷 ♿

THIS ANCIENT LEGAL centre and law school goes back to the 14th century. Like many of the buildings in this area, it was badly damaged by World War II bombs but much of it has been rebuilt. At least one of Shakespeare's plays *(A Comedy of Errors)* was first performed in Gray's Inn hall in 1594. The hall's 16th-century interior screen still survives.

More recently, the young Charles Dickens was employed as a clerk here in 1827–8. Today the garden, once a convenient site for staging duels, is open to lunchtime strollers for part of the year, and typifies the cloistered calm of the four Inns of Court. The buildings may be visited only by prior arrangement.

THE CITY

Lᴏɴᴅᴏɴ's ғɪɴᴀɴᴄɪᴀʟ district is built on the site of the original Roman settlement. Its full title is the City of London, but it is usually referred to as the City. Most traces of the early City were obliterated by the Great Fire of 1666 and World War II *(see pp22–3 and 31)*. Today glossy modern offices stand among a plethora of banks, with marbled halls and stately pillars. It is the

Traditional bank sign on Lombard Street

contrast between dour, warren-like Victorian buildings and shiny new ones that gives the City its distinctive character. Though it hums with activity in business hours, few people have lived here since the 19th century, when it was one of London's main residential centres. Today only the churches, many of them by Christopher Wren *(see p47)*, are a reminder of those past times.

SIGHTS AT A GLANCE

Historic Streets and Buildings
Mansion House ❶
Royal Exchange ❸
Old Bailey ❼
Apothecaries' Hall ❽
Fishmongers' Hall ❾
Tower of London pp154-7 ⓰
Tower Bridge ⓱
Lloyd's of London ㉒
Stock Exchange ㉔
Guildhall ㉕

Museums and Galleries
Bank of England Museum ❹
Tower Hill Pageant ⓳

Historic Markets
Billingsgate ⓬
Leadenhall Market ㉓

Monuments
Monument ⓫

Churches and Cathedrals
St Stephen Walbrook ❷
St Mary-le-Bow ❺
St Paul's Cathedral pp148-51 ❻
St Magnus the Martyr ❿
St Mary-at-Hill ⓭
St Margaret Pattens ⓮
All Hallows by the Tower ⓯
St Helen's Bishopsgate ⓴
St Katharine Cree ㉑

Docks
St Katharine's Dock ⓲

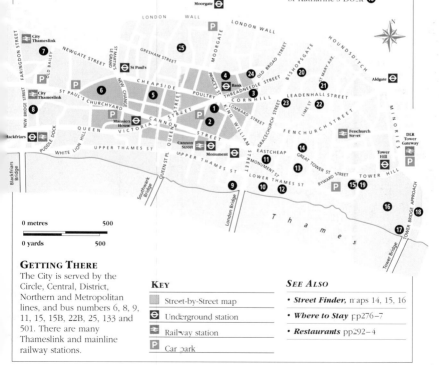

GETTING THERE
The City is served by the Circle, Central, District, Northern and Metropolitan lines, and bus numbers 6, 8, 9, 11, 15, 15B, 22B, 25, 133 and 501. There are many Thameslink and mainline railway stations.

KEY
▢ Street-by-Street map
⊖ Underground station
⊛ Railway station
P Car park

SEE ALSO
• *Street Finder,* maps 14, 15, 16
• *Where to Stay* pp276–7
• *Restaurants* pp292–4

St Paul's Cathedral with the NatWest Tower (1980) to its left

Street-by-Street: The City

THIS IS THE BUSINESS CENTRE of London, home to vast financial institutions such as the Stock Exchange and the Bank of England. But in contrast to these 19th- and 20th-century buildings are the older survivors. A walk through the City is in part a pilgrimage through the architectural visions of Christopher Wren, England's most sublime and probably most prolific architect. After the Great Fire of 1666 he supervised the rebuilding of 52 churches within the area, and enough survive to testify to his genius.

St Mary-le-Bow
Anyone born within earshot of the bells of this Wren church (the historic Bow Bells) is said to be a true Londoner or Cockney **5**

The Temple of Mithras is an important Roman relic whose foundations were revealed by a World War II bomb.

★ **St Paul's**
Wren's masterpiece still dominates the City skyline **6**

St Paul's station

N E W   C H A N G E

W A T L I N G   S T R E E T

B R E A D   S T R E E T

ST PAUL'S CHURCHYARD

C A N N O N   S T R E E T

F R I D A Y   S T

Q U E E N   V I C T O R

Mansion House station

COLLEGE · OF · ARMS

The College of Arms received its royal charter in 1484 from Richard III. Still active today, it assesses who has a legitimate claim to a British family coat of arms.

St Nicholas Cole was the first church Wren built in the City (in 1677). Like many others, it had to be restored after World War II bomb damage.

St James Garlickhythe contains unusual sword rests and hat stands, beneath Wren's elegant spire of 1717.

STAR SIGHTS

★ **St Paul's**

★ **St Stephen Walbrook**

★ **Bank of England Museum**

KEY

– – –　Suggested route

0 metres　　　　　100

0 yards　　　　　100

Skinners' Hall is the Italianate 18th-century guild hall for the leather trade.

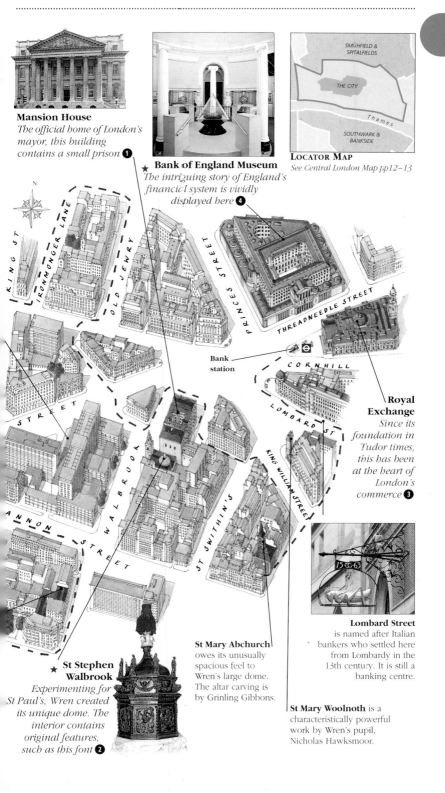

Mansion House
The official home of London's mayor, this building contains a small prison ❶

Bank of England Museum
The intriguing story of England's financial system is vividly displayed here ❹

LOCATOR MAP
See Central London Map pp12–13

SMITHFIELD & SPITALFIELDS

THE CITY

Thames

SOUTHWARK & BANKSIDE

N

KING ST

IRONMONGER LANE

OLD JEWRY

PRINCES STREET

THREADNEEDLE STREET

STREET

WALBROOK

CANNON STREET

ST SWITHINS

Bank station

CORNHILL

LOMBARD ST

KING WILLIAM STREET

Royal Exchange
Since its foundation in Tudor times, this has been at the heart of London's commerce ❸

15·G·63

Lombard Street
is named after Italian bankers who settled here from Lombardy in the 13th century. It is still a banking centre.

St Mary Abchurch
owes its unusually spacious feel to Wren's large dome. The altar carving is by Grinling Gibbons.

★ **St Stephen Walbrook**
Experimenting for St Paul's, Wren created its unique dome. The interior contains original features, such as this font ❷

St Mary Woolnoth is a characteristically powerful work by Wren's pupil, Nicholas Hawksmoor.

Mansion House ❶

Walbrook EC4. **Map** 15 B2.
☎ 020-7626 2500. ⊖ Bank, Mansion
House. **Open** to the public by
appointment only (call to arrange).

THE OFFICIAL RESIDENCE of the
Lord Mayor, it was
completed in 1753 to the
design of George Dance the
Elder, whose designs are now
in John Soane's Museum *(see
pp136–7)*. The Palladian front
with its six large Corinthian
columns is one of the most
familiar City landmarks. The
state rooms have a dignity
appropriate to the office of
mayor, one of the most
spectacular being the 27-m
(90-ft) Egyptian Hall.

Hidden from view are 11
holding cells (10 for men and
1, "the birdcage", for women),
a reminder of the building's
other function as a magistrate's court; the Mayor is
chief magistrate of the City
during his year of office.
Emmeline Pankhurst, who
campaigned for women's
suffrage in the early 20th
century, was once held here.

Egyptian Hall in Mansion House

St Stephen Walbrook ❷

39 Walbrook EC4. **Map** 15 B2. ☎
020-7283 4444. ⊖ Bank, Cannon St.
Open 10am–4pm Mon–Thu, 10am–
3pm Fri. ⛪ 12.45pm Thu. sung
Mass. 📷   **Organ recitals** Fri.

THE LORD MAYOR's parish
church was built by
Christopher Wren in 1672–9.
Architectural writers consider
it to be the finest of his City
churches *(see p47)*. The deep,
coffered dome, with its ornate
plasterwork, was a forerunner
of St Paul's. St Stephen's airy
columned interior comes as a
surprise after its plain
exterior. The font cover and
pulpit canopy are decorated
with exquisite carved figures
that contrast strongly with the
stark simplicity of Henry
Moore's massive white stone
altar (1987).

However, perhaps the most
moving monument of all is a
telephone in a glass box. This
is a tribute to Rector Chad
Varah who, in 1953, founded
the Samaritans, a voluntarily
staffed telephone help-line for
people in emotional need.

*The Martyrdom of St
Stephen*, which hangs on the
north wall, is by American
painter Benjamin West, who
became a Royal Academician
(see p90) in 1768.

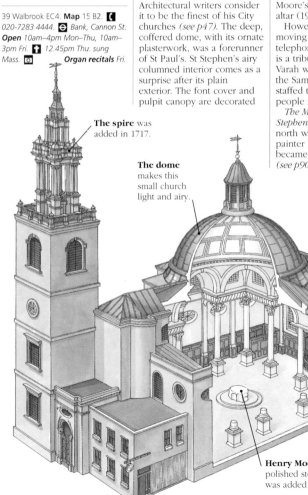

The spire was
added in 1717.

The dome
makes this
small church
light and airy.

Wren's
original altar
and screen
are still here.

Wren's pulpit
has a delicate
canopy.

Henry Moore's
polished stone altar
was added in 1987.

Royal Exchange ❸

EC3. **Map** 15 C2. ☎ 020-7623 0444.
🚇 *Bank*. **Not open** to the public.

Sir Thomas Gresham, the
Elizabethan merchant and
courtier, founded the Royal
Exchange in 1565 as a centre
for commerce of all kinds.
The original building was
centred on a vast courtyard
where merchants and tradesmen did business. Queen
Elizabeth I gave it its Royal
title and it is still one of the
sites from which new kings
and queens are announced.
Dating from 1844, this is the
third splendid building on the
site since Gresham's.
   Britain's first public lavatories
were built in the forecourt
here in 1855. Exclusively for
male use, they symbolized the
era's unenlightened attitudes.

The façade of William Tite's Royal Exchange of 1844

Bank of England Museum ❹

Bartholomew Lane EC2. **Map** 15 B1.
☎ 020-7601 5545. 📠 020-7601
5792. 🚇 *Bank*. **Open** 10am–5pm
Mon–Fri. **Closed** public hols. ♿
♿ (loop system). 📷 📹
Filmshows, lectures.

**The Duke of Wellington (1884)
opposite the Bank of England**

The bank of england was
set up in 1694 to raise
money for foreign wars. It
grew to become Britain's
central bank, and also issues
currency notes.
   Sir John Soane (see
pp136–7) was the architect of
the 1788 bank building on this
site, but only the exterior wall
of his design has survived.
The rest was destroyed in the
1920s and 1930s when the

Bank was enlarged. There is
now a reconstruction of
Soane's stock office of 1793.
   Glittering gold bars, silver
plated decoration and a Roman
mosaic floor, discovered
during the rebuilding, are
among the items on display.
The museum illustrates the
work of the Bank and the
financial system. The gift shop
sells paperweights which are
made out of used banknotes.

St Mary-le-Bow ❺

(Bow Church) Cheapside EC2.
Map 15 A2. ☎ 020-7248 5139.
🚇 *Mansion House*. **Open** 6.30am–6pm
Mon–Wed, 6.30am–6.30pm Thu,
6.30am–4pm Fri. 🕆 5.45pm Thu. 🎵

The church takes its name
from the bow arches in
the Norman crypt. When
Wren rebuilt the church (in
1670–80) after the Great Fire
(see pp22–3), he continued
this architectural pattern
through the graceful arches
on the steeple. The weathervane, dating from 1674, is an
enormous dragon.
   The church was bombed in
1941 leaving only the steeple
and two outer walls standing.
It was restored in 1956–62
when the bells were recast
and rehung. Bow bells are
important to Londoners:
traditionally only those born
within their sound can lay
claim to being true Cockneys.

St Paul's ❻

See pp 148–51.

Old Bailey ❼

EC4. **Map** 14 F1. ☎ 020-7248 3277.
🚇 *St Paul's*. **Open** 10.30am–1pm,
2–4.30pm Mon–Fri (but opening
hours vary from court to court).
Closed Christmas, New Year, Easter,
public hols. 📷

Old Bailey's rooftop Justice

This short street has a long
association with crime and
punishment. The new Central
Criminal Courts opened here
in 1907 on the site of the
notorious and malodorous
Newgate prison (on special
days in the legal calendar
judges still carry small posies
to court as a reminder of
those times). Across the road,
the Magpie and Stump served
"execution breakfasts" until
1868, when mass public
hangings outside the prison
gates were stopped.
   Today, when the courts are
in session, they are open to
members of the public.

St Paul's Cathedral ❻

FOLLOWING THE Great Fire of London in 1666, the medieval cathedral of St Paul's was left in ruins. The authorities turned to Christopher Wren to rebuild it, but his ideas met with considerable resistance from the conservative and tightfisted Dean and Chapter. Wren's 1672 Great Model plan was not at all popular with them, and so a watered-down plan was finally agreed in 1675. Wren's determination paid off though, as can be seen from the grandeur of the present cathedral.

Stone statuary outside the South Transept

★ **The Inner and Outer Dome**
At 110 m (360 ft) high it is the second biggest dome in the world, after St Peter's in Rome, as spectacular from inside as outside.

The balustrade along the top was added in 1718 against Wren's wishes.

The pediment carvings, dating from 1706, show the Conversion of St Paul.

★ **The West Front and Towers**
The towers were not on Wren's original plan – he added them in 1707, when he was 75 years old. Both were designed to have clocks.

Flying buttresses support the nave walls and the dome.

STAR SIGHTS

★ **West Front and Towers**

★ **Inner and Outer Dome**

★ **Whispering Gallery**

The West Portico comprises two tiers of columns rather than the single colonnade that Wren intended.

The West Porch, approached from Ludgate Hill, is the main entrance to St Paul's.

Queen Anne's Statue
An 1886 copy of Francis Bird's 1712 original now stands on the forecourt.

The lantern weighs a massive 850 tonnes.

The brick cone located inside the outer dome supports the heavy lantern.

The oculus is an opening through which the lantern can be seen.

The stone gallery offers a splendid view over London.

A false upper storey masks the huge flying buttresses.

★ **Whispering Gallery**
The unusual acoustics here cause whispers to echo around the dome.

The North and South Transepts cross the nave in a medieval style that contrasts with Wren's original plan *(see p150).*

South Porch
Wren took the idea of a semi-circular porch from a Baroque church in Rome.

TIMELINE

604 Bishop Mellitus built the first St Paul's. It burned down in 1087

Detail on Tijou gate (see p151)

1666 St Paul's reduced to a burnt ruin after the Great Fire

1708 Wren's son Christopher lays the last stone on the lantern

600	800	1000	1200	1400	1600	1800

1087 Bishop Maurice began Old St Paul's: a Norman cathedral of stone

1675 Foundation stone of Wren's design laid

1940–1 Slight bomb damage to the cathedral

1981 Prince Charles marries Lady Diana Spencer

A Guided Tour of St Paul's

THE VISITOR TO ST PAUL'S will be immediately impressed by its cool, beautifully ordered and extremely spacious interior. The nave, transepts and choir are arranged in the shape of a cross, as in a medieval cathedral, but Wren's Classical vision shines through this conservative floor plan, forced on him by the cathedral authorities. Aided by some of the finest craftsmen of his day, he created an interior of grand majesty and Baroque splendour, a worthy setting for the many great ceremonial events that have taken place here. These include the funeral of Winston Churchill in 1965 and the wedding of Prince Charles and Lady Diana Spencer in 1981.

The mosaics on the choir ceiling were completed in the 1890s by William Richmond.

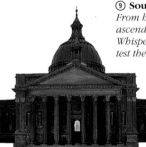

① **The Nave**
Take in the full glory of the massive arches and the succession of saucer domes that open out into a huge space below the main dome.

② **The North Aisle**
As you walk along the North Aisle, look above: the aisles are vaulted with small domes mimicking those of the nave ceiling.

⑨ **South Aisle**
From here the brave can ascend the 259 steps to the Whispering Gallery and test the acoustics.

Entrance to
Whispering
Gallery

⑧ **The Great Model**
A model of Wren's original design was carved in 1672. The plan was rejected as being too revolutionary for its time.

Main entrances

The Geometrical Staircase is a spiral of 92 stone steps giving access to the cathedral library.

SUBTUS CONDITUR
HUIUS ECCLESIÆ ET VRBIS CONDITOR
CHRISTOPHORUS WREN,
QUI VIXIT ANNOS ULTRA NONAGINTA,
NON SIBI SED BONO PUBLICO.
LECTOR, SI MONUMENTUM REQUIRIS,
CIRCUMSPICE.
Obiit XXV Feb: Anᵒ MDCCXXIII Ætᵃ XCI.

⑦ **Wren's Tomb**
Wren's burial place is marked by a slab. The inscription states: "Reader, if you seek his memorial look all around you."

KEY

– – – Tour route

③ The Crossing
The climax of Wren's interior is this great open space. The vast dome is decorated with monochrome frescoes by Sir James Thornhill, the leading architectural painter of Wren's time.

Entrance to crypt

④ The Choir
Jean Tijou, a Huguenot refugee, created much of the cathedral's fine wrought ironwork, such as these screens in the choir aisles.

John Donne's tomb, from 1631, was the only monument to survive the Great Fire of 1666. The poet posed for it in his lifetime.

⑤ The High Altar
The canopy over the altar was replaced after World War II. It is based on Wren's original Baroque drawings.

Grinling Gibbons's work can be found on the choir stalls, with typically intricate carvings of cherubs, fruits and garlands.

Lawrence of Arabia, the adventurer, is commemorated by this bust in the crypt.

⑥ The Crypt
Memorials to famous figures and popular heroes, such as Lord Nelson, can be seen in the crypt.

Apothecaries' Hall ❽

Blackfriars Lane EC4. **Map** 14 F2.
C 020-7236 1189. **❷** *Blackfriars.*
Courtyard open 9am–5pm Mon–Fri.
Closed public hols. **Phone Hall** for
appt to visit (for groups only) ♿

Apothecaries' Hall, rebuilt in 1670

LONDON HAS had livery companies, or guilds, to protect and regulate specific trades since early medieval times. The Apothecaries' Society was founded in 1617 for those who prepared, prescribed or sold drugs. It has some surprising alumni, including Oliver Cromwell and the poet John Keats. Now nearly all the members are physicians or surgeons.

Fishmongers' Hall ❾

London Bridge EC4. **Map** 15 B3.
C 020-7626 3531. **❷** *Monument.*
Not open to the public.

THIS IS ONE of the oldest livery companies, established in 1272. Lord Mayor Walworth, a member of the Fishmongers' Company, killed Wat Tyler, leader and prime motivator of the Peasants' Revolt, in 1381 *(see p162).* Today it still fulfils its original role; all the fish sold in the City must be inspected by Company officials. The building dates from 1834.

St Magnus the Martyr ❿

Lower Thames St EC3. **Map** 15 C3.
C 020-7626 4481. **❷** *Monument.*
Open 10am–4pm Tue–Fri, 10.15am–2pm Sun. ⬛ 11am Sun.

THERE HAS BEEN a church here for over 1,000 years.

Its patron saint, St Magnus, Earl of the Orkney Islands and a renowned Norwegian Christian leader, was brutally murdered in 1110.

When Christopher Wren built this church in 1671–6, it was at the foot of old London Bridge, until 1738 the only bridge across the Thames in London. Anyone going south from the city would have passed under Wren's magnificent arched porch spanning the flagstones leading to the old bridge.

Highlights of the church include the carved musical instruments that decorate the organ case. Wren's pulpit, with its slender supporting stem, was restored in 1924.

Monument ⓫

Monument St EC3. **Map** 15 C2.
C 020-7626 2717. **❷** *Monument.*
Open 10am–5.40pm Mon–Fri.
Closed 25–26 Dec, 1 Jan.
Adm charge. ⬛

THE COLUMN, designed by Christopher Wren to commemorate the Great Fire of London which devastated the original walled city in September 1666, is the tallest isolated stone column in the world. It is 62 m (205 ft) high and is said to be 62 m west of where the fire started in Pudding Lane. It was sited on the direct approach to old London Bridge, which was a few steps downstream from the present one. Reliefs around the column's base

The altar of St Magnus the Martyr

show Charles II restoring the city. The 311 steps to the top lead to a viewing platform. In 1842 this was enclosed with railings after a suicide, and has never reopened.

Billingsgate ⓬

Lower Thames St EC3. **Map** 15 C3.
❷ *Monument.* **Not open** to the public.

Fish weathervane at Billingsgate

LONDON'S MAIN fish market was based here for 900 years, on one of the city's earliest quays. During the 19th and early 20th centuries 400 tonnes of fish were sold here every day, much of it delivered by boat. It was London's noisiest market, renowned, even in Shakespeare's day, for foul language. In 1982 the market moved from this building (1877) to the Isle of Dogs.

St Mary-at-Hill ⓭

Lovat Lane EC3. **Map** 15 C2.
C 020-7626 4184. **❷** *Monument.*
Concerts. Open 10am–3pm Mon–Fri.

THE INTERIOR and east end of St Mary-at-Hill were Wren's first church designs (1670–6). The Greek cross design was a prototype for his St Paul's proposals.

Ironically, the delicate plasterwork and rich 17th-century fittings, which had survived both the Victorian mania for refurbishment and the bombs of World War II, were lost in a fire in 1988.

The building was then restored to its original appearance, only to be damaged again, this time by an IRA bomb in 1992.

St Margaret Pattens ⓮

Rood Lane and Eastcheap EC3.
Map 15 C2. 📞 020-7623 6630.
🚇 Monument. **Open** 8am–4pm
Mon–Fri. **Closed** Christmas week.
✝ 1.15pm Thu.

W REN'S CHURCH from 1684–7 was named after a type of overshoe made near here. Its Portland stone walls are a good contrast to the Georgian stucco shopfront in the forecourt. The simple interior retains 17th-century canopied pews and an ornate font.

All Hallows by the Tower ⓯

Byward St EC3. **Map** 16 D3.
📞 020-7481 2928. 🚇 Tower Hill.
Open 9am–5.30pm Mon–Fri, 10am–5pm Sa –Sun. **Closed** 26–27 Dec, 1 Jan. ♿ ✝ 11am Sun. 🅿

T HE FIRST CHURCH on this site was Saxon. The arch in the southwest corner, which contains Roman tiles, dates from that period and so do some crosses now in the crypt. There is also a well-preserved Roman pavement in the crypt, but this is irregularly open to the public. Most of the interior has been altered by restoration, but a limewood font cover, carved by Grinling Gibbons in 1682, still survives. William Penn

Roman tile from All Hallows

(founder of Pennsylvania) was baptized here in 1644 and John Quincy Adams married in 1797 before he was US president. Samuel Pepys watched the Great Fire from the church tower.

Tower of London ⓰

See pp154–7.

Tower Bridge ⓱

SE1. **Map** 16 D3.
📞 020-7378 1928. 🚇 Tower Hill.
The Tower Bridge Experience
Open Apr–Oct: 10am–6.30pm daily (last adm: 5.15pm); Nov–Mar: 9.30am–6pm daily (last adm: 4.45pm). **Closed** 24–26 Dec, 1 Jan. **Adm charge.**
📷 ♿ 🅿 Video.

C OMPLETED IN 1894, this flamboyant piece of Victorian engineering quickly became a symbol of London. Its pinnacled towers and linking catwalk support the mechanism for raising the roadway when big ships have to pass through, or for special and historic occasions.

The bridge now houses The Tower Bridge Experience, with interactive displays bringing the bridge's history to life, river views from the catwalk and a close-up look at the steam engine which powered the lifting machinery until 1976, when the system was electrified.

The catwalk, which is now open to the public, affords a beautiful view along the river.

When raised, the bridge is 40 m (135 ft) high and 60 m (200 ft) wide. In its heyday it was opened five times a day.

There are nearly 300 stairs to the top of the towers.

The Victorian winding machinery was powered by steam until 1976.

Tower of London ⓰

FOR MUCH OF ITS 900-year history the Tower was an object of fear. Those who had offended the monarch were held within its dank walls. A lucky few lived in comparative comfort, but the majority had to put up with appalling conditions. Many did not get out alive, and were tortured before meeting cruelly violent deaths on nearby Tower Hill.

★ **The White Tower**
When it was finished, c.1097, it was the tallest building in London – 30 m (90 ft) high.

★ **The Jewel House** is where the magnificent English Crown Jewels are housed *(see p156)*.

"Beefeaters"
Forty Yeoman Warders guard the Tower and live there.

Beauchamp Tower
Many high-ranking prisoners were held here, often with their own retinues of servants

Tower Green was where the most favoured prisoners were executed, away from the ghoulish crowds on Tower Hill. Only seven people died here – including two of Henry VIII's six wives – but hundreds had to bear more public executions.

STAR BUILDINGS

★ **White Tower**

★ **Jewel House**

★ **Chapel of St John**

★ **Traitors' Gate**

Main entrance

THE RAVENS

The Tower's most celebrated residents are a colony of seven ravens. It is not known when they first settled here, but there is a legend that should they desert the Tower, the kingdom will fall. In fact the birds have their wings clipped on one side, making flight impossible. The Ravenmaster, one of the Yeoman Warders, looks after the birds.

A memorial in the moat commemorates some of the ravens who have died at the Tower since the 1950s.

Queen's House
This is the official residence of the Tower's governor.

★ **Chapel of St John**
Stone for this austerely beautiful Romanesque chapel was brought from France.

Wakefield Tower, part of the Medieval Palace, has been carefully refurbished to match its original appearance in the 13th century.

VISITORS' CHECKLIST

Tower Hill EC3. **Map** 16 D3.
📞 020-7709 0765. 🚇 Tower Hill, London Bridge. 🚌 15, X15, 25, 42, 78, 100. 🚆 Fenchurch Street. **Docklands Light Railway** Tower Gateway. **Open** Mar–Oct: 9am–6pm Tue–Sat, 10am–6pm Sun; Nov–Feb: 9am–5pm Mon–Sat, 10am–5pm Sun & Mon. **Tower closed** 24–26 Dec, 1 Jan. **Adm charge.** ♿ 🚫 Ceremony of the Keys 9.30pm daily (tickets to be booked in advance). See pp53–5. 🖥 🚻

The Bloody Tower is associated with the two princes who disappeared from here in 1483 *(see p157).*

★ **Traitors' Gate**
Prisoners, many on their way to die, entered the Tower by boat here.

Medieval Palace
This was created by Henry III in 1220. It was enlarged by his son, Edward I, who added Traitors' Gate.

TIMELINE

1050	1250	1450	1650	1850	1950

1078 White Tower started

1536 Anne Boleyn executed

1483 Princes probably murdered in the Tower

1553–4 Lady Jane Grey held and executed

1810–15 Mint moves from the Tower and arms stop being manufactured here

1066 William I erects a temporary castle

1534–5 Thomas More imprisoned and executed

1603–16 Walter Raleigh imprisoned in Tower

1671 "Colonel Blood" tries to steal Crown Jewels

1834 Menagerie moves out of Tower

1941 Rudolph Hess is the last prisoner held in Queen's House

Inside the Tower

The Orb, symbolizing
the power and
Empire of Christ
the Redeemer

T HE TOWER HAS been a tourist attraction since the reign of Charles II (1660–85), when both the Crown Jewels and the collection of armour were first shown to the public. They remain powerful reminders of royal might and wealth.

THE CROWN JEWELS

T HE CROWN JEWELS comprise the regalia of crowns, sceptres, orbs and swords used at coronations and other state occasions. They are impossible to price but their worth is irrelevant beside their enormous significance in the historical and religious life of the kingdom. Most of the Crown Jewels date from 1661, when a new set was made for the coronation of Charles II; Parliament had destroyed the previous crowns and sceptres after the execution of Charles I in 1649. Only a few pieces survived, hidden by the clergy of Westminster Abbey until the Restoration.

The Coronation Ceremony

Many elements in this solemn and mystical ceremony date from the days of Edward the Confessor. The king or queen proceeds to Westminster Abbey, accompanied by parts of the regalia, including the State Sword which represents the monarch's own sword. He or she is then annointed with holy oil, to signify divine approval, and invested with ornaments and royal robes. Each of the jewels represents an aspect of the monarch's role as head of the state and church. The climax comes when St Edward's Crown is placed on the sovereign's head; there is a cry of "God Save the King" (or Queen), the trumpets sound, and guns at the Tower are fired. The last coronation was Elizabeth II's in 1953.

The Imperial State Crown, containing more than 2,800 diamonds, 273 pearls as well as other gems

The crowns

There are 10 crowns on display at the Tower. Many of these have not been worn for years, but the Imperial State Crown is in constant use. The Queen wears it at the Opening of Parliament (see p73). The crown was made in 1937 for George VI, and is similar to the one made for Queen Victoria. The sapphire set in the cross is said to have been worn in a ring by Edward the Confessor (ruled 1042 – 66).

The most recent crown is not at the Tower, however. It was made for Prince Charles's investiture as Prince of Wales at Caernavon Castle in north Wales in 1969, and is kept at the Museum of Wales in Cardiff. The Queen Mother's crown was made for the coronation of her husband, George VI, in 1937. It is the only one to be made out of platinum – all the other crowns on display at the Tower are made of gold.

Other regalia

Apart from the crowns, there are other pieces of the Crown Jewels that are essential to coronations. Among these are three Swords of Justice, symbolizing mercy, spiritual and temporal justice. The orb is a hollow gold sphere encrusted with jewels and weighing about 1.3 kg (3 lbs). The Sceptre with the Cross contains the biggest cut diamond in the world, the 530-carat First Star of Africa. The rough stone it comes from weighed 3,106 carats.

The Sovereign's Ring, sometimes referred to as "the wedding ring of England"

Plate Collection

The Jewel House also holds a collection of elaborate gold and silver plate. The Maundy Dish is still used on Maundy Thursday when the monarch distributes money to selected old people. The Exeter Salt (a very grand salt cellar from the days when salt was a valuable commodity) was given by the citizens of Exeter, in west England, to Charles II; during the 1640s' Civil War Exeter was a Royalist stronghold.

The Sceptre with the Cross (1660), rebuilt in 1910 after Edward VII was presented with the First Star of Africa diamond

The hilt and solid-gold scabbard of the Jewelled State Sword, one of the most valuable swords in the world

THE WHITE TOWER

THIS IS THE OLDEST surviving building in the Tower of London, begun by William I in 1077 and completed before 1100. For centuries it served as an armoury, and much of the national collection of arms and armour was held here. In the 1990s many exhibits moved to Leeds or Portsmouth but some of the most historic items, especially those connected with the history of the Tower, have stayed here. The extra space allows the remaining exhibits to be displayed more effectively, and also highlights architectural features of the building itself.

The Royal Castle and Armour Gallery

These two chambers on the first floor were the main ceremonial rooms of the original Norman castle. The first one, to the east, is the smaller, probably an antechamber to the banqueting Hall beyond, and contains exhibits setting out the history of the White Tower. It adjoins St John's Chapel, a rare surviving early Norman tower virtually intact, a powerfully solid interior with little ornamentation. Originally the two main rooms were twice their present height; a pitched roof was removed in 1490 to allow extra floors to be built on top. Suits of armour from Tudor and Stuart times are here, including three made for Henry VIII, one covering his horse as well. A suit made in Holland for Charles I is decorated in gold leaf.

Japanese armour presented to James I in 1613

The Ordnance Gallery

This and the temporary exhibition gallery next door were chambers created in 1490 when the roof was raised. They were used chiefly for storage and in 1603 a new floor was installed to allow gunpowder to be kept here: by 1667 some 10,000 barrels of it were stored in the Tower. Among the displays are gilt panels and ornament from the barge of the Master of the Ordnance built in 1700.

The Small Armoury and Crypt

The westerly room on the ground floor may originally have been a living area, and has traces of the oldest fireplaces known in England. Pistols, muskets, swords, pikes and bayonets are mounted on the walls and panels in elaborate symmetrical patterns based on the kind of displays popular in the Tower armouries in the 18th and 19th centuries. They were shown in the Grand Storehouse until it burned down in 1841; there is a model of it on the west wall. A collection of weapons taken from the men who planned to assassinate William III in 1696 is on show, and next door is a wooden block made in 1747 for the execution of Lord Lovat – the last public beheading in England.

The Line of Kings

The Line of Kings, ten life-size carvings of prominent English Monarchs, wearing armour and seated on horseback, originated in Tudor times, when eight such figures adorned the royal palace at Greenwich. Two more had been added by the time they first appeared in the Tower in 1660, celebrating the Restoration of Charles II. In 1688, 17 new horses and heads were commissioned, some from the great carver Grinling Gibbons (the third from the left is reputed to be his work).

Henry VIII's armour (1540)

THE PRINCES IN THE TOWER

One of the Tower's darkest mysteries concerns two boy princes, sons and heirs of Edward IV. They were put into the Tower by their uncle, Richard of Gloucester, when their father died in 1483. Neither was seen again and Richard was crowned later that year. In 1674 the skeletons of two children were found nearby.

The yacht haven of the restored St Katharine's Dock

St Katharine's Dock ⓲

E1. **Map** 16 E3. **C** 020-7488 0555. **⊖** Tower Hill. **♿ ⚑ ▣ ▢**

THIS MOST CENTRAL of all London's docks was designed by Thomas Telford and opened in 1828 on the site of St Katharine's hospital. Commodities as diverse as tea, marble and live turtles (turtle soup was a Victorian delicacy) were unloaded here.

During the 19th and early 20th centuries the docks flourished, but by the mid-20th century cargo ships were delivering vast, bulky cargoes in massive containers. The old docks became too small and new ones had to be built downstream. St Katharine's closed in 1968 and the others followed within 15 years.

St Katharine's is now one of London's most successful developments, with its commercial, residential and entertainment facilities, including a hotel and a yacht

St Helen's Bishopsgate

haven. Old warehouse buildings have shops and restaurants on their ground floors, and offices above.

On the north side of the dock is LIFFEE Commodity Products, trading in commodities such as coffee, sugar and oil. There is no public gallery but, if you ask at the door, you may be able to look down from the glass-walled reception area on to the frenzied trading floors. The dock is worth wandering through after visiting the Tower or Tower Bridge (see pp154–7 and p153).

Tower Hill Pageant ⓳

Tower Hill Terrace EC3. **Map** 16 D2. **C** 020-7709 0081. **⊖** Tower Hill. **Closed** for refurbishment until further notice. Phone for latest information. **Adm charge. ♿ ▣ ▢ Filmshows.**

THIS UNDERGROUND ride offers a whirlwind account of London's history, with an emphasis on its role as a port. The story is told through life-sized tableaux with visual and sound effects. After the ride, the viewing cars deposit visitors in a fascinating small exhibition, organized by the Museum of London. It shows objects dug up from the river (including long-sunken boats) and explains how archaeologists can make deductions from them about life in earlier times. In many ways, the exhibition is of more interest (for adults at least) than the ride itself. A large shop sells, among many other things, reproductions of Roman jewellery found in London.

St Helen's Bishopsgate ⓴

Great St Helen's EC3. **Map** 15 C1. **C** 020-7283 2231. **⊖** Liverpool St. **Open** 9am–5pm Mon, Wed–Fri. **⚑** 12.35pm & 1.15pm Tue, 10.15am & 7pm Sun. **♿**

THE CURIOUS, bisected appearance of this 13th-century church is due to its origins as two places of worship: one a parish church, the other the chapel of a long-gone nunnery next door. (The medieval nuns of St Helen's were notorious for their "secular kissing".)

Among its monuments is the tomb of Sir Thomas Gresham, who founded the Royal Exchange (see p147).

St Katharine Cree ㉑

86 Leadenhall St EC3. **Map** 16 D1. **C** 020-7283 5733. **⊖** Aldgate, Tower Hill. **Open** 10.30am–4.30pm Mon–Tue, Thu–Fri. **Closed** Christmas, Easter. **Ø** in services. **⚑** 1.05pm Thu.

The organ at St Katharine Cree

A RARE PRE-WREN 17th-century church with a medieval tower, this was one of only eight churches in the City to survive the fire of 1666. Some of the elaborate plasterwork on and beneath the high ceiling of the nave portrays the coats of arms of the guilds, with which the church has special links. The 17th-century organ, supported on magnificent carved wooden columns, was played by both Purcell and Handel.

Lloyd's of London 22

1 Lime St EC3. **Map** 15 C2.
(020-7327 1000. **e** Bank,
Monument, Liverpool St, Aldgate.
Not open to the public.

L LOYD'S WAS FOUNDED in the
late 17th century and takes
its name from the coffee
house where underwriters
and shipowners used to meet
to arrange marine insurance
contracts. Lloyd's soon
became the world's main
insurers, issuing policies on
everything from oil tankers to
Betty Grable's legs.

The present building, by
Richard Rogers, dates from
1986 and is one of the most
interesting modern buildings
in London (see p30). Its
exaggerated stainless steel
external piping and high-tech
ducts echo Rogers's forceful
Pompidou Centre in Paris.
Lloyd's is a far more elegant
building and particularly
worth seeing floodlit at night.

Leadenhall Market 23

Whittington Ave EC3. **Map** 15 C2.
e Bank, Monument. **Open**
7am–4pm Mon–Fri. See **Shops and Markets** pp322–3.

T HERE HAS BEEN a food
market here, on the site of
the Roman forum (see pp16–
17), since the Middle Ages. Its
name derives from a lead-
roofed mansion that stood
near here in the 14th century.
The ornate, Victorian covered
shopping precinct that is here
today was designed in 1881
by Sir Horace Jones, the
architect of Billingsgate fish
market (see p152). The
shopping precinct is at its
best at Christmas time when
all the stores are decorated.

Stock Exchange 24

Old Broad St EC4. **Map** 15 B1.
e Bank. **Not open** to the public.

T HE FIRST STOCK exchange
was established in
Threadneedle Street in 1773.
Before that, in the 17th and

Leadenhall Market in 1881

18th centuries, stockbrokers
met and dealt in City coffee
houses. Until 1914 the
London Stock Exchange was
the biggest in the world; now
it is third to Tokyo and New
York. The building, which
dates from 1969, used to
house the frenzied trading
floor, but in 1986 the business
was computerized and the
floor effectively made
redundant. The former public
viewing gallery stayed open
for a while, but was closed
after a terrorist bomb attempt.

Guildhall 25

Gresham St EC2. **Map** 15 B1.
(020-7606 3030. **e** St Paul's.
Not open to the public. **Clock
Museum** Aldermanbury St EC2.
Open 9.30am–4.45pm Mon–Fri. **&**

T HIS HAS BEEN the admin-
istrative centre of the City
for at least 800 years. The
crypt and great hall in the
present building date from
the 15th century.

For centuries the hall was
used for trials and many
people were condemned to
death here, including Henry
Garnet, one of the Gun-
powder Plot conspirators (see
p22). Today its role is less
bloody; in November, a few
days after the Lord Mayor's
parade takes place (see
pp54–5), the Prime Minister
addresses a banquet here.

In the adjoining public
library is the collection of the
Clockmakers' Company. This
includes some 600 watches
and 30 clocks dating from the
16th to the 19th centuries.
Mary Queen of Scots's skull-
shaped watch is also here.

Richard Rogers's Lloyd's building illuminated at night

SMITHFIELD AND SPITALFIELDS

THE AREAS JUST north of the City walls have historically provided refuge for people and institutions that did not want to come under the City's jurisdiction, or were not welcome there. These included religious orders, dissenters, the earliest theatres, French Huguenots in the 17th century, and, in the 19th and 20th centuries, other immigrants from Europe and, later, Bengal. They established workshops and small factories and brought with them their ethnic restaurants and places of worship. The name Spitalfields derives from the medieval priory of St Mary Spital. Middlesex Street off Aldgate became known as Petticoat Lane in the 16th century, when a market for clothing was established there; it remains the hub of a popular and crowded Sunday morning street market that spreads as far east as Brick Lane, today lined with aromatic Bengali food shops. The wholesale fruit and vegetable market at Spitalfields survived until 1991, when it moved to the eastern suburbs. The meat market at Smithfield, however, is still going strong. The area around Smithfield adjoining the City is dominated by the Barbican, a modern residential complex with an arts and conference centre.

Tower: Smithfield Market

Columbia Road flower and plant market

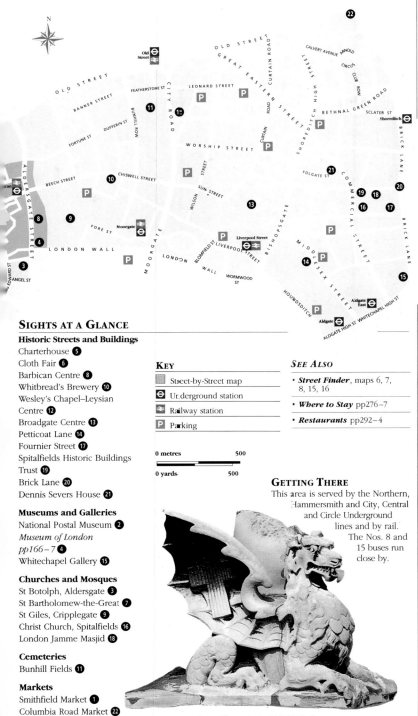

N

SIGHTS AT A GLANCE

Historic Streets and Buildings
Charterhouse ❺
Cloth Fair ❻
Barbican Centre ❽
Whitbread's Brewery ❿
Wesley's Chapel–Leysian
Centre ⓬
Broadgate Centre ⓭
Petticoat Lane ⓮
Fournier Street ⓱
Spitalfields Historic Buildings
Trust ⓲
Brick Lane ⓳
Dennis Severs House ㉑

Museums and Galleries
National Postal Museum ❷
Museum of London
pp166–7 ❹
Whitechapel Gallery ⓯

Churches and Mosques
St Botolph, Aldersgate ❸
St Bartholomew-the-Great ❼
St Giles, Cripplegate ❾
Christ Church, Spitalfields ⓰
London Jamme Masjid ⓲

Cemeteries
Bunhill Fields ⓫

Markets
Smithfield Market ❶
Columbia Road Market ㉒

KEY

▨	Street-by-Street map
Ⓔ	Underground station
➡	Railway station
🅿	Parking

0 metres   500
0 yards   500

SEE ALSO

• *Street Finder*, maps 6, 7,
  8, 15, 16

• *Where to Stay* pp276–7

• *Restaurants* pp292–4

GETTING THERE

This area is served by the Northern,
Hammersmith and City, Central
and Circle Underground
lines and by rail.
The Nos. 8 and
15 buses run
close by.

Stone dragon in Smithfield Market

Street-by-Street: Smithfield

THIS AREA IS AMONG the most historic in London. It contains one of the capital's oldest churches, some rare Jacobean houses, vestiges of the Roman wall (near the Museum of London) and central London's only surviving wholesale food market.

Smithfield's long history is also bloody. In 1381 the rebel peasant leader, Wat Tyler, was killed here by an ally of Richard I, as he presented the king with demands for lower taxes. Later, in the reign of Mary I (1553–8), scores of Protestant religious martyrs were burned at the stake here.

The Fat Boy:
the Great Fire
ended here

The Fox and Anchor pub
is open from 7am for hearty breakfasts, washed down with ale by the market traders of Smithfield.

★ **Smithfield Market**
A contemporary print shows Horace Jones's stately building for the meat market when it was completed in 1867 **❶**

SITE OF THE
SARACEN'S HEAD
INN
DEMOLISHED
1868

Fat Boy

The Saracen's Head, an historic inn, stood on this site until the 1860s when it was demolished to make way for Holborn Viaduct *(see p140).*

CHARTERHOUSE STREET

LINDSEY S

LON

WEST SMITHFIELD

SMITHFIELD STREET

COCK LANE

SNOW HILL

GILTSPUR STREET

St Bartholomew-the-Less has a 15th-century tower and vestry. Its links to the hospital are shown by this early-20th-century stained glass of a nurse; a gift of the Worshipful Company of Glaziers.

St Bartholomew's
Hospital has stood on this site since 1123. Some of the existing buildings date from 1759.

KEY

– – – Suggested route

0 metres 100

0 yards 100

Charterhouse

The square contains the remnants of a medieval monastery and a school where John Wesley (see p168) studied **5**

Barbican station

LOCATOR MAP
See Central London Map pp12–13

★Barbican Centre

World War II bombs flattened this immense site, rebuilt as a housing development in the 1960s. It has a major arts complex inside **8**

Cloth Fair

Two of its houses are survivors of the 1666 Great Fire **6**

St Bartholomew-the-Great

It has the best-preserved medieval interior of any London church **7**

★ Museum of London

The city's history is told vividly through fascinating and colourful exhibits **4**

Christ Church tower is all that remains of one of Wren's most splendid churches (1704).

~ To St Paul's station

National Postal Museum

The statue of Rowland Hill, inventor of the Penny Post, is outside **2**

STAR SIGHTS
★ Museum of London
★ Barbican Centre
★ Smithfield Market

Smithfield Market ❶

Charterhouse St EC1. **Map** 6 F5.
🚇 *Farringdon, Barbican.* **Open**
5–9am Mon–Fri.

L IVE CATTLE WERE sold here
until the mid-19th century.
Then it was the smooth field
from which its name probably
derives. Smithfield is still
London's main meat market
but, since 1855, the market
has confined itself to mainly
wholesale trading in dead
meat and poultry. The old
buildings are by Sir Horace
Jones, the Victorian architect
who specialized in markets,
but there are 20th-century
additions. Some pubs in the
area keep market hours and,
from dawn, serve substantial
breakfasts, washed down with
ale, to market traders and
early-rising office workers.

Smithfield Market central tower

National Postal Museum ❷

King Edward Bldg, King Edward St
EC1. **Map** 15 A1. **Enquiries** 📞 020-
7239 2570. 🚇 *Barbican, St Paul's.*
Opening times *currently uncertain,
phone main enquiries line in advance
of a visit to check.*

T HE FORMER HEADQUARTERS of
the Post Office stands on
the site of the old Bull and
Mouth Inn, behind St Paul's,

Stamp commemorating the 1953 Coronation: National Postal Museum

where in the 18th century the
first mail coaches would leave
for cities across the country.
The 8 million stamps and
10,000 artefacts that make up
the collection will be moving
at an uncertain date to the
Post Office Archive Centre,
Phoenix Place WC1, so be
sure to check before visiting.

St Botolph, Aldersgate ❸

Aldersgate St EC1. **Map** 15 A1.
📞 *020-7606 0684.* 🚇 *St Paul's.*
Open *11am–3pm Wed–Fri*
🕐 *1.10pm Thu.* ♿

A MODEST LATE Georgian
exterior (completed 1791)
conceals a flamboyant, well-
preserved interior which has
a finely-decorated plaster
ceiling, a rich brown wooden
organ case and galleries, and
an oak pulpit resting on a
carved palm tree. The original
box pews have been kept in
the galleries but not in the
body of the church. Some
memorials come from a 14th-
century church on the site.
  The former churchyard
alongside was converted
in 1880 into a relaxing green
space known as Postman's
Park, because it was used by
workers from the nearby Post
Office headquarters. In the
late 19th century, Victorian
artist G F Watts dedicated one
of the walls to a quirky
collection of plaques that
commemorate acts of bravery
and self-sacrifice by ordinary
people; some of these are still
there. In 1973 a powerful,
modern bronze minotaur, the
work of sculptor Michael
Ayrton, was erected.

Museum of London ❹

See pp166–7.

Charterhouse ❺

Charterhouse Sq EC1. **Map** 6 F5.
📞 *020-7253 9503.* 🚇 *Barbican.*
Open *Apr–Jul: 2.15pm Wed.* **Adm
charge.** 📷 ✏

T HE 14TH-CENTURY gateway
on the north side of the
square leads to the site of a
former Carthusian monastery
dissolved under Henry VIII.
In 1611 the buildings were
converted into a hospital
for poor pensioners, and
a charity school – called
Charterhouse – whose pupils
included John Wesley (*see
p168*), writer William
Thackeray and Robert
Baden-Powell, the
founder of the Boy
Scouts.
In 1872 the
school, now a
boarding
school for fee-
paying boys,
moved to
Godalming
in Surrey.
The site was
subsequently
taken over by St
Bartholomew's
Hospital medical
school. Some of
the old buildings
survived, including
the chapel and
part of the
cloisters.

**Charterhouse:
stone carving**

Cloth Fair ❻

EC1. **Map** 6 F5. 🚇 *Barbican.*

THIS PRETTY STREET is named after the notoriously rowdy Bartholomew Fair, which was the main cloth fair in medieval and Elizabethan England, held annually at Smithfield until 1855. Nos. 41 and 42 are fine 17th-century houses and have distinctive two-storeyed wooden bay windows, although their ground floors have since been modernized. The former poet laureate John Betjeman, who died in 1984, lived in No. 43 for most of his life. It has now been turned into a wine bar named after him.

17th-century houses: Cloth Fair

St Bartholomew-the-Great ❼

West Smithfield EC1. **Map** 6 F5. 📞 020-7606 5171. 🚇 *Barbican.* **Open** 8.30am–5pm (4pm in winter) Mon–Fri, 10.30am–1.30pm Sat, 2–6pm Sun. 🕐 9am, 11am, 6.30pm Sun. 📷 ♿ 📹 🎵 *Concerts.*

ONE OF LONDON'S OLDEST churches was founded in 1123 by a monk named Rahere whose tomb is inside. He had been Henry I's court jester until he had a dream in which St Bartholomew saved him from a winged monster.

The 13th-century arch used to be the door to the church until the nave of that earlier building was pulled down when Henry VIII dissolved the priory. Today the arch leads from Little Britain to the small burial ground – the gatehouse above it is from a later period. The present building retains the crossing and chancel of the original, with its round arches and other fine Norman detailing. There are also good examples of Tudor and other monuments. The painter William Hogarth *(see p257)* was baptized here in 1697.

From time to time parts of the church were used for secular purposes, including housing a blacksmith's forge and a hop store. In 1725 US statesman Benjamin Franklin worked for a printer in the Lady Chapel.

Barbican Centre ❽

Silk St EC2. **Map** 7 A5. 📞 020-7638 8891. 📠 020-7628 9760. 🚇 *Barbican, Moorgate.* **Open** 9am–10.30pm Mon–Sat, noon–11pm Sun, public hols. ♿ *induction loop.* 📷 🖥 🍴 📹 *Filmshows, concerts, exhibitions. See Entertainment pp324–37.*

AN AMBITIOUS PIECE of 1960s city planning, this large residential, commercial and arts complex was begun in 1962 on a site devastated by World War II bombs, and not completed for nearly 20 years. Tall residential tower blocks surround an arts centre, which also includes an ornamental lake, fountains and lawns.

The old city wall turned a corner here and substantial remains are still clearly visible (particularly so from the Museum of London – *see pp166–7*). The word barbican means a defensive tower over a gate – perhaps the architects

St Bartholomew's gatehouse

were trying to live up to the name when they designed this self-sufficient community with formidable defences against the outside world. Obscure entrances and raised walk-ways remove pedestrians from the cramped bustle of the City, but, in spite of the signposts, and yellow lines on the pavement, the centre can be difficult to navigate.

As well as two theatres and a concert hall, the Barbican includes cinemas, one of London's largest art galleries for major touring exhibitions, a convention and exhibition hall, a library and a music school (the Guildhall School of Music). There is also a surprising conservatory above the arts centre.

The well-stocked conservatory at the Barbican Centre

Museum of London ❹

OPENED IN 1976 on the edge of the Barbican, the museum provides a lively account of London life from prehistoric times to the present day. Reconstructed interiors and street scenes are alternated with displays of original domestic artefacts and items found in the museum's archaeological digs. Look out for the working model of the Great Fire of 1666, accompanied by readings from Samuel Pepys's eyewitness account.

GALLERY GUIDE
The chronological arrangement of the galleries creates an easy route, which takes about 90 minutes to complete.

The London Plate
This early English delft plate, made in 1602 at Aldgate, in the City, bears an inscription praising Elizabeth I.

Ramp to lower galleries

★ Roman Wall-Painting
The Romans left several brightly coloured wall-paintings. This fine 2nd-century example came from a Southwark bath house.

Main entrance

Lift to lower galleries

Museum entrance

ALDERSGATE STREET

LONDON WALL

To St Paul's station

STAR EXHIBITS

- **★ Roman Wall-Painting**
- **★ Late Stuart Interior**
- **★ Victorian Shop Fronts**

ORIENTATION
The museum is in a modern building above street-level where Aldersgate Street meets London Wall. Access is by signposted steps and ramps.

KEY
- ☐ Museum buildings
- ■ Raised walkways
- ☐ Roads

VISITORS' CHECKLIST

London Wall EC2. **Map** 15 A1.
📞 0120-7600 3699.
🚇 Barbican, St Paul's, Moorgate.
🚌 4, 6, 8, 9, 11, 15, 22, 25, 141, 279A, 501, 513, 502.
🚆 City Thameslink.
Open 10am–5.50pm Mon–Sat, noon–5.50pm Sun.
Closed 24–26 Dec. **Adm charge.** 📷 ♿ Induction loops fitted. 🍴 📷 🎁 **Lectures, film presentations.**

Twentieth-century London is illustrated by displays exploring the major historical events of this century. Votes for women, World War II, the rise of cinema and Swinging London are all here.

★ **Victorian Shop Fronts**
The atmosphere of 19th-century London is recreated by several authentic shop interiors, like this grocer's.

Garden

18th-Century Dress
Luxuriously worked Spitalfields silk was used to make this dress in 1753. It was worn over light-weight cane hoops.

Lift to upper galleries

KEY TO FLOORPLAN

- ☐ Prehistoric London
- ☐ Roman London
- ☐ Dark Age and Saxon London
- ☐ Medieval London
- ☐ Tudor and Early Stuart London
- ☐ Late Stuart London
- ☐ 18th-century London
- ☐ Victorian London and the Imperial Capital
- ☐ 20th-century London
- ☐ Lord Mayor's coach
- ☐ Temporary exhibitions
- ☐ Non-exhibition space

★ **Late Stuart Interior**
Outstanding features from several grand houses of the late 17th century were used to reconstruct this room.

St Giles, Cripplegate **9**

Fore St EC2. **Map** 7 A5. **C** 020-7606 3630. **E** Barbican, Moorgate. **Open** 9.15am–5.15pm Mon–Fri, 9am–1pm Sat. **A** 8am, 10am Sun (family service 11.30am third Sun of each month). **&** **C** 2–5pm Tue.

COMPLETED IN 1550, this church managed to survive the ravages of the Great Fire in 1666, but was so badly damaged by a World War II bomb that only the tower survived. St Giles was refurbished during the 1950s to serve as the parish church of the Barbican development, and now stands awkwardly amid the uncompromising modernity of the Barbican.

Oliver Cromwell married Elizabeth Bourchier here in 1620 and the poet John Milton was buried here in 1674. Well-preserved remains of London's Roman and medieval walls are on view to the south.

Whitbread's Brewery **10**

Chiswell St EC1. **Map** 7 B5. **E** Barbican, Moorgate. **Not open** to the public.

IN 1736, WHEN HE was aged just 16, Samuel Whitbread became an apprentice brewer in Bedford. By the time of his death in 1796, his Chiswell Street brewery (which he had

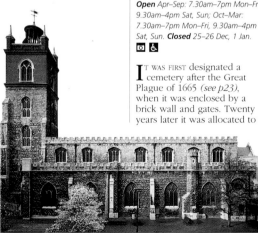
St Giles, Cripplegate

Blake's gravestone at Bunhill Fields

bought in 1750) was brewing 909,200 litres (200,000 gal) a year. The building has not been used as a brewery since 1976 when it was converted into rooms hired out for private functions – they are no longer open to the public. The Porter Tun room, which is now used as a banqueting suite, boasts the largest timber post roof in Europe, and has a huge span of 18 m (60 ft).

The streets 18th-century buildings are well-preserved examples of their period, and are worth a look from the outside. A plaque on one commemorates a visit to the brewery in 1787 by George III and Queen Charlotte.

Bunhill Fields **11**

City Rd EC1. **Map** 7 B4. **C** 020-8472 3584. **E** Old St. **Open** Apr–Sep: 7.30am–7pm Mon–Fri, 9.30am–4pm Sat, Sun; Oct–Mar: 7.30am–7pm Mon–Fri, 9.30am–4pm Sat, Sun. **Closed** 25–26 Dec, 1 Jan. **[o]** **&**

IT WAS FIRST designated a cemetery after the Great Plague of 1665 (see p23), when it was enclosed by a brick wall and gates. Twenty years later it was allocated to

Nonconformists. who were banned from being buried in churchyards because of their refusal to use the Church of England prayer book. Visitors to this spot, which is situated on the edge of the City, and shaded by large plane trees, can see monuments to the writers Daniel Defoe, John Bunyan and William Blake, as well as to members of the Cromwell family.

John Milton wrote his famous epic poem *Paradise Lost* while he lived in Bunhill Row, on the west side of the cemetery, in the years leading up to his death in 1674.

Wesley's Chapel-Leysian Centre **12**

49 City Rd EC1. **Map** 7 B4. **C** 020-7253 2262. **E** Old St. **House, chapel and museum open** 10am–4pm Mon–Sat, noon– 2pm Sun. **Adm charge** (except Sun). **&** **A** 9.45am, 11am Sun, 12.45pm Tue. **C** **[]** **Films, exhibitions.**

Wesley's Chapel

JOHN WESLEY, the founder of the Methodist church, laid the chapel's foundation stone in 1777. He preached here until his death in 1791, and is buried behind the chapel. Next door is the house where he lived, and today some of his furniture, books and other assorted possessions can be seen on display there.

The chapel, adorned in a spartan style, in accordance with Wesley's austere religious principles, has columns made from ships' masts. Beneath it is a small museum that explores the history of the Methodist church. Baroness Thatcher, the first British woman Prime Minister, in office from 1979 to 1990, was married in the chapel.

Broadgate Centre ⑬

Exchange Sq EC2. **Map** 7 C5.
📞 020-7588 6565. 🔁 *Liverpool St.*
♿ 🍴 🖥 🛗

Broadgate Centre skating rink

S ITUATED ABOVE and around Liverpool Street station, the terminus for trains to eastern England, this is one of the most successful recent (1985–91) shop and office developments. Each of the squares has its own distinctive character. Broadgate Arena emulates New York's Rockefeller Center, doubling as a skating rink in winter and a venue for refreshments and entertainment in summer.

Among the many sculptures dotted about the complex are George Segal's *Rush Hour Group*, and Barry Flanagan's *Leaping Hare on Crescent and Bell*. Don't miss the spectacular view of Liverpool Street station and its glass-roofed train shed, seen from Exchange Square to the north.

Petticoat Lane ⑭

Middlesex St E1. **Map** 16 D1.
🔁 *Aldgate East, Aldgate, Liverpool St.* **Open** *9am–2pm Sun. See* **Shops and Markets** *pp322–3.*

I N QUEEN VICTORIA'S prudish reign the name of this street, long famous for its market, was changed to the respectable but colourless Middlesex Street. That is still its official designation, but the old name, derived from its many years as a centre of the clothing trade, has stuck, and

is now applied to the market held every Sunday morning in this and the surrounding streets. Numerous attempts have been made to stop the market, but with no success. An enormous variety of goods is sold but there is still a bias towards clothing, especially leather coats. The atmosphere is noisy and cheerful, with Cockney stall-holders making use of their wit and insolence to attract custom. There are scores of snack bars, and many of these sell traditional Jewish food such as salt beef sandwiches and bagels with smoked salmon.

Whitechapel Art Gallery ⑮

Whitechapel High St E1. **Map** 16 E1.
📞 020-7522 7878. 🔁 *Aldgate East, Aldgate.* **Open** *11am–5pm Tue–Sun, 11am–8pm Wed.* **Closed** *25–26 Dec, 1 Jan, for exhibition installations.* **Occasional adm charge.** ♿ 📷 🍴
🖥 🎞 *Films, lectures.*

A STRIKING ART NOUVEAU facade by C Harrison Townsend fronts this light, airy gallery founded in 1901.

Entrance to Whitechapel Gallery

Its aim is to bring art to the people of East London. Today this independent gallery enjoys an excellent international reputation for high-quality shows of major contemporary artists; these are interspersed with exhibitions reflecting the rich cultural origins of the people in the local community. In the 1950s and 1960s the likes of Jackson Pollock, Robert Rauschenberg, Anthony Caro and John Hoyland all displayed their work here. In 1970 David Hockney's first exhibition was held here.

The gallery also has a well-stocked arts bookshop, and there is a café here, serving a range of appetizing and healthy wholefoods in a relaxed atmosphere.

Bustling Petticoat Lane Market

18th-century Fournier Street

Christic Church, Spitalfields ⑯

Commercial St E1. **Map** 8 E5
☎ 020-7247 7202. **⊜** Aldgate East,
Liverpool St. **Open** noon–2.30pm
Mon–Fri,. **⛪** 10.30am, 7pm Sun.
♿ Concerts in June.

THE FINEST of Nicholas
Hawksmoor's six London
churches, started in 1714
and completed in 1729, was
mauled by Victorian alterations.
Christ Church still dominates
the surrounding streets,
however. Its portico and spire
are best seen from the western
end of Brushfield Street,
showing the four Tuscan
columns on pediments
supporting the arched roof of
the church's portico.

Christ Church was com-
missioned by parliament in
the Fifty New Churches Act of
1711. The act's purpose was
to combat the spread of Non-
conformism (to the established
Church of England) and a
church needed to make a
strong statement here, in an
area that was fast becoming a
Huguenot stronghold. The
Protestant Huguenots had fled
from religious persecution in
Catholic France and came to
Spitalfields to work in the
local silkweaving industry.

The church's impression of
size and strength is reinforced
inside by the high ceiling, the
sturdy wooden canopy over
the west door and the gallery.
In Hawksmoor's original plan
the gallery extends around the
north and south sides joining
the organ gallery at the west

end. The organ dates from
1735; the royal coat of arms,
in Coade stone, from 1822.

. During the 19th century the
hand silkweaving industry
declined as machinery took
over, leaving Spitalfields too
poor to maintain a church. By
the early 20th century Christ
Church was in disrepair. In
1958 it was closed for worship
because it was dangerous.
Restoration began in 1964
and the church reopened in
1987. Since 1965 the crypt has
provided shelter to recovering
alcoholics.

Fournier Street ⑰

E1. **Map** 8 E5. **⊜** Aldgate East,
Liverpool Street.

THE 18TH-CENTURY houses
on the north side of this
street have attics with broad
windows that were designed
to give maximum light to the
silkweaving French Huguenot
community who lived here.
Even now, the textile trade
lives on, in this and nearby
streets, still dependent on
immigrant labour. Today it is
Bengalis who toil at sewing
machines in workrooms that
are as cramped as they were
when the Huguenots used
them. Working conditions are
improving, however, and
many of the sweatshops have
been converted into show-
rooms for companies which
now have modern factories
away from the town centre.

Christ Church, Spitalfields

Bengali sweet factory: Brick Lane

London Jamme Masjid ⑱

Brick Lane E1. **Map** 8 E5.
⊜ Liverpool St, Aldgate East.

LOCAL MUSLIMS NOW worship
here, in a building whose
life story as a religious site
reflects the fascinating history
of immigration into the area.
Built in 1743 as a Huguenot
chapel, it became a synagogue
in the 19th century, was used
as a Methodist chapel in the
early 20th century, and is
now a mosque. The sundial
above the entrance bears the
Latin inscription *Umbra
sumus* – "we are shadows".

Spitalfields Historic Buildings Trust ⑲

19 Princelet St E1. **Map** 8 E5.
☎ 020-7247 0971. **⊜** Aldgate East,
Liverpool St. **Closed** for renovation
until 2000.

THIS HOUSE, built in 1719, still
has a silkweavers' attic. Its
most intriguing feature is a
synagogue built in the garden
in 1870 and used for worship
until the 1960s. Its balconies
are inscribed with Hebrew
texts and names of benefactors.

Brick Lane ⑳

E1. **Map** 8 E5. **⊜** Liverpool St,
Aldgate East, Old St. **Market open**
dawn–noon Sun. See **Shops and
Markets** pp322–3.

ONCE A LANE running through
brickfields, this is now
the busy centre of London's
Bengali district. Its shops and

The grand bedroom of Dennis Severs House

houses, some dating from the 18th century, have seen waves of immigrants of many nationalities, and most now sell food, spices, silks and sarees. The first Bengalis to live here were sailors who came in the 19th century. In those days it was a predominantly Jewish quarter, and there are still a few Jewish shops left, including a popular 24-hour bagel shop at No. 159.

On Sundays a large market is held here and in the surrounding streets, complementing Petticoat Lane *(see p169).* At the northern end of Brick Lane is the former Black Eagle Brewery, a medley of 18th- and 19th-century industrial architecture, now reflected in, and set off by, a sympathetic mirror-glassed extension.

Dennis Severs House ㉑

18 Folgate St E1. **Map** 8 D5.
☎ 020-7247 4013. ⊖ *Liverpool St.*
Open first Sun of month 2–5pm, first Mon of month, eve (book in advance) **Adm charge. Evening performances.**

AT NO. 18 Folgate Street, built in 1724, Dennis Severs, a designer and performer, has recreated an historical interior, that takes you an a journey from the 17th to the 19th centuries. It offers what he calls "an adventure of the imagination,… a visit to a time-mode rather than… merely a look at a house". The rooms are like a series of *tableaux vivants,* as if the occupants had simply left for a moment. There is broken

18th-century portrait: Dennis Severs House

bread on the plates, wine in the glasses, fruit in the bowl; the candles flicker and horses' hooves clatter on the cobbles outside. This highly theatrical experience is quite removed from more usual museum re-creations and is not suitable for children under 12. Praised by many, including artist David Hockney, it is truly unique. The house's motto is "you either see it or you don't".

Around the corner on Elder Street are two of London's earliest surviving terraces, also built in the 1720s, where many of the orderly Georgian red-brick houses have been carefully restored.

Columbia Road Market ㉒

Columbia Rd E2. **Map** 8 D3.
⊖ *Liverpool St, Old St, Bethnal Green.* **Open** 8.30am–1pm Sun. See **Shops and Markets** pp322–3.

A VISIT TO this flower and plant market is one of the most delightful things to do on Sunday mornings in London, whether you want to take advantage of the exotic species on offer there or not. Set in a well-preserved street of small Victorian shops, it is a lively, sweet-smelling and colourful event. Apart from the stalls, there are several shops selling, among other things, home-made bread and farmhouse cheeses, antiques and interesting objects, many of them flower-related. There is also a Spanish delicatessen and an excellent snack bar that sells bagels and welcome mugs of hot chocolate on chilly winter mornings.

Columbia Road flower market

SOUTHWARK AND BANKSIDE

SOUTHWARK ONCE offered an escape route from the City, where many forms of pleasure were banned. Borough High Street was lined with taverns: the medieval courtyards that still run off it mark where they stood. The George survives as the only galleried London inn. Prostitution thrived in houses facing the river, and theatres and bear gardens *(see picture p178)* were established here in the late 16th century. Shakespeare's company was based at the Globe Theatre and also played at the Rose nearby. The palace of the Bishops of Winchester – from which a magnificent rose window survives – was best known for its notorious Clink prison. Today the wharves are closed and the river is lined with a pleasant walkway linking its attractions and giving tremendous views over the river to the City.

Shakespeare window at Southwark Cathedral

SIGHTS AT A GLANCE

Historic Streets and Buildings
Hop Exchange **2**
The Old Operating Theatre **5**
Cardinal's Wharf **9**

Museums and Galleries
Clink Prison Museum **6**
Shakespeare's Globe **8**
Tate Bankside **10**

Bankside Gallery **11**
London Dungeon **13**
Design Museum **14**

Cathedrals
Southwark Cathedral **1**

Pubs
George Inn **4**
The Anchor **7**

Markets
Borough Market **3**
Bermondsey Antiques Market **12**

Historic Ships
HMS Belfast **15**

0 metres		500
0 yards		500

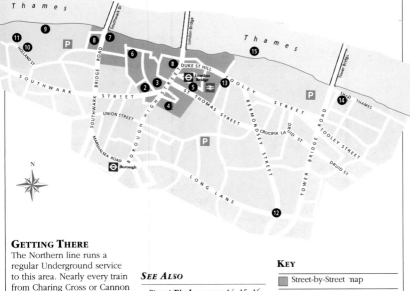

GETTING THERE
The Northern line runs a regular Underground service to this area. Nearly every train from Charing Cross or Cannon Street stops at London Bridge. Taking a bus from the city centre is very confusing as you have to change.

SEE ALSO
• *Street Finder*, maps 14, 15, 16
• *Where to Stay* pp276–7
• *Restaurants* pp292–4

KEY

▢	Street-by-Street map
⊖	Underground station
⊞	Rail station
P	Parking

View from the riverside walkway

Street-by-Street: Southwark

F ROM MEDIEVAL TIMES until the 18th century Southwark was a popular venue for the pursuit of illicit pleasures – including the Elizabethan theatre. It was south of the Thames and out of the jurisdiction of the City authorities. The 18th and 19th centuries brought docks, warehouses and factories, while railways carved a swathe through the area. Today it has been developed with offices.

Southwark Bridge
was opened in 1912
to replace a bridge
of 1819.

★ **Tate Bankside**
The former Bankside Power Station is now a powerhouse of contemporary art, its spectacular open spaces showing off exhibits to perfection ⓫

★ **Shakespeare's Globe**
This brilliant recreation of an Elizabethan theatre has open-air performances in the summer months ❽

STAR SIGHTS

★ **Southwark
Cathedral**

★ **Tate Bankside**

★ **Shakespeare's
Globe**

0 metres   100

0 yards   100

KEY

– – –   Suggested route

Southwark Quayside

LOCATOR MAP
See Central London Map pp12–13

The Anchor
For centuries it has been a favourite riverside pub with fine views ❼

Clink Prison Museum
A museum on the site of the notorious old prison looks back at Southwark's colourful past ❻

Rose window

★Southwark Cathedral
Despite major alterations, it still contains medieval elements ❶

London Bridge, in its various forms, was the only river crossing in London from Roman times until 1750. The present bridge, completed in 1972, replaced the one of 1831 now in the US.

Borough Market
There has been a market on or near this site since 1276. Now it sells wholesale fruit and vegetables ❸

The War Memorial, commemorating soldiers who fell in World War I, was erected in 1924 on Borough High Street where it has become a powerful landmark.

George Inn
This is London's only surviving traditional, galleried inn ❹

Southwark Cathedral **1**

Montague Close SE1. **Map** 15 B3.
(020-7407 2939. **&** *London Bridge.* **Open** *9am–6pm daily.* **+**
11am Sun. **♬** *Concerts.*

T HIS CHURCH DID not become
a cathedral until 1905.
However, some parts date
back to the 12th century,
when the building was
attached to a priory, and
many of its medieval features
remain. The memorials are
fascinating. The wooden
effigy of a knight is late 13th-
century, and another gem is
the tomb, dating from 1408,
of John Gower, poet and
contemporary of Geoffrey
Chaucer *(see p39)*.

The monument to William
Shakespeare, shown in front
of a relief of 17th-century
Southwark, was carved in
1912. His brother Edmond is
buried here, and so is Philip
Henslowe, who was in charge
of the nearby Rose Theatre
in Shakespeare's day. John
Harvard, who went on to
found Harvard University in
the United States, was baptized here in 1607 and there
is a chapel named after him.

Shakespeare Window in Cathedral

Hop Exchange **2**

Southwark St SE1. **Map** 15 B4. **&**
London Bridge. **Not open** *to the public.*

S OUTHWARK, with its easy
access to Kent where hops
are grown, was a natural
venue for brewing beer and
trading hops. In 1866 this
building was constructed as
the centre of that trade. Now

The George Inn, now owned by the National Trust

offices, it retains its original
pediment complete with
carved scenes showing the
hop harvest, and iron gates
with a hop motif.

Borough Market **3**

Stoney St SE1. **Map** 15 B4.
& *London Bridge.* **Open** *midnight–
10am Mon–Sat.*

T HIS SMALL WHOLESALE fruit
and vegetable market
spreads out in an L-shape
beneath the railway tracks.
It is the successor to a medieval market, held on London
Bridge, which was moved to
Borough High Street in 1276
to avoid congestion. It was
moved again in 1756, for the
same reason, to its present
location where the buildings
date from 1851. Today its
future is uncertain.

George Inn **4**

77 Borough High St SE1. **Map** 15 B4.
(020-7407 2056. **&** *London
Bridge, Borough.* **Open** *11am–11pm
Mon–Sat, noon–10.30pm Sun.* **♬**
*See **Restaurants and Pubs** pp308–9.*

D ATING FROM THE 17th-
century, this building is
the only example of a traditional galleried coaching inn
left in London. It was rebuilt
after the Southwark fire of
1676 in a style that dates back
to the Middle Ages. Originally
there would have been three

wings around a courtyard
where plays were staged in
the 17th century. In 1889 the
north and east wings were
demolished to create room
for the railway, so there is
only one wing remaining.

The inn, now owned by the
National Trust, is still a pub
and restaurant. Plays, morris
dancing and other culturally
fascinating traditional and
modern entertainments are
sometimes performed in the
yard on fine days during the
summer months.

The Old Operating Theatre **5**

9a St Thomas St SE1. **Map** 15 B4.
(020-7955 4791. **&** *London
Bridge.* **Open** *10am–4.30pm daily.*
Closed *Christmas week–New Year.*
Adm charge. **+**

S T THOMAS'S HOSPITAL, one of
the oldest in Britain, stood
here from its foundation in
the 12th century until it was
moved west in 1862. At this
time nearly all of its buildings
were demolished in order to
make way for the railway.
The women's operating

19th-century surgical tools

theatre (The Old Operating Theatre Museum and Herb Garret) survived only because it was located away from the main buildings, in a garret over the hospital church (now the Chapter House of Southwark Cathedral). It lay, bricked over and forgotten, until the 1950s. It has now been fitted out just as it would have been in the early 19th century, before the discovery of either anaesthetics or antiseptics. The display shows how patients were blindfolded, gagged and bound to the wooden operating table, while a box of sawdust underneath was used to catch the blood.

Pub sign at the Anchor Inn

the area *(see pp22–3)*. The present building is 18th-century but traces of much earlier hostelries have been found beneath it. The inn was once connected with a brewery on the other side of the road that belonged to Henry Thrale, a close friend of Dr Samuel Johnson *(see p140)*. When Thrale died in 1781, Dr Johnson went to the brewery sale and encouraged the bidders with a phrase that has passed into the English language: "The potential of growing rich beyond the dreams of avarice".

Shakespeare's Globe ❽

New Globe Walk SE1. **Map** 15 A3.
📞 020-7902 1500. ⊖ *London Bridge, Mansion House.* **Open** mid-May–Sep: 9.15am–12.15pm; Oct–mic–May: 10am–5pm daily. **Performances** mid-May–Sep. **Adm charge.** 📷 🎫 every 30 mins. 🚻

A DETAILED REPRODUCTION of an Elizabethan theatre has been built on the riverside a few hundred metres from the site of the original Globe, Shakespeare's "wooden O" where many of his plays were first performed. Open to the elements (although the seats are protected), the theatre operates only in summer, and seeing a play here can be a lively experience, with the "groundlings" standing just in

front of the stage encouraged to cheer or jeer. When there is no performance, visitors are taken on an informative tour of the theatre by resting actors who talk of the struggle of the late Sam Wanamaker to get the project completed against enormous odds. An exhibition and video tell the story of Shakespeare and other Elizabethan dramatists, and of the Globe itself.

Cardinal's Wharf ❾

SE1. **Map** 15 A3. ⊖ *London Bridge.*

A SMALL GROUP OF 17th-century houses today survives here in the shadow of the new Tate Bankside *(see p178)*. A plaque commemorates Christopher Wren's stay while St Paul's Cathedral *(see pp148–51)* was being built. He would have had a particularly fine view of the works.

Davies Amphitheatre, on the site of Shakespeare's Globe Museum

Replica of Civil War trouper's pot helmet, made in the Clink

Clink Prison Museum ❻

1 Clink St SE1. **Map** 15 B3.
📞 020-7378 1558. ⊖ *London Bridge.* **Open** 10am–6pm daily. **Closed** 25 Dec. **Adm charge.**
📷 🚻 🎫 for groups (phone first).

T HE CLINK was the popular name for the prison attached to the medieval palace of the Bishops of Winchester, of which the lovely rose window east of the museum formed part. The displays tell the story of the prison, the prostitutes who were among its inmates, and the armory that later occupied the site.

The Anchor ❼

34 Park St SE1. **Map** 15 A3.
📞 020-7407 1577. ⊖ *London Bridge.* **Open** 11am–11pm Mon–Sat, noon–10.30pm Sun. 🍴

T HIS IS ONE OF London's most famous riverside pubs. It dates from after the Southwark fire of 1676, which devastated

Tate Gallery of Modern Art at Bankside ⑪

Holland St SE1. **Map** 15 A3.
020-7401 7302. Blackfriars,
Waterloo. **Open** 10am–5.50pm daily.
Closed 24–26 Dec. **Adm charge** for
major exhibitions only.
Lectures, video presentations.

Farms at Auvers by Vincent van Gogh (1890)

O NE OF THE WORLD'S premier collections of 20th-century art now has a home worthy of its importance in this classic power station designed in 1947 by Sir Giles Gilbert Scott, the architect of Waterloo Bridge and of London's red telephone kiosks. Until 2000 the collection shared the Tate Gallery, Millbank *(see pp82–5)* with the national collection of British art. The huge Bankside Power Station, disused since 1981, was acquired by the Tate, with funding from the Millennium Commission, and an architectural competition was held to spark ideas for its conversion. The winning design, by Swiss architects Herzog & de Meuron, allows the artworks

Untitled by
Mark Rothko
(c.1951–2)

to be displayed in a dynamic style more suited to their period and innovative spirit.

From the main entrance on the west side of the building, visitors go down a ramp into the huge hall that used to contain the turbines. It has been designed to resemble a covered street and also houses large works of art. Escalators up from here lead to the display areas where the works are shown in three large suites of galleries, giving a broad chronological account of the modern movement. The paintings and sculptures embrace surrealism, abstract expressionism, pop art, minimal and conceptual art. Far more of them are on display than was possible in

The Three Dancers by
Pablo Picasso (1925)

the restricted space available at Millbank. Among many famous international works in the collection are Picasso's *The Three Dancers*, Dali's *The Metamorphosis of Narcissus* and Warhol's *Marilyn Diptych*. Paintings and sculpture by British 20th-century artists are divided between the two sites. Notable British artists with works on show include Francis Bacon, David Hockney, Henry Moore, Stanley Spencer and Barbara Hepworth.

On top of the building are two new floors, enclosed in glass. One is a restaurant with superb views. Their light filters through to the galleries below giving, together with cathedral-like windows on the river side, optimum viewing conditions.

Spectacular downstream view of the Tate's Bankside gallery, from Blackfriars

Bankside Gallery ⓬

48 Hopton St SE1. **Map** 14 F3.
☎ *020-7928 7521.* 🚇 *Blackfriars,
Waterloo.* **Open** *10am–8pm Tue,
10am–5pm Wed–Fri,1–5pm Sat &
Sun.* **Closed** *Christmas week–2 Jan.*
Adm charge. ♿ 🏛 *Lectures.*

THIS MODERN RIVERSIDE
gallery is the headquarters
of the Royal Watercolour
Society and the Royal Society
of Painter-Printmakers. Its
permanent collection is not
on show here but there are
temporary exhibitions of
watercolours and engravings,
many of which are for sale.
There is also an excellent
specialist shop that sells
books and materials.
　There is an unparalleled
view of St Paul's Cathedral
from the nearby Founders'
Arms – built on the site of the
foundry where St Paul's bells
were cast. South of here, on
Hopton Street, are some
almshouses dating from 1752.

Bermondsey Antiques Market ⓭

(New Caledonian Market) Long Lane
and Bermondsey St SE1. **Map** 15 C5.
🚇 *London Bridge, Borough.* **Open**
5am–3pm Fri, starts closing midday.
See **Shops and Markets** *pp322–3.*

ONE OF LONDON'S main
markets for antiques,
Bermondsey market was
established here in the 1960s
when the old Caledonian
Market site in Islington was
redeveloped. Each Friday at
dawn, serious antique
dealers trade their latest
acquisitions at Ber-
mondsey. The press
reports the occasional
long-lost masterpiece
changing hands here for
a song, and early-rising
optimists can try their
luck and judgment.
However, trading starts
very early, and the best
bargains go long before
most people are awake.
　Several nearby antique
shops are open all week.
The most interesting of
these are situated in a
row of old warehouses
on Tower Bridge Road.

View from the Founders' Arms

London Dungeon ⓮

Tooley St SE1. **Map** 15 C3. ☎ *0171-
403 7221.* 📞 *020-7403 0606.* 🚇
London Bridge. **Open** *10am–6pm
daily (last adm: 5pm).* **Closed** *25 Dec.*
Adm charge. ♿ 🖥 🏛

IN EFFECT a much expanded
version of the chamber of
horrors at Madame Tussaud's
(see p 220), this museum is
a great hit with ghoulish
children. It illustrates the most
bloodthirsty events in British
history. It is played strictly for
terror, and screams and
moans abound as Druids
perform a human sacrifice at
Stonehenge, Anne Boleyn is
beheaded on the orders of
her husband Henry VIII, and
a room full of people die in
agony during the Great Plague
of 1665. Torture, murder and
witchcraft fill the gaps
between these spectacles.

Antiques stall at Bermondsey Market

Design Museum ⓯

Butlers Wharf, Shad Thames SE1.
Map 16 E4. 📞 *020-7378 6055.*
🚇 *Tower Hill, London Bridge.* **Open**
*11.30am–6pm daily (last adm:
5.30pm).* **Closed** *24–26 Dec.* **Adm
charge.** ♿ 🛍 🏛 🖥 🏛

THIS MUSEUM was the first in
the world to be devoted
solely to the design of mass-
produced everyday objects.
This permanent collection
offers a nostalgic look at
furniture, office equipment,
cars, radio and TV sets, and
household utensils from the
past. Temporary exhibitions
of international design in
the Review and Collections
galleries provide a taste of
what may become familiar to
us in the future.
　On the first floor of the
museum is the Blueprint Café,
that has a wonderful view of
the Thames, especially when
the river is lit up at night.

**Eduardo Paolozzi sculpture (1986),
outside Design Museum**

HMS Belfast ⓰

Morgan's Lane, Tooley St SE1.
Map 16 D3. 📞 *020-7940 6328.*
🚇 *London Bridge, Tower Hill.*
⛴ *Tower Pier.* **Open** *10am–5pm
daily.* **Closed** *24–26 Dec.* **Adm
charge.** ♿ *except for café.*
📷 🖥 🏛

SINCE 1971, this Royal Navy
cruiser has been used as a
floating naval museum. Part
of it has been atmospherically
recreated to show what the
ship was like in 1943 when it
participated in sinking the
German cruiser *Scharnhorst.*
Other displays portray life on
board during World War II
and there are general exhibits
relating to the history of the
Royal Navy.

SOUTH BANK

FOLLOWING the Festival of Britain in 1951, the South Bank arts centre grew up around the newly erected Royal Festival Hall. The architecture of some buildings has been criticized, especially the chunky concrete Hayward Gallery. But the area functions well, and is crowded with culture-seekers most evenings and afternoons. The bordering areas of Waterloo and Lambeth are both down-to-earth, working class areas. Lambeth is celebrated in the song *The Lambeth Walk* from the 1930s musical *Me and My Girl*. The gatehouse of Lambeth Palace, situated on the southern edge of the area, is one of London's finest Tudor buildings.

Signpost at the South Bank Centre

SIGHTS AT A GLANCE

Historic Streets and Buildings
London Aquarium **6**
Lambeth Palace **9**
Waterloo Station **12**
Gabriel's Wharf **14**

Museums and Galleries
Museum of the Moving Image **2**
Hayward Gallery **3**
Florence Nightingale Museum **7**
Museum of Garden History **8**
Imperial War Museum **10**

Churches
St John's, Waterloo Road **13**

Gardens
Jubilee Gardens **5**

Theatres and Concert Halls
National Theatre **1**
Royal Festival Hall **4**
Old Vic **11**

Pubs
Doggett's Coat and Badge **15**

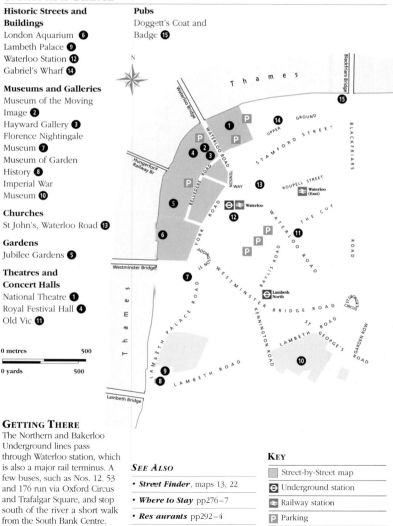

GETTING THERE

The Northern and Bakerloo Underground lines pass through Waterloo station, which is also a major rail terminus. A few buses, such as Nos. 12, 53 and 176 run via Oxford Circus and Trafalgar Square, and stop south of the river a short walk from the South Bank Centre.

SEE ALSO

• *Street Finder*, maps 13, 22
• *Where to Stay* pp276–7
• *Restaurants* pp292–4

KEY

▢	Street-by-Street map
Ⓔ	Underground station
⇄	Railway station
Ⓟ	Parking

Thameside promenade at the South Bank Centre

Street-by-Street: South Bank Centre

ORIGINALLY THIS WAS an area of wharves and
factories which was much damaged by
bombing during World War II. In 1951 it was
chosen as the site of the Festival of Britain
(see p30), celebrating the centenary of the
Great Exhibition *(see pp26–7)*. The Royal
Festival Hall is the only building from 1951 to
remain, but since then London's main arts
centre has been created around it, including
the national showplaces for theatre, music
and film, and a major art gallery.

**Memorial to
the International Brigade
of the Spanish Civil War**

To the Strand

The National Film Theatre
was established in 1953 to
show historic films *(see pp328–9)*.

Festival Pier

The Queen Elizabeth Hall
stages more intimate
concerts than the Festival
Hall. The adjoining Purcell
Room is for chamber music
(see pp330–1).

Hayward Gallery
*The concrete interior of
this venue for important
exhibitions is well suited to
many modern works* ❸

★ **Royal National Theatre**
*Its three auditoriums offer a
choice of plays ranging
from the classics to the
sharpest modern writing* ❶

★ **Royal Festival Hall**
*The London Philharmonic
is one of many world-class
orchestras to perform here
in the focal point of the
South Bank Centre* ❹

Hungerford Bridge
was built in 1864 to
carry both trains and
pedestrians to
Charing Cross.

★ **Museum of the
Moving Image**
*This all-action history
of the cinema offers a
lively family outing* ❷

STAR SIGHTS

★ **Museum of the
Moving Image**

★ **Royal National
Theatre**

★ **Royal Festival Hall**

KEY

– – –   Suggested route

0 metres   100

0 yards   100

Waterloo Bridge was completed in 1945 to Sir Giles Gilbert Scott's design. It replaced Rennie's bridge of 1817.

LOCATOR MAP
See Central London Map pp12–13

The Struggle is My Life is a bronze of Nelson Mandela, the South African leader. Made by Ian Walters, it was unveiled here in 1985.

The Shell Building, headquarters of the international oil company, was completed in 1963. Its architectural merit is still hotly debated.

Jubilee Gardens
Often crowded with picnickers, it was laid out in 1977 to celebrate Queen Elizabeth's silver jubilee ❺

London Aquarium
A lion carved in 1837 guards the former County Hall, now the London Aquarium ❻

To Westminster station

The stark concrete facade of the Hayward Gallery

Royal National Theatre ❶

South Bank Centre SE1. **Map** 14 D3.
📞 020-7452 3000. 🚇 *Waterloo.*
Open *10am–11pm Mon–Sat.* **Closed**
24–25 Dec. 📷 *during performances.*
♿ 🍽 🖥 🎧 **Concerts** *at 6pm,*
exhibitions. *See* **Entertainment**
pp326–7.

E VEN IF YOU DON'T want to see
a play, this well-appointed
complex is worth a visit. Sir
Denys Lasdun's building was
opened in 1976 after 200 years
of debate about whether there
should be a national theatre
and where it should be sited.
The company was formed in
1963, under Laurence (later
Lord) Olivier, Britain's leading
20th-century actor. The largest
of the three theatres is named
after him – the others, the
Cottesloe and the Lyttelton,
commemorate administrators.

Museum of the Moving Image ❷

South Bank Centre SE1. **Map** 14 D3.
📞 020-7401 2636. 🚇 *Waterloo.*
Open *10am–6pm daily (last adm:*
5pm). **Closed** *24–26 Dec.* **Adm**
charge. ♿ 🍽 🖥 🎧 **Events,**
lectures, filmshows.

M OMI is an enthralling
experience for both
adults and children as well
as an invaluable resource
for television and cinema
students. The museum traces
the history of film from the
first experiments with
zoetropes, magic lanterns,
lenses and cameras. The
exhibition bursts into life with
the coming of silent cinema.
A display devoted to Charlie
Chaplin, born in nearby
Kennington *(see p37),* is
illustrated with clips from his
films and artefacts from his
era. In small viewing areas
visitors watch historic scenes
from films in different *genres*
including French and Russian
cinema, documentaries and
newsreels. Actors wander
round in the guise of starlets,

A "Dalek" robot: MOMI

cowboy heroes and ushers,
engaging visitors in banter
and luring them to take part
in movie scenes. You can be
interviewed on screen in a
studio, draw your own cartoons, read the news from an
autocue and watch yourself
fly over the Thames. You
should allow at least two
hours for a visit here.

Hayward Gallery ❸

South Bank Centre SE1. **Map** 14 D3.
📞 020-7928 3144. 🚇 *Waterloo.*
Open *10am–8pm Tue–Wed, 10am–*
6pm Thu–Mon. **Closed** *24–26 Dec,*
1 Jan, Good Fri, May Day, between
exhibitions. **Adm charge.** 📷 ♿ 🎧
🖥 🛗

T HE HAYWARD GALLERY is one
of London's main venues
for large art exhibitions. Its
slabby grey concrete exterior
is too starkly modern for
some tastes and there has
been pressure for it to be
pulled down or severely
modified almost ever since it
opened in October 1968.
Hayward exhibitions cover
classical and contemporary
art, but the work of British
contemporary artists is particularly well represented.
You may have to queue,
especially at weekends.

Royal Festival Hall ❹

South Bank Centre SE1. **Map** 14 D4.
📞 020-7928 3191. 🚇 *Waterloo.*
Open *10am–10pm daily.* **Closed** *25*
Dec. 📷 *during performances.* ♿
🍽 🖥 🎧 **Pre-concert talks,**
exhibitions, free concerts. *See*
Entertainment *p330.*

T HIS WAS THE ONLY structure
in the 1951 Festival of
Britain *(see p30)* designed for
permanence. Sir Robert
Matthew and Sir Leslie
Martin's concert hall was the
first major public building in
London following World War
II. It has stood the test of time
so well that many of the
capital's major arts institutions
have gathered round it. The
hall's interior has always
attracted much admiration; its
sweeping staircases lead up

majestically from the lobby to create a tremendous sense of occasion while also remaining highly functional. The stage has hosted the likes of the cellist, Jacqueline du Pré, and the conductor, Georg Solti. The organ was installed in 1954. There are a variety of cafés, bars, music and book stalls on the lower floors and backstage tours are available.

Festival of Britain: symbol of 1951

Jubilee Gardens 5

South Bank SE1. **Map** 14 D4.
🚇 Waterloo. **London Eye** open from Dec 1999. **Adm charge.**

THIS PLEASANT riverside space was laid out in 1977 to mark the Queen's Silver Jubilee. The sculpture-dotted gardens are a popular summer venue for open air concerts. London Eye – a 135-m (443-ft) ferris wheel – installed to mark the Millennium, offers visitors a 30-minute ride with breath-taking views over the city.

London Aquarium 6

County Hall, York Rd SE1. **Map** 13 C4.
🚇 Waterloo, Westminster. **Open** 10am–6pm daily. **Adm charge.**

THIS MODERN aquarium, one of the largest in Europe, occupies part of the grandiose former headquarters of the Greater London Council. That London-wide authority was abolished in 1986 and the building stood empty for years. Now, fish and other

aquatic creatures are shown in tanks that as far as possible simulate their native habitats, the two largest devoted to the Atlantic and Pacific Oceans. Other parts of County Hall have been converted into a hotel and apartments, and football fans will want to visit the FA Premier League Hall of Fame, opened there in 1999.

Florence Nightingale Museum 7

2 Lambeth Palace Rd SE1. **Map** 14 D5.
📞 020-7620 0374. 🚇 Waterloo, Westminster. **Open** 10am–5pm Tue–Sun, public hols (last adm: 4pm). **Closed** 24–26 & 31 Dec, 1 Jan, Good Fri, Easter Sun. **Adm charge.** 🚫 ⑁
🎥 **Videos, lectures.**

THIS DETERMINED woman captured the nation's imagination as the "Lady of the Lamp", who nursed the wounded soldiers of the Crimea War (1853–6). She also founded Britain's first school of nursing at old St Thomas's Hospital in 1860. Obscurely sited near the entrance to the new St Thomas's Hospital, the museum is worth seeking out. It gives a truly fascinating account of Florence Nightingale's career through displays of original documents, photographs and

Florence Nightingale

personal memorabilia. They illustrate her life and the developments she pioneered in health care and sanitation, until her death in 1910, aged 90.

Museum of Garden History 8

Lambeth Palace Rd SE1. **Map** 21 C1.
📞 0171-261 1891. 🚇 Waterloo, Vauxhall, Lambeth North, Westminster. **Open** 10.30am–4pm Mon–Fri, 10.30am–5pm Sun. **Closed** 2nd Sun Dec–1st Sun Mar. 📷 small charge. ⑁ ⑁ ⑁ **Lectures, filmshows.**

HOUSED IN AND AROUND the 14th-century tower of St Mary's Church, this museum opened in 1979. In the churchyard is the tomb of a father and son both called John Tradescant. The Tradescants were gardeners to the 17th-century monarchs and were also pioneer plant hunters in the Americas, Russia and Europe. Their collection of rarities formed the basis of the Ashmolean Museum, in Oxford.

The museum here consists of a history of gardening in Britain, illustrated by ancient implements, plans and documents. A knot garden outside is devoted to plants from the Tradescants' era. There is a shop with a stock of garden-related items, for freshly-inspired gardeners.

Shark in a scenic tank at the London Aquarium

The Tudor gatehouse

Lambeth Palace ❾

SE1. **Map** 21 C1. ⊖ *Lambeth North, Westminster, Waterloo, Vauxhall.* **Not open** to the public.

Tʜɪs ʜᴀs ʙᴇᴇɴ the London base of the Archbishop of Canterbury, the senior cleric in the Church of England, for 800 years. The chapel and its undercroft contain elements from the 13th century, but a large part of the rest of the building is far more recent. It has been frequently restored, most recently by Edward Blore in 1828 –34. The Tudor gatehouse, however, dates from 1485 and is one of London's most pleasing and familiar riverside landmarks.

Until the first Westminster Bridge was built, the horse ferry that operated between here and Millbank was a principal river crossing. The revenues from it went to the Archbishop, who received compensation for loss of business when the bridge opened in 1750.

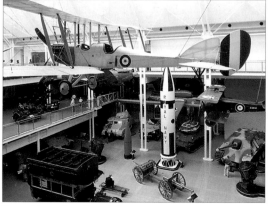

The machinery of war through the ages

Imperial War Museum ❿

Lambeth Rd SE1. **Map** 22 E1.
📞 020-7416 5000. 📠 020-7820 1683. ⊖ *Lambeth North, Elephant & Castle.* **Open** 10am–6pm daily. **Closed** 24–26 Dec. **Adm charge**, free after 4.30pm. 📷 ♿ 🍽
🎞 📷 *Filmshows, lectures.*

Iɴ sᴘɪᴛᴇ ᴏғ ᴛʜᴇ ᴛᴡᴏ colossal guns that point up the drive from the main entrance, this is not just a display of the engines of modern warfare. Massive tanks, artillery, bombs and aircraft *are* on show, yet some of the most fascinating exhibits in the museum relate more to the social effects of 20th-century wars and their impact on the lives of people at home than to the actual business of fighting. There are displays about food rationing, air raid precautions, censorship and morale-boosting.

The arts are well represented, with extracts from wartime films, radio programmes and literature, plus many hundreds of photographs, paintings by Graham Sutherland and Paul Nash, and sculpture by Jacob Epstein. Henry Moore did some evocative drawings of life during the Blitz of 1940, when many Londoners slept in underground stations in order to protect themselves from falling bombs.

The museum is kept up to date with exhibits relating to recent military engagements of British forces, including the Gulf War of 1991. It is housed in part of what used to be Bethlehem Hospital for the Insane ("Bedlam"), built in 1811. In the 19th century, visitors would come for the afternoon to enjoy the antics of the patients. The hospital moved out to new premises in Surrey in 1930, leaving this vast building empty. Its two large, flanking wings were pulled down and this central block converted into the museum which moved here from its former South Kensington site in 1936.

Old Vic ⓫

Waterloo Rd SE1. **Map** 14 E5.
📞 020-7928 7616. 📠 020-7928 7618. ⊖ *Waterloo.* **Open** for performances only. 📷 *See* **Entertainment** *pp326–7.*

The Old Vic's facade from 1816

Tʜɪs sᴘʟᴇɴᴅɪᴅ building dates from 1816, when it was opened as the Royal Coburg Theatre. In 1833 the name was changed to the Royal Victoria in honour of the future queen. Shortly after this the theatre became a centre for "music hall", the immensely popular Victorian entertainment in which singers, comedians and other acts were introduced by a chairman, who needed a booming voice to control unruly audiences.

In 1912 Lillian Baylis took over as manager and in 1914 introduced Shakespearean plays to the Old Vic. Between 1963 and 1976 it was the first home of the National Theatre *(see p184)*. In 1983 it was restored, since when it has operated as a conventional West End theatre.

Waterloo Station ⑫

York Rd SE1. **Map** 14 D4.
☎ 020-7928 5100 ⊖ Waterloo.
See **Getting to London** pp358–9.

THE TERMINUS FOR trains to southwest England, it has been superbly enlarged to serve as London's first Channel Tunnel rail link to Europe. It was originally built in 1848 but completely remodelled in the early 20th century, with a grand formal entrance on the northeast corner. Today the spacious concourse, lined with shops, makes it one of the most practical of the London rail termini.

St John's, Waterloo Road ⑬

SE1. **Map** 14 E4. ☎ 020-7633 9819.
⊖ Waterloo. **Open** 11am–4pm
Mon–Fri, 10am–noon Sat; at other
times phone first. ✝ 10.30am Sun.

ST JOHN'S IS ONE of four "Waterloo churches" that were commissioned in 1818, after the Napoleonic Wars. They are often thought to have been built as a thanksgiving for Britain's victory in these wars, but it is more likely that they were built to serve Lambeth's rapidly growing population. The church's portico, with its six Doric columns supporting a pediment, is in the Greek Revival style that was then popular. Damaged by wartime bombing, it was restored in time to become the official church for the Festival of Britain in 1951 *(see p30).*

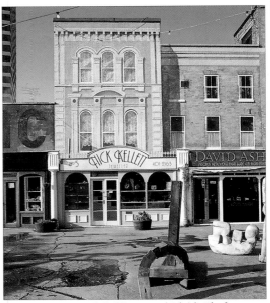

Illusionistic painting on the buildings around Gabriel's Wharf

Gabriel's Wharf ⑭

56 Upper Ground SE1. **Map** 14 E3.
⊖ Waterloo. See **Shops and Markets** pp322–3.

THIS PLEASANT enclave of boutiques, craft shops and cafés was the product of a long and stormy debate over the future of what was once an industrial riverside area. Residents of Waterloo strongly opposed various schemes for office developments before a community association was able to acquire the site in 1984 and build co-operative housing around the wharf. Adjoining the market is a small garden and a riverside walkway with marvellous views to the north of the City. The "OXO tower" to the east, built in 1928 surreptitiously to advertise a meat extract by means of its window shapes, is now the setting for a fine restaurant *(see p298).*

Doggett's Coat and Badge ⑮

1 Blackfriars Bridge SE1. **Map** 14 F3.
☎ 020-7633 9081. ⊖ Blackfriars.
Open 11am–11pm Mon–Fri. **Closed**
25–26 Dec, 1 Jan. 🎫 See
Ceremonial London p55.

A MODERN RIVERSIDE pub next to Blackfriars Bridge, it is named after an historic annual boat race. The race was instituted in 1716 for the boatmen who used to row passengers across the river. Its patron was Thomas Doggett, an actor who was grateful for the services of the watermen; they were held in low esteem because of their vulgarity and coarse language.
   The coat and ceremonial arm badge are still competed for today in a boat race between London Bridge and Cadogan Pier, Chelsea.

The memorial to the dead of World War I at Waterloo Station

CHELSEA

THE SHOWY young shoppers who paraded along the King's Road from the 1960s until the 1980s have more or less gone, along with Chelsea's reputation for extreme behaviour established by the bohemian Chelsea Set of writers and artists in the 19th century. Formerly a riverside village, Chelsea became fashionable in Tudor times. Henry VIII liked it so much that he built a small palace (long vanished) here. Artists, including Turner, Whistler and Rossetti, were attracted by the river views from

Cow's head outside the Old Dairy on Old Church Street

Cheyne Walk. The historian Thomas Carlyle and the essayist Leigh Hunt arrived in the 1830s and began a literary tradition continued by writers such as the poet Swinburne. Yet Chelsea has always had a raffish element, too: in the 18th century the pleasure gardens were noted for beautiful courtesans and the Chelsea Arts Club has had riotous balls for nearly a century. Chelsea is too expensive for most artists now, but the artistic connection is maintained by many galleries and antique shops.

SIGHTS AT A GLANCE

Historic Streets and Buildings
King's Road ❶
Carlyle's House ❷
Cheyne Walk ❺
Royal Hospital ❽
Sloane Square ❾

Museums
National Army Museum ❼

Churches
Chelsea Old Church ❸

Gardens
Roper's Garden ❹
Chelsea Physic Garden ❻

GETTING THERE
The District and Circle Underground lines serve Sloane Square; the Piccadilly line passes just outside this area, through South Kensington. Buses 11, 19 and 22 all stop on the King's Road.

SEE ALSO

- *Street Finder*, maps 19, 20

- *Where to Stay* pp276–7

- *Restaurants* pp292–4

- *Chelsea and Battersea Walk* pp266–7

No. 56 Oakley Street, where the polar explorer, R F Scott, once lived

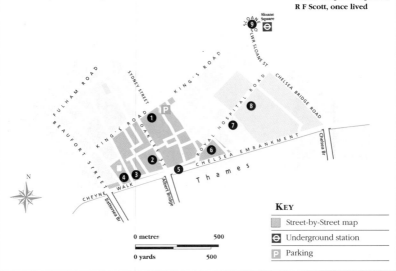

KEY

▢	Street-by-Street map
Ⓔ	Underground station
🅿	Parking

Picturesque Chelsea residences in a cul-de-sac off the King's Road

Street-by-Street: Chelsea

ONCE A PEACEFUL riverside village, Chelsea has been fashionable since Tudor times when Sir Thomas More, Henry VIII's Lord Chancellor, lived here. Artists, including Turner, Whistler and Rossetti, were attracted by the views from Cheyne Walk, before a busy main road disturbed its peace. Chelsea's artistic connection is maintained by its galleries and antique shops, while enclaves of 18th-century houses preserve its old village atmosphere.

King's Road
In the 1960s and 1970s it was the boutique-lined centre of fashionable London and is still a main shopping street ❶

The Old Dairy, at 46 Old Church Street, was built in 1796, when cows still grazed in the surrounding fields. The tiling is original.

To Kings Road

Carlyle's House
The historian and philosopher lived here from 1834 until his death in 1882 ❷

Chelsea Old Church
Although severely damaged during World War II, it still holds some fine Tudor monuments ❸

Roper's Garden
It includes a sculpture by Jacob Epstein who had a studio here ❹

Thomas More, sculpted in 1969 by L Cubitt Bevis, gazes calmly across the river near where he lived.

STAR SIGHT

★ **Chelsea Physic Garden**

KEY

- - -   Suggested route

0 metres   100

0 yards   100

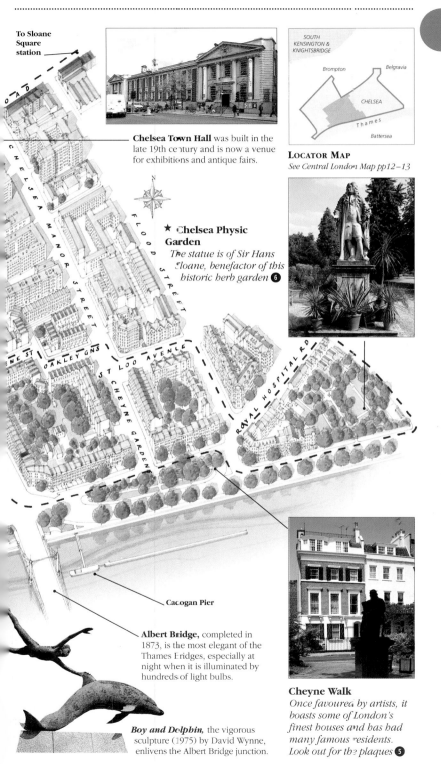

To Sloane Square station

Chelsea Town Hall was built in the late 19th century and is now a venue for exhibitions and antique fairs.

★ Chelsea Physic Garden
The statue is of Sir Hans Sloane, benefactor of this historic herb garden 6

Cadogan Pier

Albert Bridge, completed in 1873, is the most elegant of the Thames Bridges, especially at night when it is illuminated by hundreds of light bulbs.

Boy and Dolphin, the vigorous sculpture (1975) by David Wynne, enlivens the Albert Bridge junction.

Cheyne Walk
Once favoured by artists, it boasts some of London's finest houses and has had many famous residents. Look out for the plaques 5

The Pheasantry, King's Road

King's Road **❶**

SW3 and SW10. **Map** 19 B3.
🚇 *Sloane Square. See **Shops and Markets** pp310–23.*

THIS IS CHELSEA's central artery, with its wealth of small fashion shops packed with young people looking for avant-garde fashions. The mini-skirt revolution of the 1960s began here and so have many subsequent style trends, perhaps the most famous of them being punk.

Look out for the Pheasantry at No. 152, with its columns and statuary. It was built in 1881 as the shop-front of a furniture maker's premises but now conceals a modern restaurant. Antique-lovers will find three warrens of stalls on the south side of the King's Road: Antiquarius at No. 137, the Chenil Galleries at Nos. 181–3 and the Chelsea Antiques Market at No. 253.

Carlyle's House **❷**

24 Cheyne Row SW3. **Map** 19 B4.
📞 020-7352 7087. 🚇 *Sloane Square, South Kensington.* **Open** *Apr–Oct: 11am–5pm Wed–Sun, public hols (last adm: 4.30pm).* **Closed** *Good Fri.* **Adm charge.** 🚫 🖐 *by arrangement.*

THE HISTORIAN, and founder of the London Library *(see St James's Square p96)*, Thomas Carlyle moved into this modest 18th-century house in 1834, and wrote many of his best-known books here, most notably *The French Revolution*

and *Frederick the Great*. His presence made Chelsea more fashionable and the house became a mecca for some of the great literary figures of the 19th century. The novelists Charles Dickens and William Thackeray, poet Alfred Lord Tennyson, naturalist Charles Darwin and philosopher John Stuart Mill were all regular visitors here. The house has been restored so that it looks as it did during Carlyle's lifetime, and is now a museum dedicated to his life and work.

Chelsea Old Church **❸**

Cheyne Walk SW3. **Map** 19 A4. 📞 020-7352 7978. 🚇 *Sloane Sqare, South Kensington.* **Open** *10am–1pm, 2–5pm Mon–Sat, 1.30–6pm Sun.* ♿ 📷 *most days.* ✝ *10am, 11am Sun.*

Chelsea Old Church in 1860

REBUILT AFTER World War II, this square-towered building does not look old from the outside. However, early prints confirm that it is a careful replica of the medieval church that was destroyed by World War II bombs.

The glory of this church are its Tudor monuments. One to Sir Thomas More, who built a chapel here in 1528, contains an inscription he wrote (in Latin), asking to be buried next to his wife. Among other monuments is a chapel to Sir Thomas Lawrence, who was an Elizabethan merchant, and a 17th-century memorial to Lady Jane Cheyne, after whose husband Cheyne Walk was named. Outside the church is a statue in memory of Sir Thomas More, "statesman, scholar, saint", gazing piously across the river.

Roper's Garden **❹**

Cheyne Walk SW3. **Map** 19 A4.
🚇 *Sloane Square, South Kensington.*

THIS IS A SMALL PARK outside Chelsea Old Church. It is named after Margaret Roper, Sir Thomas More's daughter, and her husband William, who wrote More's biography. The sculptor Sir Jacob Epstein worked at a studio on the site between 1909 and 1914, and there is a stone carving by him commemorating the fact. The park also contains a figure of a nude woman by Gilbert Carter.

Cheyne Walk **❺**

SW3. **Map** 19 B4. 🚇 *Sloane Square, South Kensington.*

UNTIL CHELSEA Embankment was constructed in 1874, Cheyne Walk was a pleasant riverside promenade. Now it overlooks a busy road that has destroyed much of its charm. Many of the 18th-century houses remain, though, bristling with blue plaques celebrating some of the famous people who have lived in them. Most were writers and artists, including J M W Turner who lived incognito at No. 119, George Eliot who died at No. 4 and a clutch of writers (Henry James, T S Eliot and Ian Fleming) in Carlyle Mansions.

Thomas More on Cheyne Walk

Chelsea Physic Garden ❻

Swan Walk SW3. **Map** 19 C4.
📞 020-7352 5646. ⊖ *Sloane
Square.* **Open** *Apr–Oct: noon–5pm
Wed, 2–6pm Sun.* **Adm charge**.
♿ 🔲 *3.15–4.45pm.* 🔲 **Annual
exhibition** *during Chelsea Flower
Show, see p56.*

Established by the Society of Apothecaries in 1673 to study plants for medicinal use, this garden has survived to the present day. It was saved from closure in 1722 by a gift from Sir Hans Sloane, whose statue adorns it. The garden has since broadened its range of plants but parts of it would be recognizable to Sir Hans today.

Many new varieties have been nurtured in its glasshouses, including cotton sent to the plantations of the southern United States. Today, visitors can see ancient trees, an historical walk and one of Britain's first rock gardens, installed in 1772.

A Chelsea Pensioner in uniform

Chelsea Physic Garden in spring

National Army Museum ❼

Royal Hospital Rd SW3. **Map** 19 C4.
📞 020-7730 0717. ⊖ *Sloane
Square.* **Open** *10am–5.30pm daily.*
Closed *24–26 Dec, 1 Jan, Good Fri,
May Day.* ♿ 🔲 📷

A vivid and lively account of the history of British land forces from 1485 to the present day can be found here. Tableaux, dioramas and archive film clips illustrate major engagements and give a taste of what life behind the lines was like. There are fine paintings of battle scenes as well as portraits of soldiers. The attached museum shop offers a good range of military books and model soldiers.

Royal Hospital ❽

Royal Hospital Rd SW3. **Map** 20 D3.
📞 020-7730 0161. ⊖ *Sloane
Square.* **Open** *8.30am–12.30pm,
2.30–4.30pm Mon–Sat, 2–4pm Sun.*
Closed *public hols.*

This graceful complex was commissioned by Charles II from Christopher Wren in 1682 as a retirement home for old or wounded soldiers, who have been known as Chelsea Pensioners ever since. The hospital opened ten years later and is still home to about 400 retired soldiers, who are instantly recognizable in their scarlet coats and tricorne hats, a distinctive uniform which dates from the 17th century.

Flanking the northern entrance are Wren's two main public rooms: the chapel, which is notable for its wonderful simplicity, and the panelled Great Hall, still used today as the dining room. A small museum explains the history of the Pensioners.

A statue of Charles II by Grinling Gibbons is to be found on the terrace outside, and there is a fine view of the remains of Battersea Power Station across the river.

Sloane Square ❾

SW1. **Map** 20 D2. ⊖ *Sloane Square.*

Sloane Square fountain

This pleasant small square (rectangle to be precise) has a paved centre with a flower stall and fountain depicting Venus. Laid out in the late 18th century, it was named after Sir Hans Sloane, the wealthy physician and collector who bought the manor of Chelsea in 1712. Opposite Peter Jones, the 1936 department store on the square's west side, is the Royal Court Theatre, which for over a century has fostered new drama.

SOUTH KENSINGTON AND KNIGHTSBRIDGE

RISTLING WITH embassies and consulates, South Kensington and Knightsbridge remain among London's most desirable and salubrious areas. The proximity of Kensington Palace, still a royal residence, means the area has remained relatively unchanged. It vies with Mayfair as the most expensive place to live in London. The elite shops of Knightsbridge, led by Harrod's, serve its wealthy residents. With Hyde Park to the north and the museums that once celebrated Victorian learning and self-confidence at its heart, visitors to this part of London can expect to find a unique combination of the serene and the grandiose.

Facade of the Victoria and Albert Museum

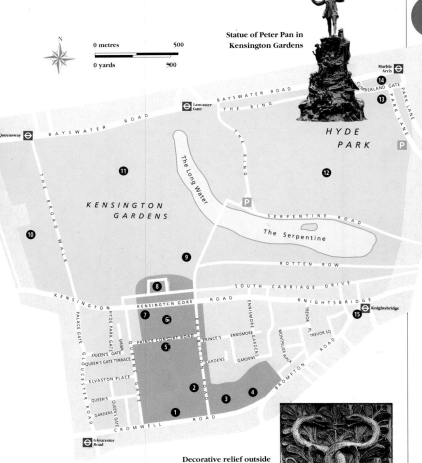

Statue of Peter Pan in Kensington Gardens

Decorative relief outside the Natural History Museum

SIGHTS AT A GLANCE

Historic Streets and Buildings
Royal College of Music **5**
Royal College of Art **7**
Kensington Palace **10**
Speakers' Corner **13**

Churches
Brompton Oratory **4**

Museums and Galleries
Natural History Museum pp204–5 **1**
Science Museum pp208–9 **2**
Victoria and Albert Museum pp198–201 **3**
Serpentine Gallery **9**

Parks and Gardens
Kensington Gardens **11**
Hyde Park **12**

Monuments
Albert Memorial **8**
Marble Arch **14**

Concert Halls
Royal Albert Hall **6**

Shops
Harrod's **15**

SEE ALSO
• *Street Finder*, maps 10, 11, 19
• *Where to Stay* pp276–7
• *Restaurants* pp292–4

GETTING THERE
South Kensington station is on the Piccadilly, Circle and District lines; only the Piccadilly line passes through Knightsbridge. The No. 14 bus runs direct from Piccadilly Circus to South Kensington, via Green Park and Knightsbridge.

KEY
Street-by-Street map
Underground station
Parking

Street-by-Street: South Kensington

A CLUTCH OF MUSEUMS and colleges provide this area with its dignified character. The Great Exhibition of 1851 in Hyde Park was so successful that in the following years smaller exhibitions were held here, just to its south. By the end of the 19th century some of these had become permanent museums, housed in grandiose buildings celebrating Victorian self-confidence.

Royal College of Art
David Hockney and Peter Blake are among the great artists who trained here ❼

The Royal College of Organists was decorated by F W Moody in 1876.

★ **Royal Albert Hall**
Opened in 1870, the Hall was partly funded by selling seats on a 999-year lease ❻

Royal College of Music
Historic musical instruments, like this harpsichord (1531) are exhibited here ❺

★ **Natural History Museum**
The dinosaur exhibits are one of the museum's most popular attractions ❶

★ **Science Museum**
Visitors here can experiment with the interactive displays ❷

Albert Memorial
This memorial was built to commemorate Queen Victoria's consort **8**

The Albert Hall Mansions, built by Norman Shaw in 1879, started a fashion for red brick.

Paddington

SOUTH KENSINGTON & KNIGHTSBRIDGE

Earl's Court

Brompton

LOCATOR MAP
See Central London Map pp12–13

KEY

— — — Suggested route

0 metres 100
0 yards 100

The Royal Geographical Society was founded in 1830. Scottish missionary and explorer David Livingstone (1813–73) was a member.

Imperial College, part of London University, is one of the country's leading scientific institutions.

★ Victoria and Albert Museum
A range of objects and a stunning photo gallery illustrate the nation's history of design and decoration **3**

Brompton Oratory
The Oratory was built during the 19th-century Catholic revival **4**

Brompton Square, begun in 1821, established this as a fashionable residential area.

Holy Trinity church dates from the 19th-century and is located in a calm backwater among cottages.

To Knightsbridge station

STAR SIGHTS

★ Victoria and Albert Museum

★ Natural History Museum

★ Science Museum

★ Royal Albert Hall

Victoria and Albert Museum ❸

Main entrance

T HE VICTORIA AND ALBERT (or V&A) contains one of the world's widest collections of fine and applied arts. The exhibits range from early Christian devotional objects to Doc Marten boots, from the paintings of John Constable to the mystical art of southeast Asia. The V&A also houses collections of sculpture, watercolours, jewellery and musical instruments. For the new millennium a stunning new building – the Spiral – will house modern design exhibits.

★ **Twentieth-Century Gallery**
This gallery shows modern design like Daniel Weil's Radio in a Bag *(1983).*

GALLERY GUIDE

The V&A consists of 7 miles (11 km) of galleries which occupy four main floor levels. The key to understanding the labyrinthine layout is in the division of galleries devoted to art and design and those concentrating on materials and techniques. In the former, many different kinds of artefacts are assembled to illustrate the art and design of a particular period or place – for example Europe 1600–1800. The materials and techniques galleries contain collections of particular forms of art – porcelain, tapestries and so on. The art and design galleries occupy most of the ground floor, with British arts situated on the first floor. The Henry Cole Wing is situated on the northwest side of the main building, and contains the museum's collections of paintings, drawings, prints and photographs. It also houses the new Frank Lloyd Wright Gallery.

European Ornament Gallery
Over 500 years of decorative art is shown here. This sculpture, made for Marie Antoinette, represents the five orders of Classical architecture.

Henry Cole Wing

Exhibition Road entrance

Constable Collection
John Constable (1776–1837) vividly captured the East Anglian landscape. This painting is called A Windmill Among Houses.

KEY TO FLOORPLAN

☐	Lower ground floor
☐	Ground floor
☐	Upper ground floor
☐	First floor
☐	Upper first floor
☐	Second floor
☐	Henry Cole Wing

STAR EXHIBITS

★ **Medieval Treasury**

★ **Nehru Gallery of Indian Art**

★ **Dress Collection**

★ **Morris and Gamble Rooms**

★ **Twentieth-Century Gallery**

★ **Morris and Gamble Rooms**
The Victorian decorations here draw on past styles and the modern materials of an industrial age.

T T Tsui Gallery of Chinese Art
This ancestor portrait, in watercolour on silk, is from the Qing Dynasty (1644–1912).

Pirelli Garden

★ **Medieval Treasury**
The Eltenberg Reliquary (c.1180) is one of the museum's masterpieces of medieval craftsmanship.

★ **Nehru Gallery of Indian Art**
Much of this collection dates from when Britain ruled India. The Emperor Shah Jehan's jade wine cup was made in 1657.

Main entrance

★ **Dress Collection**
Clothing here dates from 1600 to the present. This dress is from the 1880s.

Exploring the V&A's Collections

THE V&A WAS FOUNDED in 1852 as a Museum of Manufactures to
inspire students of design. It was renamed by Queen Victoria, in
memory of Prince Albert, in 1899. Many of the exhibits originate
from parts of the British Empire, and among the wealth of artefacts
is the greatest collection of Indian art outside India. The museum
houses the National Art Library, which contains works on aspects
of art and design, items illustrating the art of book production from
the Middle Ages onwards, and artists' diaries and correspondence.

**German Castle
Cup (15th
century)**

SCULPTURE

THERE ARE 26 galleries
devoted to Post-Classical
sculpture, alabasters and
ivories, bronzes and casts.
The superb Renaissance
collection includes a marble
relief of *The Ascension* by
Donatello. At the museum's
Exhibition Road entrance
stand 17 pieces by Auguste
Rodin, presented by the
sculptor in 1914. There are
also collections of sculpture
from India, the Middle East
and the Far East.

CERAMICS AND GLASS

EXAMPLES OF 2,000
years of crafts-
manship in pottery,
porcelain and glass
from Europe and the
Near and Far East are
exhibited across 21
galleries. These contain
superb porcelain from
all the major European
china factories such as
Meissen, Sèvres, Royal
Copenhagen and Royal
Worcester; stained glass
including some lovely
medieval "Labours of
the Months"; studio

pottery, with rare pieces by
masters such as William De
Morgan, Picasso and Bernard
Leach; rich and intricately
patterned Persian and Turkish
tiles; and a wide selection of
Chinese pieces.

FURNITURE AND DESIGN

THERE ARE 37 galleries
containing a vast array of
furniture and interior design,
with especially outstanding
collections of 18th-century
French and English pieces.
Fully furnished interiors offer
a vivid re-creation of social
life through their displays of
furniture, paintings, pottery
and other domestic
objects – one
fine example is a
room from La
Tournerie, near
Alençon, in France
(Room 3A). The V&A
also has a wide
collection of musical
instruments including
virginals, lutes, flutes,
barytons, musical boxes,
harps and a Dutch
"giraffe" piano with six
percussion pedals that ring
bells, drum and buzz.

Russian porcelain (1862)

METALWORK

INTRICATELY WROUGHT CUPS and
decanters, medals, arms and
armour, hunting horns, watches
and clocks are among more
than 35,000 objects from
Europe and the Near East
which are on display across
22 of the museum's galleries.
Highlights include the 16th-
century Burghley Nef (Room
26), a great silver salt cellar
which was used to indicate
the position of the host at the
dinner table; and the 15th-
century German Castle Cup
(Room 27), a castellated,
turreted copper gilt extravaganza. The new English Silver
galleries also explore the
history and techniques of
silver making.

THE GREAT BED OF WARE

Made in about 1590 of oak with inlaid and painted
decoration, the Great Bed of Ware measures some
3.6 by 3.6 m (12 by 12 ft) and is 2.6 m (8 ft 9 inches)
high. It is the V&A's most celebrated piece of
furniture. Elaborately carved and decorated, the bed
is a superb example of the art of the English wood-
worker. Its name derives from the town of Ware in
Hertfordshire, about a day's ride north of London,
where it resided in a number of inns. The Great
Bed's enormous size made it an early tourist
attraction, and no doubt interest in it was boosted
by Shakespeare's reference to it in *Twelfth Night*,
which he wrote in 1601.

The bed was draped
with curtains when in use.

Tippoo's Tiger, carved in wood for the Sultan of Mysore in about 1790, is depicted mauling a European soldier.

INDIAN ART

THE NEHRU GALLERY of Indian Art forms the centrepiece of the museum's extensive collection of Indian art from 1550 to 1900, a period that includes the opulent Mughal Empire and the India of the British Raj. Textiles, weapons, jewellery, metalwork, glass and paintings, both secular and religious, are on display. Highlights of the collection include a Mughal tent of hanging painted cotton (1640) decorated with birds, trees and a double-headed eagle (Room 41). Also look out for an 11th-century bronze depicting the Hindu deity Shiva as Lord of the Eternal Dance (Room 47B).

Indian panel of painted and dyed cotton from the 18th century

TEXTILES AND DRESS

THE WORLD-RENOWNED Dress Collection, displayed in Room 40, is devoted to fashionable clothing from about 1600 to the present day. The figures are fully dressed, complete with accessories; in addition, small cases display collections of such items as buttons, shoes, hats and parasols. The scope of the textile collection, displayed in 18 galleries, is very broad,

starting with ancient Egypt. English textiles of the last three centuries are particularly well represented.

The four great medieval tapestries in Room 94, from the collection of the Duke of Devonshire, depict fascinating scenes of courtly pastimes, while the Syon Cope, from 1300–20, is an exquisite example of *opus anglicanum*, a type of English embroidery which was popular in Europe during the Middle Ages.

FAR EASTERN ART

EIGHT GALLERIES are devoted to the arts of China, Japan, Korea and other Far Eastern countries. Under a dramatic arc of burnished steel fins representing the spine of a Chinese dragon, the T T Tsui Gallery of Chinese Art shows how the artefacts displayed would have been used in everyday life. Among the highlights of the collection are a giant Buddha's head from 700–900 AD, a huge Ming canopied bed, and rare jade and ceramics (Room 44). Japanese art is concentrated in the Toshiba Gallery, which is particularly notable for lacquer, ceramics, textiles,

Mantle for Buddhist priest from the mid-19th century

Samurai armour and woodblock prints. Especially fine exhibits include a 17th-century wooden writing table inlaid with gold and silver lacquer and the Akita Armour, dating from 1714, both in Room 38A.

PAINTINGS, PRINTS, DRAWINGS AND PHOTOGRAPHS

THESE COLLECTIONS are housed in the Henry Cole Wing. Highlights include British paintings from 1700 to 1900, English portrait miniatures, European paintings between 1500 and 1900, and the largest collection of works by John Constable. The Raphael Gallery displays seven tapestry designs by the Renaissance artist. The Print Room is a public study room for a collection of more than half a million watercolours, engravings, etchings and ephemera.

Nicholas Hilliard's *A Young Man Among Roses* (1588)

Natural History Museum ❶

See pp204–5.

Relief: Natural History Museum

Science Museum ❷

See pp208–9.

Victoria and Albert Museum ❸

See pp198–201.

Brompton Oratory ❹

Brompton Rd SW7. **Map** 19 A1.
📞 020-7589 4811. 🚇 South
Kensington. **Open** 6.30am–8pm daily.
✝ 11am Sun sung Latin Mass. ♿

T HE ITALIANATE Oratory is a rich (some think a little too rich) monument to the English Catholic revival of the late 19th century. The Oratory was established by John Henry Newman (who later became Cardinal Newman). Father Frederick William Faber (1814–63) had already founded a London community of priests at Charing Cross. The community had moved to Brompton, then an outlying London district, and this was to be its oratory. Newman and Faber (both Anglican converts to Catholicism) were following the example of St Philip Neri, who established a community of secular priests living without vows and based in large cities.

The present church was opened in 1884. Its facade and dome were added in the 1890s, and the interior has been progressively enriched ever since. Herbert Gribble, the architect, who was yet another new convert to Catholicism, was only 29 when he triumphed in the highly prestigious competition to design it. Inside, all the most eye-catching treasures predate the church – many of them were transported here from Italian churches. Giuseppe Mazzuoli carved the huge marble figures of the 12 apostles for Siena Cathedral in the late 17th century. The beautifully elaborate Lady Altar was originally created in 1693 for the Dominican church in Brescia, and the 18th-century altar in St Wilfrid's Chapel was actually imported from Rochefort in Belgium.

The Oratory has always been famous for its splendid musical tradition.

Royal College of Music ❺

Prince Consort Rd SW7. **Map** 10 F5.
📞 020-7589 3643. 🚇 High St
Kensington, Knightsbridge, South
Kensington. **Museum of Musical
Instruments open** 2–4.30pm Wed
in term time. **Adm charge**.
🚫 📷

S IR ARTHUR BLOMFIELD designed the turretted Gothic palace, with Bavarian overtones, that has housed this distinguished institution since 1894. The college was founded in 1882 by George Grove, who also compiled the famous *Dictionary of Music*; famous pupils have included English composers Benjamin Britten and Ralph Vaughan Williams.

You have to be smart to catch the Museum of Musical Instruments, which is rarely open; but, if you do manage to get in, you will see instruments from the earliest times and from many parts of the world. Some of the exhibits were played by such greats as Handel and Haydn.

**17th-century viol at the
Royal College of Music**

The sumptuous interior of Brompton Oratory

Joseph Durham's statue of Prince Albert (1858) by the Royal Albert Hall

Royal Albert Hall ❻

Kensington Gore SW7. **Map** 10 F5.
📞 020-7589 3203. ⊖ *High St
Kensington, South Kensington
Knightsbridge.* **Open** *for
performances.* 📷 ♿ 🖥 *See
Entertainment pp330–1.*

DESIGNED BY AN engineer,
Francis Fowke, and
completed in 1871, this huge
concert hall was modelled on
Roman amphitheatres and is
easier on the eye than most
Victorian structures. On the
red-brick exterior the only
ostentation is a pretty frieze
symbolizing the triumph of
arts and science. In plans the
building was called the Hall
of Arts and Science but
Queen Victoria changed it to
the Albert Hall, in memory of
her husband, when she laid
the foundation stone in 1868.
 The hall is often used for
Classical concerts, most
famously the "Proms", but it
also accommodates every

other kind of large gathering
such as boxing matches (first
held here in 1919), comedy
shows, rock concerts and
major business conferences.

Royal College of Art ❼

Kensington Gore SW7. **Map** 10 F5.
📞 020-7590 4444. ⊖ *High St
Kensington, South Kensington,
Knightsbridge.* **Open** *10am–6pm
Mon–Fri (phone first).* 🖥 📷
*Lectures, events, film
presentations, exhibitions.*

SIR HUGH CASSON's mainly
glass-fronted building
(1973) is in stark contrast to
the Victoriana around it. The
college was founded in 1837
as a school of design and
practical art for the manufacturing industries. It became
noted for modern art in the
1950s and 1960s when David
Hockney, Peter Blake and
Eduardo Paolozzi were there.

Albert Memorial ❽

South Carriage Drive, Kensington
Gdns SW7. **Map** 10 F5. ⊖ *High St
Kensington, Knightsbridge, South
Kensington.*

THIS GRANDIOSE but dignified
memorial to Queen
Victoria's beloved consort was
completed in 1876, 15 years
after his death. Albert was a
German prince and a cousin
of Queen Victoria's. When he
died from typhoid in 1861 he
was 41 and they had been
happily married for 21 years,
producing nine children. It is
fitting that the monument is
near the site of the 1851
Exhibition *(see pp26–7)*, for
Prince Albert was closely
identified with the Exhibition
itself and with the scientific
advances it celebrated. The
larger than life statue, by John
Foley, shows him with an exhibition catalogue on his knee.
 The desolate Queen chose
Sir George Gilbert Scott to
design the monument which
stands 55 m (175 ft) high. It is
loosely based on a medieval
market cross – although many
times more elaborate, with a
black and gilded spire, multi-
coloured marble canopy,
stones, mosaics, enamels,
wrought iron and nearly 200
sculpted figures. The steps
around it are guarded by four
groups symbolizing Europe,
Africa, America and Asia. In
the corners Engineering,
Agriculture, Manufacturing
and Commerce are shown.

**Victoria and Albert at the Great
Exhibition opening (1851)**

Natural History Museum ❶

Museum's main entrance

L IFE ON EARTH and the Earth itself are vividly explained at The Natural History Museum. Combining the latest interactive techniques with traditional displays, the exhibits tackle some fundamental issues, such as the delicate ecology of our planet and its gradual evolution over millions of years, the origin of species and how humans beings evolved. The vast, cathedral-like museum building is a masterpiece in itself. It opened in 1881 and was designed by Alfred Waterhouse using revolutionary Victorian building techniques. It is built on an iron and steel framework concealed behind arches and columns, richly decorated with sculptures of plants and animals.

★ **Creepy Crawlies**
Eight out of ten animal species are arthropods from the world of insects and spiders, like this tarantula.

First floor

Ground floor

★ **Dinosaur Exhibition**
The killer dinosaur Deinonychus is one of the life-size robotic models in the display.

GALLERY GUIDE

The museum is divided into two sets of galleries, the Life Galleries and the Earth Galleries. A 26-m (85-ft) skeleton of the dinosaur Diplodocus dominates the entrance hall (10) in the Life Galleries – the Dinosaur Exhibition (21), together with Human Biology (22) and Mammals (23–24), is to the left of the hall, with Creepy Crawlies (33) and Ecology (32) to the right. Reptiles and Fish (12) are behind the main hall. On the first floor are found Origin of Species (105) and Minerals and Meteorites (102–3).

The giant escalator in Visions of Earth (60) leads through a stunning rotating globe to Earth Galleries highlights The Power Within (61) and Earth's Treasury (64).

Cromwell Road entrance – Life Galleries

Access to basement

★ **Ecology Gallery**
A small rainforest buzzing with the sounds of life begins an exploration of the complex web of the natural world and man's role in it.

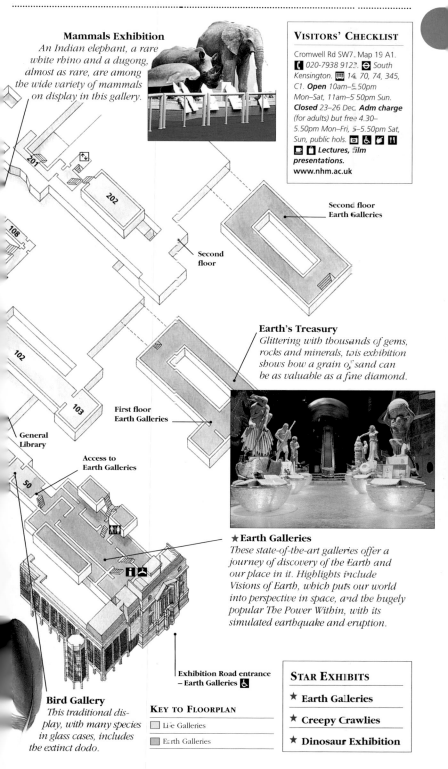

Mammals Exhibition
An Indian elephant, a rare white rhino and a dugong, almost as rare, are among the wide variety of mammals on display in this gallery.

VISITORS' CHECKLIST

Cromwell Rd SW7. Map 19 A1.
020-7938 9123. South Kensington. 14, 70, 74, 345, C1. **Open** 10am–5.50pm Mon–Sat, 11am–5.50pm Sun. **Closed** 23–26 Dec. **Adm charge** (for adults) but free 4.30– 5.50pm Mon–Fri, 5–5.50pm Sat, Sun, public hols. **Lectures, film presentations.**
www.nhm.ac.uk

Second floor Earth Galleries

Second floor

Earth's Treasury
Glittering with thousands of gems, rocks and minerals, this exhibition shows how a grain of sand can be as valuable as a fine diamond.

First floor Earth Galleries

General Library

Access to Earth Galleries

★ Earth Galleries
These state-of-the-art galleries offer a journey of discovery of the Earth and our place in it. Highlights include Visions of Earth, which puts our world into perspective in space, and the hugely popular The Power Within, with its simulated earthquake and eruption.

Exhibition Road entrance – Earth Galleries

Bird Gallery
This traditional display, with many species in glass cases, includes the extinct dodo.

KEY TO FLOORPLAN

☐ Life Galleries
☐ Earth Galleries

STAR EXHIBITS

★ Earth Galleries

★ Creepy Crawlies

★ Dinosaur Exhibition

Statue of young Queen Victoria by her daughter Princess Louise outside Kensington Palace

Serpentine Gallery ❾

Kensington Gdns W2. **Map** 10 F4.
☎ 020-7402 6075. **●** Lancaster
Gate, South Kensington. **Open**
10am–6pm daily. **Closed** for
exhibition installations, Christmas
week. **♿ ▯ Lectures** on current
exhibition 3pm Sun.

IN THE SOUTHEAST corner of
Kensington Gardens is the
Serpentine Gallery, which
houses temporary exhibitions
of contemporary painting and
sculpture. The building is a
former tea pavilion built in
1912; exhibits often spill out
into the surrounding park. Its
tiny bookshop has a remarkable stock of art books.

Kensington Palace ❿

Kensington Palace Gdns W8.
Map 10 D4. **☎** 020-7937 9561.
● High St Kensington, Queensway.
Open Summer: 10am–6pm daily;
Winter: 10am–5pm daily (last adm: 1
hr earlier). **Closed** 22–26 Dec, 1 Jan,
Good Fri. **Adm charge**. **Ø ♿**
ground floor only. **▯ ▯**
Exhibitions, holiday activities.

HALF OF THIS SPACIOUS palace
is used as lavish royal
apartments; the other half,
which includes the 18th-
century state rooms, is open
to the public. When William III
and his wife Mary came to the
throne in 1689 they bought a
mansion, dating from 1605,
and commissioned Christopher

Wren to convert it into a royal
palace. He created separate
suites of rooms for the king
and queen, and today visiting
members of public use the
queen's entrance.

Highlights include the finely
decorated state rooms and, on
the ground floor, an exhibition of court dress from
1760 to the present.

The palace has seen some
important royal events. In
1714 Queen Anne died
here from a fit of apo-
plexy brought on by
over-eating and, on
20 June 1837, Princess
Victoria of Kent was
woken at 5am to be
told that her uncle
William IV had
died and she was
now queen – the
start of her 64-
year reign. After
the death in 1997
of Diana, Princess
of Wales, the
gates became a focal point for
mourners in their thousands,
who turned the surrounding
area into a field of bouquets.

Detail of the Coalbrookdale
gate, Kensington Gardens

Henry Moore's *Arch* (1979),
Kensington Gardens

Kensington Gardens ⓫

W8. **Map** 10 E4. **☎** 020-7262 5484.
● Bayswater, High St Kensington,
Queensway, Lancaster Gate.
Open dawn–dusk daily.

THE FORMER GROUNDS of
Kensington Palace became
a public park in 1841. There
are plans to dedicate a small
part of it as a memorial
garden to Diana, Princess
of Wales. The gardens
are full of charm, start-
ing with Sir George
Frampton's statue
(1912) of J M Barrie's
fictional Peter Pan,
the boy who never
grew up, playing
his pipes to the
bronze fairies and
animals that
cling to the
column below.
Often surrounded
by parents, nan-
nies and their charges, the
statue stands near the west
bank of the Serpentine, not
far from where Harriet, wife
of the poet Percy Bysshe
Shelley drowned herself in
1816. Just north of here are
the ornamental fountains and
statues, including Jacob
Epstein's *Rima*, at the lake's
head. George Frederick
Watts's statue of a muscular
horse and rider, *Physical
Energy*, stands to the south.
Not far away are a summer
house designed by William
Kent in 1735, and the
Serpentine Gallery.

The Round Pond, created in 1728 just east of the palace, is often packed with model boats navigated by children and older enthusiasts. In winter it is occasionally fit for skating. In the north, near Lancaster Gate, is a dogs' cemetery, started in 1880 by the Duke of Cambridge while mourning one of his pets.

Hyde Park ⓬

W2. **Map** 11 B3. 020-7262 5484. Hyde Park Corner, Knightsbridge, Lancaster Gate, Marble Arch. **Open** 5am– midnight daily. **Sporting facilities**.

Riding on Rotten Row, Hyde Park

THE ANCIENT MANOR of Hyde was part of the lands of Westminster Abbey seized by Henry VIII at the Dissolution of the Monasteries in 1536. It has remained a royal park ever since. Henry used it for hunting but James I opened it to the public in the early 17th century, and it became one of the city's most prized public spaces. The Serpentine, an artificial lake used for boating and bathing, was created when Caroline, George II's queen, dammed the flow of the Westbourne River in 1730.

In its time the park has been a venue for duelling, horse racing, highwaymen, political demonstrations, music (Mick Jagger and Luciano Pavarotti have each had a concert here) and parades. The 1851 Exhibition was held here in a vast glass palace *(see pp26–7)*. The aristocracy drove their carriages on the outer roads.

Speakers' Corner ⓭

Hyde Park W2. **Map** 11 C2. Marble Arch.

AN 1872 LAW made it legal to assemble an audience and address them on whatever topic you chose; since then this corner of Hyde Park has become the established venue for budding orators and a fair number of eccentrics. It is well worth spending time here on a Sunday: speakers from fringe groups and one-member political parties reveal their plans for the betterment of mankind while the assembled onlookers heckle them without mercy.

Marble Arch ⓮

Park Lane W1. **Map** 11 C2. Marble Arch.

JOHN NASH designed the arch in 1327 as the main entrance to Buckingham Palace. It was, however, too narrow for the grandest coaches and was moved here in 1851. Now, only senior members of the Royal Family and one of the royal artillery regiments are allowed to pass under it.

The arch stands near the site of the old Tyburn gallows (marked by a plaque), where until 1783 the city's most notorious criminals were hanged in front of crowds of bloodthirsty spectators.

An orator at Speakers' Corner

Harrod's ⓯

Knightsbridge SW1. **Map** 11 C5. 020-7730 1234. Knightsbridge. **Open** 10am–6pm Mon, Tue, Sat, 10am–7pm Wed–Fri. See **Shops and Markets** p311.

LONDON'S MOST FAMOUS department store had beginnings in 1849 when Henry Charles Harrod opened a small grocery shop nearby on Brompton Road. By concentrating on good quality and impeccable service (rather than on low prices) the store was soon popular enough to expand over the surrounding area.

It used to be claimed that Harrod's could supply anything from a packet of pins to an elephant – not quite true today, but the range of stock is still phenomenal.

Harrod's at night, lit by 11,500 lights

Science Museum **❷**

CENTURIES OF CONTINUING scientific and technological development lie at the heart of the Science Museum's massive collections. The hardware displayed is magnificent: from steam engines, to aeroengines; spacecraft to the very first mechanical computers. Equally important is the social context of science – what discoveries and inventions mean for day-to-day life – and the process of discovery itself. Exciting interactive displays enable visitors to take part in scientific enquiry themselves.

Science Museum facade

★ Launch Pad
A plasma ball is one of many hands-on exhibits for children in this first-floor gallery where basic scientific principles are demonstrated.

★ Glimpses of Medical History
A 17th-century Italian vase for storing snake bite potion is part of this fascinating collection.

Computing Then and Now reveals the history of counting machines and computers from the abacus onwards.

GALLERY GUIDE
There are seven floors. The Basement features The Garden *and* Things, *for younger children, as well as* The Secret Life of the Home *tracing the history of domestic appliances. Steam power dominates the ground floor; here too is the* Space Gallery. *The first floor has the award-winning* Challenge of Materials *gallery as well as* Food for Thought. *On the second floor is a range of such diverse galleries as nuclear power, ships, printing and computing. On the third floor is* Flight *with the interactive* Flight Lab, *as well as* Health Matters *and the* Science in the 18th Century *galleries. The fourth and fifth floors house the medical galleries, featuring the* Science and Art of Medicine *and* Veterinary History.

★ The Exploration of Space
Apollo 10 took US astronauts around the moon in May 1969, and now forms part of an exhibition on people and space.

Main entrance

Visitors' Checklist

Exhibition Rd SW7. **Map** 19 A1.
☎ 020-7938 8000.
🚇 South Kensington. 🚌 9, 10,
45, 49, 52, 74, 345, C1. **Open**
10am–6pm daily. **Closed** 24–26
Dec. **Adm charge.** 📷 ♿
**Lectures, films, workshops,
demonstrations.** 🖥 🎫
www.nmsi.ac.uk

★ Flight
*A replica of one of Otto Lilienthal's
gliders (1895) is one of the displays
that range from man's early
dreams of flight to today's jets.*

Navigation and Surveying
*The display of navigational
and surveying aids includes
this ornately decorated
circumferentor (1676) by the
architect Joannes Macarius.*

Food for Thought
*The science of food is explored
through demonstrations and
historic reconstructions, such as
this 18th-century kitchen.*

Meteorology
*There is a rich collection of
weather instruments and other
exhibits, like this 16th-century
watercolour of a comet.*

Key to Floorplan

☐	Basement
☐	Ground floor
☐	First floor
☐	Second floor
☐	Third floor
☐	Fourth floor
☐	Fifth floor

★ Challenge of Materials
*Our expectations of materials
are confounded with exhibits
like this steel wedding dress,
or a bridge made of glass.*

Star Exhibits

★ **Launch Pad**

★ **Exploration of
   Space**

★ **Challenge of
   Materials**

★ **Flight**

★ **Glimpses of
   Medical History**

KENSINGTON AND HOLLAND PARK

Tiled crest from Holland House

THE WESTERN and northern perimeters of Kensington Gardens are a rich residential area including many foreign embassies. Here, the shops on Kensington High Street are almost as smart as the ones on Knightsbridge, and Kensington Church Street is a good source of quality antiques. Around Holland Park are some magnificent late Victorian houses, two of them open to the public. But as you cross into Bayswater and Notting Hill you enter a more vibrant, cosmopolitan part of London. Its stucco terraces are lined with medium-priced hotels and a huge number of inexpensive restaurants. There has always been something rather furtive about Bayswater. Victorian men would keep mistresses in its terraces; the Profumo sex scandal (1963) that toppled a government occurred here and today prostitution remains a major, if discreet, local industry. Its high street, Queensway, is a centre of club life and café society, while further west Portobello Road is a popular street market. Many West Indians settled in Notting Hill in the 1950s and for three days every August its streets are home to a lively Caribbean carnival *(see p57)*.

SIGHTS AT A GLANCE

Historic Streets and Buildings
Holland House **2**
Leighton House **3**
Commonwealth Experience **4**
Linley Sambourne House **5**
Kensington Square **6**
Kensington Palace Gardens **7**
Queensway **8**

Parks and Gardens
Holland Park **1**

Markets
Portobello Road **9**

Historic Areas
Notting Hill **10**

GETTING THERE
The District, Circle and Central lines serve the area. Bus numbers 9, 10, 73, 27, 28, 49, 52, 70, C1, 31 stop on Kensington High Street; 12, 27, 28, 31, 52, 70, 94, go to Notting Hill Gate; and 70, 7, 15, 23, 27, 36, 12, 94 cross Bayswater.

KEY

☐ Street-by-Street map
🚇 Underground station

0 metres   500
0 yards   500

SEE ALSO
- **Street Finder**, maps 9, 17
- **Where to Stay** pp276–7
- **Restaurants** pp292–4

Entrance to a house in Edwardes Square, Kensington

Street-by-Street: Kensington and Holland Park

ALTHOUGH NOW PART OF central London, as recently as the 1830s this was a country village of market gardens and mansions. Outstanding among these was Holland House; part of its grounds are now Holland Park. The area grew up rapidly in the mid-19th century and most of its buildings date from then – mainly expensive apartments, mansion flats and fashionable shops.

Holland House
The rambling Jacobean mansion, started in 1605 and pictured here in 1795, was largely demolished in the 1950s ❷

★ **Holland Park**
Parts of the old formal gardens of Holland House have been retained to grace this delightful public park ❶

The Orangery, now a restaurant, has parts that date from the 1630s when it was in the grounds of Holland House.

Melbury Road is lined with large, Victorian houses. Many were built for fashionable artists of the time.

Commonwealth Experience
Exhibits give a flavour of the countries that were British colonies ❹

The Victorian letter box on the High Street is one of the oldest in London.

★ **Leighton House**
It is preserved as it was when the Victorian painter, Lord Leighton, lived here. He had a passion for Middle Eastern tiles ❸

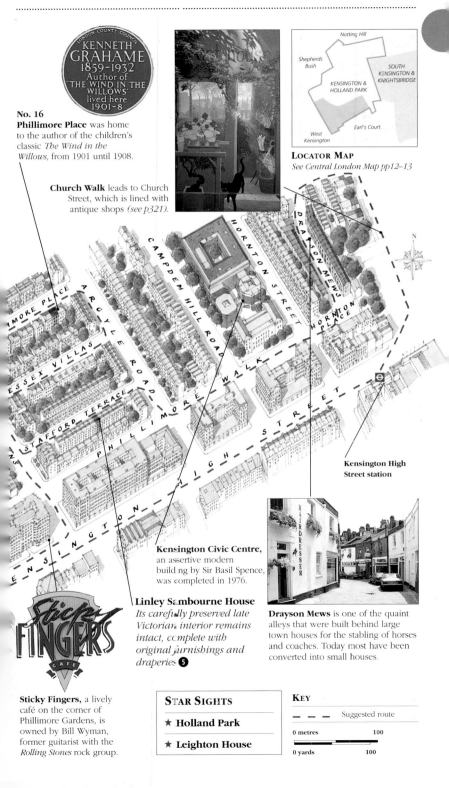

KENNETH
GRAHAME
1859–1932
Author of
"THE WIND IN THE
WILLOWS"
lived here
1901–8

No. 16
Phillimore Place was home to the author of the children's classic *The Wind in the Willows,* from 1901 until 1908.

LOCATOR MAP
See Central London Map pp12–13

Church Walk leads to Church Street, which is lined with antique shops *(see p321).*

Kensington High Street station

Kensington Civic Centre, an assertive modern building by Sir Basil Spence, was completed in 1976.

Linley Sambourne House
Its carefully preserved late Victorian interior remains intact, complete with original furnishings and draperies ⑤

Drayson Mews is one of the quaint alleys that were built behind large town houses for the stabling of horses and coaches. Today most have been converted into small houses.

Sticky Fingers, a lively café on the corner of Phillimore Gardens, is owned by Bill Wyman, former guitarist with the *Rolling Stones* rock group.

STAR SIGHTS
★ **Holland Park**
★ **Leighton House**

KEY

– – – Suggested route

0 metres   100

0 yards   100

Holland Park ●

Abbotsbury Rd W14. **Map** 9 B4.
☎ 020-7602 9487. **⊖** *Holland Park,
High St Kensington, Notting Hill Gate.*
Open *Apr–late Oct: 7.30am–10pm
daily (but flexible); late Oct–Mar:
7.45am–4.30pm (11pm floodlit areas).*
🚻 □ *Open-air opera, theatre,
dance. Art exhibitions Apr–Oct.
See* **Entertainment** *pp326–7.*

THIS SMALL but delightful
park, more wooded and
intimate than the large royal
parks to its east (Hyde Park
and Kensington Gardens,
see pp206–7), was opened in
1952 on what remained of the
grounds of Holland House –
the rest had been sold off in
the late 19th century for the
construction of large houses
and terraces to the north and
west. The park still contains
some of the formal gardens,
laid out in the early 19th
century for Holland House.
There is also a Japanese
garden, created for the 1991
London Festival of Japan. The
park has an abundance of
wildlife, including peacocks.

Holland House ●

Holland Park W8. **Map** 9 B5. **Youth
Hostel ☎** 020-7937 0748. **⊖**
Holland Park, High St Kensington. See
Where to Stay *p275.* **♿**

Original tiling in Holland House

DURING ITS HEYDAY in the
19th century, this was a
noted centre of social and
political intrigue. Statesmen
such as Lord Palmerston
mixed here with the likes of
the poet Byron. The remains
of the house are now used as
a youth hostel.
    The outhouses are put to
various uses: exhibitions are
held in the orangery and the
ice house (a forerunner of the
fridge), and the old Garden
Ballroom is now a restaurant.

The café in Holland Park

Leighton House ●

12 Holland Park Rd W14. **Map** 17 B1.
☎ 020-7602 3316. **⊖** *High St
Kensington.* **Open** *11am–5.30pm
Mon–Sat.* **Closed** *public hols.* **🚻**
*noon Wed–Thu or by prior arrange-
ment* **🔲** *Concerts, exhibitions.*

BUILT FOR Pre-Raphaelite
painter Lord Leighton in
1866, the house has been
preserved with its opulent
decoration almost intact, as
an extraordinary monument
to the Victorian Aesthetic
movement. The highlight is
the Arab hall, added in 1879
to house Leighton's fabulous
collection of Islamic tiles,
some of which are inscribed
with pieces from the Koran.
The best paintings, including
some by Edward Burne-Jones,
John Millais and Leighton
himself, can be seen in the
downstairs reception rooms.

Commonwealth Experience ●

Kensington High St W8. **Map** 9 C5.
☎ 020-7603 4535. **⊖** *High St
Kensington.* **Closed** *for refurbishment
until 2002.* **🔲 🚻 📷 ♿**

IN 1962, the Commonwealth
Institute (as it was then
called) replaced the old
Imperial Institute (founded in
1887). It is housed in a striking,
tent-like building and includes
many displays on the history,
industries and culture of the
50 member nations of the
Commonwealth. There are
permanent displays, temporary
art exhibitions and music
from Commonwealth groups.
The building in currently un-
dergoing an extensive facelift.

Linley Sambourne House ●

18 Stafford Terrace W8. **Map** 9 C5.
☎ 020-8994 1019. **⊖** *High St
Kensington.* **Open** *1 Mar–31 Oct:
10am–4pm Wed, 2–5pm Sun.* **Closed**
1 Nov–28 Feb. **Adm charge.** **Ø 🔲**

THE HOUSE, built in about
1870, has hardly changed
since Linley Sambourne
furnished it in the cluttered
Victorian manner, with china
ornaments and heavy velvet
drapes. Sambourne was a
cartoonist for the satirical
magazine *Punch* and drawings,
including some of his own,
cram the walls. Some rooms
have William Morris wallpaper
(see p245), and even the
lavatory is a Victorian gem.

**Logo for *Punch*
magazine
(1841–1992)**

Kensington Square **6**

W8. **Map** 10 D5. 🚇 *High St Kensington.*

THIS IS ONE of London's oldest squares. It was laid out in the 1680s, and a few early 18th-century houses still remain. (Nos. 11 and 12 are the oldest.) The renowned philosopher John Stuart Mill lived at No. 18, and the Pre-Raphaelite painter and illustrator Edward Burne-Jones at No. 41.

JOHN STUART
MILL
1806-1873
Philosopher
Lived Here

Resident's plaque in Kensington Square

Kensington Palace Gardens **7**

W8. **Map** 10 D3. 🚇 *High St Kensington, Notting Hill Gate, Queensway.*

THIS PRIVATE ROAD of luxury mansions is on the site of the former kitchen gardens of Kensington Palace *(see p206).*

It changes its name half-way down; the southern part is known as Palace Green. It is open to pedestrians but closed to cars, unless they have specific business here. Most of the houses are occupied by embassies and their staff. At the cocktail hour, watch the black limousines with their diplomatic number plates sweep beneath the raised barriers at each end of the road.

Queensway **8**

W2. **Map** 10 D2. 🚇 *Queensway, Bayswater.*

ONE OF LONDON'S most cosmopolitan streets, Queensway has the heaviest concentration of eating places anywhere except Soho. At newsagents, you may see more Arabic and European than British newspapers on sale. At the northern end is the comed Whiteley's shopping centre. Founded by

Queensway shopfront

William Whiteley, who was born in Yorkshire in 1863, it was probably the world's first department store. The present building dates from 1911.

The street is named after Queen Victoria, who rode here as a princess.

Portobello Road **9**

W11. **Map** 9 C3. 🚇 *Notting Hill Gate, Ladbroke Grove.* **Antiques market open** 9.30am – 4pm Fri, 8am–5pm Sat. See also **Shops and Markets** *p323.*

THERE HAS been a market here since 1837. The southern end today consists almost exclusively of stalls selling antiques, jewellery, souvenirs and many other collectables popular with tourists. The market is crowded on summer weekends, but is worth visiting for its bustling and cheerful atmosphere even if you don't intend to buy. If you do, you are unlikely to get a real bargain, since the stallholders have a sound idea of the value of what they sell.

Notting Hill **10**

W11. **Map** 9 C3. 🚇 *Notting Hill Gate.*

NOW THE HOME of Europe's biggest street carnival, most of this area was farmland until the 19th century. In the 1950s and 1960s Notting Hill became a centre for the Caribbean community, many of whom lived here when they first arrived in Britain. The carnival started in 1966 and takes over the area every August over the holiday weekend *(see p57)* when costumed parades flood through the streets.

Antique shop on Portobello Road

REGENT'S PARK AND MARYLEBONE

THE AREA south of Regent's Park, incorporating the medieval village of Marylebone, has London's highest concentration of quality Georgian housing. It was developed by Robert Harley, Earl of Oxford, as London shifted west in the 18th century. Terraces by John Nash adorn the southern edge of Regent's Park, the busiest of the royal parks, while to its northwest lies St John's Wood, a smart inner suburb.

GETTING THERE
Regent's Park and Great Portland Street are the nearest tube stations. Marylebone is served by tube and British Rail. Buses 13, 139 and 159 run from Trafalgar Square to near Baker Street, and numerous buses run along Oxford Street.

SIGHTS AT A GLANCE

Historic Streets and Buildings
Harley Street ④
Portland Place ⑤
Broadcasting House ⑥
Cumberland Terrace ⑮

Museums and Galleries
Wallace Collection ⑩
Sherlock Holmes Museum ⑪

Churches and Mosques
St Marylebone Parish Church ③
All Souls, Langham Place ⑦
London Central Mosque ⑫

Parks and Gardens
Regent's Park ②

Entertainment
Madame Tussauds and the Planetarium ①
Wigmore Hall ⑨
London Zoo ⑭

Historic Hotels
Langham Hilton Hotel ⑧

Historic Waterways
Regent's Canal ⑬

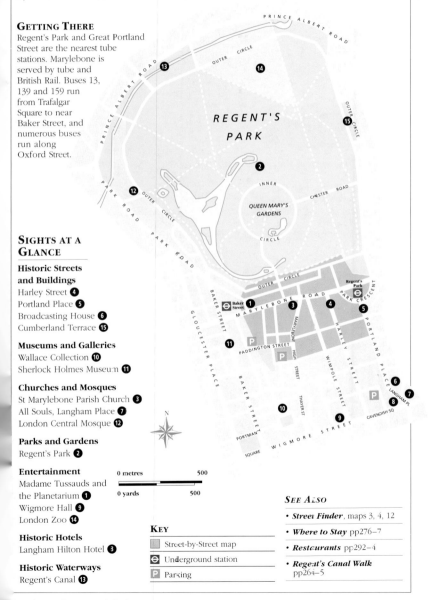

KEY
Street-by-Street map
⊖ Underground station
P Parking

SEE ALSO
• **Street Finder**, maps 3, 4, 12
• **Where to Stay** pp276–7
• **Restaurants** pp292–4
• **Regent's Canal Walk** pp264–5

St Andrew's Place, Regent's Park

Street-by-Street: Marylebone

SOUTH OF REGENT'S PARK, the medieval village of
Marylebone (originally Maryburne, the stream by
St Mary's church) has London's highest concentration of genteel Georgian housing. Until the 18th
century it was surrounded by fields and a pleasure
garden, but these were built over as fashionable
London drifted west. In the mid-19th century,
professional people, especially doctors,
used the spacious houses to receive
wealthy clients. The area has maintained
both its medical connection and its elegance.

Tiananmen
Square
memorial:
Portland Place

★ Regent's Park
*John Nash laid out the
royal park in 1812 as
a setting for Classically
designed villas and
terraces* ②

**The Royal Academy of
Music,** England's first
music academy, was
founded in 1774. The
present brick building,
with its own concert
hall, is from 1911.

**★ Madame Tussauds and the
Planetarium**
*The wax museum of famous people,
historical and contemporary, is one
of London's most popular attractions.
Next door, a planetarium shows
models of the sky at night* ①

To Regent's
Park

**St Marylebone Parish
Church**
*Poets Robert Browning
and Elizabeth Barrett
married in this church* ③

KEY

- - - Suggested route

Baker Street
station

0 metres   100

0 yards   100

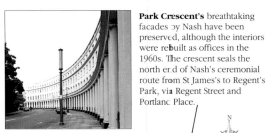

Park Crescent's breathtaking facades by Nash have been preserved, although the interiors were rebuilt as offices in the 1960s. The crescent seals the north end of Nash's ceremonial route from St James's to Regent's Park, via Regent Street and Portland Place.

LOCATOR MAP
See Central London Map pp12–13

The London Clinic is one of the best-known private hospitals in this medical district.

Regent's Park station

Portland Place
In the centre of this broad street stands a statue of Field Marshal Sir George Stuart White, who won the Victoria Cross for gallantry in the Afghan War of 1879 ❺

The Royal Institute of British Architects is housed in a controversial Art Deco building designed by Grey Wornum in 1934.

Harley Street
Consulting rooms of eminent medical specialists have been here for more than a century ❹

STAR SIGHTS

★ **Madame Tussauds and the Planetarium**

★ **Regent's Park**

Mme Tussauds and the Planetarium ❶

Marylebone Rd NW1. **Map** 4 D5.
📞 020-7935 6861. ⊖ Baker St.
Open 10am–5.30pm Mon–Fri,
9.30am–5.30pm Sat, Sun. **Closed** 25
Dec. **Adm charge.** ♿ phone first.
📷 🖥 📱

Traditional wax-modelling at Madame Tussauds

MADAME TUSSAUD began her wax-modelling career rather morbidly, taking death masks of many of the best-known victims of the French Revolution. In 1835 she set up an exhibition of her work in Baker Street, not far from the collection's present site.

The 1990s collection still relies upon traditional wax-modelling techniques to recreate politicians, film and television actors, rock stars and sporting heroes.

The main sections of the exhibition are the "Garden Party", where visitors mingle with extraordinarily lifelike models of celebrities; "Super Stars", devoted to the giants of the entertainment world; and

the "Grand Hall", containing a collection of royalty, statesmen and world leaders, writers and artists. Where else on earth could Lenin, Martin Luther King and William Shakespeare all rub shoulders?

The Chamber of Horrors is the most renowned part of Madame Tussauds. It includes recreations of the most gruesome episodes in the grim catalogue of crime and punishment: the murderers Dr Crippen and Ethel le Nève;

Gary Gilmore facing a firing squad; and the chill gloom of a Victorian street in Jack the Ripper's London.

The "Spirit of London" is the finale. Visitors travel in stylized London taxi-cabs and participate in momentous events of the city, from the Great Fire of 1666 to 1960s Swinging London.

Situated next door, and part of the same great complex, is the London Planetarium, where a spectacular star show explores and reveals some of the mysteries of the planets and the solar system. The interactive Space Trail exhibition contains many detailed models of the planets, satellites and spacecraft.

Waxwork of Elizabeth II

Tulip time at Queen Mary's Gardens in Regent's Park

Regent's Park ❷

NW1. **Map** 3 C2. 📞 020-7486 7905.
⊖ Regent's Park, Baker St, Great
Portland St. **Open** 5am–dusk daily.
♿ 🖥 **Open air theatre.** See
Entertainment pp326–8.

THIS AREA OF land became enclosed as a park in 1812. John Nash designed the scheme and originally envisaged a kind of garden suburb, dotted with 56 villas in a variety of Classical styles,

with a pleasure palace for the Prince Regent. At the end of the day only eight villas – but no palace – were built inside the park (three survive round the edge of the Inner Circle).

The boating lake, which has many varieties of water birds, is marvellously romantic, especially when music drifts across from the bandstand in the distance. Queen Mary's Gardens are a mass of wonderful sights and smells in summer, when visitors

can enjoy Shakespeare productions at the Open Air Theatre nearby. Broad Walk provides a picturesque stroll north from Park Square.

Nash's master plan for Regent's Park continues just beyond its north-eastern edge in Park Village East and West. These captivating buildings in elegant stucco were completed in 1828, some adorned with Wedgwood-style medallions.

St Marylebone Parish Church ❸

Marylebone Rd NW1. **Map** 4 D5.
📞 020-7935 7315. ⊖ Regent's Park.
Open 12.30–1.30pm Mon–Fri, Sun
mornings. ♿ 📷 🕐 11am Sun. 📱

THIS IS WHERE the poets Robert Browning and Elizabeth Barrett were married in 1846 after eloping from her strict family home on nearby Wimpole Street. The large, stately church by Thomas Hardwick was consecrated in 1817 after the former church, where Lord Byron was christened in 1778, had become too small. Hardwick was determined that the same should not happen to his new church – so everything is on a grand scale.

Commemorative window in St Marylebone Parish Church

Harley Street ❹

W1. **Map** 4 E5. ⊖ *Regent's Park, Oxford Circus, Bond St, Great Portland St.*

THE LARGE HOUSES on this late 18th-century street were popular with successful doctors and specialists in the middle of the 19th century when it was a rich residential area. The doctors' practices stayed and lend the street an air of hushed order, unusual in central London. There are very few private houses or apartments here now, but William Gladstone lived at No. 73 from 1876 to 1882.

Portland Place ❺

W1. **Map** 4 E5. ⊖ *Regent's Park.*

THE ADAM BROTHERS, Robert and James, originally laid this street out in 1773. Only a few of their original houses remain, the best being Nos. 27 to 47 on the west side, south of Devonshire Street. John Nash added the street to his processional route that ran from Carlton House to Regent's Park and sealed its northern end with the Park Crescent. The building of the Royal Institute of British Architects (1934) at No. 66 is adorned with symbolic statues and reliefs. Its bronze front doors depict London's buildings and the River Thames.

Broadcasting House ❻

Portland Place W1. **Map** 12 E1.
⊖ *Oxford Circus.* **BBC Experience**
❏ *0870-603 0304.* **Open**
10.30am–4.30pm Tue–Sun, 1–3.30pm Mon. **Adm charge.** ♿ 🚻

BROADCASTING HOUSE was built in 1931 as a suitably modern Art Deco headquarters for the brand-new medium of broadcasting. Its front, curving with the street, is dominated by Eric Gill's stylized relief of Prospero and Ariel, and more of the sculptor's distinctive ornament can be seen higher up. The lobby has been carefully restored to its 1930s appearance.

In the 1990s most BBC studios migrated to west London and the building is now occupied by management. The move has left room for a high-tech exhibition using the latest interactive techniques. Visitors can try their skills in various functions, including sports commentary, presenting a weather forecast, directing a soap opera and acting in a play.

The history of broadcasting is highlighted by the Marconi collection of early radio equipment and memorabilia, and there are numerous recordings and video clips of favourite programmes of all eras.

Relief on the Royal Institute of British Architects on Portland Place

All Souls, Langham Place ❼

Langham Place W1. **Map** 12 F1.
❏ *020-7580 3522.* ⊖ *Oxford Circus.* **Open** *9.30am–6pm Mon–Fri, 9am–9pm Sun.* ♿ 🚻 *11am Sun.* 🚻

JOHN NASH designed this church in 1824. Its quirky round frontage is best seen from Regent Street. When it was first built, the spire was ridiculed as it appeared too slender and flimsy.

The only Nash church in London, it had close links with the BBC, formerly based opposite at Broadcasting House, and has often doubled as a recording studio for the daily broadcast service.

Langham Hilton Hotel ❽

1 Portland Place W1. **Map** 12 E1.
❏ *020-7636 1000.* ⊖ *Oxford Circus. See **Where to Stay** p284.*

THIS WAS LONDON'S grandest hotel after it was opened in 1865. The writers Oscar Wilde and Mark Twain and composer Antonin Dvořák were among its many distinguished guests. The hotel was, for a time, used by the BBC, but since then has been restored behind its original facade. Its marble-lined entrance hall leads into the Palm Court, where there is piano music at tea-time. Colonial days are recalled in the Memories of the Empire restaurant and the Chukka bar.

All Souls, Langham Place (1824)

Wigmore Hall 9

36 Wigmore St W1. **Map** 12 E1.
☎ 020-7935 2141. ⊖ Bond St.
See **Entertainment** p331.

Tʜɪꜱ ᴀᴘᴘᴇᴀʟɪɴɢ little concert hall for chamber music was designed by T E Collcutt, architect of the Savoy Hotel *(see p285)*, in 1900. At first it was called Bechstein Hall because it was attached to the Bechstein piano showroom: the area used to be the heart of London's piano trade. Opposite is the white-tiled Art Nouveau emporium built in 1907 as Debenham and Freebody's department store – the forerunner of today's Debenham's on Oxford Street.

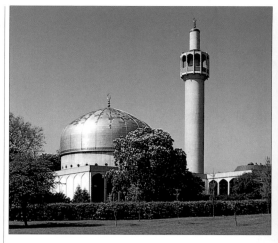
The Mosque on the edge of Regent's Park

Wallace Collection 10

Hertford House, Manchester Square W1. **Map** 12 D1. ☎ 020-7935 0687. ⊖ Bond St. **Open** 10am–5pm Mon–Sat, 2–5pm Sun. **Closed** 24–26 Dec, 1 Jan, Good Fri. 🚫 ♿ 📷 🅿 **Lectures.**

16th-century Italian dish from the Wallace Collectiom

Tʜɪꜱ ɪꜱ ᴏɴᴇ ᴏꜰ the world's finest private collections of art. It has remained intact since it was bequeathed to the government in 1897 with the stipulation that it should go on permanent public display with nothing added or taken away. The product of passionate collecting for four generations of the Hertford family, it is a must for anyone with even a passing interest in the progress of European art up to the late 19th century.

Most of its highlights are in gallery 22, which contains some 70 master works. Frans Hals's *The Laughing Cavalier*

is here, and Rembrandt's *Titus*, along with Titian's *Perseus and Andromeda* and Nicolas Poussin's *A Dance to the Music of Time*. There are also superb English portraits by Reynolds, Gainsborough and Romney. The 25 galleries contain fine Sèvres porcelain and sculpture by Houdon, Roubiliac and Rysbrack. There is also an armour collection.

Sherlock Holmes Museum 11

221b Baker St NW1. **Map** 3 C5.
☎ 020-7935 8866. ⊖ Baker St. **Open** 9.30am–6pm daily. **Closed** 25 Dec. **Adm charge.** 📷 🍴 🅿

Sɪʀ ᴀʀᴛʜᴜʀ ᴄᴏɴᴀɴ ᴅᴏʏʟᴇ's fictional detective was supposed to have lived at 221b Baker Street – this

Conan Doyle's Sherlock Holmes

museum, which boasts the right number, actually sits between Nos. 237 and 239. Visitors are greeted by Holmes's "housekeeper" and shown to his recreated rooms on the first floor. The fourth floor shop sells copies of the stories and deerstalker hats.

London Central Mosque 12

146 Park Rd NW8. **Map** 3 B3.
☎ 020-7724 3363. ⊖ Marylebone, St John's Wood, Baker St. **Open** dawn–dusk daily. ♿ 🅿 **Lectures.**

Sᴜʀʀᴏᴜɴᴅᴇᴅ ʙʏ ᴛʀᴇᴇꜱ on the edge of Regent's Park, this large, golden-domed mosque was designed by Sir Frederick Gibberd and completed in 1978. It was built to cater for the increasing number of Muslim residents and visitors in London. The mosque's main hall of worship, which is capable of holding 1,800 people, is a plain square chamber with a domed roof. It is sparsely furnished apart from a magnificent carpet and a colossal chandelier. The dome is lined in a traditional Islamic pattern of broken shapes, predominantly blue. Visitors must remove their shoes before entering the mosque, and women, for whom there is a separate gallery, should also remember to cover their heads.

Regent's Canal ⑬

NW1 & NW8. **Map** 3 C1. 🚇 020-7482 0523. 🅴 *Camden Town St John's Wood, Warwick Ave.* **Canal towpaths open** *dawn – dusk daily.* See **Three Guided Walks** *pp264–5.*

A boat trip on Regent's Canal

JOHN NASH was extremely enthusiastic about this waterway, opened in 1820 to link the Grand Junction Canal, which ended at Little Venice in Paddington in the west, with the London docks at Limehouse in the east. He saw it as an added attraction for his new Regent's Park, and originally wanted the canal to run through the middle of that park. He was persuaded out of that by those who thought that the bargees' bad language would offend the genteel residents of the area. Perhaps this was just as well – the steam tugs that hauled the barges were dirty and sometimes dangerous.

In 1874 a barge carrying gunpowder blew up in the cutting by London Zoo, killing the crew, destroying a bridge and terrifying the populace, and the animals. After an initial period of prosperity the canal began to be hit by increasing competition from the new railways and so gradually slipped into decline.

Today it has been revived as a leisure amenity; the towpath is paved as a pleasant walkway and short boat trips are offered between Little Venice and Camden Lock, where there is a thriving crafts market. Visitors to the zoo can use the landing stage that is situated alongside it.

London Zoo ⑭

Regent's Park NW1. **Map** 4 D2. 🆔 020-7722 3333. 🅴 *Camden Town.* **Open** *10am – 4pm daily.* **Closed** *25 Dec.* **Adm charge**.

OPENED IN 1828, the zoo has been one of London's biggest tourist attractions ever since, and is also a major research and conservation centre. However, spectacular TV programmes on wildlife, and doubts about the ethics of keeping animals in cages, have caused attendances at the zoo to drop from their 1950s

London Zoo's aviary designed by Lord Snowdon (1964)

peak of 3 million visitors a year. In recent years the future of London zoo has been subject to a great deal of uncertainty.

Cumberland Terrace ⑮

NW1. **Map** 4 E2. 🅴 *Great Portland St, Regent's Park.*

JAMES THOMSON is credited with the detailed design of this, the longest and most elaborate of the Nash terraces around Regent's Park. Its imposing central block of raised Ionic columns is topped with a decorated triangular pediment. Completed in 1828, it was designed to be visible from the palace Nash planned for the Prince Regent (later George IV). The palace was never built because the Prince was too busy with his plans for Buckingham Palace *(see pp94–5).*

Nash's Cumberland Terrace, dating from 1828

HAMPSTEAD

H AMPSTEAD HAS ALWAYS stayed aloof from London, looking down from its site on the high ridge north of the metropolis. Today it is essentially a Georgian village. The heath separating Hampstead from Highgate reinforces its appeal, isolating it further from the hurly-burly of the modern city. A stroll around the charming village streets, followed by a tramp across the heath, makes for one of the finest walks in London.

SIGHTS AT A GLANCE

Historic Streets and Buildings
Flask Walk and Well Walk ①
Church Row ⑤
Downshire Hill ⑥
Vale of Health ⑬

Museums and Galleries
Burgh House ②
Fenton House ④
Keats House ⑦
Kenwood House ⑩

Parks and Gardens
Hampstead Heath ⑧
Parliament Hill ⑨
The Hill ⑫

Pubs and Restaurants
Jack Straw's Castle ③
Spaniards Inn ⑪

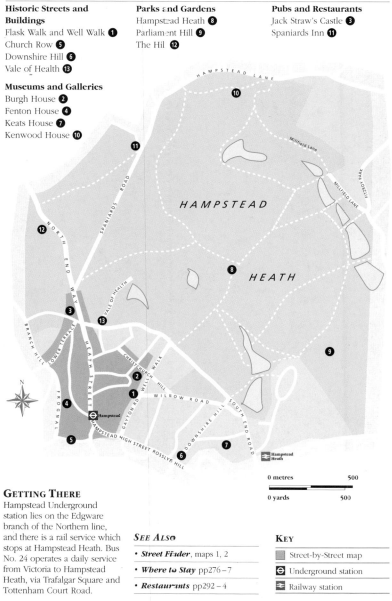

GETTING THERE
Hampstead Underground station lies on the Edgware branch of the Northern line, and there is a rail service which stops at Hampstead Heath. Bus No. 24 operates a daily service from Victoria to Hampstead Heath, via Trafalgar Square and Tottenham Court Road.

SEE ALSO
• *Street Finder*, maps 1, 2
• *Where to Stay* pp276–7
• *Restaurants* pp292–4

KEY
▢ Street-by-Street map
⊖ Underground station
⧎ Railway station

0 metres 　 500
0 yards 　 500

View across Hampstead Heath from Holly Hill

Street-by-Street: Hampstead

Perched awkwardly on a hilltop, with its broad heath to the north, Hampstead has kept its villagey atmosphere and sense of being aloof from urban pressures. This has attracted artists and writers since Georgian times and made it one of London's most desirable residential areas. Its mansions and town houses are perfectly maintained and a stroll through Hampstead's narrow streets is one of London's quieter pleasures.

Jack Straw's Castle
The pub on the edge of the Heath is named after a 14th-century rebel ❸

★ Hampstead Heath
A welcome retreat from the city, its broad open spaces include bathing ponds, meadows and lakes ❽

Whitestone Pond takes its name from the old white milestone nearby. It is 4.5 miles (7 km) from Holborn *(see pp132–41)*.

Grove Lodge was home to novelist John Galsworthy (1867–1933), author of the *Forsyte Saga*, for the last 15 years of his life.

Admiral's House dates from about 1700. Built for a sea captain, its name derives from its external maritime motifs. No admiral ever actually lived in it.

STAR SIGHTS

- ★ **Burgh House**
- ★ **Hampstead Heath**
- ★ **Fenton House**
- ★ **Church Row**

KEY

– – – Suggested route

0 metres	100
0 yards	100

★ Fenton House
Summer visitors should seek out this late 17th-century house and its exquisite walled garden, which are well hidden in the jumble of streets near the heath ❹

★ Burgh House
Built in 1702 but much altered since, the house contains an intriguing local history museum and a café overlooking the small garden ❷

LOCATOR MAP
See Greater London Map pp10–11

The New End Theatre
produces rare but significant work. The building used to be a morgue.

No. 40 Well Walk is where artist John Constable lived while working on his many Hampstead pictures.

Flask Walk and Well Walk
An alley of charming specialist shops broadens into a residential village street ❶

Hampstead station

The Everyman Cinema
has been an art cinema since 1933.

★ Church Row
The tall houses are rich in original detail. Notice the superb iron-work on what is probably London's finest Georgian street ❺

Jack Straw's Castle in the 19th century

Flask Walk and Well Walk ❶

NW3. **Map** 1 B5. ⊖ *Hampstead.*

Flask walk is named after the Flask pub. Here, in the 18th century, therapeutic spa water from what was then the separate village of Hampstead was put into flasks and sold to visitors or sent to London. The water, rich in iron salts, came from nearby Well Walk where a disused fountain now marks the site of the well. The Wells Tavern, almost opposite the spring, used to be a hostelry that specialized in accommodating those who engaged in the illicit liaisons for which the spa became notorious.

In later times, there have been many notable residents of Well Walk including artist John Constable (at No. 40), novelists D H Lawrence and J B Priestley and the poet John Keats, before he moved to his better-known house in what is now Keats Grove.

Site of the well on Well Walk

At the High Street end, Flask Walk is narrow and lined with old shops. Beyond the pub (note the Victorian tiled panels outside) it broadens into a row of Regency houses, one of which used to belong to the novelist Kingsley Amis.

Burgh House ❷

New End Sq NW3. **Map** 1 B4.
📞 020-7431 0144. ⊖ *Hampstead.*
Open *noon–5pm Wed–Sun, 2–5pm public hols.* **Closed** *Christmas week.*
📷 🍴 ♿ **Music recitals.**

The last private tenant of Burgh House was the son-in-law of the writer Rudyard Kipling, who visited here occasionally in the last years of his life until 1936. After a period under the ownership of Hampstead Borough Council, the house was let to the independent Burgh House Trust. Since 1979 the Trust has run it as the Hampstead Museum, which illustrates the history of the area and concentrates on some of its most celebrated residents.

One room is devoted entirely to the life of John Constable, who painted an extraordinary series of studies of clouds from Hampstead Heath. The house also has sections on Lawrence, Keats, the artist Stanley Spencer and others who lived and worked in the area. There is a display about Hampstead as a spa in the 18th and 19th centuries, which is also well worth a visit. Burgh House regularly accomodates exhibitions by contemporary local artists. The house itself was built in

1703 but is named after a 19th-century resident, the Reverend Allatson Burgh. It has been much altered inside, and today the marvellously carved staircase is a highlight of the interior. Also worth seeing is the music room which was reconstructed in 1920, but contains good 18th-century pine panelling from another house. In the 1720s Dr William Gibbons, chief physician to the then thriving Hampstead spa, lived here.

There is a moderately priced café in the basement, with a terrace that overlooks the house's pretty garden.

Burgh House staircase

Jack Straw's Castle ❸

12 North End Way NW3. **Map** 1 A3.
📞 020-7435 8374 ⊖ *Hampstead.*
Open *licensing hours (see p308).*
♿

This pub is named after one of Wat Tyler's lieutenants in the Peasants' Revolt of 1381 *(see p162)*. Jack Straw is believed to have built an encampment here, from which he planned to march on London. Instead, he was captured and hanged by the king's men. There has certainly been a pub here for many years – Charles Dickens was a customer – but the present building, a mock castle, dates only from 1962. It is a huge place, and there are good views across the Heath from the restaurant and Turret Bar on the second floor.

Fenton House ❹

20 Hampstead Grove NW3.
Map 1 A4. 📞 020-7435 3471.
🚇 Hampstead. **Open** 2–5pm
Wed–Fri, 11am–5pm Sat, Sun, public
hols. **Closed** Nov–mid-Mar. **Adm
charge.** 🎫 **Summer concerts**
8pm Wed.

BUILT IN 1693, this splendid William and Mary house is the oldest mansion in Hampstead. It contains two specialized exhibitions that are open to the public during the summer: the Benton-Fletcher collection of early keyboard instruments, which includes a harpsichord dating from 1612, said to have been played by Handel; and a fine collection of porcelain. The instruments are kept in full working order and are actually used for concerts held in the house. The porcelain collection was largely accumulated by Lady Binning, who, in 1952, bequeathed the house and all of its contents to the National Trust.

Church Row ❺

NW3. **Map** 1 A5. 🚇 Hampstead.

THE ROW IS ONE of the most complete Georgian streets in London. Much of its original detail has survived, notably the ironwork.

At the west end is St John's, Hampstead's parish church, built in 1745. The iron gates are earlier and come from Canons Park in Edgware. Inside the church is a bust of John Keats. John Constable's grave is in the churchyard, and many Hampstead luminaries are buried in the adjoining cemetery.

Downshire Hill ❻

NW3. **Map** 1 C5. 🚇 Hampstead.

A BEAUTIFUL STREET of mainly Regency houses, it lent its name to a group of artists, including Stanley Spencer and Mark Gertler, who would gather at No. 47 between the two World Wars. That same

house had been the meeting-place of Pre-Raphaelite artists, among them Dante Gabriel Rossetti and Edward Burne-Jones. A more recent resident, at No. 5, was the late Jim Henson, the creator of the television puppets, *The Muppets*.

The church on the corner (the second Hampstead church to be called St John's) was built in 1823 to serve the Hill's residents. Inside, it still has its original box pews.

Keats House ❼

Keats Grove NW3. **Map** 1 C5.
📞 020-7435 2062. 🚇 Hampstead,
Belsize Park. **Closed** for long periods
of time until further notice for major
structural renovation. Phone in
advance for further information. 📷
Poetry readings, talks.

Lock of John Keats's hair

ORIGINALLY TWO semi-detached houses built in 1816, Keats was persuaded to move into the smaller one in 1818 by his friend, Charles

St John's, Downshire Hill

Armitage Brown. Keats spent two productive years here: *Ode to a Nightingale*, perhaps his most celebrated poem, was written under a plum tree in the garden. The Brawne family moved into the larger house a year later and Keats became engaged to their daughter, Fanny However, the marriage never took place because Keats died of consumption in Rome before two years had passed. He was only 25 years old.

One of Keats's love letters to Fanny, the engagement ring he offered her, and a lock of her hair are among the mementoes that are now exhibited at the house – it was first opened to the public in 1925. Visitors are also able to see some of Keats's original manuscripts and books, part of a collection that serves as an evocative and memorable tribute to his life and work.

Fenton House's 17th-century facade

View over London from Hampstead Heath

Hampstead Heath 🎱

NW3. **Map** 1 C2. 🎱 020-8348 9945.
🎱 Belsize Park, Hampstead. **Open**
24hrs daily. **Special walks on**
Sundays. **Concerts, poetry readings,**
children's activities in summer.
Sports facilities, bathing ponds.
Sports bookings 🎱 020-8458 4548.

T HE BEST TIME to stride
across these broad 3 sq
miles (8 sq km) is Sunday
afternoon, when the local
residents walk off their roast
beef lunches, discussing the
contents of the Sunday
papers. Separating the hilltop
villages of Hampstead and

Highgate *(see p242)*, the Heath
was made from the grounds
of several, formerly separate,
properties and embraces a
variety of landscapes –
woods, meadows, hills, ponds
and lakes. It remains
uncluttered by the haphazard
buildings and statues that
embellish the central London
parks, and its open spaces
have become increasingly
precious to Londoners as
the areas around it get more
crowded. There are ponds for
bathing and fishing and, on
three holiday weekends –
Easter, late spring and late
summer – the southern part
of the Heath is taken over by
a popular funfair *(see pp56–9)*.

Parliament Hill 🎱

NW5. **Map** 2 E4. 🎱 020-7485 4491.
🎱 Belsize Park, Hampstead.
🎱 **Concerts, children's activities** in
summer. **Sporting facilities**. 🎱

A N UNLIKELY BUT romantic
explanation for the area's
name is that it is where Guy
Fawkes's fellow-plotters
gathered on 5 November 1605
in the vain hope of watching
the Houses of Parliament
blow up after they had
planted gunpowder there *(see
p22)*. More probably it was a
gun emplacement for the
Parliamentary side during the
Civil War 40 years later. The
gunners would have enjoyed

Kenwood House 🎱

Hampstead Lane NW3. **Map** 1 C1.
🎱 020-8348 1286. 🎱 Highgate,
Archway. **Open** Apr–Sep: 10am–6pm
daily; Oct–Mar: 10am–4pm daily.
Closed 24–25 Dec. 🎱 🎱
Lakeside concerts in summer.
Exhibitions, poetry readings,
recitals. 🎱 🎱 See **Entertainment**
pp330–31.

T HIS IS A MAGNIFICENT Adam
mansion, filled with Old
Master paintings, including
works by Vermeer, Turner and
Romney (who lived in
Hampstead). It is situated in
landscaped grounds high on
the edge of Hampstead Heath.
There has been a house here
since 1616 – the present one

was remodelled by Robert
Adam in 1764 for the Earl of
Mansfield, the Lord Chancellor.
Adam refitted existing rooms
and added to the original
building. Most of his interiors
have survived, the highlight
being the library. A Rembrandt
self-portrait is the star attraction
of the collection, and there
are also works by Van Dyck,
Hals, Reynolds and others.

The orangery is
now used for
occasional concerts
and recitals.

a broad view across London: even today, when many tall buildings have intervened, it provides one of the most spectacular views over the capital. From here the dome of St Paul's is prominent.

Parliament Hill is also a popular place for flying kites or sailing model boats.

Spaniards Inn ⑪

Spaniards Rd NW3. **Map** 1 B1.
📞 020-8731 6571. 🚇 *Hampstead, Golders Green.* **Open** *11am–11pm Mon–Sat, noon–10.30pm Sun.* ♿
See **Restaurants and Pubs** *pp308–9.*

The historic Spaniards Inn

DICK TURPIN, the notorious 18th-century highwayman, is said to have frequented this pub. When he wasn't holding up stage coaches on their way to and from London, he stabled his horse, Black Bess, at the stables nearby. The building certainly dates from Turpin's

time and, although the bar downstairs has been altered frequently, the small upstairs Turpin Bar is original. A pair of guns over the bar were reputedly taken from anti-Catholic rioters, who came to Hampstead to burn the Lord Chancellor's house at Kenwood during the Gordon Riots of 1780. The landlord detained them by offering pint after pint of free beer and, when they were drunk, disarmed them.

Among the pub's noted patrons have been the poets Shelley, Keats and Byron, the actor David Garrick and the artist Sir Joshua Reynolds.

The toll house has been restored; it juts into the road so that, in the days when tolls were levied, traffic could not race past without paying.

The Hill ⑫

North End Way NW3. **Map** 1 A2
📞 020-8455 5183. 🚇 *Hampstead, Golders Green.* **Open** *9am–one hour before dusk daily.*

THIS CHARMING garden was created by the Edwardian soap manufacturer and patron of the arts, Lord Leverhulme. It was originally the grounds to his house, and is now part of Hampstead Heath. It boasts a pergola walkway, best seen in summer when the plants are in flower; the garden also has a beautiful formal pond.

The pergola walk at The Hill

Vale of Health ⑬

NW3. **Map** 1 B4. 🚇 *Hampstead.*

THIS AREA was famous as a distinctly unhealthy swamp before it was drained in 1770; until then it was known as Hatches Bottom. Its newer name may derive from people fleeing here from cholera in London at the end of the 18th century. Alternatively, the name could have been the hype of a property developer, when it was first recorded in 1801.

The poet James Henry Leigh Hunt put it on the literary map when he moved here in 1815, and played host to Coleridge, Byron Shelley and Keats.

D H Lawrence lived here and Stanley Spencer painted in a room above the Vale of Health Hotel, demolished in 1964.

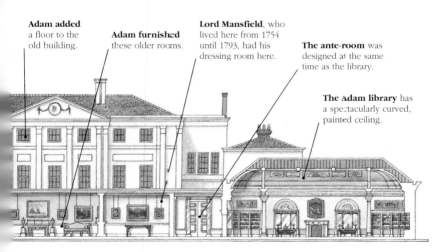

Adam added a floor to the old building.

Adam furnished these older rooms.

Lord Mansfield, who lived here from 1754 until 1793, had his dressing room here.

The ante-room was designed at the same time as the library.

The Adam library has a spectacularly curved, painted ceiling.

GREENWICH AND BLACKHEATH

BEST KNOWN AS the place from which the world's time is measured, Greenwich marks the historic eastern approach to London by land and water. Home to the National Maritime Museum and the exquisite Queen's House, Greenwich avoided the industrialization of its neighbours in the 19th century and today remains an elegant oasis of bookshops, antique shops and markets. Blackheath lies just to its south.

SIGHTS AT A GLANCE

Historic Streets and Buildings
Queen's House **2**
Royal Naval College **7**
Old Royal Observatory **9**
Croom's Hill **12**

Museums
National Maritime Museum **1**
Fan Museum **13**
Millennium Dome (see pp246–9)

Churches
St Alfege Church **3**

Parks and Gardens
Greenwich Park **10**
Blackheath **11**

Walkway
Greenwich Foot Tunnel **6**

Pubs and Restaurants
Trafalgar Tavern **8**

Ships
Gipsy Moth IV **4**
Cutty Sark **5**

GETTING THERE

The best way is by rail from Charing Cross, Cannon Street or London Bridge stations. The 188 bus goes five times an hour to Greenwich from Euston. There are also numerous river boats (pp60–5).

SEE ALSO

• **Street Finder**, maps 23, 24
• **Where to Stay** pp276–7
• **Restaurants** pp292–4

KEY

▨	Street-by-Street map
⬆	Railway station
P	Parking

View across the Thames from Greenwich Park, overlooking Queen's House

Street-by-Street: Greenwich

THIS HISTORIC TOWN marks the eastern approach to London and is best visited by river *(see pp60–5)*. In Tudor times it was the site of a palace much enjoyed by Henry VIII, near a fine hunting ground and his naval base. He and his daughters Elizabeth I and Mary were born here but the old palace is gone, leaving Inigo Jones's exquisite Queen's House, built for James I's wife. Museums, book and antique shops, markets, Wren's architecture and the magnificent park make Greenwich an enjoyable day's excursion.

Greenwich Foot Tunnel
Leading to the Isle of Dogs, this is the only Thames tunnel built solely for pedestrians ❻

Greenwich Pier provides a boarding point for boat services to Westminster and the Thames Barrier.

Gipsy Moth IV
Sir Francis Chichester sailed single-handedly round the world in this little yacht ❹

Cutty Sark
Majestic clipper ships, such as this, once traded across the oceans ❺

Goddard's Pie and Eel House is a rare survivor of a London tradition *(see p307)*.

Greenwich Market sells crafts, antiques and books at weekends. It is especially popular on Sundays.

St Alfege Church
There has been a church here since 1012 ❸

Spread Eagle Yard was a stopping point for horse-drawn carriages. The ticket office is now a second-hand book shop.

LOCATOR MAP
See Greater London Map pp10–11

★ **Royal Naval College**
Wren's stately structure was built in two halves so that the Queen's House would keep its river view ❼

The George II Statue was sculpted by John Rysbrack in 1735 and depicts the king as a Roman emperor.

The Painted Hall contains 18th-century murals by Sir James Thornhill, who painted the interior of the dome at St Paul's Cathedral.

N

★ **Queen's House**
On his return from Italy, this was the first building Inigo Jones designed in the Palladian style ❷

National Maritime Museum
Real and model boats, paintings and instruments, like this 18th-century compass, illustrate naval history ❶

STAR SIGHTS

★ **Royal Naval College**

★ **Queen's House**

KEY

‒ ‒ ‒ Suggested route

0 metres 100

0 yards 100

National Maritime Museum ❶

Romney Rd SE10. **Map** 23 C2.
☎ *020-8858 4422*. ⊞ *Maze Hill*.
Open *10am–5pm daily (last adm: 30 mins before closing).* **Closed** *24–26 Dec.* **Adm charge.**
⛱ *to most of museum.* **Lectures, exhibitions**. ▣ ▢

THE SEA HAS ALWAYS played an extremely important role in British history as a means of both defence and expansion, and this museum celebrates the "island nation's" seafaring heritage. Exhibits include everything from the earliest coracles (primitive hollow canoes) made from wood and leather, through early models of Elizabethan galleons to modern cargo, passenger and naval ships. There are sections devoted to trade and empire, the exploratory expeditions of Captain Cook and others, and the Napoleonic Wars.

One of the star exhibits is the uniform that Lord Horatio Nelson was wearing when he was shot at the Battle of Trafalgar in October 1805: you can easily see the bullet hole and the bloodstains.

Rather more spectacular, however, are the royal barges in the basement, most notably one that was built for Prince Frederick in 1732, elaborately decorated with gilded mermaids, shells, garlands and his Prince of Wales's feathers on the stern. Throughout the museum, which was built in the 19th century as a school for sailors' children, are scores of exquisitely crafted models of ships and historic paintings.

St Alfege's altar with rails by Jean Tijou

Prince Frederick's barge at the National Maritime Musueum

Queen's House ❷

Romney Rd SE10. **Map** 23 C2.
☎ *020-8858 4422*. ⊞ *Maze Hill, Greenwich.* **Open** *10am–5pm daily (last adm: 4.30pm).* **Closed** *until 2000 for renovation.* **Adm charge.** ⛱ ▥
▣ ▢ **Lectures, concerts, exhibitions.**

THE HOUSE WAS designed by Inigo Jones after his return from Italy and was completed in 1637. It was originally meant to be the home of Anne of Denmark, wife of James I, but she died while it was still being built and it was finished for Charles I's queen, Henrietta Maria. She fell in love with it and called it her house of delights. After the Civil War it was briefly occupied by Henrietta as dowager queen, but was not much used by the royal family after that.

The house is furnished as it would have been in the late 17th century, with brightly coloured wallhangings and fabrics. It was built as two halves, with one on each side of the road from Woolwich to Deptford, and linked by a bridge. Later the road was diverted; its former course is marked by cobbles in the courtyard. The main hall is a perfect cube, 12 m (40 ft) in all three dimensions. Another feature is the spiral "tulip staircase" (named after the design on its balustrades), curving sinuously upwards without a central support.

St Alfege Church ❸

Greenwich Church St SE10.
Map 23 B2. ☎ *020-8853 0687.*
⊞ *Greenwich.* **Open** *12.30–4pm Mon, Wed & Fri, 9am–11pm Sat..* ✚ *9.30am, 11.15am Sun.* ▣ ⛱ ▨
Concerts, exhibitions.

THIS IS ONE OF Nicholas Hawksmoor's distinctive and powerful designs, with its gigantic columns and pediments topped by urns. It was completed in 1714 on the site of an older church which marked the martyrdom of St Alfege, the then Archbishop of Canterbury, killed on this spot by Danish invaders in 1012.

Some of the carved wood inside is by Grinling Gibbons, but much of it was badly damaged by a World War II bomb and has been restored. The wrought iron of the altar and gallery rails is original, attributed to Jean Tijou. There is a reproduction of the register entry recording the baptism of Henry VIII in the former church, and a brass plate denoting the tomb of General Wolfe, who died fighting the French in Quebec in 1759. A window commemorates Thomas Tallis, the 16th-century composer and organist, who is buried here.

Gipsy Moth IV ❹

King William Walk SE10.
Map 23 B2. [020-8858 3445.
Greenwich, Maze Hill.
Greenwich Pier.
Not open to the public.

Gipsy Moth IV

S IR FRANCIS CHICHESTER sailed single-handed around the world in this little yacht. The journey, in 1966–7, took 226 lonely days to cover the 30,000 miles (48,000 km). He had to endure very cramped conditions on this 16-m (54-ft) vessel. The Queen knighted him on board using the sword with which Elizabeth I had knighted that earlier English seaman, Sir Francis Drake.

The domed terminal of the Greenwich Foot Tunnel

Cutty Sark ❺

King William Walk SE10. **Map** 23 B2.
[020-8858 3445. [020-8853 3589. Greenwich, Maze Hill.
Greenwich Pier. **Open** 10am–5pm daily (last adm: 4.30pm). **Closed** 24–26 Dec. **Adm charge**. restricted. Filmshows, videos.

T HIS MAJESTIC vessel is a survivor of the clippers that crossed the Atlantic and Pacific Oceans in the 19th century. Launched in 1869 as a tea carrier, it was something of a speed machine in its day, winning the annual clippers' race from China to London in 1871, in a time of 107 days. It made its final voyage on the high seas in 1938 and was put on display here in 1957. On board you can see where the merchant seamen slept, ate, worked and pursued their interests. Exhibits show the history of sail and the Pacific trade, and there is a thrilling collection of carved ships' figureheads.

Greenwich Foot Tunnel ❻

Between Greenwich Pier SE10 and Isle of Dogs E14. **Map** 23 B1. Maze Hill, Greenwich. **Docklands Light Railway** Island Gardens.
Greenwich Pier. **Open** 24hrs daily.
Lifts open 5am–9pm daily.
when lifts open.

T HIS 370-M (1,200-FT) long tunnel was opened in 1902 to allow south London labourers to walk to work in

Millwall Docks. Today it is worth crossing for the wonderful views, across the river, of Christopher Wren's Royal Naval College and Inigo Jones's Queen's House.

Matching round red-brick terminals, with glass domes, mark the top of the lift shafts on either side of the river. The tunnel is about 2.5 m (9 ft) high and is lined with 200,000 tiles. The north end, on the southern tip of the Isle of Dogs, is close to the terminus of the Docklands Light Railway, with trains to Canary Wharf (see p245), Limehouse, East London and the City. Although there are security cameras, the tunnel can be eerie at night.

A late 19th-century figurehead in the Cutty Sark

Royal Naval College ❼

Greenwich SE10. **Map** 23 C2.
📋 *020-8858 2154.* 🚤 *Greenwich,
Maze Hill.* **Open** *2.30–5pm daily (last
adm: 4.45pm).* **Closed** *public hols.* 🚫

THESE AMBITIOUS buildings
by Sir Christopher Wren
were built on the site of the
old 15th-century royal palace,
where Henry VIII, Mary I and
Elizabeth I lived. The chapel
and hall are the only parts of
the college that are open to
the public. The west front
was completed by Vanbrugh.

The chapel, by Wren, was
destroyed by fire in 1779.
The present Rococo interior,
designed by James Stuart, is
marvellously light and airy,
and has dainty plasterwork
decorations on the ceilings
and walls. The altar rail and
communion table, as well as
the candelabra, are gilded.

The Painted Hall was
opulently decorated by Sir
James Thornhill in the first
quarter of the 18th century.
The magnificent ceiling
paintings are supported by
his illusionistic pillars and
friezes. At the foot of one of
his paintings on the west
wall, the artist himself is
shown, apparently extending
his hand for more money.

Thornhill's painting of King William in the Hall of the Naval College

Trafalgar Tavern ❽

Park Row SE10. **Map** 23 C1.
📋 *020-8858 2437. See* **Restaurants
and Pubs** *pp308–9.*

THIS CHARMING panelled pub
was built in 1837 and
quickly became established,
along with other waterside
inns in Greenwich, as a
venue for "whitebait dinners".
Government ministers, legal
luminaries and the like would
arrive from Westminster and
Charing Cross by water on
celebratory occasions and
feast on the tiny fish, which
could in those days be caught
locally. The last such meeting
of government ministers was
held here in 1885. Whitebait
still features, when in season,
on the menu at the pub's
restaurant, though they no
longer come from the now
somewhat polluted Thames.

This is another of Charles
Dickens's haunts. He drank
here with one of his novels'
most famous illustrators, the
engraver George Cruickshank.

In 1915 the pub became an
institution for old merchant
seamen. It was restored in 1965
after a spell when it was used
as a club for working men.

Old Royal Observatory ❾

Greenwich Park SE10. **Map** 23 C3.
📋 *020-8858 4422.* 🚤 *Maze Hill,
Greenwich.* **Open** *10am–5pm daily
(last adm: 4.30pm).* **Closed** *23-26
Dec.* **Adm charge.** 🚫 📷

THE MERIDIAN (0° longtitude)
that divides the earth's
eastern and western hemi-
spheres passes through here,
and millions of visitors have
taken the opportunity of being
photographed standing with a
foot on either side of it. In
1884, Greenwich Mean Time
became the basis of time
measurement for most of the
world, following an important
international agreement.

The original building, still
standing, is Flamsteed House,
designed by Wren. It has a
distinctive octagonal room at
the top, hidden by square
outer walls and crowned with
two turrets. Above one of
them is a ball on a rod which
has dropped at 1pm every
day since 1833, so that sailors
on ships on the Thames, and
makers of chronometers
(navigators' clocks), could set
their clocks by it.

Flamsteed was the first
Astronomer Royal, appointed
by Charles II, and this was
the official government
observatory from 1675 until
1948, when the lights of

Trafalgar Tavern viewed from the Thames

London became too bright and the astronomers moved to darker Sussex. Today the Astronomer Royal is based in Cambridge and in the old Observatory there is housed an intriguing exhibition of astronomical instruments, chronometers and clocks.

A rare 24–hour clock at the Old Royal Observatory

his plan. There are great river views from the hilltop and on a fine day most of London can be seen. To the south-east of the park is the Ranger's House (1688), allotted in 1815 to the Park Ranger, but

Ranger's House in Greenwich Park

today housing an architectural study centre, the fine Suffolk Collection of 17th-century English portraits by Larkin, Lely and others, and a display of historic musical instruments.

Blackheath **①①**

SE3. **Map** 24 D5. ⬆ Blackheath.

THIS OPEN HEATH used to be a rallying point for large groups entering London from the east, including Wat Tyler's band of rebels at the time of the Peasants' Revolt in 1381. It is also the place where James I introduced the game of golf, from his native Scotland, to the then largely sceptical English.

Today the heath is well worth exploring for the stately Georgian houses and terraces that surround it. In the prettily-named Tranquil Vale to the south there are shops selling books, prints and antiques.

Croom's Hill **①②**

SE10. **Map** 23 C3. ⬆ Greenwich.

THIS IS ONE of the best kept 17th- to early 19th-century streets in London. The oldest buildings are at the southern end, near

Blackheath: the Manor House of 1695; near it, No. 68, from about the same date; and No. 66 the oldest of all.

Famous residents of Croom's Hill have included General James Wolfe (buried in St Alfege), and the Irish actor Daniel Day Lewis.

Fan Museum **①③**

12 Croom's Hill SE10. **Map** 23 B3. 🕻 020-8858 7879. ⬆ Greenwich. **Open** 11am–4.30pm Tue–Sat, noon–4.30pm Sun (5pm in summer). **Adm charge** but reductions for pensioners and disabled. 🔲 ⬇ 🖫 🖺 **Lectures, fan-making workshops.**

ONE OF LONDON'S most unlikely museums – the only one of its kind in the world – was opened here in 1989. It owes its existence and appeal to the enthusiasm of Helene Alexander, whose personal collection of 2,000 fans from the 17th century onwards has been augmented by gifts from others, including several fans that were made for the stage. The exhibitions are changed regularly in order to highlight a wide-ranging craft which embraces design, miniature painting, carving and embroidery. If there, Ms Alexander will guide you around the exhibits.

Greenwich Park **①⓪**

SE10. **Map** 23 C3. 🕻 020-8858 2608. ⬆ Greenwich, Blackheath, Maze Hill. **Open** 6am–dusk daily. ⬇ 🔲 **Children's shows, music, sports. Ranger's House,** Chesterfield Walk, Greenwich Park SE10. **Map** 23 C4. 🕻 020-8853 0035. **Open** 1 Apr–30 Sep: 10am–6pm daily; 1–21 Oct: 10am–5pm daily; 22 Oct–31 Mar 10am–4pm Wed–Sun. **Closed** 24–25 Dec. 🖌 book in advance. 🖺

ORIGINALLY THE GROUNDS of a royal palace and still owned by the Crown, the park was enclosed in 1433 and its brick wall built in the reign of James I. Later, in the 17th century, the French royal landscape gardener André Le Nôtre, who laid out the gardens at Versailles, was invited to design one at Greenwich. The broad avenue, rising south up the hill, was part of

Stage fan used in a D'Oyly Carte operetta

FURTHER AFIELD

MANY OF THE GREAT houses originally built as country retreats for London's high and mighty were overrun by sprawling suburbs in the Victorian era. Fortunately several have survived as museums in these now less-rustic surroundings. Most are less than an hour's journey from central London. Richmond Park and Wimbledon Common give a taste of the country, while a trip to the Millennium Dome is an adventure.

SIGHTS AT A GLANCE

Historic Streets and Buildings
Sutton House ⑪
Charlton House ⑲
Eltham Palace ⑳
Ham House ㉙
Orleans House ㉚
Hampton Court pp254–7 ㉘
Marble Hill House ㉛
Syon House ㉝
Osterley Park House ㉟
Pitshanger Manor Museum ㊱
Strand on the Green ㊴
Chiswick House ㊵
Fulham Palace ㊷

Churches
St Mary, Rotherhithe ⑬
St Mary's, Battersea ㉔
St Anne's, Limehouse ⑭

Museums and Galleries
Lord's Cricket Ground ①
Saatchi Collection ②
Freud Museum ③
St John's Gate ⑦
Crafts Council Gallery ⑧
Geffrye Museum ⑩
Bethnal Green Museum of Childhood ⑫
William Morris Gallery ⑯
Horniman Museum ㉑
Dulwich Picture Gallery ㉒
Wimbledon Lawn Tennis Museum ㉕
Wimbledon Windmill Museum ㉖
Musical Museum ㉞
Kew Bridge Steam Museum ㊲
Hogarth's House ㊶
London Toy and Model Museum ㊹

Parks and Gardens
Battersea Park ㉓
Richmond Park ㉗
Kew Gardens pp260–1 ㊳

Cemeteries
Highgate Cemetery ⑤

Modern Architecture
Canary Wharf ⑮
Millennium Dome ⑱
Chelsea Harbour ㊸

Historic Districts
Highgate ④
House of Detention ⑥
Islington ⑨
Richmond ㉜

Modern Technology
Thames Barrier ⑰

All the sights in this section lie inside the M25 motorway (see pp10–11).

KEY

Main sightseeing areas

Motorway

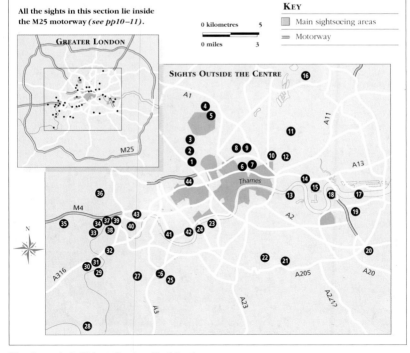

GREATER LONDON

M25

0 kilometres 5

0 miles 3

SIGHTS OUTSIDE THE CENTRE

Thames

Victorian tombs in Highgate Cemetery, North London

North of the Centre

Lord's Cricket Ground ❶

NW8. **Map** 3 A3. 📞 *020-7289 1611.*
🚇 *St John's Wood.* **Open** *for guided tours and ticket-holders to matches only.* **Closed** *25 Dec.* **Adm charge**.
📷 ♿ 🎥 *Mid-Sep–mid-Apr: noon, 2pm; mid-Apr–mid-Sep: 10am, noon, 2pm.* 🎟 *See* **Entertainment** *pp336–7.*

THE HEADQUARTERS of Britain's chief summer sport contains a museum, including a stuffed sparrow killed by a cricket ball as well as the Ashes (burned wood in an urn), the object of ferocious competition between the English and Australian national teams. The museum explains the history of the game, while paintings and mementoes of notable cricketers make it a place of pilgrimage for devotees of the sport.

Cricket pioneer Thomas Lord moved his ground here in 1814. The Pavilion (1890), with its weather vane depicting Old Father Time, is late Victorian. There are guided tours of Lord's even when there is no game being played.

The Ashes at Lord's

Saatchi Collection ❷

98a Boundary Rd NW8. 📞 *020-7624 8299.* 🚇 *St John's Wood, Swiss Cottage.* **Open** *noon–6pm Thu–Sun.* **Adm charge** *(except Thu).* 🎥 *(phone to arrange).* 🎟 **Lectures**.

CHARLES SAATCHI, who is an advertising executive, and his former wife established this gallery of contemporary art in a converted warehouse. (There is no sign outside so take care not to miss it.) He owns approximately 600 works by artists such as Andy Warhol, Carl André and Frank Stella, and selections are put on display in exhibitions that are changed every few months.

Sigmund Freud's famous couch

Freud Museum ❸

20 Maresfield Gdns NW3.
📞 *020-7435 2002.* 🚇 *Finchley Rd.*
Open *noon–5pm Wed–Sun.* **Closed** *24–26 Dec.* **Adm charge**. 📷 ♿ 🎟
Lectures, videos.

IN 1938 SIGMUND FREUD, the founder of psychoanalysis, fled from Nazi persecution in Vienna to this Hampstead house. Making use of the possessions he brought with him, his family recreated the atmosphere of his Vienna consulting rooms. After Freud died in 1939 his daughter Anna (who was a pioneer of child psychoanalysis) kept the house as it was. In 1986 the house was opened to the public as a museum dedicated to Freud. The most famous item is the couch on which patients lay for analysis. A compilation of 1930s home movies shows cheerful moments with his dog as well as scenes of Nazi attacks on his apartment. The museum's bookshop has a large collection of his works.

Highgate ❹

N6. 🚇 *Highgate.*

THERE HAS BEEN a settlement here since at least the early Middle Ages, when an important staging post on the Great North Road from London was established here with a gate to control access. Like Hampstead across the Heath *(see pp228–31)*, it soon became fashionable for its unpolluted air, and noblemen built country houses here. It still has an exclusive feel, with a Georgian High Street and expensive houses. On Highgate Hill, a statue of a black cat marks the spot where a dejected Richard Whittington and his pet are said to have paused. He was about to leave London, when he heard the sound of Bow Bells telling him to turn back – to become Lord Mayor three times *(see p39)*.

Highgate Cemetery ❺

Swain's Lane N6. 📞 *020-8340 1834.*
🚇 *Archway.* **Eastern Cemetery open** *Apr–Oct: 10am–5pm daily; Nov–Mar: 10am–4pm daily.* **Western Cemetery open** 🎥 *only Apr–Oct: noon, 2pm, 4pm Mon–Fri, 11am–4pm Sat, Sun; Nov–Mar: 11am–3pm Sat, Sun.* **Closed** *25–26 Dec, during funerals.* **Adm charge**. ♿

THE WESTERN part of this early Victorian delight opened in 1839. Its graves and tombs perfectly reflect high Victorian taste. For many years it lay neglected until a voluntary group, called the Friends of Highgate Cemetery stepped in to save it from further decline. They have restored the Egyptian Avenue, a street of family vaults, built in a style based on that of ancient Egyptian tombs, and the Circle of Lebanon, more vaults in a ring, topped by a cedar tree. In the eastern section lies Karl Marx, beneath a gigantic black bust of himself. The novelist George Eliot (real name, Mary Anne Cross) is also buried here.

George Wombwell's Memorial at Highgate Cemetery

Cells in the House of Detention

House of Detention ❻

Clerkenwell Close, EC1. **Map** 6 D4.
📞 020-7253 9494. ⊖ *Farringdon.*
Open *10am–6pm daily.* **Adm charge.**

CLERKENWELL'S NAME refers to a well in Farringdon Lane where medieval city clerks staged passion plays. The area has a chequered history. Dominated by St John's Priory until Henry VIII dissolved the monasteries in 1536, it briefly became a fashionable suburb but declined after the Plague of 1665 *(see p22)* and Huguenot refugees moved in, setting up workshops for jewellery and silverwork. At the same time a large new prison was built here because Newgate was getting overcrowded. This put a blight on the surrounding streets, and they grew notorious as some of the worst slums in Victorian London, described by Dickens in *Oliver Twist.*

The prison was rebuilt in 1845 and has since been largely demolished, but some of its rooms are preserved in this museum on the site, including the basement kitchen, wash-house and a few cells. The accompanying exhibition tells its story graphically.

Nearby on Rosebery Avenue is the famous Sadler's Wells Theatre *(see p332).*

St John's Gate ❼

St John's Lane EC1. **Map** 6 F4.
📞 020-7253 6644. ⊖ *Farringdon.*
Museum open *9am–5pm Mon–Fri, 10am–4pm Sat.* **Closed** *public hol weekends.* **Adm charge.** 🚫 ♿
📷 *11am, 2.30pm Tue, Fri, Sat.* 📷

THE TUDOR GATEHOUSE and parts of the 12th-century church are all that remain of the priory of the Knights of St John, which flourished here for 400 years and was the precursor of the St John Ambulance. Over the years, the priory buildings have had many uses, including as offices for Elizabeth I's Master of the Revels, a pub, a coffee shop run by artist William Hogarth's father, and the offices of the *Gentlemen's Magazine* (1731–54). A museum of the order's history is open daily, but to see the rest of the building, join a guided tour.

The Crafts Council Gallery

Crafts Council Gallery ❽

44a Pentonville Rd N1. **Map** 6 D2.
📞 020-7278 7700. ⊖ *Angel.*
Open *11am–6pm Tue–Sat, 2–6pm Sun.* **Closed** *25–26 Dec, 1 Jan.* ♿
💻 📷 *Lectures.*

THE COUNCIL is the national body for promoting the creation and appreciation of crafts in Britain. It has a collection of contemporary British crafts, some of which is displayed here, along with special exhibitions. There is a reference library and information service and a bookshop which also sells many good examples of modern crafts.

Islington ❾

N1. **Map** 6 E1. ⊖ *Angel, Highbury & Islington.*

ISLINGTON WAS ONCE a highly fashionable spa, but the rich began to move out in the late 18th century, and the area deteriorated rapidly. During the 20th century, writers such as Evelyn Waugh, George Orwell and Joe Orton lived here. Now Islington has again returned to fashion as one of London's first areas to become "gentrified", with many young professionals buying and refurbishing old houses.

An older relic is Canonbury Tower, the remains of a medieval manor house converted into apartments in the 18th century. Writers such as Washington Irving and Oliver Goldsmith lived here and today it houses the Tower Theatre. On Islington Green there is a statue of Sir Hugh Myddleton, who built a canal through Islington in 1613 to bring water to London from Hertfordshire; today a pleasant landscaped walk along its banks runs between Essex Road and Canonbury stations. There are two markets close to the Angel station *(see p322)*: Chapel Road selling fresh food and cheap clothing, and the nearby Camden Passage, selling expensive antiques.

St John's Priory: today, only the gatehouse remains intact

East of the Centre

Geffrye Museum's Victorian Room

Geffrye Museum ⓾

Kingsland Rd E2. [020-7739 9893.
⊖ Liverpool St, Old St. **Open** 10am–
5pm Tue–Sat, noon–5pm Sun. (also
noon–5pm Mon public hols,. **Closed**
24–26 Dec, 1 Jan, Good Fri. ⓰ ⓱
⬛ Exhibitions, lectures, events.

T HIS DELIGHTFUL MUSEUM is
housed in an attractive set
of almshouses built in 1715
on land bequeathed by Sir
Robert Geffrye, a 17th-century
Lord Mayor of London who
made his fortune through
trade, including the slave
trade. The almshouses (built
for ironworkers and their
widows) have been adapted
into typical room settings of
specific periods, and provide
an insight into the history of
family life and the evolution
of interior design. The historic
room settings begin with
Elizabethan (which contains
magnificent panelling) and
run through various major
styles, including Art Nouveau,
while an airy, glass and red-
brick extension houses more
modern settings, such as an
example of 1990s "loft living".
Each room contains superb
examples of the furniture
of the period collected from
all over Britain. In the
middle, the chapel has not
been altered significantly
from its original appear-
ance, with box pews. There
are attractive garden settings
outside the museum, which
include a walled herb garden.

Sutton House ⓫

2–4 Homerton High St E9.
[020-8986 2264. ⊖ Bethnal
Green then bus 253. **Open** Feb–Nov:
11.30am–5pm Wed, Sun. **Closed** Dec,
Jan, Good Fri. **Adm charge**. ⬛ ⓰
⬛ ⬛ ⬛ **Concerts, lectures**.

O NE OF THE FEW London
Tudor merchants' houses
to survive in something like
its original form, it is now
being restored. Built in 1535
for Ralph Sadleir, a courtier to
Henry VIII, it was owned by
several wealthy families before
becoming a girls' school in
the 17th century. In the 18th
century the front was altered,
but the Tudor fabric remains
surprisingly intact, with much
original brickwork, large fireplaces and linenfold panelling.

Bethnal Green Museum of Childhood ⓬

Cambridge Heath Rd E2.
[020-8983 5200. ⟹ Hackney
Central. ⊖ Bethnal Green. **Open**
10am–5.50pm Mon–Thu, Sat,
2.30–5.50pm Sun. **Closed** 24–26
Dec, 1 Jan, May Day. ⬛ ⬛ ⬛
Workshop, children's activities.

T HIS BRANCH of the Victoria
and Albert Museum (see
pp198–201) is more usefully
described as a toy museum,
although there are plans to
broaden its range by showing
exhibits on the social history
of childhood. Its array of
dolls, lavish dolls' houses
(some donated by royalty),

Tate "Baby" house made in 1760

games, model trains, theatres,
puppets and some large play
equipment are well explained
and enticingly displayed to
make a veritable trove of fun.
The purpose-built museum
building was erected on the
V&A site. In 1872, when the
V&A was extended, it was
dismantled and reassembled
here to bring the light of
learning to the East End. The
toy collection began early this
century and Bethnal Green
became a dedicated toy
museum in 1974.

St Mary, Rotherhithe ⓭

St Marychurch St SE16.
[020-7231 2465. ⊖ Rotherhithe.
Open 7.30am–6pm daily. ⬛
9.30am, 6pm Sun. ⬛ ⬛ restricted.

St Mary, Rotherhithe

T HIS BRIGHT CHURCH was
built in 1715 on the site of
a medieval church, traces of
which remain in the tower. It
has nautical connotations,
most notably a memorial to
Christopher Jones, captain of
the *Mayflower* on which the
Founding Fathers sailed to
North America. The barrel
roof resembles an inverted
hull. The communion table
is made from the timbers
of the *Temeraire*, a warship
whose final journey to the
breaker's yard at Rotherhithe
was evocatively recorded in
Turner's painting at the
National Gallery (see pp104–7).

William Morris tapestry (1885)

St Anne's, Limehouse ⓐ

Commercial Rd E14.
C 020-7987 1502. **Docklands Light Railway** Westferry. **Open** 2–4pm Mon–Fri, 2.30–5pm Sat, Sun (key from rectory at other times, 5 Newell St, E14). ♦ 10.30am, 6pm Sun. ⬚ ⬚ **Concerts, lectures**.

T HIS IS ONE of the group of East End churches designed by Nicholas Hawksmoor. It was completed in 1724. Its 40-m (130-ft) tower very soon became a landmark for ships using the East End docks – St Anne's still has the highest church clock in London. The church was damaged by fire in 1850 and, while it was being restored, the architect Philip Hardwick Victorianized its interior. It was bombed in World War II and is today in need of further restoration.

Canary Wharf ⓑ

E14. **Docklands Light Railway** Canary Wharf. ⬚ ⬚ ⬚ ⬚ **Information centre, concerts, exhibitions**. See **The History of London** pp30 –1.

L ONDON'S MOST ambitious commercial development opened in 1991, when the first tenants moved into the

50-storey Canada Tower, designed by Argentine architect Cesar Pelli. At 250 m (800 ft) it dominates the city's eastern skyline and is the tallest office building in Europe. It stands on what was the West India Dock, closed, like all the London docks, between the 1960s and the 1980s, when trade moved to the modern container port down river at Tilbury. After almost a decade of recession-related uncertainly, Canary Wharf is growing and thriving. When completed, it will have 21 office buildings plus shops and leisure facilities.

William Morris Gallery ⓒ

Lloyd Park, Forest Rd E17. **C** 020-8527 3782. ⊖ Walthamstow Central. **Open** 10am–1pm, 2–5pm Tue–Sat, 10am–1pm, 2–5pm first Sun each month. **Closed** 24–26 Dec and public hols. ⬚ ⬚ **Lectures**.

T HE MOST influential designer of the Victorian era, born in 1834, lived in this imposing 18th-century house as a youth. It is now a beguiling and well-presented museum giving a full account of William Morris the artist, designer, writer, craftsman and pioneer socialist. It has choice examples of his work and that of various other members of the Arts and Crafts movement that he inspired – furniture by A H Mackmurdo, Kelmscott Press books, tiles by de Morgan, and paintings by the Pre-Raphaelites.

Thames Barrier ⓓ

Unity Way SE18. **C** 020-8854 1373. ⇌ Charlton. **Open** 10am–5pm Mon–Fri (Oct–Feb 10am–4pm), 10.30am–5.30pm Sat, Sun. **Closed** 25–26 Dec. **Adm charge**. ⬚ ⬚ ⬚ ⬚ **Multi-media show, exhibition**.

Thames Barrier

I N 1236 THE THAMES rose so high that people rowed across Westminster Hall in boats; London was flooded again in 1663 and 1928. A tidal surge in 1953 caused great damage in the estuary below London. Something had to be done, and in 1965 the Greater London Council (see County Hall p183) invited proposals – nine years later work began on the barrier. It is 520 m (1,700 ft) across, and its 10 gates, which pivot from their normal position flat on the river bed, swing up to 1.6 m (6 ft) above the level reached by the tide in 1953. The barrier was opened in 1984 and seldom has to be raised more than once or twice a year. It is best visited by boat (see pp60–65).

Canada Tower at Canary Wharf

Millennium Dome ⓘ

THE MILLENNIUM DOME is the focal point for Britain's celebration of the year 2000. From its spectacular opening ceremony on December 31, 1999 its vast interior is home to a year-long exhibition that welcomes and examines the choices facing humanity in the 21st century and beyond. Offering fourteen unique zones to explore, the Dome is above all an experience to be enjoyed, with elements to astonish, inspire, and enlighten.

Self Portrait is a view of all things British, from attitudes and icons to people, places, and objects. Visitors can give their opinions on the Dome and other current hot issues.

Talk explores interaction of every sort, from smoke signals to a holographic telephone.

Faith is a zone for personal reflection as 2,000 years of Christian history is celebrated in today's multi-faith Britain.

Mind is an imagination-expanding experience hosted by intelligent artificial life forms.

Rest offers visitors time to switch off and relax in a dream-like world. Its serene ride is a break from the stimulating experiences of the other zones.

Cables and Masts
Over 43 miles (70 km) of steel cable form the netting that supports the canopy. Abseilers spent three months rigging it to the twelve 328-ft (100-m) masts.

Money and the way we use it faces huge changes in the 21st century. Visitors can find out just how easy it is to spend £1 million.

Ventilator for the Blackwall Tunnel

Work explores the changing world of earning a living and looks at the scope for breaking away from the "9-to-5". A vast kinetic machine links it to the Learn zone.

Learning Life is magical proof that learning is an adventure to be continued and enjoyed throughout a lifetime.

Dome Statistics
The base of the Dome is ten times that of St. Paul's Cathedral. Nelson's Column could stand beneath its roof and the Eiffel Tower could lie on its side within. The roof could take the weight of a airplane.

Roof Panels
The 72 panels that form the canopy are made of Teflon-coated spun glass fiber. More than 109,000 sq yards (100,000 sq m) of fabric was needed to cover the Dome.

Home Planet greets new arrivals to our world at the **Earth Visitor Center**, and takes them on a virtual tour around the globe.

Living Island brings ecology home in the context of a lively beachside setting. A Victorian-style pier houses a play arcade with games conveying environmental messages amid the fun.

Journey offers a virtual reality ride to see the transportation systems and vehicles of the future.

Shared Ground looks at personal and community space and how we can improve and protect them. A highlight is the Crystal City – a pulsating time-lapse view of 24 hours in the life of a great city.

One of twelve hoppers for recycled water

Millennium Show
A spectacular multimedia show plays up to six times a day to 12,000 spectators in the heart of the Dome. Many young people have been specially trained in acrobatic skills for this event.

Entrance

Body is centered in the astonishing **Giant Body Sculpture**, through which visitors move to find out about just how amazing and complex the "human machine" really is.

Play combines the age-old traditions of fun and games with the breathtaking advances of the digital playground. Absorbing, entertaining, interactive, and personally challenging games make this a hard zone to leave behind, at any age.

STAR ATTRACTIONS

★ **Giant Body Sculpture**

★ **Millennium Show**

★ **Earth Visitor Center**

Exploring the Millennium Dome

THE OVERARCHING THEME of the Dome is an examination of the choices facing the human race in the 21st century and beyond. The individual zones converge at the Millennium Show arena in the center.

MIND ZONE

AN ADVENTURE playground of the brain is contained within eight spheres, apparently suspended in space, connected by moving walkways. In the spheres you can play mind games involving optical and other illusions. A "morphing machine" will allow you to simulate changing age, sex, or race. The zone is peopled by robots and other intelligent artificial life forms.

BODY ZONE

DIAMETRICALLY OPPOSITE the Mind Zone, this part of the Dome is dominated by a 200-ft (61-m) long sculpture of two bodies, the largest representation of the human form in the world. Walking through it you can see how the body functions. Multimedia displays show how diet, exercise, and other lifestyle choices affect it. The interactive Explore area looks forward to developments in medicine in the 21st century.

PLAY ZONE

THE AGE-OLD traditions of playtime are harnessed to computer technology in an examination of leisure pursuits and what extra options will be available in the new millennium. The Parallax Ride carries you up on a moving walkway past huge multimedia displays. From the top you can descend by abseiling or climbing down in "Spiderman" suits. An elevator serves the unadventurous.

SHARED GROUND ZONE

A HOUSE MADE OF recycled materials has rooms that show how people of seven different age groups go about creating their own private space. Outside the house is a "nightmare street," showing the very worst of what we can do to ruin our neighborhoods. The Crystal City is a fascinating walk-through, three-dimensional portrayal of life in a city over the course of a 24-hour period.

JOURNEY ZONE

ONE OF THE MOST persistent human instincts is the desire to travel, to be on the move. This zone examines the future of travel, with new transportation systems and new energy-efficient vehicles. You can take control of an entire city's transit network and see if you can run it more efficiently than the professionals. A virtual reality journey offers the excitement of long-distance travel without leaving the Dome.

LIVING ISLAND ZONE

THE THEME OF our relationship to the environment is explored in a seaside setting, with a sandy beach, waves, a lighthouse, and a Victorian-style pier. Passing through a tunnel in the cliff (made of recycled crushed cans) you reach a promenade complete with bandstand, deckchairs, ice cream stands, seagulls, rides, and beach huts. The slot machines in the traditional amusement arcade, and the games in the Future Scenario Casino, all convey ecological messages with a spirit of fun.

HOME PLANET ZONE

YOU ARE FROM another universe, visiting Earth for the first time. At the Earth Visitor Center you are taken on a journey around the world. Here are sights, sounds, and sensations of the planet in all its rich diversity, showing what men and women have done to create societies in which they can live in harmony and personal fulfilment.

SELF PORTRAIT ZONE

A CELEBRATION OF the things regarded as "typically British," the contents selected by millions of members of the public. Here is the National Portrait, 260-ft (80-m) long – a montage of photographs of millions of British citizens, added to each day with pictures of Dome visitors.

Flourishing reedbeds near the Dome

THE LAND AROUND THE DOME

The peninsula on which the Millennium Dome stands was once the polluted site of a vast gasworks. As part of this project it has been entirely cleaned up, and will provide habitats for a wide variety of wildlife. One element of the new sanctuary has been created between the Dome and the river, where local children have planted young reeds to encourage birds, mammals, and wild plantlife to return – a boardwalk allows visitors to take a closer look. In all, 15 acres have been landscaped and 12,000 trees planted in the new riverside park and along the Thames-side walk.

FAITH ZONE

IN A STRIKING tentlike structure, the many faiths held by British people today are explored in photographs and movies. The zone is designed to encourage personal reflection on belief and the spirit, and on the common values that underpin the great religions of the world.

TALK ZONE

A CELEBRATION OF the ways in which we communicate, from smoke signals to the cellphone, the zone includes an interactive walk tracing how we learn to relate verbally from the time we utter our first words. On the technology deck you can try out the latest phones and leave a message for future generations.

REST ZONE

THIS MAY BE one of the most popular zones, as visitors retreat from the bustle and frenzy of the Dome's other experiences. Board a restful ride and relax as it takes you through a series of dreamlike worlds, like a mental flotation tank. Try not to visit this zone until you are at least half way through your visit.

MONEY ZONE

WHILE OTHER ZONES promote spiritual values and good citizenship, this one is based on the premise that money makes the world go round. You can see £1 million in cash and are allowed to spend it in an interactive fantasy department store, as well as learning how the state of the global economy impacts on your personal finances.

WORK ZONE

CHANGES TO COME in the new millennium is a theme that runs right through the Dome, but nowhere is it more apparent than in the world of work. This zone juxtaposes the old-style workplace, complete with nightmare boss, with ones of the future. A huge kinetic machine, linking with the next zone, symbolizes the interdependence of work and learning.

LEARNING LIFE ZONE

LEARNING IS a lifelong quest. As well as watching a magic show full of illusions revealing unexpected facets of learning, you can access the Internet Domesday Book. This holds children's ideas of what future generations need to know about Britain today, based on their own experiences and those of their parents and grandparents.

OUR TOWN STORY

CHILDREN PLAY a major role in this event, which adds another dimension to the Dome. Local communities have come together to enact a story from the history of their town or village in drama and music. As many groups as possible will perform in a purpose-built theater. Taken together, these mini-dramas illustrate the enormous cultural diversity that exists within the British Isles.

THE DOME PENINSULA

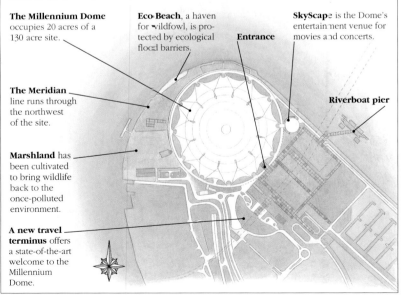

The Millennium Dome occupies 20 acres of a 130 acre site.

The Meridian line runs through the northwest of the site.

Marshland has been cultivated to bring wildlife back to the once-polluted environment.

A new travel terminus offers a state-of-the-art welcome to the Millennium Dome.

Eco-Beach, a haven for wildfowl, is protected by ecological flood barriers.

Entrance

SkyScape is the Dome's entertainment venue for movies and concerts.

Riverboat pier

South of the Centre

A Jacobean fireplace at Charlton House

Charlton House ⓲

Charlton Rd SE7. [020-8856 3951. ⇌ Charlton. **Open** 9am–10pm Mon–Fri, 10am–5pm Sat (phone to arrange). **Closed** public hols. ⬜ ⬜ ⬜

T HE HOUSE was completed in 1612 for Adam Newton, tutor to Prince Henry. It has good river views and is the best-preserved Jacobean mansion in the London area – well worth the tricky journey for enthusiasts of that period. It is now used as a community centre but many of the original ceilings and fireplaces survive intact, as does the carved main staircase, all with an astonishing quantity of ornament. Some parts of the wood panelling, too, are original, and the ceilings have been restored using the original moulds. In the grounds is a summer house that, according to tradition, was designed by Inigo Jones, and a mulberry tree (probably the oldest in England) said to have been planted by James I in 1608 as part of his failed attempt to start an English silk industry.

Eltham Palace ⓴

Court Yard SE9. [020-8294 2548. ⇌ Eltham, then a 15-minute walk. **Open** Wed–Fri, Sun. Apr–Sep: 10am–6pm; Oct: 10am–5pm; Nov–Mar: 10am–4pm. **Adm charge.** ⬜ ⬜ ⬜

T HIS UNIQUE property lets visitors relive the grand life of two very different eras. In the 14th century, English kings spent Christmas in a splendid palace here. The Tudors used it as a base for deer-hunting but it fell to ruin after the Civil War (1642–8). In 1932 Stephen Courtauld, a film director and member of the wealthy textile family, restored the hall which, apart from the bridge over the moat, was the only part of the medieval palace to survive. Next to it he built a house described as "a wonderful combination of Hollywood glamour and Art Deco design". This has now been superbly restored and is open in addition to the old hall, the carp-filled moat and the superb 1930s garden, with its marvellous London views.

Horniman Museum ㉑

100 London Rd SE23. [020-8699 1872. ⇌ Forest Hill. **Gardens open** 8am–dusk daily. **Museum open** 10.30am–5.30pm Mon–Sat, 2–5.30pm Sun. **Closed** 24–26 Dec. ⬜ ⬜ ⬜ **Concerts, lectures, events**.

F REDERICK HORNIMAN, the tea merchant, had this museum built in 1901 to house the curios he had collected on his travels. It has a distinctly Victorian feel, from the inspirational mosaic on the front (representing Humanity in the House of Circumstance) to the overstuffed walrus inside. As you would expect, there is also an exhibition of tea-making paraphernalia.

Dulwich Picture Gallery ㉒

College Rd SE21. [020-8693 8000. ⇌ West Dulwich, North Dulwich. **Open** 10am–5pm Tue–Fri, 11am–5pm Sat, 2–5pm Sun (last adm: 4.45pm). **Closed** all public hols except Bank Holiday Mondays. **Adm charge.** ⬜ ⬜ ⬜ ⬜ ⬜ **Concerts, events, lectures, art classes.**

E NGLAND'S OLDEST public art gallery, it was opened in 1817 and designed by Sir John Soane (see pp136–7). Its imaginative use of skylights

Rembrandt's *Jacob II de Gheyn* **at Dulwich Picture Gallery**

made it the prototype of most art galleries built since. The gallery was commissioned to house the collection of nearby Dulwich College. (The College, by Charles Barry, was opened in 1870.).

This superb collection has works by Rembrandt (whose *Jacob II de Gheyn* has been stolen from here four times), Canaletto, Poussin, Watteau, Claude, Murillo and Raphael.

The building houses Soane's mausoleum to Desenfans and Bourgeois, original founders of the collection.

Tennis racket and net from 1888, Wimbledon Lawn Tennis Museum

Battersea Park ㉓

Albert Bridge Rd SW11. **Map** 19 C5. **(** 020-8871 7530. **⊖** *Sloane Square then bus 137.* **⊟** *Battersea Park.* **Open** *dawn–dusk daily.* 🅿 ♿ **Horticultural Therapy Garden (** 0171-720 2212. 🖼 **Events.** See **Three Guided Walks** pp266–7.

Peace Pagoda, Battersea Park

THIS WAS THE second public park created to relieve the growing urban stresses on Victorian Londoners (the first was Victoria Park in the East End). It opened in 1858 on the former Battersea Fields – a swampy area notorious for every kind of vice, centred around the Old Red House, a disreputable pub.

The new park immediately became popular, especially for its man-made boating lake, with its romantic rocks, gardens and waterfalls. Later it became a great site for the new craze of cycling.

In 1985 a peace pagoda – one of more than 70 built throughout the world – was opened in the park. Buddhist nuns and monks took 11 months to complete the 35-m (100-ft) high monument.

St Mary's, Battersea ㉔

Battersea Church Rd SW11. **(** 020-7228 9648. **⊖** *Sloane Square then bus 19 or 219.* **Open** *noon–3pm Tue & Wed, or by prior arrangement.* 🕐 *11am, 6.30pm Sun.* 🅿 **Concerts.**

THERE HAS BEEN a church here since at least the 10th century. The present brick building dates from 1775; but the 17th-century stained glass, commemorating Tudor monarchs, comes from the former church.

In 1782 the poet and artist William Blake was married in the church to the daughter of a Battersea market gardener. Later J M W Turner was to paint some of his marvellous views of the Thames from the church tower. Nearby is Old Battersea House (1699).

Wimbledon Lawn Tennis Museum ㉕

Church Rd SW19. **(** 020-8946 6131. **⊖** *Southfields.* **Open** *10.am–5pm daily (not during Championships except to ticket holders).* **Closed** *Good Fri, 25 Dec, 1 Jan.* **Adm charge.** ♿ 🖼 🅿 **Exhibitions.**

EVEN THOSE with only a passing interest in the sport will find plenty to enjoy at this lively museum. It traces tennis's development from its invention in the 1860s as a diversion for country house parties, to the sport it is today. Alongside strange 19th-century equipment are film clips showing the great players of the past. More recent matches may be viewed in the video theatre.

Wimbledon Windmill Museum ㉖

Windmill Rd SW19. **(** 020-8947 2825. **⊖** *Wimbledon then 30-min walk.* **Open** *Easter–31 Oct: 2–5pm Sat–Sun.* **Closed** *1 Nov–Easter (except groups, by arrangement).* **Adm charge.** 🅿 🖼 🅿 🖼 *by arrangement.*

THE MILL on Wimbledon Common was built in 1817. The building at its base was converted into cottages in 1864. Lord Baden-Powell, founder of the Boy Scouts, lived in the mill house. Now the site is a windmill museum.

St Mary's, Battersea

West of the Centre

Ham House

Richmond Park 🟤

Kingston Vale SW15. 📞 020-8948 3209. 🔵 🚆 Richmond then bus 65 or 71. **Open** Oct–Mar: 7.30am–dusk daily; Apr–Sep: 7am–dusk daily. **Fishing, golf, riding, cycling**.

Deer in Richmond Park

CHARLES I, WHEN he was Prince of Wales in 1637, built a wall 8 miles (13 km) round to enclose the royal park as a hunting ground. Deer still graze warily among the chestnuts, birches and oaks, no longer hunted but still discreetly culled. They have learned to co-exist with the many thousands of human visitors who stroll here on fine weekends.

In late spring the highlight is the Isabella Plantation with its spectacular display of rhododendrons, while the nearby Pen Ponds are very popular with optimistic anglers. (Adam's Pond is for model boats.) The rest of the park is heath, bracken and trees. Richmond Gate, in the northwest corner, was designed by the landscape gardener Capability Brown in 1798. Nearby is Henry VIII Mound, where in 1536 the

king, staying in Richmond Palace, awaited the signal that his former wife, Anne Boleyn, had been executed. The Palladian White Lodge, built for George II in 1729, is home to the Royal Ballet School.

Hampton Court 🟤

See pp254–7.

Ham House 🟤

Ham St, Richmond. 📞 020-8940 1950. 🔵 🚆 Richmond then bus 65 or 371. **Open** Apr–Oct: 1–5pm Sat–Wed. **Closed** Nov–Mar. **Adm charge**. ♿ 📷 by prior arrangement only. 🍴 🏠

THIS MAGNIFICENT HOUSE by the Thames was built in 1610 but had its heyday later, when it was the home of the Duke of Lauderdale, confidant to Charles II and Secretary of

Marble Hill House

State for Scotland. His wife, the Countess of Dysart, inherited the house from her father who had been Charles I's "whipping boy" – meaning that he was punished for the future king's misdemeanours. From 1672 the Duke and Countess started to modernize the house, and it was soon regarded as one of the finest in Britain. The diarist John Evelyn admired their garden, which has now been restored to its 17th-century form.

On some days in summer, a foot passenger ferry runs from here to Marble Hill House and Orleans House at Twickenham.

Orleans House 🟤

Orleans Rd, Twickenham. 📞 020-8892 0221. 🔵 🚆 Richmond then bus 33, 90, 290, R68 or R70. **Open** Apr–Sep: 1–5.30pm Tue–Sat, 2–5.30pm Sun, public hols. Oct–Mar: 1.30–4.30pm Tue–Sat, 2–4.30pm Sun, public hols. **Closed** 24–26 Dec, Good Fri. ♿ restricted. 🏠 **Concerts, lectures**.

ONLY THE OCTAGON, designed by James Gibbs for James Johnson in 1720, remains of this early 18th-century house. It is named after Louis Philippe, the exiled Duke of Orleans, who lived here between 1800 and 1817, before becoming king of France in 1830. The lively interior plasterwork of the Octagon still remains intact. The adjacent gallery shows temporary exhibitions, and these include some local history displays of the area.

Marble Hill House 🟤

Richmond Rd, Twickenham. 📞 020-8892 5115. 🔵 🚆 Richmond then bus 33, 90, 290, R68 or R70. **Open** Apr–Sep: 10am–6pm daily; Oct–Mar: 10am–4pm daily. **Closed** 24–26 Dec. 📷 ♿ restricted. 🏠 🍴 🏠 **Concerts, fireworks** on summer weekends. See **Entertainment** p331.

BUILT IN 1729 for George II's mistress, the house and its grounds have been open to the public since 1903. It has now been largely restored to its

Georgian appearance, but is not yet fully furnished. There are paintings by William Hogarth and a view of the river and house in 1762 by Richard Wilson, who is regarded as the father of English landscape painting.

Richmond ㉜

SW15. 🚇 🚊 *Richmond.*

Richmond side street

T HIS ATTRACTIVE London village took its name from the palace that Henry VII built here in 1500. Many early 18th-century houses survive near the river and off Richmond Hill, notably Maids of Honour Row, which was built in 1724. The beautiful view of the river from the top of the hill has been captured by many artists, and is largely unspoiled.

Syon House ㉝

London Rd, Brentford. 📞 020-8560 0881. 🚇 *Gunnersbury then bus 237 or 267.* **House open** *mid-Mar–Oct: 11am–5pm Wed–Thu, Sun (last adm 4.15pm).* **House closed** *Nov–mid-Mar.* **Gardens open** *10am–6pm (or dusk, whichever is earlier) daily.* **Adm charge**. 🚫 🚻 *to gardens only.* ⬛ ⬛ ⬛ ⬛

T HE EARLS and Dukes of Northumberland have lived here for 400 years – it is the only large mansion in the entire London area still in its

hereditary ownership. The outbuildings accommodate a butterfly house, an art centre, a garden centre, a National Trust souvenir and gift shop and two restaurants. The house itself will always be the star exhibit, with lavish interiors by Robert Adam. Some rooms even have Spitalfields silk wall-hangings and there are many beautiful pictures. The tranquil gardens include a rosarium and an enchanting conservatory which was built in 1830.

Musical Museum ㉞

368 High St, Brentford. 📞 020-8560 8108. 🚇 *Gunnersbury, South Ealing then bus 65, 237 or 267.* **Open** *Apr–Jun, Sep–Oct: 2–5pm Sat, Sun; Jul & Aug: 2–4pm Wed–Fri, Sat, Sun; 2–5pm.* **Closed** *Nov–Mar.* **Adm charge**. 🔲 🚻 🚫 🔲

T HE COLLECTION comprises chiefly large instruments, including player (or automatic) pianos and organs, miniature and cinema pianos, and what is thought to be the only surviving self-playing Wurlitzer organ in Europe.

Drawing room: Osterley Park House

Osterley Park House ㉟

Isleworth. 📞 020-8560 3918. 🚇 *Osterley.* **Open** *1–4.30pm Wed–Sun (last adm: 4pm).* **Closed** *1 Nov –31 Mar, Good Fri.* 🔲 🔲 **Garden open** *9am–dusk.*

O STERLEY is ranked among Robert Adam's finest works, and its colonnaded portico and multi-coloured library ceiling are the proof. Much of the furniture was designed by Adam, and the garden and its temple are by William Chambers, architect of Somerset House *(see p117).* The greenhouse is by Adam.

Robert Adam's red drawing room at Syon House

Hampton Court ㉗

CARDINAL WOLSEY, powerful Archbishop of York to Henry VIII, began building Hampton Court in 1514. Originally it was not a royal palace, but was

Ceiling decoration from the Queen's Drawing Room intended as Wolsey's riverside country residence. Later, in 1525, in the

hope of retaining royal favour, Wolsey offered it to the king. After the royal takeover, Hampton Court was twice rebuilt and extended, first by Henry himself and then, in the 1690s, by William and Mary, who employed Christopher Wren as architect.

There is a striking contrast between Wren's Classical royal apartments and the Tudor turrets, gables and chimneys elsewhere. The inspiration for the gardens as they are today comes largely from the time of William and Mary, for whom Wren created a vast, formal Baroque landscape, with radiating avenues of majestic limes and many collections of exotic plants.

★ The Maze
Lose yourself in one of the garden's most popular features.

Royal tennis court

Main entrance

River Thames

★ The Great Vine
The vine was planted in 1768, and, in the 19th century, produced up to 910 kg (2,000 lbs) of black grapes.

The Pond Garden
This sunken water garden was part of Henry VIII's elaborate designs.

Privy Garden

River boat pier

★ The Mantegna Gallery
Andrea Mantegna's nine canvases depicting The Triumph of Julius Caesar *(1490s) are housed here.*

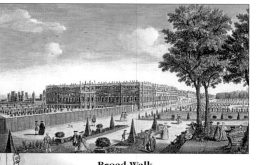

Broad Walk
A contemporary print shows the East Front and the Broad Walk during the reign of George II (1727–60).

Long Water
A man-made lake runs parallel to the Thames, from the Fountain Garden across the Home Park.

Fountain Garden
A few of the clipped yews here were planted in the reign of William and Mary.

The East Front
The windows of the Queen's Drawing Room, designed by Wren, overlook the central avenue of the Fountain Garden.

STAR FEATURES

★ **The Great Vine**

★ **The Mantegna Gallery**

★ **The Maze**

Exploring the Palace

Carving on the roof of the Great Hall

AS AN HISTORIC royal palace, Hampton Court bears traces of many of the kings and queens of England from Henry VIII to the present day. The building itself is an harmonious blend of Tudor and English Baroque architecture. Inside, visitors can see the Great Hall, built by Henry VIII, as well as state apartments of the Tudor court. Many of the state apartments, including those above Fountain Court by Christopher Wren, are decorated with furniture, tapestries and old masters from the Royal Collection.

Tudor Chimneys
Ornate chimneys, some original, some careful restorations, adorn the roof of the Tudor palace.

Queen's Presence Chamber

Queen's Guard Chamber

★ Chapel Royal
The Tudor chapel was fitted by Wren except for the carved and gilded vaulted ceiling.

Haunted gallery

★ Great Hall
The stained-glass window in the Tudor Great Hall shows Henry VIII flanked by the coats of arms of his six wives.

STAR FEATURES

★ **Great Hall**

★ **Fountain Court**

★ **Clock Court**

★ **Chapel Royal**

★ Clock Court
Anne Boleyn's Gateway is at the entrance to Clock Court. The Astronomical Clock, created for Henry VIII in 1540, is also located here.

King's Great Bedchamber
William III bought the crimson bed from his Lord Chamberlain.

Wren's east facade

Queen's Gallery
This marble chimneypiece by John Nost adorns the Queen's Gallery, where entertainments were often staged.

CARDINAL WOLSEY
Thomas Wolsey (c.1475–1530), simultaneously a cardinal, Archbishop of York and chancellor, was, after the king, the most powerful man in England. However, when he was unable to persuade the pope to allow Henry VIII to divorce his first wife, Catherine of Aragon, Wolsey fell from royal favour. He died while making his way to face trial for treason.

★ **Fountain Court**
The windows of state apartments are visible above the cloisters of Fountain Court.

King's Staircase
Leading to the state apartments, the King's Staircase has wall paintings by Antonio Verrio.

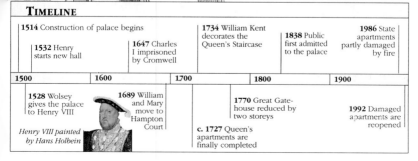

TIMELINE

1500	1600	1700	1800	1900
1514 Construction of palace begins		**1734** William Kent decorates the Queen's Staircase	**1838** Public first admitted to the palace	**1986** State apartments partly damaged by fire
1532 Henry starts new hall	**1647** Charles I imprisoned by Cromwell			
1528 Wolsey gives the palace to Henry VIII	**1689** William and Mary move to Hampton Court	**1770** Great Gatehouse reduced by two storeys		**1992** Damaged apartments are reopened
Henry VIII painted by Hans Holbein		**c. 1727** Queen's apartments are finally completed		

Pitshanger Manor and Gallery ㊱

Mattock Lane W5. ☎ 020-8567 1227. ⊖ *Ealing Broadway.* **Open** *10am–5pm Tue–Sat.* **Closed** *public hols.* 📷 ♿ *Exhibitions, concerts, lectures.*

S IR JOHN SOANE, architect of the Bank of England *(see p147)*, designed this house on the site of an earlier one. Completed in 1803 it was to become his own country residence. There are clear echoes of his elaborately constructed town house in Lincoln's Inn Fields *(see pp136–7)*, especially in the library, with its imaginative use of mirrors, in the darkly-painted breakfast room opposite and in the "monk's dining room" which is located on the basement level.

Soane retained two of the principal formal rooms: the drawing room and the dining room. These were designed in 1768 by George Dance the Younger, with whom Soane had worked before establishing his own reputation.

A sympathetic 20th-century extension has been refurbished as a gallery offering a wide range of contemporary art exhibitions and associated events.

The house also contains a large exhibition of Martinware, highly decorated glazed pottery made in nearby Southall between 1877 and

Martinware bird at Pitshanger Manor

1915 and fashionable in late Victorian times. The gardens of Pitshanger Manor are now a pleasant public park and provide a welcome contrast to the bustle of nearby Ealing.

Kew Bridge Steam Museum ㊲

Green Dragon Lane, Brentford. ☎ 020-8568 4757. ⊖ *Kew Bridge, Gunnersbury then bus 237 or 267.* **Open** *11am–5pm daily.* **Closed** *week to Christmas, Good Fri.* **Adm charge.** 📷 ♿ 🖥 🚻 🎁 *book in advance.*

T HE 19TH-CENTURY water pumping station, near the north end of Kew Bridge, is now a museum of steam power. Its chief exhibits are five giant Cornish beam engines which used to pump the water here from the river, to be distributed throughout London. The earliest engines, which date from 1820, were designed to pump water out of the Cornish tin and copper mines. See them in operation at weekends and on public holidays.

Kew Gardens ㊳

See pp260–1.

City Barge: Strand on the Green

Strand on the Green ㊵

W4. ⊖ *Gunnersbury then bus 237 or 267.*

T HIS CHARMING Thames-side walk passes some fine 18th-century houses as well as rows of more modest cottages once inhabited by fishermen. The oldest of its three pubs is the City Barge *(see pp308–9)*, parts of which date from the 15th century: the name is older and derives from when the Lord Mayor's barge was moored on the Thames outside.

Chiswick House ㊴

Burlington Lane W4. ☎ 020-8995 0508. ⊖ *Chiswick.* **Open** *Easter–Oct: 10am–6pm daily; Nov–Good Friday: 10am–4pm Wed–Sun.* **Adm charge.** ✗ 🖥 🎁

C OMPLETED IN 1729 to the design of the third Earl of Burlington, this is a textbook example of a Palladian villa. Burlington revered both Palladio and his disciple Inigo

Chiswick House

Jones, and their statues stand outside. Built round a central octagonal room, the house is packed with references to ancient Rome and Palladian devices, such as rooms whose dimensions form perfect cubes.

Chiswick was Burlington's country residence and this house was built as an annexe to a larger, older house, which was later demolished. It was designed for recreation and entertaining – Lord Hervey, Burlington's enemy, dismissed it as "too little to live in and too big to hang on a watch chain". Some of the ceiling paintings are by William Kent, who also laid out the gardens.

The house was a private mental home from 1892 until 1928 when a long process of restoration began. The restorers are still searching for pieces of its original furniture, but the layout of the garden, now a public park, is much as Kent designed it.

Hogarth's House ❹

Hogarth Lane, W4. **☎** *020-8994 6757.* **🚇** *Turnham Green.* **Open** *Apr–Oct: 1–5pm Tue–Fri, 1–6pm Sat, Sun; Nov–Dec & Feb–Mar: 1–4pm Tue–Fri, 1–5pm Sat, Sun.* **Closed** *Jan.* 🖥 📷 **♿** *ground floor only.* 🚻

W HEN THE PAINTER William Hogarth lived here from 1749 until his death in 1764, he called it "a little country box by the Thames" and painted bucolic views from its windows – he had moved from Leicester Square *(see*

Tudor entrance to Fulham Palace

p103). Today heavy traffic roars by along the Great West Road, on its way to and from Heathrow Airport – rush hour traffic is also notoriously bad here. In an environment as hostile as this, and following years of neglect and then bombing during World War II, the house has done well to survive. It has now been turned into a small museum and gallery, which is filled mostly with a collection of engraved copies of the moralistic cartoon-style pictures with which Hogarth made his name. Salutary tales, such as *The Rake's Progress* (in Sir John Soane's Museum – *see pp136–7), Marriage à la Mode, An Election Entertainment* and many others, can all be seen here.

WILLIAM HOGARTH
Painter & Engraver
1697–1764
LIVED AND WORKED HERE FOR 15 YEARS
COUNTY OF MIDDLESEX

Plaque on Hogarth's House

Fulham Palace ❹

Bishop's Ave SW6. **☎** *020-7736 3233.* **🚇** *Putney Bridge.* **Open** *Wed–Sun, public hol Mon, Mar–Oct: 2–5pm; Nov–Mar: 1–4pm Thu–Sun.* **Closed** *Good Fri, 25–26 Dec.* **Park open** *daylight hrs.* **Adm charge** *for museum.* **♿** 📷 🅿 🚻 **Events, concerts, lectures.**

T HE HOME of the Bishops of London from the 8th century until 1973, the oldest parts of Fulham Palace date from the 15th century. The rest of the building has been embellished in a mixture of styles by successive bishops. The palace stands in its own gardens northwest of Putney Bridge, where the annual Oxford versus Cambridge Boat Race begins *(see p56).*

1940s wind-up cycle, London Toy and Model Museum

Chelsea Harbour ❹

SW10. **🚇** *Fulham Broadway.* **♿** **Exhibitions.** 🖥 🚻

T HIS IS AN impressive development of modern apartments, shops, offices, restaurants, a hotel and a marina. It is near the site of Cremorne Pleasure Gardens, which closed in 1877 after more than 40 years as a venue for dances and circuses. The centrepiece is the Belvedere, a 20-storey apartment tower with an external glass lift and pyramid roof, topped with a golden ball on a rod that rises and falls with the tide.

London Toy And Model Museum ❹

21–23 Craven Hill W2. **Map** 10 E2. **🔲** *020-7402 5222.* **🚇** *Paddington.* **Open** *9am–5.30pm daily (last adm 4.30pm).* **Closed** *25–26 Dec, 1 Jan.* **Adm charge.** 🅿 *by arrangement only.* 🖥 **♿** 🚻

A N ENORMOUS NUMBER of toys models and dolls, dating from the 18th century up to the present, are crammed into this house near Paddington station. There is a room of model trains and another of cars; a teddy bears' picnic; and dolls' houses, the biggest of which is 2.4 m (8 ft) long and has 16 rooms. In the garden are a carousel and two model railways, one of which offers rides. The museum provides many delights and activities for children, and much nostalgia for adults.

Kew Gardens ⓸

THE ROYAL BOTANIC GARDENS at Kew are the most complete public gardens in the world. Their reputation was first established by Sir Joseph Banks, the British naturalist and plant hunter, who worked here in the late 18th century. In 1841 the former royal gardens were given to the nation and now display about 40,000 different kinds of plant. Kew is also a centre for scholarly research into horticulture and botany and garden enthusiasts will want a full day for their visit.

Princess Augusta
King George III's mother established the first garden on a nine-acre (3.6 ha) site here in 1759.

Queen Charlotte's Cottage

★ **Temperate House**
The building dates from 1899. Delicate woody plants are arranged here according to their geographical origins.

★ **Pagoda**
Britain's fascination with the Orient influenced William Chambers's pagoda, built in 1762.

HIGHLIGHTS

Spring
Flowering cherries ①
Crocus "carpet" ②

Summer
Rock Garden ③
Rose Garden ④

Autumn
Autumn foliage ⑤

Winter
Alpine House ⑥
Witch Hazels ⑦

Lion Gate entrance

Evolution House
gives a detailed history of plant life on Earth.

Flagpole

Marianne North Gallery
The Victorian flower painter, Marianne North, gave her works to Kew and paid for this gallery of 1882.

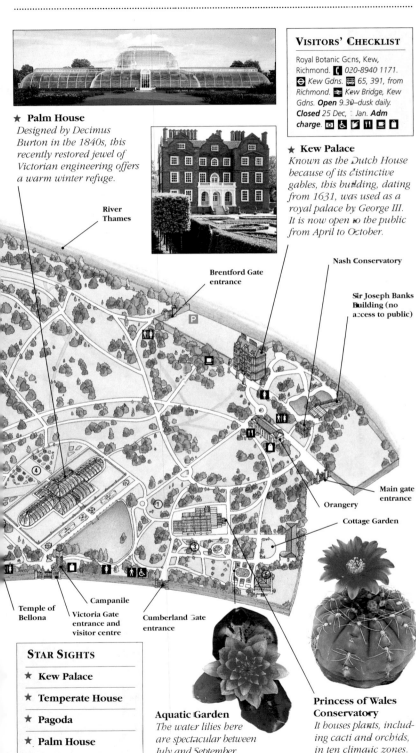

★ Palm House
Designed by Decimus Burton in the 1840s, this recently restored jewel of Victorian engineering offers a warm winter refuge.

River Thames

★ Kew Palace
Known as the Dutch House because of its distinctive gables, this building, dating from 1631, was used as a royal palace by George III. It is now open to the public from April to October.

Brentford Gate entrance

Nash Conservatory

Sir Joseph Banks Building (no access to public)

Main gate entrance

Orangery

Cottage Garden

Temple of Bellona

Campanile

Victoria Gate entrance and visitor centre

Cumberland Gate entrance

Aquatic Garden
The water lilies here are spectacular between July and September.

Princess of Wales Conservatory
It houses plants, including cacti and orchids, in ten climatic zones.

THREE GUIDED WALKS

LONDON IS AN EXCELLENT city for walkers. Although it is much more spread out than most European capitals, many of the main tourist attractions are fairly close to each other *(see pp12–13)*. Central London is full of parks and gardens *(see pp48–51)*, and there are also several walk routes planned by the tourist board and local history societies. These include footpaths along canals and the Thames, and the Silver Jubilee Walk. Planned in 1977 to commemorate the Queen's Silver Jubilee, the walk runs for 12 miles (19 km) between Lambeth Bridge in the west and Tower Bridge in the east; the London Tourist Board *(see p345)* has maps of the route, which is marked by silver-coloured plaques placed at intervals on the pavement.

Statue of boy and dolphin in Regent's Park

Each of the 16 areas described in the *Area-by-Area* section of this book has a short walk marked on its *Street-by-Street* map. These walks will take you past many of the most interesting sights in that area. On the following six pages are routes for three walks that take you through areas of London not covered in detail elsewhere. These range from the bustling, fashionable King's Road *(see pp266–7)* to the wide open spaces of riverside Richmond and Kew *(see pp268–9)*.

Several companies offer guided walks *(see below)*. Most of these have themes, such as ghosts or Shakespeare's London. Look in listings magazines *(see p324)* for details.

Useful numbers The Original London Walks
020-7624 3978. City Walks 020-7700 6931.

CHOOSING A WALK

The Three Walks
This map shows the location of the three guided walks in relation to the main sightseeing areas of London.

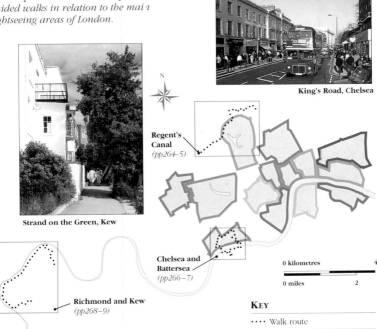

King's Road, Chelsea

Strand on the Green, Kew

Regent's Canal
(pp264–5)

Chelsea and Battersea
(pp266–7)

Richmond and Kew
(pp268–9)

0 kilometres   4

0 miles   2

KEY

···· Walk route

Houseboats on Regent's Canal, Little Venice

A Two-Hour Walk along the Regent's Canal

MASTER BUILDER John Nash wanted the Regent's Canal to pass through Regent's Park, but instead it circles north of the park. Opened in 1820, it is long defunct as a commercial waterway but is today a valuable leisure amenity. This walk starts at Little Venice and ends at Camden Lock market, diverting briefly to take in the view from Primrose Hill. For more details on the sights near the Regent's Canal, see pages 216–23.

Houseboat on the canal ③

From Little Venice to Lisson Grove

At Warwick Avenue station ① take the left-hand exit and walk straight to the traffic lights by the canal bridge at Blomfield Road. Turn right and descend to the canal through an iron gate ② opposite No. 42, marked "Lady Rose of Regent". The pretty basin with moored narrow boats is Little Venice ③. At the foot of the steps turn left to walk back beneath the blue iron bridge ④. You soon have to climb up to street level again because this stretch of the towpath is reserved for access to the

The Warwick Castle, near Warwick Avenue

barges. Cross Edgware Road and walk down Aberdeen Place. When the road turns to the left by a pub, Crockers ⑤, follow the signposted Canal Way down to the right of some modern flats. Continue your route along the canal towpath, crossing Park Road at street level. The scenery along this stretch is unremarkable, but it is not long before a splash of green to your right announces that you are now walking alongside Regent's Park ⑥.

Houseboats moored at Little Venice ③

TIPS FOR WALKERS

Starting point: Warwick Avenue Underground station.
Length: 3 miles (5 km).
Getting there: Warwick Avenue and Camden Town Underground stations are at either end of the walk. Buses 16, 16A and 98 go to Warwick Avenue; 24, 29 and 31 go to Camden Town.
Stopping-off points: Crockers, Queens and The Princess of Wales (corner of Fitzroy and Chalcot Roads) are good pubs. At the junction of Edgware Road and Aberdeen Place is Café La Ville. Camden Town has many cafés, restaurants and sandwich shops.

KEY

— Walk route

⁂ Good viewing point

🚇 Underground station

🚆 Railway station

(Map showing route through Maida Vale, St John's Wood, Edgware Road, Lisson Grove and surrounding streets)

0 metres   500
0 yards   500

Regent's Park

Soon you see four mansions ⑦. A bridge on huge pillars marked "Coalbrookdale" ⑧ carries Avenue Road into the park. Cross the next bridge, with London Zoo ⑨ on your right, then turn left up a slope. A few steps later, take the right fork, and turn left to cross Prince Albert Road. Turn right before entering Primrose Hill through a gate ⑩ on your left.

Mansion with riverside gardens ⑦

Primrose Lodge, Primrose Hill ⑩

Primrose Hill

From here there is a view of the zoo aviary ⑪, designed by Lord Snowdon and opened in 1965. Inside the park, keep to the left-hand path that climbs to the top of the hill. Soon you fork right to the summit, which offers a fine view of the city skyline. A viewing panel ⑫ helps identify the landmarks but it does not include the 1990 skyscraper at Canary Wharf, with its pyramid crown, on the left. Descend on the left, making for the park gate at the junction of Regent's Park Road and Primrose Hill Road.

Indoor market, Camden Lock ⑲

Towards Camden

Almost opposite the gate is the Queens ⑬, a Victorian pub and, just to the left, is No. 122 Regent's Park Road ⑭. This was for 24 years the home of the communist philosopher Friedrich Engels; he was often visited there by his friend Karl Marx.

Turn right and walk down Regent's Park Road for 135 m (150 yd) then turn left up Fitzroy Road. On the right, between Nos. 41 and 39, is

the entrance to Primrose Hill Studios ⑮, built in 1882. Residents have included the musician Sir Henry Wood and illustrator Arthur Rackham, famous for his fairy pictures.

Continue down Fitzroy Road past No. 23 ⑯, once home to the poet W B Yeats, then go right into Chalcot Road and left down Princess Road, past a Victorian board school ⑰. Turn right and rejoin the canal down steps across Gloucester Avenue. Turn left under the railway bridge and past the Pirate Castle ⑱, a water sports centre. Cross a hump bridge and enter Camden Lock Market ⑲ *(see p.322)* through an arch on your left. After browsing there you can take the water bus ⑳ back to Little Venice or turn right into Chalk Farm Road and walk up to Camden Town Underground station.

Pedestrian bridge over the canal at Camden Lock ⑲

A Three-Hour Walk in Chelsea and Battersea

Royal Hospital ③

T HIS DELIGHTFUL CIRCULAR WALK ambles through the grounds of the Royal Hospital and across the river to Battersea Park, with its romantic Victorian land-scaping. It then returns to the narrow village streets of Chelsea and the stylish shops on the King's Road. For more details on the sights in Chelsea see pages 188–93.

Sloane Square to Battersea Park

From the station ①, turn left and walk down Holbein Place. The Renaissance painter's connection with Chelsea stems from his friendship with Sir Thomas More who lived nearby. Pass the cluster of good antique shops ② as you turn on to Royal Hospital Road. Enter the

grounds of the Royal Hospital ③, designed by Christopher Wren, and turn left into the informal Ranelagh Gardens ④. The small pavilion by John Soane ⑤ displays a history of the gardens as a Georgian pleasure resort – it was the most fashionable meeting place for London society.

Galleon on Chelsea Bridge

Charles II statue in Royal Hospital ⑥

LING CHARLES II

Leave the gardens for fine views of the hospital and Grinling Gibbons's bronze of Charles II ⑥. The granite obelisk ⑦ commemorates the 1849 battle at Chilianwalla, in what is now Pakistan, and forms the centre-piece of the main marquee at the Chelsea Flower Show *(see p56)*.

Battersea Park

When crossing the Chelsea Bridge ⑧ (1937), look up at the four gilded galleons on top of the pillars at each end. Turn into Battersea Park ⑨ *(see p247)*, one of London's liveliest, and follow the main path along the river to enjoy the excellent views of Chelsea. Turn left at the exotic Buddhist Peace Pagoda ⑩ to the main part of the park.

Past the bowling greens lies Henry Moore's carving of *Three Standing Figures* ⑪ (1948) and the lake, a favoured spot for wildfowl. (There are boats for hire.) Just beyond the sculpture head northwest and, after crossing the central avenue, fork right and make for the wooden gate into the rustic Old English Garden ⑫. Leave the garden by the metal gate and return to Chelsea via the Victorian Albert Bridge ⑬.

***Three Standing Figures* by Henry Moore ⑪**

KEY

— Walk route

✲ Good viewing point

Ⓔ Underground station

TIPS FOR WALKERS

Starting point: Sloane Square.
Length: 4 miles (6.5 km).
Getting there: Sloane Square is the nearest tube. There are frequent buses 11, 19, 22 and 349 to Sloane Square and along the King's Road.
Royal Hospital Grounds are open only 10am–6pm Mon–Sat, 2–6pm Sun.
Stopping-off points: There is a café in Battersea Park, by the lake. The King's Head and Eight Bells, on Cheyne Walk, is a well known local pub. There are several other pubs, restaurants and sandwich shops to be found along the King's Road. The Chelsea Farmers' Market on Sydney Street has several cafés.

Old English Garden in Battersea Park ⑫

Albert Bridge ⑬

much of its original character. Where Glebe Place meets the King's Road are three pretty, early 18th-century houses ㉓. Cross Dovehouse Green opposite (it used to be a burial ground), to Chelsea Farmers' Market ㉔, an enclave of cafés and craft shops.

The King's Road

Leave the market on Sydney Street and cross into the garden of St Luke's Church ㉕, where the writer Charles Dickens was married. The walk then winds through pretty back streets until it rejoins the King's Road ㉖ *(see p192)*, which was very fashionable in the 1960s. On the left is The Pheasantry ㉗. Look down the side streets on both left and right to see the squares and terraces: Wellington Square ㉘, then Royal Avenue ㉙, intended as a triumphal way to the Royal Hospital, and Blacklands Terrace ㉚, where book-lovers will want to visit John Sandoe's shop. The Duke of York's Territorial Headquarters ㉛ (1803) on the right marks the approach to Sloane Square ㉜ and the Royal Court Theatre *(see Sloane Square p193).*

Thomas Carlyle statue ⑮

The Back Streets of Chelsea

Over the bridge is David Wynne's sculpture of a boy and dolphin ⑭ (1975). Pass the sought-after residences on Cheyne Walk and the statues of historian Thomas Carlyle ⑮, and Sir Thomas More ⑯. The area was renowned for gatherings of intellectuals. Past Chelsea Old Church ⑰ is Roper's Gardens ⑱ with

its carving by Jacob Epstein. Just beyond these is the old, medieval Crosby Hall ⑲. Justice Walk ⑳ has a nice view of two early Georgian houses – Duke's House and Monmouth House. Turn left to pass the site of the Chelsea porcelain factory ㉑, which used to make highly fashionable (and today very highly collectable) wares in the late 18th century. Glebe Place ㉒ has retained

Royal Court Theatre ㉜

A 90-Minute Walk around Richmond and Kew

THIS DELIGHTFUL RIVERSIDE walk begins in historic Richmond by the remains of Henry VII's once-splendid palace and ends at Kew, Britain's premier botanic garden. For more details on the sights in Richmond and Kew, turn to pages 248–54.

The river at low tide

Richmond Green

From Richmond station ①, proceed to Oriel House ②, which is practically opposite. Take the alleyway beneath it, and turn left towards the red-brick and terracotta Richmond Theatre ③, built in 1899. The remarkable Edmund Kean, whose brief, meteoric career in the early 19th century had a lasting impact on English acting, was closely associated with the previous theatre on the site. Opposite is Richmond Green ④. Cross it diagonally and go through the entrance arch ⑤ of the old Tudor palace, which is adorned with the arms of Henry VII.

Old Palace: carving over entrance ⑤

remnants, much modified, of the 16th-century buildings.

Leave Old Palace Yard at the right-hand corner ⑥, following a sign "To the River", and turn left to pass the White Swan pub ⑦. At the river, go right along the towpath under the iron railway bridge and then the concrete Twickenham Bridge ⑧, completed in 1933, to reach Richmond Lock ⑨, with its cast-iron footbridge built in 1894. The Thames is tidal as far as Teddington, some 3 miles (5 km) upstream, and the lock is used to make the river continuously navigable.

The Riverside

Do not cross the bridge but continue along the wooded path by the river to Isleworth Ait ⑩, a large island where herons may be standing warily on the river bank. Just beyond it, on the far shore, is All Saints' Church ⑪, where the 15th-century tower has survived several rebuildings, most recently in the 1960s. Further round the inlet, Isleworth ⑫, once a small riverside village with a busy harbour, is now a dormitory for central London. Here there will be river traffic to watch: barges, yachts and, in summer, the passenger boats that ply up-river to Hampton Court (see pp60–1). Rowers are out at most times of year, training for races and regattas. The most prestigious occasions are the Henley Regatta in July and the Oxford v Cambridge boat race, every spring from Putney to Mortlake (see p56).

Richmond Theatre ③

Richmond

Richmond owes much of its importance – as well as its name – to Henry, victor of the Wars of the Roses and the first Tudor monarch. On becoming king in 1485 he spent a lot of time at an earlier residence on this site, Sheen Palace, dating from the 12th century. The palace burned down in 1499 and Henry had it rebuilt, naming it Richmond after the town in Yorkshire where he held an earldom. In 1603 Henry's daughter, Elizabeth I, died here. The houses inside the archway on the left contain

Herons fish the river

THE AVENUE

KEY

—	Walk route
☀	Good viewing point
⊖	Underground station
⊟	Railway station

Kew

After a while the appearance of iron railings on your right marks where Old Deer Park ⑬ turns into Kew Gardens ⑭ (more correctly the Royal Botanic Gardens – *see pp260–1*). There used to be a riverside entrance for visitors arriving on foot or by water, but the gate ⑮ is now

Kew Palace in Kew Gardens ⑲

Just beyond are modern waterside apartments at Brentford ⑰. This was originally an industrial suburb, sited where the Grand Union Canal runs into the Thames, and its residential potential has only recently been exploited. You can pick out the tall chimney of the waterworks ⑱, now a museum dedicated to steam power. On the right, behind the Kew Gardens car park, there is soon a view of Kew Palace ⑲, a gloomy edifice in red brick built in 1631.

Beyond the car park, leave the river by Ferry Lane on to Kew Green ⑳. Now you could spend the rest of the day in Kew Gardens or cross Kew Bridge and turn right on to Strand on the Green ㉑, a fine riverside walkway with atmospheric pubs, the oldest of them the City Barge ㉒ *(see p258)*. Head south down Kew Road if you need to get back, then turn left at Kew Gardens Road to depart from Kew Gardens underground station (District line).

TIPS FOR WALKERS

Starting point: Richmond station.
Length: 3 miles (5 km).
Getting there: Richmond Underground or railway station. Bus 415 comes from Victoria, 391 and R68 from Kew.
Stopping-off points: There are many cafés, pubs and tearooms in Richmond. The famous Maids of Honour tearoom is at Kew, as is Jasper's Bun in the Oven, a good restaurant.

Steam Museum ⑱

| 0 metres | 500 |
| 0 yards | 500 |

closed and the nearest entrance is to the north, near the car park.

Across the river, there are magnificent views of Syon House ⑯, seat of the Dukes of Northumberland since 1594. Part of the present house dates from the 16th century but it was largely redesigned by Robert Adam in the 1760s. You are looking at it across the garden Capability Brown laid out in the 18th century.

The river bank between Richmond and Kew

TRAVELLERS'
NEEDS

WHERE TO STAY

LONDON'S HOTELS have had one of the worst reputations for value in Europe, but things are improving rapidly. At the top end of the market, there are the reliable, if expensive, international establishments and the pedigree hotels, such as the Savoy and the Ritz, for which London is renowned. Many of the mid-range hotels offer better value for money, although they tend to be slightly further out of the centre of town. There is, however, a distinct lack of appealing hotels at the lower end of the market, and budget hotels can be rather seedy and run down.

Hilton doorman

We have inspected more than 200 hotels across a wide range of price brackets and have selected 84 of them as offering visitors particularly good value for money. *Choosing a Hotel* on pages 276–7 will help you to narrow down your choice of hotel; for further details on each of the hotels turn to the listings found on pages 278–85.

Apart from hotels, there are other options worth considering. Self-catering apartments and private homes *(see pp274–5)* are available at a wide range of prices, and there are camping sites, halls or hostels for students and budget travellers *(see p275)*.

WHERE TO LOOK

THE MOST EXPENSIVE hotels tend to be in smart West End areas such as Mayfair and Belgravia. Often large and opulent, with uniformed flunkies, they are not always the most relaxing places to stay. For smaller, but still luxurious hotels, head for South Kensington or Holland Park.

The streets off Earl's Court Road are full of hotels at the bottom of the price range. Several of the big railway stations are well served with smaller hotels too. Try Ebury Street near Victoria, or Sussex Gardens near Paddington. From Euston, head for Bloomsbury (avoiding the insalubrious area behind King's Cross), where several modern hotels offer sensibly priced accommodation.

There are inexpensive hotels in the suburbs, such as Ealing, Hendon, Wembley or Harrow, where you can leave your car, and get into town easily on public transport (although it may take an hour or more to do so).

If you get stranded at an airport or have to catch a very early morning flight, consult the list on pages 356–7.

For further information, advice and booking services, contact the **London Tourist Board** which offers useful leaflets about all sorts of accommodation in central and Greater London.

DISCOUNT RATES

PRICES TEND to be high all year round, but there are usually bargains to be had. Many hotels, including the big groups, reduce their rates at weekends and for special breaks *(see p274)*. Others work on a more ad hoc basis, depending on how busy they are. If a hotel isn't full, it is always worth trying to negotiate a discount.

Hotels in the lower price brackets often offer rooms without attached showers or bathrooms. These cost about 20% less than the full tariff.

HIDDEN EXTRAS

THERE IS A tendency to quote tariffs exclusive of VAT (currently 17.5% – *see p310*), and the final bill can come as a shock. Read the small print carefully. Most hotels give room rates rather than rates per person, but check. You should also check the service charge, which is usually included in the quoted price but in some cases is added on. Beware of extras, such as a mark-up on telephone calls.

The Tearoom at the Waldorf Hotel *(see p284)*

The Hampshire Hotel *(see p283)*

Breakfast is likely to be charged on top of the room rate in more expensive hotels, but tends to be included in the price in cheaper ones. Continental breakfast usually consists of coffee, fruit juice and a roll, toast or croissants with jam. English (or full) breakfast will see you through the busiest mornings of sight-seeing. At its most basic it consists of cereal and fruit juice, followed by bacon, eggs and toast *(see p288)*.

Tipping is expected in the more expensive hotels. There is generally no need to tip staff other than porters, the exception being the concierge if, for example, he or she books theatre tickets for you.

Single travellers are usually charged a "supplement" and end up paying about 80% of the double room rate, even if they are occupying a "single" room – so try to make sure you get a good one.

The elegant hallway of the Gore Hotel in Kensington *(see p279)*

FACILITIES

ROOMS AT ALL prices can be small (see the chart on pages 276–7 for hotels with larger than average rooms), but all except the most basic provide at least a telephone and television. In general, recently modernized hotels provide the most facilities at any price level, although in some small and very smart hotels you pay for atmosphere and pampering rather than for mini-bars and electronic gadgetry.

Whatever the hotel, you will be expected to vacate your room by noon on the day you leave, and sometimes even earlier.

HOW TO BOOK

IT IS ALWAYS advisable to book well in advance, as room availability fluctuates. Booking directly with the hotel can be done by letter, phone or fax, and usually entails giving some kind of guarantee: either a credit card number from which a can-cellation fee can be deducted, or a one-night deposit (some hotels will expect more for longer stays).

The **London Tourist Board** provides a free booking service. To take advantage of this, write, at least six weeks in advance, to the Accommodation Service's Advance Booking Office stating how much you want to spend. Remember to confirm any bookings they make for you. If you give less than six weeks notice, a small booking fee is charged, plus a deposit for your stay which is deducted from the final bill. You can book by credit card over the phone, or turn up at an LTB Tourist Information Centre in Victoria or Liverpool Street stations or at Heathrow (on the underground station concourse for terminals 1, 2 and 3). The LTB also has branches at Harrods, Selfridges and the Tower of London.

Accommodation booking services are also available at the **British Travel Centre** on Regent Street. A number of non-LTB booking agencies

A distinctive London hotel

operate from booths in the major railway stations too. Unidentified touts, who hang around at railway and coach stations offering cheap accommodation to tourists, should be avoided.

USEFUL BOOKING ADDRESSES

British Hotel Reservation Centre
13 Grosvenor Gdns,
SW1 0BD.
(020-7828 2425

British Travel Centre
1 Lower Regent St,
SW1Y 4XT.
(020-8846 9000.

Holiday Care Service
2 Old Bank Chambers, Station Rd, Horley, Surrey.
(01293-774535 *Accommodation Service for disabled travellers (see also p274).*

London Accommodation Centre
70 Tottenham Court Rd, W1P 9PA.
(020-7436 6091.

London Tourist Board (LTB)
Accommodation Service's Advance Booking Office (credit cards only).
26 Grosvenor Gdns, SW1W 0DU.
(020-7932 2020.

Thomas Cook Hotel and Travel Reservations Ltd
5–11 Lavington St, SE1 0NZ.
(020-7945 6000.

SPECIAL BREAKS

Many travel agencies carry brochures from the major hotel chains listing special offers, which are usually costed on a minimum two-night stay. Some are extraordinarily good value compared to the usual tariff. For most travellers, this is the best way to take advantage of London hotels.

Other brochures are produced by specialist city-break operators, not tied to a single chain, and many privately owned hotels produce their own special-break brochures. Ferry companies and airlines offer packages including hotel breaks. Sometimes the same hotel may be featured in several brochures at widely differing prices and with different perks. It's worth asking the hotel directly what special rates they offer

1920s Savoy poster

DISABLED TRAVELLERS

Our information about wheelchair access to hotels was gathered by questionnaire and depends on the hotels' own assessment of their suitability. The **LTB** provide two useful leaflets: *Accessible Accommodation in London* and *London for All*. A booklet, *Access in London*, can be obtained from RADAR, City Forum, 250 City Road EC1V 8AF (0171) 250 3222.

TRAVELLING WITH CHILDREN

London hotels have long been notorious child-free zones, but some of them now try to accommodate children's needs. It is worth asking about deals for children; some hotels have special rates, or allow children to stay free in their parents' rooms. See *Choosing a Hotel* on pages 276–7 for hotels with facilities for children.

SELF-CATERING FLATS

Many agencies offer self-catering accommodation in flats, usually for stays of a week or more. Prices, depending on size and location, start at about £300 per week.

The **Landmark Trust** rents apartments in historic or unusual buildings. These include rooms in Hampton Court *(see pp254–7)* and flats in a pretty 18th-century terrace in the City: one of them was the home of the late poet laureate, Sir John Betjeman. A handbook of Landmark properties is available from them for a small charge.

SELF-CATERING AGENCIES

Ashburn Gardens Apartments
3 Ashburn Gdns, SW7 4DG.
📞 020-7370 2663.

Astons Budget Studios/Designer Studios
39 Rosary Gdns, SW7 4NQ.
📞 020-7370 0737.

Ealing Tourist Flats
94 Gordon Rd, W13 8PT.
📞 020-8566 8187.

The Landmark Trust
Shottesbrooke, Maidenhead, Berkshire, SL6 3SW.
📞 01628-825925.

Service Suites
42 Lower Sloane St, SW1W 8BP.
📞 020-7730 5766.

STAYING IN PRIVATE HOMES

A number of agencies organize stays in private homes, several are registered with the **LTB**. Prices depend on the location, and range from £15 to £60 per person per night. Sometimes you will stay with the family, but this isn't guaranteed, so it's as well to make your preference clear when you book. Even though you are not making a hotel booking, the same rules about deposits and cancellation fees may apply. Reservations can be made by credit card through LTB's telephone booking service *(see p273)*, or through any of the information centres listed under Self-Catering. Several agencies have minimum stays of anything up to a week.

Wolsey Lodges, a consortium of private homes, offers interesting hospitality and often a good dinner. It has four London properties.

AGENCIES FOR STAYS IN PRIVATE HOMES

Alma Tourist Services
21 Griffiths Rd, SW19 1SP.
📞 & ꜰᴀx 020-8540 2733.

Anglo World Travel
123 Shaftesbury Ave, WC2H 8AD.
📞 020-7379 7477.

At Home in London
70 Black Lion Lane, W6 9BE.
📞 020-8748-1943.

Host and Guest Service
Harwood House, 27 Effie Rd, SW6 1EN.
📞 020-7731 5340.

Classical opulence at Claridge's Hotel *(see p282)*

London Home to Home
19 Mount Park Crescent, W5 2RN
C & **FAX** *020-8567 2998.*

Wolsey Lodges
9 Market Place, Hadleigh, nr. Ipswich,
Suffolk, IP7 5DL.
C *01473 822058.*

BUDGET ACCOMMODATION

DESPITE THE generally high cost of accommodation in London, budget possibilities do exist, and they are not only for the young.

Dormitory accommodation and youth hostels
These can be booked through LTB's information centre at Victoria *(see p273)* for a small fee plus a refundable deposit. There are private hostels near Earl's Court, where a dormitory bed with breakfast can cost as little as £10 a night. Don't expect anything too elaborate for prices like this.

More upmarket is the **Central Club**, a Lutyens building in the heart of the West End. It is run by the YWCA but open to all. Single rooms here cost about £30, much less if you share.

There are seven **Youth Hostels Association** hostels in London. Despite the name, there is no age limit on staying in these. One of the most interesting is Holland House, a Jacobean mansion in Holland Park *(see p214)*, to the west of the city centre. Book well in advance, as it is deservedly popular.

HOSTEL ADDRESSES

Central Club
16–22 Great Russell St,
WC1B 3LR.
C *020-7636 7512.*

London Hostel Association
54 Eccleston Sq,
SW1V 1PG.
C *020-7834 1545.*

Youth Hostels Association
Trevelyan House,
8 St Stephen's Hill,
St Albans, Herts,
AL1 2DY.
C *017278 55215.*

City of London Youth Hostel

Camping Sites
Tent City in East Acton (open June-September) is close to the underground, has basic facilities and a 400-bed tented hostel but can't take caravans. Hackney, Edmonton, Leyton, Chingford, Abbey Wood and Crystal Palace sites are further from transport, but have more facilities and caravan spaces. The **LTB** has a camping leaflet.

CAMPING SITES

Tent City
Old Oak Common Lane, W3 7DP.
C *020-8749 9074.*

Halls of residence
Student rooms are available from July to September at very reasonable prices. Some of these are in central locations such as South Kensington. It is best to book in advance, but **King's College** or **Imperial College** can sometimes find a place at short notice.

BOOKING ADDRESSES FOR RESIDENCE HALLS

City University Accommodation and Conference Service
Northampton Sq, EC1V 0HB.
C *020-7477 8037.*

Imperial College Summer Accommodation Centre
Watts Way, Princes Gdns,
SW7 1LL.
C *020-7594 9507.*

King's Campus Vacation Bureau
127 Stamford St,
SE1 9NQ
C *020-7928 3777.*

USING THE LISTINGS
The hotels on pages 278–85 are listed according to area and price category. The symbols summarize the facilities at each hotel.

⌨ all rooms have bath and/or shower unless otherwise indicated
1 single-rate rooms available
♯ rooms for more than two people available, or an extra bed can be put in a double room
24 24-hour room service
TV television in all rooms
Y minibar in all rooms
🚭 non-smoking rooms available
👁 rooms with good views
▤ air-conditioning in all rooms
🏋 gym/fitness facilities
🏊 swimming pool in hotel
🖥 business facilities: message-taking service, fax machine for guests, desk and telephone in all rooms and a meeting room within the hotel
🧒 children's facilities *(see p277).*
♿ wheelchair access
⇅ lift
🐾 pets allowed in bedrooms (confirm with the management). Most hotels accept guide dogs regardless of rulings on pets. NB: Animals brought into the UK are subject to six months quarantine.
P hotel parking available
🌿 garden or terrace open to guests
Y bar
🍴 restaurant
ℹ tourist information point
💳 credit and charge cards accepted:
AE American Express
DC Diners Club
MC Mastercard/Access
V Visa
JCB Japanese Credit Bureau
Price categories for a standard double room per night, including breakfast, tax and service:
£ under £70
££ £70–£100
£££ £100–£150
££££ £150–£200
£££££ over £200

Choosing a Hotel

THE 84 HOTELS listed in the following pages have all been inspected and assessed. This choosing chart shows a selection of factors affecting the choice of hotel. For more information on each hotel see pages 278–85. The hotels are listed by area and alphabetically within their price categories.

	Price	Number of Rooms	Large Rooms	Business Facilities	Children's Facilities	Recommended Restaurant	Close to Shops and Restaurants	Quiet Location	24-Hour Room Service
BAYSWATER, PADDINGTON (see p278)									
Byron	££	45			●			■	
Delmere	££	39							
Mornington	£££	68			●			■	●
Whites	£££££	54	●	■	●				●
KENSINGTON, HOLLAND PARK, NOTTING HILL (see p278)									
Abbey House	£	16						●	■
Abbey Court	£££	22		■				■	●
Pembridge Court	£££	20			●			■	●
Portobello	£££	24						■	
Copthorne Tara	£££££	825		■			●	■	●
Halcyon	£££££	43		■	●	■		■	●
SOUTH KENSINGTON, GLOUCESTER ROAD (see pp278–9)									
Swiss House	££	16		■					
Aster House	£££	12			●			■	
Cranley	£££	37						■	●
Five Sumner Place	£££	13						■	●
Harrington Hall	£££	200	●	■	●		●	■	●
Number Sixteen	££££	36			●			■	
Blakes	£££££	51	●	■		■	●	■	●
Gore	£££££	54		■	●	■		■	
Pelham	£££££	50		■	●				●
Rembrandt	£££££	195	●	■	●				●
Sydney House	££££	21					●	■	●
KNIGHTSBRIDGE, BROMPTON, BELGRAVIA (see pp279–81)									
Executive	£££	27					●		
Knightsbridge Green	£££	28			●		●		
The London Outpost	££££	11		■	●		●		●
Basil Street	£££££	93		■	●		●		●
Beaufort	£££££	28		■	●		●	■	
Berkeley	£££££	158	●	■			●		●
Capital	£££££	48		■	●	■		■	●
Cliveden Town House	£££££	35		■	●		●	■	●
Egerton House	£££££	28		■			●	■	●
Eleven Cadogan Gardens	£££££	62		■			●	■	●
Halkin	£££££	41	●	■		■		■	●
Hyatt Carlton Tower	£££££	220	●	■	●	■	●		●
Lowndes	£££££	78		■			●	■	●
WESTMINSTER, VICTORIA (see p281)									
Collin House	£	13							
Elizabeth	£	30			●			■	
Woodville House	£	12							
Windermere	££	22		■					●
Tophams Belgravia	£££	29		■					●
Holiday Inn	££££	210	●		●				●
Stakis London St Ermins	££££	290		■	●			■	●
Goring	£££££	75	●					■	●
Royal Horseguards	£££££	280		■				■	●

Price categories for a standard double room per night including breakfast, tax and service:
£ under £70
££ £70–£100
£££ £100–£150
££££ £150–£200
£££££ over £200

CLOSE TO SHOPS AND RESTAURANTS Within a 5-minute walk of a good centre for shops and restaurants.

CHILDREN'S FACILITIES Family rooms and/or an extra bed in a double room, child cots and chairs in the breakfast room or restaurant.

BUSINESS FACILITIES Message-taking service, fax machine for guests, desk and telephone in each room and a meeting room within the hotel.

		NUMBER OF ROOMS	LARGE ROOMS	BUSINESS FACILITIES	CHILDREN'S FACILITIES	RECOMMENDED RESTAURANT	CLOSE TO SHOPS AND RESTAURANTS	QUIET LOCATION	24-HOUR ROOM SERVICE
PICCADILLY, MAYFAIR *(see pp281–2)*									
Athenaeum	£££££	157	●	■	●		●		●
Brown's	£££££	157	●	■			●		●
Claridge's	£££££	197	●	■			●		●
Connaught	£££££	90	●			■	●		●
Dorchester	£££££	251	●	■	●	■			●
Dukes	£££££	83	●	■				●	●
Forty-Seven Park Street	£££££	52	●	■		■		●	●
Four Seasons	£££££	227		■	●		●		●
Grosvenor House	£££££	586	●	■	●	■	●		●
Ritz	£££££	131	●	■			●		●
Twenty-Two Jermyn St	£££££	18	●	■			●	■	●
SOHO, LEICESTER SQUARE, OXFORD STREET *(see p283)*									
Concorde	££	26			●		●		●
Edward Lear	££	30			●		●		
Parkwood	££	18			●		●		●
Bryanston Court	£££	54		■			●		●
Durrants	£££	92		■				●	●
Hazlitt's	£££	23					●		
Hampshire	£££££	125	●	■	●		●		●
Marble Arch Marriott	£££££	240	●	■	●				●
REGENT'S PARK, MARYLEBONE *(see pp283–4)*									
Blandford	££	33						■	
Hotel La Place	££	24		■	●			■	●
Dorset Square	£££	38	●		●			■	●
White House	££££	584		■	●			■	●
Langham Hilton	£££££	379	●	■	●		●		●
BLOOMSBURY, FITZROVIA, COVENT GARDEN, STRAND *(see pp284–5)*									
Fielding	££	24		■			●	■	●
Mabledon Court	££	30							
Academy	£££	48			●				●
Bonnington	£££	215		■	●				●
Hotel Russell	££££	329	●	■	●				●
Covent Garden Hotel	£££££	50	●	■	●		●		●
Howard	£££££	135	●	■	●				●
Mountbatten	£££££	127	●	■	●		●		●
Savoy	£££££	207	●	■	●	■	●		●
Waldorf	£££££	292		■	●		●		●
THE CITY *(see p285)*									
Tower Thistle	££££	900		■				■	●
FURTHER AFIELD *(see p285)*									
Chase Lodge	££	12			●			■	
La Reserve	££	41		■					
Swiss Cottage	££	75		■	●				
Kingston Lodge	£££	62		■	●				
Cannizaro House	££££	45	●	■				■	
Sheraton Skyline	£££££	351	●	■	●				●

BAYSWATER
PADDINGTON

Byron

36–38 Queensborough Terrace, W2 3SH. **Map** 10 E2. **📞** 020-7243 0987. **FAX** 020-7792 1957. **TX** 263431 BYRON G. **Rooms:** 45.

AE, DC, MC, V. **£££**

The decor is generally pleasant, ranging from a quite traditional country house style in the small cosy lounge to unfussy neutrality in the bedrooms. Staff are young and unstarchy, and the setting is peaceful. A few scuffs here and there are forgivable in such a friendly, unpretentious hotel.

Delmere

130 Sussex Gdns, W2 1UB. **Map** 11 A2. **📞** 020-7706 3344. **FAX** 020-7262 1863. **TX** 8953857. **Rooms:** 39.

DC, MC, V, JCB. **££**

This well-kept building stands out amid a line of drab neighbours. Furnishings can be pretentious in places, and some bedrooms have been shoe-horned into scarcely adequate spaces. Nonetheless, the hotel is very well-run and civilized. The comfortable, homely sitting room downstairs has a cosy gas powered coal fire and supplies of the main daily newspapers.

Mornington

12 Lancaster Gate, W2 3LG. **Map** 10 F2. **📞** 020-7262 7361. **FAX** 020-7706 1028. **TX** 24281. **Rooms:** 68.

AE, DC, MC, V. **£££**

This quiet hotel is run with old-world courteous efficiency. The clubby intimacy of the book-lined library lounge provides a good contrast to the cool, almost chilly, stark Scandinavian austerity of the bedrooms. The steamy, relaxing sauna and smorgasbord buffet breakfast are reminders of the hotel Swedish parentage.

Whites

90 Lancaster Gate, W2 3NR. **Map** 10 F2. **📞** 020-7262 2711. **FAX** 020-7262 2147. **TX** 24771. **Rooms:** 54.

AE, DC, MC, V. **£££££**

This large 19th-century hotel overlooking Kensington Gardens has an almost seasidey feel to its wedding-cake exterior. Inside, pretty chandeliers give the attractive public areas a festive and cheering air. The crystal look even extends to the bedrooms, where the decor is a mixture of Oriental, Louis XV and Belle Epoque themes. The historic appearance of these rooms is preserved by having hidden television sets that rise magically from cupboards at the press of a button when required.

KENSINGTON
HOLLAND PARK
NOTTING HILL

Abbey House

11 Vicarage Gate, W8 4AG. **Map** 10 D4. **📞** 020-7727 2594. **Rooms:** 16. **£**

The outside of this attractively located, Victorian family home looks charming, and the proportions of the plant-filled stairwell hint at gracious living. But no-frills bed and breakfast is what Abbey House offers. Bedrooms, though spacious, are very simply furnished. The only public area is a bright, cheerful breakfast room in the basement.

Abbey Court

20 Pembridge Gdns, W2 4DU. **Map** 9 C3. **📞** 020-7221 7518. **FAX** 020-7792 0858. **TX** 262167 ABBYCT. **Rooms:** 22.

AE, DC, MC, V, JCB. **£££**

This lavishly decorated and well-kept town house provides a successful brand of luxury bed and breakfast. An elegant reception lounge and a conservatory breakfast room form the public areas. Bedrooms vary, but all include handsome Victorian-style bathroom fittings and antiques. An unusually high proportion are singles – handy for lone travellers.

Pembridge Court

34 Pembridge Gdns, W2 4DX. **Map** 9 C3. **📞** 020-7229 9977. **FAX** 020-7727 4982. **TX** 298363. **Rooms:** 20.

AE, DC, MC, V, JCB. **££££**

This elegant town house hotel, situated in a smart quiet street near Notting Hill Gate is privately owned. Throughout, it is comfortable and civilized, and its unique decorative identity comes from gorgeous displays of accessories: gloves, fans, purses, in all the rooms. Caps Restaurant downstairs is a rather suave evening-only wine-bar.

Portobello

22 Stanley Gdns, W11 2NG. **Map** 9 B2. **📞** 020-7727 2777. **FAX** 020-7792 9641. **Rooms:** 24.

AE, DC, MC, V. **£££**

This eccentric place has a darkish and sophisticated decor which is a mix of Victorian Gothic and Edwardian. The tiniest single rooms have box-like beds and minute, spartan bathrooms. Larger rooms are available, and for an exotic touch there is the Round Room (a round bed beneath free-flying drapes). A casually chic restaurant is downstairs.

Copthorne Tara

Scarsdale Pl, Wright's Lane, W8 5SR. **Map** 10 D5. **📞** 020-7937 7211. **FAX** 020-7937 7100. **TX** 918834 TARAHL G. **Rooms:** 825.

AE, DC, MC, V, JCB. **£££££**

The location, in a quiet sidestreet just off Kensington High Street, is a strong point. Inside, the style and facilities of this modern chain hotel are predictably comfortable and include a number of themed bars.

Halcyon

81 Holland Park, W11 3RZ. **Map** 9 A4. **📞** 020-7727 7288. **FAX** 020-7229 8516. **TX** 266721. **Rooms:** 43.

AE, DC, MC, V, JCB. **£££££**

This is a luxurious hotel in the heart of Holland Park. Within the splendid Belle Epoque exterior, the beautifully proportioned reception rooms retain all their original features. The bedrooms are hedonistic fantasies filled with canopies, swags and drapes of fabric. Bathrooms have whirlpool baths and bidets. The hotel cannot be described as good value, but it gives a feeling of opulence.

SOUTH KENSINGTON
GLOUCESTER ROAD

Swiss House

171 Old Brompton Rd, SW5 0AN. **Map** 18 E3. **📞** 020-7373 2769. **FAX** 020-7373 4983. **Rooms:** 16.

AE, DC, MC, V. **££**

Trailing plants at the entrance give this tall, terraced guesthouse an immediately welcoming look. Inside, the impression is reinforced by the cheerful, cottagey breakfast room – pine dresser with china and dried flower arrangements – and neat bedrooms, some of which are surprisingly spacious.

Aster House

3 Sumner Pl, SW7 3EE. **Map** 19 A2.
【 020-7581 5888. **FAX** 020-7584 4925. **Rooms:** 12. ⬛ 1️⃣ TV Y
🌀 🚼 🅿 ⬆ MC, V. ⓔⓔⓔ

Several houses in this elegant South Kensington terrace are discreet, upmarket hotels, but few have such reasonable tariffs. L'Orangerie, the hotel's stylish conservatory restaurant, serves health-conscious breakfasts. The bedrooms, all non-smoking, are individually decorated in varying degrees of sumptuousness. Children over 12 catered for.

Cranley

10–12 Bina Gdns, SW5 0LA.
Map 18 E2. 【 020-7373 0123.
FAX 020-7373 9497. **TX** 991503.
Rooms: 37. ⬛ 1️⃣ ⬛ TV ⬆
⬆ AE, DC, MC, V, JCB. ⓔⓔⓔⓔ

Antiques and designer fabrics abound in this grand American-owned town house hotel, although not all of the rooms are particularly large. Discreetly concealed kitchenettes with fridge and microwave are an unusual and practical feature of the bedrooms. The drawing room is exceptionally attractive.

Five Sumner Place

5 Sumner Pl, SW7 3EE. **Map** 19 A2.
【 020-7584 7586. **FAX** 020-7823 9962. **Rooms:** 13. ⬛ 1️⃣ ⬛ TV
⬆ 🅿 ⬆ AE, MC, V. ⓔⓔⓔ

A past winner of the British Tourist Association's Best Bed and Breakfast Award, this Victorian terraced town house is elegant and stylish. An eye-catching conservatory set with blue-skirted breakfast tables and fresh flowers overlooks a pretty patio garden. Upstairs, 13 bedrooms, all individually decorated, provide quiet, civilized havens from the bustle and noise of central London.

Harrington Hall

5–25 Harrington Gdns, SW7.
Map 18 E2. 【 020-7396 9696.
FAX 020-7396 9090. **Rooms:** 200.
⬛ 🈂 1️⃣ ⬛ TV ⬆ 🍴 ⬛ 🍽
🚼 ⬆ Y 🍴 ⬆ AE, DC, MC, V.
ⓔⓔⓔⓔ

Understated elegance is the order of the day in this large hotel, set discreetly behind carefully restored 19th-century townhouse façades. Every modern comfort is

available, from air conditioning in the rooms to fully equipped fitness and business centres for the use of its guests. Spacious bedrooms are furnished in a mix of Victorian prints and almost-convincing reproduction furniture.

Number Sixteen

16 Sumner Pl, SW7 3EG. **Map** 19 A2.
【 020-7589 5232. **FAX** 020-7584 8615. **TX** 266638. **Rooms:** 36. ⬛
34. 1️⃣ ⬛ TV Y ⬆ ⬆ 🅿
⬆ AE, DC, MC, V. ⓔⓔⓔⓔ

The unmarked entrance is typical of the classy little hotels along this smart, white-painted Kensington street. Inside, the ambience is understated but luxurious. Number Sixteen scores over its neighbours with better facilities and more extensive public areas, including a conservatory leading on to a charming garden of dribbling fountains. The bedrooms are surprisingly spacious and imaginatively decorated, while the bathrooms are in the process of being upgraded. Children over 12 catered for.

Blakes

33 Roland Gdns, SW7 3PF. **Map** 18 F3. 【 020-7370 6701. **FAX** 020-7373 0442. **TX** 8813500. **Rooms:** 51. ⬛ 1️⃣ ⬛ 24 TV Y ⬆ ⬆
🅿 Y 🍴 ⬆ AE, DC, MC, V, JCB. ⓔⓔⓔⓔ

Designer Anouska Hempel's dashing establishment is a London legend. The racing green facade distinguishes it instantly, and one glimpse of the exotic, scented interior declares this is no ordinary hotel. Each bedroom is a unique, extravaganza of deep colours, rich silks, and opulent furnishings such as brocaded four-posters and antique lacquered chests.

Gore

189 Queen's Gate, SW7 5EX.
Map 18 F5. 【 020-7584 6601.
FAX 020-7589 8127. **TX** 296244.
Rooms: 54. ⬛ 1️⃣ ⬛ TV Y ⬆
🚼 ⬆ Y 🍴 ⬆ AE, DC, MC, V, JCB. ⓔⓔⓔⓔ

This idiosyncratic Victorian hotel is a sister to Hazlitt's *(see p283)*. The trendy Kensington crowd hustle for tables at the chic Bistrot 190. Its Restaurant 190, under chef Shaun Rowlands, is highly regarded, with seafood considered a speciality. Bedrooms vary from tiny singles with pine washstands to Tudor fantasies complete with their own minstrel's galleries; many bathrooms have Victorian and Edwardian furniture. Service is endearingly laid-back but always charming, and the tariff need not make you gasp.

Pelham

15 Cromwell Pl, SW7 2LA. **Map** 19 A1.
【 020-7589 8288. **FAX** 020-7584 8444. **TX** 881 4714 TUDOR G.
Rooms: 50. ⬛ 1️⃣ 24 TV Y
⬛ ⬆ 🚼 ⬆ Y 🍴 ⬆ AE, MC, V.
ⓔⓔⓔⓔ

Less than a minute from South Kensington tube, the Pelham looks straight from the pages of a glossy magazine. From the 18th-century panelling in the drawing room to the flowers in the bedrooms, everything shows perfect house-keeping and exquisite (if opulent) taste. The restaurant (which also functions as lounge and bar) is particularly comfortable.

Rembrandt

11 Thurloe Pl, SW7 2RS. **Map** 19 A1.
【 020-7589 8100. **FAX** 020-7225 3363.
TX 295828. **Rooms:** 195. ⬛ 1️⃣ ⬛
24 TV ⬆ 🍴 ⬛ ⬆ 🚼 ⬆ Y 🍴
⬆ AE, DC, MC, V, JCB.
ⓔⓔⓔ

The corporate style of this large hotel opposite the Victoria and Albert Museum does not preclude the restful atmosphere throughout its refurbished interior.

Sydney House

9–11 Sydney St, SW3 6PU.
Map 19 A1. 【 020-7376 7711. **FAX** 020-7376 4233. **Rooms:** 21. ⬛ 24
TV Y ⬆ ⬆ Y 🍴 ⬆ AE, DC, MC, V, JCB. ⓔⓔⓔⓔ

The palazzo wall treatments, Bugatti furniture, and Baccarat chandeliers of the foyer set the tone here. Each room is a self-contained mini-world: Biedermeier here, Paris fabrics there. The dining room is deep sunshine and navy wicker. For this kind of style, the tariff is remarkably reasonable.

KNIGHTSBRIDGE
BROMPTON
BELGRAVIA

Executive

57 Pont St, SW1X 0BD. **Map** 19 C1.
【 020-7581 2424. **FAX** 020-7589 9456. **TX** 9413498 EXECUT G.
Rooms: 27. ⬛ 1️⃣ ⬛ TV ⬆ Y
⬆ AE, DC, MC, V. ⓔⓔ

This unobtrusive listed town house lies a short stroll from some of London's most exclusive shops. Beyond the gracious entrance hall, bedrooms are modern and agreeably furnished, if not strong on personality. Downstairs, buffet breakfast is served in a room of pink Chinese Chippendale.

For key to symbols *see p275*

Knightsbridge Green

159 Knightsbridge, SW1X 7PD.
Map 11 C5. 020-7584 6274.
FAX 020-7225 1635. **Closed** 24–26
Dec. **Rooms:** 28. AE, DC, MC, V. ££££

Its proximity to Harrods, coupled with its reassuring ambiance, makes this long-established, up-market bed and breakfast popular with women. Tea and coffee are available all day long in the Club Room. Most bedrooms have attached sitting rooms where breakfast is served. Decor is restful, and the practical details of lighting, sound-proofing, and storage space are considered.

The London Outpost

69 Cadogan Gdns, SW3 2RB.
Map 19 C2. 020-7589 7333.
FAX 020-7581 4958. **Rooms:** 11.
AE, DC, MC, V. ££££

Hidden in a maze of Victorian mansions, this quietly grand bed and breakfast has the air of a private home. Paintings, antiques and fine china fill the house and many of the building's original features remain, including fireplaces, cornices, and huge windows. Breakfast is served in the peaceful bedrooms, and light meals can be ordered at other times of the day. There's a health club upstairs to help trim back the pounds. The Biedermeier Suite is top of the range, with some exquisitely finished high-quality reproduction furnishings.

Basil Street

Basil St, SW3 1AH. **Map** 11 C5.
020-7581 3311. FAX 020-7581 3693. TX 28379. **Rooms:** 93. 76.
AE, DC, MC, V. ££££

The civilized but unintimidating atmosphere of this privately owned hotel with its unpretentious Edwardian air explains its enduring popularity. The comfortable lounge bar is a perfect place to relax for afternoon tea. Its wine-bar and upper carvery are excellent value for the area, and the unique Parrot Club for women (which men can visit by invitation only) is a plucky, interesting riposte to the leathery male bastions found elsewhere in some of London's hotels.

Beaufort

33 Beaufort Gdns, SW3 1PP.
Map 19 B1. 020-7584 5252.
FAX 020-7589 2834. TX 929200.
Rooms: 28. AE, DC, MC, V, JCB.
£££££

Sheer elegance at least partially excuses the high tariffs of this classy little place tucked away in a leafy cul-de-sac near Harrods. Fresh flowers, stylish fabrics and floral watercolours characterize its delightful bedrooms. Downstairs, Bunter (the resident ginger cat) may be found monopolizing one of the luxurious sofas. Personal service and pampering are what you are paying for here, and neither is in short supply. Children over 10 are catered for.

Berkeley

Wilton Pl, SW1X 7RL. **Map** 12 D5.
020-7235 6000. FAX 020-7235 4330. TX 919252. **Rooms:** 158.
AE, DC, MC, V, JCB. £££££

The discreet main entrance to this august member of the Savoy Group of hotels leads to a dignified hallway of marble and Lutyens panelling. The Buttery and Bar downstairs are slightly less formal, while bedrooms display unusual individuality.

Capital

22–24 Basil St, SW3 1AT. **Map** 11 C5.
020-7589 5171. FAX 020-7225 0011. **Rooms:** 48. AE, DC, MC, V.
£££££

The Capital is a small but perfectly-formed and distinctly luxurious hotel with a noted restaurant. Furnishings are imaginative and elaborate in a French *fin de siècle* mode. Its sister next door at No. 28, the equally stylish L'Hôtel (020-7589 6286), offers somewhat less expensive rooms but has fewer facilities than the Capital – take your choice.

Cliveden Town House

24–26 Cadogan Gdns, SW3 2RP.
Map 19 C2. 020-7730 6466.
FAX 020-7730 0236. **Rooms:** 35.
AE, DC, MC, V, JCB. £££££

As you would expect from the London base of one of Britain's finest hotels, service and comfort here are of the highest order. The most modern of today's facilities sit discreetly alongside the elegance and charm of another age. Rooms have open fireplaces, and many overlook the gardens, as does the delightful drawing room. The Breakfast Room – the alternative to room service – is decorated with masks designed by celebrities.

Egerton House

17–19 Egerton Terrace, SW3 2BX.
Map 19 B1. 020-7589 2412.
FAX 020-7584 6540. **Rooms:** 29.
AE, DC, MC, V. £££££

This smart, town house provides high standards of both service and comfort. The style is urbane and professional. Although some of the furnishings have not yet quite achieved the patina of age, they certainly look easily good enough to stand alongside what are very obviously genuine antiques.

Eleven Cadogan Gardens

11 Cadogan Gdns, SW3 2RJ. **Map** 19 C2. 020-7730 3426. FAX 020-7730 5217. TX 8813318. **Rooms:** 62. AE, DC, MC, , JCB. £££££

From the outside you would never guess that this redbrick mansion is a hotel. Perhaps it explains why so many famous people retreat here for peace and privacy when they become tired of being lionized by the public. A relaxing atmosphere of quiet good taste and unobtrusive service matches the panelling on the walls and the crisp sheets on the beds. Furnished with dignity and conservative elegance, the more mundane of hotel-type trappings are largely absent from this establishment.

Halkin

5 Halkin St, SW1X 7DJ. **Map** 12 D5.
020-7333 1000. FAX 020-7333 1100. **Rooms:** 41. AE, DC, MC, V, JCB. £££££

For those weary of artificial period charm, the minimalism of the Halkin will come as a breath of fresh air. A restrained palette of blue and grey, black and white creates a cool, sophisticated and utterly contemporary look. The bedrooms luxuriate in tawny marble, state-of-the-art bedside consoles, and fitted furniture in coppery veneers.

Hyatt Carlton Tower

Cadogan Pl, SW1X 9PY. **Map** 19 C1.
020-7235 1234. FAX 020-7245 6570. TX 21944. **Rooms:** 220.
AE, DC, MC, V, JCB. £££££

This large chain hotel avoids the usual soullessness of its type. The staff are well-trained and friendly. In some places the furnishings are too predictable, but the Chinoiserie Lounge, where a harpist plays, is a wonderful place to rest weary feet after battling round shops or museums.

Lowndes

Lowndes St, SW1X 9ES. **Map** 20 D1.
C 020-7823 1234. **FAX** 020-7235 1154. **TX** 919065. **Rooms:** 78.
AE, DC, MC, V.
£££££

This little sister of the Hyatt Carlton Tower just round the corner has a pleasant, small-scale feel, and guests can use the larger hotel's excellent facilities at no extra cost. The designer country-house reception lounge provides a relaxing place to read papers over coffee. Bedrooms contain a panoply of excellent facilities amid smart contemporary decor.

WESTMINSTER
VICTORIA

Collin House

104 Ebury St, SW1W 9QD.
Map 20 E2. **C** & **FAX** 020-7730 8031. **Closed** 2 weeks at Christmas. **Rooms:** 13. 8. **£**

This small, non-smoking guest-house distinguishes itself from many similar neighbours by its pleasant welcome, and if decor is scarcely fashionable the rooms are fresh and clean. A tiny breakfast room downstairs, cheered up by landscape photographs and honey pine, is the only public room.

Elizabeth

37 Eccleston Sq, SW1V 1PB. **Map** 20 F2. **C** 020-7828 6812. **FAX** 020-7828 6814. **Rooms:** 38. 32. V, MC.

Refurbishment has made the Elizabeth even better value for money than in the past – and the price has always been surprisingly low for the area. As a bonus, guests also have access to the pleasant, leafy gardens and the tennis courts of Eccleston Square.

Woodville House

107 Ebury St, SW1W 9QU.
Map 20 E2. **C** 020-7730 1048.
FAX 0717-730 2574. **Rooms:** 12.
£

Though neither spacious nor luxurious, this guesthouse, in a Georgian building, is civilized, personal and much frequented by budget-conscious visitors. The breakfast room is screened off

into intimate spaces; the bedrooms have tiny armchairs and other neat fittings.

Windermere

142–144 Warwick Way, SW1V 4JE. **Map** 20 E2. **C** 020-7834 5163.
FAX 020-7630 8831. **TX** 94017182 **WIRE** G **Rooms:** 22. 20. AE, MC, V, JCB. **££**

The well-kept Victorian exterior of this inexpensive, friendly hotel stands out on a busy road. Inside the illusion is not broken: it is as neat as a pin, with a pleasant breakfast room, that doubles as a coffee shop, downstairs where snacks and drinks are available all day. Light, clean bedrooms have curtains of heavy glazed chintz and modern fittings.

Tophams Belgravia

28 Ebury St, SW1W 0LU. **Map** 20 E1.
C 020-7730 8147. **FAX** 020-7823 5966. **Rooms:** 42. 39. AE, DC, MC, V, JCB. **£££**

Several adjacent town houses make up this classy, privately owned hotel. Family heirlooms and pictures deck cosy public rooms. Labyrinthine passages and stairways connect the rooms, most of which are small and plain. The price is very good for the area.

Holiday Inn

2 Bridge Pl, SW1V 1QA. **Map** 20 F2.
C 020-7834 8123. **FAX** 020-7828 1099. **TX** 914973. **Rooms:** 212.
AE, DC, MC, V, JCB. **££££**

This uncompromising modern block, that overlooks the train marshalling yards of nearby Victoria station, is Swedish-owned. The slight starkness of its chrome, glass and plastic coffee shop is more than offset by the friendly, efficient Scandinavian welcome and the stylish, well-equipped bedrooms. One of the hotel's special attractions is the panoply of health facilities that is available.

Stakis London
St Ermin's

Caxton St, SW1H 0QW. **Map** 13 A5.
C 020-7222 7888. **FAX** 020-7222 6914.
TX 917731. **Rooms:** 290. 1
AE, DC, MC, V, JCB. **££££**

This institutional-looking, late-Victorian hotel is close enough to Westminster to have once had its own tunnel-link to the House of Commons. The most striking

interior feature is a grand Baroque staircase rearing from the main lounge up towards the glittering chandeliers, curving balustrades, and ornate plaster ceilings. The bedrooms are quite comfortably furnished in a less overbearing style than the rest of the hotel.

Goring

Beeston Pl, Grosvenor Gdns, SW1W 0JW. **Map** 20 E1. **C** 020-7396 9000.
FAX 020-7834 4393. **TX** 919166.
Rooms: 75. 1 P AE, DC, MC, V.
£££££

This imposing Edwardian building is a rare beast – a central London hotel that is both grand and family-run. The third-generation Gorings maintain immaculate standards, with meticulous attention to every detail. The hotel exudes an air of understated elegance. Exceptional points include the bar-lounge and a delightful formal garden, which is, alas, only for looking at.

Royal Horseguards

2 Whitehall Court, SW1A 2EJ.
Map 13 C4. **C** 020-7839 3400.
FAX 020-7925 2263. **TX** 917096.
Rooms: 280. 1 AE, DC, MC, V, JCB. **£££££**

This grand 19th-century hotel overlooks the river not far from the Houses of Parliament. Potted palms, chandeliers and ornate plasterwork fill the lobby. Beyond, the comfortable public rooms include Granby's Restaurant, smart and formal in green leather, and a haunt of well-known political faces. The style of the bedrooms varies from Classica opulence to contemporary smartness.

PICCADILLY
MAYFAIR

Athenaeum

116 Piccadilly, W1V 0EJ. **Map** 12 E4.
C 020-7499 3464. **FAX** 020-7493 1860. **TX** 261589. **Rooms:** 157.
AE, DC, MC, V, JCB. **£££££**

Despite the prestigious Mayfair location of this smart hotel, the welcome is friendly, personal and unforbidding. Tea or coffee in the relaxing Windsor lounge is a particular strong point. So, too, is the vast range of malt Scotch whiskies in the clubby cocktail bar. Some bedrooms are a little insipid, but all are extremely comfortable and well-furnished.

Brown's

30 Albemarle St, W1X 4BP.
Map 12 F3. 【 *020-7493 6020.*
FAX *020-7493 9381.* **TX** *28686.*
Rooms: *157.* 🛏 1 ♿ TV 🍸
🛳 ▤ 🐕 ♨ 🏃 ⚓ 🍸 🍽
⊗ *AE, DC, MC, V, JCB.*
ⓔⓔⓔⓔⓔ *See* **Restaurants and Pubs** *pp306–7.*

Some of the urbane charm of the original Mr Brown (who must have been the perfect gentleman's gentleman) still lingers here in one of London's oldest and most traditional hotels. The legendary afternoon teas are served in the chintzy lounge. Bedrooms are mostly large, with charming, slightly outmoded decor.

Claridge's

55 Brook St, W1A 2JQ. **Map** 12 E2.
【 *020-7629 8860.* **FAX** *020-7499 2210.* **TX** *218762 CLRDGS G.*
Rooms: *197.* 🛏 1 ♿ 24 TV 🍸
🛳 ▤ 📺 🐕 🏃 ♨ 🍸 🍽
AE, DC, MC, V, JCB.
ⓔⓔⓔⓔⓔ

So much part of the establishment that it functions virtually as an annexe to Buckingham Palace, Claridge's favours the traditional approach – yet the atmosphere is surprisingly unstarchy.

Art Deco blends with the Classical grandeur of fine marble mosaic, chandeliers, and a staircase wide enough for two complete ballgowns to pass unhindered. Hungarian musicians weave their magic in the foyer; waiters, valets and maids can be summoned to the vast, bedrooms at the touch of a button.

Connaught

16 Carlos Pl, W1Y 6AL. **Map** 12 E3.
【 *020-7499 7070.* **FAX** *020-7495 3262.* **Rooms:** *90.* 🛏 1 ♿ TV 🍸
♨ ⚓ 🍸 🍽 ⊗ *AE, DC, MC, V, JCB.* ⓔⓔⓔⓔⓔ

So self-confident is this famous hotel that it provides neither brochure nor tariff. (Terms – not the highest in Mayfair – are available "on application".) The hotel is not large and its decor is unshowy. Utter discretion is the watchword: guests' privacy is jealously guarded and every last whim is noted for future reference. Those outside the charmed circle may feel they are being excluded from the club of Connaught residents. Many are gently informed that the hotel is quite, quite full. To make a reservation, don't simply try ringing up – and under no circumstances just turn up and expect a room. Write, courteously, a long time in advance.

Dorchester

53 Park Lane, W1A 2HJ. **Map** 12 D3.
【 *020-7629 8888.* **FAX** *020-7495 7342.* **TX** *887704 DORCH G.* **Rooms:** *251.* 🛏 1 ♿ 24 TV 🍸 🛳 🍽
▤ 📺 🐕 🏃 ♿ ♨ P 🍸 🍽 ⊗
AE, DC, MC, V, JCB. ⓔⓔⓔⓔⓔ

Soft, pale gold gleams on marble pillars and super scalloped ceiling domes, towering arrangements of flowers deck the Promenade where teas are served, and all is conspicuous, flamboyant grandeur in this old hotel. Eating places include the famous Grill Room, the calmer Terrace, and the exotically themed Oriental restaurants. Suites and bedrooms, which have triple-glazing on the Park Lane side, are – needless to say – sybaritic.

Dukes

35 St James's Pl, SW1A 1NY.
Map 12 F4. 【 *020-7491 4840.*
FAX *020-7493 1264.* **TX** *28283.*
Rooms: *83.* 🛏 1 ♿ 24 TV 🍸
▤ 📺 🐕 🏃 ♨ 🍸 🍽 ⊗ *AE, DC, MC, , JCB..* ⓔⓔⓔⓔⓔ

This fine Edwardian building is wedged into a minute secluded courtyard where the gas-lamps are still lit by hand. Though expensive and exclusive, Dukes is notably friendly and cheering. The bar has a masculine look: monumentally-priced cognacs are dispensed beneath the stern gaze of three ducal portraits (Wellington, Marlborough, Norfolk). Children over 5 are catered for.

Forty-Seven Park Street

47 Park St, W1Y 4EB. **Map** 12 D2.
【 *020-7491 7282.* **FAX** *020-7491 7281.* **TX** *22116 LUXURY.* **Rooms:** *52.* 🛏 1 ♿ 24 TV 🍸 🛳 🐕
♨ P 🍸 🍽 ⊗ *AE, DC, MC, V, JCB.* ⓔⓔⓔⓔⓔ

Many have heard of the Roux's celebrated restaurant, Le Gavroche. Fewer realize that you can, if you are wealthy enough, stagger just next door to recover from gastronomic excess. Here 52 luxurious suites, each one different, feature French-style clocks and bronzes on fireplaces, finely crafted furniture, downy duvets, and thick fluffy towels. Room service from the restaurant is also available.

The Four Seasons

Hamilton Pl, Park Lane, W1A 1AZ.
Map 12 D4. 【 *020-7499 0888.*
FAX *020-7493 6629.* **TX** *227711.*
Rooms: *227.* 🛏 1 ♿ 24 TV 🍸
🛳 🍽 📺 🐕 🏃 ♿ ♨ P ✒
🍸 🍽 ⊗ *AE, DC, MC, V, JCB.*
ⓔⓔⓔⓔⓔ

The Four Seasons prides itself on individual service and understated luxury, and the overall effect is firmly traditional. In the opulent, well-equipped rooms, quieter styles are gradually replacing the Oriental birds and heavy chintzes, and the foyer and lounge areas glitter with Venetian crystal. Up the grand staircase the elegant Four Seasons Restaurant and the less formal Lanes buffet provide worthy arenas for splendid food.

Grosvenor House

86–90 Park Lane, W1A 3AA. **Map** 12 D3. 【 *020-7499 6363.* **FAX** *020-7493 3341.* **TX** *24871.* **Rooms:** *586.*

🛏 1 ♿ 24 TV 🍸 🛳 🍽 🍽
▤ 🏃 ♿ ♨ P 🍸 🍽 ⊗
AE, DC, MC, V, JCB. ⓔⓔⓔⓔⓔ

This establishment is perhaps most famous as host to grand occasions. The Great Room is the largest banqueting room in Europe, with space for 2,000 people. Behind the Lutyens facade overlooking Hyde Park, the hotel is formal and luxurious but thoroughly cosy and comfortable. Several very different restaurants include the suavely elegant Nico at 90 *(see p296).*

Ritz

55 Piccadilly, W1V 9DG. **Map** 12 F3.
【 *020-7493 8181.* **FAX** *020-7493 2687.* **TX** *267200.* **Rooms:** *131.* 🛏
1 ♿ 24 TV 🍸 🛳 ▤ 🍽 🏃
♿ ♨ ⚓ 🍸 🍽 ⊗ *AE, DC, MC, , JCB.* ⓔⓔⓔⓔⓔ *See p91.*

Cunard's flagship still draws the crowds, especially for afternoon teas in the Palm Court – perhaps the closest most of us can get to sampling Life at the Top. The Ritz's marbled, Frenchified rooms are undeniably grand – especially the restaurant, where gilded chandeliers are suspended from a fresco of clouds above the diners' heads. If you don't look up, look out over the Italian Garden towards the tree-filled oasis of Green Park.

Twenty-Two Jermyn Street

22 Jermyn St, St James's, SW1Y 6HL.
Map 12 F3. 【 *020-7734 2353.* **FAX** *020-7734 0750.* **Rooms:** *18.* 🛏 1
♿ 24 TV 🍸 🍽 🍽 ⊗
AE, DC, MC, V, JCB. ⓔⓔⓔⓔⓔ

An unobtrusive entrance leads to a warren of luxurious suites and studios, perfectly kitted out for the business visitor. They are very comfortable for anyone else, too, lavishly decorated and beautifully maintained. Round-the-clock room service, use of a nearby health club and an emphasis on security and privacy justify the hotel's apparently steep tariffs.

SOHO
LEICESTER SQUARE
OXFORD STREET

Concorde

50 Great Cumberland Pl, W1H 7FD.
Map 11 C1. **C** 020-7402 6169.
FAX 020-7724 1184. **TX** 262076.
Rooms: 27. ▢ ▢ ▢ ▢ ▢
▢ ▢ *AE, DC, MC, V.* ⓔⓔ

This hotel shares the pleasantly
bygone but cared-for ambience
of its bigger sister next door *(see
Bryanston Court)*. The facilities,
however, are simpler, and the
tariff is correspondingly lower –
representing remarkably good
value this close to Oxford Street.

Edward Lear

28–30 Seymour St, W1H 5WD.
Map 11 C2. **C** 020-7402 5401. **FAX**
020-7706 3766. **Rooms:** 31 ▢ 18.
▢ ▢ ▢ ▢ *MC, V.* ⓔⓔ

Once the home of humourist
Edward Lear, this clean, simple
bed and breakfast is not too far
from Oxford Street. It caters for
single people and families as well
as for the orderly couples most
hotels seem meant for. There are
two small lounges (one full of
Edward Lear books and limericks),
and a light breakfast room. Rear
rooms are free of traffic noise.

Parkwood

4 Stanhope Pl, W2 2HB. **Map** 11 B2.
C 020-7402 2241. **FAX** 020-7402
1574. **Rooms:** 18. ▢ 12. ▢ ▢ ▢
▢ ▢ *MC, V.* ⓔⓔ

This friendly, cosy family bed and
breakfast is in a tidy house, with
Classical portico and jet black
railings, just a block from Marble
Arch. The lounge-cum-reception
has a gracious air, but bedrooms
are not at all luxurious and show
some signs of wear. Downstairs is
a small, cheerful breakfast room
with simple bentwood chairs.

Bryanston Court

56–60 Great Cumberland Pl, W1H 7FD.
Map 11 C1. **C** 020-7262 3141.
FAX 020-7262 7248. **Rooms:** 54. ▢
▢ ▢ ▢ ▢ ▢ ▢
▢ *AE, DC, MC, V, JCB.* ⓔⓔⓔ

Blue awnings add a continental
jauntiness to this well-kept hotel.
Inside, soft lighting quietly gleams
on oil portraits and gently battered
brown leather. The atmosphere is
civilized and old-fashioned, but
personal – as few West End hotels
are these days. The bedrooms are
simple, smallish, and functional.

Durrants

George St, W1H 6BJ. **Map** 11 B1.
C 020-7935 8131. **FAX** 020-757487
3510. **Rooms:** 92. ▢ ▢ ▢ ▢ ▢
▢ ▢ ▢ ▢ ▢ ▢ *AE, MC,
V.* ⓔⓔⓔ

This well-loved Georgian hotel
still has the feel of the old country
coaching inn it once was. The
restaurant is a place of crisp linen
and silver domed tureens. Bars
and sitting rooms full of leather
and oak panelling reinforce the
distinct impression of old-fashioned,
masculine taste. Bedrooms are
unfussy, and smallish at the rear.

Hazlitt's

6 Frith St, W1V 5TZ. **Map** 13 A2.
C 020-7434 1771. **FAX** 020-7439
1524. **Closed** 24–26 Dec. **Rooms:** 23.
▢ ▢ ▢ ▢ ▢ *AE, DC, MC, V.*
ⓔⓔⓔⓔ

One of London's most beguiling
and individual hotels is set in
three 18th-century houses – the
critic and essayist William Hazlitt
(1778–1830) once lived in one of
them. Although not luxurious, it is
resoundingly civilized. Pictures
deck every wall, but bedrooms
are restfully plain in greens and
creams, with solid, interesting
antiques. Palms and ferns, and
sometimes a Classical bust, perch
on Victorian baths with huge
claw feet. Apart from a small fire-
lit sitting-room behind reception,
there are no public areas.

Hampshire

Leicester Sq, WC2H 7LH. **Map** 13 B3.
C 020-7839 9399. **FAX** 020-7930
8122. **TX** £14848 HAMPS G.
Rooms: 123. ▢ ▢ ▢ ▢ ▢ ▢
▢ ▢ ▢ ▢ ▢ ▢ ▢ ▢ ▢
▢ *AE, DC, MC, V, JCB.* ⓔⓔⓔⓔⓔ

Few suspect such lavishness could
possibly be concealed on one of
London's seedier squares, in the
unlikely setting of the former
Dental Hospital. Inside, this
imposing brick building is plush
enough to please the most
exacting of American executives
(the core of its trade). It is a chain
hotel (part of the Edwardian
group), and stylishly immaculate.
A slightly colonial air prevails
among the Hampshire's ceiling
fans and vast Chinese jars.

Marble Arch Marriott

134 George St, W1H 6DN.
Map 11 B1. **C** 020-7723 1277.
FAX 020-7402 0666. **TX** 27983.
Rooms: 240. ▢ ▢ ▢ ▢ ▢ ▢
▢ ▢ ▢ ▢ ▢ ▢ ▢ ▢
▢ ▢ ▢ *AE, DC, MC, V, JCB.*
ⓔⓔⓔⓔⓔ

This modern box just off Edgware
Road has remarkably good
facilities and a cared-for, relaxing
atmosphere. Rooms contain one or
two comfortable queen-sized beds,
American-style. There is also a
health club with gym and
swimming pool, and – unusual for
the centre of town – free parking.

REGENT'S PARK
MARYLEBONE

Blandford

80 Chiltern Street, W1M 1PS.
Map 4 D5. **C** 020-7486 3103.
FAX 020-7487 2786. **TX** 262594
BLANFD G. **Rooms:** 33 ▢ ▢ ▢
▢ ▢ ▢ ▢ *AE, DC, MC, V.*
ⓔⓔ

The Blandford has won numerous
awards for its welcoming brand of
inexpensive bed and breakfast. It
is a family-run establishment
offering simple, unassuming, and
practical accommodation, and a
lavish breakfast, in a quiet sidestreet near Baker Street station.

Hotel La Place

17 Nottingham Pl, W1M 3FF.
Map 4 D5. **C** 020-7486 2323.
FAX 020-7486 4335. **Rooms:** 24. ▢
▢ ▢ ▢ ▢ ▢ ▢ ▢ ▢ ▢
▢ ▢ ▢ *DC, MC, V.* ⓔⓔⓔ

Just a stone's throw away from
Madame Tussauds in central
London, this is a real find –
a pleasant town house, well-
appointed and producing simple
meals in its basement restaurant.
A plant-filled bar of blonde
bentwood and rattan skilfully
suggests a garden setting.
Bedrooms are very well-furnished
and equipped with many more
features than you would expect
for these prices. The care that is
taken about security makes this
an attractive hotel for women
travelling alone.

Dorset Square

39–40 Dorset Sq, NW1 6QN.
Map 3 C5. **C** 020-7723 7874.
FAX 020-7724 3328. **TX** 263964.
Rooms: 38. ▢ ▢ ▢ ▢ ▢ ▢
▢ ▢ ▢ ▢ ▢ ▢ ▢ ▢ *AE,
MC, V.* ⓔⓔⓔⓔ

This beautifully restored Regency
building has enormous panache:
antiques, bold fabrics, *objets d'art*,
and interesting paintings happily
mingle. Each room is different.
Downstairs, a restaurant and bar,
with games like backgammon in
progress, provide a relaxed
alternative to the carefully
plumped sitting rooms.

For key to symbols see p275

White House

Albany St, NW1 3UP. **Map** 4 E4.
(020-7387 1200. **FAX** 020-7388
0091. **TX** 24111. **Rooms:** 584.
AE, DC, MC,
V, JCB. ⓔⓔⓔⓔ

Once touched by the Profumo
Affair (a political sex scandal of
the 1960s), this large, impressive
complex of suites and apartments
today provides high standards of
accommodation and a varied
range of public rooms. The smart,
classic restaurant and comfortably
chintzy cocktail lounge are well
complemented by a popular, cool
basement wine bar with beams
and copper knickknacks, and the
spacious Garden Café. An extra
advantage is the hotel's proximity
to Euston mainline railway station
(see p358–9).

Langham Hilton

1c Portland Pl, W1N 4JA. **Map** 4 E5.
(020-7636 1000. **FAX** 020-7323
2340. **Rooms:** 379.
AE, DC, MC, V, JCB.
ⓔⓔⓔⓔⓔ See p221.

Reopened as a hotel in 1991, after
long tenure by the BBC who used
it for radio broadcasting, the
Langham offers a lavish, Hilton-
style re-creation of its former
Victorian splendour, in addition to
all the contemporary "mod cons"
anyone could possibly wish for.
The public rooms reflect a
fashionable nostalgia for the days
of the British Empire. The spacious
bedrooms are sumptuous, as is the
famous ballroom, decked with
glittering Italian chandeliers and
pompously ornate plasterwork.

BLOOMSBURY

FITZROVIA

COVENT GARDEN

THE STRAND

Fielding

4 Broad Court, Bow St, WC2B 5QZ.
Map 13 C2. **(** 020-7836 8305.
FAX 020-7497 0064. **Rooms:** 24.
AE,
DC, MC, V, JCB. ⓔⓔ

As an inexpensive, personally
run bed and breakfast in a
fascinating part of London, the
Fielding is hard to beat. Smoky the
parrot may well be the first to
greet you in a small bar of pink
plush. Upstairs, a miscellany of
bedrooms rambles in all
directions, some split-level and

oddly shaped, all small, none
luxurious. Several have useful
desks for working visitors; shower-
rooms with minuscule basins are
ingeniously squeezed into
impossible spaces.

Mabledon Court

10–11 Mabledon Pl, WC1H 9BA.
Map 5 B3. **(** 020-7388 3866.
FAX 020-7387 5686. **Rooms:** 30.
AE, MC, V. ⓔⓔ

There's nothing fancy about this
rather plain building, or its
surroundings, but the tariff doesn't
give itself airs either, and the hotel
is handily placed for both King's
Cross and St Pancras railway
stations. The small rooms are clean
and neat, with a tiny lounge and a
stylishly modern breakfast room in
the basement.

Academy

17–25 Gower St, WC1E 6HG.
Map 5 A5. **(** 020-7631 4115.
FAX 020-7636 3442. **Rooms:** 48.
AE, DC, MC, V, JCB. ⓔⓔⓔ

Sentinel bay trees mark these
three Georgian town houses near
the heart of London University.
Inside the Academy, the ambience
is sophisticated without excess.
French windows by the book-
shelves of a cosy sitting room lead
to an inviting patio garden. A
basement restaurant offers very
interesting food served in intimate
surroundings, sometimes
accompanied by live music.

Bonnington

92 Southampton Row, WC1B 4BH.
Map 5 C5. **(** 020-7242 2828.
FAX 020-7831 9170. **TX** 261591.
Rooms: 215. AE,
DC, MC, V, JCB. ⓔⓔⓔ

This family-run hotel is one
of the most useful in Bloomsbury.
The furnishings are mostly quite
unremarkable, but the managerial
style is politely personal and
quietly assured. The lounge-bar
and restaurant are pleasant and
modern. Weekend deals are
excellent value for families.

Hotel Russell

Russell Sq, WC1B 5BE. **Map** 5 B5.
(020-7837 6470. **FAX** 020-7837
2857. **TX** 24615. **Rooms:** 329.
AE, DC, MC, V, JCB.
ⓔⓔⓔⓔ

The portentous exterior of this
grand, late-Victorian pile is
matched by the foyer, a maze of
tawny marble with an imposing

stairway leading off it. Wood
panelling, leather chesterfields,
rich dark fabrics, and chandeliers
set the tone elsewhere. The nicest
rooms overlook the gardens. The
Virginia Woolf brasserie serves
pre-theatre dinners.

Covent Garden Hotel

10 Monmouth St, WC2 9HB. **Map** 13
B2. **(** 020-7806 1000. **FAX** 020-
7806 1100. **Rooms:** 50.
AE, MC, V. ⓔⓔⓔⓔⓔ

Another example of the continuing
gentrification of the Covent Garden
area, this charming hotel opened
in 1996 in a no-expense-spared
conversion of a former French
hospital. Its interior manages to
combine luxury with coziness to
such an extent that it's tempting
simply to relax in the stylish,
wood-panelled drawing room and
library and never stray outside at
all. But with the best of London's
shops, entertainment and streetlife
all around, it's worth tearing
yourself reluctantly away.

Howard

Temple Pl, Strand, WC2R 2PR.
Map 14 D2. **(** 020-7836 3555.
FAX 020-7379 4547. **TX** 268047.
Rooms: 135.
AE, DC, MC, V, JCB. ⓔⓔⓔⓔⓔ

The building is unmistakably
modern, but the authoritative
polish of the hotel's staff soon
transports you to a bygone era.
The foyer is an ornate Classical
pastiche, with *diamanté*
chandeliers and riotous plasterwork painted in ice-cream shades.
Other notable features are a
landscaped interior garden visible
from restaurant and bar, and
splendid river views from many
of the pleasant, traditionally
furnished bedrooms.

Mountbatten

20 Monmouth St, WC2H 9HD.
Map 13 B2. **(** 020-7836 4300.
FAX 020-7240 3540. **TX** 298087.
Rooms: 127.
AE, MC, V, JCB.
ⓔⓔⓔⓔⓔ

Well-located for theatreland or
Covent Garden, the hotel is filled
with memorabilia of World War II
veteran, Lord Mountbatten. Public
areas have the ease and style of
Edwardian drawing rooms and
are pleasantly decked out with
colonial and Oriental touches:
ceiling fans, rugs, huge potted
palms. The popular wine bar
downstairs serves a very good
range of snacks, and pre-theatre
dinners can also be arranged.

Savoy

Strand, WC2R 0EU. **Map** 13 C2.
020-7836 4343. FAX 020-7240
6040. TX 24234. *Rooms: 207.*
AE, DC,
MC, V, JCB. €€€€€ See p116.

On its dais above the Thames,
Richard D'Oyly Carte's dream
hotel still lords it over this part
of London. Inside, the Savoy Grill
is a time-honoured institution for
political and journalistic *tête-à-
têtes*, and piano-accompanied tea
in the lovely Thames Foyer is
ever-popular. Art Deco features
give the Savoy much of its
distinctive elegance. Many of
the bedrooms have old-fashioned
bathrooms with enormous
watering-can shower-heads. Some
particularly appealing balconied
singles have views upriver. But it
is the little touches that give the
Savoy its excellent reputation:
those mattresses with 836 springs,
the bells by the beds for instant
service, and the managing
director's quaint belief that
"standardization is not part of
hotel-keeping". The skylighted
rooftop swimming pool and the
fitness centre are as stylish as
one would expect.

Waldorf

Aldwych, WC2B 4DD. **Map** 14 D2.
020-7836 2400. FAX 020-7836
7244. TX 24574. *Rooms: 292.*
AE, DC, MC, V, JCB.
€€€€€

Still smart, this superior Forte hotel
is no longer quite the exclusive
haunt of its heyday. However, the
tea dances for which it was once
so famous still take place at
weekends, and afternoon tea
beneath the famous scrolled
balcony where the band plays is
a popular pastime. The Aldwych
Brasserie provides a less formal
setting for pre-theatre dinners.
Some of the bedrooms are a bit
glum, but they are gradually
being refurbished.

THE CITY

Tower Thistle

St Katherine's Way, E1 9LD.
Map 16 E3. 020-7481 2575.
FAX 020-7481 3799. TX 885934.
Rooms: 802.
AE, DC, MC, V, JCB.
€€€€

This 1970s concrete ziggurat
commands a splendid piece of
river frontage, just below Tower

Bridge and looking across to
Butler's Wharf. Inside, the foyer is
cool and spacious, with running
water and plants. Restaurants
range from the expensive Princes
and a hearty Carvery to the chic
Which Way West, which
transforms into a nightclub.
Bedrooms are not very large, but
all have good views, modern
decor and excellent facilities.

FURTHER AFIELD

Chase Lodge

10 Park Rd, Hampton Wick, KT1 4AS.
020-8943 1862. FAX 020-8943 9363.
Rooms: 13.
AE, DC, MC, V. €€

This modest Victorian house has
an airy conservatory where
excellent breakfasts and dinners
are served. There is also a small,
smart bar and sitting room. The
bedrooms, though small, are
prettily done out in cottagey
styles with pine or Victorian
furnishings, and bathrooms are
fitted in where possible.

La Reserve

422–428 Fulham Rd, SW6 1DU.
Map 18 E5. 020-7385 8561.
FAX 020-7385 7662. *Rooms: 43.*
AE, DC, MC, V. €€

Although the frontage is Classical,
the hotel is determinedly different
inside. The austere, ultra-modern
furnishings may not appeal to
everyone, but the minimalist
bedrooms have smart bedspreads
and good bathrooms. The
restaurant serves a short but
spirited menu of ethnic specialities
all day long.

Swiss Cottage

4 Adamson Rd, NW3 3HP.
020-7722 2281. FAX 020-7483
4588. TX 297232 SWISSCO G.
Rooms: 59. 4. AE, DC, MC, V.
€€

This well-kept Victorian house
in a quiet street not far from
Swiss Cottage underground
station offers a pleasantly old-
fashioned stay. Antiques and a
grand piano mingle with the
reproduction furniture and an
interestingly unusual collection
of paintings and antiquated
wallpapers. Bedrooms are
spacious and comfortable, the
more expensive rooms boasting
velvet sofas or *chaises longues*.
The restaurant's short menu is
supplemented by sandwiches
and simple snacks served in the
bar and lounge.

Kingston Lodge

Kingston Hill, Kingston-upon-Thames,
KT2 7NP. 020-854 4481. FAX 020-
8547 1013. TX 936C34. *Rooms: 62.*
AE, DC, MC, V. €€€

This small-scale, suburban hotel,
which is part of the Forte chain, is
light and homely. It is on a fairly
busy road, but there are plenty of
quieter rooms at the rear. The
open-plan but nicely intimate,
split-level public areas ramble
from the reception desk. A gas
coal fire burns cheerfully in a
wooden Adam-look surround, and
billowy blinds shield diners from
the sun in the glass-walled
restaurant. There are a few signs
of wear and tear, but generally the
comfortable effects are sustained.

Cannizaro House

West Side, Wimbledon Common,
SW19 4UE. 020-8379 1464.
FAX 020-8879 7338. TX 941 3837.
Rooms: 45. AE,
DC, MC, V, JCB. €€€€€

King George III (reigned
1760–1820) once breakfasted in
this merchant's mansion, originally
dating from 1705, and the hotel
has an ostentatious style that is
appropriate to its royal connection.
Plaster ceilings, stark, imposing
fireplaces, complex flower
arrangements, and windows
ornamented with swagged curtains
all add to an air of grandeur. The
splendour continues upstairs in the
bedrooms. But the best feature of
Cannizaro House is its splendid
secluded gardens, which give it
the feel of a country house.

Sheraton Skyline, Heathrow Airport

Bath Rd, Hayes, Middlesex, UB3 5BP.
020-8759 2535. FAX 020-8750
9150. TX 934254. *Rooms: 351.*
AE, DC,
MC, V, JCB. €€€€€

If you are looking for something
in the vicinity of Heathrow Airport
which is more than just an air-
conditioned, soundproofed box,
try the Sheraton Skyline. One of its
main attractions is the amazing
Patio Caribe, an extraordinary
indoor pool amid a jungle of
tropical foliage, which makes a
nice setting for cocktails or buffet
lunch. Other features conform to
the smart chain hotel pattern.
Courtesy transport to the airport
and free parking are provided.
*For a list of other hotels that are
close to Gatwick or Heathrow
airports see pages 355–7.*

For key to symbols *see p275*

RESTAURANTS AND PUBS

A pre-theatre menu board

EATING OUT IN London is like taking a gastronomic world tour. In the space of just a few days you can travel from America to Africa, taking in all the European countries, and the Near, Middle and Far East on the way. Over the past 30 years, and particularly the last decade, London has been transformed into a veritable United Nations of cuisine.

afield have also been included. *Choosing a Restaurant* on pages 292–4 summarizes key features of the restaurants, and is organized by area so that you can locate one close by. More details can be found in the individual listings on pages 295–305, grouped according to the type of cuisine.

In recent years, London's cafés have taken on a new look and are among the most lively places in town. As for pubs, for which Britain is famed, many now serve tasty meals, ranging from simple snacks to popular ethnic dishes. Some mainly more informal places to eat and drink, including pubs, are on pages 306–9.

CHOOSING YOUR TABLE

The restaurants listed in this book offer a high standard of cooking, value for money and an enjoyable evening out, and represent a huge range of styles and prices. They are spread across the main tourist areas; a few that merit a special trip further

LONDON RESTAURANTS

COVENT GARDEN, Piccadilly, Soho and Leicester Square are the areas where you will find the widest choice of eating places. Kensington and Chelsea also boast a good range of restaurants, and Butler's Wharf on the south bank of the Thames has been regenerated with several excellent restaurants near the waterfront.

You can still get traditional British roast beef and stodgy puddings at the likes of Simpson's *(see p295)* but the most significant trend is a new style of British cooking which

marries a lighter approach to a variety of culinary influences. Home-grown chefs like Sally Clarke (of Clarke's, *see p298*), Alastair Little *(see p297)* and Marco Pierre White (The Oak Room, *see p296*) are leading the way.

London is a real paradise for lovers of Indian food, with countless tandoori, balti and bhel poori houses serving cheap food. Two very popular cuisines are Thai and Italian; Soho has a couple of the best-known Thai venues, alongside Japanese, Indonesian, and some of the best Chinese chefs and restaurants outside Hong Kong. Some modern Italian restaurants, epitomized by Riva *(see p299)* and the River Café *(see p299)*, offer a lighter style of cooking than the traditional trattorias. French cooking, the longest-established "guest" cuisine in the city, accounts for a sizeable percentage of the high-class establishments in The City and around Mayfair.

Most restaurants provide at least one vegetarian option and some offer a separate vegetarian menu. A number of specialist vegetarian restaurants offer more adventurous dishes, such as The Place Below *(see p301)*. Seafood is a London speciality, with both new-style and traditional fish restaurants being well represented.

Coast *(see p298)*

OTHER PLACES TO EAT

MANY LONDON hotels have excellent restaurants open to non-residents. Some hotel restaurants can be stuffy and rather over-priced, but others offer top-quality food prepared by star chefs.

There are a number of pizza and pasta chains serving decent meals in branches across the city. Many pubs are now rivalling wine bars and serving a range of food from standard pub fare to Thai curries or Mediterranean char-grilled food, with excellent wine lists to match. French-style café-brasseries have caught on and a number of coffee houses-pâtisseries are worth a visit. Otherwise, you can grab a quick, cheap snack from a sandwich bar, pizza stand or all-night bagel bakery.

Commissionaire at the Hard Rock Café *(see p302)*

Bibendum *(see p297)*

TIPS ON EATING OUT

Most London restaurants serve lunch between 12.30pm and 2.30pm and dinner from 7pm until 11pm. Last orders are usually at 11pm. Ethnic restaurants tend to stay open slightly longer; often until midnight or even later. Many restaurants close on Sunday and Monday. All-day café brasseries (11am–11pm) may only be licensed to serve alcohol at certain times or with a meal. The traditional British Sunday lunch *(see p289)* appears in almost every pub and many restaurants, so unless that is what you want, it is worth checking first as even high-class restaurants may suspend their normal menu on Sundays.

Only the most expensive spots demand a collar and tie; the preferred dress is usually "smart casual". Booking is advisable, especially at newly-opened or celebrity-chef-run venues.

PRICE AND SERVICE

An average three-course meal with wine at a medium-priced restaurant in central London can be had for between £25 and £35 per head. Lower prices (£5–£15 a head) prevail at small ethnic and vegetarian cafés, wine bars and pubs. Many restaurants have set-price menus which generally offer much better value than the *à la carte* menu. In central London pre- and post- theatre set

menus have also become increasingly popular, and are geared towards quick service.

Before ordering, check the small print at the bottom of the menu. Prices will include Value Added Tax (VAT) and may add an optional service charge (between 10 and 15%). In addition, some restaurants may impose a cover charge (£1–£2 a head); some may have a minimum charge during their busiest periods, and some refuse to accept certain credit cards. Beware of the old trick where service is included in the bill but staff leave the "total" box on your credit slip blank, hoping you will add another 10%.

Expect different types of service in different types of restaurant: cheerful and breezy in fast-food joints; discreet yet attentive in high-class places. At peak times you will usually have to wait longer.

EATING WITH CHILDREN

Except in Italian restaurants, fast-food places and a few other places, children are generally tolerated rather than warmly welcomed in London restaurants. However, many do offer a special children's menu, small portions and high chairs *(see pp292–4)* and some actively encourage children and teenagers by offering entertainments, music and activities. Turn to page 339 for a suggestion of places that cater particularly well to children of various ages.

USING THE LISTINGS
Key to symbols in the listings on pp295–305.

🍴	fixed-price menu
L	lunch
D	dinner
🚭	no-smoking tables
V	vegetarian options
🧒	children's portions and/or high chairs
♿	wheelchair access
👔	jacket and tie required
🎵	live music
🪑	tables outside
🍷	good wine list
★	highly recommended
💳	credit cards accepted:
AE	American Express
DC	Diners Club
MC	Mastercard/Access
V	Visa
JCB	Japanese Credit Bureau

Price categories for a three-course dinner for one including a half-bottle of house wine and all unavoidable extra charges (eg cover and service):
£ under £15
££ £15–£25
£££ £25–£35
££££ £35–£50
£££££ over £50

Clarke's Restaurant *(see p298)*

London's top Hungarian restaurant *(see p301)*

What to Eat in London

T HE TRADITIONAL SUNDAY lunch displays what is best about British food – good ingredients prepared simply but well. A joint of roast meat (usually lamb or beef) served with appropriate accompaniments (mint sauce or redcurrant jelly for lamb, mustard or horseradish sauce for beef) is the centrepiece of the meal;

Fish and Chips
The battered fish (usually haddock or cod) and chips are deep fried.

wonderful homely puddings and fine British cheeses served with cheese biscuits are obligatory "afters". Sunday lunch is still an institution for Londoners and you will find versions of it in many restaurants and cafés as well as in hotels and pubs all over the capital. The legendary English breakfast may be less ambitious than the five-course feast enjoyed by the Victorians, but it is still a hearty meal and the perfect start to a hard day's sightseeing. Afternoon tea (which is usually taken at around 4pm) is another treat, when the British genius for cakes and their fondness for tea-drinking come together. The smell of fish and chips will often greet you as you wander around the city, and this classic British meal is best eaten in the open air, direct from its paper wrapping.

Full English Breakfast
This favourite meal consists of bacon, egg, tomato, fried bread and a variety of sausages.

Toast and Marmalade
Breakfast is usually finished off with slices of toast spread with orange marmalade.

Ploughman's Lunch
Crusty bread, cheese and sweet pickle are at the heart of this simple pub lunch.

Cheeses
British cheeses are mostly hard or semi-hard, such as Cheshire, Leicester and the most famous of all, Cheddar. Stilton is blue-veined.

Cheddar

Sage Derby

Cheshire

Stilton

Red Leicester

Bread and Butter Pudding
Served hot, the layers of bread and dried fruit are baked in a creamy custard.

Strawberries and Cream
Strawberries served with sugar and cream are a favourite summer dessert.

Summer Pudding
The outer bread lining is soaked in the juice of the many soft fruits inside.

Cucumber Sandwiches
Wafer-thin cucumber sandwiches are a traditional part of an English tea.

Jam and Cream Scones
Halfway between a cake and a bun, scones are served with cream and jam.

Tea
A cup of tea, served with milk or lemon, is still the British national drink.

Meat dishes are usually served with at least one green vegetable.

Horseradish sauce

Yorkshire pudding

Roast beef

Roast potatoes

Roast Beef and Yorkshire Pudding
Yorkshire pudding, a savoury batter baked in the oven, is the traditional accompaniment to roast beef along with horseradish sauce, roast potatoes and a meat gravy.

Steak and Kidney Pie
Chunks of beef and pigs' kidneys are braised in a thick gravy and topped off with a browned pastry crust.

Shepherd's Pie
This is made with stewed minced lamb, vegetables and a mashed potato topping.

What to Drink
Beer is the British drink. The many different kinds (see p308) range from light lager to stout and bitter. Gin originally came from London. Pimms, usually mixed with lemonade, fruit and mint, is a cooling drink on those hot summer days.

Stout (Guinness)   Bitter   Lager

Pimms   Gin and tonic

London's Best: Restaurants and Pubs

THE SHEER VARIETY of eating and drinking places in London is overwhelming. There are elegant high-class restaurants offering the most *haute* of *haute cuisine,* exotic ethnic specialists (from the Indian sub-continent to the Caribbean), cheap and cheerful cafés, friendly neighbourhood pubs, and fish and chip shops. There is something for every taste, pocket and occasion. See pages 295–305 for the full restaurant listings, pages 306–7 for more informal eating places and pages 308–9 for pubs.

L'Odéon
This grand restaurant is celebrated for its exciting dishes using unusual food and flavour combinations.
(See p296.)

Sea Shell
One of the best fish and chip shops in London, this busy restaurant and take-away has customers who come from far and wide.
(See pp306–7.)

Regent's Park and Marylebone

Kensington and Holland Park

South Kensington and Knightsbridge

The Chapel
A modern pub catering to a discerning clientele, The Chapel has superb food, an excellent wine list and friendly staff. (See pp308–9.)

Chelsea

Brown's
Afternoon tea is a speciality of this traditional hotel.
(See pp306–7.)

Tamarind
This Indian restaurant serves up meticulously prepared curry dishes created by top chefs. (See p304.)

Aubergine
This charming French restaurant prepares faultless dishes combining rich flavours with great delicacy and finesse. (See p296.)

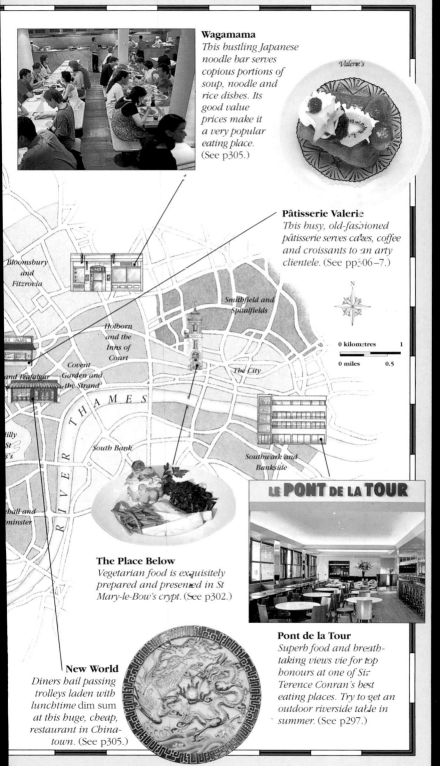

Wagamama
This bustling Japanese noodle bar serves copious portions of soup, noodle and rice dishes. Its good value prices make it a very popular eating place. (See p305.)

Pâtisserie Valerie
This busy, old-fashioned pâtisserie serves cakes, coffee and croissants to an arty clientele. (See pp306–7.)

Valerie's

Bloomsbury
and
Fitzrovia

Smithfield and
Spitalfields

Holborn
and the
Inns of
Court

Covent
Garden and
the Strand

and Trafalgar

The City

0 kilometres 1

0 miles 0.5

Piccadilly
St
's

South Bank

Southwark and
Bankside

RIVER THAMES

hall and
minster

The Place Below
Vegetarian food is exquisitely prepared and presented in St Mary-le-Bow's crypt. (See p302.)

LE **PONT** DE LA **TOUR**

Pont de la Tour
Superb food and breath-taking views vie for top honours at one of Sir Terence Conran's best eating places. Try to get an outdoor riverside table in summer. (See p297.)

New World
Diners hail passing trolleys laden with lunchtime dim sum at this huge, cheap, restaurant in China-town. (See p305.)

Choosing a Restaurant

THE RESTAURANTS IN this section have been selected for their good value or exceptional food. This chart highlights some of the main factors which may influence your choice. For more details about the restaurants see pages 295–305; light meals and snack places are on pages 306–7; and pubs on pages 308–9.

	Page Number	Set-Price Lunches	Set-Price Dinners	Late Opening	Children's Facilities	Tables Outside	No-Smoking Tables	Vegetarian Options
BAYSWATER, PADDINGTON								
Magic Wok (*Chinese*) £££	305	●						●
Veronica's (*British*) £££	295	●	■			●		●
KENSINGTON, HOLLAND PARK, NOTTING HILL								
Mandola (*Caribbean*) ££	302	●	■		■			●
The Abingdon (*French*) £££	296	●			■	●		●
Kensington Place (*Modern International*) ★ £££	298	●		●	■			●
Wódka (*Polish*) £££	301	●						
Bali Sugar (*Modern International*) ££££	297							●
Dakota (*Americas*) ££££	302	●			■			●
Clarke's (*Modern International*) ££££	298	●	■					●
SOUTH KENSINGTON, GLOUCESTER ROAD								
Bibendum (*Modern International*) £££££	298	●		●	■			
KNIGHTSBRIDGE, BROMPTON, BELGRAVIA								
Nippon Tuk (*Japanese*) ££	304	●	■		■			●
Emporio Armani Express (*Italian*) £££	299							●
Bombay Brasserie (*Indian*) ££££	303	●		●			■	●
Le Suquet (*Fish and Seafood*) ££££	301	●						
Salloos (*Indian*) ★ ££££	303	●	■					●
Memories of China (*Chinese*) £££££	305	●	■					●
CHELSEA, FULHAM								
Cactus Blue (*Americas*) £££	302	●	■				■	●
Chutney Mary (*Indian*) £££	303	●		●			■	●
Vama (*Indian*) £££	304	●	■				■	●
Albero & Grana (*Spanish*) ££££	300			●	■			●
Bluebird (*Modern International*) ££££	298			●		●		●
Nikita's (*Russian*) ££££	301		■	●				●
Aubergine (*French*) ★ £££££	296	●	■					●
PICCADILLY, MAYFAIR, BAKER STREET								
Al Hamra (*Lebanese*) £££	300			●	■			●
Hard Rock Café (*Americas*) £££	302			●	■	●	■	●
Mulligan's of Mayfair (*Irish*) £££	298	●	■					●
Singapore Garden (*Southeast Asian*) £££	304	●	■					●
Sofra (*Turkish*) £££	300	●	■	●				●
Stephen Bull (*Modern International*) £££	299							●
Vong (*Thai*) £££	304	●	■	●			■	●
Zafferano (*Italian*) ★ £££	299	●			■			
The Avenue (*Modern International*) ££££	297	●		●	●			●
Coast (*Modern International*) ★ ££££	298	●		●	■			
Criterion Brasserie (*French*) ★ ££££	296	●		●	■			
Miyama (*Japanese*) ££££	304	●	■					
L'Odéon (*French*) ★ ££££	296	●		●	■			●
Quaglino's (*Modern International*) ££££	298	●		●				
Tamarind (*Indian*) ★ ££££	303	●	■	●	■			●
Chez Nico (*French*) £££££	296	●	■					●
The Connaught (*British*) £££££	295	●	■		■			●

Price categories include a three-course dinner for one, half a bottle of house wine, and all unavoidable extra charges such as cover and service (10–15%).
£ under £15
££ £15–£25
£££ £25–£35
££££ £35–£50
£££££ over £50.

★ Means highly recommended.

SET-PRICE LUNCHES AND DINNERS
Restaurants offering set-price meals at lunch, dinner or both. These usually represent very good value.
LATE OPENING
Last orders taken at or after 11.30pm excluding Sunday.
CHILDREN'S FACILITIES
Children's portions and/or high chairs.
VEGETARIAN OPTIONS
A vegetarian restaurant, or a restaurant with a number of vegetarian main courses on the menu.

		Page Number	Set-Price Lunches	Set-Price Dinners	Late Opening	Children's Facilities	Tables Outside	No-Smoking Tables	Vegetarian Options
Le Gavroche (French)	£££££	296	●						
The Greenhouse (British)	£££££	295	●			■			●
The Lindsay House (British)	£££££	295	●	■					●
Oak Room (French) ★	£££££	296	●						
The Oriental (Chinese)	£££££	305	●			■			
Stefano Cavallini (Italian)	£££££	299	●				■		●
La Tante Claire (French)	£££££	297	●						
SOHO									
Mildred's (Vegetarian)	£	301					●	■	●
Tokyo Diner (Japanese)	£	305			●			■	●
Fung Shing (Chinese)	££	305	●	■	●	■			●
Harbour City (Chinese) ★	££	305	●	■	●	■			●
Melati (Indonesian)	££	304	●	■	●	■			●
Momo (Greek)	££	300	●						●
New World (Chinese)	££	305	●	■	●	■		■	●
Yo! Sushi (Japanese)	££	305				■			●
Blue's Bistro and Bar (Americas)	£££	302	●	■	●				●
Café Fish (Fish and Seafood)	£££	301			●			■	●
The Gay Hussar (Hungarian)	£££	300	●						●
Mezzo (Modern International) ★	£££	298	●		●	■			●
Royal China (Chinese)	£££	305	●	■					●
Sri Siam (Thai)	£££	304	●		●				●
Veeraswamy (Indian)	£££	304	●		●	●			●
Alastair Little (Modern International)	££££	297	●						●
Chor Bizarre (Indian)	££££	303	●		●	■		■	●
Nobu (Japanese)	£££££	305	●	■		■		■	●
The Sugar Club (Modern International) ★	£££££	299	●		●	■			●
COVENT GARDEN, THE STRAND									
Calabash (African)	£	302			●	■			●
Food for Thought (Vegetarian)	£	301					●	■	●
World Food Café (Vegetarian) ★	£	302				■		■	●
Plummers (British)	££	295	●	■	●	■			●
Alfred (British) ★	£££	295	●	■	●	■	●		●
Bank (Modern International)	£££	297	●	■	●	■			●
Belgo Centraal (Belgian) ★	£££	300	●	■	●				●
Christopher's (Americas)	£££	302			●	■			
Orso (Italian)	£££	299			●			■	●
Palais du Jardin (French)	£££	297	●	■	●	■	●		●
Simpson's (British)	£££	295	●						●
Bertorelli's (Italian)	££££	299			●			■	●
Mon Plaisir (French)	££££	296	●	■					●
Quo Vadis (French)	££££	297	●	■	●				●
Rules (British)	££££	295	●			■			●
The Ivy (Modern International) ★	££££	298			●	■			●
BLOOMSBURY, FITZROVIA									
Table Café (Italian)	£	299				■			●
Wagamama (Japanese) ★	£	305	●	■	●			■	●
Chutneys (Indian)	££	303	●		●			■	●

Price categories include a three-course dinner for one, half a bottle of house wine, and all unavoidable extra charges such as cover and service (10–15%).
£ under £15
££ £15–£25
£££ £25–£35
££££ £35–£50
£££££ over £50.

★ Means highly recommended.

SET-PRICE LUNCHES AND DINNERS
Restaurants offering set-price meals at lunch, dinner or both. These usually represent very good value.
LATE OPENING
Last orders taken at or after 11.30pm excluding Sunday.
CHILDREN'S FACILITIES
Children's portions and/or high chairs.
VEGETARIAN OPTIONS
A vegetarian restaurant, or a restaurant with a number of vegetarian main courses on the menu.

Restaurant	Price	Page Number	Set-Price Lunches	Set-Price Dinners	Late Opening	Children's Facilities	Tables Outside	No-Smoking Tables	Vegetarian Options
CAMDEN TOWN, HAMPSTEAD									
Daphne (Greek)	££	300	●		●	■	●		●
Lemonia (Greek)	££	300	●		●	■			●
Cottons Rhum Shop (Caribbean)	£££	302			●			■	●
ISLINGTON									
Anna's Place (Swedish)	£££	300				■	●		●
SPITALFIELDS, CLERKENWELL									
Nazrul (Indian)	£	303	●	■	●				●
Cicada (Spanish)	£££	304						■	●
Moro (Portuguese)	£££	301							●
Quality Chop House (British)	£££	295			●			■	●
Maison Novelli (French)	££££	296							●
THE CITY, SOUTH BANK									
Moshi Moshi Sushi (Japanese)	£	304	●	■				■	●
The Place Below (Vegetarian) ★	££	301	●	■				■	●
Café Spice Namaste (Indian)	£££	303	●	■					●
Livebait (Fish and Seafood)	££££	301	●	■				■	●
RSJ (French)	£££	297	●	■					●
Sweetings (Fish and Seafood)	£££	301							
The People's Palace (Modern International)	££££	298	●		●	■		■	●
Le Pont de la Tour (French)	£££££	297	●		●	■	●		●
Oxo Tower (Modern International)	££££	298	●			■			●
FURTHER AFIELD									
Istanbul Iskembecisi, N16 (Turkish)	££	300	●	■	●	■			
Madhu's Brilliant, Southall (Indian)	££	303	●	■	●	■		■	●
Rasa, N16 (Indian) ★	££	303		■		■		■	●
Riva, SW13 (Italian)	£££	299	●						●
Wilson's, W14 (Scottish)	£££	296						■	●
Spread Eagle, SE10 (French)	££££	297	●	■					●
River Café, W6 (Italian) ★	£££££	299					●	■	

St Paul's Cathedral

VISITOR INFORMATION

acoustiguide

**audio
tours
available**

The Shop

You can buy a lasting reminder of your visit in our Cathedral Shop.

Here, you will find CDs and tapes of the magnificent Cathedral Choir together with the handsomely-designed official Guidebook. The shop also stocks a fine range of stationery, clothing, books & Bibles, jewellery, religious products and toys & games, all of which have been hand-selected for their quality and value.

Our friendly, knowledgeable staff will provide any help you may need, including guidance on tax free shopping.

www.stpaulsshop.co.uk

The Café

Serving a wide range of drinks and food, the Crypt Café is the perfect place to enjoy a snack or light lunch in a comfortable atmosphere or simply to relax and watch the world go by.

The Refectory

This beautifully-restored restaurant provides morning coffee, lunch and traditional afternoon tea. Children are welcome and tables may be reserved by personal visit or telephoning 020 7246 8358.

Further current information can be found on our website www.stpauls.co.uk or telephone 020 7246 8348

BRITISH

British food has an unenviable reputation and is increasingly irrelevant to the British daily diet, which has become a medley of ingredients and styles from around the world. However, there are restaurants which take pride in producing authentic British food at its best *(see pp288–9)*, and these have a very loyal following.

Alfred

245 Shaftesbury Avenue WC2. **Map** 13 B1. 020-7240 2566. **Open** noon–3.30pm Mon–Fri, 6–11.30pm Mon–Sat. **Closed** 24 Dec–2 Jan. ☎ V ☂ ⊞ ★ 💳 AE, DC, MC, V, JCB. ££££

Opened in 1994, this is one of a new breed of restaurants that avoids the "starch and two veg" formula of many traditional British restaurants. The minimal decor is retro, reminiscent of a post-war café, tastefully decorated with carefully-chosen details in Bakelite and Formica. The menu changes seasonally to make the best use of market produce. Simple classics and imaginative modern dishes are immaculately prepared and presented. Staff are polite and purposeful, and there's a varied and excellent selection of beers, ciders and English country wines.

The Connaught

Carlos Pl W1. **Map** 12 E3. 020-7499 7070. **Open** 7.30–10am (for breakfast), 12.30–2.30pm, 6.30–10.45pm daily. **Grill open** 12.30–2.30pm, 6.30–10.45pm Mon–Fri. **Grill closed** public hols. ☎ V ☂ ⊞ T 💳 AE, DC, MC. £££££

The Connaught Hotel possesses London's grandest old-fashioned dining room. Here French flair is seamlessly joined with British formality, both in the food and the surroundings. Immaculate staff serve indigenous specialities like mixed grill and bread-and-butter pudding; or Gallic treats like *feuilleté d'oeufs brouillés aux truffes* (pastries filled with scrambled eggs and truffles), *homard grillé aux herbes* (grilled lobster with herbs) and *crème brûlée*. The same menu is served in the Grill Room during the week; book well in advance for both restaurants.

The Greenhouse

27a Hay's Mews W1. **Map** 12 E3. 020-7499 3331. **Open** noon–2.30pm Mon–Fri, 6.30pm–11pm Mon–Sat, 12.30–3pm, 6.30–10pm Sun. ☎ V ☂ 💳 AE, DC, MC, V. ££££££

Worth seeking out, in a quiet Mayfair mews, is this elegant, low-ceilinged restaurant, serving British food with confidence. Dishes such as boiled bacon with lentils, grilled lamb burger on spiced couscous with lemon chutney or cod in batter with mushy peas are raised to the level of smart, dinner-party fare. The atmosphere buzzes, the lighting glows warmly, and the ambience created by the sublime steamed sultana, ginger and syrup sponge never ceases to amaze.

The Lindsay House

21 Romilly St, W1. **Map** 12 E4. 020-7439 0450. **Open** noon–3pm, 6–11pm Mon–Fri, 6–11pm only Sat. ☎ V 💳 AE, DC, MC, V, JCB. £££££

This fine Georgian town house with its simple interior flourishes under the expert stewardship of talented Irish chef Richard Corrigan. Offal lovers flock here to try Corrigan's flavour combinations in dishes such as the starter of mushroom risotto garnished with pig's ears, or a main course of pan-roasted veal sweetbreads. There's a wide choice of non-meat food too, a good wine list and superb service.

Plummers

33 King St WC2. **Map** 13 C2. 020-7240 2534. **Open** noon–2.30pm Mon–Fri, 5.30–11.30pm Mon–Sat, noon–2.30pm, 5.30–10pm Sun. **Closed** public hols. ☎ V ☂ 💳 AE, DC, MC, V. ££

In an area full of transient restaurants, Plummers has stayed in business by serving good food in sizeable portions, from a menu which offers set prices for one, two or three courses. Diners can choose from a menu that has changed very little over the past 15 years: chunky British food such as steak and kidney pie and pork and apple casserole, alongside equally chunky American dishes such as clam chowder, Cajun meatloaf, and hamburgers with a choice of sauces.

Quality Chop House

94 Farringdon Road EC1. **Map** 6 E4. 020-7837 5093. **Open** noon–3pm Mon–Fri, 6.30pm–11.30pm Mon–Sat, noon–4pm, 7–11.30pm Sun. **Closed** 24 Dec–2 Jan. ⚡ V £££

"Progressive working class caterer" says the sign on the etched glass window of this beautiful Victorian diner with its original 1869 fittings wonderfully intact. But the workers these days are more likely to hail from the City than the factory. Sausage and mash may still appear on the bill of fare, but the sausages are meaty veal and the mash is

perfectly fluffy and creamy. Other upgraded stalwarts of British cuisine include salmon fishcakes (with sorrel sauce), liver and bacon, scrambled egg and smoked salmon, and, of course, chops.

Rules

35 Maiden La WC2. **Map** 13 C2. 020-7836 5314. **Open** noon–11.15pm Mon–Sat, noon–10.15pm Sun. **Closed** 24–25 Dec. ☎ L. V ☂ 💳 AE, DC, MC, V. £££££

London's oldest surviving restaurant has been serving staunchly traditional British food since 1798. Long a haunt of actors and aristocrats (historical cartoons and photographs signed by the great luminaries of British theatre cover the walls), it now attracts tourists, businessmen, and a few "hunting-shooting-fishing" types visiting town. Specialities of the house include beef, venison and feathered game (grouse, woodcock, partridge). (*See also p112*.)

Simpson's

100 Strand WC2. **Map** 13 C2. 020-7836 9112. **Open** 7am–10am (for breakfast), noon–2.30pm, 3–5pm, 5.30–11pm Mon–Sat, noon–2.30pm, 6–9pm Sun. **Closed** public hols. ☎ V ☂ 🎵 💳 AE, DC, MC, V, JCB. £££

This is a vast, open dining hall, with more than a hint of British public school (men are asked to wear jackets and ties, but the atmosphere is not in imidately stuffy). Go there to have the roast beef, carved in thick slices from giant, silver-domed trolleys. A recommended starter is the quail's eggs in haddock and cheese sauce, and, for the truly British experience, finish with bread and butter pudding or even get to grips with spotted dick.

Veronica's

3 Hereford Rd W2. **Map** 10 D2. 020-7229 5079. **Open** noon–3pm Mon–Fri, 6–11pm Mon–Sat. **Closed** public hols. ☎ V ☂ ⊞ 💳 AE, DC, MC, V. ££££

Veronica's specializes in a style of British regional and historical cooking that is unique among London restaurants. Dishes might include calves' liver and beetroot (1940), spring lamb with crabmeat (19th-century) or Hannah Woolley chicken and mustard (1644). Every couple of months, proprietress Veronica Shaw changes both the menu and the decor to tie in with a different theme, such as Scottish, Irish or Tudor food, the Middle Ages or World War II.

Wilson's

236 Blythe Road, W14. **Map** 17 A1.
(020-7603 7267. **Open** noon–
2.30pm Sun–Fri, 7.30–10pm
Mon–Sat. **Closed** Christmas week,
public hols. **V** ⚡ ⚹ **MC**, V.
£££

Bob Wilson runs the best "Scottish"
restaurant in London. It's not a
theme park, though; dishes from
the daily-changing menu are
mostly Anglo-Gallic, though there
are a few Scottish dishes such as
haggis, Athol brose (a dessert of
cream with oats, whisky and
honey), plus of course Scotch beef
and salmon. There are also half a
dozen malt whiskies to choose
from. After dinner Mr Wilson will
serenade patrons via the beauty of
the bagpipes, if requested.

FRENCH

As London's longest established
"guest" cuisine, French food is
readily available throughout the
capital, and the quality can be
superb. Top British chefs such as
Marco Pierre White (The Oak
Room) and Gordon Ramsay
(Aubergine) have achieved
celebrity status. You'll find most
types of French food well represented, from *haute cuisine*,
through the modern, lighter style,
to traditional, regional cuisines.

The Abingdon

54 Abingdon Rd W8. **Map** 17 C1.
(020-7937 3339. **Open** noon–
2.30pm, 6.30–11pm Mon–Sat, noon–
3pm, 6.30–10pm Sun. ⚹🍴 L. **V** ⚡
⚡ ⚹⚡ AE, MC, V, JCB. £££

A stylish, yet relaxed, neighbourhood bar and restaurant close to
Kensington High Street. Well-off
locals come here to sip wine while
poring over the Modern European
menu. Fish, such as steamed fillet
of sea bass with roasted red
peppers, is a strong point. The
service is welcoming and friendly.

Aubergine

11 Park Walk SW10. **Map** 18 F4.
(020-7352 3449. **Open** 12.15–
2pm Mon–Fri, 7–10.30pm Mon–Sat.
Closed 19 Dec–6 Jan, Easter Fri &
Mon. 🍴 only. **V** ⚡ ⚡ ★
⚡ AE, DC, MC, V, JCB.
£££££

This modern French restaurant
has a comfortable, well organized
interior, charming and attentive
service and, above all, faultless
cooking. *Cappuccinos* (frothy
soups) may include *haricots
blancs* with truffle oil or roasted
langoustines, brilliantly combining
lightness with rich, intense flavours.

Main courses include giant ravioli
of seafood, perfectly-cooked fish,
or a few meat and offal dishes. All
are beautifully presented. The only
drawbacks are the prices and the
necessity of booking in advance.

Chez Nico

90 Park Lane W1. **Map** 12 D3.
(020-7409 1290. **Open** noon–
2pm, 7–11pm Mon–Sat. **Closed**
public hols, 10 days at Christmas.
🍴🍴 L. **V** ⚡ ⚡ ⚡ AE, DC,
MC, V. £££££

Chez Nico is the three-star Michelin
HQ of superstar chef Nico Ladenis.
In these spacious surroundings,
Nico's artistry runs riot. *Foie gras*
is a recurring theme, adding a
richness and strength of flavour
that is balanced by delicate touches.
Dishes such as grilled sea bass
with celeriac purée and poached
fennel are superb. Nico's other
venues, Nico Central on Great
Portland Street (020-7436 8846)
and Simply Nico near Victoria
Station (020-7630 8061), allow you
to enjoy less complicated creations.

Criterion Brasserie

Piccadilly Circus W1. **Map** 13 A3.
(020-7930 0488. **Open** noon–
2.30pm, 6pm–midnight Mon–Sat,
noon–4pm, 6–10pm Sun. 🍴 L.
⚹ ⚡ ★ ⚡ AE, DC, MC, V, JCB.
££££

Part of Marco Pierre White's chain,
this venture was intended to bring
his cooking to the proletarians. Its
Piccadilly location and the interior,
a stunning neo-Byzantine hall with
a vaulted mosaic ceiling, are the
highlights. The cooking is good,
though it sometimes fails to match
Marco's reputation. Avoid the set
menus, which can be disappointing.
The *cappuccino* (frothy soup) of
chicken is divine, a main course of
shelled and sautéed langoustines
impressive, and a lemon tart tangy
and quite perfectly moist.

Le Gavroche

43 Upper Brook St W1. **Map** 12 D2.
(020-7408 0881or 020-7499 1826.
Open noon–2pm, 7–11pm Mon–Fri.
Closed public hols. 🍴 L. ⚡ ⚡
⚡ AE, DC, MC, V. £££££

This is the high temple of *haute
cuisine*, with prices to match.
However, the standard of cooking
set by Michel and Albert Roux is
consistently superb. The Roux
philosophy is to create a perfect
marriage between ingredients,
cooking methods and flavourings
for example, sautéed scallops in a
soy and spice sauce, served with
crisp, fried vegetable strips. Décor,
like the food, is tasteful and firmly
traditional, the service relentlessly

formal, the menu written entirely
in French, and the wine list vast
and daunting (800 wines). If you
want to experience Le Gavroche
on a budget, there are set meals
which work out half the price of
going *à la carte* – if you're lucky,
two people might even get some
change from a hundred pounds.

Maison Novelli

29 Clerkenwell Green EC1. **Map** 6 E4
(020-7251 6606. **Open** noon–
3pm, 6.30–11pm Mon–Fri. **Closed**
25 Dec, 1 Jan. **V** ⚡ AE, DC, MC, V.
££££

Jean-Christophe Novelli's
background is haute cuisine, and
it shows; dishes are sometimes too
fussy, but the flavours are never
compromised. Offal is one of his
signatures – hot salted pork
knuckle served with green lentils,
pigeon glazed with honey, or
stuffed braised pig's trotter are
always a terrific treat.

Mon Plaisir

21 Monmouth St WC2. **Map** 13 B2.
(020-7836 7243. **Open** noon–
2.15pm, 5.50–11.15pm Mon–Sat.
🍴 ⚡ AE, DC, MC, V, JCB.
££££

A long-standing fixture of Covent
Garden's theatreland, Mon Plaisir
retains its reputation for reliable,
unpretentious French provincial
food, cooked and served with care
and courtesy. The menu changes,
but you will usually find the likes
of fish soup, goat's cheese salad,
snails in garlic, *coq au vin, daube
de boeuf* and one of the best
cheeseboards in London.

The Oak Room

Hotel Meridien, 21 Piccadilly W1.
Map 12 E4. **(** 020-7465 1640.
Open noon–2.30pm, 7–11.15pm
Mon–Sat. **Closed** 24–26 Dec, 1 Jan,
some public hols.🍴 L. **V** ⚡ ⚡
⚡ AE, MC, V. £££££

This is another outpost of the
empire whose ruler's title consists
of three little words which have
come to represent culinary élan –
Marco Pierre White. Mr White's
cooking may well have found its
natural habitat in the glorious
surroundings of the Meridien; it
would be unfair to single out
dishes when the quality of the
cooking is so consistently high.

L'Odéon

65 Regent St W1. **Map** 12 F2.
(020-7287 1400. **Open** noon–
2.45pm, 5.30–11.30pm, Mon–Sat.
Closed 1 Jan, Easter Mon. 🍴 L.
V ⚹ ⚡ 🎵 ★ ⚡ AE, DC, MC, V,
JCB. ££££

Chef and owner, Bruno Loubet, is known for his ingredient and flavour combinations such as starter of carrot-coloured lasagne squares layered with ceps and pumpkin; potted shrimps in herb butter, served on toasted brioche and topped with slivers of endive and french beans. Asian influences are incorporated; stuffed pig's trotter glazed with barbecue sauce and steamed sea bass served with a black bean and garlic dressing.

Palais du Jardin

136 Long Acre. **Map** 13 B2.
(020-7379 5353. **Open** noon–3pm, 5.30–midnight Mon–Sat, noon–midnight Sun. ¶◎¶ ♨ ♿ 🔲
♟ ⊘ AE, DC, MC, V. €€€€

What looks from the outside like a small brasserie is in fact a multi-levelled 300-seater. Splash out on the dramatically presented *fruits de mer* or go for the ultra-fishy fishcakes. House wine is from the Jura region of France – an unusual but successful choice.

Le Pont de la Tour

Butlers Wharf SE1. **Map** 16 E4.
(020-7403 8403. **Bar and grill open** 11.30am–11.30pm Mon–Sat, 11.30am–11pm Sun. **Restaurant open** noon–3pm Sun–Fri, 6–11.30pm Mon–Sat, 6–11pm Sun. ¶◎¶ L. 🔲
♿ ♫ 🔲 ♟ ⊘ AE, DC, MC, V, JCB. €€€€€

This riverside Terence Conran creation boasts wonderful views of Tower Bridge. Set in a converted warehouse, the interior has the look of an ocean liner. The food is streamlined, too: pea risotto with mint; scallops with garlic butter; calves' liver with red onions. There is also a bar, and a grill serving seafood, steaks, and salads.

Quo Vadis

26-29 Dean St W1. **Map** 13 C2.
(020-7437 9585. **Open** noon–2.30pm, 6–11.30pm Mon–Fri, 6–11.30pm Sat, 6–10.30pm Sun. ¶◎¶ Mon–Fri. 🔲 ⊘ AE, DC, MC, V, JCB. €€€€

This beautiful restaurant has a comforting feel, complemented by proficient service and food which has the right balance of comfort and challenge, such as Cornish dressed crab with avocado and hot toast, ravioli of langoustine.

RSJ

13a Coin St SE1. **Map** 14 E3.
(020-7928 4554. **Open** noon–2pm Mon–Fri, 5.30–11pm Mon–Sat. **Closed** public hols. ¶◎¶ L & D. 🔲
♟ ⊘ AE, DC, MC, V. €€€€

RSJ serves a mixture of unspec-tacular but well-executed dishes. Salmon, lamb, duck and chicken are the most commonly featured, served both plain and with sauces. An extraordinarily good wine list specializes in some of the beautiful wines of the Loire region in the west of France.

Spread Eagle

1–2 Stockwell St SE10. **Map** 23 B2.
(020-8853 2333. **Open** noon–2.30pm, 6.30–10.30pm Mon–Sat, noon–5pm Sun. ¶◎¶ not Sat D. 🔲
♿ ⊘ AE, DC, MC, V. €€€€

The Spread Eagle is one of the few reliable and reasonably-priced restaurants in Greenwich. Set meals of hearty, no-nonsense food are served in this dark and rather quaint 17th-century coaching inn: generous mussel soup, seafood sausage, veal kidneys in mussel sauce and the excellent lamb with tomatoes and black olives.

La Tante Claire

The Berkeley Hotel, Wilton Place SW1.
Map 12 D5. **(** 020-7828 2003.
Open 12.30–2pm, 7–11pm Mon–Sat. **Closed** Christmas, Easter week, last three weeks Aug & public hols. ¶◎¶ L. ♿ 🔲 ♟ ⊘ AE, DC, MC, V, JCB. €€€€€

You must book well ahead at this small, smart, top-notch, expensive establishment. Gascon owner-chef Pierre Koffman likes to cook rich dishes, using goose fat and *foie gras* liberally. Stuffed pig's trotter, *tournedos Rossini* and kid with chocolate and raspberry vinegar sauce give an idea of the style.

MODERN
INTERNATIONAL

These restaurants represent an approach to cooking that has appeared in the last decade and continues to evolve. Its main feature is a willingness to borrow ingredients and styles from various cuisines all over the world and to create something new: a dish might include a cut of British lamb, some oriental spices, and a few preserved lemons from Morocco. The lightness of touch and innovative use of fresh ingredients is much favoured by adventurous and thrusting young chefs such as Sally Clarke and Alastair Little.

Alastair Little

49 Frith St W1. **Map** 13 A2.
(020-7734 5183. **Open** noon–3pm Mon–Fri, 6–11pm Mon–Sat. **Closed** public hols. ¶◎¶ ⊘ AE, MC, V. €€€€

Alastair Little was one of the first to usher in Modern International cooking. The menu is somewhat Italian in style, serving such innovative dishes as Scottish mussels with a hot and sour salsa, carpaccio of pancetta loin with rocket and Parmesan, or roast sea bass with pickled samphire, saffron butter sauce and chives. A new branch, where Alastair is now based, has opened at 136 Lancaster Road, W11 (0171 243 2220).

The Avenue

7-9 St James's St SW1. **Map** 12 F3.
(020-7321 2111. **Open** noon–3pm, 6–midnight Mon–Sat, noon–3.30pm, 7.30–10pm Sun. ¶◎¶ L. 🔲 ♿ 🔲 ♫ 🔲 ⊘ AE, DC, MC, V, JCB. €€€€

This huge white room, with its wall of TV screens showing videos, looks more like a gallery of modern art than a bar and restaurant. The long bar gets busy with Mayfair suits in the early evening, only some sliding along to a table later. Dish prices are high, but the food is flawlessly prepared. Starters might include a perfectly caramelized endive tart; main courses, brill simmered in bacon broth with white beans.

Bali Sugar

33a All Saint's Road, W11. **Map** 9 B1.
(020-7437 7776. **Open** 12.30–3pm, 6.30–11pm daily. **Closed** 24–26 Dec. 🔲 ⊘ AE, DC, MC, V. €€€€

A Notting Hill terraced house has been rather cleverly converted into a split-level restaurant, tastefully decorated in shades of straw and sand. Starters might include grilled scallops with sweet chilli sauce and crème fraîche, while main courses are even more globally inspired – duck leg braised in tamarind and star anise with *soba* noodles, *hijiki* and pickled plums. The braised chicken breast with fufu (plantain mash) and green beans is well worth a nibble.

Bank

1 Kingsway, Aldwych, WC2. **Map** 13 C1. **(** 020-7379 9797. **Open** 7–10.30am, noon–3pm, 5.30–11.00pm Mon–Fri, 11.30am–3.30pm, 5.30–11.30pm Sat, noon–3.30pm, 5.30-10pm Sun. ¶◎¶ L & D. 🔲 ♿ ⊘ AE, DC, MC, V, JCB. €€€

This former bank building has been given a stunning makeover. The postmodern interior has a funky showcase bar, while diners nibble under huge sheets of glass. The dishes – which range from fish and chips to rump of lamb with white bean casserole are toothsome in the extreme.

For key to symbols see p287

Bibendum

Michelin House, 81 Fulham Rd, SW3.
Map 19 A2. **☎** 020-7581 5817.
Open noon–2.30pm Sun–Fri,
noon–3pm Sat, 7–11pm Mon–Sat,
7–10.30pm Sun. **Closed** Easter Mon,
4 days Christmas. ¶❸ L. ⚑ ▼ ☝ ⚒
♟ ⌷ AE, DC, MC, V. ⓔⓔⓔⓔⓔ

Well-heeled diners come to feast
in the glorious, stained-glass
setting of the restored Michelin
building. The cooking is good, as
it should be when a meal for two
costs over £100. Dishes include
calf's sweetbreads with mushroom
en croûte and Madeira sauce, roast
rabbit with tomatoes, black olives
and pancetta, or cold lobster with
fennel salad and tarragon dressing.

Bluebird

The King's Road Gastrodome, 350
King's Rd SW3. **Map** 19 A4. **☎** 020-
7559 1000. **Open** noon–3.30pm
Mon–Fri, 6–11.30pm Mon–Sat,
11am– 4.30pm Sat & Sun, 6–10.30pm
Sun. **Closed** 25 Dec, 1 Jan. ⚑ ⛶
⌷ AE, DC, MC, V, JCB. ⓔⓔⓔⓔ

Sir Terence Conran's renovation of
this huge garage is amazing. His
latest blockbuster covers all bases
with a restaurant, small café, cook
shop, food hall, outdoor fruit and
veg stall and bar. The cooking, by
Australian–trained chef Michael
Moore, is not as faultless as the
prices suggest; but the extensive
menu of Mediterranean influences
is well worth investigating.

Clarke's

124 Kensington Church St W8.
Map 10 D4. **☎** 020-7221 9225.
Open 12.30–2pm, 7–10pm Mon–Fri.
Closed 2 weeks summer, Christmas,
Easter, public hols. ¶❸ L & D. ☝
♟ ⌷ AE, MC, V. ⓔⓔⓔⓔ

Britain, California and Italy meet
in the kitchens of talented chef-
proprietress Sally Clarke. There is
a set dinner menu that changes
daily and is always superb. Food
is light but tasty; recurring ingredients are Mediterranean vegetables,
corn-fed chicken, salmon, bream,
fresh herbs and wild plants such as
dandelion and elderflower.

Coast

26B Albemarle St W1. **Map** 12 F3.
☎ 020-7495 5999. **Open** noon–
3pm, 6pm–midnight Mon–Sat, noon–
3.30pm, 6pm–11pm Sun. ⚑ ☝ ☝
♟ ★ ⌷ AE, MC, V, JCB. ⓔⓔⓔⓔ

This is possibly London's most
extraordinary restaurant, not just
for the ruthlessly daring goldfish-
bowl interior, but also for Bruno

Loubet's cooking which pushes
forward expectations of what will
and won't work in the kitchen.
Dishes such as *pavé* of tomato
risotto with avocado, artichoke
heart, goat's cheese and tomato
oil redefine the risotto. Even more
amazing, how about a pudding of
vanilla cream topped with a *confit*
of sweetly-glazed tomato. The
wine list is good, but expensive,
and worth dunking into.

The Ivy

1 West St WC2. **Map** 13 B2.
☎ 020-7836 4751. **Open** noon–
3pm Mon–Sat, noon–3.30pm Sun,
5.30pm– midnight daily. ⚑ ☝ ☝
★ ⌷ AE, DC, MC, V. ⓔⓔⓔⓔⓔ

The Ivy has long been a land-mark
of the theatre district and a venue
for first-night parties. Stars – some
fading, others in the ascendant –
cluster in the oak-panelled, interior
to dine on reliable fare like salmon
fishcakes with sorrel sauce, tomato
and basil ravioli with shaved
Pecorino, or even corned beef
hash with fried egg. Booking is
virtually impossible unless you're
something of a 'name'.

Kensington Place

201–205 Kensington Church St W8.
Map 9 C3. **☎** 020-7727 3184.
Open noon–3pm, 6.30–11.45pm
Mon–Sat, 6.30–10.15pm Sun. **Closed**
Christmas, Good Friday, Aug public hol.
¶❸ L. ⚑ ☝ ★ ⌷ MC. ⓔⓔⓔ

This austerely-decorated restaurant
attracts a vibrant crowd. The fare
is at the very cutting edge of
Modern International cuisine; sea
kale with poached eggs and
truffles may well be followed
by grilled spiced quails with
butternut squash, lamb steaks
cooked in sage butter, or wild sea
trout with lentils and champagne
sauce. The wine list is fairly priced.

Mezzo

100 Wardour St W1. **Map** 13 A2.
☎ 020-7314 4000. **Open** noon–
2.30pm Mon–Fri, 12.30–2.30pm Sun,
6–11.30pm Mon–Thu, 6pm–12.30am
Fri & Sat, 6–10.30pm Sun. ¶❸ L. ⚑
☝ ☝ ♫ ★ ⌷ AE, DC, MC, V, JCB.
ⓔⓔⓔⓔ (Mezzonine ⓔⓔⓔ)

Mezzo is the largest restaurant in
the capital. Upstairs is Mezzonine,
a fast-turnover refectory you may
need to queue for, with slightly
longer hours, while more leisurely,
contemplative meals are served
downstairs. Mezzonine has food in
oriental style; downstairs the dishes
are both modern and European.
With its sweeping staircase, vast
bar and army of staff, Mezzo is the
brightest jewel in Conran's crown.

Mulligan's of Mayfair

13–14 Cork St W1. **Map** 12 F3.
☎ 020-7409 1370. **Open** 12.30–
3pm Mon–Fri, 6.30–9.30pm
Mon–Sat. **Closed** public hols. ¶❸
⚑ ⌷ AE, DC, MC, V, JCB. ⓔⓔⓔ

An Irish basement restaurant
offering hearty dishes such as
turnip and brown bread soup,
black pudding, ox tongue, and a
good range of fish dishes. Sample
specialities such as *colcannon*
(mashed potatoes and cabbage)
and *boxty* (potato pancake).

Oxo Tower

Oxo Tower Wharf, Barge House St,
SE1. **Map** 14 E3. **☎** 020-7803 3888.
Restaurant open noon–3pm Sun–Fri,
6–11.30pm daily. **Brasserie open**
11am–11.30pm daily. ¶❸ L (brasserie).
⚑ ☝ ☝ ⌷ AE, DC, MC, V, JCB.
Restaurant ⓔⓔⓔⓔ. **Brasserie**
ⓔⓔⓔ

This landmark South Bank
building has been completely
renovated, with a Harvey Nichols-
owned restaurant, brasserie and
bar near the top, serving Asian-
influenced food and offering
superb views and a large terrace
for summer dining.

The People's Palace

Level 3, Royal Festival Hall, South
Bank Centre, SE1. **Map** 14 D4.
☎ 020-7928 9999. **Open** noon–
3pm, 6–10.45pm daily. **Closed**
25 Dec, 1 Jan. ¶❸ L. ⚑ ▼ ⚒ ⚑ ☝
♟ ⌷ AE, DC, MC, V. ⓔⓔⓔ

This retro 1950's dining room
within the Royal Festival Hall has
lovely Thames views. There are
daily-changing set menus at
extremely reasonable prices. *A la
carte* dishes include grilled breasts
of pigeon with sauerkraut and
chorizo sausage, spiced pork
wonton with pak choi, garlic and
ginger, or fillet of sea bream with
courgettes, garlic, lemon and
thyme. Try to avoid peak times
before and after performances to
avoid eating in a crowd.

Quaglino's

16 Bury St SW1. **Map** 12 F3. **☎** 020-
7930 6767. **Open** noon–3pm daily,
5.30pm–midnight Mon–Thu, 5.30pm–
1am Fri & Sat, 5.30– 10.30pm Sun.
Closed 25 Dec, 1 Jan. ¶❸ L. ⚑ ▼ ♫
♟ ⌷ AE, DC, MC, V. ⓔⓔⓔⓔ

Quaglino's is an elegant and glamorous place to dine, but not ideal
for an intimate or especially relaxing
meal, as 200 heads will turn as you
enter down the sweeping staircase. The seafood is particularly
recommended; the service can be
just a tiny bit on the brusque side.

The Sugar Club

21 Warwick St W1. **Map** 12 F2.
(020-7437 7776. **Open** noon–
3pm, 6–10.30pm daily. **|O|** L. **&**
e AE, MC, V. **£££££**

Chef Peter Gordon has moved to
more spacious premises from his
original All Saints Road venue, and
is producing ever greater food for
his delighted customers. Pacific
Rim is too limited a term now for
his scope of cooking, but if you
love lively Asian flavours put to
innovative use with top quality
ingredients then you will join the
ranks of satisfied diners. Fish,
seafood and duck dishes are
especially recommended, and the
desserts are unmissable.

Stephen Bull

5–7 Blandford St W1. **Map** 12 D1.
(020-7486 9696. **Open** 12.15–
2.30pm Mon–Fri, 6.30–10.30pm
Mon–Sat. **☆** **&** **e** AE, DC, MC, V.
££££

This stylish venue offers contemporary fare: goat's cheese soufflé;
tortellini of crab and ginger with
citrus dressing; soya-glazed sea
trout with orange and sorrel sauce.
The fish dishes are good, and the
wine list reasonable. There's a
bistro and bar (020-7490 1750)
near Smithfield Market (see p164),
offering cheaper food in a striking
setting, and a slightly more expensive but even better outpost in the
heart of theatreland at 12 St Martin's
Lane, WC2 (020-7379 7811).

ITALIAN

Italian cuisine in London has
undergone a renaissance and now
resembles real Italian food. A
move away from the pizza, pasta,
and veal standards, towards a style
that combines traditional home
cooking with a modern lightness
of touch, has captivated the
capital's restaurant-goers. Seafood,
beans, mixed-leaf salads, char-
grilled vegetables and pan-roasted
meats, toasted breads, polenta and
wild mushrooms feature strongly.

Bertorelli's

44a Floral St WC2. **Map** 13 C2.
(020-7836 3969. **Open** noon–3pm,
5.30–11.30pm Mon–Sat. **↗** **V** **&**
restaurant only. **e** AE, DC, MC, V,
JCB. **££££**

This slick operation near the Opera
House in Covent Garden is used to
dealing with rushed pre-theatre
diners. Upstairs there is a grand
restaurant, while downstairs there
is a simpler café concentrating on
reliable pasta and pizza dishes.

Emporio Armani Express

191 Brompton Rd SW3. **Map** 11 B5.
(020-7823 8818. **Open** 10am–7pm
Mon–Sat. **V** **&** **e** AE, DC, MC, V,
JCB. **£££**

This is a specialist venue for those
who need to refuel between shopping bouts. Design is cool, service
warm, and the food is refreshing.
Go for any chicken or fish dish
before you venture out again.

Orso

27 Wellington St WC2. **Map** 13 C2.
(020-7240 5269. **Open** noon–
midnight daily. **Closed** Christmas. **↗**
V **£££**

At this gathering point for media
and theatre types, the food
changes constantly. Orso is noted
for innovative pasta and meat and
fish in bold sauces. The interior is
attractive but can be noisy; the
service may be brisk. The Holland
Park branch, Orsino (020-7221
3299), is a touch more relaxed.

River Café

Thames Wharf Studios, Rainville Rd
W6. **(** 020-7381 8824. **Open**
12.30–2.45pm Sun–Fri, 7–11pm
Mon–Fri, 12.30–2.30pm, 7–11.15pm
Sat. **Closed** public hols. **☆** **&** **▥**
★ **e** MC, V. **£££££**

Praise has been heaped on this
HQ of the Italian new-wave
movement. Both the food and the
surroundings are pleasantly clean,
light and crisp. Mozzarella, sage,
sun-dried tomatoes, Parmesan, pine
nuts, basil, thyme and garlic are
the flavours that accompany delicious char-grilled fish and meats.

Riva

169 Church Rd SW13. **(** 020-8748
0434. **Open** noon–2.30pm Sun–Fri,
7–11pm Mon–Thu, 7–11.30pm Fri,
Sat, 7–9.30pm Sun. **V** **☆** **&** **♟**
e AE, MC, V. **£££**

Southwest Londoners are devoted
to the regional Italian cooking
served here. The emphasis is on
top-quality ingredients combined
in imaginative ways. Seafood and
fish are well-represented on the
menu, which changes regularly.

Stefano Cavallini Restaurant at The Halkin

5-6 Halkin St SW1. **Map** 12 D5.
(020-7333 1234. **Open** 12.30–
2.30pm, 7.30–11pm Mon–Sat, 7–
10pm Sun. **Closed** 24-26 Dec, New
Year. **|O|** L. **V** **☆** **&** **e** AE, DC,
MC, V, JCB. **£££££**

This fine Italian establishment has
the subdued tones and impeccable
taste which appeals to all jet-
setters. The cooking is modern,
and exquisitely light with well-
judged flavours – antipasti of
breaded saddle of rabbit with
rosemary and artichoke sauce, or a
main dish of sea bass *tortelloni*
with asparagus and black truffle.
Prices may seem steep, but cooking
this good seldom comes cheap.

Table Café

Habitat, Tottenham Court Rd W1.
Map 5 A5. **(** 020-7636 8330.
Open 10.30am–5.30pm Mon–Wed,
Fri, Sat, 10am–7.30pm Thu. **V** **↗**
only. **☆** **&** **e** AE, DC, MC, V. **£**

In the basement of a home interior
shop is this brightly-lit, delightful
café serves a short, daily-changing
menu of appealing food. The
antipasto plate is simple, but it
usually has a good assembly of
fine ingredients; salads are always
superb, and the Italianate cakes
are definitely worth seeking out.

Zafferano

15 Lowndes St SW1. **Map** 20 D1.
(020-7235 5800. **Open** noon–
2.30pm, 7–11pm daily. **|O|** L. **☆**
& **★** **e** AE, DC, MC. **£££**

This is one of the very best of the
capital's Italian restaurants, thanks
to Giorgio Locatelli's mastery of his
culinary genre. The interior looks
like an unfussy, unpretentious
trattoria, belying the standard of
the cuisine, which could be
launched into space to give aliens
a taste of everything that is great
about our planet's food. Locatelli
takes pasta to new heights and has
an instinctive flair for adding to the
ecstasy with just the right sauce.
The fish and meat dishes are every
bit as good, and the *tiramisu* is
reckoned to be the best in London.
The service is attentive and discreet.

GREEK AND MIDDLE EASTERN

Cuisines from all over the Middle
and near East (Greece, Turkey,
Lebanon and North Africa) are
increasingly popular in London.
They have a lot in common, dishes
tending to be lightly rather than
heavily spiced – barbecued meats,
herby stews, salads and vegetable
dips such as *taramasalata* (cod's
roe), *houmous* (chick pea paste)
and *tabouleh* (minced parsley and
bulgar wheat with tomatoes and
onions) are often prominent. The
cheapest way to eat is with a set-
price *meze* – a selection of such
dishes: it's particularly good for
those new to this food.

Daphne

83 Bayham St NW1. **Map** 4 F1. *020-7267 7322.* ***Open*** *noon–2.30pm, 6pm–11.30pm Mon–Sat.* ***Closed*** *25–26 Dec, 1 Jan. L. MC, V.* ££

Daphne is a welcoming, friendly place offering all that's best about Greek hospitality and good Greek food: simple and fresh ingredients, flavoured with herbs and at a very reasonable price. Good meat and fish dishes predominate but there is also a frequently-changing list of vegetarian specials. The *meze* is particularly good value.

Al Hamra

31–33 Shepherd Market W1. **Map** 12 E4. *020-7493 1954.* ***Open*** *noon–midnight daily. AE, DC, MC, V, JCB.* £££

On arrival at this smart Lebanese restaurant you will be brought a plate of olives, fresh Middle Eastern bread and raw vegetables to accompany the *meze* dishes, of which there are over 40. Try the *moutabal*, made with aubergine and sesame, or for a warm dish, the *houmous kawarmah* (chick pea paste topped with lamb and pine nuts). The service is a little brusque and charmless.

Istanbul Iskembecisi

9 Stoke Newington Rd N16. *020-7254 7291.* ***Open*** *5pm–5am daily. MC, V.* ££

This is one of several cheap Turkish restaurants in this part of Dalston, and it's certainly worth a visit. It serves offal dishes such as grilled lamb intestines and boiled brains with salad. It also serves excellent dishes for the fainter of heart, such as char-grilled meats. It's lively spot, with charming staff, low prices, and it stays open until 5am, so you can have either a very late supper or a very early breakfast.

Lemonia

89 Regent's Park Rd NW1. **Map** 3 C1. *020-7586 7454.* ***Open*** *noon–3pm Sun–Fri, 6.30–11.30pm Mon–Sat. L. MC, V.* ££

This enormously popular Greek restaurant serves beautifully prepared food in a bustling, lively atmosphere. The menu includes good vegetarian options such as stuffed vegetables and bean and lentil dishes; the *meze* dishes include a fine *tabouleh* and a delicious aubergine dip. You should book evenings well in advance. If you can't get a table, try the sister restaurant, Limani (020-7483 4492), opposite.

Momo

25 Heddon St, W1. **Map** 12 F2. *020-7434 4040.* ***Open*** *12.30–3pm Mon–Fri, 7–11pm Mon–Sat.* ***Closed*** *Sun & public hols. AE, MC, V, JCB.* ££

Momo's menu is traditional and unadulterated Maghreb food, set in tasteful North African decor of rough walls the colour of the Sahara, Islamic lanterns and low brass tables and leather chairs. Try the pigeon *pastilla*, ground pigeon meat layered into a parcel of filo pastry topped with icing sugar, the *tagines* or the *couscous* dishes.

Sofra

18 Shepherd St W1. **Map** 12 E4. *020-7493 3320.* ***Open*** *noon–midnight daily. AE, DC, MC, V.* £££

Sofra is one of London's best-known and most delicious Turkish restaurants. The meat grills are good but the main attractions are the delicious but tiny *meze* dishes: *kisir* (a crushed wheat salad), *imam biyaldi* (stuffed aubergine), *böreks* (filled pastries) and so on. There are also two bustling Covent Garden branches, at Tavistock Street (020-7240 3773) and Garrick Street (020-7240 6688), and a Soho Café at 33 Old Compton Street, W1 (020-7494 0222).

Other European

Although most national and international cuisines can be found in London, some are restricted to only one or two establishments of any note. The British generally favour food from climates more southern and exotic than their own, but there are a few Northern and Eastern European restaurants well worth a visit.

Albero & Grana

89 Sloane Ave SW3. **Map** 20 D2. *020-7225 1048.* ***Tapas bar open*** *5.30pm–midnight Mon–Sat, 6–10.30pm Sun.* ***Restaurant open*** *7.30–11pm Mon–Sat.* ***Closed*** *public hols. AE, DC, MC, V, JCB.* ££££

This Spanish tapas bar and restaurant is the rendezvous for many wealthy expatriate Spaniards and for all lovers of Spanish cuisine. The jewel-coloured interior is complemented by the neat and presentable bar staff and the discreetly glamorous clientele. If you're merely peckish, you can eat well (for under £20 per head) at the tapas bar which does classic dishes such as escalivada (*ragoût* of grilled peppers and aubergines) and *chorizo* (Spanish sausage) cooked with chick peas. In the more formal restaurant, you should expect to pay at least double this for excellent modern Spanish cuisine.

Anna's Place

90 Mildmay Pk N1. *020-7249 9379.* ***Open*** *12.15–2.15pm Tue–Sat, 7–11pm Mon–Sat.* ***Closed*** *20 Dec–8 Jan, Easter, Aug.* £££

Virtually everything in this airy Swedish restaurant is home-made, including the bread and the sorbets. With the attentive service, and Anna herself often stopping by your table for a chat, it is like eating in a friend's kitchen. The menu is short, with marinated fish and meat featuring strongly. The main courses include some quite simple dishes – roast lamb in a herb crust, grilled fish and more traditional Swedish specialities. The puddings, in particular, are unmissable. Booking in advance is essential, especially if you want to sit outside on the pretty terrace.

Belgo Centraal

50 Earlham St WC2. **Map** 13 B2. *020-7813 2233.* ***Open*** *noon–11.30pm Mon–Sat, noon–10.30pm Sun.* ***Closed*** *25 Dec, 1 Jan. ★ AE, DC, MC, V, JCB.* £££

Take the industrial-strength space-age lift down to this modern but monastic dungeon run by young staff who are dressed in monk's habits but have dispensed with monastic reticence. This stylish subterranean canteen is distracting enough in itself, but the Belgian food and beer also merit further investigation. The filling dishes are centred around *moules* and *frites*, while the Belgian beer list has many extraordinary lambic and wheat bottled beers.

The Gay Hussar

2 Greek St W1. **Map** 13 B2. *020-7437 0973.* ***Open*** *12.30–2.30pm, 5.30–10.45pm Mon–Sat.* ***Closed*** *public hols. L. AE, DC, MC, V.* £££

The atmosphere in the city's only Hungarian restaurant is masculine and library-like. For many years politicians and literary figures have gathered in the wood-panelled and velvet-upholstered interior to feast on specialities such as the renowned chilled wild cherry soup, stuffed cabbage, pork schnitzel with smoked sausage, cold pike and of course the rich goulash with egg dumplings, spiked with Hungarian paprika.

Moro

34–36 Exmouth Market, Clerkenwell, EC1. **Map** 6 E4. 020-7833 8336. **Open** 12.30–2.30pm, 7–10.30pm Mon–Fri. V AE, MC, V. ££££

Moro is a spartan room serving dishes which are mostly modern interpretations of Spanish, Moorish and north African dishes and ingredients – *falafel* with bread and chopped salad, a plate of mixed vegetable *meze*, wood-roasted cod with tahini, cumin, caramelized onions, rice and cucumber. Be warned, the acoustics are terrible – you may need to raise your voice in order to make yourself heard over the dinner-time uproar.

Nikita's

65 Ifield Rd SW10. **Map** 18 E4. 020-7352 6326. **Open** 7.30–11.30pm Mon–Sat. **Closed** public hols. D. V AE, DC, MC, V. ££££

This exotic basement restaurant serves excellent Russian food: *borscht* (beetroot soup), *pirozhki* (meat pastries), *blinis* (yeast pancakes) with smoked salmon and sour cream, chicken Kiev, beef stroganoff and salmon *coulibiac* (stuffed with rice and egg and encased in pastry). Stars of the show are the numerous vodkas in 17 different flavours. Diners are fervently advised not to try them all in one visit, for fear of compromising the palate.

Wódka

12 St Alban's Gro W8. **Map** 10 E5. 020-7937 6513. **Open** 12.30–2.30pm Mon–Fri, 7–11.15pm Mon–Sat. L. AE, DC, MC, V. £££

A mixture of heavy traditional and light modern Polish food is served in a small, bare, but friendly setting. Alongside the bulky standards – meat-stuffed cabbage (*golabki*) and olive-stuffed beef (*zrazy*) – you can find such delights as marinated peppers and cheese or rye toast, warm salad of smoked eel with new potatoes and capers, or *shashlik* of lamb fillet with *casza* (roasted buckwheat).

London boasts a thriving, though fairly small, collection of fish restaurants, the best of which get their produce fresh every morning at the crack of dawn from local markets. Many of the older, stuffier fish restaurants have now been overtaken by Modern International chefs serving top-quality fish at much lower prices.

Café Fish

36–40 Rupert St SW1. **Map** 13 A2. 020-7287 8989. **Open** 12.30–3pm Mon–Fri, 5.30–11.30pm Mon–Sat, noon–10.30pm Sun. V AE, DC, MC, JCB. £££

New owners Livebait have moved this perennial favourite around the corner and given it a new lease of life. Starters are still quite straightforward (oysters, whitebait, smoked salmon, fish soup), and main courses are innovative yet simple, relying less on rich cream sauces than in the past. The seafood platter is good value.

Livebait

43 The Cut SE1. **Map** 14 D4. 020-7928 7211. **Open** noon–3pm Mon–Fri, 5.30–11.15pm Mon–Sat. **Closed** 24–26 Dec, 1 Jan. AE, DC, MC, V, JCB. ££££

This former pie-and-mash shop has been spruced up in the original Victorian style and is currently the most charming and popular place to eat on the South Bank. The service is pleasant and the seafood and fish are second-to-none. An ice-filled seafood counter lets you choose from the day's catch. The *plateau de fruits de mer* allows you to try the lot – oysters, clams, prawns, cockles, whelks, and a monstrous hen crab. Livebait also has a branch in Covent Garden (020-7836 7161).

Le Suquet

104 Draycott Ave SW3. **Map** 19 B2. 020-7581 1785. **Open** noon–2.30pm, 7–11.30pm daily. L. AE, DC, MC, V. ££££

Le Suquet is a lively but relaxed French hang-out. It is at its best on balmy summer nights, when the windows open out onto Draycott Avenue. Highlights are foil-wrapped sea bream, scallops in garlic and the seafood platter – a seaweed-fronded cornucopia of marine life.

Sweetings

30 Queen Victoria St EC4. **Map** 14 F2. 020-7248 3062. **Open** 11.30am–3pm Mon–Fri. **Closed** 24 Dec–2 Jan. £££

An old fish restaurant in the City with a wonderful Victorian interior and ancient feel. Dishes include old favourites like potted shrimps, prawn cocktail and even real turtle soup; main courses are various fish grilled, fried or poached. Desserts, such as steamed pudding with lashings of custard, are staunchly British and traditional.

Vegetarians can enjoy a wide selection of top-quality food at many London restaurants, but there are still relatively few places that offer a completely vegetarian menu. The restaurants in this section specialize in food without meat or fish, though Mildred's sneaks in the occasional seafood dish. Menus often indicate which dishes are suitable for vegans.

Food for Thought

31 Neal St WC2. **Map** 13 B2. 020-7836 0239 or 9072. **Open** noon–8.15pm Mon–Sat, noon–4pm Sun. only. V only. £

The short but imaginative menu features stir-fries, Japanese tofu dishes and European casseroles and soups, plus interesting quiches and indulgent puddings and cakes (raspberry scrunch or orange and coconut scones with whipped cream are good for the soul, if not for the arteries). It's very reasonably priced for Covent Garden, which partly explains the size of the crowds, especially at lunchtimes.

Mildred's

58 Greek St W1. **Map** 13 B2. 020-7494 1634. **Open** noon–11pm Mon–Sat, noon–5pm Sun. only. V £

This is one of the few vegetarian restaurants offering a range of dishes to match its meat-serving rivals. Soups range from Japanese miso to Polish vegetable and barley; main courses may include Brazilian vegetable and coconut casserole or Chinese black bean vegetables with fresh pineapple and noodles. Cramped surroundings mean you may be asked to share a table.

The Place Below

St Mary-Le-Bow Church EC2. **Map** 15 A2. 020-7329 0789. **Open** 7.30am–2.30pm Mon–Fri. only. V ★ ££

At lunchtimes, city workers pack the crypt of Wren's famous "Bow Bells" church *(see p147)* for tasty soups, quiches and hot dishes. After olive bread, there might be red pepper and almond soup, then courgette, feta and mint tartlets with tomato gravy and an avocado and plum tomato salad. This can be followed by a dessert of seasonal fruits, home-made ice-cream or something indulgent like dark and white chocolate truffle cake. You can bring your own wine (free corkage) or sample the heady sparkle of the delicious home-made lemonade.

For key to symbols *see p287*

World Food Café

14 Neal's Yard WC2. **Map** 13 B1. [C]
020-7379 0298. **Open** noon–5pm
Mon–Sat. **Closed** public hols. [symbols]
only. [V] only. [symbols] ★ [£]

This New Age centre is the natural
home of one of London's best
vegetarian restaurants. The mellow
atmosphere and airy feel make it
a perfect spot to try some good
global food. You can choose
between Mexican, West African,
Indian or Turkish dishes, all carefully prepared and with generous
portions. The fresh juice mixtures
are superb, and the desserts worth
the money. Try and avoid busy
lunchtimes. Unlicensed, and,
pehaps, all the better for it.

THE AMERICAS

Apart from the long-standing
flood of burger bars (see pp306–7),
American food – especially of
a reasonably good standard – is
comparatively new to London.
Joints like the Hard Rock Café
make some concessions to the
healthy-eating trend, but as a rule
big is beautiful. Standard fare is
hamburgers, fried chicken, BBQ
spare ribs and BLTs (bacon,
lettuce and tomato sandwiches),
all under a mountain of French
fries and followed by rich cakes
and ice-cream sundaes. Most of
the restaurants throw in a few
dishes from Mexico and Louisiana,
and service is polite and obliging
at almost every venue.

Blue's Bistro and Bar

42–43 Dean St W1. **Map** 13 A1.
[C] 020-7494 1966. **Open** noon–midnight Mon–Thu, noon–1am Fri, Sat.
[symbols] [V] [symbols] AE, MC, V.
[£][£][£]

Blue's presents modern food in an
appealing Soho environment – the
windowless restaurant is painted
white and decorated with bright
art college oil paintings. Try the
very good tuna salad; you could
follow this with Manhattan clam
chowder and pan-fried scallops
with wilted spinach and chilli jam.
The set-price meals served on
Monday and Tuesday evenings are
a steal.

Cactus Blue

86 Fulham Rd, SW3. **Map** 19 A2.
[C] 020-7823 7858. **Open** 5.30–
11.45pm Mon–Fri, noon–midnight
Sat, noon–11pm Sun. **Closed** 1 Jan,
25–26 Dec. [symbols] [V] [symbols] AE, DC, MC,
V, JCB. [£][£][£]

This stunning interior is decorated
in desert colours, but is much
more sophisticated than the Tex-

Mex name suggests. A starter of
baked pumpkin *tamale* is
cornmeal and Parmesan baked
inside the husks of a sweetcorn;
roast squash *quesadilla* is triangles
of warm, soft bread filled with
pumpkin on a green chilli relish.
The staff are young and fun but
still manage to be attentive, polite
and highly professional. The bar is
well-stocked with many tequilas.

Christopher's

18 Wellington St WC2. **Map** 13 C2.
[C] 020-7240 4222. **Open** 11.30–
11pm Mon–Sat, noon–3.30pm Sun.
Closed Public hols. [symbols] [symbols] AE, DC,
MC, V, JCB. [£][£][£] or [£][£][£]
pre-theatre menu (6–7pm).

From the ground floor sports-style
bar leads a frescoed spiral staircase up to the elegantly draped
palatial dining room. Huge
portions of surprisingly modern
food include a fine Caesar salad –
an enormous plate of young
cos lettuce topped with robust
shavings of Parmesan and chunky
croutons. Main courses, such as
the grilled salmon with herbs and
olive oil sauce, are simple and
perfectly executed. Puddings
are also served in vast portions –
the lemon meringue is delicious
and wonderfully light.

Dakota

127 Ledbury Rd, W11. **Map** 9 C2.
[C] 020-7792 9191. **Open** noon–
3.30pm daily, 7–11pm Mon–Sat,
7–10.30pm Sun. **Closed** 25–26 Dec.
[symbols] L (Mon–Fri). [V] [symbols] AE, MC,
V, JCB. [£][£][£][£]

This is the latest "southwestern"
American restaurant of chef Daniel
MacDowell. Daniel has an instinct
for this cuisine's vibrant flavours –
dishes such as pan-fried *annatto*
marinated blackleg chicken with
pumpkin salad and a pumpkin seed
sauce are innovative and delightful.
You would never find most of the
dishes in the US or Mexico, but
some might claim that they're all
the better for that.

Hard Rock Café

150 Old Park Lane W1. **Map** 12 E4.
[C] 020-7629 0382. **Open** 11.30am–
12.30am Sun–Thu, 11.30am–1am
Fri–Sat. **Closed** 25 Dec. [symbols] [V] [symbols]
[symbols] AE, MC, V. [£][£]

This is one of the few eating
places in London where a queue
is a permanent feature. Rock fans
flock from all over the planet to
eat burgers here beneath such rock
memorabilia as Jimi Hendrix's
guitar and Ringo's stick, or beside
such ambient features as Ozzie
Osborne's aromatic white leather
shoes. A rock museum, a place of

pilgrimage, a marketing outlet –
this is definitely a place that
people either love or hate. There
is a surprisingly good selection of
vegetarian dishes, devised by the
late Linda McCartney.

AFRICAN
AND CARIBBEAN

Given London's multi-ethnic
population, there are fewer Afro-
Caribbean restaurants than you
might expect; the style of cooking
has not caught on like Indian and
Chinese. African and Caribbean
cooking have basic foods in
common – fibrous root vegetables
like sweet potato and cassava, rice
and flat breads, pumpkin, beans
and peas and sweet, fleshy fruits
like guava and mango. Common
dishes are fried plantain (a type of
banana) with a hot sauce, spicy
stews and soups and curried goat.

Calabash

The Africa Centre, 38 King St WC2.
Map 13 C2. [C] 020-7836 1976.
Open 12.30–3pm Mon–Fri, 6–
11.30pm Mon–Sat. **Closed** public
hols. [V] [symbols] AE, DC, MC, V. [£]

As authentically African as you can
find in Covent Garden, this restaurant, with its friendly unrushed staff,
has a menu that roams nomadic-
ally around the continent, with a
variety ranging from pounded
yams to couscous and Algerian
wine to Namibian Rhino Beer. The
club upstairs is one of London's
liveliest African music venues.

Cottons Rhum Shop,
Bar and Restaurant

55 Chalk Farm Rd NW1. [C] 020-7482
1096. **Open** noon–midnight Mon–Sat,
noon–11pm Sun. **Closed** 24–26 Dec.
[V] [symbols] AE, MC, V. [£][£][£]

The loud reggae music announcing
Cottons' presence doesn't bother
the smart young crowd that flocks
to this intimately lit bar-restaurant
for cocktails. On the menu, jokily
named dishes such as "rasta pasta"
and "ragga prawns" sit beside such
staples of Jamaican cooking as
curried goat and fried chicken.

Mandola

139–141 Westbourne Grove W11.
Map 9 B2. [C] 020-7229 4734.
Open noon–11.30pm daily. [symbols] [V]
[symbols] [£][£]

A Sudanese café and restaurant
which is cheap, full of character,
and serves good, unusual food
cooked to a high standard.
Sudanese food resembles a mixture
of Lebanese-style *meze* and East

African ingredients and stews, with many vegetarian dishes. *Tipalia* is an East African freshwater fish with a white fish taste, fried in a spice mixture which is mouth-watering.

INDIAN

Indian food is a true delight of eating out in London. There is a vast number of Indian restaurants, and many of them specialize in specific styles of food. Dishes range from mildly spicy (*korma*) through medium-hot (*bhuna, dansak, dopiaza*) to very hot (*madras, vindaloo*). Indian meals in the West may begin with soup or a starter, and main course dishes (with rice or flat breads such as *chapati* or *nan*) are often shared. "Balti" dishes, fast-cooked dishes served in a small wok, are a recent import from the Midlands.

Bombay Brasserie

Courtfield Cl, Courtfield Rd SW7. **Map** 18 E2. **(** 020-7370 4040. **Open** 112.30–3pm, 7.30pm–midnight daily. **Closed** 25–26 Dec. **Y@Y** D. ♨ **V** **&** 🎵 **⊆** DC, MC, V. £££££

This is one of the most acclaimed Indian restaurants outside Asia. It has an impressive colonial atmosphere, redolent of the Raj. The mainly North Indian menu includes some unusual regional specialities. The execution of the regional dishes (including Parsi and Goan) is second to none. There's a much less expensive buffet at lunchtime.

Café Spice Namaste

16 Prescot St E1. **Map** 16 E2. **(** 020-7488 9242. **Open** noon–3pm, 6.30–10.30pm Mon–Fri, 6.30–10pm Sat. **Closed** public hols. **Y@Y** **V** **&** ⊆ AE, DC, MC, V, JCB. £££

This edge-of-City upmarket Indian boldly goes where no curry house has gone before. How about emu tikka masala? Despite the occasional gimmick, Cyrus Todiwala's masterful cooking is often enticing and truly inventive for a cuisine that's all too often backward-looking. Of the traditional dishes, Parsi and Goan food – such as the *dansak* (lamb with spiced, puréed lentils) or *sorpotel* (Goan diced pork offal) – are his particular strengths. One thing's for sure: whatever you order, it'll be different from anything you've had before.

Chutney Mary

Plaza 535, Kings Rd SW10. **Map** 18 E5. **(** 020-7351 3113. **Open** 12.30–2.30pm, 7–11.30pm Mon–Sat, 12.30–3pm, 7–10.30pm Sun. **Y@Y** L. ♨ **V** ⊆ AE, DC, MC, V, JCB. £££

"Chutney Mary" is an Indian term used to describe women who straddle two cultures: Indian and British. It neatly sums up the cookery of this smart restaurant. There are Indian staples such as *roghan josh* (lamb braised in yoghurt) and *chicken tikka*, but the majority of the cooking is a unique blend of Indian and Western.

Chutneys

124 Drummond St NW1. **Map** 4 F4. **(** 020-7388 0604. **Open** noon–2.45pm, 6–11.30pm Mon–Sat, noon–10.30pm Sun. **Closed** Christmas. **Y@Y** L. ♨ **V** ⊆ MC. ££

Pale and cool, this is the smartest of the clutch of good-value Indian vegetarian restaurants lining Drummond Street. At the buffet lunches you are faced with the glorious greed-challenge of helping yourself to as much as you like from a table groaning with *dals* (lentils), vegetable curries, rice, chutneys, breads and a sweet – all for about £5.

Madhu's Brilliant

39 South Rd, Southall, Middx UB1. **(** 020-8574 1897 or 020-8571 6380. **Open** 12.30–3pm, 6–11.30pm Mon–Fri, 6pm–midnight Sat, Sun. **Closed** Tue. **Y@Y** **V** **&** ⊆ AE, DC, MC, V. ££

Authentic food and outstanding value for money – half the price (or less) than you might expect. The accent is on strongly flavoured Indian and Pakistani meat dishes and it is well worth the effort of making the detour to Southall.

Nazrul

130 Brick Lane E1. **Map** 8 E5. **(** 020-7247 2505. **Open** noon–3pm, 5.30pm–midnight Mon–Sat, noon–midnight Sun. **Y@Y** **V** £

Nazrul is one of the best of the scores of cheap Bangladeshi-run cafés and restaurants in the Brick Lane area. Decor and furnishings are very basic, prices very low and the atmosphere very lively. Portion sizes can be gargantuan, so do exercise restraint when ordering. The venue is unlicensed, but you can bring along your own alcohol.

Chor Bizarre

16 Albermarle St W1. **Map** 12 F3. **(** 020-7629 9802. **Open** noon–3pm daily, 6–11.30pm Mon–Sat, 6–10.30pm Sun. **Closed** Christmas. **Y@Y** **V** **&** ⊆ AE, MC, V, JCB. ££££

Chor Bizarre's interior is a charming jumble of fine Indian antiques. There are many unusual dishes on the menu – genuine regional Indian dishes prepared with care, such as *gazab ka tikka* (chicken pieces imbued with a cheesy aroma) and Keralan prawn curry (hot orange stew with pepper and mustard seeds).

Rasa

55 Stoke Newington Church St N16. **(** 020-7249 0344. **Open** noon–2pm Fri–Sun, 6–11pm Mon–Thu, Sun, 6pm–midnight Fri, Sat. **Closed** 25–26 Dec. ♨ only. **Y@Y** **V** **&** ★ ⊆ AE, DC, MC, V, JCB. ££

This is the only restaurant outside India to serve the vegetarian home cooking of the state of Kerala. The colourful dishes are gently flavoured and aromatic with the many spices indigenous to the region (cardamom, pepper, curry leaves, turmeric, cloves). Principal ingredients include the Keralan staples of rice, coconut, plantain and tapioca root. The cooking is completely authentic, and of a very high standard, with great attention to detail. The service is charming.

Salloos

62–64 Kinnerton St SW1. **Map** 11 C5. **(** 020-7235 4444. **Open** noon–2.30pm, 7–11.15pm Mon–Sat. **Closed** public hols. **Y@Y** **V** ★ ⊆ AE, DC, MC, V. ££££

Almost certainly the best Indian restaurant in town isn't Indian at all – it's Pakistani, and it's worth tasting the difference. There's a predominance of meat (lamb, chicken, quails) which is grilled; baked in the tandoori oven and curried. The wine list is impressive and the cooking precise and fresh, but the high prices reflect this. The set lunch, however, is a bargain. The atmosphere here is upmarket and the service is always faultlessly polite and professional.

Tamarind

20 Queen St W1. **Map** 12 E4. **(** 020-7629 3561. **Open** noon–3pm Sun–Fri, 6–11.30pm daily. **Y@Y** **V** **&** ★ ⊆ AE, DC, MC, V, JCB. ££££

Stairs lead down from a discreet concealed entrance into a gilded basement with sumptuous, linerlike decor. The menu doesn't stray much from the dishes found in hundreds of curry houses in London, but the quality of the food, fastidiously prepared by top chefs from India, is far superior to most. Mayfair is one of the few areas where a restaurant can get away with these prices, but don't let this discourage you, especially if you want to discover just how good a *biriani* or a *roghan josh* can be.

For key to symbols *see p287*

Vama

438 King's Rd, SW10. **Map** 18 E5.
[020-7351 4118. **Open** noon–3pm
daily, 6.30–11pm Mon–Sat, 6.30–
10.30pm Sun. **Closed** Christmas.
🍴 **€** 🎵 🏃 🕎 **V** 🚭 MC, V, JCB.
€€€

The decor here is sumptuous, and
so is the the food, which is quite
stylishly copied from the kitchens
of Iran, Pakistan and Afghanistan.
Meat is to the fore in grilled and
tandoor-cooked lamb and chicken
dishes which are quite refreshingly
different from the norm.

Veeraswamy

Victory House, 101 Regent St W1.
Map 12 F1. **[** 020-7734 1401.
Open noon–2.30pm, 5.30–11.30pm
Mon–Sat, 12.30–3pm, 6.30–10pm
Sun. 🍴 **€** **V** 🕎 AE, DC, MC, V,
JCB. **€€€€**

Founded in 1927, this is the oldest
Indian restaurant in London. The
walls are bright sari colours and
the pillars are gilded. The menu is
as modern as modern Indian gets.
Malabar fresh kingfish curry is
unlike any you'll find in Kerala,
with tidy presentation and the
sauce poured on fish steaks. The
service is extremely friendly.

SOUTHEAST ASIAN

Southeast Asian food, especially
Thai, has made a distinctive mark
on the London restaurant scene.
The majority of restaurants in this
section tend to emphasize Thai,
Singaporean, Malaysian or
Indonesian cuisine but also offer a
combination of them all. A sharp,
tangy taste comes from lime juice,
kaffir lime leaves and lemongrass;
a sour note from tamarind; ginger
and garlic; a variety of chillies
provide the heat; coconut milk the
coolant. Rice or noodles are the
basis of any southeast Asian meal,
the preferred cooking methods are
steaming and stir-frying, and the
food is usually served lukewarm.

Cicada

132-136 St John St EC1. **Map** 6 E2.
[020-7720 5433. **Open** noon–
11pm Mon–Fri, 6pm–midnight Sat.
Closed Christmas. **V** 🚭 🕎
🚭 AE, DC, MC, V, JCB. ★ **€€€**

This is one of the best places to
eat in London. The spacious
layout is designed to make you
feel that you've got room to relax
while you eat, and what you eat is
bound to be good. The fare blends
influences from every kind of
Southeast Asian cuisine. One almost
gets the feeling that a superb new
hybrid is being created here. While

you really should try the seared
salmon presented on a bed of
leaves, you can rest assured that
there are no disappointing dishes.
The service adds to the joy.

Melati

21 Gt Windmill St W1. **Map** 13 A2.
[020-7437 2745. **Open** noon–
midnight daily. **Closed** Christmas.
🍴 **€** **V** 🏃 🎵 🚭 AE, DC, MC, V,
JCB. **€€**

Booking is advisable in this
bustling Indonesian restaurant if
you don't want to queue. The
service is swift and polite (if a little
rushed at times) and the preparation
of dishes is very authentic. The
Singapore laksa – an aromatic
vermicelli noodle soup – is
particularly good, the satays (small
spicy kebabs) are moist and tasty.
Desserts such as kue dadar (a
green pancake roll stuffed with
coconut) are unmissable.

Singapore Garden

154-156 Gloucester Place NW1.
Map 3 C4. **[** 020-7723 8233. **Open**
noon–2.30pm daily, 6–10.30pm Sun–
Thu, 6–11pm Fri & Sat. **Closed** 24–26
Dec. 🍴 **€** **V** 🚭 AE, DC, MC, V.
€€€

This delightful restaurant serves
the best Singaporean food in
central London. The relative calm
of this hotel dining room allows
you to fully appreciate the superbly-
prepared Nonya dishes – a fusion
of Malay spices and Chinese cooking styles. Typical dishes to try
include chilli crab, stir-fried
noodles such as kway teow (flat
rice noodles with prawns, egg,
pork and fish cake), and the daily
seafood specials which might
include soft-shell crab, lemongrass
chicken, or beef rendang.

Sri Siam

16 Old Compton St W1. **Map** 13 A2.
[020-7434 3544. **Open** noon–3pm,
6–11.15pm Mon–Sat, 6–10.30pm
Sun. **Closed** 24–26 Dec, 1 Jan. 🍴 **€**
V 🚭 AE, DC, MC, V. **€€€**

This stylish restaurant is a perfect
place for your first taste of Thai
food; the heat is toned down, but
the flavours aren't. Try the mixed
starters, and any of the seafood
dishes. There is an extensive
vegetarian menu, which contains
exquisite hot and sour soups and
salads, as well as satay, curries,
deep-fried beancurd, and more.
The set lunch menu is good value.

Vong

Berkeley Hotel, Wilton Place, SW1.
Map 12 D5. **[** 020-7235 1010.

Open noon–2.30pm, 6–11.30pm
Mon–Sat, 6–10pm Sun. 🍴 **€** **V** 🚭
🏃 🚭 AE, DC, MC, V, JCB.
€€€€€

Vong is certainly an experience:
postmodernists admire the clean
architecture and powerbrokers
come to impress their guests. The
edges of the Pacific rim are drawn
into dishes such as lobster daikon
roll with a rosemary ginger dip,
raw tuna and vegetables wrapped
in rice paper, or a steaming
dessert of exotic fruit soup.

JAPANESE

Japanese restaurants are renowned
for being simply but stylishly
decorated. Some have teppan-yaki
tables (where diners surround a
chef who cooks on a hotplate)
and a bar where you can snack on
sushi – raw fish or vegetables on
vinegared rice. The most expensive
places have tatami rooms, where
parties eat seated on straw mats.

Miyama

38 Clarges St W1. **Map** 12 E3.
[020-7499 2443. **Open** noon–
2.30pm Mon–Fri, 6–10.30pm daily.
🍴 **€** 🕎 🚭 AE, DC, MC, V, JCB.
€€€€

Close to the Japanese Embassy
just off Piccadilly, Miyama is an
elegant place for meticulously
prepared and presented Japanese
food. Besides sushi and sashimi
meals, the teppan-yaki counter is
popular for meats and seafood
grilled before your admiring eyes
and your slavering mouth.

Moshi Moshi Sushi

Unit 24, Liverpool Street Station, EC2.
Map 7 C5. **[** 020-7247 3227. **Open**
11.30am–9pm Mon–Fri. **V** 🚭 only.
🎵 🚭 MC, V. **€**

A sushi bar set in a brightly austere
shop unit overlooking Liverpool
Street Station. A conveyor belt
whisks a selection of fish-and-rice
nibbles past as you sit at the
counter. This is an ideal place to
try salmon roe, grey mullet, yellow-
tail, conger eel or sea urchin.
There's a branch at 7–8 Limeburner
Lane, EC4 (020-7248 1808).

Nippon Tuk

165 Draycott Ave SW3. **Map** 19 B2.
[020-7589 8464. **Open** noon–
3pm Mon–Sat, 6.–11pm Mon–Sun.
🍴 **€** **V** 🏃 🕎 🚭 MC, V, JCB. **€€**

This friendly sushi restaurant may
be at the lower end of the price
scale, but it's very high in terms
of quality and service. A little on
the snug side, but none the worse

for that, this is the place for surreptitious conversations over some excellent salads, sushi and noodles. It's in with the in-crowd, but don't let that put you off.

Nobu

19 Old Park Lane, W1. **Map** 11 E4.
(020-7447 4747. **Open** noon–2.15pm Mon–Fri, 6–10.30pm Mon–Sat, 6–9.45pm Sun. **Closed** public hols.
🍴🇪 V 🌿 ♿ 🍷 AE, DC, MC, V, JCB. ££££££

Nobu is inside the Metropolitan Hotel. Dishes are unique: there are Japanese elements – the *bonsai* portion sizes, the clever use of fish and seafood, tastes such as *miso* paste, *wasabi* or *shoyu* – but the ingredient combinations and preparations are special, and include Peruvian influences.

Tokyo Diner

2 Newport Place, WC1. **Map** 13 B2.
(020-7287 8777. **Open** noon–midnight daily. 🌿 🍷 V ♿ MC, V. £

The low prices and convenient location make this restaurant a very useful bolt-hole. In true Japanese fashion, the door is electric, the taps in the restrooms automatic, and tips are not accepted. The extensive, clearly annotated menu covers sushi, sashimi, noodle soups, and Japanese curries; accompany these with Japanese lager. The cooking may not be first-rate, but the bill is a pleasant surprise.

Wagamama

4 Streatham St WC1. **Map** 13 E1.
(020-7323 9223. **Open** noon–11pm Mon–Sat, 12.30–10pm Sun.
🍴🇪 👫 🌿 only. V ★ 🍷 AE, V. £

This bustling high-tech noodle bar just off Coptic Street is immensely popular. The food is cheap, filling and interesting: large bowls of soup, or pan-fried noodles or rice with seafood and vegetables. Studiously cool waiting staff take orders on handsets which resemble Nintendo Game Boys. The queue looks very daunting, but it's fast-moving. There is also a branch at 10a Lexington Street, W1 (020-7292 0990), with shorter queues.

Yo! Sushi

52-53 Poland St, W1. **Map** 13 A2.
(020-7287 0433. **Open** noon–midnight daily. **Closed** Christmas. 🌿 V 👫 🍷 AE, DC, MC, V, JCB. ££

This isn't the first, but it is the most startling revolving sushi bar outside Japan. Huge TV screens show satellite TV and pop videos, and the walls are lit by stage lights.

The sushi quality is secondary to the atmosphere, but that's not to say it's bad – it certainly isn't expensive. Following Japanese tradition, there is no service charge and tips are not accepted.

CHINESE

The cuisine most common to London's Chinese restaurants is Cantonese, which has rice as its staple food and favours steaming or stir-frying. However, some offer north Chinese cooking which relies more on thick noodles, steamed bread and lamb dishes. The chilli-hot food of Sichuan and Hunan is popular here, too. At lunchtime (and never later than 6pm) in many Cantonese restaurants in Soho's Chinatown, you can eat *dim sum*, a series of inexpensive, delicious snacks, mostly steamed or fabulously deep-fried dumplings.

Fung Shing

15 Lisle St WC2. **Map** 13 A2.
(020-7437 1539. **Open** noon–11.45pm daily. **Closed** 24–25 Dec.
🍴🇪 V 🌿 🍷 AE, DC, MC, V. ££

For many, Fung Shing is the best restaurant in Chinatown. The new furnishings are markedly more elegant than many you'll find in the vicinity and food from the breadth of the Cantonese repertoire is on the menu. The hot-pot dishes (hearty stews in delicious stock) are recommended.

Harbour City

46 Gerrard Street W1. **Map** 13 A2.
(020-7439 7859. **Open** noon–11.15pm Mon–Thu, noon–midnight Fri, Sat, 11am–10.30pm Sun. 🍴🇪 👫 ★ 🍷 AE, DC, MC, V, JCB. ££

One of many establishments on Gerrard Street serving an extensive *dim sum* selection, Harbour City stands out because the *dim sum* menu is carefully translated into English, and because the staff are very gracious. As with Chinese food vegetarian dishes are limited, but all the dishes taste superb.

Magic Wok

100 Queensway W2. **Map** 10 D2.
(020-7792 9767 or 020-7221 9953.
Open 11am–11pm daily. 🍴🇪 L. 🍷 ★ 🍷 AE, DC, MC, V. £££

Magic Wok is one of the finest of Queensway's many Chinese restaurants. The list of specials changes regularly, yet invariably contains some of the most interesting Cantonese dishes. Deep-fried soft-shell crab with garlic and spicy chilli always makes an excellent starter.

Memories of China

67–69 Ebury St SW1. **Map** 20 E1.
(020-7730 7734. **Open** noon–2.30pm, 7–10.45pm Mon–Sat, 7–10.15pm Sun. **Closed** public hols.
🍴🇪 V ♿ 🍷 AE, DC, MC, V, JCB. ££££

At this restaurant, decorated in a light, minimalist style, the menu aims to guide Western diners through China's major cuisines. Set meals provide a sound (if a little expensive) introduction to many types of regional food, gently tailored to Western tastes.

New World

1 Gerrard Pl W1. **Map** 13 B2.
(020-7734 0396. **Open** 11am–11.45pm Sun–Thu, 11–12.15am Fri, Sat. **Closed** 25–26 Dec.
♿ 🌿 🍷 AE, DC, MC, V, JCB. ££

This is one of the most authentic restaurants serving *dim sum* in Chinatown. Flag down a trolley and take your pick. Many staff have shaky English so there's an element of chance in what you'll receive and it adds to the fun. The full menu is as long as the Great Wall, though rather more modern, and its content features items to tempt both the meek and the more adventurous diner.

The Oriental

The Dorchester Hotel, Park La W1.
Map 12 D4. **(** 020-7317 6328.
Open noon–2.30pm Mon–Fri, 7–11pm Mon–Sat. 🍴🇪 V ♿ 🍷 🍷 AE, DC, MC, V JCB. £££££

The Dorchester Hotel unveiled its Chinese restaurant with much aplomb in 1991. Battalions of skilful chefs were shipped in to meticulously prepare the Cantonese food. The expensive ingredients and exquisite presentation find favour with the business and social elite that gather here. Whatever you do, don't miss out on the full Chinese tea service. Parties of up to 12 can hire the sumptuous private rooms.

Royal China

40 Baker St W1. **Map** 12 D1.
(020-7487 4688. **Open** noon–11pm Mon–Sat, noon–10pm Sun. **Closed** Christmas. 🍴🇪 V 🍷 AE, MC, V. £££

An excellent *dim sum* venue, usefully located near Madame Tussauds. Try the *cheung fun*, translucent steamed prawn dumpling with chives or the roast pork buns. Also succumb to the temptation of the many more unusual dishes such as steamed scallop with mini-melon.

For key to symbols see p287

Light Meals and Snacks

SOMETIMES YOU HAVE neither the time nor the money to sit down for a full meal. Fortunately, London has a wonderful range of places offering simple, quick and sometimes cheap food. The places listed here are ideal for hungry tourists on a tight sightseeing schedule.

BREAKFAST

A GOOD BREAKFAST IS essential preparation for a hard day's sightseeing. Many hotels *(see pp272–85)* will serve breakfast to non-residents, and you can get a taste of luxury by breakfasting in one of the stately old English dining rooms such as **Simpson's-on-the-Strand**. Here wonderful English breakfasts *(see pp288–9)* include oddities such as pig's nose with parsley and onion sauce. If a mug of tea with eggs and baked beans on toast is more your scene, there are "greasy spoons" all over the city. A more cosmopolitan option is a pastry and a cappuccino from a café. If you're late to bed or early to rise, **Harry's** is open from 11pm to 6am, and several pubs around Smithfield market, including the **Cock Tavern**, serve good-value fare from 5.30am.

COFFEE AND TEA

I F YOU'RE OUT SHOPPING, many of London's department stores have their own cafés, the most stylish being the new-wave Italian **Emporio Armani Express**. Patisseries such as **Patisserie Valerie** and **Maison Bertaux** are a particular delight and also have mouthwatering window displays. Afternoon tea is an English institution not to be missed. Top hotels like the **Ritz** and **Brown's** *(see p282)* offer pots of tea, scones with jam and cream, delicious, thin cucumber sandwiches and cakes galore. Superbly moreish cakes (and coffee) can also be found at the **Coffee Gallery**, near the British Museum. **Fortnum and Mason** *(see p311)* serves both afternoon and high teas (a more substantial meal). The **Seattle Coffee Company** serves drinks from the city that never sleeps. In Kew, the **Maids of Honour** tea-room offers pastries, reputedly enjoyed here by King Henry VIII.

GALLERY AND THEATRE CAFÉS

M OST GALLERIES HAVE cafés: the one at the **British Museum** *(see p126–9)* has lots of vegetarian dishes; the **Café de Colombia** at the Museum of Mankind *(see p91)* offers excellent coffee accompanied by chocolate coffee beans. If you are visiting the Young Vic Theatre, **Konditor & Cook** serves wonderful cakes of scrumptious substance.

DINERS

L ONDON IS LITTERED with burger bars, where the food consists of burgers, fries, fried chicken, apple pie, milk shakes and cola. **Maxwell's** is a Covent Garden institution, serving great burgers and cocktails, while at the **Rock Island Diner** staff leap on to tables for rock 'n' roll routines. Try the tasty burgers and fun atmosphere at the branches of **Ed's Easy Diner**.

PIZZA AND PASTA

I TALIAN FAST FOOD IS sold all over London. The best pizza chain is **Pizza Express**; try its branches in a converted dairy *(see p122)* as well as at the elegant **Kettners**. For pasta, go for family-run trattorias like **Centrale**, **Lorelei** and **Pollo**; these have character and are very good value.

SANDWICH BARS

S ANDWICH BARS are where many Londoners buy their lunch. A few of these are upmarket; the many branches of **Prêt à Manger** and **Aroma** are two of the best, serving unusual and tasty sandwiches.

FISH AND CHIPS

F ISH AND CHIPS is a British experience you should not miss. Visit local "chippies" for fish deep-fried in batter, with thick potato chips, smothered in salt and vinegar. Traditional accompaniments are bread baps and pickled onions. For a higher-class supper, try a sit-down restaurant that offers a range of fresh fish such as lemon sole, skate and cod. Three of the best are the **Sea Shell**, **Faulkner's** and the **Upper Street Fish Shop**.

BARS

I F YOU FANCY A drink, the obvious venue is one of London's many pubs *(see pp308–9)*. A more elegant and decadent option is to visit one of London's smart hotel like **Claridge's** and to relax in a comfortable armchair in the foyer while a waiter brings your drinks. Wine bars such as the popular and busy **Cork and Bottle** are good for a snack, meal or just a glass of wine. Old Compton Street in Soho has a growing gay and gay-ish bar scene, where straight people are welcome. Tables spill out on to the pavements and a trendy crowd ensure a lively atmosphere. The best for a mixed crowd are **Freedom** and **Mondo**, both packed with beautiful people and offering loud House music and pricey drinks. There's also a new crop of stylish straight bars in London, the best of these being **Ny-lon**, **Detroit** and the **R Bar**. If rum is a particular passion, then Afro-Caribbean **Cottons** *(see p303)* and the **Brixtonian** *(see p302)* both have large selections.

BRASSERIES

W HERE LONDON was once bound by strict meal times, it has increasingly become an all-day grazing ground. Brasserie chains such as the stylish **Dôme** and **Café Rouge** dominate; **Boulevard** is one of the best of the independent brasseries.

INTERNET CAFÉS

CYBER CAFÉS are cool places to have a coffee and a bite to eat in between surfing the Internet. **Cyberia Cyber Café** is in Fitzrovia, while **Café Internet** is near Victoria.

STREET FOOD

HOT ROASTED CHESTNUTS are an autumnal delight. Shellfish stalls, which sell ready-to-eat potted shrimps, crab, whelks and jellied eels

are a feature of every street market. At Camden Lock and Spitalfields you can wander from stall to stall choosing between falafels, satay chicken, vegeburgers, Chinese noodles and honey balls. If you're in the East End, Jewish bakeries such as **Brick Lane Beigel Bake** and **Ridley Bagel Bakery** are open 24 hours a day; they're great fun and very cheap. During a hot summer, try **Marine Ices**, which serves some of the most delicious ice cream in town.

If you feel tempted to have a nibble of the quintessential Cockney cuisine, you can still find pie and mash shops all over London (though maybe not so readily in the smart areas). You can have a very satisfying nosh-up of jellied eels and potatoes, or meat pie with mash and liquor (green parsley sauce) and still have change from a fiver. For the real experience, you should drench your food in vinegar and wash it all down with a couple of mugs of tea.

DIRECTORY

BREAKFAST

Cock Tavern
East Poultry Market, Smithfield Market EC1.
Map 6 F5.

Harry's Bar
19 Kingly St W1.
Map 12 F2.

Simpson's
100 Strand WC2.
Map 13 C2.

COFFEE AND TEA

Brown's Hotel
Albermarle St W1.
Map 12 F3.

Coffee Gallery
23 Museum St WC1.
Map 13 B1.

Emporio Armani Express
191 Brompton Rd SW3.
Map 19 B1.

Fortnum and Mason
181 Piccadilly W1.
Map 12 F3.

Maids of Honour
288 Kew Rd, Richmond.

Maison Bertaux
28 Greek St W1.
Map 13 A1.

Patisserie Valerie
215 Brompton Rd SW3.
Map 19 B1.

Ritz
Piccadilly W1. Palm Court. Ritz Bar. **Map** 12 F3.

Seattle Coffee Co.
51-54 Long Acre WC2.
Map 13 B2.

GALLERY AND THEATRE CAFÉS

British Museum
Great Russel St WC1.
Map 5 B5.

Café de Colombia
Museum of Mankind, 6 Burlington Gardens W1.
Map 12 F3.

Konditor & Cook
Young Vic Theatre, 66 The Cut SE1. **Map** 14 E4.

DINERS

Ed's Easy Diner
12 Moor St W1.
Map 13 B2.
One of several branches.

Maxwell's
89 James St WC2.
Map 13 C2.

Rock Island Diner
2nd Floor, London Pavilion, Piccadilly Circus W1.
Map 13 A3.

PIZZA AND PASTA

Centrale
16 Moor St W1.
Map 13 B2.

Kettners
(Pizza Express) 29 Romilly St W1. **Map** 13 A2.

Lorelei
21 Bateman St W1.
Map 13 A2.

Pizza Express
30 Coptic St WC1.
Map 13 B1.
One of several branches.

Pollo
20 Old Compton St W1.
Map 13 A2.

SANDWICH BARS

Aroma
1b Dean St W1. **Map** 13 A1.
One of several branches.

Prêt à Manger
421 Strand WC2.
Map 13 C3.
One of many branches.

FISH AND CHIPS

Faulkner's
424-426 Kingsland Rd E8.

Sea Shell
49-51 Lisson Grove NW1.
Map 3 B5.

Upper St Fish Shop
324 Upper St N1.
Map 6 F1.

BARS

Claridge's
Brook St W1.
Map 12 E2.

Cork and Bottle
44-46 Cranbourn St WC2.
Map 13 B2.

Detroit
35 Earlham St WC2.
Map 13 B2.

Freedom
60-66 Wardour St W1.
Map 13 A2.

Mondo
12-13 Greek St W1.
Map 13 A2.

Ny-lon
84-86 Sloane Ave SW3.
Map 19 B2.

R Bar
4 Sydney St SW3.
Map 19 A3.

BRASSERIES

Boulevard
38-40 Wellington St WC2. **Map** 13 C2.

Café Rouge
27 Basil St SW3.
Map 11 C5.

Dôme
34 Wellington St WC2.
Map 13 C2.

INTERNET CAFÉS

Café Internet
22-24 Buckingham Palace Rd SW1.
Map 20 E2.

Cyberia Cyber Café
39 Whitfield St W1.
Map 4 F4.

STREET FOOD

Brick Lane Beigel Bake
159 Brick La E1.
Map 8 E5.

Marine Ices
8 Haverstock Hill NW3.

Ridley Bagel Bakery
13-15 Ridley Rd E8.

London Pubs

PUBLIC HOUSES OR PUBS were originally just that – houses where the public could eat, drink, and stay the night. Large inns with courtyards, such as the **George Inn** *(see p176)*, were originally the interchanges for horse-drawn coach services. Some pubs stand on age-old ale-house sites, like the **Ship**, the **Lamb and Flag** *(see p116)*, and the **City Barge** *(see p258)*. But many of the finest pubs date from the emergence in the late 1800s of "gin palaces", where Londoners escaped from the misery of the slums into lavish interiors, often with stunning mirrors (the **Salisbury**) and elaborate decoration (the **Tottenham**). Near Little Venice *(see pp264–5)* you will find **Crockers**, probably the finest surviving gin palace to be found in London.

RULES AND CONVENTIONS

IN THEORY, PUBS can now open between 11am–11pm on Monday to Saturday and noon–10.30pm on Sunday, but some may close in the afternoon or early evening and also at weekends. You must be at least 18 to buy or drink alcohol, and at least 14 to enter a pub without an adult. Children can be taken into pubs that serve food, or can use outside areas. Order at the bar, and pay when you are served; tips are not usual unless you are served food and drink at a table. "Last orders" are usually called 10 minutes before closing, then "time" is called, and a further 20 minutes are then allowed for finishing up drinks.

BRITISH BEER

THE MOST TRADITIONAL British beers come in many different strengths and tastes, they are flat (not fizzy), and are only lightly cooled. The spectrum of bottled beers goes from "light" ale, through "pale", "brown" and up to the strong "old". A sweeter, lower alcohol, alternative is shandy, a mixture of draught beer or lager with lemonade.

Many traditional methods of brewing and serving beer have been preserved over the years, and there is a great variety of "real ale" in London pubs. Serious beer drinkers should look for "Free Houses", pubs that are not tied to any particular brewery. The main

London brewers are Young's (try the strong "Winter Warmer" beer) and Fuller's. Small micro-breweries are uncommon, but the **Orange Brewery** not only serves a good pint and excellent food, it also offers tours of the brewery.

OTHER DRINKS

ANOTHER TRADITIONAL English drink found in every London pub is cider. Made from apples, it comes in a range of strengths and levels of dryness. A truly local London spirit is gin, usually drunk with tonic water. In winter, mulled wine (warm and spicy) or hot toddies (brandy or whisky with hot water and sugar) may be served. Non-alcoholic drinks like mineral water and fruit juices are always available, too.

FOOD IN PUBS

PUB FOOD has undergone a revolution in the last few years. While the majority of pubs still serve traditional meals at lunchtimes, such as Ploughman's Lunch (cheese, salad and bread), Shepherd's Pie or roast beef lunch on Sundays *(see pp288–9)*, pubs serving more adventurous evening meals have become fashionable. The **Chapel**, **Cow**, **Eagle**, **Engineer**, **Crown and Goose**, **Fire Station**, **Lansdowne** and **Prince Bonaparte** are the best of these new-wave pubs, offering interesting food at reasonable prices. Booking a table in advance is essential.

HISTORIC PUBS

NEARLY EVERY PUB in London has a fascinating history. The buildings might contain beamed medieval snugs, extravagant Victorian fantasies, or the stunning Arts and Crafts style interior of the **Black Friar**. At the **Bunch of Grapes** (SW3), the bar is divided by "snobscreens", a feature once found in many pubs that allowed the upper classes to enjoy a drink without having to mix with their servants. The 16th-century **King's Head and Eight Bells** has a display of antiques. Many pubs have strong literary associations, such as the **Fitzroy Tavern** (a meeting place for writers and artists: *see p131*), **Ye Olde Cheshire Cheese** (associated with Dr Johnson: *see p140*) and the **Trafalgar Tavern** *(see p238)* where Charles Dickens was a regular customer. On a less literary note, the **Bull and Bush** in North London was the subject of an old music-hall song.

Other pubs have more violent associations – victims of Jack the Ripper were found near the **Roebuck** and the **Ten Bells**. The 18th-century highwayman Dick Turpin refreshed himself between robberies at **Spaniards Inn** in north London *(see p231)*, and the **French House** *(see p109)* in Soho was once a meeting point for the French Resistance in World War II.

THEMED PUBS AND BARS

THEMED PUBS are a recent phenomenon. Self-styled "Irish" pubs such as **Filthy McNasty's** and the cavernous **Waxy O'Connor's** do not attract many people from the Emerald Isle, but enough drinking goes on to give them a certain credibility. In a similar vein are "Australian" bars such as **Sheila's**. Sports bars have so far failed to grip the imagination of Londoners in quite the same way. The **Sports Café**, near Piccadilly, has three bars, a dance floor – and 120 television sets showing satellite TV.

OUTDOOR DRINKING

THERE ARE relatively few pubs in the centre of London with outdoor seating areas and the better choices tend to be further out of town. The **Freemason's Arms** in Hampstead, for example, has a very pleasant garden. Some pubs enjoy riverside locations with fine views. From the **Grapes** down in Limehouse to the **White Cross** in Richmond, there are many choices along the length of the River Thames in London.

PUBS WITH ENTERTAINMENT

ENTERTAINMENT is on offer in many of London's pubs. There are fringe theatre productions (see p328) at the **King's Head**, the **Bush**, the **Latchmere**, and the **Prince Albert**. Other pubs have live music (see pp333–5): English folk at the **Archway Tavern**; modern jazz at the **Bulls Head** and a wide variety of music styles at the popular **Mean Fiddler** which regularly draws a full house.

PUB NAMES

Signs have hung outside public houses since 1393, when King Richard II decided they should replace the older practice of having a bush outside the door. Most people were illiterate, so names were chosen that could easily be pictured: coats of arms (Freemasons' Arms), historical figures (Princess Louise) or heraldic animals (White Lion).

DIRECTORY

Key to symbols:
🔲 stage in bar area or special room for live performers (phone for details)
🔲 offers more than standard bar snacks
🎵 regular live music (phone for details)
🔲 outside drinking area

SOHO, TRAFALGAR SQUARE

French House
49 Dean St W1.
Map 13 A2. 🔲

Sports Café
80 Haymarket SW1.
Map 13 A3.

Tottenham
6 Oxford St W1.
Map 13 A1.

Waxy O'Connor's
14-16 Rupert St W1.
Map 13 A2.

COVENT GARDEN, STRAND

Lamb and Flag
33 Rose St WC2.
Map 13 B2. 🔲

Salisbury
90 St Martin's Lane
WC2. **Map** 13 B2.

Sheila's
14 King St WC2.
Map 13 B2.

BLOOMSBURY, FITZROVIA

Fitzroy Tavern
16 Charlotte St W1.
Map 13 A1. 🔲

HOLBORN

Ye Olde Cheshire Cheese
145 Fleet St EC4.
Map 14 E1. 🔲

THE CITY, CLERKENWELL

Black Friar
174 Queen Victoria St EC4.
Map 14 F2.

Eagle
159 Farringdon Rd EC1.
Map 6 E4. 🔲

Filthy McNasty's
68 Amwell St EC1.
Map 6 E3.

Ship
23 Lime St EC3. **Map** 15 C2.

Ten Bells
84 Commercial St E1.
Map 16 E1.

SOUTHWARK AND SOUTH BANK

Bunch of Grapes
St Thomas St SE1.
Map 15 C4. 🔲 🔲

Fire Station
150 Waterloo Rd SE1.
Map 14 E4. 🔲

George Inn
77 Borough High St SE1.
Map 15 B4. 🔲 🔲

CHELSEA, SOUTH KENSINGTON

King's Head and Eight Bells
50 Cheyne Walk SW3.
Map 19 A5. 🔲

Orange Brewery
37 Pimlico Rd SW1.
Map 20 D2. 🔲

CAMDEN TOWN, HAMPSTEAD

Bull and Bush
North End Way NW3.
Map 1 A3.

Chapel
48 Chapel St NW1.
Map 3 B5. 🔲 🔲

Crown and Goose
100 Arlington Rd NW1.
Map 4 F1. 🔲

Engineer
65 Gloucester Ave NW1.
Map 4 D1. 🔲 🔲

Freemasons Arms
32 Downshire Hill NW3.
Map 1 C5. 🔲

Landsdowne
90 Gloucester Ave NW1.
Map 4 D1. 🔲

Spaniards Inn
Spaniards Rd NW3.
Map 1 A3. 🔲

NOTTING HILL, MAIDA VALE

Cow
89 Westbourne Park Rd
W11. **Map** 23 C1. 🔲 🔲

Crockers
24 Aberdeen Pl NW8.

Prince Albert
11 Pembridge Rd W11.
Map 9 C2. Gate Theatre:
🔲 020-7229 0706. 🔲

Prince Bonaparte
80 Chepstow Rd W2.
Map 9 C1. 🔲

FURTHER AFIELD

Archway Tavern
1 Archway Close N19.
🎵

Bull's Head
373 Lonsdale Rd SW13.
🎵

Bush
Shepherd's Bush Green
W12. Theatre: 🔲 020-
8743 3383. 🔲

City Barge
27 Strand-on-the-Green
W4. 🔲 🔲

Grapes
76 Narrow St E14. 🔲

King's Head
115 Upper St N1. **Map** 6
F1. Theatre: 🔲 020-
7226 1916. 🔲 🎵 🔲

Latchmere
503 Battersea Park Rd
SW11. Grace Theatre
🔲 020-7228 2620. 🔲

Mean Fiddler
28a High St NW10. 🎵

Roebuck
27 Brady St E1.

Trafalgar Tavern
Park Row SE10.
Map 23 C1. 🎵 🔲

White Cross
Cholmondeley Walk,
Richmond. 🔲 🔲

SHOPS AND MARKETS

LONDON IS STILL one of the most lively shopping cities in the world. Within just a few minutes' walk you can find both vast department stores, with glittering window displays, and tiny, cluttered rooms where one customer almost fills the entire shop. Many of the most famous London shops are in Knightsbridge or Regent Street, where prices can be steep, but Oxford Street, which is packed with a huge number of shops offering quality

Bags from two of the most famous West End shops

goods at a range of prices, is also worth a visit. All over London, there are plenty of places tucked away down side-streets – and don't forget to try the markets for antiques, crafts, household goods, food and clothing. You can buy virtually anything in London; specialities include clothes (from Burberry raincoats and traditional tweeds to "street fashion"); floral scents and soaps; art and antiques; and craft goods such as jewellery, ceramics and leather.

WHEN TO SHOP

IN CENTRAL LONDON, most shops open somewhere between 9am and 10am and close between 5pm and 6pm on weekdays; some earlier on Saturdays. The "late night" shopping (until 7pm or 8pm) is on Thursdays in Oxford Street and the rest of the West End, and on Wednesdays in Knightsbridge and Chelsea; some shops in tourist areas, such as Covent Garden *(see pp110–19)* and the Trocadero, are open until 7pm or later every day, including Sundays. A few street markets *(see pp322–3)* and a slowly growing number of other shops are also open on Sundays.

HOW TO PAY

MOST SHOPS WILL accept the following major credit cards: Access (Mastercard), American Express, Diners Club, Japanese Credit Bureau and Visa. Some, however, do not, notably the John Lewis stores and Marks and Spencer, as well as street markets and some smaller shops. Some of the stores do accept traveller's cheques, especially if they're in sterling; for other currencies the rate of exchange is less favourable than in a bank. You need your passport with you. Very few shops accept personal cheques drawn against foreign banks, unless they are Eurocheques.

RIGHTS AND SERVICES

IF YOUR PURCHASE is defective you are usually entitled to a refund if you have proof of purchase and return the goods. This isn't always the case with sales goods, so inspect them carefully before you buy.

Most large stores, and some small ones, will pack goods up for you and also send them anywhere in the world.

VAT EXEMPTION

VAT (VALUE ADDED tax) is a sales tax of 17.5% which is charged on virtually all goods sold in Britain (the notable exceptions are books, food and all children's clothes). VAT is nearly always included in the advertised or marked price, although often business suppliers, including some stationers and electrical goods shops, charge it separately.

Non-European Community visitors to Britain who stay no longer than three months may claim back VAT. If you plan to do this, make sure you take along your passport when shopping. You must complete a form in the store when you buy the goods and then give a copy to customs when you leave the country. (You may have to show your purchases to customs, so do pack them somewhere accessible.) The tax refund may be returned to you by cheque or attributed to your credit card, but then a service charge will usually be

Harrod's elaborate Edwardian tiled food halls

deducted and most stores have a minimum purchase threshold (often £50 or £75). If you arrange to have your goods shipped directly home from the store, VAT should be deducted before you pay.

TWICE-YEARLY SALES

THE TRADITIONAL sale season is from January to February and June to July, when virtually every shop cuts its prices and sells off imperfect or unwanted stock. The department stores have some of the best reductions; one of the most famous sales is at **Harrod's** *(see p207)* where queues start to form outside long before opening.

BEST OF THE DEPARTMENT STORES

THE KING OF London's department stores, by tradition, is **Harrod's**, with its 300 departments and staff of 4,000. Prices are not always as high as you may well expect. The spectacular food hall, decorated with Edwardian tiles, has splendid displays of fish, cheese, fruit and vegetables; other specialities include fashions for all ages, china and glass, electronics and kitchenware. Though Harrod's is still just as popular, especially with well-heeled visitors, Londoners often head instead for nearby **Harvey Nichols**, which aims to stock the best of everything with the price tags to match. Clothes are particularly strong, with the emphasis firmly on very high fashion, with many talented British, European and American represented. There is also an impressive menswear section. The food hall, opened in 1992, is one of the most stylish in London.

Selfridge's vast building on Oxford Street houses everything from Gucci bags and Hermès scarves to household gadgets and bed-linen. **Miss Selfridge**, the popular high street fashion chain, also has a branch in the store.

The original **John Lewis** was a draper and his shop still has a gorgeous selection of fabrics and haberdashery. Its china, glass and household items make John Lewis, and its well-known Sloane Square partner, Peter Jones, equally popular with Londoners.

Liberty *(see p109)*, the last privately owned department store in London, still sells the hand-blocked silks and other oriental goods it was famed for when it opened in 1875. Look out for the famous scarf department.

Fortnum and Mason's ground floor provisions department is so engrossing that the upper floors of classic fashion remain peaceful. The food section stocks everything from baked beans to the beautifully prepared hampers.

Some of the best-known names in British clothes design today

DEPARTMENT STORES

Fortnum and Mason
181 Piccadilly W1. **Map** 12 F3.
📞 020-7734 8040.

Harrod's
87–135 Brompton Rd SW1.
Map 11 C5.
📞 020-7730 1234.

Harvey Nichols
109–125 Knightsbridge SW1.
Map 11 C5.
📞 020-7235 5000.

John Lewis
278–306 Oxford St W1. **Map** 12 E1.
📞 020-7629 7711.

Liberty
210–220 Regent St W1. **Map** 12 F2.
📞 020-7734 1234.

Selfridge's
400 Oxford St W1. **Map** 12 D2.
📞 020-7629 1234.

Doorman at Fortnum and Mason

MARKS AND SPENCER

MARKS AND SPENCER has come a long way since 1882 when Russian emigré Michael Marks had a stall in Leeds's Kirkgate market under the sign, "Don't ask the price – it's a penny!" It now has over 680 stores worldwide and everything in them is "own label". It stocks reliable versions of more expensive clothes – Marks and Spencer's underwear in particular is a staple of the British wardrobe. The food department concentrates entirely on upmarket convenience foods. The main Oxford Street branches at the Pantheon (near Oxford Circus) and Marble Arch are the most interesting and well stocked.

Penhaligon's for scents *(see p318)*

London's Best: Shopping Streets and Markets

LONDON'S BEST shopping areas range from the elegance of Knightsbridge, where porcelain, jewellery and *couture* clothes come at the highest prices, to colourful markets such as Brick Lane and Portobello Road. Meccas for those who enjoy searching for a bargain, London's markets also reflect the vibrant street life engendered by its enterprising multi-racial community. The city is fertile ground for specialist shoppers: there are streets crammed with antique shops, antiquarian booksellers and art galleries. Turn to pages 316–23 for more details of shops, grouped according to category.

Kensington Church Street
The small book and furniture shops on this winding street still provide old-fashioned service. (See p321.)

Regent's Park and Marylebone

N

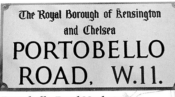

Portobello Road Market
Over 200 stalls sell objets d'art, jewellery, medals, paintings and silverware – plus fresh fruit and vegetables. (See p323.)

See inset map

Kensington and Holland Park

South Kensington and Knightsbridge

Picca and Jame

Knightsbridge
Exclusive designer-wear is on sale here, at Harrod's as well as smaller stores. (See p207.)

Chelsea

King's Road
A centre for avant-garde fashion in the 1960s and 1970s, the street is still popular with West London shoppers. There is also a good antiques market. (See p192.)

LONDON'S WEST END SHOPS

Oxford Street is sometimes called London's
High Street and many of the shops that line it are
branches of national or international chains. The
big department stores such as Selfridge's and John
Lewis also loom along this street, as do smaller
shops selling clothes and tourist souvenirs. South of
Oxford Street, on Regent Street, Piccadilly and Bond
Street, prices rise and shoppers search for specialized
purchases among the designer clothes and accessories
shops, jewellers and art and antique dealers.

Brick Lane Market
In this East End street, everything from old books to new trainers is on sale. (See p322.)

Gabriel's Wharf
The wharf has been converted into small shops selling art, jewellery and crafts. (See p187.)

Petticoat Lane
London's most famous market has leather, clothes, watches, jewellery and toys. (See p323.)

Charing Cross Road
Crammed shops selling old and new books line this long street. (See p316.)

Covent Garden and Neal Street
Street entertainers perform in this lively and historic market. The specialist shops of Neal Street are nearby. (See p115.)

Clothes

LONDON OFFERS the clothes-shopper a seemingly inexhaustible range of styles, price levels, quality and areas to shop in. The world's top designers are here, clustered around Knightsbridge, Bond Street and Chelsea, as are familiar chains such as Benetton and The Gap. But it is the wealth of home-based style that makes London such an exciting place to buy clothes. British designers excel in the opposite extremes of the market – traditional tailoring and street fashions.

TRADITIONAL CLOTHING

THE RUGGED country look is best found in the Regent Street/Piccadilly area. Waxed Barbour jackets are available from Farlow's (see Royal Opera Arcade p92) of Pall Mall and riding accessories from **Swaine Adeney**. **Kent and Curwen** is the place for cricket jumpers and **Captain Watts**, guernsey sweaters and oilskins. Try the Knightsbridge branch of **The Scotch House** for traditional tartan clothing, cashmere, Aran jerseys and Shetland shawls.

Classic town and business wear is another speciality of this area. **Burberry** sells the famous trenchcoats as well as checked clothing and some distinctive luggage from their shop on Haymarket. **Hackett** stocks traditionally tailored men's clothing. For shirts visit Jermyn Street, where you can order them made-to-measure or choose the more reasonably priced off-the-shelf ones. Many manufacturers now also sell classic women's blouses.

Liberty (see p109) use their famous patterned prints to make scarves, ties, blouses, pretty English rose dresses and some unusual trimmed denim jackets. **Laura Ashley** is also well renowned for its floral print dresses and frilly blouses.

For the ultimate in luxury, visit Savile Row, home of the top few tailors, including the famous **Gieves and Hawkes**.

MODERN BRITISH DESIGN AND STREET FASHION

LONDON IS one of the world's capitals for street fashion – designer **Jean Paul Gaultier** prefers it to Paris because, he says, the street fashion is "free from the constraints of good taste". In Britain, quirky

Vivienne Westwood won the Fashion Designer of the Year Award (1991). Other over-the-top British designers can be found in **Browns**. For more wearable styles, try the shops around Newburgh Street, West Soho. Most are predominantly for women, but **The Duffer of St George** is among the trailblazers for men. New designers often start out with a small stall at **Hype DF** or **Kensington Market** – both very good for whacky or unusual clothing. Nowadays Oxford Street shops such as **Top Shop** and **Mash** excel at copying street fashions at very low prices.

Paul Smith is one of the best shops for British high fashion. For women only, try **Browns**, **Whistles**, **Jasper Conran**, **Katharine Hamnett** and finally **Caroline Charles**.

KNITWEAR

FROM Fair Isle jumpers to Aran knits, the traditional British knitwear is famous. The best places for these are in Piccadilly – where you will find **N Peal** – and in Regent Street and Knightsbridge. Top designers such as **Patricia Roberts** and **Joseph Tricot**, and small shops such as **Jane and Dada**, stock a range of quite unusual and innovative machine- and hand-knits.

CHILDREN'S CLOTHES

YOU can get traditional hand-smocked dresses and romper suits from Liberty, **Young England** and **Anthea Moore Ede**, which stock

SIZE CHART

For Australian sizes follow British and American convention

Children's clothing

British	2–3	4–5	6–7	8–9	10–11	12	14	14+ (years)
American	2–3	4–5	6–6X	7–8	10	12	14	16 (size)
Continental	2–3	4–5	6–7	8–9	10–11	12	14	14+ (years)

Children's shoes

British	7^{1}	8	9	10	11	12	13	1	2
American	$7^{1/2}$	$8^{1/2}$	$9^{1/2}$	$10^{1/2}$	$11^{1/2}$	$12^{1/2}$	$13^{1/2}$	$1^{1/2}$	$2^{1/2}$
Continental	24	$25^{1/2}$	27	28	29	30	32	33	34

Women's dresses coats and skirts

British	6	8	10	12	14	16	18	20
American	4	6	8	10	12	14	16	18
Continental	38	40	42	44	46	48	50	52

Women's blouses and sweaters

British	30	32	34	36	38	40	42
American	6	8	10	12	14	16	18
Continental	40	42	44	46	48	50	52

Women's shoes

British	3	4	5	6	7	8
American	5	6	7	8	9	10
Continental	36	37	38	39	40	41

Men's suits

British	34	36	38	40	42	44	46	48
American	34	36	38	40	42	44	46	48
Continental	44	46	48	50	52	54	56	58

Men's shirts

British	14	15	$15^{1/2}$	16	$16^{1/2}$	17	$17^{1/2}$	18
American	14	15	$15^{1/2}$	16	$16^{1/2}$	17	$17^{1/2}$	18
Continental	36	38	39	41	42	43	44	45

Men's shoes

British	7	$7^{1/2}$	8	9	10	11	12
American	$7^{1/2}$	8	$8^{1/2}$	$9^{1/2}$	$10^{1/2}$	11	$11^{1/2}$
Continental	40	41	42	43	44	45	46

nostalgically styled clothes such as smocks, gowns, and tweed coats with smart velvet collars. **Trotters**, just behind Sloane Square, offers everything from shoes to haircuts.

SHOES

WITH SHOES, again it's the very traditional or the very trendy British designers and manufacturers who excel.

Their ready-made traditional brogues and Oxfords are the mainstay of **Church's Shoes**. For hand-made, classic footwear, try the Royal Family's shoe-maker **John Lobb**. At the other end of the scale, **Shelly's** sells the utilitarian, trendy Dr Martens, originally designed as hard-wearing work boots but now the shoe to be seen in. **Red or Dead** designs and produces some

really extravagant designs in shoes as well as clothes, while for something a little more elegant, try **Johnny Moke** of the King's Road or **Emma Hope** in east London. If you are on the look-out for more exquisite women's shoes visit **Manolo Blahnik**. Cheaper and less exclusive, but often equally original, designs can be found either in **Hobbs** or **Pied à Terre.**

DIRECTORY

TRADITIONAL

Burberry
18–22 Haymarket SW1.
Map 13 A3.
[020-7930 3343.
One of two branches.

Captain Watts
7 Dover St W1.
Map 12 E3.
[020-7493 4633.

Gieves & Hawkes
1 Savile Row W1.
Map 12 E3.
[020-7434 2001.

Hackett
87 Jermyn St SW1.
Map 13 A3.
[020-7930 1300.
One of several branches.

Kent and Curwen
39 St James's St SW1.
Map 12 F3.
[020-7409 1955.

Laura Ashley
256–258 Regent St W1.
Map 12 F1.
[020-7437 9760.
One of several branches.

The Scotch House
2 Brompton Rd SW1.
Map 11 C5.
[020-7581 2151.
One of several branches.

Swaine Adeney
54 St James St SW1.
Map 12 F3.
[020-7409 7277.

MODERN/STREET FASHION

Browns
23–27 South Molton St W1. **Map** 12 E2.
[020-7514 0000.
One of several branches.

Caroline Charles
56–57 Beauchamp Pl SW3.
Map 19 B1.
[020-7589 5850.

The Duffer of St George
29 Shorts Gardens W2.
Map 13 B2.
[020-7379 4660.

Hype DF
48–52 Kensington High St W8. **Map** 10 D5.
[020-7938 3801.

Jean-Paul Gaultier
171–5 Draycott Ave SW3.
Map 19 B2.
[020-7584 4648.

Katharine Hamnett
20 Sloane St SW1.
Map 11 C5.
[020-7823 1002.

Kensington Market
49–53 Kensington High St W8. **Map** 10 D5.
[020-7938 4343.

Mash
73 Oxford St W1.
Map 13 A1.
[020-7434 9609.

Koh Samui
50 Monmouth St WC2.
Map 13 B2.
[020-7240 4280.

Nicole Farhi
158 New Bond St W1.
Map 12 E2.
[020-7499 8368.

Paul Smith
40–44 Floral St WC2.
Map 13 B2.
[020-7379 7133.

Top Shop
Oxford Circus W1.
Map 12 F1.
[020-7636 7700.
One of several branches.

Vivienne Westwood
6 Davies St W1.
Map 12 E2.
[020-7629 3757.

Whistles
12–14 St Christopher's Pl W1. **Map** 12 D1
[020-7487 4484.

KNITWEAR

Jane and Dada
20–21 St Christopher's Pl W1. **Map** 12 D1.
[020-7486 0977.

Joseph Tricot
28 Brook St W1.
Map 12 E2.
[020-7629 6077.

N Peal
Burlington Arcade,
Piccadilly, W1. **Map** 12 F3.
[020-7493 9220.
One of several branches.

Patricia Roberts
60 Kinnerton St SW1.
Map 11 C5.
[020-7235 4742.

CHILDREN'S

Anthea Moore Ede
16 Victoria Grove W8.
Map 18 E1.
[020-7584 8826.

Trotters
34 King's Rd SW3.
Map 19 C2.
[020-7259 9620.

Young England
47 Elizabeth St SW1.
Map 20 E2.
[020-7259 9003.

SHOES

Church's Shoes
163 New Bond St W1.
Map 12 E2.
[020-7499 9449.
One of several branches.

Emma Hope
33 Amwell St EC1.
Map 6 E3.
[020-7833 2367.

Hobbs
47 South Molton St W1.
Map 12 E2
[020-7629 0750.
One of several branches.

Johnny Moke
396 King's Rd SW10.
Map 18 F4.
[020-7351 2232.

John Lobb
9 St James's St SW1.
Map 12 F4.
[020-7930 3664.

Manolo Blahnik
49–51 Old Church St,
Kings Road SW3.
Map 19 A4.
[020-7352 3863.

Pied à Terre
19 South Molton St W1
Map 12 E2.
[020-7493 3637.
One of several branches.

Red or Dead
33 Neal St WC2.
Map 13 B2.
[020-7379 7571.
One of several branches.

Shelly's
19–21 Foubert's Pl,
Carnaby Street, W1.
Map 12 F2
[020-7287 0593.
One of several branches.

Specialist Shops

Lof the grand department stores
such as Harrod's, but there are many specialist
shops which should also figure on the visitor's itinerary.
Some have expertise built up over a century or more,
while others cater for the new and fashionable.

FOODS

Bmaligned but there are
many specialities that are well
worth sampling, such as teas,
cheeses, chocolates, biscuits
and preserves *(see pp288–9)*.
The food halls of Fortnum
and Mason, Harrod's and
Selfridge's are good for all of
these. Otherwise, head for
Paxton and Whitfield, a
delightful shop dating from
1830 and stocking over 300
cheeses, including baby
Stiltons and Cheshire truckles,
along with pork pies, elegant
biscuits, oils and preserves.

For chocolates, the ultimate
extravagance is **Charbonnel
et Walker**. Despite the name
it is an English manufacturer,
and the chocolates are all
handmade. **Bendicks** on
Curzon Street stands 50 yards
from the original 1921
premises. They make dark
chocolates in Winchester by
hand, and the classic dessert
mint is still the speciality.

TEAS

THAT MOST famous of British
drinks comes in all kinds
of flavours, from the delicate
gunpowder green to the rich,
strong and dark English
breakfast types. An interesting
selection, including fruit-
flavoured teas, is available at
the **Tea House** in Covent
Garden. Jolly tea pots are also
stocked here. The **Algerian
Coffee Stores** sells more tea
than coffee, including herbal
and fruity ones. The selection
of coffees is still excellent,
however, and there are many
luxury grocery items in stock.

ONE-OFFS

THERE ARE hundreds of odd
shops in London that
specialize in just one sort of
thing. **The Bead Shop**, for
example, sells a massive

selection of beads, and also
stocks the equipment for
making them into jewellery.
**The Covent Garden Candle
Company** supplies, candles
of every imaginable shape
and size, along with candle
holders and candle-making
equipment. Demonstrations of
the art take place outside.
Halcyon Days specializes in
little enamelled copper boxes,
the products of a revived
English 18th-century craft.

Astleys sells pipes but not
tobacco; the range is quite
bewildering, from simple
handturned straightgrains to
weird-looking slope-domed
calabashes and Sherlock
Holmesian meerschaums. For
serious collectors of antique
scientific instruments, **Arthur
Middleton** has a fascinatingly
cluttered shop full of ancient
globes and early microscopes.
For equally serious collectors
of dolls' houses, the **Singing
Tree** has the ultimate in
English dolls' houses, and
many beautifully crafted tiny
things to put inside them, all
replicated to precise scale in
accurate period style.

Finally, at **Anything Left-
Handed** in Soho, everything
is designed to make life easier
for the left-hander. Scissors,
corkscrews, cutlery, pens and
kitchen and garden tools are
the main sellers.

BOOKS AND MAGAZINES

Bookshops are high among
London's specialities.
Charing Cross Road *(see p108)*
is the focal point for those
searching for new, antiquarian
and second-hand volumes,
and is the home of **Foyle's**,
with its massive but notoriously
badly organized stock. Large
branches of chains such as
Books Etc and **Waterstone's**
are also here; so are many
specialist bookshops such as
Murder One for crime
books, **Silver Moon** for

women's and feminist writing,
and **Zwemmer** for art books.

Stanford's *(see p112)*, with
maps and guides to cover the
globe, is in Long Acre; more
travel books can be found at
the **Travel Bookshop**. Nearby
is **Books for Cooks**, complete
with café and demonstration
kitchen. Adult comics are the
speciality at **Comic Showcase**
in Neal Street, while fantasy,
science fiction and graphic
novels abound at **Forbidden
Planet**. For gay writing, visit
the pioneering **Gay's The
Word**, near Russell Square.
The best selection of books
on movies is found at the
Cinema Bookshop.

The **PC Bookshop** sells a
huge range of books on all
aspects of computers, while
its sister shop nearby stocks
multimedia packages.

Two of the best general
bookshops are **Hatchard's** in
Piccadilly and the flagship
Dillons store in Gower
Street, both of which offer a
well-organized and extensive
choice. **Compendium**, an
alternative bookstore near
Camden Market, features
hard-to-obtain titles. **The
Banana Bookshop** in Covent
Garden must be the world's
most endearing remainder
shop, with jungle murals and
a waterfall running beside the
stairs.

The Charing Cross Road
area is the best hunting
ground for antiquarian books.
Many shops offer a book-
finding service if the title you
want is no longer in print.

If you're looking for newspapers and magazines from
abroad, the basement of
Tower Records has the best
selection of US newspapers,
while **Capital Newsagents**
stocks (among others) Italian,
French, Spanish and Middle
Eastern publications. **Gray's
Inn News** is also worth a
visit for publications from
overseas *(see pp352–3)*.

RECORDS AND MUSIC

As one of the world's
greatest centres of
recorded music, London has a
huge and excellent selection

of record shops catering to all manner of musical styles. The **Music Discount Centre** has a very good range of classical music, as do the mega-stores such as **HMV**, **Virgin** and **Tower Records**, which are best for mainstream platters

from pop to punk to peaceful easy listening. The small specialist shops tend to cater to the more esoteric tastes. For jazz take a trip to **Ray's Jazz** and **Honest Jon's**, while reggae fans should skank down to **Daddy Kool**. HMV

has a good selection of world music, and **Stern's** is peerless when it comes to African music. For 12-inch singles, the medium of club and dance music, **Trax** and **Black Market** are two of the most central places to look.

DIRECTORY

FOODS

Bendicks of Mayfair
7 Aldwych WC2.
Map 13 C2.
☎ 020-7836 1846.

Charbonnel et Walker
1 Royal Arcade, 28 Old Bond St W1. **Map** 12 F3.
☎ 020-7491 0939.

Paxton and Whitfield
93 Jermyn St SW1.
Map 12 F3.
☎ 020-7930 0259.

TEAS

Algerian Coffee Stores
52 Old Compton St W1.
Map 13 A2.
☎ 020-7437 2480.

The Tea House
15 Neal St WC2.
Map 13 B2.
☎ 020-7240 7539.

ONE-OFFS

Anything Left-Handed
57 Brewer St W1.
Map 9 A2.
☎ 020-7437 3910.

Arthur Middleton
12 New Row, Covent Garden WC2.
Map 13 B2.
☎ 020-7836 7042.

Astleys
16 Piccadilly Arcade SW1.
Map 13 A3.
☎ 020-7499 9950.

The Bead Shop
43 Neal Street WC2.
Map 13 B1.
☎ 020-7240 0931.

The Covent Garden Candle Company
30 The Market, Covent Garden Piazza WC2.
Map 13 C2.
☎ 020-7836 9815.

Halcyon Days
14 Brook St W1.
Map 12 E2.
☎ 020-7629 8811.

The Singing Tree
69 New King's Rd SW6.
☎ 020-7736 4527.

BOOKS AND MAGAZINES

The Banana Bookshop
10 The Market, Covent Garden Piazza WC2.
Map 13 C2.
☎ 020-7379 7650.

Books Etc
120 Charing Cross Rd WC2.
Map 13 B1.
☎ 020-7379 6838.

Books for Cooks
4 Blenheim Crescent W11.
Map 9 B2.
☎ 020-7221 1992.

Capital Newsagents
48 Old Compton St W1.
Map 13 A2.
☎ 020-7437 2479.

Cinema Bookshop
13–14 Great Russell St WC1. **Map** 13 B1.
☎ 020-7637 0206.

Comic Showcase
76 Neal St WC2. **Map** 13 B1.
☎ 020-7240 3664.

Compendium
234 Camden High St NW1.
☎ 020-7485 8944.

Dillons
82 Gower St WC1.
Map 5 A5.
☎ 020-7636 1577.

Forbidden Planet
71 New Oxford St WC1.
Map 13 B1.
☎ 020-7836 4179.

Foyle's
113–119 Charing Cross Rd WC2. **Map** 13 B1.
☎ 020-7437 5660.

Gay's The Word
66 Marchmont St WC1.
Map 5 B4.
☎ 020-7278 7654.

Gray's Inn News
50 Theobald's Rd WC1.
Map 6 D5.
☎ 020-7405 5241.

Hatchard's
187 Piccadilly W1.
Map 12 F3.
☎ 020-7439 9921.

Murder One
71–73 Charing Cross Rd WC2. **Map** 13 B2.
☎ 020-7734 3485.

PC Bookshop
21 Sicilian Ave WC1.
Map 13 1C.
☎ 020-7831 0022.

Silver Moon
64–68 Charing Cross Rd WC2. **Map** 13 B2.
☎ 020-7836 7906.

Stanford's
12–14 Long Acre WC2.
Map 13 B2.
☎ 020-7836 1321.

Travel Bookshop
13 Blenheim Crescent W11. **Map** 9 B2.
☎ 020-7229 5260.

Waterstone's
121–125 Charing Cross Rd WC2. **Map** 13 B1.
☎ 020-7434 4291.

The Women's Book Club
34 Great Sutton St EC1.
Map 6 F4.
☎ 020-7251 3007.

Zwemmer
26 Litchfield St WC2.
Map 13 B2.
☎ 020-7379 7886.

RECORDS AND MUSIC

Black Market
25 D'Arblay St W1.
Map 13 A2.
☎ 020-7437 0478.

Daddy Kool Music
12 Berwick St W1.
Map 13 A2.
☎ 020-7437 3535.

HMV
150 Oxford St W1.
Map 13 A1.
☎ 020-7631 3423.

Honest Jon's Records
278 Portobello Rd W10.
Map 9 A1.
☎ 020-7969 9822.

The Music Discount Centre
33–34 Rathbone Pl W1.
Map 13 A1.
☎ 020-7637 4700.

Ray's Jazz
180 Shaftesbury Ave WC2. **Map** 13 B1.
☎ 020-7240 3969.

Rough Trade
130 Talbot Rd W11.
Map 9 C1.
☎ 020-7229 8541.

Stern's
293 Euston Rd NW1.
Map 5 A4.
☎ 020-7387 5550.

Tower Records
1 Piccadilly Circus W1.
Map 13 A3.
☎ 020-7439 2500.

Trax
55 Greek St W1.
Map 13 A2.
☎ 020-7734 0795.

Virgin Megastore
14–30 Oxford St W1.
Map 13 A1.
☎ 020-7631 1234.

Gifts and Souvenirs

LONDON IS A WONDERFUL PLACE to shop for presents. As well as an impressive array of original ceramics, jewellery, perfume and glassware, there is exotic merchandise from around the world, including jewellery from India and Africa, stationery from Europe and kitchenware from France and Italy. The elegant, Regency-period Burlington Arcade (see p91) is a popular shopping destination selling high-quality gifts, clothes, art and crafts, many of which are made in the UK.

The shops at big museums, such as the Victoria and Albert (see p198–201), the Natural History (see p204–5) and the Science Museum (see p208–9) often have unusual and original items to take home as mementoes of your visit, while **Contemporary Applied Arts**, **Thomas Neal's** shopping complex and the market in Covent Garden Piazza (see p114) all sell a good range of British pottery, jewellery, knitwear and other crafts. If you want to buy all your presents under one roof, go to Liberty (see p311), where beautiful stock from all over the globe fills every department.

JEWELLERY

JEWELLERY SHOPS in London range from the extremely traditional to the tiny shops and stalls that huddle in areas like Covent Garden (see pp110–19), Gabriel's Wharf (see p187), and Camden Lock (see p322), which specialize in unusual pieces. **Butler and Wilson** has some of the most eye-catching costume jewellery in town, while next door **Electrum** keeps less bold but equally innovative pieces.

Past Times sells modern reproductions of ancient British designs, including Celtic, Roman and Tudor, as do the shops at the British Museum (see p126–9) and the V&A. The **Lesley Craze Gallery** sells new designs, while **Contemporary Applied Arts** has stylish craft jewellery. The essential place for Gothic jewellery is **The Great Frog** on Carnaby Street. Liberty stocks spectacular ethnic, costume and fashion jewellery. **Manquette** is also worth visiting, for its elegant, one-off pieces in lapis lazuli, amber, coral, gold and silver.

HATS AND ACCESSORIES

TRADITIONAL MEN'S hats, from flat caps to trilbies and pith helmets, can be found at **Edward Bates** and **Herbert Johnson**. For women, truly distinctive creations come from **Herald and Heart Hatters**, while **Stephen Jones** has a wide range of designs from the everyday to the extravagant and will make hats to match any outfit if you supply your own fabric.

For a selection of the best in British accessories, try the shops on Jermyn Street or in the arcades off Piccadilly. Elsewhere, **James Smith & Sons** produces wonderful umbrellas, ideal for wet London weather. For walking sticks, canes and riding crops, pay a visit to Swaine Adeney (see p315).

Mulberry Company stocks classically English luggage, as well as accessories such as belts, purses and wallets, and **Janet Fitch** sells a wide range of bags, belts, jewellery, hats and other essential accessories.

At the cheaper end of the market, the **Accessorize** chain sells all manner of beads and baubles, grouped by colour to help co-ordinate your outfit.

PERFUMES AND TOILETRIES

MANY BRITISH perfumeries use recipes that are hundreds of years old. **Floris** and **Penhaligon's**, for example, still manufacture the same flower-based scents and toiletries for men and women that they sold in the 19th century. The same goes for **Czech and Speake**, and for men's specialists **Truefitt and Hill** and **George F Trumper**, where you can buy some wonderful reproductions of antique shaving equipment as well. Both **Culpeper** and **Neal's Yard Remedies** employ traditional herbal and floral remedies as bases for their natural, therapeutic toiletries.

Other manufacturers have a more contemporary approach to their wares; the **Body Shop**, for example, uses recyclable plastic packaging for its natural cosmetics and toiletries and encourages staff and customers alike to take an interest in environmental issues. **Molton Brown** sells a range of natural cosmetics, body and haircare products, from both its own shops in South Molton Street and Hampstead and from other outlets.

STATIONERY

SOME OF THE most interesting wrapping paper on sale in London is designed by **Tessa Fantoni**, whose paper-covered boxes, photo frames and albums are sold in several specialist stationery and gift shops, as well as the Conran Shop and her own shop in Clapham.

Falkiner Fine Papers stocks a range of handmade and decorative papers. Their marbled paper makes glorious giftwrapping for a very special gift. To find luxurious writing paper, pens, pencils and desk accessories, try the Queen's stationer, **Smythson** of Bond Street. Fortnum and Mason (see p311) does handsome leather-bound diaries, blotters and pencil holders, while Liberty embellishes desk accessories with its famous Art Deco prints. For personal organizers covered in anything from vinyl to iguana skin there's the **Filofax Centre** or the more original **Lefax**. The minuscule shop **Pencraft** is the place for pens by Mont Blanc, Watermans, Parker, or Sheaffer. Finally, for cards, pens, wrapping paper and stationery, pop into one of the branches of **Paperchase**.

INTERIORS

WEDGWOOD STILL makes the famous pale blue Jasper china that Josiah Wedgwood designed in the 18th century. You can buy it, as well as Irish Waterford crystal and Coalport bone china, at **Waterford Wedgwood** on Piccadilly. For a fine selection of original pottery, visit the **Craftsmen Potters Association** of Great Britain and **Contemporary Applied Arts**. Everything sold by **The Holding Company** holds something, and does so in a funkier fashion than ordinary crates and boxes. Personalized gifts are also available. **Heal's**, the **Conran Shop** and **Freud's** all offer a great selection of stylish, well-designed accessories for the home. For a wealth of good-quality kitchen and various household items, **Divertimenti** and **David Mellor** are the places to go.

Art and Antiques

LONDON'S ART AND antique shops are spread across the capital. While the more fashionable (and more expensive) dealers are concentrated in a relatively small area bounded by Mayfair and St James's, other shops and galleries catering to a more modest budget are scattered over the rest of the city. Whether your taste is for Old Masters or young modern artists, Boule or Bauhaus, you are bound to find something of beauty in London that is within your financial means.

MAYFAIR

CORK STREET is the centre of the British contemporary art world. Walk up from Piccadilly and pass, on your left, the **Piccadilly Gallery**, which sells modern British pictures. Next come several galleries, including **Boukamel Contemporary Art**, offering work in varying degrees of the avant-garde. The biggest name to look out for is **Waddington**, and if you want to discover the flavour of the month a stop here is a must. However, purchasing is only for the serious (and rich) collector. **Chat Noir** in nearby Albemarle Street is committed to selling contemporary work at a more affordable price. Before retracing your steps down Cork Street, look into Clifford Street, where **Maas Gallery** excels in Victorian masters. Make your way back via a wide variety of artistic styles, from traditional British sporting pictures and sculpture at **Tryon and Swann** to **Mayor's** Surrealism and mainstream art at **Redfern**.

Nearby, Old Bond Street is the centre of the fine antiques trade in London. If it's Turner watercolours or Louis XV furniture you're after, this is the place. A walk up from Piccadilly takes you past the lush portals of **Richard Green** and the **Fine Art Society**, among other extremely smart galleries. For furniture and decorative arts visit **Bond Street Antiques Centre** and **Asprey**; for silver go to **S J Phillips**; and for Victorian art try **Christopher Wood's** gallery. Even if you are not a buyer these galleries are fascinating places to visit, so don't be afraid to walk in – you can learn more from an hour spent here than you can from weeks of studying text books. Also on Old Bond Street are two of the big four London auction houses, **Phillips** and **Sotheby's**. In Bury Street the well-heeled can visit the **Malcolm Innes** gallery, where there are sporting watercolours on show.

ST JAMES'S

SOUTH OF Piccadilly lies a maze of 18th-century streets. This is gentlemen's club country *(see Pall Mall p92)* and the galleries mostly reflect the traditional nature of the area. The centre is Duke Street, home of Old Master dealers **Johnny van Haeften** and **Harari and Johns**. At the bottom is King Street, with that leviathan of antiques dealers, **Spink**. A few doors down you will find the main salerooms of **Christie's**, the well-known auction house where Van Goghs and Picassos change hands for millions.

Walk back up Bury Street past several interesting galleries and duck into Ryder Street to take in **Chris Beetle's** gallery of works by illustrators and caricaturists.

WALTON STREET

CLOSE TO fashionable and expensive Knightsbridge, the art galleries and antique shops along this elegant little street have prices to match. A short walk away in nearby Montpelier Street is **Bonham's** the auctioneers, fourth in line of the big four and recently redecorated in chic style. Of course, fourth in line does not necessarily mean fourth in quality, and you may be lucky enough to find a bargain here.

PIMLICO ROAD

THE ANTIQUE shops that line this road tend to cater predominantly for the pricey requirements of the interior decorator – this is where to come if you are searching for an Italian leather screen or a silver-encrusted ram's skull. Of particular fascination is **Westenholz**. Nearby, **Henry Sotheran** offers fine prints.

BELGRAVIA

THIS AREA HAS a reputation for good British pictures. The real hub of art activity is Motcomb Street, which caters for most tastes. Those seeking fine but well-priced British pictures should head towards **Michael Parkin's** gallery, while Oriental-art enthusiasts will luxuriate in the **Mathaf Gallery**, with its 19th-century British and European paintings of the Arab world.

AFFORDABLE ART

THE HUGELY popular Contemporary Art Society's market takes place every autumn at the **Royal Festival Hall**, with work on sale from £100. London's East End, a growth area for contemporary art, has a cluster of small galleries as well as the magnificent **Flowers East**, which is strong on work by young artists. For sometimes brilliant shows of contemporary art, step along to Portobello and the **East-West Gallery**. A lot of the work on offer here is reasonably-priced, too. **Purdey Hicks** is a great place to go for affordable contemporary British painting.

PHOTOGRAPHY

THE LARGEST collection of original photographs for sale in the country is at the **Photographers' Gallery**. The **Special Photographers' Company** is well known for selling top-quality work – by unknown artists as well as famous photographic names. **Hamilton's** is worth visiting during its major exhibitions.

BRIC-A-BRAC AND COLLECTABLES

For smaller, more affordable pieces, it's worth going to one of the markets, such as Camden Lock *(see p322)*, Camden Passage *(p322)* or Bermondsey *(p322)*, which is the main antiques market, catering to the trade. Many high streets out of the centre of town have covered markets of specialist stalls. Finally, a browse along Kensington Church Street in west London will reveal everything from Arts and Crafts furniture to Staffordshire dogs in a concentration of small emporia.

AUCTIONS

If you are confident enough, auctions are a cheaper way to buy art or antiques but be sure to read the small print in the catalogue (which usually costs around £15). Bidding is simple – you simply register, take a number, then raise your hand when the lot you want comes up. The auctioneer will see your bid. It's as easy as that, and can be great fun. The main auction houses are Christie's, Sotheby's, Phillips and Bonham's. Don't forget Christie's saleroom in South Kensington, which offers art and antiques for the more modest budget.

DIRECTORY

MAYFAIR

Asprey
165–169 New Bond St W1. **Map** 12 E2.
020-7493 6767.

Bond Street Antiques Centre
124 New Bond St W1. **Map** 12 F3.
020-7351 5353.

Boukamel Contemporary Art
9 Cork St W1. **Map** 12 F3.
020-7734 6444.

Chat Noir
35 Albemarle St W1. **Map** 12 F3.
020-7495 6710.

Christopher Wood Gallery
20 Georgian House, 10 Bury St W1. **Map** 12 F3.
020-7499 7411.

Fine Art Society
148 New Bond St W1. **Map** 12 E2.
020-7629 5116.

Maas Gallery
15a Clifford St W1. **Map** 12 F3.
020-7734 2302.

Malcolm Innes
7 Bury St SW1. **Map** 12 F3.
020-7839 8083.

Mayor Gallery
22a Cork St W1. **Map** 12 F3.
020-7734 3558.

Piccadilly Gallery
16 Cork Street W1. **Map** 12 F3.
020-7629 2875.

Redfern Art Gallery
20 Cork St W1. **Map** 12 F3.
020-7734 1732.

Richard Green
4 New Bond St W1. **Map** 12 E2.
020-7491 3277.

S J Phillips
139 New Bond St W1. **Map** 12 E2.
020-7629 6261.

Tryon and Swann
23-24 Cork St W1. **Map** 12 F3.
020-7734 6961.

Waddington Galleries
11, 12, 34 Cork St W1. **Map** 12 F3.
020-7437 8611.

ST JAMES'S

Chris Beetle
8 & 10 Ryder St SW1. **Map** 12 F3.
020-7839 7429.

Harari and Johns
12 Duke St SW1. **Map** 12 F3.
020-7839 7671.

Johnny van Haeften
13 Duke St SW1. **Map** 12 F3.
020-79303062.

Spink & Son
5 King St SW1. **Map** 12 F4.
020-7930 7888.

PIMLICO ROAD

Henry Sotheran Ltd
80 Pimlico Rd SW1. **Map** 20 D3.
020-7730 8756.

Westenholz
76 Pimlico Rd SW1. **Map** 20 D2.
020-7824 8090.

BELGRAVIA

Mathaf Gallery
24 Motcomb St SW1. **Map** 12 D5.
020-7235 0010.

Michael Parkin Gallery
11 Motcomb St SW1. **Map** 12 D5.
020-7235 8144.

AFFORDABLE ART

East-West Gallery
8 Blenheim Cres W11. **Map** 9 A2.
020-7229 7981.

Flowers East
199–205 Richmond Rd E8.
020-8985 3333.

Purdey Hicks
65 Hopton St SE1. **Map** 14 F3.
020-7401 9229.

Royal Festival Hall
South Bank Centre SE1. **Map** 14 D4.
020-7928 3191.

PHOTOGRAPHY

Hamiltons
Unit 9, The Courtyard, St John's on the Hill, Haydon Way SW11.
020-8874 7007.

Photographers' Gallery
5 & 8 Great Newport St WC2. **Map** 13 B2.
020-7831 1772.

Special Photographers Company
21 Kensington Park Rd W11. **Map** 9 B2.
020-7221 3489.

AUCTIONS

Bonhams, W & F C, Auctioneers
Montpelier St SW7. **Map** 11 B5.
020-7584 9161

Also: Chelsea Galleries, 65–69 Lots Road SW10. **Map** 18 F5.
020-7351 7111.

Christie's Fine Art Auctioneers
8 King St SW1. **Map** 12 F4.
020-7839 9060.

Also: 85 Old Brompton Road SW7. **Map** 18 F2.
020-7581 7611.

Sotheby's Auctioneers
34–35 New Bond St W1. **Map** 12 E2.
020-7493 8080.

Phillips Auctioneers & Valuers
101 New Bond St W1. **Map** 12 E2.
020-7629 5602.

Markets

LONDON STREET MARKETS have an air of exuberant irreverence which in itself provides sufficient reason to pay them a visit. At many you'll also find some of the keenest prices in the capital. Keep your wits about you and your hand on your purse and join in the fun.

Bermondsey Market (New Caledonian Market)

Long Lane and Bermondsey St SE1. **Map** 15 C5. ⊖ *London Bridge, Borough.* **Open** *5am–2pm Fri.* **Starts closing** *midday. See p179.*

Bermondsey is the gathering point for London's antique traders every Friday. Serious collectors start early and scrutinize the paintings, the silver and the vast array of old jewellery. Browsers might uncover some interesting curiosities but most bargains go before 9am.

Berwick Street Market

Berwick St W1. **Map** 13 A1. ⊖ *Piccadilly Circus, Leicester Sq.* **Open** *9am–6pm Mon–Sat. See p108.*

The spirited costermongers of Soho's Berwick Street sell the cheapest and most attractive fruit and vegetables in the West End. Spanish black radish, star fruit and Italian plum tomatoes are among the produce you might find here; Dennis's vegetable stall sells a massive range of interesting edible fungi, all immaculately presented. The market is good for fabrics and cheap household goods too, as well as for leather handbags and delicatessen. Separated from Berwick Street by a seedy passageway is Rupert Street market, where prices tend to be higher and the traders quieter.

Brick Lane Market

Brick Lane E1. **Map** 8 E5. ⊖ *Shoreditch, Liverpool St, Aldgate East.* **Open** *daybreak to 1pm Sun. See pp170–1.*

This massively popular East End jamboree is at its best around its gloriously frayed edges. Explore the Cheshire Street lock-ups, packed with tatty furniture and old books, or the mish-mash of junk sold on Bethnal Green Road. East End spivs huddle together on Bacon Street proffering gold rings and watches, while much of Sclater Street is given over to pet foods and provisions. On the wasteland off Cygnet Street, new bicycles, fresh meat and frozen food are among the myriad of goods up for grabs. Brick Lane itself is rather more prosaic, with new goods such as handbags, sports shoes and jeans on sale, but look out too for the wonderful range of spice shops and curry restaurants in this centre for London's Bangladeshi community.

Brixton Market

Electric Ave SW9. ⊖ *Brixton.* **Open** *8.30am–5.30pm Mon, Tue, Thu–Sat; 8.30am–1pm Wed.*

This market offers a wonderful assortment of Afro-Caribbean food, from goats' meat, pigs' tails and salt fish to plantain, yams and breadfruit. The best food is to be found in the old Granville and Market Row arcades, where exotic fish are a highlight. Afro style wigs, strange herbs and potions, religious tracts sold by Rastafarian priests and, on Brixton Station Road, cheap second-hand clothes are also to be had. From record stalls, the bass of raw reggae pounds through this cosmopolitan market like a heartbeat.

Camden Lock Market

Buck St NW1. ⊖ *Camden Town.* **Open** *9.30am–5.30pm Mon–Fri, 10am–6pm Sat and Sun.*

Camden Lock Market has grown swiftly since its opening in 1974. Handmade crafts, new and second-hand street fashions, wholefoods, books, records and antiques form the bulk of the goods that are on sale, although thousands of young people come here simply for the atmosphere, especially at weekends. This is enhanced by the buskers and street performers who draw the crowds to the attractive cobbled area around the canal.

Camden Passage Market

Camden Passage N1. **Map** 6 F1. ⊖ *Angel.* **Open** *10am–2pm Wed, 10am–5pm Sat.*

Camden Passage is a quiet walkway where bookshops and restaurants nestle among bijou antique shops. Prints, silverware, 19th-century magazines, jewellery and toys are among the many collectables that are on show. There aren't very many bargains to be picked up here, as most of the traders tend to be specialists. However, it is an ideal market for those who want to indulge in some genteel browsing.

Chapel Market

Chapel Market N1. **Map** 6 E2. ⊖ *Angel.* **Open** *9am–3.30pm Tue, Wed, Fri, Sat; 9am–1pm Thu, Sun.*

This is one of London's most traditional and exuberant street markets. Weekends are best; the fruit and vegetables are varied and cheap, the fish stalls are the finest in the area, and there's a wealth of bargain household goods and clothing to be had.

Church Street and Bell Street Markets

Church St NW8 and Bell St NW1. **Map** 3 A5. ⊖ *Edgware Rd.* **Open** *8.30am–4pm Mon–Thu, 8.30am–5pm Fri, Sat.*

Like many of London's markets, Church Street reaches a crescendo at the weekend. On Friday, stalls selling electrical goods, cheap clothes, household goods, fish, cheese and antiques join the everyday fruit and vegetable stalls. Alfie's Antique Market at Nos. 13–25 houses over 300 small stalls selling anything from jewellery to old radios and gramophones. Bell Street, running parallel, has its own market where second-hand clothes, records and antiquated electrical goods are sold for a song on Saturdays.

Columbia Road Market

Columbia Rd E2. **Map** 8 D3. ⊖ *Shoreditch, Old St.* **Open** *8am–12.30pm Sun. See p171.*

This is the place to come to buy greenery and blossoms or just to enjoy the fragrances and colours. Cut flowers, plants, shrubs, seedlings and pots are all sold at about half normal prices in this charming Victorian street on a Sunday morning.

East Street Market

East St SE17. ⊖ *Elephant and Castle.* **Open** *8am–5pm Tue, Wed, Fri, Sat; 8am–2pm Thu, Sun.*

East Street Market's high spot is Sunday, when over 250 stalls fill the narrow street and a small plant and flower market is set up on Blackwood Street. Fruit and vegetable stalls are in a minority as traders of clothes (mainly new), electrical and household goods swing into action, while furtive street-hawkers proffer shoelaces and razor blades from old suitcases. Many locals come here more for the entertainment than to buy, as did the young Charlie Chaplin (*see p37*) at the beginning of the century.

Gabriel's Wharf and Riverside Walk Markets

56 Upper Ground and Riverside Walk SE1. **Map** 14 E3. 🚇 *Waterloo.* ***Gabriel's Wharf open*** *9.30am–6pm Fri–Sun;* ***Riverside Walk open*** *10am–5pm Sat, Sun and irregular weekdays. See p187.*

Little shops filled with ceramics, paintings and jewellery surround a bandstand in Gabriel's Wharf where jazz groups sometimes play in the summer. A few stalls are set up around the courtyard, selling ethnic clothing and handmade jewellery and pottery. The nearby book market, to be found under Waterloo Bridge, includes a good selection of new and old Penguin paperbacks, as well as new and second-hand hardbacks.

Greenwich Market

College Approach SE10. **Map** 23 B2. 🚂 *Greenwich.* ***Open*** *9am–5pm Sat, Sun.*

At weekends, the area west of the Hotel Ibis accommodates dozens of trestle tables piled with coins, medals and banknotes, second-hand books, Art Deco furniture, and assorted bric-a-brac. The covered crafts market specializes in wooden toys, clothes made by young designers, handmade jewellery and accessories.

Jubilee and Apple Markets

Covent Gdn Piazza WC2. **Map** 13 C2. 🚇 *Covent Gdn.* ***Open*** *9am–5pm daily.*

Covent Garden has become the centre of London street-life, with some of the capital's best busking. Both these markets sell lots of interesting crafts and designs. The Apple Market, inside the Piazza where the famous fruit and vegetable market was housed (see p114) has chunky knitwear, leather jewellery and novelty goods; a nearby open-air section has cheap army-surplus clothes, old prints and more jewellery. Jubilee Hall sells antiques on Monday, crafts at the weekend, and a large selection of clothes, handbags, cosmetics and tacky mementoes in between.

Leadenhall Market

Whittington Ave EC3. **Map** 15 C2. 🚇 *Bank, Monument.* ***Open*** *7am–4pm Mon–Fri. See p159.*

Leadenhall Market is a welcome culinary oasis in the City and houses some of the best food shops in the capital. The market's

traditional strengths of poultry and game have been well maintained: mallard, teal, partridge and woodcock are all available when in season. There is also a fabulous display of sea food, including excellent oysters, at Ashdown. Other stores stock high-class delicatessen, cheeses and chocolate – an expensive but mouth-watering display of goods that is hard to beat.

Leather Lane Market

Leather Lane EC1. **Map** 6 E5. 🚇 *Chancery Lane.* ***Open*** *10.30am–2pm Mon–Fri.*

This ancient street has played host to a market for over 300 years. The history of the Lane has nothing to do with leather (it was originally called Le Vrune Lane), but it is in this commodity that some of the best buys are to be had in modern times. The stalls selling electrical goods, cheap tapes and CDs, clothes and toiletries are also worth having a browse through.

Petticoat Lane Market

Middlesex St E1. **Map** 16 D1. 🚇 *Liverpool St, Aldgate, Aldgate East.* ***Open*** *9am–2pm Sun (Wentworth St 10am–2.30pm Mon–Fri). See p169.*

Probably the most famous of all London's street markets, Petticoat Lane continues to attract many thousands of visitors and locals every Sunday. The prices may not be as cheap as some of those to be found elsewhere, but the sheer volume of leather goods, clothes (the Lane's traditional strong point), watches, cheap jewellery and toys more than makes up for that. A variety of fast-food sellers do a brisk trade catering for the bustling crowds.

Piccadilly Crafts Market

St James's Church, Piccadilly W1. **Map** 13 A3. 🚇 *Piccadilly Circus, Green Park.* ***Open*** *10am–5pm Thu–Sat.*

Many of the markets in the Middle Ages were held in churchyards and Piccadilly Crafts Market is rekindling that ancient tradition. It is aimed mostly at visitors to London rather than locals, and the merchandise on display ranges from tacky T-shirts to genuine 19th-century prints. Warm Aran woollens, handmade greetings cards and, on a few of the stalls, antiques also compete for custom and attention. All are spread out in the shadow of Wren's beautiful church (see p90).

Portobello Road Market

Portobello Rd W10. **Map** 9 C3. 🚇 *Notting Hill Gate, Ladbroke Grove.* ***Open*** *antiques and junk: 7am–5.30pm Sat. General market: 9am–5pm Mon–Wed, Fri, Sat; 9am–1pm Thu. See p215.*

Portobello Road is really three or four markets rolled into one. The Notting Hill end has over 2000 stalls displaying a compendium of objets d'art, jewellery, old medals, paintings and silverware. Most stalls are managed by experts, so bargains are rare. Further down the gentle hill, antiques give way to fruit and vegetables. The next transformation comes under the Westway flyover, where cheap clothes, bric-a-brac and tacky jewellery take over. From this point on the market becomes increasingly shabby.

Ridley Road Market

Ridley Rd E8. 🚂 *Dalston.* ***Open*** *9am–3pm Mon–Wed. 9am–noon Thu. 9am–5pm Fri, Sat.*

Early this century Ridley Road was a centre of the Jewish community. Since then, Asians, Greeks, Turks and West Indians have also settled in the area and the market is a lively celebration of this cultural mix. Highlights include the 24-hour bagel bakery, the shanty-town shacks selling green bananas and reggae records, the colourful drapery stalls and the very cheap fruit and vegetables.

St Martin-in-the-Fields Market

St Martin-in-the-Fields Churchyard WC2. **Map** 13 B3. 🚇 *Charing Cross.* ***Open*** *11am–5pm Mon–Sat; noon–5pm Sun. See p102.*

This crafts market was started in the late 1980s. T-shirts and football scarves are among the unremarkable selection of London mementoes; more interesting are the Russian dolls, the South American handicrafts and the assorted knitwear.

Shepherd's Bush Market

Goldhawk Rd W12. 🚇 *Goldhawk Road, Shepherd's Bush.* ***Open*** *9.30am–5pm Mon–Wed, Fri, Sat. 9.30am–2.30pm Thu.*

Like Ridley Road and Brixton, Shepherd's Bush Market is a focal point for many of the local ethnic communities. West Indian food, Afro wigs, Asian spices and cheap household and electrical goods are just some of the attractions.

ENTERTAINMENT IN LONDON

Café sign advertising
free live music

LONDON HAS THE ENORMOUS, multi-layered variety of entertainment that only the great cities of the world can provide, and, as always, the city's historical backdrop adds depth to the experience. While few things could be more contemporary than dancing the night away in style at a famed disco such as Stringfellows or Heaven, you could also choose to spend the evening picturing the ghosts of long-dead Hamlets pacing ancient boards in the shadow of one of the living legends that grace the West End theatres today. There's a healthy, innovative fringe theatre scene too, plus world-class ballet and opera in fabled venues such as Sadler's Wells, the Royal Opera House and the Coliseum. In London you'll be able to hear the best music, ranging from classical, jazz and rock to rhythm and blues, while dedicated movie buffs can choose from hundreds of different films each night, both in large, multi-screen complexes and excellent small independent cinemas. Sports fans can watch a game of cricket at Lords, cheer on oarsmen on the Thames or eat strawberries and cream at Wimbledon. Should you be feeling adventurous and sporty yourself, you could try going for a horse ride along Rotten Row in Hyde Park. There are festivals, celebrations and sports to attend, and there's plenty for children to do, too – in fact, there's plenty for everyone to do. Whatever you want, you'll be sure to find it on offer in London; it's just a question of knowing where to look.

Cultural classics: a concert at Kenwood House *(top)*; open-air theatre at Regent's Park *(above left)*; *The Mikado* at the Coliseum *(above right)*

INFORMATION SOURCES

FOR DETAILS OF events in London, check the comprehensive weekly listings and review magazine *Time Out* (published every Wednesday), sold at most newsagents and many bookshops. The weekly *What's On and Where to Go In London* (Wednesdays) is also useful, and London's evening newspaper, the *Evening Standard*, gives brief daily listings with a detailed supplement, "Hot Tickets", every Thursday. The *Independent* has daily listings and also reviews a different arts sector every day, plus a weekly round-up section, "The Information"; the *Guardian* has arts reviews in its G2 section every day and weekly listings on Saturday. The *Independent*, *Guardian* and *The Times* all have lists of ticket availability.

Specialized news sheets, brochures and advance listings are distributed free in the foyers of theatres, concert halls, cinemas and arts complexes such as the South Bank and Barbican. Tourist information offices and hotel foyers often have the same publications. Fly posters advertise forthcoming events on billboards everywhere.

The Society of West End Theatres (SWET) publishes an informative free broadsheet every fortnight, available in many theatre foyers. It tends to concentrate on mainstream theatres, but does provide invaluable information about what's on. The National Theatre and the Royal Shakespeare Company also publish free broadsheets detailing future performances, distributed at the theatres.

Each SWET theatre has a phone-in "Theatreline" with details of seat availability updated daily. Note that these calls cost three times as much as a standard local call, and five times as much in peak hours. The general SWET line (0171-836 0971) provides daily updates on seat availability as well as more general information on choice of shows.

BOOKING TICKETS

SOME OF THE more popular shows and plays in London's West End – the latest Lloyd Webber musical for instance – can be totally booked out for weeks and even months ahead and you will find it impossible to purchase any tickets. This is not the norm, though, and most tickets will be available on the night, especially if you would be prepared to queue in front of the theatre for returns. However, for a stress-free holiday it helps to book tickets in advance; this will ensure that you get the day, time and seats that you want. You can book tickets from the box office in person, by telephone or by post. Quite a few hotels have concierges or porters who will give advice on where to go and arrange tickets for you.

Box offices are usually open from about 10am–8pm, and accept payment by cash, credit card, traveller's cheque or else a personal UK cheque

Line-up from the Royal Ballet, on stage at Covent Garden

when supported by a cheque guarantee card. Many venues will now sell unclaimed or returned tickets just before the performance; ask at the box office for the queuing times. To reserve seats by telephone, call the box office and either pay on arrival or send payment – seats are usually held for three days. Some venues now have separate phone numbers for your credit card bookings – check before you call. Reserve your seat, and always take your credit card with you when you collect your ticket. Some smaller venues do not accept credit cards.

Palace Theatre plaque

DISABLED VISITORS

MANY LONDON venues are old buildings and were not originally designed with disabled visitors in mind, but

recently many facilities have been updated, particularly to give access to those using wheelchairs, or for those with hearing difficulties.

Telephone the box office prior to your visit to reserve the special seating places or equipment, which are often limited. It is also worth your while enquiring about any special discounts that might be available for disabled people and for their party.

TRANSPORT

NIGHT BUSES are now the preferred late-night mode of transport or phone for a cab from the venue. If you find yourself outside the city centre late at night, do not rely on being able to hail a taxi quickly in the street. The Underground usually runs until just after midnight but the times of last trains vary according to the lines. Check timetables in the stations (see p362–3).

BOOKING AGENCIES

Tickets are also available from agencies. Try the theatre box office first; if no seats are available there, find out the standard prices before going to an agency. Most, but not all, are reputable. Agencies advertising top show tickets for "tonight" may really have them, and they may be a fair price. If you order by phone, tickets will be posted to you or sent to the theatre for you to collect. Commission should be a standard 22%. Some shows waive the agency fee by paying the commission themselves; this is usually advertised, and agencies should then charge standard box office prices. Always compare prices, try to avoid agencies in bureaux de change, and buy from ticket touts in the street only in desperation.

Ticket booth in Shaftesbury Avenue

London's Theatres

LONDON OFFERS AN extraordinary range of theatrical entertainment – this is one of the world's great stages, and, at its best, standards of quality are extremely high. Despite their legendary reputation for reserve, the British are passionate about theatre and London's theatres reflect every nuance of this passion. You can stroll along a street of West End theatres and find a sombre Samuel Beckett, Brecht or Chekhov play showing next door to some absurdly frothy farce like *No Sex Please, We're British!* Amid such diversity there is always something to appeal to everyone.

WEST END THEATRE

THERE IS A distinct glamour to the West End theatres. Perhaps it is the glittering lights of the foyer and the impressively ornate interiors, or maybe it is their hallowed reputations – but whatever it is, the old theatres retain a magic all of their own.

The West End billboards always feature a generous sprinkling of world-famous performers such as Judi Dench, Vanessa Redgrave, John Malkovich, Richard Harris and Peter O'Toole.

The major commercial theatres cluster along Shaftesbury Avenue and the Haymarket and around Covent Garden and Charing Cross Road. Unlike the national theatres, most West End theatres survive only on profits; and do not receive any state subsidy. They rely on an army of ever-hopeful "angels" (financial backers) and producers to keep the old traditions alive.

Many theatres are historical landmarks, such as the classic **Theatre Royal Drury Lane**, established in 1663 *(see p115)*, and the elegant **Theatre Royal Haymarket** – both superb examples of early 19th-century buildings. Another to note is the **Palace** *(see p108)*, with its terracotta exterior and imposing position right on Cambridge Circus.

NATIONAL THEATRE

THE **Royal National Theatre** is based in the South Bank Centre *(see p330)*. Here, the large, open-staged Olivier, the proscenium-staged Lyttelton and the small, flexible Cottesloe offer a range of size and style, making it possible to produce every kind of theatre from large, extravagant works to miniature masterpieces. The complex is also a lively social centre. Enjoy a drink with your friends before your play begins; watch the crowds and the river drift by; wander around the many free art exhibitions; relax during the free early evening concerts in the foyer or browse through the theatre bookshop.

The **Royal Shakespeare Company**, Britain's national theatre company, has its London home at the Barbican Centre. While this unique company centres its work mainly on Shakespeare's many plays its repertoire also includes some classic Greek tragedies, gems of the Restoration theatre and a multitude of modern works. Vast productions of superb quality are staged in the magnificent Barbican Theatre, and smaller performances can be seen on the more intimate stage of The Pit, which is contained in the same complex. The centre's layout is known to be somewhat confusing so go a little early to ensure you arrive before the performance. Use any spare time to enjoy the free art and craft exhibitions in the foyer, often complementary to the plays being staged at the time, and the free musical entertainments which range from classical opera to chamber music, samba to the sound of the big brass band.

The Barbican can also supply information about RSC productions at their theatres in Stratford-upon-Avon.

NATIONAL THEATRE BOOKING ADDRESSES

Royal National Theatre
(Lyttelton, Cottesloe, Olivier) South Bank SE1. **Map** 14 D3.
C 020-7452 3000.

Royal Shakespeare Company
Barbican Centre, Silk St EC2.
Map 7 A5.
C 020-7638 8891.

PANTOMIME

SHOULD YOU HAPPEN to be visiting London between December and February, one unmissable experience for the whole family is pantomime. Part of nearly every British child's upbringing, "panto" is an absurd tradition in which major female characters are played by men and principal male roles are played by women and the audience has to participate, shouting encouragement and stage directions to a set formula. Adults may find the whole experience rather strange, but most children love the experience.

OPEN-AIR THEATRE

A PERFORMANCE OF one of Shakespeare's airier creations such as *Comedy of Errors, As You Like It* or *A Midsummer Night's Dream*, takes on an atmosphere of pure enchantment and magic among the green vistas of Regent's Park *(see p220)* or Holland Park *(see p214)*. Be sure to take a blanket and, to be safe, an umbrella.

Refreshments are available, or you can take a picnic.

OPEN-AIR THEATRE BOOKING ADDRESSES

Holland Park Theatre
Holland Park. **Map** 9 B4.
C 020-7602 7856.
Open Jun–Aug.

Open-Air Theatre
Inner Circle, Regent's Park NW1.
Map 4 D3.
C 020-7935 5756.
F 020-7486 1933.
Open May–Sep.

WEST END THEATRES

Adelphi 🄴
Strand WC2.
📞 020-7344 0055.

Albery 🄰
St Martin's Lane WC2.
📞 020-7369 1730.

Aldwych 🄷
Aldwych WC2.
📞 020-7416 6003.

Ambassadors 🄔
West St WC2.
📞 020-7836 1171.

Apollo 🄚
Shaftesbury Avenue W1.
📞 020-7494 5054.

Cambridge 🄢
Earlham St WC2.
📞 020-7494 5040.

Comedy 🄸
Panton St SW1.
📞 020-7369 1731.

Criterion 🄼
Piccadilly Circus W1.
📞 020-7369 1747.

Duchess 🄕
Catherine St WC2.
📞 020-7494 5075.

Duke of York's 🄓
St Martin's Lane WC2.
📞 020-7836 5122.

Fortune 🄙
Russell St WC2.
📞 020-7836 2238.

Garrick 🄕
Charing Cross Rd WC2.
📞 020-7494 5085.

Gielgud 🄩
Shaftesbury Ave W1.
📞 020-7494 5065.

Her Majesty's 🄝
Haymarket SW1.
📞 020-7494 5400.

Lyric 🄛
Shaftesbury Ave W1.
📞 020-7494 5045.

New London 🄴
Drury Lane WC2.
📞 020-7405 0072.

Palace 🄒
Shaftesbury Ave W1.
📞 020-7434 0909.

Phoenix 🄙
Charing Cross Rd WC2.
📞 020-7369 1733.

Piccadilly 🄑
Denman St W1.
📞 020-7369 1734.

Playhouse 🄛
Northumberland Ave WC2.
📞 020-7839 4401.

Prince Edward 🄬
Old Compton St W1.
📞 020-7447 5400.

Prince of Wales 🄖
Coventry St W1.
📞 020-7839 5972/5987.

Queen's 🄤
Shaftesbury Ave W1.
📞 020-7494 5040.

Shaftesbury 🄤
Shaftesbury Ave WC2.
📞 020-7379 5399.

Strand 🄖
Aldwych WC2.
📞 020-7930 8800.

St Martin's 🄦
West St WC2.
📞 020-7336 1443.

Theatre Royal:
–Drury Lane 🄘
Catherine St WC2.
📞 020-7494 5062.
–Haymarket 🄚
Haymarket SW1.
📞 020-7930 8800.

Vaudeville 🄔
Strand WC2.
📞 020-7336 9987.

Whitehall 🄘
Whitehall SW1.
📞 020-7369 1735.

Wyndham's 🄒
Charing Cross Rd WC2.
📞 020-7369 1736.

WEST END THEATRES

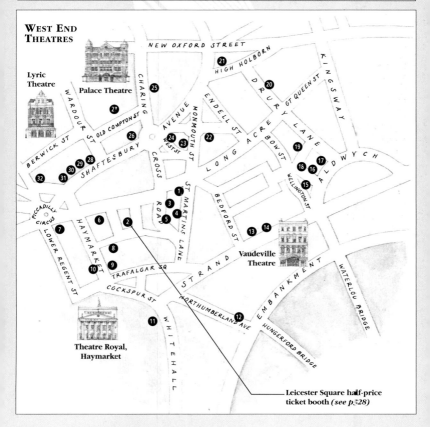

Leicester Square half-price
ticket booth *(see p328)*

FRINGE THEATRE

Lattchmere pub
ONDON'S FRINGE theatre acts
as an outlet for new,
adventurous writing and for
writers from other cultures
and lifestyles – works by Irish
writers appear regularly, as
do plays by Caribbean and
Latin American and
feminist and gay writers.

The plays are usually staged
in tiny theatres based in pubs,
such as the **Gate Theatre**
above the Prince Albert pub
in Notting Hill, the **King's
Head** in Islington and the
Grace in the Latchmere pub
in Battersea (see p309), or in
warehouses and spare space
in larger theatres, such as the
Donmar Warehouse and the
Studio in the Lyric.

Venues like the **Bush**, the
Almeida and the **Theatre
Upstairs** at the Royal Court
have earned their reputations
for discovering outstanding
new works, some of which
have subsequently transferred
successfully to the West End.

Foreign-language plays are
sometimes performed at
national cultural institutes; for
example you might be able to
catch Molière at the **French
Institute** or Brecht at the
Goethe Institute; check the
listings magazines.

For alternative stand-up
comedy and cabaret, where
you can encounter the sharp
edge of satire with its brash,
newsy style, try the **Comedy
Store**, the birthplace of so-
called "alternative" comedy,
or the **Hackney Empire**, a
former Victorian music hall
which is well worth visiting
for its magnificent well-
preserved interior.

BUDGET TICKETS

There is a wide range of
prices for seats in London
theatres. The cheaper West
End tickets, for example, can
cost under £10, whereas the
best seats for musicals hover
around the £30 mark. However,
it is usually quite possible to
obtain cheaper tickets.

The Leicester Square Half
Price Ticket Booth (see p327)
sells tickets on the day of the
performance for a wide range
of mainstream shows. Situated
in Leicester Square, the booth
is open Monday to Saturday,
from noon for matinees and
from 2.30–6.30pm for evening
performances. Payment is by
cash and there is a strict limit
of only four tickets for each
purchaser. There is also a
small service charge to pay.

You can sometimes get
reduced price seats for matinee
performances, press and
preview nights – it is always
worth checking with the box
office to see what they
currently have on offer.

CHOOSING SEATS

If you go to the theatre in
person, you will be able to
see its seating plan and note
where you can get a good
view at an affordable price. If
you book by telephone, you
should note the following:
stalls are in front of the stage
and expensive. The back stalls
are slightly cheaper; dress,
grand or royal circles are
above the stalls and cheaper
again; the upper circle or
balcony are the cheapest seats
but you will have to climb
several flights of stairs; the

slips are seats that run
along the very edges of the
theatre; boxes are the most
expensive option.

It is also as well to bear
in mind that some of the
cheapest seats may have a
restricted view of the stage.

THEATRE-RELATED ACTIVITIES

If you are curious about
how the mechanics of the
theatre work, you would
probably enjoy a back-stage
tour. The National Theatre
and the RSC both organize
these tours (contact the box
office – see p326 – for details).
If you enjoy a good walk,
London Theatre Walks (020-
7839 7438) may interest you.
The Theatre Museum (see
p115) is well worth a visit.

IRATE GHOSTS

Many London theatres are
reputed to have ghosts;
however, the two most
famous spectres haunt the
environs of the Garrick
and the Duke of York's
(see p327). The Garrick is
heavily atmospheric and
the ghost of Arthur
Bourchier, a manager at
the turn of the century, is
reputed to make fairly
regular appearances. He
hated critics and many
believe he is still trying to
frighten them away. The
ghost occupying the Duke
of York's theatre was
Violet Melnotte, an actress
manager during the 1890s,
who was famed for her
extremely fiery temper.

FRINGE THEATRE

Almeida
Almeida St N1.
📞 020-7359 4404.

Bush
Shepherds Bush Green
W12.
📞 020-7602 3703.

Comedy Store
28a Leicester Sq WC2.
Map 13 B3.
📞 020-7344 0234.

Donmar Warehouse
41 Earlham St WC2.
Map 13 B2.
📞 020-7369 1732.

French Institute
17 Queensberry Pl SW7.
Map 18 F2.
📞 020-7589 6211.

Gate Theatre
The Prince Albert,
11 Pembridge Rd W11.
Map 9 C3.
📞 020-7229 0706.

Goethe Institute
50 Prince's Gate,
Exhibition Rd SW7.
Map 11 A5.
📞 020-74596 4000.

Grace
503 Battersea Park Rd
SW11.
📞 020-7228 2620.

Hackney Empire
291 Mare St E8.
📞 020-8985 2424.

King's Head
115 Upper St N1.
Map 6 F1.
📞 020-7226 1916.

Studio
Lyric, Hammersmith,
King St W6.
📞 020-8741 2311.

Theatre Upstairs
Royal Court,
Sloane Sq SW1.
Map 19 C2.
📞 020-7730 2554.

Cinemas

IF YOU CAN'T FIND a movie you like in London, then you don't like movies. The huge choice of British, American, foreign-language, new, classic, popular and special-interest films makes London a major international film centre, with about 250 different films showing at any one time. There are about 50 cinemas in the central district of London alone, many of them ultra-modern multi-screened complexes. The big commercial chains show current smash-hits and a healthy number of independent cinemas offer some inventive programmes drawing on the whole history of film. London's listings magazines carry full details of what's on, where.

WEST END CINEMAS

WEST END is a loose term for the main cinemas in the West End of London which show new releases, such as the **Odeon Leicester Square** and the **ABC** Shaftesbury Avenue, but it also includes the cinemas found in Chelsea, Fulham and Notting Hill. Programmes normally begin around midday and are then repeated every two or three hours, with the last show around 8.30pm; there are late-night screenings on Fridays and Saturdays at most of the central cinemas.

West End cinemas are very expensive and a seat in front of the best screens will cost you twice what you would pay to see the same film at a local cinema outside central London. The price of admission is often cheaper for the afternoon performances or on Mondays. It is a good idea to reserve your seats well in advance for screenings of the more popular films on Friday and Saturday evenings and Sunday afternoon. Most of the larger cinemas now take credit card reservations for seats over the telephone.

REPERTORY CINEMAS

THESE CINEMAS OFTEN show foreign-language and slightly more "off-beat" art films and sometimes change programmes daily or even several times each day. Some cinemas show two or three films, often on the same theme, for one entrance charge.

These include the **Prince Charles**, which is situated centrally, close to Leicester Square, the **Everyman** in north London, the ICA in the Mall, the newly refurbished **Ritzy** in South London and the National Film Theatre.

NATIONAL FILM THEATRE

THE NATIONAL FILM Theatre (NFT) and the Museum of the Moving Image (MOMI) *(see p184)* are both located in the South Bank Arts Complex, near Waterloo Station. The NFT has two cinemas of its own, both of which offer a huge and diverse selection of films. The NFT also holds regular screenings of rare and restored films and television programmes taken from the National Film Archive. A must for movie buffs.

FOREIGN-LANGUAGE FILMS

THESE ARE screened at the repertory and independent cinemas, including the **Renoir**, the **Prince Charles**, the **Lumière**, the Curzon in Shaftsbury Avenue, the **Minema** and the **Screen** cinemas chain. Films are shown in original language, with English subtitles.

FILM CERTIFICATES

CHILDREN ARE ALLOWED to go to a cinema unaccompanied by an adult to films which have been awarded either a U (universal) or a PG (parental guidance advised) certificate for viewing.

With other films, the numbers 12, 15 or 18 quite simply denote the minimum ages allowed for admission to the cinema. These classifications are always clearly advertised in the publicity for the film.

LONDON FILM FESTIVAL

THE MOST important cinema event in Britain is held every November when over 100 films – some of which will have already won awards abroad – from a number of countries are screened. The NFT, several of the repertory cinemas and some of the big West End cinemas will have special showings of these films. Details are published in the listings magazines. Tickets are quite hard to come by but some "standby" tickets will generally be available to the public 30 minutes before the start of a performance.

CINEMA ADDRESSES

ABC
135 Shaftesbury Ave WC2.
Map 13 B2.
[020-7836 8606.

Everyman
Hollybush Vale NW3.
Map 1 A5.
[020-7435 1525.

Lumière
49 St Martin's Lane WC2.
Map 13 B2.
[020-7836 0691.
[020-7379 3014.

Minema
45 Knightsbridge SW1.
Map 12 D5.
[020-7369 1723.

National Film Theatre
South Bank Centre, SE1.
Map 14 D3.
[020-7928 3232.

Odeon Leicester Sq
Leicester Sq, WC2.
Map 13 B2.
[020-8315 4215.

Prince Charles
Leicester Pl, WC2.
Map 13 B2
[020-7437 8181.

Renoir
Brunswick Sq WC1.
Map 5 C4.
[020-7837 8402.

Ritzy
Brixton Rd SW2.
[020-7737 2121.

Screen Cinemas
96 Baker St NW1
Map 3 C5.
[020-7935 2772.

Opera, Classical and Contemporary Music

UNTIL RECENTLY, OPERA enjoyed a somewhat elitist reputation. However, televised concerts and free outdoor concerts in Hyde Park and the Piazza, Covent Garden, have greatly increased its popularity. London is home to five world-class orchestras and a veritable host of smaller music companies and contemporary music ensembles; it also houses three permanent opera companies and numerous smaller opera groups and leads the world with its period orchestras. It is a major centre for the classical recording industry, which helps to support a large community of musicians and singers. Mainstream, obscure, traditional and innovative music are all to be found in profusion. *Time Out* magazine *(see p324)* has the most comprehensive listings of the classical music on offer around the capital.

Royal Opera House

Floral Street WC2. **Map** 13 C2.
📞 020-7304 4000. See p115.

The building, with its opulent, elaborate red, white and gold interior, is very glamorous; it looks, and is, expensive. It is the home of the Royal Opera, but very often visiting opera and ballet companies also perform here. Many productions are shared with foreign opera houses, so if you are a visitor to England check that you haven't already seen the same production at home. Works are always performed in the original language, but English translations are flashed up above the stage.

Seats are usually booked well in advance, particularly if major stars such as Placido Domingo, Luciano Pavarotti or Kiri Te Kanawa are performing. The sound is best in the seats centre of stage, right in the front. Tickets range from about £5 to £200 or more for a world-class star. The cheapest seats tend to be bought first, although a number of these tickets are reserved for sale on the day. (Remember some of the cheaper seats in the Royal Opera House have extremely restricted views of the stage.) Standing passes can often be obtained right up to the time of a performance. Standby information is available on the day of the performance on 020-7836 6903 and there are often concessions on tickets. It is also worthwhile queuing for last-minute returns.

London Coliseum

St Martin's Lane WC2. **Map** 13 B3.
📞 020-7836 0111.
📠 020-7632 8300. See p119.

The Coliseum, home of the English National Opera (ENO), has rather faded decor but the musical standards are extremely high. The company trains its own singers for its productions and they rehearse in the setting in which they will perform. ENO productions of the classics are nearly all sung in English. The productions are often adventurous and critics have been known to complain that the clarity of the storyline is impaired. The audiences tend to be younger than at the Royal Opera House, the seats are much cheaper and there is less corporate entertaining. The cheapest seats are infamous for being real backbreakers.

Sadler's Wells

Rosebery Ave EC1. **Map** 6 E3.
📞 020-7314 8800.

Less glamorous, expensive and central than the other opera houses, Sadler's Wells does not have its own company but it provides a useful venue for many visiting companies. Among these, three have a regular season here, each presenting two works: the D'Oyly Carte company, formed in 1875 specifically to perform works by Gilbert and Sullivan, has its season in April and May; Opera 80, with a cast of 22 singers and an orchestra of 27, offers opera in English at a reasonable price in the last two weeks of May; and the British Youth Opera performs here each year in early September.

South Bank Centre

South Bank Centre SE1. **Map** 14 D4.
📞 020-7921 0600. See p182.

The South Bank Centre houses the Royal Festival Hall (RFH), the Queen Elizabeth Hall and the Purcell Room. There are nightly performances, mostly of classical music, interspersed with opera, ballet and modern dance seasons, jazz, festivals of contemporary and ethnic music and other one-off events running throughout the year. The largest concert hall on the South Bank is the RFH, which is ideal for the major national and international orchestras and large-scale choral works. The Purcell Room is comparatively small and tends to host string quartets and contemporary music in addition to many debut recitals of young artists. The Queen Elizabeth Hall lies somewhere in between. It stages medium-sized ensembles whose audiences, while too large for the Purcell Room, would not fill the Festival Hall. Jazz and ethnic music are performed here and the very innovative and often controversial Opera Factory makes several appearances throughout the year. It performs a range of modern interpretations of the classics, and often also commissions and performs new works. The acoustics are very good throughout the complex.

The London Philharmonic Orchestra is resident at the South Bank. The Royal Philharmonic, the Philharmonia and the BBC Symphony Orchestra are frequent visitors, along with leading ensembles and soloists such as Shura Cherkassky, Stephen Kovacevich and Anne-Sofie von Otter.

The Academy of St Martin-in-the-Fields, the London Festival Orchestra, Opera Factory, the London Classical Players and the

LONDON MUSIC FESTIVALS

The London Opera Festival takes place in June. Venues include the Place Theatre, the Lilian Baylis Theatre (Sadler's Wells), the Purcell Room, St John's Smith Square and the Royalty Theatre. Singers and companies from all over the world come to London to perform in this festival. For tickets and general information, contact the individual theatres. The City of London Festival is held annually in July, when churches and public buildings in the City host a range of varied musical events. Venues such as the Tower of London *(see p154)* and Goldsmiths' Hall can themselves lend much atmosphere to the events. Many concerts are free. For more details, apply to the box office (020-7606 7010) from May onwards.

London Mozart Players all have regular seasons. There are also frequent free foyer concerts, and throughout the summer the centre is well worth visiting as musical events take place on the terraces when the weather permits.

Barbican Concert Hall

Silk Street EC2. **Map** 7 A5.
C 020-7638 8891. See p165.

This stark concrete building is the permanent home of the London Symphony Orchestra, (LSO), which concentrates on the work of one composer each season. The LSO Summer Pops features an impressive line-up of stars from stage, television, film and the recording world, which in the past has included famous artists such as Victor Borge and the jazz singer Barbara Cook.

The English National Opera makes regular appearances, and the Royal Philharmonic Orchestra has a spring season.

The Barbican is also renowned for its concerts of contemporary music: the BBC Symphony Orchestra holds an annual festival of 20th-century composers here and the London Sinfonietta, which specializes in 20th-century music, performs most of its London concerts at the same venue. There are free foyer concerts too.

Royal Albert Hall

Kensington Gore SW7. **Map** 10 F5.
C 020-7589 3203. See p203.

The beautiful Royal Albert Hall is the venue for a wide variety of events from fashion and pop shows to wrestling. However, from mid-July to mid-September it is devoted solely to the Henry Wood Promenade Concerts, the "Proms". Organized by the BBC, the season features the BBC Philharmonic Orchestra, which performs some modern symphonic music as well as classics. Visiting orchestras from around the United Kingdom and worldwide, such as the City of Birmingham Orchestra, the Chicago Symphony Orchestra and the Boston Symphony Orchestra, make up a very varied programme. Tickets for the Proms can be bought on the day of performance but long queues build up early in the day so experienced Promenaders take cushions to sit on. Tickets sell out weeks ahead for the "Last Night of the Proms", which has become a national institution. The audience wave flags and sing. Some people may consider it an evening of nationalistic fervour, although the majority just like singing the traditional *Land of Hope and Glory* without giving much thought to its possibly jingoistic words.

OUTDOOR MUSIC

London has many outdoor musical events in summer. At Kenwood House on Hampstead Heath *(see p230)*, a grassy hill leads down to a lake, beyond which is the concert platform. Arrive early as the concerts are popular, particularly if fireworks are to accompany the music. Deck-chairs tend to be booked up early, so most people sit on the grass. Take a sweater and a picnic. Purists beware – people walk around, eat and talk throughout and the music is amplified so it can be a little distorted. You don't get your money back if it rains, as they have never abandoned a performance yet.

Other venues include Marble Hill House in Twickenham *(see p248)*, with practices similar to Kenwood, Crystal Palace Park and Holland Park.

Wigmore Hall

36 Wigmore St W1. **Map** 12 E1.
C 020-7935 2141. See p222.

Because of its excellent acoustics the Wigmore Hall is a favourite with visiting artists, and attracts international names such as Jessye Norman and Julian Bream for a very wide-ranging programme of events. It presents seven evening concerts a week, and a Sunday morning concert from September through to July.

St Martin-in-the-Fields

Trafalgar Sq WC2. **Map** 13 B3.
C 020-7930 1862. See p102.

This elegant Gibbs church is home to the Academy of St Martin-in-the-Fields and the famous choir of the same name. These and orchestras as disparate as the Henry Wood Chamber Orchestra, the Penguin Café Orchestra and the St Martin-in-the-Fields Sinfonia provide evening concerts. The choice of each programme is, to a degree, dictated by the religious year; for example, Bach's *St John Passion* is played at Ascensiontide and Handel's *Messiah* at Christmas.

Free lunchtime concerts are given on Mondays, Tuesdays and Fridays by young artists.

St John's, Smith Square

Smith Sq SW1. **Map** 21 B1.
C 020-7222 1061. See p81.

This converted Baroque church has good acoustics and provides comfortable seating, making it a marvellous setting. It hosts varied concerts and recitals by groups such as the Wren Orchestra, the Vanbrugh String Quartet and the London Sonata Group. A daily series of BBC Radio lunchtime concerts covers the music and song recitals.

Broadgate Arena

3 Broadgate EC2. **Map** 7 C5.
C 020-7588 6565. See p169.

This is the new City-based venue for a summer season of lunchtime concerts offering varied programmes, often from up-and-coming musicians.

MUSIC VENUES

Orchestral

Barbican Concert Hall
Broadgate Arena
Queen Elizabeth Hall
Royal Albert Hall
Royal Festival Hall
St Martin-in-the-Fields
St John's, Smith Square

Chamber and Ensemble

Barbican Concert Hall
Broadgate Arena
Purcell Room
Royal Festival Hall foyer
St Martin-in-the-Fields
St John's, Smith Square
Wigmore Hall

Soloists and Recitals

Barbican Concert Hall
Purcell Room
Royal Albert Hall
St Martin-in-the-Fields
St John's, Smith Square
Wigmore Hall

Children's

Barbican Concert Hall
Royal Festival Hall

Free

Barbican Concert Hall
National Theatre foyer *(see p326)*
Royal Festival Hall foyer
St Martin-in-the-Fields (lunchtime)

Early Music

Purcell Room
Wigmore Hall

Contemporary Music

Barbican Concert Hall
South Bank Complex

Dance

LONDON-BASED DANCE companies present a range of styles from classical ballet to mime, jazz, experimental and ethnic dance. London is also host to visiting companies as diverse as the classic Bolshoi Ballet and the innovative Jaleo Flamenco. Most dance companies (with the exception of the resident ballets) have short seasons that seldom last longer than a fortnight and often less than a week – check the listings magazines for details *(see pp324)*. Theatres that regularly feature dance are the **Royal Opera House**, the **London Coliseum**, **Sadler's Wells** and **The Place Theatre**. There are also performances at the **South Bank Centre** and other arts centres throughout the city.

BALLET

THE **Royal Opera House** *(see p115)* and the **London Coliseum** in St Martin's Lane are by far the best venues for classical ballet; providing the stage for foreign companies when they visit London. The Opera House is home to the Royal Ballet, which usually invites major international guest artists to take up residence. Book well in advance for classics such as *Swan Lake* and *Giselle*. The company also has an unusual repertoire of modern ballet; triple bills provide a mixture of new and old and seats are normally quite readily available.

The English National Ballet holds its summer season at the **London Coliseum**. It has a similar repertoire to the Royal Ballet and stages some very popular productions.

Visiting companies also perform at **Sadler's Wells** *(see p330)*, where the London City Ballet has its annual season during December and January. This company has a mainly classical repertoire.

CONTEMPORARY

A PLETHORA OF new and young companies is flourishing in London, each with its own distinctive style. **Sadler's Wells** is one of the main venues, with short seasons featuring visiting and local companies. Attached to Sadler's Wells is the Lilian Baylis Studio, a venue for smaller and often more experimental productions.

The Place Theatre is the home of contemporary and ethnic dance companies and has a year-round programme of performances from these and visiting dancers. The London Contemporary Dance Theatre, the largest of Britain's contemporary dance companies, is based here.

The **Island Theatre** was designed as a theatre/cinema and has only recently been used for dance. During the summer, Rambert Dance performs its season of works by internationally acclaimed choreographers. Rambert has another short season and runs a week of choreographic

workshops in April at the **Riverside Studios**. Other venues that are sometimes used include the **Institute of Contemporary Arts** (ICA) *(see p92)* and the **Shaw Theatre** as well as a new East End venue, the **Chisenhale Dance Space**, a centre for small and independent companies currently regarded as on the experimental fringe of contemporary dance.

ETHNIC

THERE IS A constant stream of visiting groups coming to perform traditional dance from all over the world. Both **Sadler's Wells** and the **Riverside Studios** are major venues, while classical ethnic dance companies, including Indian and Far Eastern, have seasons at the South Bank Centre, often in the **Queen Elizabeth Hall**. Check the listings magazines for details.

DANCE FESTIVALS

THERE ARE TWO major contemporary dance festivals each year in London, featuring many different companies. Spring Loaded runs from February to April, while Dance Umbrella runs from early October to early November. The listings magazines carry all details.

Other smaller festivals include Almeida Dance, from the end of April to the first week of May at the **Almeida Theatre**, and The Turning World, a festival running in April and May offering dance from all over the world.

Rock, Pop, Jazz, Reggae and World Music

YOU WILL FIND THE WHOLE range of popular music being strummed and hummed, howled, growled or synthesized in London. There may be as many as 80 listed concerts on an ordinary weeknight, featuring rock, reggae, soul, folk, country, jazz, Latin and world music. In addition to the gigs, there are music festivals in the summer at parks, pubs, halls and stadiums throughout the capital (see p335). Check the listings magazines and keep your eyes open for publicity posters (see p324).

MAJOR VENUES

THE LARGEST venues in London are host to an extraordinary variety of music. Stars who are guaranteed to fill thousands of seats play **Wembley Stadium** in the summer when the football season is over. In winter, the pop idols tend to prefer the cavernous indoor **Wembley Arena**, the **Labatt's Apollo**, or, if they take themselves rather seriously, the **Royal Albert Hall**.

The **Brixton Academy** and the **Town and Country Club** are next in prominence and size. Each can take well over 1,000 people, and for many Londoners these former cinemas are the capital's best venues, with seating upstairs, large dance-floors downstairs and accessible bars.

ROCK AND POP

INDIE MUSIC is one of the mainstays of London's live music output. Following the leads of Manchester and Bristol, the capital has a healthy, cross-fertilized rock scene: venues all over town offer Britpop, bratpop, hip-hop, trip-hop and the many other variations on pop which have yet to be labelled for the mass market. Kentish Town's **Bull and Gate** and the **Powerhaus** in Islington are good for goth, while rock rules at the **Astoria** in the West End, **The Shepherd's Bush Empire** and the **National Ballroom Kilburn**, among many others.

The **Mean Fiddler** in Harlesden is one of the best of the mid-sized venues and is famous for being the place that bands play twice – once on the way up, and again on the way down. London is the home of pub-rock, which is a vibrant blend of rhythm and blues, rock and punk that has been evolving since the 1960s as a genre in which bands frequently develop before finding their real musical identity. Such diverse bands as the Clash, Dr Feelgood and Dire Straits all started as pub rockers. The **Station Tavern** in West London hosts many of the best pub-rock bands around; and while there's usually no entrance fee, drinks are surcharged. The **Sir George Robey** near Finsbury Park and many other pubs tend to follow suit.

New bands have a popular showcase at the **Rock Garden** in Covent Garden most week nights, while **Borderline**, near to Leicester Square, is frequented by record company talent scouts. **Subterania** in Ladbroke Grove holds new songwriter nights. The **Camden Palace** is very good value for money, especially on Tuesdays, with the finest established indie pop both before and after live performances from up-and-coming indie bands.

JAZZ

THE NUMBER of jazz venues in London has grown in the last few years – both the music and the lifestyle which is romatically imagined to go with it are officially hip once again. **Ronnie Scott's** in the West End is still the pick of the vintage crop, and since the 1950s many of the finest performers in the world have come to play here. The **100 Club** in Oxford Street is another very popular venue for confirmed jazzniks.

Jazz and food have formed a partnership at venues such as the **Palookaville** in Covent Garden, the **Dover Street Wine Bar** and the largely vegetarian **Jazz Café**. Others include the **Pizza Express** on Dean Street and the **Pizza on the Park**, by Hyde Park Corner.

The **South Bank Centre** (see p182) and also the **Barbican** (see p165) feature formal jazz concerts and free jazz in the foyers.

REGGAE

LONDON'S LARGE West Indian community has made the city the European reggae capital. At the **Notting Hill Carnival** (see p57), late in August, many top bands perform free.

Reggae has now become integrated with the mainstream rock music scene, and bands appear at most of London's rock venues.

WORLD MUSIC

MUSICIANS FROM every corner of the globe live in London. "World music" includes African, Latin, South American, anything exotic, and its popularity has sparked a revitalization of British and Irish folk music. **Cecil Sharp House** has regular shows for folk purists, while the **ICA** (see p92) hosts innovative acts. **The Weavers Arms**, near Newington Green, has a reputation for Cajun, African and Latin American music. Hot Latin nights can be found at **Down Mexico Way** near Piccadilly and at **Cuba Libre** in Islington. For all French Caribbean and African sounds you could check **Le Café de Piaf** inside Waterloo Station; and for the widest selection of African sounds and food in town, try visiting the **Africa Centre** in Covent Garden. The **Barbican Centre**, the **Royal Festival Hall** and the **Queen Elizabeth Hall** at the South Bank Centre all offer plenty of world music.

Clubs

THE OLD CLICHÉ that London dies when the pubs shut no longer holds true. Europe has long scoffed at Londoners going to bed at 11pm when the night is only just beginning in Paris, Madrid and Rome, but London has caught on at last and you can revel all night if you want to. The best clubs are not all confined to the city's centre – initial disappointment that your hotel is a half-hour tube-ride from Leicester Square can be offset by the discovery of a trendy club right on your doorstep.

ETIQUETTE

FASHIONS and club nights change very rapidly and nightspots open and close down all the time. Some of the best club nights are one-nighters – check the listings magazines (see p324). Style magazines like The Face can help you avoid humiliating comments from bouncers who don't like your appearance. Some clubs change the dress policy with each evening, so it is best to check in advance.

A few clubs require that you arrange membership 48 hours in advance, and you may also find that you have to be introduced by a member. Again, check these details in the listings magazines. Groups of men may not be welcome, so split up and find a woman to go in with; expect to queue to get in. Entrance fees may seem reasonable, but drinks tend to be over-priced.

Opening times are usually 10pm–3am Monday to Saturday, although many clubs stay open until 6am at the weekend and some open on Sunday from about 8pm to midnight.

MAINSTREAM

LONDON IS HOME to one of the best-known discos in the world: **Stringfellows** is as much a part of the tourist circuit as Madame Tussaud's. It's glitzy and expensive so jeans are out of the question. The nearby **Hippodrome** is similar. One of the world's largest discos, it has stunning lighting, several bars and also serves food.

Most of the more upmarket nightclubs in London, for example, **Annabel's**, have a strict members-only policy; they require nominations by current members and have long waiting lists, so unless you mix in privileged circles you are unlikely to get in.

Traditional West End disco-type clubs which are easier to enter include **Limelight**, the sleek club **Legends** and **Café de Paris**, where you can dine and boogie the night away.

Further north, the **Forum** hosts popular club nights, which feature classic soul, funk and rhythm and blues. Similar clubs are **Equinox** in Leicester Square and the **Tattershall Castle**, a disco boat moored on the Thames.

FASHIONABLE VENUES AND CLUB NIGHTS

OVER THE LAST few years London has become one of the most innovative club capitals in the world, a major stage where trends are set. **Heaven** hosts England's premier "house" night. With its huge dance floor, excellent lasers, sound systems and lightshows it's very popular, so start queuing early. The **Ministry of Sound** is a New York-style club that set the pattern for others to follow, but it has no alcohol licence and is very hard to get into. If you are feeling energetic house nights are also run at the **Gardening Club** and **Woody's**, home to garage as well as hardcore house and the young and trendy **Wag Club**. LA2 hosts an alternative dance night with "Popscene" for "indie" music sounds.

As with many clubs, **Bar Rhumba** has different themes on different evenings, but if you like your dancing with a dash of spice and a lot of sauce, sashay along to its salsa night. Another multi-faceted fun palace is the **Blue Note**.

"Talkin' Loud" club night at the **Fridge** offers some of the funkiest jazz-based sounds. **Turnmills** is London's first 24-hour club; it's cheap, plays funky jazz and also boasts a decent restaurant. For 1970s nostalgists, **Le Scandale** hosts "Carwash" – disco was never such fun There is also cheap admission for those brave enough to dress in seventies style so what you lose in fashion points, you can re-coup for your bar budget.

There are surprisingly few regular reggae nights. **Gossips** has the best dance reggae on Saturday and a tremendous toe-tapping tripartite rhythm riot of ska, classic soul and R 'n' B on Thursday.

GAY

LONDON HAS a number of gay nightclubs. The best-known and most popular is **Heaven**, with its huge dance floor and bar and video lounge. The **Fridge** and the **Gardening Club** host mixed gay nights, and the Fridge holds women-only nights.

TRANSVESTITE

WATCH for the occasional "Kinky Gerlinky" night in the listings magazines, an outrageously kitsch collection of drag queens and assorted exotica. In Soho, **Madame Jojo**'s revue is a fabulous whirl of glittering colour and extreme high camp.

CASINOS

TO GAMBLE in London you must be a member, or at least the guest of a member, of a licensed gaming club. Most clubs are happy to let you join but membership must be arranged 48 hours in advance. Many will let you in to use facilities other than the gambling tables until about 4am, when most close. Try the excellent restaurants and bars, which are often subject to the usual licensing laws (see p308). Many clubs also have "hostesses" – beware the cost of their company.

DIRECTORY

MAJOR MUSIC VENUES

Brixton Academy
211 Stockwell Rd SW9.
020-7924 9999.

Labatt's Apollo
Queen Caroline St W6.
0870-505 0007.

Royal Albert Hall
See p203.

Forum
9–17 Highgate Rd NW5.
020-7284 1001.
020-7284 2200.

Wembley Arena and Stadium
Empire Way, Wembley, Middlesex HA9.
0870-840 1111.

ROCK AND POP VENUES

Astoria
157 Charing Cross Rd WC2. **Map** 13 B1.
020-7434 9592.

Borderline
Orange Yard, Manette St WC2. **Map** 13 B1.
020-7734 2095.

Bull and Gate
389 Kentish Town Rd NW5. 020-7485 5358.

Camden Palace
1a Camden High St NW1. **Map** 4 F2.
020-7387 0428.

LA2
157 Charing Cross Rd WC2. **Map** 13 B2.
020-7734 6963.

Limelight
136 Shaftesbury Ave WC2. **Map** 13 B2.
020-7434 0572.

Mean Fiddler
22–28a High St NW10.
020-8961 5490.
020-8963 0940.

National Ballroom Kilburn
234 Kilburn High Rd NW6.
020-7328 3141.

Rock Garden
6–7 The Piazza, Covent Garden WC2. **Map** 13 C2.
020-7836 4052.

Shepherd's Bush Empire
Shepherd's Bush Green W12.
020-8740 7474.

Station Tavern
41 Bramley Rd W10.
020-7727 4053.

Subterania
12 Acklam Rd W10.
020-8960 4590.
020-8284 2200.

Woody's
41–43 Woodfield Rd W9.
020-7286 5574.

JAZZ VENUES

100 Club
100 Oxford St W1.
Map 13 A1.
020-7636 0933.

Barbican Hall
See p165.

Dover Street Wine Bar
8–10 Dover St W1.
Map 12 F3.
020-7629 9813.

Jazz Café
5 Parkway NW1. **Map** 4 E1.
020-7916 6060.

Pizza Express
10 Dean St W1. **Map** 13 A1
020-7437 9595.

Pizza on the Park
11 Knightsbridge SW1.
Map 12 D5.
020-7235 5550.

Ronnie Scott's
47 Frith St W1. **Map** 13 A2.
020-7439 0747

Royal Festival Hall
See p184.

Vortex Jazz Bar
Stoke Newington Church St N16. 020-7254 6516.

WORLD MUSIC

Africa Centre
38 King St WC2.
Map 13 C2.
020-7836 1973.

Barbican Centre
See p165.

Cecil Sharp House
2 Regent's Park Rd NW1.
Map 4 D1.
020-7485 2206.

Cuba Libre
72 Upper St N1. **Map** 6 F1.
020-7354 9998.

Down Mexico Way
25 Swallow St W1.
Map 12 F3.
020-7437 9895.

ICA
See p92.

Mean Fiddler
22-28A High St NW10.
020-8961 5490.

Queen Elizabeth Hall
South Bank Centre SE1.
Map 14 D4.
020-7960 4242.

Royal Festival Hall
See pp184–5.

Weavers Arms
98 Newington Green Rd N1.
020-7226 6911.

CLUBS

Annabel's
44 Berkeley Sq W1.
Map 12 E3.
020-7629 1096.

Bar Rhumba
36 Shaftesbury Ave WC2.
Map 6 E2.
020-7287 2715.

Blue Note
1-5 Parkfield St N1.
Map 7 C3.
020-7729 8440.

Café de Paris
3 Coventry St W1.
Map 13 A3.
020-7734 7700.

Club 180
180 Earl's Court Rd SW5.
Map 18 D2.
020-7835 1826.

Equinox
Leicester Sq WC2.
Map 13 B2.
020-7437 1446.

Fridge
Town Hall Parade, Brixton Hill SW2.
020-7326 5100.

Gardening Club
4 The Piazza, Covent Garden WC2.
Map 13 C2.
020-7497 3154.

Gossips
69 Dean St W1.
Map 13 A2.
020-7434 4480.

Heaven
Under the Arches, Villiers St WC2.
Map 13 C3.
020-7930 2020.

Hippodrome
Cranbourn St WC2.
Map 13 B2.
020-7437 4311.

Legends
29 Old Burlington St W1.
Map 12 F3
020-7437 9933.

Madame Jojo
8–10 Brewer St W1.
Map 13 A2.
020-7734 2473.

Ministry of Sound
103 Gaunt St SE1.
020-7378 6528.

Scandale
53–54 Berwick St W1.
Map 13 A1.
020-7437 6830.

Stringfellows
16 Upper St Martin's Lane WC2.
Map 13 B2
020-7240 5534.

Tattershall Castle
Victoria Embankment, SW1.
Map 13 C3.
020-7839 6548.

Turnmills
63 Clerkenwell Road EC1.
Map 6 E5.
020-7250 3409.

Wag Club
35 Wardour St W1.
Map 13 A2.
020-7437 5534.

Sport

THE RANGE OF SPORTS on offer in London is quite phenomenal. Should you feel the urge to watch a game of medieval tennis or go scuba-diving in the city centre, you've come to the right place. More likely, you'll just want to watch a football or rugby match, or play a set of tennis in a park. With far more public facilities than most European capitals, London is the place to enjoy cheap, accessible sport.

AMERICAN FOOTBALL

THE LONDON MONARCHS play teams from Europe and America in March and April. The NFL Bowl, in which two top American football teams compete in an exhibition match, is held in August, also at Wembley.

ATHLETICS

ATHLETES WILL find a good choice of running tracks, often with free admission. **West London Stadium** has good facilities; **Regent's Park** is free; try also **Parliament Hill Fields**. For a sociable jog, meet the Bow Street Runners at **Jubilee Hall** on Tuesdays at 6pm.

CRICKET

FIVE-DAY TEST MATCHES and one-day internationals are played in summer at Lord's (see p242) and the Oval, near Vauxhall. Tickets for the first four days of tests and for one-day games are hard to get, but you may get in on the last day and see a thrilling finish. When Middlesex and Surrey play county games at these grounds there are always seats.

FOOTBALL

THIS IS THE MOST popular spectator sport in Britain, its season running from August to May, with matches on week-ends and weekday evenings. It is the most common topic of conversation in pubs, where games are often shown live on TV. Premier League and FA Cup games may sell out in advance but you can usually get seats for internationals at Wembley. London's top clubs include **Arsenal**, **Chelsea**, **West Ham** and **Tottenham**.

GOLF

THERE ARE NO golf courses in Central London, but a few are scattered around the outskirts. The most accessible public courses are **Hounslow Heath**, **Chessington** (nine holes, train from Waterloo) and **Richmond Park** (two courses, computerized indoor teaching room). If you didn't pack your clubs, sets can be hired at a reasonable price.

GREYHOUND RACING

AT A NIGHT "down the dogs" you can follow the races on a screen in the bar, stand by the track or watch from the restaurant (book in advance) at **Walthamstow Stadium**, **The Embassy London Stadium** or **Wimbledon Stadium**.

HORSE RACING

HIGH CLASS FLAT RACING in summer and steeple-chasing in winter can be seen at **Ascot**, **Kempton Park** and **Sandown Park**., all less than an hour from central London by train. Britain's most famous race, the Derby, is run at **Epsom** in June.

HORSE-RIDING

FOR CENTURIES, fashionable riders have exercised their steeds in Hyde Park; **Ross Nye** will provide you with a horse so that you can follow a long tradition.

ICE-SKATING

ICE-SKATERS SHOULD head for London's best-known rink, **Queens**, where you can hire skates. The most attractive ice rink, open only in winter, is in the **Broadgate** complex in the heart of the City.

RUGBY

THE PROFESSIONAL Rugby League has 13 players a side and plays cup final matches at **Wembley**; Rugby Union, or rugger, is a 15-a-side amateur game, and its internationals are played at **Twickenham Rugby Football Ground**. The season runs from September to April and you can watch "friendly" week-end games at local grounds. Top London teams **Saracens** and **Rosslyn Park** can be seen at their own grounds outside the centre of town.

SQUASH

SQUASH COURTS tend to be busy, so try to book at least two days ahead. Many sports centres have squash facilities and will hire out equipment, including **Swiss Cottage Sports Centre** and **Saddlers Sports Centre**.

SWIMMING

BEST INDOOR pools include **Chelsea Sports Centre** and **Porchester Baths**; for outdoor, try **Highgate** (men), **Kenwood** (women) and **Hampstead** (mixed bathing).

TENNIS

THERE ARE hundreds of tennis courts in London's public parks, most of them cheap and easily reserved. It can be busy in the summer, so book your court two or three days ahead. You must supply your own racquet and balls. Good public tennis courts include the following: **Holland Park**, **Parliament Hill** and **Swiss Cottage**.

Tickets for the Centre Court of the **All England Lawn Tennis Club** at Wimbledon are hard to obtain – it is possibly easier to enter the tournament as a player than to obtain tickets for Centre Court; try queueing overnight, or queue for return tickets after lunch on the day – for a bargain price, you can still enjoy a good four hours of tennis. (See p247.)

TRADITIONAL SPORTS

An OLD LONDON tradition is the University Boat Race, held in March or April, when teams from Oxford and Cambridge row from Putney to Mortlake *(see p56)*; a newer tradition is the London Marathon, which is run from Greenwich to Big Ben at Westminster *(see p56)* on an April Sunday. You can watch croquet at the **Hurlingham Club** and medieval tennis at **Queen's Club**.

WATER SPORTS

There are facilities for a wide variety of water sports at the **Docklands Sailing and Water Sports Centre**. You can choose from sports such as windsurfing, dinghy sailing, powerboating, waterskiing and canoeing. Rowing boats are also available for hire by the hour on the calmer, central London waters of the **Serpentine** in Hyde Park and **Regent's Park Lake**.

WORKING OUT

Most sports centres have gymnasiums, work-out studios and health clubs. If you are a member of the YMCA, you'll be able to use the excellent facilities at the **Central YMCA**. **Jubilee Hall** and **Swiss Cottage Sports Centre** both offer a variety of aerobic classes, keep-fit and weight training. For those who have overdone it, the **Chelsea Sports Centre** has a sports injury clinic.

DIRECTORY

General Sports Information Line
C 020-7222 8000.

Greater London Sports Council
C 020-7273 1500.

All England Lawn Tennis and Croquet Club
Church Rd, Wimbledon SW19. C 020-8946 2244.

Arsenal Stadium
Avenell Rd, Highbury N5.
C 020-7704 4000.

Ascot Racecourse
Ascot, Berkshire.
C 01344 22211.

Broadgate Ice Rink
Broadgate Circle EC2.
Map 7 C5.
C 020-7505 4608.

Central YMCA
112 Great Russell St WC1. **Map** 13 B1.
C 020-7637 8131.

Chelsea Football Club
Stamford Bridge SW6.
C 020-7385 5545.

Chelsea Sports Centre
Chelsea Manor St SW3.
Map 19 B3.
C 020-7352 6985.

Chessington Golf Course
Garrison Lane, Surrey.
C 020-8391 0948.

Docklands Sailing and Watersports Centre
235a Westferry Rd, E14.
C 020-7537 2626.

The Embassy London Stadium
Waterden Rd, E15 2EQ.
C 020-8986 3511.

Epsom Racecourse
Epsom Downs, Surrey.
C 01372 726311.

Hampstead Ponds
off East Heath Rd NW3.
Map 1 C4.
C 020-7435 2366.

Holland Park Lawn Tennis Courts
Kensington High St W8.
Map 9 B5.
C 020-7602 2226.

Hounslow Heath Golf Course
Staines Rd, Hounslow, Middlesex.
C 020-8570 5271.

Hurlingham Club
Ranelagh Gdns SW6
C 020-7736 8411.

Jubilee Hall Sports Centre
30 The Piazza, Covent Garden WC2. **Map** 13 C2.
C 020-7836 4007.

Kempton Park Racecourse
Sunbury on Thames, Middx.
C 01932 782292.

Kenwood and Highgate Ponds
Millfield Lane N6. **Map** 2 E3.
C 020-8340 4044.

Linford Christie Stadium
Du Cane Rd W12.
C 020-8749 6758.

Lord's Cricket Ground
St John's Wood NW8.

Map 3 A3.
C 020-7289 1611.

Oval Cricket Ground
Kennington Oval SE11.
Map 22 D4.
C 020-7582 6660.

Parliament Hill
Highgate Rd NW5.
Map 2 E4.
C 020-7435 8998 (athletics).
C 020-7485 4491 (tennis).

Porchester Centre
Queensway W2.
Map 10 D1.
C 020-7792 2919.

Queen's Club (Real Tennis)
Palliser Rd W14.
Map 17 A3.
C 020-7385 3421.

Queens Ice Skating Club
17 Queensway W2.
Map 10 E2.
C 020-7229 0172.

Regent's Park Lake
Regent's Park NW1.
Map 3 C3.
C 020-7486 7905.

Richmond Park Golf
Roehampton Gate, Priory Lane SW15.
C 020-8876 3205.

Rosslyn Park Rugby
Priory Lane, Upper Richmond Rd SW15.
C 020-8876 1879.

Ross Nye
8 Bathurst Mews W2.
Map 11 A2.
C 020-7262 3791.

Saddlers Sports Centre
Goswell Rd EC1.
Map 6 F3.
C 020-7253 9285.

Sandown Park Racecourse
Esher, Surrey.
C 01372 463072.

Saracens Rugby Football Club
5 Vicarage Rd, Watford, Hertfordshire, WD1.
C 01923 496 200

Serpentine
Hyde Park W2.
Map 11 B4.
C 020-7262 3751.

Swiss Cottage Sports Centre
Winchester Rd NW3.
C 020-7413 6490

Tottenham Hotspur
White Hart Lane, 748 High Rd N17.
C 020-7365 5050

Twickenham Rugby Ground
Whitton Rd.
Twickenham, Middlesex.
C 020-8892 8161.

Walthamstow Stadium
Chingford Rd E4.
C 020-8531 4255

Wembley Stadium
Wembley, Middlesex.
C 020-8900 1234.

West Ham United
Boleyn Ground, Green St, Upton Park E13.
C 020-8548 2700.

CHILDREN'S LONDON

LONDON OFFERS children a potential goldmine of fun, excitement and adventure. Each year finds new attractions and sights opening up and older ones being updated.

First-time visitors may want to watch traditional ceremonies *(see pp52–5)* or visit famous buildings *(see p35)*, but these are merely the tip of the iceberg. While London's parks, zoos and adventure playgrounds provide outdoor activities there are also loads of workshops, activity centres and museums providing quizzes, hands-on experiments and interactive displays. A day out needn't be costly: children are entitled to reduced fares on London Transport and lower admission prices at museums. Some of London's star attractions, for instance all the ceremonies, are free.

Humpty Dumpty doll

PRACTICAL ADVICE

A LITTLE PLANNING is the key to a successful outing. You may want to check the opening hours of the places you plan to visit in advance, by telephone. Work out your journey thoroughly using the tube map at the end of this book. If you are travelling with very young children remember that there will be queues at the Underground stations or bus stops near popular sights. These will be long during peak hours, so buy your tickets or a Travelcard in advance *(see p360).*

Children under 5 can travel free on buses and tubes and child fares operate for all children between the ages of 5 and 15. (Children of 14 and 15, and those who look older than they are, need to have a Photocard.) Children very often enjoy using public transport, especially when it's

Punch and Judy show in the Piazza, Covent Garden

a novelty, so plan your outing carefully using one form of transport for the outward journey and another for the journey home. You can get around London easily by bus, Underground, taxi, train and riverboat *(see pp 360–7).* Visiting all the exhibitions and museums as a family doesn't have to be

Covent Garden clowns

as expensive as it sounds. An annual family season ticket, usually for two adults and up to four children, is available at many of the museums and often costs only marginally more than the initial visit. In some cases you can buy a family ticket that covers a group of museums; for instance the Science, Natural History and Victoria and Albert Museums in South Kensington *(see pp194–209).* Being able to visit a sight more than once means that you won't exhaust your children and put them off museums for life by trying to see absolutely everything over one long, tiring day.

If your children want a break from sightseeing, most borough councils provide information on activities for children such as playgroups, theatres, fun fairs and activity centres in their area. Leaflets are usually available from libraries and leisure centres, as well as local town halls. During the long summer school holidays (July to the beginning of September) there are organized activity programmes all over London.

CHILDREN AND THE LAW

CHILDREN UNDER 14 are not allowed into British pubs and wine bars (unless there is a special family room or garden) and only people over 18 can drink or buy any alcohol. In restaurants, only those over 16 can drink wine and beer with their meal (over 18 for spirits).

EATING OUT WITH CHILDREN

The choosing chart (see pp292–4) in the front of the restaurants section of this book shows establishments that welcome children. But as long as your offspring are reasonably well-behaved, most of London's more informal and ethnic restaurants will be happy to serve a family. Some can also provide highchairs and booster cushions, as well as colouring mats to keep children quiet while waiting for their food to arrive. Many will also offer special children's menus with small helpings which, although fairly unadventurous, will cut the cost of your meal.

Over the weekend some restaurants (such as **Smollensky's Balloon** and **Sweeny Todds**) provide live entertainment for children in the form of clowns, storytellers and magicians. A number accept bookings for children's parties. It is always worth trying to book in advance (especially for Sunday lunch), so that you don't have to hang around waiting with tired and hungry children.

London has a number of restaurants ideal for older children. Among these are the Rock Island Diner (see p306) and the **Hard Rock Café** on Old Park Lane.

For budget eating, try the Café in the Crypt, St Martin-in-the-Fields (see p102).

Coming up for air at Smollensky's Balloon

Colourful service at the Rock Island Diner

USEFUL ADDRESSES

Haagen-Dazs
14 Leicester Square WC2. **Map** 13 B2.
(020-7287 9577.

Hard Rock Café
150 Old Park Lane W1. **Map** 12 E4.
(020-7629 0382.

Smollensky's Balloon
1 Dover St W1. **Map** 12 F3.
(020-7491 1199.

Sweeny Todds
3–5 Tooley St SE1. **Map** 15 C3.
(020-7407 5267.

Some films are classed as unsuitable for children (see p329), and young children are rarely welcome anywhere they might create a nuisance.

If you want to take your children by car, you must use seat belts wherever they are provided. Babies will need a special child seat. If you are in doubt, ask at any police station.

GETTING THEM OFF YOUR HANDS

MANY OF London's great museums (see pp40–3) and theatres (see pp326–8) provide weekend and holiday activities and workshops where you can leave children for a few hours or even for a whole day, and the children's theatres are a great way to spend a rainy afternoon. A day at the fair is always a success – try Hampstead fair on summer bank holidays.

London has a great many sports centres (see pp336–7), which usually open daily and often have special clubs and activities to occupy children of every age.

From 4pm to 6pm Kids Line (020-7222 8070) details children's events in London.

If you want a total break, contact **Childminders**, **Babysitters Unlimited**, **Universal Aunts** or **Pippa Pop-Ins**, London's hotel for children between 2 and 12.

CHILDMINDING

Babysitters Unlimited
2 Napoleon Road, Twickenham.
(020-8892 8888.

Childminders
9 Nottingham Street W1. **Map** 4 D5.
(020-7487 5040.

Pippa Pop-Ins
430 Fulham Road SW6.
Map 18 D5.
(020-7385 2458.

Universal Aunts
PO Box 304, SW4.
(020-7738 8937.

Airborne at the Hampstead fair

Bathtime fun at Pippa Pop-Ins

SHOPPING

All children love a visit to **Hamleys** toy shop or Harrod's toy department *(see p311)*. **Davenport's Magic Shop** and **The Doll's House** are smaller and more specialized.

Both the **Early Learning Centre**, with its many branches, and the **Children's Book Centre** have good selections of books. Some bookshops organize readings and signings by children's authors, especially during Children's Book Week which is held in October. **Useful numbers** Children's Book Centre **C** 020-7937 7497; Davenport's Magic Shop **C** 020-7836 0408; The Doll's House **C** 020-7240 6075; Early Learning Centre **C** 020-7937 0419; Hamleys **C** 020-7734 3161.

Bears at Hamleys toy shop

MUSEUMS AND GALLERIES

LONDON HAS a wealth of museums, exhibitions and galleries; more information on those listed here is to be found on pages 40–43. Most have been updated over the last few years to incorporate some exciting modern display techniques. It's unlikely that you'll have to drag reluctant children around an assortment of lifeless and stuffy exhibits.

The Bethnal Green Museum of Childhood (the children's branch of the Victoria and Albert Museum), the London Toy and Model Museum, with its garden and steam railway, and Pollock's Toy Museum are especially good for young children.

For older children try one of London's Brass Rubbing Centres: the great Brass Rubbing Centre in the Crypt of St Martin-in-the-Fields *(p102)*, Westminster Abbey *(pp76–9)* or St James's Church, Piccadilly *(p90)*. The Guinness World of Records Exhibitions *(p100)* at the Trocadero, the Museum of the Moving Image *(p184)*, Madame Tussauds *(p220)* or Tower Bridge *(p153)* are all firm favourites with children too.

The British Museum has fabulous treasures from all over the world, and the Commonwealth Experience and the Horniman Museum have colourful displays from many different cultures. The Science Museum, with over 600 working exhibits, is one of London's best attractions for children – its Launch Pad gallery will help keep them amused for hours. If you have the stamina, the Natural History Museum next door contains hundreds of amazing objects and animals from the world of nature, including a fabulous Dinosaur Exhibition complete with sound effects.

Shirley Temple doll at Bethnal Green Museum

Suits of armour built for knights and monarchs can be seen at the Tower of London. More up-to-date armoury and weapons, including aircraft and the tools of modern warfare, can be seen at the National Army Museum, and the Imperial War Museum. Also worth a visit is the Guards' Museum located on Birdcage Walk. London's colourful past is brought alive at the Museum of London.

The superb **London Aquarium** *(p185)*, on the bank of the Thames, offers close-up encounters with sea life from starfish to sharks.

THE GREAT OUTDOORS

LONDON IS FORTUNATE in having many parks and open spaces *(see pp48–51)*. Most local parks contain conventional playgrounds for children, many with modern, safe equipment. Some parks also have One O'Clock Clubs (specially enclosed areas for children under 5 with activities supervised by play-workers) as well as adventure playgrounds, nature trails,

Puppets at the Little Angel Marionette Theatre, Highbury

Playground at Gunnersbury Park

boating ponds and athletic tracks for older children and energetic adults.

Kite-flying on Blackheath *(p239)*, Hampstead Heath or Parliament Hill can be great fun, as can boating in Regent's Park. A trip to Primrose Hill *(pp262–3)* can be combined with a visit to London Zoo and Regent's Canal *(p223)*.

The large parks are one of London's greatest assets for parents who have energetic children. For a good walk or cycle ride, there is quite an abundance of parks all over London. For instance, there's Hyde Park in the city centre; Hampstead Heath up in the north; Wimbledon Common in southwest London; and Gunnersbury Park in west London. Cyclists should be sure to watch out for pedestrians and remember that some paths may be out of bounds.

Battersea Park has a children's zoo and Crystal Palace Park (Thicket Rd, Penge SE20) has a children's farm. Greenwich and Richmond Parks have herds of deer. If you want a relaxing trip, why not go and feed the ducks on the pond in St James's Park?

Tuojiangasaurus skeleton at the Natural History Museum

CHILDREN'S THEATRE

INTRODUCING CHILDREN to the theatre can be great fun for adults too. Get involved with the froth and mania at the **Little Angel Theatre,** or the floating fantasy of the **Puppet Theatre Barge** in Little Venice. **The Unicorn Theatre** offers the best range of children's theatre and the **Polka Children's Theatre** has some good shows.
Useful numbers Little Angel Theatre **(** 020-7359 8581. Polka Children's Theatre **(** 020-8543 3741. Puppet Theatre Barge Marionette Performers **(** 020-7249 6876. The Unicorn Theatre **(** 020-7379 3280.

Deer at Richmond Park

SIGHTSEEING

FOR SEEING the sights of London you can't beat the top of a double-decker bus *(see pp364–5)*. It's a cheap and easy way of entertaining children, and if they get restless you can always jump off the bus at the next stop. London's colourful ceremonies are detailed on pages 52–5.

Children will also enjoy such spectacles as the summer fun fairs in London's parks, the firework displays throughout London on

Boating lake near Winfield House in Regent's Park

Guy Fawkes Night (every 5 November) and the Christmas decorations in Regent Street and Trafalgar Square.

BEHIND THE SCENES

OLDER CHILDREN in particular will love the opportunity to look "behind the scenes" and see how famous events or institutions are run.

If you have a brood of sports enthusiasts, you should visit the impressive Wembley Stadium, Twickenham Rugby Football Ground *(see p337)*, Lord's Cricket Ground *(p242)*, or the Wimbledon Lawn Tennis Museum *(p247)*.

For budding theatre buffs, the Royal National Theatre *(p184)*, the Royal Opera House *(p115)*, and Sadler's Wells *(p330)* all offer tours.

Other good buildings for children to visit include the Tower of London *(pp154–7)*, the Old Bailey law courts *(p147)* and the Houses of Parliament *(pp72–3)*.

If none of the above satisfy the children, the London Fire Brigade (020-7587 4063) and the London Diamond Centre (020-7629 5511) offer more unusual guided tours.

SURVIVAL
GUIDE

PRACTICAL INFORMATION

LONDON HAS RESPONDED well to the demands of tourism. The range of facilities on offer to travellers, from cashpoint machines and bureaux de change to medical care and late-night transport, has expanded very quickly over the last few years. Whether or not you find London an expensive city will depend on the prevailing exchange rate between the pound and your own cur-rency. It is known for its high hotel prices but even here there are budget options *(see pp272–5)*. Nor need you spend a lot on food if you choose care-fully: for the price of a single meal at some Mayfair restaurants you could feed yourself, albeit modestly, for sev-eral days *(see pp306–7)*. The following tips will help you to make the most of your visit.

A walking tour of the City

AVOIDING THE CROWDS

MUSEUMS AND GALLERIES can be crowded with school parties, particularly at the end of terms, so it might be best to plan your visit to start after 2.30pm during term-time. At other times of the year, visit early in the day and try and avoid weekends if you can.
• Coach parties are another source of congestion. They do, however, tend to follow a predictable path. To miss them, it is wise to steer well clear of Westminster Abbey in the morning, and St Paul's around the afternoon. The Tower of London is usually busy all day.

A lot of London can be seen on foot. Brown signs indicate sights and facilities of interest to tourists. Look out, too, for the blue plaques attached to many buildings *(see p39)* showing where famous citizens have lived in the past.

GUIDED TOURS

A GOOD WAY to enjoy London, weather permitting, is from the top of a traditional open-topped double-decker bus. The **London Transport Sight-seeing Tour** lasts around 90 minutes, and leaves every half-hour or so (10am–6pm) from various central locations. Commercial rivals, including **Frames Rickards** and **Harrod's**, offer tours lasting anything from an hour to a full day. You can buy your tickets just before boarding, or in advance (sometimes more cheaply) at Tourist Informa-tion Centres. Private tours can also be arranged with many companies, for instance **Tour Guides Ltd** or **British Tours.** The best tour guides receive a Blue Badge qualification from the London Tourist Board.

You can also explore London by joining a walking tour *(see p259)*. Themed tours range from pub crawls to a jaunt in the steps of Charles Dickens. Check for details of the walks at tourist offices, or in listings magazines *(see p324)*.

Cruise boats operate on the River Thames – an excellent way of travelling the breadth of London *(see pp60–5)*.
Useful numbers British Tours 020-7734 8734; Frames Rickards 020-7837 3111; Harrod's 020-7581 3603; London Transport Sightseeing Tour 020-7828 7395; Tour Guides Ltd 020-7495 5504; information for the disabled: 020-7495 5504.

OPENING HOURS

OPENING TIMES for sights have been listed in the *Area by Area* section of this book. Core visiting times in London are 10am–5pm daily, though many places stay open longer, especially in summer. Some major sights, like the British Museum, also stay open late on certain evenings. There are variations at week-ends and public holidays. Opening times on Sundays are often restricted and a few museums close on Mondays.

Double-decker sightseeing bus with an open top

Queueing for a bus

ADMISSION CHARGES

MANY MAJOR sights, including London's cathedrals and some churches, have recently started either to charge for admission or to ask for a voluntary contribution upon entry. Charges vary greatly, from the cheap (only a few pounds for the Florence Nightingale Museum, *see p185*) to the more expensive (over £6.00 for the Tower of London, *see pp154–7*). The *Area by Area* listings tell you which museums charge for admission.

Some sights have reduced-price visiting times and offer concessions. It is best to telephone if you think you might be eligible.

Signposted information for tourists

ETIQUETTE

SMOKING IS NOW forbidden in many of London's public places. These include the bus and Underground transport systems, taxis, some British Rail stations, all theatres and most cinemas. Many London restaurants now have no-smoking sections. The great exception to the anti-smoking trend is pubs. ASH (Action on Smoking and Health) can give advice on smoke-free venues (020-7935 3519). Consult the Hotels and Restaurants listings *(pp278–85* and *pp295–305)* for details of places that cater for non-smokers.

Londoners queue for anything from shops, buses and post offices to theatre tickets,

takeaway food and taxis. Anyone barging in will encounter frosty glares and acid comments. The exceptions are commuter rail and rush-hour tube services, when the laws of the jungle prevail.

The words "please", "thank you" and "sorry" are used regularly in London; people sometimes apologize if you step on their feet. It may seem unnecessary to thank a barman for simply doing his job, but it should improve your chances of decent service.

Like any big city, London can seem alienating to newcomers, but Londoners are usually helpful, and most will respond generously to your request for directions. The stalwart British bobby (police constable on the beat) is also always patiently ready to help stranded tourists *(see p346)*.

DISABLED VISITORS

MANY SIGHTS HAVE access for wheelchairs. Again, this information is listed in the *Area by Area* section of this book, but phone first to check that your special needs are catered for. Useful guides to buy include *Access in London*, published by Nicholson, *London for All*, published by the London Tourist Board, and a booklet from London Transport called *Access to the Underground*, available at main tube stations. **Artsline** gives free information on facilities for disabled people at cultural events and venues. **Holiday Care Service** offers many facts on hotel facilities for the disabled. **Tripscope** provides free information on transport for the elderly and the disabled.

Useful numbers Artsline [020-7388 2227; Holiday Care Service [01293 771500; Tripscope [020-8994 9294.

Box for voluntary contributions in lieu of admission charges

TOURIST INFORMATION CENTRES

THESE OFFER ADVICE on anything from day trips and guided tours to accommodation.

Tourist information symbol

If you need tourist information, including free leaflets on current events, look for the large blue symbol at the following locations:

Heathrow Airport
Location The Underground station. ⊖ *Heathrow, 1, 2, 3.* **Open** 8am–6pm daily.

Liverpool Street Station
EC2. **Map** 7 C5.
Location The Underground station. ⊖ *Liverpool Street.* **Open** 8.15am–7pm Mon, 8.15am–6pm Tue–Sat, 8.15am–4.45pm Sun.

Selfridge's
400 Oxford St. W1. **Map** 12 D2.
Location The basement.
⊖ *Bond Street.* **Open** 9.30am–7pm Fri–Wed, 9.30–8pm Thu.

Victoria Station
SW1. **Map** 20 F1.
Location The railway station forecourt. ⊖ *Victoria.*
Open 8am–7pm daily.

You can also telephone the London Tourist Board on [020-7932 2000.

Another service exists for information about the City of London area only (see pp143–59):

City of London Information Centre
St Paul's Churchyard EC4.
Map 15 A1. [020-7332 1456.
⊖ *St Paul's.* **Open** Apr–Oct: 9.30am–5pm daily; Nov–Mar: 9.30am–12.30pm Sat only.

Personal Security and Health

LONDON IS A LARGE city which, like any other, has had its recent share of urban problems. It has also often been a terrorist target, and London life is sometimes disrupted by security alerts. Nearly all of these turn out to be false alarms, but they should always still be taken seriously. Never hesitate to approach one of London's many police constables for assistance – they are trained to help the public with any of their problems.

SUITABLE PRECAUTIONS

THERE IS LITTLE likelihood that your stay in London will be blighted at all by the spectre of violent crime. Even in the run-down and rougher parts of the town, the risk of having your pocket picked, or your bag stolen, is not very great. It is far more likely to happen right in the middle of heaving shopping crowds in areas like Oxford Street or Camden Lock, or perhaps on a very busy tube platform.

Muggers and rapists prefer poorly lit or isolated places like back-streets, parks and unmanned railway stations. If you avoid these, especially at night, or travel round in a group, you should manage to stay out of danger.

Pickpockets and thieves pose a much more immediate problem. Keep your valuables securely concealed. If you carry a handbag or a case, never let it out of your sight – particularly in restaurants, theatres and cinemas, where it is not unknown for bags to vanish from between the feet of their owners.

Although London has a small population of homeless people, they do not present a threat. The very worst they are likely to trouble you with is a request for spare change.

WOMEN TRAVELLING ALONE

UNLIKE SOME European cities, it is considered quite normal in London for women to eat out on their own or go out in a group, perhaps to a pub or a bar. However, risks do exist, and caution is essential. Stick to well-lit streets with plenty of traffic. Many women avoid travelling on the tube late at

Mounted police

night, and it is best not to travel alone on trains. If you have no companions, try to find an occupied carriage – preferably with more than one group of people. Best of all, take a taxi (see p367).

Many forms of self-defence are restricted in the UK, and it is illegal for anyone to carry various offensive weapons in public places. These include knives, coshes, guns and tear-gas canisters, all of which are strictly prohibited. Personal alarm systems are permitted.

PERSONAL PROPERTY

TAKE SENSIBLE precautions with personal property at all times. Make sure that your possessions are adequately insured before you arrive, since it is difficult for visitors to arrange once in the UK.

Don't carry your valuables around with you; take just as much cash as you need, and leave the rest in a hotel safe or lock it up in your suitcase. Traveller's cheques are the safest method of carrying large amounts of money (see p349). Never leave bags or briefcases unattended in tube or train stations – they will either be stolen or suspected of being bombs and therefore cause a security alert.

Report all lost items to the nearest police station (get the necessary paperwork if you plan an insurance claim). Each of the main rail stations has a lost property office on the premises. If you do leave something on a bus or tube, it may be better to call in at the address given below rather than to telephone.

Lost Property

Lost Property Offices
London Transport Lost Property Office, 200 Baker Street W1. **Open weekday mornings only.** [ ] 020-7486 2496, enquiries should be made in person; Black Cab Lost Property Office. [ ] 020-7833 0996.

Woman Police Constable　　**Traffic Police Officer**　　**Police Constable**

Typical London police car

London ambulance

London fire engine

EMERGENCIES

LONDON'S EMERGENCY police, ambulance and fire services are on call 24 hours a day. These, like the London hospital casualty services, are strictly for emergencies only.

Services are also available to offer help in emergencies, for instance in case of rape. If there is no appropriate number in the Crisis Information box (see right) you may be able to obtain one from the directory enquiries service (dial 142 or 192). Police stations and also hospitals with casualty wards are shown on the Street Finder maps (see pp368–9).

MEDICAL TREATMENT

VISITORS TO LONDON from all countries outside the European Community (EC) are strongly advised to take out medical insurance against the cost of any emergency hospital care, specialists' fees and repatriation. Emergency treatment in a British casualty ward is free, but additional medical care may be costly.

Residents of the EC and nationals of other European and Commonwealth countries are entitled to receive free medical treatment under the National Health Service (NHS). Before travelling, you should obtain a form confirming that your country of origin has adequate reciprocal health arrangements with Britain. Even without this form, free medical treatment can still be obtained if you offer proof of nationality, but there are exceptions for certain kinds of treatment and medical insurance is always advisable.

If you need to see a dentist while staying in London, you will have to pay at least a small amount. This will vary, depending on your entitlement to NHS treatment, and whether you can find an NHS dentist. Various institutions offer 24-hour dental treatment (see addresses right), but if you wish to visit a private dental surgeon, try looking in the Yellow Pages (see p352).

MEDICINES

YOU CAN BUY most medical supplies from chemists and supermarkets throughout London. However, many medicines are available only with a doctor's prescription. If you are likely to require drugs, either bring your own supplies or get your doctor to write out the generic name of the drug, as opposed to the brand name. If you are not eligible to receive NHS treatment, you will be charged at the medicine's cost price; remember to get a receipt to support any medical insurance claim you may wish to make.

Boots, a chain of chemists' shops

Banking and Local Currency

VISITORS TO LONDON will find that banks usually offer them the best rates of exchange. Privately owned bureaux de change have variable exchange rates, and care should be taken to check the small print details relating to commission and minimum charges before completing any transaction. Bureaux de change do, however, have the advantage of staying open long after the banks have closed.

Cashpoint machine

BANKING

BANKING HOURS vary in London. The minimum opening hours are, without exception, 9.30am–3.30pm Mon–Fri, but many stay open longer than this, especially those in the centre of London. Saturday morning opening is also more common now. All banks are closed on public holidays (known as bank holidays in the UK, *see p59*), and some may close early on the day before a holiday.

Many major banks in London have cashpoint machines that will allow you to obtain money by using your credit card and a PIN (personal identification number); some machines have clear computerized instructions in several languages. American Express cards may be used in 24-hour Lloyds Bank and Royal Bank of Scotland cash machines in London, but you must arrange to have your PIN linked by code to your personal account before you leave home. There is a 2% charge for each transaction.

Besides the main clearing banks, good places to change your traveller's cheques are **Thomas Cook** and **American Express** offices, or the bank-operated bureaux de change, which can usually be found at airports and major railway stations. Don't forget to bring along a passport if you want to change cheques.

You can find facilities for changing money all over the city centre, at main stations and tourist information offices, and in most large stores. **Chequepoint** is one of the largest bureaux de change in Britain; **Exchange International** has a number of useful late-opening branches. Since, in London, there is no consumer organization to regulate the activities of the privately run bureaux de change, their prices need to be examined carefully.

CREDIT CARDS

IT IS WORTH bringing a credit card with you, particularly for hotel and restaurant bills, shopping, car hire and booking tickets by telephone. Visa is the most widely accepted card in London, followed by Mastercard (its local name is Access), American Express, Diners Club and JCB.

It is possible to obtain cash advances (up to your credit limit) with an internationally recognized credit card at any London bank displaying the appropriate card sign. You will be charged the credit card company's interest rate, which appears on your statement with the amount advanced.

MAIN BANKS IN LONDON

England's main clearing banks (those whose dealings are processed through a single clearing house) are Barclays, Lloyds, HSBC (formerly the Midland Bank) and National Westminster (NatWest). The Royal Bank of Scotland also has a number of branches in London with exchange facilities. The commission charged by each bank for changing money can vary, so check before going ahead with your transaction.

Each bank can be easily identified by a distinctively styled sign bearing its name.

CASH AND TRAVELLER'S CHEQUES

BRITAIN'S CURRENCY is the pound sterling (£), which is divided into 100 pence (p). Since there are no exchange controls in Britain, there is no limit to how much cash you may import or export.

Traveller's cheques are the safest alternative to carrying large amounts of cash. Keep receipts from your traveller's cheques separately, and also make a note of offices where you will be able to obtain a refund if the cheques are lost or stolen. Some banks issue traveller's cheques free of commission to established customers, but the normal rate is about 1%. It is sensible to change some money into sterling before arriving in Britain, as queues at airport exchange offices can be very long. Do obtain some smaller denominations: shopkeepers may refuse to accept larger notes for small purchases.

English bank notes of all denominations always feature the Queen's head on one side.

Bank Notes

English notes used in the UK are £5, £10, £20 and £50. Scotland has its own notes which, despite being legal tender throughout the UK, are not always accepted.

£20 note

£50 note

£10 note

£5 note

Coins of the Realm

Coins in circulation are £2, £1, 50p, 20p, 10p, 5p, 2p and 1p (shown here slightly smaller than actual size). They all have the Queen's head on one side.

2 pounds (£2)

1 pound (£1)

50 pence (50p)

20 pence (20p)

10 pence (10p)

5 pence (5p)

2 pence (2p)

1 penny (1p)

Using London's Phones

YOU WILL FIND A PHONEBOX on many street corners in central London and in main bus stations and every railway station. Inland calls are most expensive from 9am to 1pm on weekdays. Cheap rate applies before 8am or after 6pm on weekdays, and all day at weekends. Cheap times for overseas calls vary from country to country, but tend to be at weekends and in the evening. You can use coins, buy prepaid phone-cards or use your credit card. British Telecom phone-cards come in £2, £4 and £10 denominations and can be bought at some newsagents as well as post offices.

REACHING THE RIGHT NUMBER

- All London codes are changing during the period 1 June 1999–22 April 2000.
- The codes shown in the edition are the new ones.
- From 22 April 2000 the 020 prefix should be omitted if calling within London. Before that date, use the entire number.
- Internal directory: 192.
- If you have any prob-lems contacting a number, call the operator on 100.
- To make an inter-national call, dial 00 followed by the country code (USA and Canada: 1; Australia: 61; New Zealand: 64), area code and the number.
- International operator: 155.
- International directory: 153. You need a phone-card with at least £2 credit for an international call.
- **In an emergency, dial 999 or 112.**

PHONEBOXES

THERE ARE two different types of BT phoneboxes found in London: old-style red phoneboxes and a new, modern style. The payphones are equipped to take either coins or cards.

In those that accept cards, you can use BT phonecards, BT charge cards and most credit cards. The newer-style phoneboxes have a display on the door indicating whether cards, coins, or both, are accepted. Instructions on

Old BT phonebox **New BT phonebox**

how to use both card and coin-operated payphones are set out below.

USING A CARD PHONE

USING A COIN PHONE

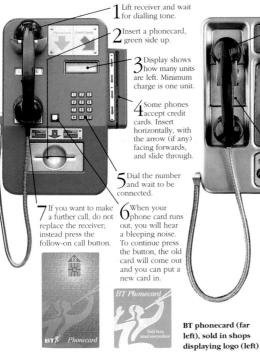

1 Lift receiver and wait for dialling tone.

2 Insert a phonecard, green side up.

3 Display shows how many units are left. Minimum charge is one unit.

4 Some phones accept credit cards. Insert horizontally, with the arrow (if any) facing forwards, and slide through.

5 Dial the number and wait to be connected.

7 If you want to make a further call, do not replace the receiver; instead press the follow-on call button.

6 When your phone card runs out, you will hear a bleeping noise. To continue press the button, the old card will come out and you can put a new card in.

BT phonecard (far left), sold in shops displaying logo (left)

1 Lift the receiver and wait for the dialling tone.

2 Insert the money. Any combination of coins can norm-ally be used except for five, two and one pence coins.

3 Dial the number and wait to be connected.

4 The display indicates how much money you have put in and the credit left. A rapid bleeping noise means your money has run out. Insert more coins.

5 If you want to make a further call, do not replace the receiver, instead press the follow-on call button.

6 When you have finished speaking, replace the receiver. Any coins that were not used will be returned. Coin phones do not give change, so use 10p and 20p coins for shorter calls.

Sending a Letter

Red and gold Post Office sign

BESIDES MAIN POST OFFICES that offer all the postal services available, London has many sub post offices, which often double as newsagents. Post offices are usually open from 9am to 5.30pm Monday to Friday, and until 12.30pm on Saturday. First- and second-class stamps are available either individually or in books of ten. First-class stamps can be used for letters and cards to the European Union. Post boxes – in all shapes and sizes but always red – are found throughout the city.

Old-style pillar box

POSTAL SERVICES

STAMPS CAN BE BOUGHT at any outlet which displays the sign "Stamps sold here". Hotels often have post boxes in their reception areas. When writing to a UK address always make sure you include the postcode, which can be found in telephone directories. Any letters posted within the UK can be sent either first or second class. The first-class service is more expensive but quicker, with most letters reaching their destination

Aerogrammes are all 1st class

2nd-class stamp   1st-class stamp

Books of ten 1st- and 2nd-class stamps

the following day (except for Sunday); second-class mail takes a day or two longer.

POSTE RESTANTE

IT IS POSSIBLE to receive mail in London by *poste restante*. This is a service where letters can be sent for collection. To use the service be sure to print the surname clearly so it will be filed away correctly. Send it to *Poste Restante* followed by the address of the post office. To collect your post you will have to show your existing passport or another form of identification. Post will be kept for one month. London's main post office is in William IV Street, WC2. Also, the American Express office at 6 Haymarket, London provides a *poste restante* service for its customers.

POST BOXES

THESE MAY BE either free-standing "pillar boxes" or wall safes, both painted bright red. Some pillar boxes have separate slots, which are clearly labelled, one slot for overseas and first-class mail, another for second-class mail. Initials found on the outside of the older style post boxes indicate the monarch at the time it was erected.

Post boxes are often embedded in post office walls. Collections are usually made

New-style post box

several times a day during weekdays (less often on Saturdays and never on Sundays); times are marked on the box.

POSTING ABROAD

AIRMAIL PROVIDES a speedy and cost-effective method of communication. Aerogrammes go first class anywhere in the world and cost the same regardless of destination. It takes about four days for them to reach cities in Europe, and between four and seven days for destinations elsewhere. Sending post by surface mail is more economical but it can take up to 12 weeks to reach its destination. Letters and parcels within the EU cost the same as posting inland.

The Post Office offers an express delivery service called **Parcelforce International**. It is comparable in price to private companies like **DHL**, **Crossflight** or **Expressair**.

Crossflight
℡ 01753 776000.

DHL
℡ 0345 100300.

Expressair
℡ 020-8897 6568.

Parcelforce International
℡ 0800 224466.

EXTRA INFORMATION

SHOULD YOU require any services that are not listed in this guide, try consulting one of London's telephone directories. The Yellow Pages comprehensively lists services throughout London, and should be available at your hotel. **Talking Pages** is a telephone service which is operated by British Telecom. It gives you the telephone number of someone who offers the service you want in any part of London (or the UK) that you specify.

Directory enquiries (dial 192) can be dialled free from payphones and will give you any telephone number in the directory. You need to know the name and address of the person or business.

CUSTOMS AND IMMIGRATION

A VALID PASSPORT is needed to enter the UK. Visitors from the EC, the US, Canada, Australia and New Zealand do not require a visa to enter, nor are any inoculations or vaccinations necessary.

When you arrive at one of Britain's airports or seaports you will find separate queues at immigration control – one for European Community (EC) nationals, several others for everyone else.

European union has led to changes in UK customs and immigration policy. Travellers entering the UK from outside the EC still have to pass through customs channels: red exit routes for people carrying goods on which a duty has to be paid; green routes for those with no payment to make (nothing to "declare"). If, however, you are travelling from within the EC you will find that these have been replaced by a blue channel – EC residents no longer have to "declare" goods. Random checks will still be made to guard against the likes of drug traffickers.

EC residents are no longer entitled to a VAT (Value Added Tax) refund on goods bought in the UK. Travellers from outside the EC can obtain one if they leave the UK within three months of the purchase date *(see p310)*.

International Student Identity Card

STUDENT TRAVELLERS

AN ISIC CARD (International Student Identity Card) entitles full-time students to discounts on things from travel to sports events. For students from the US, the ISIC also includes some medical cover,

though this may not be sufficient on its own. If you don't have an ISIC, it can be obtained (with proof of student status) from the **University of London Students' Union** (ULSU) or branches of **STA Travel**. ULSU offers many social and sports facilities to valid union card holders and reciprocating educational establishments. **International Youth Hostel Federation** membership is also worth having for cheap accommodation in London.

EC nationals do not require a permit to work in the UK. Commonwealth citizens under the age of 27 are allowed to do part-time work in the UK for up to two years. Visiting students from the US can get a blue card which enables them to work for up to six months (you must get this before you arrive). **BUNAC** is a student club organizing work exchange schemes for students from Australia, the United States, Canada and Jamaica.

USEFUL ADDRESSES AND TELEPHONE NUMBERS

BUNAC
16 Bowling Green Lane EC1.
Map 6 E4. **☎** 020-7251 3472.

International Youth Hostel Federation
☎ 01707-332 487.

STA Travel
74 and 86 Old Brompton Rd SW7.
Map 18 F2. **☎** 020-7581 1022.

Talking Pages
☎ 0800-600 900.

University of London Students' Union
Malet St WC1. **Map** 5 A5.
☎ 020-7580 9551.

NEWSPAPERS, TELEVISION AND RADIO

LONDON'S PRINCIPAL newspaper is the *Evening Standard*, available from about midday, Monday to Friday.

PUBLIC TOILETS

Although many older-style, supervised public conveniences still exist, these have largely been replaced by coin-operated "Superloos". Young children should never use these devices on their own – they will find it almost impossible to operate the inner door handle.

1 If the green "vacant" light is shown, insert the required fee. The door located on your left will slide open.

"Vacant" light   Coin slot

2 Once inside, the door slides closed and locks.

3 To exit, pull down the inner door handle.

London newspaper stand

The Friday edition is worth getting for its listings section and reviews. International newspapers are sold in many newsagents. The *International Herald Tribune* is available on the day of issue; others may appear a day or more later. Five television channels can be seen with conventional receiving equipment: two run by the BBC (BBC1 and BBC2), and three independent (ITV and Channels 4 and 5). Satellite and cable networks are both available in the UK, and some hotels have these facilities for their guests.

The BBC's local and national radio stations are supplemented by many independent local companies,

EMBASSIES AND CONSULATES

Australian High Commission
Australia House, The Strand WC2. **Map** 13 C2.
☎ 020-7379 4334.

Canadian High Commission
Haut Commissariat du Canada, Macdonald House,1 Grosvenor Square W1. **Map** 12 D2.
☎ 020-7258 6600.

New Zealand High Commission
New Zealand House, 80 Haymarket SW1. **Map** 13 A3.
☎ 020-7930 8422.

United States Embassy
24 Grosvenor Square W1.
Map 12 D2. ☎ 020-7499 9000.

like London's Capital Radio (194m/1548kHz MW; 95.8mHz FM), a pop music station.

INTERNATIONAL NEWSAGENTS

Gray's Inn News
50 Thecbald's Rd WC1. **Map** 5 C5.
☎ 020-7405 5241.

A Moroni and Son
68 Old Compton Street W1.
Map 13 A2. ☎ 020-7437 2847.

D S Radford
61 Fleet St EC4. **Map** 14 E1.
☎ 020-7583 7166.

ELECTRICAL ADAPTORS

THE ELECTRICAL supply in London is 240V AC. Plugs have three square pins and take fuses of 3, 5 and 13 amps. Visitors will need an adaptor for appliances; this is best bought before leaving home. Most hotels have two-pronged European-style sockets for shavers only.

Standard British plug

LONDON TIME

DIAL 123 TO CHECK the time on London's 24-hour **Speaking Clock** service. Clocks change for summer and winter time.

CONVERSION CHART

OFFICIALLY THE metric system is used, but imperial measures are still common.

Imperial to metric
1 inch = 2.5 centimetres
1 foot = 30 centimetres
1 mile = 1.6 kilometres
1 ounce = 28 grams
1 pound = 454 grams
1 pint = 0.6 litre
1 gallon = 4.6 litres

Metric to imperial
1 millimetre = 0.04 inch
1 centimetre = 0.4 inch
1 metre = 3 feet 3 inches
1 kilometre = 0.6 mile
1 gram = 0.04 ounce
1 kilogram = 2.2 pounds

RELIGIOUS SERVICES

THE FOLLOWING organizations can help you find a place to worship.

Church of England
St Paul's Cathedral EC4.
Map 15 A2. ☎ 020-7236 4128.

Roman Catholic
Westminster Cathedral, Victoria St SW1. **Map** 20 F1.
☎ 020-7798 9055.

Jewish
Liberal Jewish Synagogue, 28 St John's Wood Rd NW8.
Map 3 A3. ☎ 020-7286 5181.
United Synagogue (Orthodox) 735 High Rd N12.
☎ 020-8343 8989.

Moslem
Islamic Cultural Centre, 146 Park Rd NW8. **Map** 3 B3.
☎ 020-7724 3363.

Baptist
London Baptist Association, 1 Merchant St E3.
☎ 020-8980 6818.

Quakers
Religious Society of Quakers, 173–7 Euston Rd NW1.
Map 5 A4. ☎ 020-7387 3601.

Evangelical
Whitefield House, 186 Kennington Park Rd SE11.
Map 22 E4.
☎ 020-7582 0228.

Buddhist
The Buddhist Society, 58 Eccleston Sq SW1.
Map 20 F2. ☎ 020-7834 5858.

St Martin-in-the-Fields, Trafalgar Square *(see p102)*

GETTING TO LONDON

Lonnon is one of Europe's central routing points for international air and sea travel. By air, travellers face a bewildering choice of carriers serving North America, Europe and Australasia. Stiff competition on some routes means that low fares are occasionally introduced to attract new passengers. British Airways has a Concorde service, boasting the fastest flights in the world, between London and New York or Washington. Long-distance sea travel is, however, a different proposition as few transatlantic liners operate these

Concorde

days. Cunard offers the only regular services and doubt looms even over these. There are efficient and regular ferry services from Europe. About 20 passenger and car ferry routes, served by large ferries, hovercrafts, jetfoils and catamarans, cross the North Sea and the English Channel to Britain. Since 1995 the Channel Tunnel has provided a new, efficient high-speed train link running between Europe and the UK, although work on the new rail line on the English side of the Channel will not be complete for some years.

AIR TRAVEL

THE MAIN United States airlines offering scheduled flights to London include Delta, United, American Airlines and USAir. Two major British operators are **British Airways** and **Virgin Atlantic**. From Canada, the main carriers are Canadian Airlines (now incorporating WardAir) and Air Canada. Fierce competition for these prestigious transatlantic routes means that there are some excellent deals available. The flight time from New York is about six and a half hours (less on Concorde), and from Los Angeles about 10 hours.

There are regular scheduled flights to London from all the major European cities, as well as from numerous other parts of the UK itself, including northern England, Scotland and Northern Ireland.

The choice of carriers from Australasia is enormous. Well

over 20 airlines share around two dozen different routes. Journey times can vary from just over 20 hours on a big modern jet to over 100 hours via China. The more indirect your route, the cheaper the fare; but remember that three days' jet travel is bound to be stressful. **Qantas**, **Air New Zealand** and **British Airways** may be your first thoughts for comfort and speed, but all the Far Eastern operators and several European airlines offer interesting alternatives.

Getting a good deal
Cheap deals are available from good travel agents and package operators, and are advertised in newspapers and travel magazines. Airlines will quote you the regular price, but they often reduce this if seats are unsold. Students, senior citizens and regular or business travellers may well be able to obtain a discount. Children under two (who do not occupy a separate seat) pay 10% of the adult fare; older children up to 12 also travel at lower fares.

Ticket types
APEX (Advanced purchase) tickets can be good buys, but they need to be booked up to a month in advance. They are subject to restrictions and cannot be changed without penalty. There are usually

minimum (and maximum) length of stay requirements. Fares on scheduled flights are available through specialist agents at much lower rates. Charter flights offer even cheaper seats, but have less flexible departure times and can be less punctual.

If you book a cheap deal with a discount agent, check whether you will get a refund if the agent or operator ceases trading, and don't part with the full fare until you see the ticket. You will have to pay a deposit. Check with the relevant airline to ensure that your seat has been confirmed.

AIRLINE NUMBERS

Major Carriers
Air New Zealand
(020-8846 9595.

British Airways
(0345-222 111.

Qantas
(020-8846 0321.

Virgin Atlantic
(01293 562345.

Discount ticket agents
ATAB (Air Travel Advisory Bureau)
This regulatory organization will recommend a discount agency.
(020-7636 5000.

Lukas Travel *(European travel)*
(020-7734 9174.

Major Travel *(worldwide travel)*
(020-7485 7017.

Passenger jet landing at Heathrow

TRAVELLING BY RAIL

LONDON HAS EIGHT main rail stations at which InterCity express trains terminate. These are scattered in a ring around the city centre (see pp358–9). Paddington in west London serves the West Country, Wales and the South Midlands; Liverpool Street in the City covers East Anglia and Essex. In north London, Euston, St Pancras and King's Cross serve northern and central Britain. In the south, Charing Cross, Victoria and Waterloo serve the whole of southern England and are also the termini for travel by ferry and train from Europe. Since 1995, **Eurostar** has operated the Channel Tunnel rail service, with trains terminating at Waterloo International.

All of London's stations have had recent facelifts and are now smart and modern

Station concourse at Liverpool Street

with many facilities for the traveller, such as bureaux de change and shops selling books and confectionery.

Information about rail services is quite easy to find; most rail stations have an information point detailing times, prices and destinations.

In addition, constantly updated details of services are screened on to monitors scattered around the stations. Railway staff are usually helpful and courteous.

If your ferry ticket does not include the price of rail travel to the centre of London, tickets can be bought at the clearly signed ticket offices or automatic machines (see p366). You may decide to buy a Travelcard from the first day you are in London (see p360).

Eurostar London Waterloo International (0345 881 881.
National Rail Enquiries (0345 484 950.

BR information point (see p345)

COACH SERVICES

THE MAIN COACH station in London is on Buckingham Palace Road (about 10 minutes' walk from Victoria railway station). You can travel to London by coach from many European cities, but the majority of services travelling through London are from within the UK. National Express run to about 1,000 British destinations, but other companies depart from this station, too. Coach travel is cheaper than the railway, but journeys are longer and arrival times can be unpredictable. National Express Rapide coaches can be very comfortable and normally have sophisticated facilities. London Country buses operate within 40 miles (64 km) of London.

Coach numbers London Country Bus (01737-240501; Rapide (0990-808080.

CROSSING THE CHANNEL

Britain's sea links with Europe were finally joined by a landlink in 1995, when the Channel Tunnel opened. **Eurotunnel** operates a drive-on-drive-off train service for cars between Folkestone and Calais which runs about three times an hour with a journey time of 35 minutes. A network of ferry services also operates between British and Continental ports. Ferry crossings from the Continent are operated by **Stena Line, P&O European Ferries, Sally Line** and **Brittany Ferries**. Fast hovercraft services between Dover and Calais or Boulogne are run by **Hoverspeed**. **Seacat** services cross between Folkestone and Boulogne and between Newhaven and Dieppe. The shortest crossings are not necessarily the cheapest – you pay for both the speed of your journey and the convenience. If you

Cross-channel ferry

are travelling with your car you will need to check out the terms of your insurance cover.

Contact Brittany Ferries (0990 360360; Eurotunnel (0990 353535; Hoverspeed (01304 865000; P&O (0990 980 980; Sally (01843 595566; Seacat (01304 865000; Stena (0990 707070.

London's Airports

Passenger jet

LONDON'S TWO MAIN airports, Heathrow and Gatwick, are supported by Luton, Stansted and London City airport *(see pp358–9)*. Heathrow and Gatwick are both well connected with the city centre and have a range of facilities, from banks and bureaux de change to hotels, shops and restaurants. Find out which airport you'll be landing at so you can plan the last stages of your journey.

Customs channels at Heathrow

HEATHROW (LHR)

HEATHROW IN WEST London (airport information 020-8759 4321) is the world's busiest international airport. Mainly scheduled long-haul aircraft land there, and a fifth terminal is being planned to cope with the rising levels of air traffic to the UK. Money exchanging facilities are also found in all terminals.

All of the four terminals are linked to the Underground system by a variety of moving walkways, passageways and lifts. Just follow the clearly marked directions posted throughout the terminals and

you can't go wrong. London Underground runs a regular service on the Piccadilly line. The tube journey into central London normally takes about 40 minutes (add 10 minutes more from terminal 4).

The best way to travel into London from Heathrow is the

Signs for exits in Heathrow

Heathrow Express to Paddington. This operates 24 hours a day, with trains every 15 minutes from 9am until midnight and then every hour between midnight and 5.30am, and half-hourly thereafter until 9am. The journey time is 15 minutes

AIRPORT HOTELS

Forte Crest
(020-8759 2323.

Holiday Inn
(01895-445555.

Sheraton Skyline
See p285.

London Heathrow Hilton
(020-8759 7755.

Terminal 3, for long-haul flights (apart from British Airways) and SAS flights to Scandinavia, has 24-hour exchange facilities.

To M4 and A4 roads for London

Terminal 1 deals with British airlines' flights to Europe and within Britain.

Plan of Heathrow Airport
When leaving London be sure to check which terminal you need. Terminal 4 is some way from the others and therefore has its own Underground station.

Heathrow terminals 1, 2 and 3 station

Terminal 2 handles most European services of non-British airlines.

Heathrow terminal 4 station

Terminal 3 Departures

KEY

⊖ Underground station

🚌 Bus terminal (local services)

🚍 Coach station

P Short-term parking

⇌ Direction of traffic flow

Terminal 4 serves Concorde, British Airways intercontinental flights, and some flights to Paris, Athens and Amsterdam.

Sterling Hotel

GATWICK (LGW)

GATWICK AIRPORT (airport information: 0293-535 353) is located south of London, on the Surrey–Sussex border. Unlike Heathrow, it handles scheduled and charter flights.

A large volume of package holiday traffic passes through Gatwick. This can cause long queues at immigration desks and security checks, so make sure to leave plenty of time in which to check in on your return journey if you want to avoid being rushed. Make

Plan of Gatwick Airport

There are two terminals at Gatwick: north and south. They are linked by a free monorail service, and the journey between them takes only a couple of minutes. Near the railway station entrance (which, if you are not arriving by rail, is clearly marked) you will find boards that state which terminal serves your carrier.

Gatwick Express

Trains to London
Services to Victoria Station every 15 minutes; hourly throughout the night

Platform indicator for express railway service to London

certain, too, that you know which terminal your flight home leaves from.

Gatwick has fewer business facilities than Heathrow. On the positive side, however, it has a number of 24-hour restaurants, banks, exchange

KEY

✈	Railway station
🚍	Coach station
P	Short-term parking
🚓	Police station
⇒	Direction of traffic flow

facilities and duty-free shops located in both the north and south terminals.

Gatwick has convenient rail links with the capital, including Thameslink. The Gatwick Express train provides a fast, regular service into Victoria station. Allow about half an hour for the journey, but check (*see p356*) to find out off-peak variations.

Driving from Gatwick to central London can take a couple of hours. A taxi will cost from £50 to £60.

AIRPORT HOTELS

Chequers Thistle
📞 01293-786992.

Hilton International
📞 01293-518080.

Le Meridien
📞 01293-567070.

Hilton International

To A23 and M23 roads for London

Railway line

A23 road

Inter-terminal monorail link

To A23 and M23 roads for London

Forte Crest Hotel

Taxi rank

Coach station and arrivals pick-up (lower level)

Arrivals pick-up (lower level)

North terminal

South terminal

OTHER AIRPORTS SERVING LONDON

Luton and Stansted airports, both located to the north of London, are at present used principally by charter flights. Both airports have future plans for expansion. From Luton, connecting buses take passengers to the rail station, and from there trains run to King's Cross station. Alternatively, take a coach to Victoria. The half-hourly Stansted Express

train terminates at Liverpool Street station and there is a regular and efficient coach service to Victoria.

The relatively new London City Airport, in Docklands, is designed mainly for business travellers and operates short flights to Europe. It has particularly good business facilities and is only a short taxi (or helicopter) journey from the City.

One of two large hotels at Gatwick

Getting to the Millennium Dome

T HIS MAP SHOWS all the main transport links to the Dome. The site is
only 12 minutes by underground from Waterloo. There is direct
access by river boat from central London and Greenwich and a transit
link from Charlton station, plus cycle- and footpaths along the Thames.
The Dome site is entirely car-free, apart from pre-booked parking for
disabled visitors. There is a 3-km (2-mile) restricted parking zone
around the Dome.

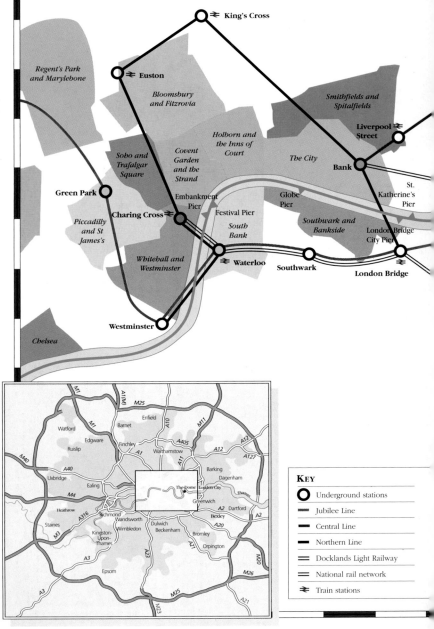

KEY

◯	Underground stations
▬	Jubilee Line
▬	Central Line
▬	Northern Line
═	Docklands Light Railway
═	National rail network
⇌	Train stations

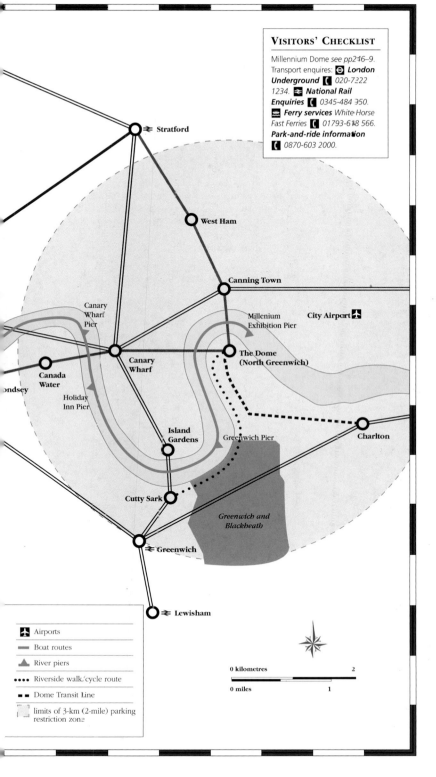

VISITORS' CHECKLIST

Millennium Dome *see pp246–9*.
Transport enquires: London
Underground 020-7222
1234. **National Rail**
Enquiries 0345-484 950.
Ferry services White-Horse
Fast Ferries 01793-618 566.
Park-and-ride information
0870-603 2000.

Stratford

West Ham

Canning Town

Canary
Wharf
Pier

Millenium
Exhibition Pier

City Airport

Canary
Wharf

The Dome
(North Greenwich)

Canada
Water

ondsey

Holiday
Inn Pier

Island
Gardens

Greenwich Pier

Charlton

Cutty Sark

*Greenwich and
Blackheath*

Greenwich

Lewisham

Airports
Boat routes
River piers
Riverside walk/cycle route
Dome Transit Line
limits of 3-km (2-mile) parking
restriction zone

0 kilometres   2

0 miles   1

Getting around London

LONDON'S PUBLIC TRANSPORT system is one of the busiest and largest in Europe, and has all the over-crowding problems to match. The worst and busiest times to travel are in the two rush hours, between 8am and 9.30am or later, from 4.30pm to 6.30pm. Within London and its suburbs, most of the public transport is organized by London Regional Transport (LRT). This consists of various types of bus, the Underground sys-

Routemaster bus

tem, and Network SouthEast (an overland train system which is operated by British Rail). For any information you require about fares, routes and timings of the various transport services, ring 020-7222 1234 *(see p345)*, or visit one of the LRT Travel Information Centres which are to be found at Euston, King's Cross and Victoria mainline stations as well as at Oxford Circus, Piccadilly Circus and Heathrow Airport.

THE TRANSPORT SYSTEM

THE UNDERGROUND (the "tube") is usually by far the quickest way of travelling around London. Services are, however, prone to delays and the trains are often crowded. Changing lines may involve a longish walk at some stations.

London is so large that some sights are a long way, even a bus journey, from any Underground station. There are also areas, often in the south, with no Underground service. Bus travel can be slow, and walking may be quicker.

Photocard and Weekly Travelcard

TRAVELCARDS

PUBLIC TRANSPORT in London is expensive compared with many cities in Europet. Short trips are relatively more expensive than the longer journeys; it is rarely worth-while getting on a tube to travel just one stop.

By far the most economical tickets are Travelcards – daily, weekly or monthly passes that allow unlimited travel on all forms of transport in the zones you require. (Six bands, called travel zones, extend from the city centre

into the outer suburbs; most of London's main sights are located in Zone One.)

Travelcards are bought in train or Underground stations *(see p362)* and at newsagents displaying a red "pass agent" sign. For weekly and monthly tickets you need a passport-sized photo for a Photocard. One-day Travel-cards (no photo needed) cannot be

used before 9.30am from Monday to Friday. There are no restrictions on weekly or monthly Travelcards. If you are in London for four days or more, a one- or two-zone weekly Travelcard is probably the most economical and convenient pass to buy.

You can also buy a "carnet" of ten single-zone tickets for roughly two-thirds full price.

LONDON ON FOOT

Once you get used to traffic driving on the left, London can be safely explored on foot but take care when crossing the road. There are two types of pedestrian crossing in London: striped zebra crossings marked by beacons, and push-button crossings at traffic lights. Traffic should stop for you if you are waiting at a zebra crossing, but at push-button crossings cars will not stop until the green man lights up. Look out for instructions written on the road; these tell you from which direction you can expect the traffic to come.

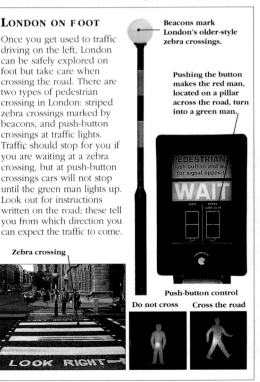

Beacons mark London's older-style zebra crossings.

Pushing the button makes the red man, located on a pillar across the road, turn into a green man.

Zebra crossing

Push-button control

Do not cross   **Cross the road**

Driving a Car in London

Sign for a car park

MOST VISITORS ARE BETTER off not driving in central London. Traffic moves at an average speed of about 11 mph (18 km/h) during the rush hour, and parking is hard to find. Many Londoners only take their car out at weekends and after 6.30pm on weekdays, when you are allowed to park on some single yellow lines and at parking meters free of charge. Remember that you must drive on the left.

Double yellow lines on road, meaning no parking at any time

PARKING REGULATIONS

PARKING IN London is scarce, and you should look closely at any restrictions (usually attached to lampposts). Meters close to the centre are expensive during working hours (usually 8.00am–6.30pm Mon–Sat). You will also need plenty of coins (see p349) to feed them. Two hours is usually the maximum time you can stay at any meter. National Car Parks (marked with the logo NCP) are available in central areas and are easy to find. NCP produces a free London Parking Guide showing its parks; write to 21 Bryanston Street, W1A 4NH or call 020-7499 7050.

You are not allowed to park along red routes or on double yellow lines at any time. Parking on single yellow lines is prohibited during working hours but you can park on them during the evenings or on Sundays provided you are not causing an obstruction. Resident permit zones are unenforceable outside office hours, but remove your car before 8am. Steer clear of any parking areas marked "card-holders only". Parking on pedestrian crossings is always forbidden. In Pay-and-Display areas, you should buy a ticket for the appropriate time span to display on your windscreen.

Parking meter

CLAMPING AND TOWING

IF YOU PARK illegally or allow a meter to run out, you may well find your car has been clamped. A large notice

slapped across your windscreen will inform you which Payment Centre you need to visit to get your car released (after paying a hefty fine). If you can't find your car at all, it is quite likely to have been removed by a team of London's feared and hated car impounders. Their speed and efficiency are remarkable, the cost and inconvenience to drivers enormous: it is rarely worth taking the risk. The main car pounds are at Hyde Park, Kensington and Camden Town. Ring 020-7747 7474 and you will be told if they do have your car and where-abouts it is being held.

Traffic Signs

Every driver should read the UK Highway Code *manual (available from bookshops) and familiarize themselves with London's traffic signs.*

Illegally parked car immobilized by wheel clamp

CAR HIRE AGENCIES

Avis
📞 020-7917 6700.

Eurodollar
📞 020-7278 2273.

Europcar
📞 08456-005 000.

Hertz
📞 020-7278 1588.

No stopping   **30 mph (48 km/h) speed limit**

No entry   **Give way to all vehicles**   **One-way traffic**   **No right turn allowed**

CYCLING AROUND LONDON

London's busy roads can be quite hazardous for cyclists, but the parks and quieter districts make excellent cycling routes. Use a solid lock to deter thieves, and wear weatherproof reflect-ive clothing. Cycle helmets are not compulsory but are strongly recommended. You might also wear a protective mask to counteract pollution. Bikes can be hired from **On Your Bike**.

Hire shop numbers and adresses On Your Bike, 52–54 Tooley St SE1. 📞 020-7378 6669.

Travelling by Underground

Underground sign outside a station

T HE UNDERGROUND system, known as the "tube" to Londoners, has 273 stations, each clearly marked with the Underground logo. Tube trains run every day, except Christmas Day, from about 5.30am until just after midnight, but a few lines or sections of lines have an irregular service. Check when the last train leaves if you are relying on it after 11.30pm. Fewer trains run on Sundays. It can occasionally be unpleasant travelling on the tube late at night.

London Underground train

Reading the Underground Map

The 11 Underground lines are colour-coded and maps (see inside cover) called Journey Planners are posted at every station. Maps of the central section are displayed in the trains. The map shows how to change lines to travel from where you are to any station on the Underground system. Some lines, such as the Victoria and Jubilee, are simple single-branch routes; others, such as the Northern line, have more than one branch. The Circle line is a continuous loop around central London. Distances shown on the map are not to scale and the routes that lines are seen to take should not be relied upon for directions.

Double circle, meaning two stations are linked

Station for changing between lines, or to British Rail train

Station serving two lines

HOW TO READ THE JOURNEY PLANNER MAPS *(see inside back cover)*

Intersection with British Rail

Intersection with other lines and British Rail

HOW TO READ CHARTS DISPLAYED IN CARRIAGES

Bakerloo
Northern
⇌ Charing Cross

BUYING A TICKET

If you are likely to be making more than two journeys a day on London's Underground, the best ticket to buy is a Travelcard *(see p360)*. You can also buy single tickets or return tickets either from the ticket office in each station or from one of the two types of automatic machines that are found in most stations. The large machines *(see below)* take coins and £5 or £10 notes, and normally give

change. You select the ticket type you need, then the station you are travelling to, and the cost of the fare is automatically displayed. The smaller machines only show a choice of fare prices from which you select the correct one for your journey. They do not take notes, seldom give change, and are geared towards regular Underground travellers, who know the cost of their journey in advance.

1 Select the type of ticket you need from those shown: adult or child, single, return, or one-day Travelcard.

2 Press the button for the station you want to travel to.

3 The fare is shown here. Also indicated is whether you need to give exact money or if change can be given.

4 Insert either coins or a bank note. The machine will give you change if it has enough coins.

5 Collect your tickets and any change.

Tickets
Keep your ticket – you will need it at the end of your journey.

MAKING A JOURNEY BY UNDERGROUND

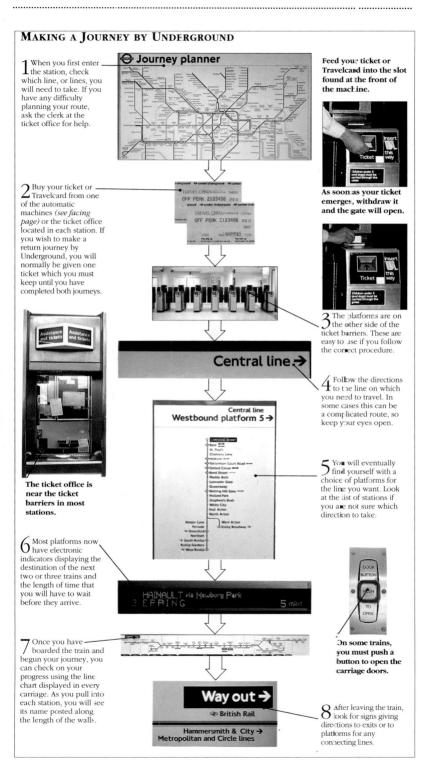

1 When you first enter the station, check which line, or lines, you will need to take. If you have any difficulty planning your route, ask the clerk at the ticket office for help.

⊖ Journey planner

Feed your ticket or Travelcard into the slot found at the front of the machine.

As soon as your ticket emerges, withdraw it and the gate will open.

2 Buy your ticket or Travelcard from one of the automatic machines (*see facing page*) or the ticket office located in each station. If you wish to make a return journey by Underground, you will normally be given one ticket which you must keep until you have completed both journeys.

3 The platforms are on the other side of the ticket barriers. These are easy to use if you follow the correct procedure.

The ticket office is near the ticket barriers in most stations.

Central line →

4 Follow the directions to the line on which you need to travel. In some cases this can be a complicated route, so keep your eyes open.

Central line Westbound platform 5 →

5 You will eventually find yourself with a choice of platforms for the line you want. Look at the list of stations if you are not sure which direction to take.

6 Most platforms now have electronic indicators displaying the destination of the next two or three trains and the length of time that you will have to wait before they arrive.

HAINAULT via Newbury Park
2 EPPING   5 mins

7 Once you have boarded the train and begun your journey, you can check on your progress using the line chart displayed in every carriage. As you pull into each station, you will see its name posted along the length of the walls.

On some trains, you must push a button to open the carriage doors.

Way out →
⇌ British Rail

Hammersmith & City →
Metropolitan and Circle lines

8 After leaving the train, look for signs giving directions to exits or to platforms for any connecting lines.

London's Buses

London Regional Transport symbol

ONE OF LONDON's most recognizable symbols is the old-fashioned, red double-decker Routemaster bus, but it is a less common sight than it once was. As a result of deregulation and privatization of the city's bus system, there are now many smaller modern buses, some single-decker and some not even red, carrying passengers on London's streets. If you are able to get a seat, a bus journey is an undemanding and enjoyable way of seeing London. If you are in a hurry, however, it can be frustrating. London's traffic is notoriously congested and slow-moving and bus journeys can take a long time, especially during rush hours (8–9.30am and 4.30–6.30pm).

FINDING THE RIGHT BUS

EACH BUS STOP in central London has a list of main destinations showing which bus routes you need. There may also be a local street plan with each nearby bus stop letter-coded. Make sure you catch a bus going in the right direction; if in doubt, check with the driver.

USING LONDON'S BUSES

BUSES PAUSE, even if nobody wants to get on or off, at stops marked with the LRT symbol *(see above)*, unless they are labelled "request" stops. Route numbers and destinations are displayed clearly on the front and rear of the bus. The newer buses have only a driver, who takes fares as passengers board. Routemaster services have both a driver and a conductor who collects fares during the journey. The driver or conductor will tell you the fare for your destination and give change (but not for large notes). You will be given a ticket valid only for that journey – if you change buses you have to pay again. Keep your ticket until the end of your journey

Bus Conductor
Conductors sell tickets on London's Routemaster buses.

in case an inspector boards. Buying a Travelcard *(see p360)* is more convenient especially if you are making several journeys.

When you want to get off the bus, ring the bell as the bus approaches the stop you require; on Routemasters the conductor will do this for you. Never get on or off a bus unless it is standing at a bus stop. If you are not sure which stop you need, ask the conductor or driver.

Bus Stops
Buses always pause at stops marked with the LRT symbol (far left). At request stops (below), hail the driver by raising your arm. In practice it pays to do this at any stop.

Tickets on Routemasters
The conductor will issue you with the right ticket for your journey. Try not to pay with a large note.

USEFUL BUS ROUTES

Several of London's bus routes are convenient for many of the capital's main sights and shops. If you arm yourself with a Travelcard and are in no particular hurry, sightseeing or shopping by bus can be great fun. The cost of a journey by public transport is far less than any of the charges levied by tour operators, but you won't have the commentary that tour companies give you as you pass sights *(see p344)*.

There are also some sights or areas in London that are inaccessible by Underground. Buses run regularly from the city centre to, for instance, the Albert Hall *(see p203)*, Chelsea *(see pp188–93)*, and Clerkenwell *(see p243)*.

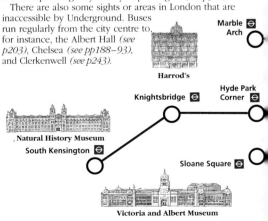

Marble Arch

Harrod's

Hyde Park Corner

Knightsbridge

Natural History Museum

South Kensington

Sloane Square

Victoria and Albert Museum

Routemaster Bus
Board these buses at the rear. The conductor asks for your fare after you have boarded and found a seat.

To stop the bus, press the bell located by the doors or near the stairs, just once.

Destinations are shown on the front and rear of buses.

To buy a ticket, have your money ready before you board.

Night Buses
These services run through the night from stops with this logo. One-day Travelcards are not valid on them.

New-Style Bus
These buses are controlled by the driver and do not have a conductor. The driver collects fares as passengers board.

NIGHT BUSES

LONDON'S NIGHT-TIME services run on several popular routes from 11pm until 6am. The routes are prefixed with the letter "N" before blue or yellow numbers. All these services pass through Trafalgar Square, so if you are out late, head there to get a ride at least part of the way home. Be sure to plan your journey carefully; London is so big that even if you board a bus going in the right direction you could end up completely lost, or a long walk from your accommodation. As always, make sure that you employ a little common sense when travelling on a night bus. Sitting all alone on the top deck is not a good idea; night buses never have a conductor. Travel information centres can supply you with details of routes and time-tables for night buses, which are also posted at bus stops.

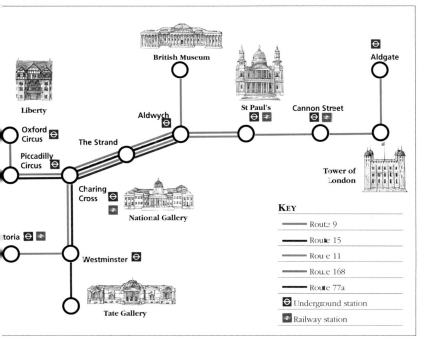

British Museum

Liberty

Aldgate

Oxford Circus

The Strand

Aldwych

St Paul's

Cannon Street

Piccadilly Circus

Charing Cross

National Gallery

Tower of London

...toria

Westminster

Tate Gallery

KEY

—— Route 9
—— Route 15
—— Route 11
—— Route 168
—— Route 77a
Ⓔ Underground station
⬱ Railway station

Seeing London by Rail

Paddington

Railway station sign

Londons's train service is used by many hundreds of thousands of commuters daily. As far as tourists are concerned, rail services are useful for trips to the outskirts of the capital, especially south of the river where the Underground hardly extends. Trains are ideal for longer excursions around Britain *(see pp358–9)*.

USEFUL ROUTES

Perhaps the most useful rail line for visitors to London is the one that starts off from Charing Cross or Cannon Street stations (services from here only run on weekdays) and goes via London Bridge to Greenwich *(see pp232–9)*.

The Thameslink service also connects Luton Airport with south London, Gatwick Airport and Brighton via West Hampstead and Blackfriars.

USING THE TRAINS

London has eight main railway stations serving the whole of the southeast and beyond *(see pp358–9)*. Rail services travel overground and vary between slow stopping trains, express services to major towns and Intercity trains which travel throughout the UK. Make sure that you study the platform indicators carefully so that you get on the most direct train to the correct destination.

Some train doors will open automatically, others at the touch of a button or else by means of a handle. To open the older-style manual doors from inside, you need to pull down the window and reach outside. Keep well away from the doors while the train is travelling, and if you have to stand, make sure you hold on firmly to a strap or hand-rail.

RAIL TICKETS

All tickets must be bought in person, either from a travel agent or from a railway station. Most credit cards are accepted. Queues for ticket offices can often be long, so use the automatic machines similar to those on the Underground *(see p362)*.

A bewildering range of train tickets exists, but two main options stand out: for travel within Greater London, Travelcards *(see p360)* offer the most flexibility, while for longer journeys, Cheap Day Return tickets offer excellent value compared to the standard return fares. However, these are both only obtainable and usable after 9.30am.

Cheap Day Return tickets

DAY TRIPS

Southeast England has a lot more besides the capital to offer visitors. Getting out of London is fast and very easy by rail. For details of sights ring the English Tourist Board *(see p345)*. Passenger Enquiries (020-7928 5100) will give you details of all their services.

Boating on the River Thames at Windsor Castle

Audley End
Village with a stunning Jacobean mansion nearby.
≷ *from Liverpool Street. 40 miles (64 km); 1 hr.*

Bath
Beautiful Georgian city which has escaped redevelopment. It also has Roman remains.
≷ *from Paddington. 107 miles (172 km); 1 hr 25 mins.*

Brighton
Lively and attractive seaside resort. See the Royal Pavilion.
≷ *from Victoria. 53 miles (85 km); 1 hr.*

Cambridge
University city with fine art gallery and ancient colleges.
≷ *from Liverpool Street or King's Cross. 54 miles (86 km); 1 hr.*

Canterbury
Its cathedral is one of England's oldest and greatest sights.
≷ *from Victoria. 84 miles (98 km); 1 hr 25 mins.*

Hatfield House
Elizabethan palace with remarkable contents.
≷ *from King's Cross or Moorgate. 21 miles (33 km); 20 mins.*

Oxford
Like Cambridge, famous for its ancient university.
≷ *from Paddington. 56 miles (86 km); 1 hr.*

Salisbury
Famous for its cathedral, Salisbury is within driving distance of Stonehenge.
≷ *from Waterloo. 84 miles (135 km); 1 hr 40 mins.*

St Albans
Once a great Roman city.
≷ *from King's Cross or Moorgate. 25 miles (40km); 30 mins.*

Windsor
Riverside town; royal castle damaged by fire in 1992.
≷ *from Paddington, change Slough. 20 miles (32 km); 30 mins.*

Getting a Taxi

LONDON'S WELL-KNOWN black cabs are almost as much of an institution as its red buses. But they, too, are being modernized, and you may well see blue, green, red or even white cabs, with some carrying advertising. Black-cab drivers have to take a stringent test on their knowledge of London's streets and its quickest traffic routes before they are awarded a licence. Contrary to popular opinion, they are also among London's safest drivers, if only because they are forbidden to drive a cab with damaged bodywork.

The modern colours of traditional London cabs

London taxi rank

FINDING A CAB

LICENSED CABS MUST carry a "For Hire" sign, which is lit up whenever they are free. You can ring for them, hail them on the streets or find them at ranks, especially near large stations and some major hotels. Raise your arm and wave purposefully. The cab will stop and you simply tell the driver your destination. If a cab stops, it must take you anywhere within a radius of 6 miles (9.6 km) as long as it is in the Metropolitan Police district, which includes most of the Greater London area and Heathrow Airport.

An alternative to black cabs are mini-cabs, saloon cars summoned by ringing a firm or going into one of their offices, which are usually open 24 hours a day. Do not take a mini-cab in the street as they often operate illegally, without proper insurance, and can be dangerous. Negotiate your fare before setting off. Mini-cab firms are listed in the Yellow Pages (see p352).

TAXI FARES

ALL LICENSED CABS have meters which will start ticking at around £1 as soon as the taxidriver accepts your custom. The fare increases by minute or for each 311 m (340 yds) travelled. Surcharges are then added for every piece of luggage, each extra passenger and unsocial hours such as late at night. Fares should be displayed in the vehicle.

USEFUL NUMBERS

Computer Cabs (licensed)
020-7286 0286.

Radio Taxis (licensed)
020-7272 0272.

Ladycabs (women-only drivers) 020-7254 3501.

Lost property
020-7833 0996.
Open 9am–4pm Mon–Fri.

Complaints
020-7230 1631.
You will need to know the cab's serial number.

The light, when lit, shows the cab is available and whether there is wheelchair access.

The meter displays your fare as it increases, and surcharges for extra passengers, luggage or unsocial hours. Fares are the same in all licensed cabs.

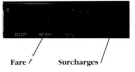

Fare / Surcharges

Licensed Cabs
London's cabs are a safe way of travelling around the capital. They have two fold-down seats, can carry a maximum of five passengers and have ample luggage space.

STREET FINDER

T HE MAP REFERENCES given with all sights, hotels, restaurants, shops and entertainment venues described in this book refer to the maps in this section *(see* How Map References Work *opposite)*. A complete index of street names and all the places of interest marked on the maps can be found on the following pages.

The key map shows the area of London covered by the *Street Finder*, with the postal codes of all the various districts. The maps include the sightseeing areas (which are colour-coded), as well as the whole of central London with all the districts important for hotels, restaurants, pubs and entertainment venues.

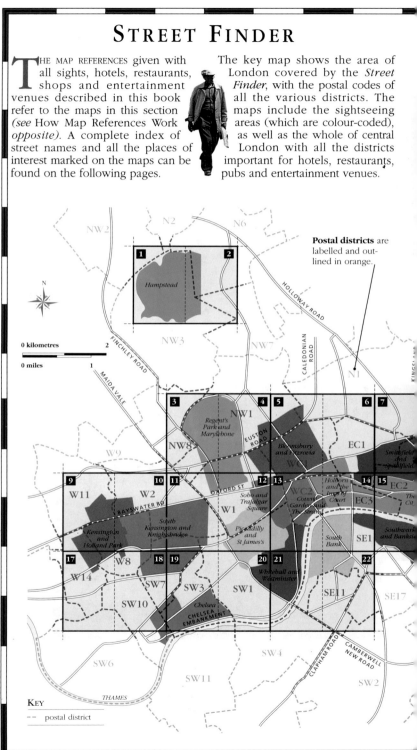

Postal districts are labelled and outlined in orange.

KEY

- - - postal district

HOW THE MAP REFERENCES WORK

The first figure tells you which Street Finder map to turn to.

Wesley's House and Chapel ⑫

49 City Rd EC1. **Map 7** **B4**.
☎ 020-7253 2262. ⊖ *Old St.*
House open *10am–4pm Mon–Sat.*
Adm charge. 📷 ⚡ ✝ *11 am Sun.*
💾 ⓘ *Films, exhibitions.*

A letter and number give the grid reference. Letters go across the map's top and bottom; figures on its sides.

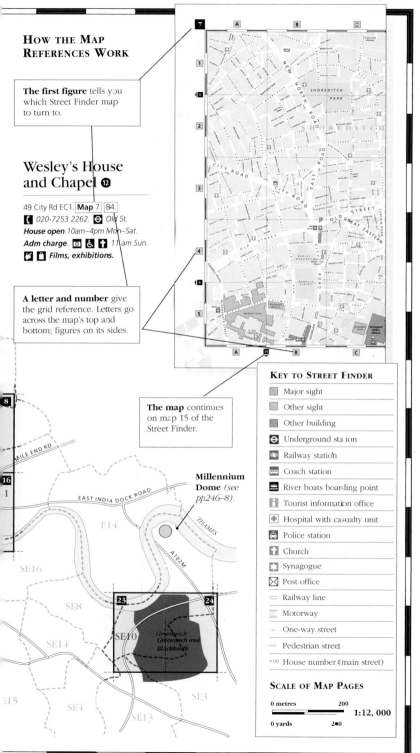

The map continues on map 15 of the Street Finder.

Millennium Dome *(see pp246–8).*

KEY TO STREET FINDER

	Major sight
	Other sight
	Other building
⊖	Underground station
⭧	Railway station
🚌	Coach station
⛴	River boats boarding point
ℹ	Tourist information office
✚	Hospital with casualty unit
🏠	Police station
✝	Church
✡	Synagogue
⊠	Post office
═	Railway line
▬	Motorway
⟶	One-way street
▬	Pedestrian street
◄130	House number (main street)

SCALE OF MAP PAGES

0 metres	200	
		1:12, 000
0 yards	200	

Street Finder Index

Dennis Severs House E1	8 D5
Denny St SE11	22 E2
Denyer St SW3	19 B2
Derbyshire St E2	8 F3
Dereham Pl EC2	8 D4
Dericote St E8	8 F1
Derry St W8	10 D5
Design Museum SE1	16 E4
Devonshire Clo W1	4 E5
Devonshire Dri SE10	23 A4
Devonshire Pl W1	4 D5
Devonshire Sq EC2	16 D1
Devonshire St W1	4 E5
Devonshire Terr W2	10 F2
Dewey St N1	6 E1
Diamond Terr SE10	23 B4
Dickens House Museum WC1	6 D4
Dilke St SW3	19 C4
Dingley Rd EC1	7 A3
Dinsdale Rd SE3	24 E2
Disbrowe Rd W6	17 A4
Disney Pl SE1	15 A4
Diss St E2	8 E2
Ditch Alley SE10	23 A4
Dock St E1	16 E2
Dockhead SE1	16 E5
Dr Johnson's House EC4	14 E1
Doddington Gro SE17	22 F3
Doddington Pl SE17	22 F4
Dodson St SE1	14 E5
Dolben St SE1	14 F4
Dolphin Sq SW1	21 A3
Dombey St WC1	5 C5
Donegal St N1	6 D2
Donne Pl SW3	19 B2
Doon St SE1	14 E3
Doric Way NW1	5 A3
Dorset Rd SW8	21 C5
	22 D5
Dorset St NW1, W1	3 C5
	3 C5
Doughty Ms W1	6 D4
Doughty St WC1	6 D4
Douglas St SW1	21 A2
Douro Pl W8	10 E5
Dove House St SW3	19 A3
Dove Row E2	8 F1
Dover St W1	12 F3
Down St W1	12 E4
Downing St SW1	13 B4
Downshire Hill NW3	1 C5
Draycott Ave SW3	19 B2
Draycott Pl SW3	19 C2
Draycott Terr SW3	19 C2
Drayton Gdns SW10	18 F3
Druid St SE1	16 D4
Drummond Cres NW1	5 A3
Drummond Gate SW1	21 B3
Drummond St NW1	4 F4
	5 A3
Drury La WC2	13 C1
Drysdale St E2	8 D3
Duchess of Bedford's Wlk W8	9 C5
Duchess St W1	4 E5
Duchy St SE1	14 E3
Dufferin St EC1	7 B4
Duke Humphrey Rd SE3	24 D5
Duke of Wellington Pl SW1	12 D5
Duke of York St SW1	13 A3
Duke St SW1	12 F3
Duke St W1	12 D2
Duke St Hill SE1	15 B3
Duke's La W8	10 D4
Duke's Rd WC1	5 B3
Duke's Pl EC3	16 D1
Dunbridge St E2	8 F4
Duncan Rd E8	8 F1
Duncan St N1	6 F2

Duncan Terr N1	6 F2
Dunloe St E2	8 E2
Dunraven St W1	11 C2
Dunston Rd E8	8 D1
Dunston St E8	8 D1
Durant St E2	8 F2
Durham St SE11	22 D3
Durham Terr W2	10 D1
Durward St E1	8 F5
Dutton St SE10	23 B4
Dyott St WC1	13 B1

E

Eagle Ct EC1	6 F5
Eagle St WC1	13 C1
Eagle Wharf Rd N1	7 A2
Eamont St NW8	3 B2
Earl St EC2	7 C5
Earlham St WC2	13 B2
Earl's Court Exhibition Centre SW5	17 C3
Earl's Court Gdns SW5	18 D2
Earl's Court Rd SW5, W8	18 D2
	17 C1
Earl's Court Sq SW5	18 D3
Earl's Terr W8	17 B1
Earl's Wlk W8	17 C1
Earlswood St SE10	24 D1
Earsby St W14	17 A2
East Ferry Rd E14	23 A1
East Heath NW3	1 B3
East Heath Rd NW3	1 B4
East Pier E1	16 F4
East Rd N1	7 B3
East Smithfield E1	16 E3
East Tenter St E1	16 E2
Eastbourne Ms W2	10 F1
Eastbourne Terr W2	10 F1
Eastcastle St W1	12 F1
	13 A1
Eastcheap EC3	15 C2
Eastney St SE10	23 C1
Eaton Gate SW1	20 D2
Eaton La SW1	20 E1
Eaton Ms SW1	20 D1
	20 E1
Eaton Ms North SW1	20 D1
Eaton Ms West SW1	20 D2
Eaton Pl SW1	20 D1
Eaton Sq SW1	20 D1
Eaton Terr SW1	20 D2
Ebbisham Dri SW8	22 D4
Ebor St E1	8 D4
Ebury Bridge SW1	20 E2
Ebury Bridge Rd SW1	20 E3
Ebury Ms SW1	20 E1
Ebury Sq SW1	20 E2
Ebury St SW1	20 E2
Eccleston Bridge SW1	20 E2
Eccleston Ms SW1	20 D1
Eccleston Pl SW1	20 E2
Eccleston Sq SW1	20 F2
Eccleston St SW1	20 E1
Edge St W8	9 C4
Edgware Rd W2	3 A5
	11 B1
Edith Gro SW10	18 E4
Edith Rd W14	17 A2
Edith Terr SW10	18 E5
Edith Vlls W14	17 B2
Edwardes Sq W8	17 C1
Effie Rd SW6	17 C5
Egerton Cres SW3	19 B1
Egerton Dri SE10	23 A4
Egerton Gdns SW3	19 B1
Egerton Pl SW3	19 B1
Egerton Terr SW3	19 B1
Elaine Gro NW5	2 E5
Elcho St SW11	19 B5
Elder St E1	8 D5
Eldon Gro NW3	1 B5
Eldon Rd W8	18 E1
Eldon St EC2	7 C5
Elgin Cres W11	9 A2

Elia St N1	6 F2
Eliot Hill SE13	23 B5
Eliot Pl SE3	24 D5
Eliot Vale SE3	23 C5
Elizabeth Bridge SW1	20 E2
Elizabeth St SW1	20 E2
Ellen St E1	16 F2
Ellerdale Clo NW3	1 A5
Ellerdale Rd NW3	1 A5
Elliott's Row SE11	22 F1
Elm Pk Gdns SW10	18 F3
	19 A3
Elm Pk Rd SW3	18 F4
	19 A3
Elm Pl SW7	18 F3
Elm St WC1	6 D4
Elsham Rd W14	9 A5
Elvaston Pl SW7	18 E1
Elverson Rd SE8	23 A5
Elverton St SW1	21 A1
Elwin St E2	8 E3
Elystan Pl SW3	19 B2
Elystan St SW3	19 B2
Emba St SE16	16 F5
Embankment Gdns SW3	19 C4
Emerald St WC1	6 D5
Emerson St SE1	15 A3
Emma St E2	8 F2
Emperor's Gate SW7	18 E1
Endell St WC2	13 B1
Enderby St SE10	24 D1
Endsleigh Gdns WC1	5 A4
Endsleigh St WC1	5 A4
Enford St W1	3 B5
English Grounds SE1	15 C4
Enid St SE16	16 E5
Ennismore Gdns SW7	11 A5
Ennismore Gdns Ms SW7	11 A5
Ensign St E1	16 F2
Epirus Rd SW6	17 C5
Epworth St EC2	7 C4
Erasmus St SW1	21 B2
Errol St EC1	7 B4
Essex Rd N1	6 F1
Essex St WC2	14 D2
Essex Vlls W8	9 C5
Estcourt Rd SW6	17 B5
Estelle Rd NW3	2 E5
Esterbrooke St SW1	21 A2
Eustace Rd SW6	17 C5
Euston Rd NW1	4 F4
	5 A4
Euston Sq NW1	5 A3
Euston St NW1	5 A4
Evelyn Gdns SW7	18 F3
Evelyn Wlk N1	7 B2
Eversholt St NW1	4 F2
Eversholt St NW1	5 A3
Ewer St SE1	15 A4
Exeter St WC2	13 C2
Exhibition Rd SW7	11 A5
	19 A1
Exton St SE1	14 E4
Eyre St Hill EC1	6 E4
Ezra St E2	8 E3

F

Fabian Rd SW6	17 B5
Fair St SE1	16 D4
Fairclough St E1	16 F1
Fairholme Rd W14	17 A3
Fakruddin St E1	8 F4
Falconwood Ct SE3	24 E5
Falkirk St N1	8 D2
Fan Museum SE10	23 B3
Fane St W14	17 B4
Fann St EC1	7 A5
Fanshaw St N1	7 C3
Faraday Museum W1	12 F3
Farm La SW6	17 C5
Farm St W1	12 E3
Farmer's Rd SE5	22 F5
Farncombe St SE16	16 F5
Farnham Royal SE11	22 D3

Farringdon La EC1	6 E4
Farringdon Rd EC1	6 E4
Farringdon St EC4	14 F1
Fashion St E1	8 E5
Faunce St SE17	22 F3
Fawcett St SW10	18 E4
Feathers Pl SE10	23 C2
Featherstone St EC1	7 B4
Felton St N1	7 B1
Fenchurch Ave EC3	15 C2
Fenchurch Bldgs EC3	15 C2
Fenchurch St EC3	15 C2
	16 D2
Fentiman Rd SW8	21 C4
	22 D5
Fenton House NW3	1 A4
Fernshaw Rd SW10	18 E4
Ferry St E14	23 B1
Festival/South Bank Pier SE1	14 D3
Fetter La EC4	14 E1
Field Rd W6	17 A4
Fieldgate St E1	16 F1
Filmer Rd SW6	17 B5
Finborough Rd SW10	18 E4
Fingal St SE10	24 F1
Finsbury Circus EC2	7 B5
	15 B1
Finsbury Mkt EC2	7 C5
Finsbury Pavement EC2	7 B5
Finsbury Sq EC2	7 B5
Finsbury St EC2	7 B5
First St SW3	19 B1
Fisherton St NW8	3 A4
Fishmongers' Hall EC3	15 B2
Fitzalan St SE11	22 D2
Fitzgeorge Ave W14	17 A2
Fitzjames Ave W14	17 A2
Fitzjohn's Ave NW3	1 B5
Fitzroy Pk N6	2 E1
Fitzroy Sq W1	4 F4
Fitzroy St W1	4 F5
Flask Wlk NW3	1 B5
Flaxman Terr WC1	5 B3
Fleet Rd NW3	2 D5
Fleet St EC4	14 E1
Fleming Rd SE17	22 F4
Fleur de Lis St E1	8 D5
Flitcroft St WC2	13 B1
Flood St SW3	19 B3
Flood Wlk SW3	19 B3
Floral St WC2	13 C2
Florence Nightingale Museum SE1	14 D5
Florida St E2	8 F3
Flower Wlk, The SW7	10 F5
Foley St W1	4 F5
Folgate St E1	8 D5
Forbes St E1	16 F2
Fordham St E1	16 F1
Fore St EC2	7 B5
Foreign & Common- wealth Office SW1	13 B4
Forset St W1	11 B1
Forston St N1	7 B2
Forsyth Gdns SE17	22 F4
Fortune St EC1	7 A4
Foster La EC2	15 A1
Foubert's Pl W1	12 F2
Foulis Terr SW7	19 A2
Fount St SW8	21 B5
Fountains, The W2	10 F3
Fournier St E1	8 E5
Foxley Rd SW9	22 E5
Foyle Rd SE3	24 E2
Frampton St NW8	3 A4
Francis St SW1	20 F1
	21 A1
Franklins Row SW3	19 C3
Frazier St SE1	14 E5
Frederick St WC1	6 D3
Friend St EC1	6 F3
Frith St W1	13 A2
Frognal NW3	1 A5
Frognal Gdns NW3	1 A5

Each place name is followed by its postal district, and then by its Street Finder reference

Each place name is followed by its postal district, and then by its Street Finder reference

Each place name is followed by its postal district, and then by its Street Finder reference

Each place name is followed by its postal district, and then by its Street Finder reference

Upper Brook St W1 12 D2
Upper Cheyne Row SW3 19 B4
Upper Grosvenor St W1 12 D3
Upper Ground SE1 14 E3
Upper Marsh SE1 14 D5
Upper Montagu St W1 3 C5
Upper Phillimore Gdns W8 9 C5
Upper St Martin's La WC2 13 B2
Upper Thames St EC4 15 A2
Upper Wimpole St W1 4 D5
Upper Woburn Pl WC1 5 B4
US Embassy W1 12 D2
Uxbridge St W8 9 C3

V

Vale,The SW3 19 A4
Vale of Health NW3 1 B3
Valentine Pl SE1 14 F5
Vallance Rd E1,E2 8 F4
Vanbrugh Fields SE3 24 E3
Vanbrugh Hill SE3 24 E2
Vanbrugh Hill SE10 24 E1
Vanbrugh Pk SE3 24 E3
Vanbrugh Pk Rd SE3 24 F3
Vanbrugh Pk Rd West SE3 24 E3
Vanbrugh Terr SE3 24 F4
Vane Clo NW3 1 B5
Vanston Pl SW6 17 C5
Varndell St NW1 4 F3
Vassall Rd SW9 22 E5
Vaughan Way E1 16 F3
Vauxhall Bridge SW1 21 B3
Vauxhall Bridge Rd SW1, SE1 20 F1
21 A2
Vauxhall Gro SW8 21 C4
Vauxhall Park SW8 21 C4
Vauxhall St SE11 22 D3
Vauxhall Wlk SE11 21 C3
Vere St W1 12 E1
Vereker Rd W14 17 A3
Vernon Rise WC1 6 D3
Vernon St W14 17 A2
Vestry St N1 7 B3
Vicarage Gate W8 10 D4
Victoria & Albert Museum SW7 19 A1
Victoria Embankment EC4 14 E2
Victoria Embankment SW1 13 C4
Victoria Embankment WC2 13 C3
Victoria Embankment Gdns WC2 13 C3
Victoria Gro W8 18 E1
Victoria Rd W8 10 E5
18 E1
Victoria St SW1 13 B5
20 F1
21 A1
Victoria Tower Gardens SW1 21 C1
Villiers St WC2 13 C3
Vince St EC1 7 C3
Vincent Sq SW1 21 A2
Vincent St SW1 21 A2
Vincent Terr N1 6 F2
Vine La SE1 16 D4
Vine St EC3 16 D2
Vintner's Pl EC4 15 A2
Virginia Rd E2 8 D3
Voss St E2 8 F3

W

Wakefield St WC1 5 C4
Wakley St EC1 6 F3
Walbrook EC4 15 B2
Walcot Sq SE11 22 E1
Waldorf Hotel WC2 13 C2
Walham Gro SW6 17 C5
Wallace Collection W1 12 D1
Walmer Rd W11 9 A3
Walnut Tree Rd SE10 24 E1
Walnut Tree Wlk SE11 22 D1
Walpole St SW3 19 C3
Walton Pl SW3 19 C1
Walton St SW3 19 B2
Wandon Rd SW6 18 E5
Wandsworth Rd SW8 21 B5
Wansdown Pl SW6 18 D5
Wapping High St E1 16 F4
Wardour St W1 13 A2
Warham St SE5 22 F5
Warner Pl E2 8 F2
Warner St EC1 6 E4
Warren St W1 4 F4
Warwick Gdns W14 17 B1
Warwick La EC4 14 F1
Warwick Rd SW5 18 D3
Warwick Rd W14 17 B1
Warwick Sq SW1 20 F2
Warwick St W1 12 F2
Warwick Way SW1 20 F2
Wat Tyler Rd SE10 23 B5
Waterford Rd SW6 18 D5
Waterloo Bridge SE1,WC2 14 D3
Waterloo Pl SW1 13 A3
Waterloo Rd SE1 14 E4
Waterson St E2 8 D3
Watling St EC4 15 A2
Weaver St E1 8 E4
Weavers La SE1 16 D4
Webb Rd SE3 24 E2
Webber Row SE1 14 E5
Webber St SE1 14 E4
15 A5
Weighouse St W1 12 D2
Welbeck St W1 12 D1
Well Rd NW3 1 B4
Well Wlk NW3 1 B4
Welland St SE10 23 B2
Weller St SE1 15 A5
Wellesley Terr N1 7 A3
Wellington Arch W1 12 D4
Wellington Bldgs SW1 20 E3
Wellington Pl NW8 3 A3
Wellington Rd NW8 3 A2
Wellington Row E2 8 E3
Wellington Sq SW3 19 C3
Wellington St WC2 13 C2
Wells Rise NW8 3 C1
Wells St W1 12 F1
Wenlock Basin N1 7 A2
Wenlock Rd N1 7 A2
Wenlock St N1 7 B2
Wentworth St E1 16 D1
Werrington St NW1 5 A2
Wesley's House & Chapel EC1 7 B4
West Sq SE11 22 F1
West St WC2 13 B2
West Cromwell Rd SW5,W14 17 B3
West Eaton Pl SW1 20 D1
West Ferry Rd E14 23 A1
West Gro SE10 23 B4
West Harding St EC4 14 E1
West Heath NW3 1 A3
West Heath Rd NW3 1 A4
West Hill Ct N6 2 E3
West Hill Pk N6 2 E2
West Pier E1 16 F4
West Smithfield EC1 14 F1
West Tenter St E1 16 E2
Westbourne Cres W2 10 F2
Westbourne Gdns W2 10 D1
Westbourne Gro W2 10 D2
Westbourne Gro W11 9 B2
Westbourne Pk Rd W2 10 D1
Westbourne Pk Rd W11 9 B1
Westbourne Pk Vlls W2 10 D1
Westbourne St W2 11 A2
Westbourne Terr W2 10 E1
Westcombe Hill SE10 24 F1
Westcombe Pk Rd SE3 24 E2
Westcott Rd SE17 22 F4
Westerdale Rd SE10 24 F1
Westgate Terr SW10 18 D3
Westgrove La SE10 23 B4
Westland Pl N1 7 B3
Westminster Abbey SW1 13 B5
Westminster Bridge SE1, SW1 13 C5
Westminster Bridge Rd SE1 14 D5
Westminster Cathedral SW1 20 F1
Westminster Hospital SW1 21 B1
Westminster School Playing Fields SW1 21 A2
Westmoreland Pl SW1 20 E3
Westmoreland St W1 4 D5
Westmoreland Terr SW1 20 E3
Weston Rise WC1 6 D3
Weston St SE1 15 C4
Westway A40(M) W10 9 A1
Wetherby Gdns SW5 18 E2
Wetherby Pl SW7 18 E2
Weymouth Ms W1 4 E5
Weymouth St W1 4 E5
Weymouth Terr E2 8 E2
Wharf Pl E2 8 F1
Wharf Rd N1 7 A2
Wharfdale Rd N1 5 C2
Wharton St WC1 6 D3
Wheatsheaf La SW8 21 C5
Wheler St E1 8 D4
Whetstone Pk WC2 14 D1
Whiston Rd E2 8 D1
Whitbread Brewery EC2 7 B5
Whitcomb St WC2 13 A3
White Lion St N1 6 E2
White's Row E1 8 D5
Whitechapel Art Gallery E1 16 E1
Whitechapel High St E1 16 E1
Whitechapel Rd E1 8 F5
16 E1
Whitechurch La E1 16 E1
Whitecross St EC1,EC2 7 A4
Whitfield St W1 4 F4
Whitefriars St EC4 14 E2
Whitehall SW1 13 B3
Whitehall Ct SW1 13 C4
Whitehall Pl SW1 13 B4
Whitehall Theatre SW1 13 B3
Whitehead's Gro SW3 19 B2
White's Grounds SE1 16 D4
Whitfield Rd SE3 23 C5
Whitfield St W1 5 A5
Whitgift St SE11 21 C2
Whitmore Rd N1 7 C1
Whitworth St SE10 24 D1
Wicker St E1 16 F2
Wickham St SE11 22 D3
Wicklow St WC1 5 C3
Wigmore Hall W1 12 E1
Wigmore St W1 12 D1
Wilcox Rd SW8 21 B5
Wild Ct WC2 13 C1
Wild St WC2 13 C1
Wild's Rents SE1 15 C5
Wildwood Gro NW3 1 A2
Wildwood Rise NW11 1 A1
Wildwood Rd NW11 1 A1
Wilfred St SW1 12 F5
Wilkinson St SW8 21 C5
William St SW1 11 C5
William IV St WC2 13 B3
William Rd NW1 4 F3
Willoughby Rd NW3 1 B5
Willow Pl SW1 20 F2
Willow Rd NW3 1 C4
Willow St EC2 7 C4
Wilmer Gdns N1 7 C1
Wilmer Gdns N1 8 D1
Wilmington Ms SW1 11 C5
Wilmington Sq WC1 6 E3
Wilsham St W11 9 A3
Wilkes St E1 8 E5
Wilson Gro SE16 16 F5
Wilson St EC2 7 C5
Wilton Cres SW1 12 D5
Wilton Pl SW1 12 D5
Wilton Rd SW1 20 F1
Wilton Row SW1 12 D5
Wilton Sq N1 7 B1
Wiltshire Row N1 7 B1
Wimborne St N1 7 B2
Wimpole Ms W1 4 E5
Wimpole St W1 4 E5
12 E1
Winchester Clo SE17 22 F2
Winchester St SW1 20 E3
Wincott St SE11 22 E2
Windmill Hill NW3 1 A4
Windmill Wlk SE1 14 E4
Windsor Terr N1 7 A3
Winfield House NW1 3 B3
Winforton St SE10 23 B4
Winnington Rd N2 1 B1
Winsland St W2 10 F1
11 A1
Woburn Pl WC1 5 B4
Woburn Sq WC1 5 B4
Woburn Wlk WC1 5 B4
Wolseley St SE1 16 E5
Wood Clo E2 8 F4
Wood St EC2 15 A1
Woodbridge St EC1 6 F4
Woodland Gro SE10 24 D1
Woodlands Pk Rd SE10 24 D2
Woods Ms W1 12 D2
Woodseer St E1 8 E5
Woodsford Sq W14 9 A4
Woodsome Rd NW5 2 F4
Woodstock St W1 12 E2
Woolwich Rd SE10 24 E1
Wootton St SE1 14 E4
Worfield St SW11 19 B5
World's End Pas SW10 18 F5
Wormwood St EC2 15 C1
Woronzow Rd NW8 3 A1
Worship St EC2 7 C4
Wren St WC1 6 D4
Wright's La W8 10 D5
Wycherley Clo SE3 24 E3
Wyclif St EC1 6 F3
Wyldes Clo NW11 1 A2
Wynan Rd E14 23 A1
Wyndham Rd SE5 22 F5
Wyndham St W1 3 C5
Wynford Rd N1 6 D2
Wynyatt St EC1 6 F3
Wyvil Rd SW8 21 B5

Y

Yardley St WC1 6 E4
Yeoman's Row SW3 19 B1
York Gate NW1 4 D4
York House Pl W8 10 D4
York Rd SE1 14 D4
York St W1 3 B5
York Ter East NW1 4 D4
York Ter West NW1 4 D4
York Way N1 5 C1
Yorkton St E2 8 E2
Young St W8 10 D5

Each place name is followed by its postal district, and then by its Street Finder reference

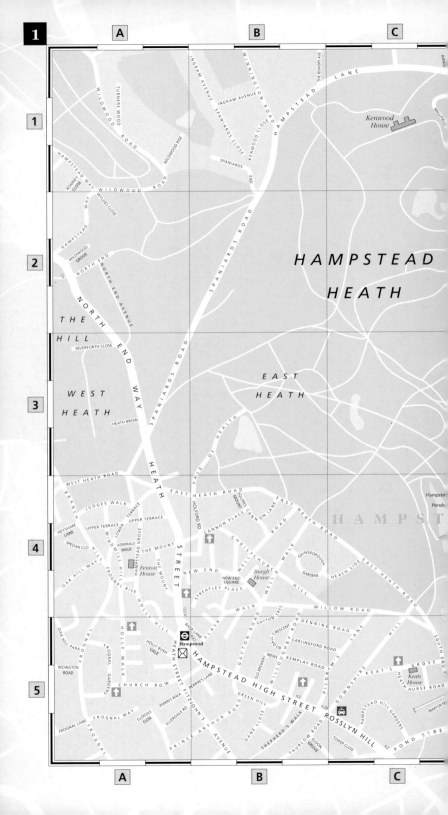

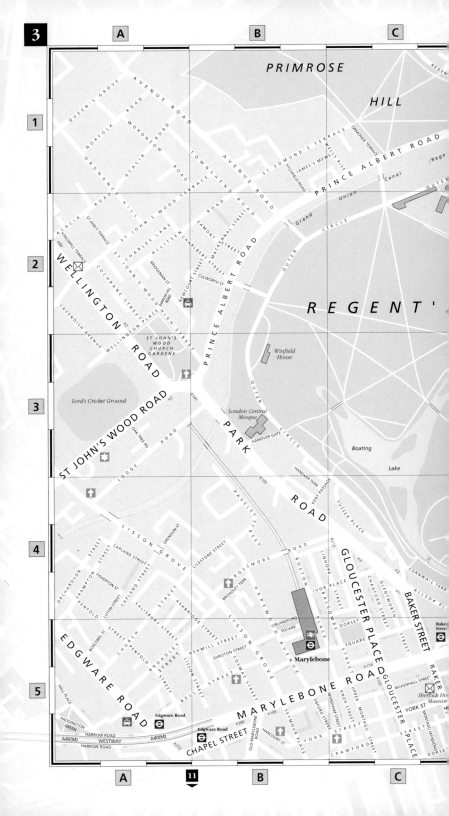

3

A　　　B　　　C

1

PRIMROSE

HILL

QUEEN'S GROVE
AVENUE ROAD
NORFOLK ROAD
WORONZOW ROAD
ORDNANCE HILL
ACACIA ROAD
TOWNSHEND ROAD
AVENUE ROAD
ST EDMUND'S TERRACE
WELLS RISE
FITCHLEY ROAD
JAMES'S MEWS
ORMONDE TERRACE
STEDMUND'S TERRACE
PRINCE ALBERT ROAD
Regent
REGEN

Union Canal

Grand

OUTER

2

WELLINGTON ROAD
ACACIA
KINGSMILL TERRACE
ST ANN'S TERRACE
ST JOHN'S WOOD TERRACE
ST CHARLES LANE
COCHRANE STREET
ST JOHN'S WOOD HIGH STREET
ALLITSEN ROAD
ALDON HILL
BRIDGEMAN ST
NEWCOURT STREET
CHARLBERT STREET
MACKENNAL STREET
EAMONT STREET
CULWORTH ST
PRINCE ALBERT ROAD
CIRCLE
OUTER

R E G E N T '

Winfield House

3

CAVENDISH AVENUE
WELLINGTON PLACE
WELLINGTON ROAD
ST JOHN'S WOOD CHURCH GARDENS
Lord's Cricket Ground
ST JOHN'S WOOD ROAD
OAK TREE RD
LODGE ROAD
London Central Mosque
HANOVER GATE
OUTER CIRCLE
P A R K
HANOVER TERR
KENT PASSAGE
Boating
Lake

4

LISSON GROVE
ORCHARDSON STREET
FRAMPTON STREET
FISHERTON ST
CAPLAND STREET
GRENDON ST
LUTON STREET
CAPLAND STREET
LILESTONE STREET
PENFOLD STREET
ASHBRIDGE STREET
SALISBURY STREET
PAVELEY STREET
ROSSMORE ROAD
BROADLEY TERR
HAREWO ROAD
BOSTON
ROAD
R O A D
SUSSEX PLACE
IVOR PLACE
LINHOPE STREET
CHAGFORD STREET
GLENWORTH STREET
BALCOMBE STREET
CORNWALL TERR
ALLSOP PL
BAKER STREET
Baker Street

5

EDGWARE ROAD
HALL PLACE
BOSCOBEL ST
CHURCH STREET
PENFOLD STREET
CHAPEL STREET
BROADLEY STREET
ASHMILL STREET
BELL STREET
LISSON STREET
SHROTON STREET
COSWAY STREET
BLANDFORD SQUARE
Marylebone
DORSET SQUARE
GLOUCESTER PLACE
BICKENHALL STREET
SherLock Holmes Museum
BAKER STREET
YORK ST
UPPER MONTAGU STREET
MONTAGU MANSIONS
KNOX STREET
WYNDHAM STREET
ENFORD STREET
SEYMOUR PLACE
YORK
HARCOURT ST
OLD MARYLEBONE ROAD
M A R Y L E B O N E   R O A D
CRAWFORD STREET
DORSE

PADDINGTON GREEN
HARROW ROAD
WESTWAY
A40(M)
HARROW ROAD
A40(M)
Edgware Road
Edgware Road
CHAPEL STREET

A　　　　　　B　　　C

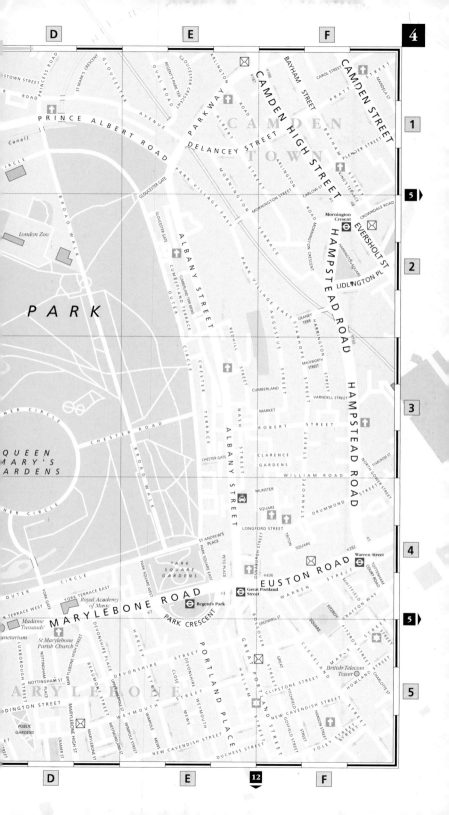

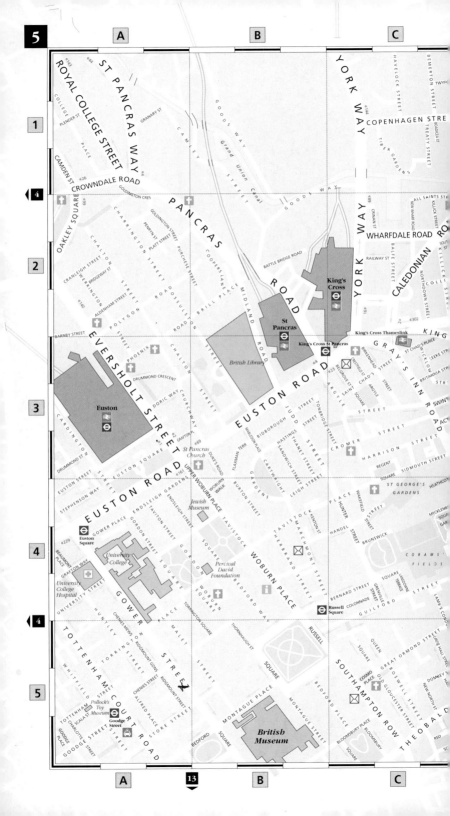

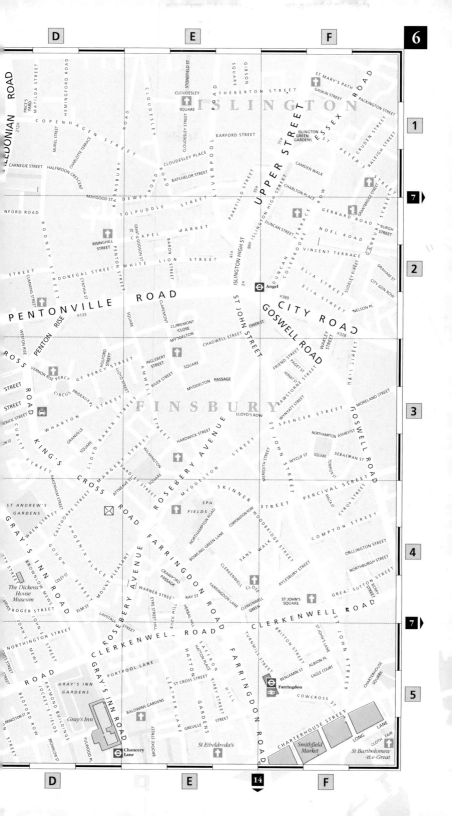

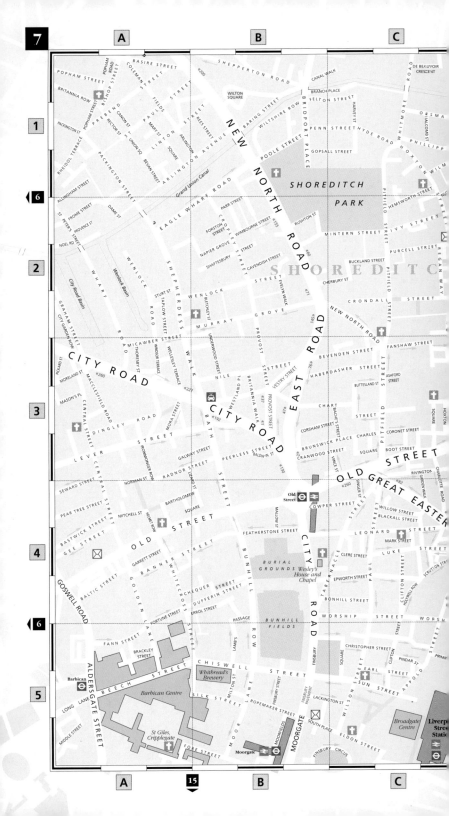

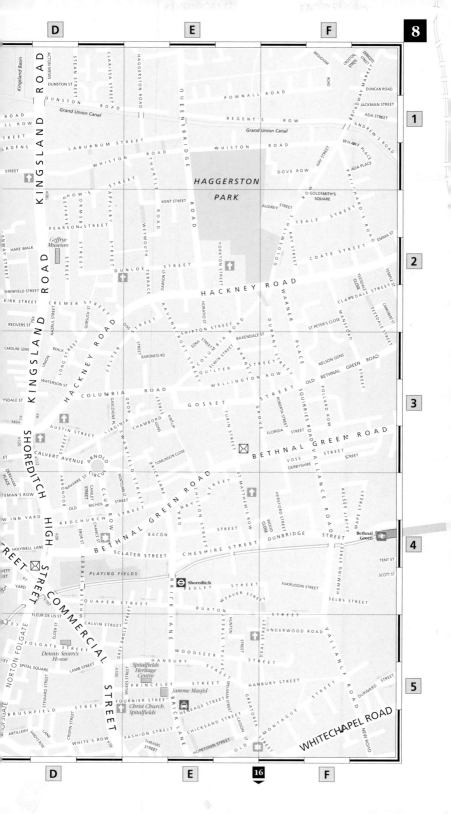

Kingsland Basin
ACTON STREET
SWAN STREET
STEAN STREET
DUNSTON ROAD
CLARISSA STREET
HAGGERSTON ROAD
BROUGHAM ROAD
CROSTON STREET
DERBYSHIRE STREET
DUNCAN ROAD

D U N S T O N   R O A D

POWNALL ROAD

BROADWAY MARKET
JACKMAN STREET

Grand Union Canal

R E G E N T ' S   R O W

ANDREW'S ROAD
ADA STREET

1

KINGSLAND ROAD

ROAD
LL ROW
STREET
ARDENS
STREET

Grand Union Canal

LABURNUM STREET

WHISTON STREET

THURTLE

HAGGERSTON ROAD

QUEENSBRIDGE ROAD

W H I S T O N   R O A D

DOVE ROW
HAY STREET
WHARF PLACE
ADA PLACE
PRITCHARD'S ROAD

HOW'S STREET
WORMSBY STREET
GEFFRYE STREET
APPLEBY STREET

HAGGERSTON PARK

AUDREY STREET
GOLDSMITH'S SQUARE

Geffrye Museum

PEARSON STREET

KENT STREET

WEYMOUTH TERRACE

YORKTON STREET

GOLDSMITH'S ROW
SHIPTON STREET
KAY STREET
TEALE STREET

COATE STREET

EMMA ST

2

KINGSLAND ROAD

HARE WALK
SHENFIELD STREET
KIRK STREET
REDVERS ST
CAROLINE GDNS

DUNLOE STREET
CREMER STREET
GORSUCH STREET
NAZRUL STREET

DUNLOE TERRACE

STREET

H A C K N E Y   R O A D

WARNER PLACE

DURANT STREET

ST PETER'S CLOSE

TEESDALE CLOSE
TEMPLE ST
CAMBERIDGE STREET
MANSFORD STREET
TEESDALE STREET
CLAPEDALE STREET

RAVENSCROFT STREET
HORATIO ST
EZRA STREET
COLUMBIA ROAD
BAXENDALE ST

ELWIN STREET
QUILTER STREET
BARNET GROVE
WELLINGTON ROW

ROBERTA STREET
SQUIRRIES STREET
OLD BETHNAL GREEN ROAD
POLLARD ROW
NELSON GDNS

SHORE
DITCH
HIGH
STREET

KINGSLAND ROAD

YSDALE ST

HACKNEY ROAD

PELTER STREET
LONG STREET
UNION WALK
WATERSON ST

C O L U M B I A   R O A D

GASCOIGNE PLACE
VIRGINIA ROAD
SWANFIELD STREET

G O S S E T   S T R E E T

CHAMBORD STREET
KIRBY STREET
TURIN STREET
GROVE STREET

FLORIDA STREET

B E T H N A L   G R E E N   R O A D

VOSS STREET
DERBYSHIRE STREET
VALLANCE ROAD

3

AUSTIN STREET
CALVERT AVENUE
ARNOLD CIRCUS
NAVARRE STREET
CAMLET STREET
OLD NICHOL STREET
CLUB ROW
MONTCLARE STREET

ROAD

TOMLINSON CLOSE

BRICK LANE

CHILTON STREET
MATTHEW'S ROW
HEREFORD STREET
WOOD CLOSE

BE
THNAL GREEN
ROAD

DERBYSHIRE PLACE
FREEMAN'S ROW
W INN YARD

BOUNDARY STREET
REDCHURCH STREET
EBOR ST
CHANCE ST

BACON STREET

GRANBY STREET

DUNBRIDGE STREET

KELSEY STREET
HEMMING STREET
MAPE STREET

Bethnal Green ⊞

4

HOLYWELL LANE
FLEET STREET YARD

HIGH STREET

COMMERCIAL STREET

WHEELER STREET
BRICK LANE

SCLATER STREET
PLAYING FIELDS

C H E S H I R E   S T R E E T

STREET

QUAKER STREET

FAKRUDDIN STREET

PEDLEY STREET
Shoreditch ⊞

WEAVER STREET

SELBY STREET
TENT ST
SCOTT ST

FLEUR DE LIS ST
NORTON FOLGATE
SPITAL SQUARE
STEWARD STREET
BRUSHFIELD

CALVIN STREET
ELDER STREET
LAMB STREET
Dennis Severs's House

B U X T O N   S T R E E T

WOODSEER STREET

HANBURY STREET

WILKES STREET
Spitalfields Heritage Centre

P R I N C E L E T   S T R E E T

HANBURY STREET

SPELMAN STREET
GREATOREX STREET

UNDERWOOD ROAD
DEAL STREET

STREET

VALLANCE ROAD

DURWARD STREET

5

BISHOPSGATE
ARTILLERY LANE
SANDYS ROW
CRISPIN STREET
FASHION STREET
FOURNIER STREET
Christ Church, Spitalfields
WHITE'S ROW
THRAWL STREET
HOPETOWN STREET

Jamme Masjid
FLEUR DE LIS STREET
HENEAGE STREET
CHICKSAND STREET
CASSON STREET

MONTAGUE STREET

OLD MONTAGUE STREET

W H I T E C H A P E L   R O A D

NEW ROAD

WESTWAY A40(M)

Royal Oak

WESTBOURNE PARK VILLAS

WESTBOURNE PARK ROAD

DURHAM TERRACE

ALEXANDER STREET

TERRACE KILDARE

SUNDERLAND TER

NEWTON ROAD

WESTBOURNE GDNS

PORCHESTER ROAD

BURDETT MEWS

QUEENSWAY

PORCHESTER SQ

GLCUCESTER TERRACE

GLOUCESTER TERRACE

ORSETT TERRACE

WESTBOURNE

BRIDGE

TERRACE

GLOUCESTER TERRACE

EASTBOURNE TERRACE

Paddington

Paddington

LONDON STREET

NORTH WHARF ROAD

WINDSOR ST

PRAED ST

HALLFIELD
ESTATE

GLOUCESTER TERRACE

CLEVELAND TERRACE

EASTBOURNE MEWS

WESTBOURNE TERRACE

CHILWORTH MEWS

GLOUCESTER MEWS

CHILWORTH STREET

ROAD

SPRING STREET

CONDUIT

MEWS

WESTBOURNE
GROVE

BISHOP'S

GROVE

MONMOUTH RD

GARWAY ROAD

REDAN PLACE

QUEENSWAY

INVERNESS

REDAN PLACE

KENSINGTON

GARDENS SQUARE

LEINSTER
SQUARE

PRINCE'S
SQUARE

MOSCOW
ROAD

PALACE

COURT

OSSINGTON STREET

ARDRE GARDENS

GATE

PRINCE'S
SQUARE

LEICESTER GDNS

PORCHESTER

SALEM ROAD

TERRACE

INVERNESS TERRACE

PORCHESTER GARDENS

QUEENSBOROUGH
TERRACE

QUEENSBOROUGH

LEINSTER GARDENS

LEINSTER TERRACE

PORCHESTER TERRACE

GLOUCESTER MEWS WEST

CLEVELAND
GARDENS

CLEVELAND SQUARE

CLEVELAND
SQUARE

QUEEN'S
GARDENS

London Toy and
Model Musium

CRAVEN HILL
GARDENS

CHILWORTH MEWS

GLOUCESTER TERRACE

DEVONSHIRE TERRACE

BROOK MEWS NORTH

CRAVEN HILL

CRAVEN HILL
MEWS

CRAVEN
TERRACE

LANCASTER
GATE

WESTBOURNE
CRESCENT

LANCASTER
GATE

Lancaster Gate

LANCASTER TERRACE

LANCASTER

BAYSWATER

Bayswater

INVERNESS
PLACE

INVERNESS TERRACE

PALACE COURT

BARK PLACE

CAROLINE PL

ORME COURT

ORME
LANE

Queensway

PALACE
SIDE

ST PETERSBURGH PLACE

MOSCOW
ROAD

PALACE GARDENS MEWS

CHISWICK GARDENS

PALACE GARDENS TERRACE

VICARAGE GATE

Kensington.
Palace

ROAD

THE

BROAD

WALK

PALACE

AVENUE

PALACE

GREEN

THE

WALK

LANCASTER
WALK

LANCASTER
WALK

The
Fountains

Peter Pan
Statue

KENSINGTON

Round Pond

GARDENS

DUKE'S LANE

HOLLAND STREET

CHURCH STREET

STREET

NTON STREET

HIGH

High Street
Kensington

AVERNA
COURT

WRIGHT'S LANE

DERRY STREET

YORK
HOUSE PLACE

OLD
COURT
PLACE

YOUNG STREET

KENSINGTON
COURT

KENSINGTON
SQUARE

CAMBRIDGE
PLACE

KENSINGTON COURT PLACE

VICTORIA
ROAD

DE VERE GARDENS

KENSINGTON
PALACE
GATE

DOURO PL

CANNING PLACE

ST ALBANS GROVE

KENSINGTON

GATE

THE

FLOWER

WALK

Albert
Memorial

ROAD

Royal College
of Art

Royal Albert
Hall

Royal College
of Music

Museum of
Instruments

HYDE PARK GATE

QUEENS GATE

HYDE PARK
GATE

QUEENS GATE MEWS

QUEENS GATE

BREMNER
RD

PRINCE

CONSORT ROAD

ALBERT COURT

D   E   F

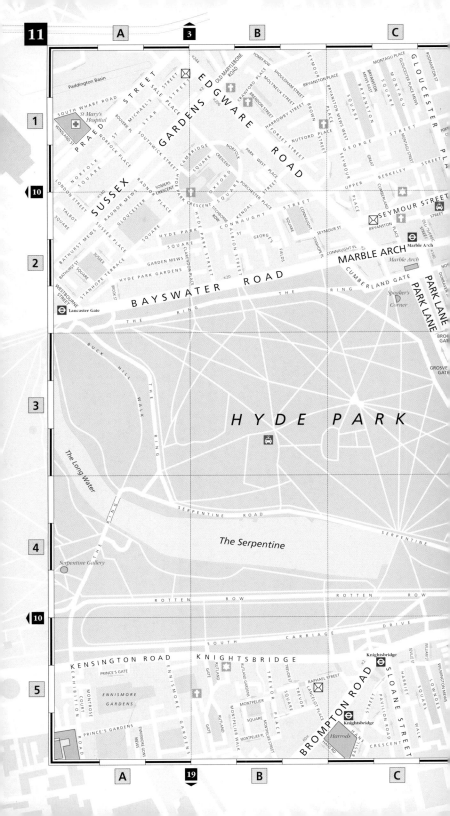

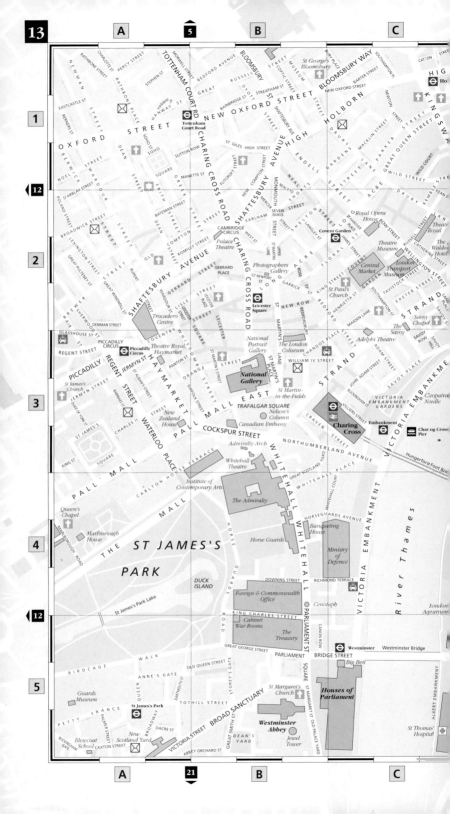

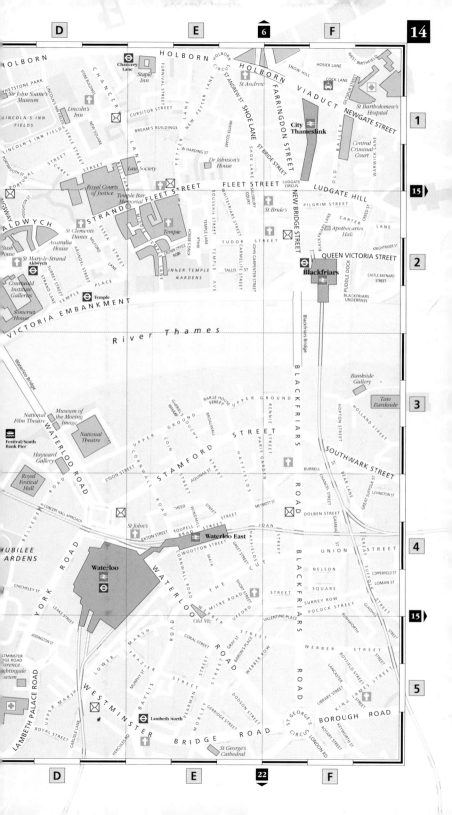

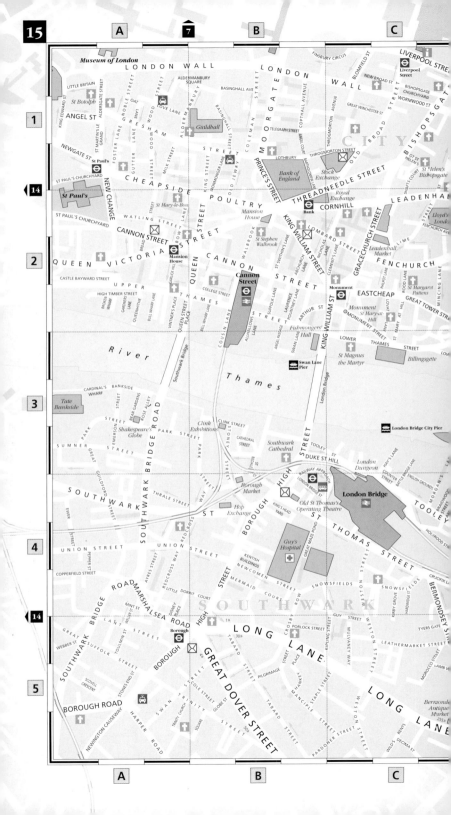

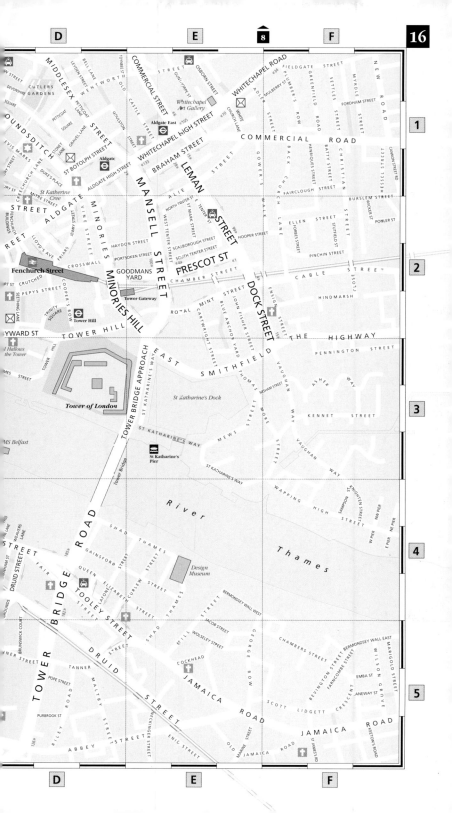

D E F

1

2

3

4

5

MIDDLESEX STREET

CUTLERS GARDENS SQUARE

DEVONSHIRE SQUARE

HOUNDSDITCH

PETTICOAT LANE

BELL LANE

TOWER ST OLD

LEYDEN ST

WENTWORTH ST

TOWERS ST

GRAVEL LANE

GOULSTON ST

CASTLE ST

STONEY LANE

COMMERCIAL STREET

OSBORN STREET

GUNTHORPE ST

White
Chapel
Art Gallery

WHITECHAPEL ROAD

FIELDGATE STREET

PLUMBER'S ROW

MULBERRY ST

GREENFIELD ROAD

SETTLES STREET

MYRDLE STREET

FORDHAM STREET

NEW ROAD

EVIS MARKS

CREECHURCH LANE

DUKE'S PLACE

ST BOTOLPH STREET

Aldgate

WHITECHAPEL HIGH STREET

Aldgate East

BRAHAM STREET

ALDGATE HIGH STREET

LEMAN STREET

ALIE STREET

GOWER'S WALK

BACK CHURCH LANE

HENRIQUES STREET

BATTY STREET

CHRISTIAN STREET

FAIRCLOUGH STREET

BURSLEM STREET

CANON STREET RD

HESSEL STREET

COMMERCIAL ROAD

St Katherine Cree

MITRE STREET

ALDGATE

JEWRY STREET

VINE STREET

MINORIES

FRIARS

HAYDON STREET

CROSSWALL

NORTH TENTER ST

WEST TENTER STREET

ST MARK STREET

SCARBOROUGH STREET

HOOPER STREET

ELLEN STREET

FORBES STREET

STUTFIELD ST

PINCHIN STREET

WICKER ST

PONLER ST

Fenchurch Street

CRUTCHED FRIARS

PEPYS STREET

COOPER'S ROW

MINORIES

PORTSOKEN STREET

GOODMANS YARD

SOUTH TENTER STREET

MANSELL STREET

PRESCOT ST

CHAMBER STREET

CABLE STREET

HINDMARSH

Tower Gateway

TRINITY SQUARE

Tower Hill

YWARD ST

TOWER HILL

ll Hallows the Tower

TOWER HILL

ROYAL MINT STREET

CARTWRIGHT STREET

BLUE ANCHOR YARD

JOHN FISHER STREET

DOCK STREET

ENSIGN STREET

THE HIGHWAY

PENNINGTON STREET

Tower of London

TOWER BRIDGE APPROACH

ST KATHARINE'S WAY

EAST SMITHFIELD

THOMAS MORE STREET

NEDHAM STREET

VAUGHAN WAY

ASHER WAY

KENNET STREET

HMS Belfast

St Katharine's Dock

ST KATHARINE'S WAY

St Katharine's Pier

Tower Bridge

MEWS STREET

ST KATHARINE'S WAY

VAUGHAN WAY

WAPPING HIGH STREET

SAMPSON ST

EIGHTEEN STREET

NW PIER

W PIER

E PIER

NE PIER

River Thames

SHAD THAMES

GAINSFORD STREET

QUEEN ELIZABETH STREET

CURLEW STREET

LAFONE STREET

Design Museum

BERMONDSEY WALL WEST

CHAMBERS STREET

BERMONDSEY WALL EAST

BEVINGTON STREET

FARNCOMBE STREET

EMBA ST

WILSON GROVE

MARIGOLD STREET

DRUID STREET

WEAVERS LANE

FAIR STREET

TOOLEY STREET

SHAD THAMES

MILL STREET

JACOB STREET

WOLSELEY STREET

GEORGE ROW

ANEWAY ST

KEETON'S ROAD

ST JAMES'S RD

TOWER BRIDGE ROAD

DRUID STREET

TANNER STREET

POPE STREET

MALTBY STREET

RILEY ROAD

PURBROOK ST

ABBEY STREET

JAMAICA ROAD

COCKHEAD

MARINE STREET

OLD JAMAICA ROAD

SCOTT LIDGETT CRESCENT

ENID STREET

JAMAICA ROAD

BRUNSWICK COURT

BRUNEL STREET

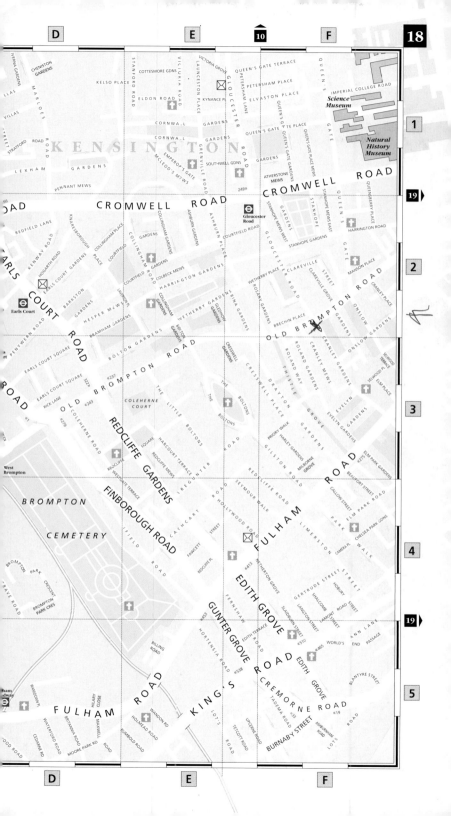

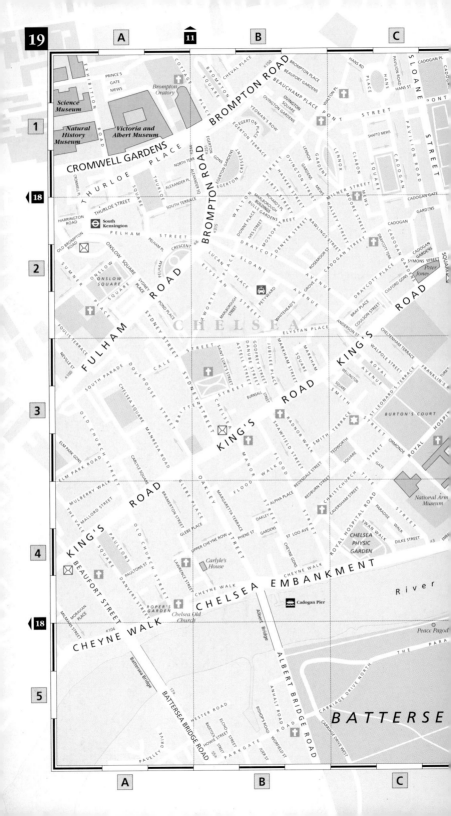

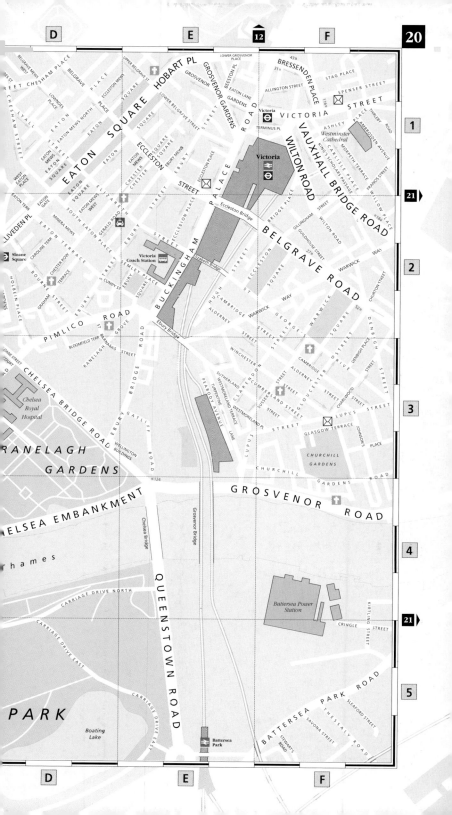

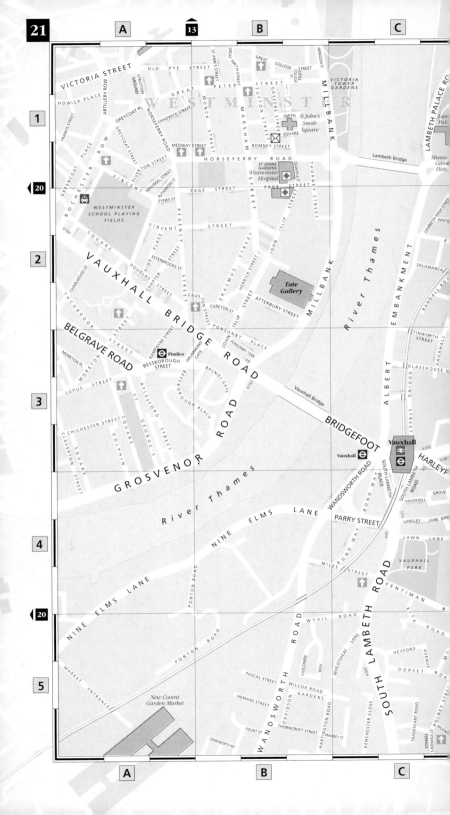

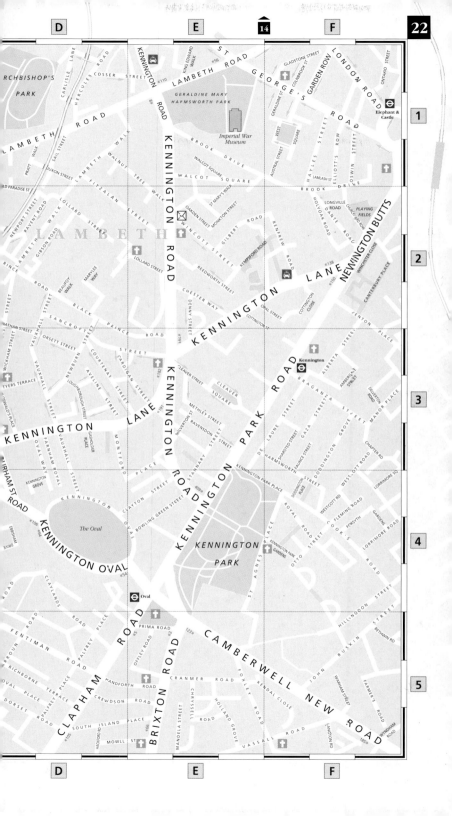

D E 14 F

1

2

3

4

5

D E F

RCHBISHOP'S
PARK

CARLISLE LANE

HERCULES ROAD

COSSER STREET

KENNINGTON ROAD

LAMBETH ROAD

KING EDWARD WALK

ST GEORGE'S ROAD

LAMBETH ROAD

GARDEN ROW

GLADSTONE STREET

GERALDINE ST

COLNBROOK ST

LONDON ROAD

ONTARIO STREET

Elephant &
Castle

GERALDINE MARY
HARMSWORTH PARK

Imperial War
Museum

LAMBETH ROAD

WALNUT TREE WALK

FITZALAN STREET

PRATT WALK

SAIL STREET

JUXON STREET

BROOK DRIVE

WALCOT SQUARE

WALCOT SQUARE

KENNINGTON ROAD

WEST SQUARE

AUSTRAL STREET

HAYLES STREET

LAMLASH ST

ELLIOTT'S ROW

BROSWIN STREET

BROOK DRIVE

RD PARADISE ST

NEWPORT STREET

LOLLARD STREET

LAMBETH WALK

RAVEN ROAD

GIBSON ROAD

L A M B E T H

ST MARY'S WALK

OAKDEN STREET

MONKTON STREET

WINCOTT STREET

GILBERT ROAD

RENFREW ROAD

KENNINGTON ROAD

LONGVILLE ROAD

DANTE ROAD

HOLYOAK ROAD

CHURCH 3RD CLOSE

PLAYING
FIELDS

NEWINGTON BUTTS

LOLLARD STREET

REEDWORTH STREET

KEMPSFORD ROAD

KENNINGTON LANE

WINCHESTER CLOSE

CANTERBURY PLACE

PRINCE

BEAUFOY WALK

MARYLEE WAY

BLACK PRINCE ROAD

SANCROFT STREET

CHESTER WAY

DENNY STREET

OPAL STREET

COTTINGTON ST

COTTINGTON CLOSE

FENTON PLACE

NATHAN STREET

VAUXHALL STREET

ORSETT STREET

NEWBURN STREET

COURTENAY STREET

CARDIGAN STREET

KENNINGTON LANE

CLEAVER STREET

CLEAVER SQUARE

KENNINGTON PARK ROAD

BRAGANZA STREET

DE LAUNE STREET

ALBERTA STREET

AMBERGATE STREET

DELVERTON ROAD

MANOR PLACE

Kennington

WICKHAM STREET

TYERS TERRACE

VAUXHALL STREET

LOUGHBOROUGH STREET

AVELINE STREET

GOSLINGER PLACE

MILVERTON ST

METHLEY STREET

RAVENSDON STREET

STANNARY STREET

SHANFORD STREET

GAZA STREET

STREATA

DODDINGTON GROVE

CHAPTER RD

OSWALD'S PLACE

FARNHAM ROYAL

OVAL WAY

MONTFORD PLACE

HARMSWORTH STREET

DODDINGTON PLACE

ROYAL ROAD

WEST-COTT RD

WEST-OTT ROAD

FORSYTH

COOK'S

LORRIMORE SQ

KENNINGTON

KENNINGTON OVAL

KENNINGTON GROVE

The Oval

CLAYTON STREET

OVAL

BOWLING GREEN STREET

KENNINGTON PARK PLACE

ST AGNES PLACE

KENNINGTON PARK GARDENS

OTTO STREET

FLEMING ROAD

GARDENS

LORRIMORE ROAD

HILLINGDON STREET

FAIRHAM ST ROAD

FEBRSHAM DRIVE

KENNINGTON OVAL

CLAYLANDS ROAD

PRIMA ROAD

Oval

OFFLEY ROAD

CAMBERWELL NEW ROAD

RUSKIN

BETHWIN RD

FENTIMAN ROAD

RICHBORNE TERRACE

PALFREY PLACE

CLAPHAM ROAD

HANDFORTH ROAD

CRANMER ROAD

FOXLEY ROAD

KENDAL CLOSE

JOHN

WARHAM STREET

FARMER'S ROAD

LANGTON ROAD

WYNDHAM ROAD

OVAL PLACE

DORSET ROAD

PALFREY PLACE

CREWDSON ROAD

BRIXTON ROAD

CHRYSSELL ROAD

MANDELA STREET

HOLLAND GROVE

VASSALL ROAD

SOUTH ISLAND PLACE

MOWLL ST

23

A   B   C

1

WYNAN ROAD
PONTERS CLOSE
WEST FERRY ROAD
MANCHESTER ROAD
EAST FERRY ROAD
FERRY STREET
MIDLAND PLACE
FERRY STREET
SAUNDERS NESS ROAD
Island Gardens
ISLAND GARDENS

River **Thames**

Greenwich Foot Tunnel

🚇 **Greenwich Pier**

2

Gipsy Moth IV

STOWAGE
COPPERAS STREET
CREEK   ROAD
THAMES   STREET
NORWAY ST
HORSEFERRY PLACE
WELLINGTON STREET
CLARENCE STREET
BARDSLEY   LANE

GREENWICH CHURCH STREET

KING WILLIAM WALK
NELSON ROAD

Cutty Sark

Royal Naval College

CRANE STREET
HIGH BRIDGE
PARK ROW
EASTNEY
OLD WOOLWICH ROAD

ROMNEY ROAD

Queen's House

FEATHERS PLACE
PARK

GRE

National Maritime Museum

ℹ️

St Alfege ✝

THORNHAM STREET
HADDO STREET
CLAREMONT STREET
ROAN STREET
RANDALL PLACE
STRAIGHTSMOUTH STREET

STOCKWELL ST
NEVADA ST

3

NORMAN ROAD
TARVES WAY
✉️
STRAIGHTSMOUTH
GREENWICH HIGH ROAD
🚉 **Greenwich**

ROYAL HILL
BURNEY STREET

Fan Museum 🏛️

CROOM'S HILL GROVE
CROOM'S   HILL
GLOUCESTER CIRCUS

GREENWICH

Old Royal Observatory

THE   AVENU

4

GREENWICH   SOUTH   STREET

DEVONSHIRE DRIVE
LANGDALE ROAD
ASHBURNHAM PLACE
CATHERINE GROVE
EGERTON DRIVE
ASHBURNHAM GROVE
GUILDFORD GROVE
BLISSET STREET
CIRCUS STREET
BRAND STREET
PRIOR STREET
ROYAL HILL
WINFORTON STREET
DABIN CRESCENT
MAIDENSTONE HILL
DIAMOND TERRACE
POINT HILL
WESTGROVE LANE
WEST GROVE
HYDE VALE
GEORGETTE PLACE
LUTON PL

CHESTERFIELD ROAD
GVOR
GENERAL WOLFE ROAD
HILL

✝ *Ranger House*

BLACKHEATH RD

DITCH ALLEY

HOLLYMOUNT CLOSE

BLACKHEATH   HILL   SHOOTERS   HILL   ROAD

DARTMOUTH HILL
DARTMOUTH ROW
DARTMOUTH GROVE
HARE AND BILLET ROAD

WHITFIELD ROAD

5

LEWISHAM   ROAD

JOHN PENN STREET
MORDEN STREET
SPARTA STREET
BECK CLOSE
BINNET GROVE
COLDBATH STREET
BLISS CRESCENT
NECTARINE WAY
ORCHARD
RAVENSBOURNE PLACE
RUSSETT WAY
ROSEWOOD GARDENS
CONINGTON RD
LETHBRIDGE CLOSE
MORDEN HILL
MORDEN CLOSE
BLACKHEATH RISE
PRINCE'S RISE
LEWISHAM HILL
ST AUSTELL ROAD
WAT TYLER ROAD
MOUNTS POND ROAD
GRANVILLE PARK
ABERDEEN TERRACE
PAGODA GARDENS
OAKCROFT ROAD
ELIOT HILL
THE ORCHARD
ELIOT

BROOKMILL ROAD
ELVERSON ROAD
LEATHWELL ROAD

A   B   C

D **E** **F**

TRAFALGAR ROAD

QUAY
ERSKINE ST
SPELTON
BELLOT ST
CHRISTCHURCH WAY
C BELLOT ST
COMMERELL ST
CONLEY STREET
BLACKWALL LANE
GLENISTER RD
ARMITAGE RD
FINGAL STREET
CHILVER ST
DENHAM ST
A102 (M)

W O O L W I C H   R O A D

GIBSON ST
ERSKINE ROAD
BRANNING STREET
HADRIAN STREET
CARADOC ROAD
WOOLWICH ROAD
WHITWORTH ST
ROAD
ROAD
COLOMB STREET
RODMERE STREET
HALSTOW ROAD
CHEVENING ROAD
KEMSING ROAD
COMBEDALE
WESTCOMBE HILL
WESTDALE ROAD
WESTCOMBE ROAD
1129

Greenwich District Hospital

ROYAL HOSPITAL CEMETERY

ORLOP STREET
WOODLAND GROVE
CARSWOOD
WALNUT TREE ROAD
VANBRUGH HILL
CALVERT ROAD
ANNANDALE ROAD
ANNANDALE ROAD
ORMISTON ROAD

Westcombe Park

TUSKAR STREET
WOODLANDS PARK
RESTELL CLOSE
DINSDALE ROAD
HUMBER ROAD
PEACHUM ROAD
COLERAINE ROAD
BEACONSFIELD
MYCENAE ROAD
RUTHIN ROAD

Maze Hill

VISTA
MAZE HILL
TOM SMITH CLOSE
ULUNDI ROAD
FOYLE ROAD
WEBB ROAD
HUMBER ROAD
BELFAST GARDENS
ROAD
INGLESIDE GROVE
BEACONSFIELD ROAD
BEACONSFIELD
CLOSE
MYCENAE ROAD

P A R K

WESTCOMBE
HIGHMORE ROAD
VANBRUGH FIELDS
LYNDALE CLOSE
MAZE HILL
PARK
VANBRUGH PARK ROAD WEST
VANBRUGH PARK ROAD
W E S T C O M B E   P A R K   R O A D
ROAD
BROADBRIDGE CLOSE

N W I C H

WYCHERLEY CLOSE
COMBE AVENUE
COMBE MEWS
PARK
MANDEVILLE CLOSE
VANBRUGH
ST
HEATH
WAY
JOHN'S   PARK
PARK
STRATHEDEN ROAD

VANBRUGH

WAY

BLACKHEATH AVENUE
POWER AVENUE
CHARLTON
WAY
MAZE HILL
CHARLTON
WAY
VANBRUGH TERRACE
ANGERSTEIN LANE
LANGTON
WAY
ST GERMANS
PLACE

S H O O T E R S   H I L L   R O A D
37ª

CHARLTON
ROAD
DUKE HUMPHREY ROAD
LONG POND ROAD
CHARLES ROAD
PRINCE OF WALES ROAD

B L A C K H E A T H
GOFFERS ROAD
TALBOT PLACE
MOUNTS POND ROAD
BLACKHEATH VALE
HARE AND BILLET ROAD
ORCHARD ROAD
ELIOT PLACE
GROTE'S PLACE
TRANQUIL VALE
ALL SAINTS DRIVE
ROYAL PARADE
MONTPELIER ROW
PRINCE OF WALES ROAD
SOUTH PARAGON PLACE
FALCONWOOD COURT
PARAGON PLACE
SQUARE
POND ROAD
RYCULFE ROAD
THE PARAGON
FULTHORP ROAD
MERRYFIELD
MAYBRIGHT
MORDEN ROAD
KIDBROOKE GARDENS
REGENT'S PLACE
MORDEN ROAD
MORDEN ROAD MEWS
THE KEEP

D **E** **F**

1
2
3
4
5

General Index

Acknowledgments

DORLING KINDERSLEY would like to thank the following people whose help and assistance contributed to the preparation of this book.

MAIN CONTRIBUTOR

Michael Leapman was born in London in 1938 and has been a journalist since he was 20. He has worked for most British national newspapers and writes about travel and other subjects for several publications, among them *The Independent, Independent on Sunday, The Economist* and *Country Life*. He has written ten books, including *London's River* (published 1991) and the award-winning *Companion Guide to New York* (1983, revised 1991). In 1989 he edited the acclaimed *Book of London*.

CONTRIBUTORS

Yvonne Deutch, Guy Dimond, George Foster, Iain Gale, Fiona Holman, Phil Harriss, Lindsay Hunt, Christopher Middleton, Steven Parissien, Christopher Pick, Bazyli Solowij, Mark Wareham, Jude Welton.

DORLING KINDERSLEY wishes to thank the following editors and researchers at Webster's International Publishers: Sandy Carr, Matthew Barrell, Siobhan Bremner, Serena Cross, Annie Galpin, Miriam Lloyd, Ava-Lee Tanner.

ADDITIONAL PHOTOGRAPHY

Max Alexander, Peter Anderson, June Buck, Peter Chadwick, Michael Dent, Philip Dowell, Mike Dunning, Andreas Einsiedel, Steve Gorton, Christi Graham, Alison Harris, Peter Hayman, Stephen Hayward, Roger Hilton, Ed Ironside, Colin Keates, Dave King, Neil Mersh, Nick Nichols, Robert O'Dea, Vincent Oliver, John Parker, Tim Ridley, Kim Sayer, Chris Stevens, James Stevenson, James Strachan, Doug Traverso, David Ward, Mathew Ward, Steven Wooster and Nick Wright.

ADDITIONAL ILLUSTRATIONS

Ann Child, Tim Hayward, Fiona M Macpherson, Janos Marffy, David More, Chris D Orr, Richard Phipps, Michelle Ross, John Woodcock.

CARTOGRAPHY

Advanced Illustration (Cheshire), Contour Publishing (Derby), Euromap Limited (Berkshire). Street Finder maps: ERA Maptec Ltd (Dublin) adapted with permission from original survey and mapping from Shobunsha (Japan).

CARTOGRAPHIC RESEARCH

James Anderson, Roger Bullen, Tony Chambers, Ruth Duxbury, Jason Gough, Ailsa Heritage, Jayne Parsons, Donna Rispoli, Jill Tinsley, Andrew Thompson, Iorwerth Watkins.

RESEARCH ASSISTANCE

Chris Lascelles, Kathryn Steve.

DESIGN AND EDITORIAL ASSISTANCE

Keith Addison, Oliver Bennett, Michelle Clark, Carey Combe, Vanessa Courtier, Lorna Damms, Simon Farbrother, Fay Franklin, Simon Hall. Marcus Hardy, Sasha Heseltine, Paul Hines, Stephanie Jackson, Nancy Jones, Stephen Knowlden, Jeanette Leung, Jane Middleton, Fiona Morgan, Louise Parsons, Leigh Priest, Liz Rowe, Simon Ryder, Susannah Steel, Anna Streiffert, Andrew Szudek, Diana Vowles, Andy Wilkinson.

SPECIAL ASSISTANCE

Christine Brandt at Kew Gardens, Shelia Brown at The Bank of England, John Cattermole at London Buses Northern, the DK picture department, especially Jenny Rayner, Pippa Grimes at the V & A, Emma Healy at Bethnal Green Museum of Childhood, Alan Hills at the British Museum, Emma Hutton and Cooling Brown Partnership, Gavin Morgan at the Musuem of London, Clare Murphy at Historic Royal Palaces, Ali Naqei at the Science Museum, Patrizio Semproni, Caroline Shaw at the Natural History Museum, Gary Smith at British Rail, Monica Thurnauer at The Tate and Alistair Wardle.

PHOTOGRAPHIC REFERENCE

The London Aerial Photo Library, and P and P F James.

PHOTOGRAPHY PERMISSIONS

DORLING KINDERSLEY would like to thank the following for their kind permission to photograph at their establishments: All Souls Church, Banqueting House (Crown Copyright by kind permission of Historic

Royal Palaces), Barbican Centre, Burgh House Trust, Cabinet War Rooms, Chapter House (English Heritage), Charlton House, Chelsea Physic Garden, Clink Exhibition, Maritime Trust (Cutty Sark), Design Museum, Gatwick Airport Ltd, Geffrye Museum, Hamleys and Merrythought, Heathrow Airport Ltd, Imperial War Museum, Dr Johnson's House, Keats House (the London Borough of Camden), London Underground Ltd, Madame Tussaud's, Old St Thomas's Operating Theatre, Patisserie Valerie, Place Below Vegetarian Restaurant, Royal Naval College, St Alfege's, St Bartholomew-the-Great, St Bartholomew-the-Less, St Botolph's Aldersgate, St James's, St John's Smith Square, The Rector and Churchwardens of St Magnus the Martyr, St Mary le Strand, St Marylebone Parish Church, St Paul's Cathedral, the Master and Wardens of the Worshipful Company of Skinners, Smolensky's Restaurants, Southbank Centre, Provost and Chapter of Southwark Cathedral, HM Tower of London, Wellington Museum, Wesley Chapel, the Dean and Chapter of Westminster, Westminster Cathedral, and Hugh Hales, General Manager of the Whitehall Theatre (part of the Maybox Theatre group). Dorling Kindersley would also like to thank all the other museums, galleries, churches, restaurants, shops, and other sights who aided us with photography at their establishments. These are too numerous to thank individually.

PICTURE CREDITS

t = top; tl = top left; tc = top centre; tr = top right; cla = centre left above; ca = centre above; cra = centre right above; cl = centre left; c = centre; cr = centre right; clb = centre left below; cb = centre below; crb = centre right below; bl = bottom left; b = bottom; bc = bottom centre; br = bottom right.

Works of art have been reproduced with the permission of the following copyright holders: © ALAN BOWNESS, HEPWORTH ESTATE: 85cla; © LUCIEN FREUD: 83b; © DAVID HOCKNEY 1970–1: 85t; © The family of ERIC H. KENNINGTON, RA: 151bl; © KATE ROTHKO PRIZEL and CHRISTOPHER ROTHKO/DACS 1999 178cla; © SUCCESSION PICASSO/DACS 1999 178cr; © ANGELA VERREN-TAUNT. All rights reserved, DACS 1999 85cr. The works illustrated on pages 45c, 85b, 206b, 266cb have been reproduced by kind permission of the HENRY MOORE FOUNDATION.

The Publishers are grateful to the following individuals, companies and picture libraries for permission to reproduce their photographs:

Printed by kind permission of THE ALBERMARLE CONNECTION: 91t; ARCAID: RICHARD BRYANT 246B; MOHAMED AL FAYED: 310b; GOVERNOR AND COMPANY OF THE BANK OF ENGLAND: 145tr; BRIDGEMAN ART LIBRARY, London: 21t, 28t; British Library, London 14, 19tr, (detail) 21br, 24cb, (detail) 32tl, 32bl; Courtesy of the Institute of Directors, London 29cla; Guildhall Art Gallery, Corporation of London (detail) 26t; Guildhall Library, Corporation of London 24br, 76c; ML Holmes Jamestown – Yorktown Educational Trust, VA (detail) 17bc; Master and Fellows, Magdalene College, Cambridge (detail) 23clb; Marylebone Cricket Club, London 242c; William Morris Gallery, Walthamstow 19tl, 251tl; Museum of London 22–3; O'Shea Gallery, London (detail) 22cl; Royal Holloway & Bedford New College 157bl; Russell Cotes Art Gallery and Museum, Bournemouth 38tr; Thyssen-Bornemisza Collection, Lugano Casta 257b; Westminster Abbey, London (detail) 32bc; White House, Bond Street, London 28cb.

BRITISH AIRWAYS: 354t, 356tl, 359t; reproduced with permission of the BRITISH LIBRARY BOARD: 125b; © THE BRITISH MUSEUM: 16t, 16ca, 17tl, 40t, 91c, 126–7 all pics except 126t, 128–9 all pics.

CAMERA PRESS, London: P. Abbey - LNS 73cb; Cecil Beaton 79tl; HRH Prince Andrew 95bl; Allan Warren 31cb; COLORIFIC!: Steve Benbow 55t; David Levenson 66–7; CONRAN RESTAURANTS 291cb; Courtesy of the CORPORATION OF LONDON: 55c, 146t; COURTAULD INSTITUTE GALLERIES, London: 41c, 117b.

PERCIVAL DAVID FOUNDATION OF CHINESE ART: 130c; Copyright: Dean & Chapter of Westminster 78bl, 79tr; DEPARTMENT OF TRANSPORT (Crown Copyright): 361b; Courtesy of the GOVERNORS AND THE DIRECTORS DULWICH PICTURE GALLERY: 43bl, 252bl.

ENGLISH HERITAGE: 258b; ENGLISH LIFE PUBLICATIONS LTD: 259b; PHILIP ENTICKNAP: 251tr; ET ARCHIVE: 19bl, 26c, 26bc, 27bl, 28br, 29cra,

29clb, 33tc, 33cr, 36bl, 185tl; British Library, London 18cr; Imperial War Museum, London 30bc; Museum of London 15b, 27br, 28bl; Science Museum, London 27cla; Stoke Museum Staffordshire Polytechnic 23bl, 25cl, 33bc; Victoria and Albert Museum, London 20c, 21bc, 25tr; MARY EVANS PICTURE LIBRARY: 16bl, 16br, 17bl, 17br, 20bl, 22bl, 24t, 25bc, 25br, 27t, 27cb, 27bc, 30bl, 32br, 33tl, 33cl, 33bl, 33br, 36t, 36c, 38tl. 39bl, 72cb, 72b, 90b, 112b, 114b, 116c, 135t, 139t, 155bl, 159t 162ca, 174ca, 177b, 203b, 212t, 222b.

Courtesy of the FAN MUSEUM (The Helene Alexander Collection) 239b; FREUD MUSEUM, London: 242t.

THE GORE HOTEL, London: 273.

ROBERT HARDING PICTURE LIBRARY: 31ca, 42c, 52ca, 169tl, 325tl, 347cb, 366b; Philip Craven 206t; Brian Hawkes 21clb; Michael Jenner 21cra, 238t; 58t, 223t; Mark Mawson 113tl; Nick Wood 63bl; HAYES-DAVIDSON (computer generated images: 174bl, 178b; HEATHROW AIRPORT LTD: 356tr; Reproduced with permission of HER MAJESTY'S STATIONARY OFFICE (Crown Copyright): 156 all pics; JOHN HESELTINE: 12tr, 13tl, 13tr, 13cb, 13br, 51tl, 63br, 98, 124b, 132, 142. 172, 216; FRIENDS OF HIGHGATE CEMETERY: 37tr. 240, 242b; HISTORIC ROYAL PALACES (Crown Copyright): 5t, 35tc, 254–5 all except 254br, 256–7 all except 257b; THE HORNIMAN MUSEUM, London: 252br; House of Detention 243t; HOVERSPEED LTD: 359b; HULTON GETTY: 24bl, 124tl, 135cr, 228t.

THE IMAGE BANK, London: Gio Barto 55b Derek Berwin 31t, 272t; Romilly Lockyer 72t, 94br; Leo Mason 56t; Simon Wilkinson 197t; Terry Williams 139b; Courtesy of ISIC, UK: 352t.

PETER JACKSON COLLECTION: 24–5.

ROYAL BOTANIC GARDENS, KEW: Andrew McRob 48cl, 56b, 244–5 all pics except 245t & 245br.

LEIGHTON HOUSE, ROYAL BOROUGH OF KENSINGTON: 212b; LITTLE ANGEL MARIONETTE THEATRE: 341tl; LONDON AMBULANCE SERVICE: 347ca; London Aquarium 185b; LONDON TOY AND MODEL MUSEUM: 261t; LONDON TRANSPORT MUSEUM: 28ca; 362–3 all maps and tickets.

MADAME TUSSAUD'S: 218c, 220t; MANSELL COLLECTION: 19br, 20t, 20br, 21bl, 22t, 22cl, 23br, 27ca, 32tr; METROPOLITAN POLICE SERVICE: 346t, 347t; MUSEUM OF LONDON: 16cb, 17tr, 17cb, 18t, 21crb, 41tc, 166–7 all pics.

NATIONAL EXPRESS LTD: 358; Reproduced by courtesy of the TRUSTEES, THE NATIONAL GALLERY, London: 35c, 104–5 all except 104t, 106–7 all except 107t; NATIONAL PORTRAIT GALLERY, London: 4t, 41tl, 101cb, (detail) 102b; NATIONAL POSTAL MUSEUM, London: 26bl, 164t; By permission of the KEEPER OF THE NATIONAL RAILWAY MUSEUM. York: 28–9; NATIONAL TRUST PHOTOGRAPHIC LIBRARY: Wendy Aldiss 23ca; John Bethell 258t, 259t; Michael Boys 38bc; NATURAL HISTORY MUSEUM, LONDON: 205t, 205cr; Derek Adams 204b; John Downs 204c; NHPA: G. I. Bernard 248; NEW MILLENNIUM EXPERIENCE COMPANY: QA Photos 246t, 247t, 247b; NEW SHAKESPEARE THEATRE CO: 324bl.

PALACE THEATRE ARCHIVE: 108t; PICTOR INTERNATIONAL, London: 61t, 174br; PIPPA POP-INS CHILDREN'S HOTEL, London: 339b.

PITSHANGER MANOR MUSEUM: 260c; POPPERFOTO: 29tl, 29crb, 30tl, 30tr, 30c, 33tr, 39br; PRESS ASSOCIATION LTD: 29bl, 29br; PUBLIC RECORD OFFICE (Crown Copyright): 18b.

BILL RAFFERTY: 324br; REX FEATURES LTD: 53tl; Peter Brooker 53tr; Andrew Laenen 54c; THE RITZ, London: 91b; ROCK CIRCUS: 100cb; ROCK ISLAND DINER: 339ca; ROYAL ACADEMY OF ARTS, London: 90tr; THE BOARD OF TRUSTEES OF THE ROYAL ARMOURIES: 41tr, 155tl, 157t, 157br; ROYAL COLLECTION, ST JAMES'S PALACE © HM THE QUEEN: 8–9, 53b, 88t, 93t, 94–5 all pics except 94br & 95bl, 96t, 254br; ROYAL COLLEGE OF MUSIC, London: 196c, 202c.

THE SAVOY GROUP: 274t, 274b; SCIENCE MUSEUM, London: 208cr, 208b, 209cl, 209 cra, 209bl, 209br; SCIENCE PHOTO LIBRARY: Maptec International Ltd 10b; SEALINK PLC: 355b; SPENCER HOUSE LTD: 88b; SOUTHBANK PRESS OFFICE: 182bl; SYNDICATION INTERNATIONAL: 31bl, 35tr, 52cb, 53c, 58bl, 59t, 136; Library of Congress 25bl.

TATE GALLERY: 43br, 82–3 all pics except 82t & 83t, 84–5 all pics, 178t, 178cla, 178cr.

The London Underground

UNDERGROUND

London Travel Information 0171-222 1234 24 hours
Minicom 0171-918 3015

© London Regional Transport

Parano 01892 786 444
NÉ Hemel Hempstead
SE Tunbridge Wells — Wadha
Victoria
m - f